Books by Walter Johnson

THE BATTLE AGAINST ISOLATION

WILLIAM ALLEN WHITE'S AMERICA

THE UNITED STATES: EXPERIMENT IN DEMOCRACY
(*with Avery Craven*)

HOW WE DRAFTED ADLAI STEVENSON

1600 PENNSYLVANIA AVENUE: PRESIDENTS AND THE PEOPLE, 1929–1959

THE FULBRIGHT PROGRAM: A HISTORY
(*with Francis J. Colligan*)

Edited by Walter Johnson

SELECTED LETTERS OF WILLIAM ALLEN WHITE

ROOSEVELT AND THE RUSSIANS: THE YALTA CONFERENCE
By Edward R. Stettinius, Jr.

TURBULENT ERA: A DIPLOMATIC RECORD OF FORTY YEARS, 1904–1945
By Joseph C. Grew

THE PAPERS OF ADLAI E. STEVENSON
Volume I: The Beginnings of Education
Volume II: Washington to Springfield, 1941–1948

The Papers of Adlai E. Stevenson

WALTER JOHNSON, *Editor*

CAROL EVANS, *Assistant Editor*

The Papers of

Advisory Committee

Adlai E. Stevenson

VOLUME II

Washington to Springfield
1941–1948

LITTLE, BROWN *and* COMPANY • *Boston* • *Toronto*

FIRST EDITION

T 02/73

The editors gratefully acknowledge the permission of the following authors, publish-
ers, individuals and institutions to reprint selected materials as noted:
Edwin C. Austin, George W. Ball, Barron's Educational Series, Inc., Jack O. Brown,
Noel F. Busch, Everett Case, Henry P. Chandler, Harlan Cleveland, Benjamin V.
Cohen, Connecticut Herald Corporation, Lauchlin B. Currie, The Curtis Publishing
Company, Milton S. Eisenhower, Thomas K. Finletter, Wilder Foote, IIT Research
Institute, Mrs. Ernest L. Ives, J. M. Juran, Mrs. R. Keith Kane, Emory Scott Land,
Walter Lippmann, Archibald MacLeish, John J. McCloy, Carl McGowan, Porter
McKeever, Loring C. Merwin, Paul Miller, George Morgenstern, Joe Alex Morris,
William Morrow and Company, Inc., James F. Oates, Jr., Oxford University Press,
Byron Price, Random House, Inc., Stanley Reed, Nelson A. Rockefeller, Hermon D.
Smith, Donald C. Stone, Walter N. Thayer, Mrs. Ronald Tree, Mrs. Carl Vrooman,
and Kenneth G. Younger for all items from their publications and writings as de-
tailed in the footnotes.
Kenneth S. Davis for excerpts from his book, *A Prophet in His Own Country: The
Triumphs and Defeats of Adlai E. Stevenson*. Copyright ©1957 by Kenneth S. Davis.
George W. Ball, William E. Stevenson, Jacob M. Arvey, Stephen A. Mitchell and
Harper & Row, Publishers for selections from the chapters, "With A.E.S. in War
and Politics," by George W. Ball, "Two Stevensons of Princeton," by William E.
Stevenson, "A Gold Nugget in Your Backyard," by Jacob M. Arvey, and "Adlai's
Amateurs," by Stephen A. Mitchell, published in *As We Knew Adlai: The Stevenson
Story by Twenty-two Friends*. Edited and with Preface by Edward P. Doyle. Copy-
right © 1966 by Harper & Row, Publishers.

Library of Congress Cataloging in Publication Data

Stevenson, Adlai Ewing, 1900-1965.
    The papers of Adlai E. Stevenson.

    CONTENTS: v. 1. The beginnings of education.--v. 2.
Washington to Springfield, 1941-1948.
    I. Title.
E748.S84A25 1972   973.921'092'4 [B]   73-175478
ISBN 0-316-467510 (v.2)

*Published simultaneously in Canada
by Little, Brown & Company (Canada) Limited*

PRINTED IN THE UNITED STATES OF AMERICA

Foreword

At the ceremony at the United Nations after Adlai E. Stevenson's death, his close friend Archibald MacLeish said:

> If his intelligence was remarkable it was remarkable, even more than for its clarity, for its modesty, its humor, its naturalness, its total lack of vanity or arrogance. If he was one of the great articulators of his time, one of the few, true voices, it was because the words he spoke were the words of his own thought, of his deepest and most personal conviction. It was himself he gave in word and thought and action, not to his friends alone but to his country, to his world. And the gift had consequences. It changed the tone and temper of political life in the United States for a generation. It humanized the quality of international dialogue throughout a great part of the world. It enlightened a darkened time.

Adlai E. Stevenson's own words — in letters, postcards, speeches, and his abortive attempts at keeping a diary — are presented in the volumes of *The Papers of Adlai E. Stevenson.*

These volumes are a documentary biography of Stevenson and, at the same time, a documentary history in his own words of the extraordinary, and often bewildering, changes that remolded the United States and the world during his lifetime from 1900 to 1965.

In selecting the materials from Stevenson's papers to be published in these volumes the editors decided to emphasize the material that helped to answer such questions as: How did he educate himself? How did he become the man he became? What were the key influences in his life? How did he understand his times? How did he articulate the problems of his time?

Deeply involved in the affairs of his own generation, Stevenson's career as special assistant to Secretary of the Navy Frank Knox, his mission to wartorn Italy, his work on a bombing survey mission to France, his collaboration with Secretary of State Edward R. Stettinius, Jr., and Assistant Secretary of State Archibald MacLeish to found the United Nations, his leadership of the United States delegation to the United Nations Preparatory Commission, his participation in the 1946 and 1947 meetings of the General Assembly of the United Nations, and his campaign for the governorship of Illinois, are chronicled in Volume II. The letters, postcards, speeches, and fragments of diary reveal how he continued to broaden his education and acquired a deeper understanding of his times. He had a mind that was at home with the culture of the past. At the same time he was in a continual quest for enlightenment about the present. Moreover, he had a profound concern that the American people constantly educate themselves in order to retain the richness of their past and be able to cope with the problems of a rapidly changing nation and world.

After he won the governorship of Illinois by the largest margin in history, Mr. Justice Felix Frankfurter wrote Stevenson on November 13, 1948:

> Considering the quality of the educational political campaign which you have conducted, it is a source of deep satisfaction that the people of Illinois have decided to have you at the head of their affairs.
>
> I watched your campaign with not merely the interest of a friend but with that of a deep believer in democracy, and the outcome heartens one's faith in democracy, and is of course a source of great rejoicing to all your friends. I have no doubt that you will prove that wisdom and humane understanding without the silly compromises of the narrowly prudent can guide political action. Indeed, wisdom and humane understanding are the only things that are truly prudent.

The editors had a larger collection of papers available for Volume II than for Volume I. Volume II is, therefore, more selective. Governor Stevenson provided in his will that material about his governorship of Illinois be deposited in the Illinois State Historical Library and the remainder be deposited in the Princeton University Library. Stevenson's most important correspondence, drafts of speeches, and fragments of diary were at his home in Libertyville when he died. The editors selected some of the material for this volume from the material at Libertyville before the collection was divided between the two depositories. Some items are still in the possession of Adlai E. Stevenson III. We collected some handwritten letters and postcards from old friends.

The editors of these volumes searched widely for handwritten documents. Stevenson enjoyed writing by hand — he must have, since he wrote so many letters and postcards. Some people, particularly before he became governor of Illinois, failed to save them. Many people were most cooperative, placing all their Stevenson items at our disposal. The location of handwritten letters, postcards or originals of typewritten letters is given in the footnote references.

We indicate in the introduction to each part of Volume II or in footnotes to individual items the location of the material used. We have provided a brief summary of Stevenson's career in these introductions as well as a description of our editorial method. We have provided editorial comment on any item where it was necessary for clarity or for continuity.

Over the years Stevenson wrote many letters to Mrs. Edison Dick and her family. Some were dictated and transcribed on the typewriter, and some were handwritten. Mrs. Dick submitted extracts to the editors from handwritten letters she received. She has indicated with ellipses material that was deleted by her. The originals of all the handwritten letters are in her possession.

Most of Stevenson's letters were signed with his full name; those signed "Ad" or "Adlai" were to close personal or political friends. Because we have had to work, in most cases, with carbon copies, it is impossible to know how these letters and memoranda were signed. Hence, signatures have been omitted from such items. Whenever we have located the original letter and it was signed "Ad" or "Adlai," we have included the signature.

When he wrote by hand, Stevenson had several idiosyncrasies. He spelled "it's" without the apostrophe; he used "thru" for "through," and so forth. We have left them as he wrote them and have not added a *sic*.

When references in a letter were not clear, the editors wrote to the recipient of the letter (or to his heirs), to seek clarification. The responses — many of them reflected in the footnotes — have been extremely valuable and add a dimension that would not have been possible to achieve unless these volumes were edited shortly after Stevenson's death.

The editors generally did not include letters written to Stevenson. Publishing letters written by people still alive or recently alive requires permission — a time-consuming task. Instead we have summarized the contents of an incoming letter where it was necessary to make Stevenson's reply understandable.

Under the legal agreement between Walter Johnson and Adlai, Borden and John Fell Stevenson, Adlai E. Stevenson III agreed to read each volume before publication. If he objected to the inclusion of any particular item of his father's papers, and Walter Johnson refused to accept the objection, the matter in dispute went to Judge Carl McGowan for final — and irrevocable — decision. No objection by Adlai III was raised to any of the items in this volume.

Contents

Illustrations

(*between pages 304 and 305*)

Part One

Special Assistant to Secretary of the Navy Frank Knox

1941–1944

On June 30, 1941, Frank Knox signed the form appointing Adlai E. Stevenson "Principal Attorney" in the "Office of the Secretary, Navy Department, with pay at the rate of $5,000 per annum." On July 21 Stevenson started work as a special assistant to Knox. During the next three years, he served as the Secretary's speech writer, attended important meetings with him, represented Knox and the Navy on various interagency committees, and handled many administrative matters for the Secretary.

In 1942 Stevenson said to a reporter: "You embarrass me by asking what I do. Let us call it odd jobs, most unpleasant." The reporter observed: "He looks as if he seems to enjoy that thought."

Stevenson also told the reporter:

> I like to live through this time in Washington. Each day I am impressed how many wiser people there are. It is good for the ego to get a little deflated and this is the right moment. It is also very stimulating to work for Secretary Knox, he is the most courageous and fearless and disinterested public servant I know. His farsightedness has few equals.[1]

In addition to Secretary Knox, Stevenson worked closely with Undersecretary James Forrestal and Assistant Secretary Ralph Bard.[2] In the Department of War he worked with Undersecretary Robert P. Patterson, Assistant Secretary John J. McCloy and Assistant Secretary Robert A. Lovett. Stevenson's service on numerous interagency committees led to close friendships with many people including Lend-Lease Administrator Edward R. Stettinius, Jr., and poet Archibald MacLeish, head of the Office of Facts and Figures and Librarian of Congress.

[1] Washington *Times-Herald*, April 14, 1942.
[2] See Julius Augustus Furer, *Administration of the Navy Department in World War II* (Washington: Department of the Navy, 1959).

[3]

*During 1941 and 1942, MacLeish developed a government informa-
tion policy and program. In order to fashion consistent policies for all
the agencies of government, he worked through the Committee on War
Information. John J. McCloy represented the Army, Attorney General
Francis Biddle the Department of Justice, Benjamin Cohen the White
House, James Dunn the Department of State, and Stevenson the Navy.*

*MacLeish told Stevenson's sister, Mrs. Ernest L. Ives, "He said little
but did a lot to increase the flow of information. It was then I began to
realize how effective he could be and so, I think, did a lot of others." [3]*

*On December 22, 1941, MacLeish wrote Stevenson, "I have absolute
confidence in your judgment," and eight days later he wrote, "I can't
tell you what it means to me to have you on the Committee on War Information and to have you take the part you are taking." [4]*

*When the Committee on War Information was terminated, MacLeish
wrote Secretary Frank Knox, June 16, 1942: "I cannot let the Committee
on War Information disappear from sight without writing you to tell
you how deeply I appreciate your kindness in appointing Adlai to this
service. . . . I know that I personally am deeply appreciative of the
Committee's work and particularly of Adlai's work." Knox replied on
June 23, 1942: "I am not at all surprised that Mr. Stevenson rendered
the kind of services you describe. He is one of the outstanding young
men of Chicago, and I am very happy, indeed, to have him associated
with me in the Navy Department." [5]*

*Stevenson's old friend George Ball, who left Chicago at Stevenson's
suggestion to work for the Lend-Lease Administration, wrote:*

> From the moment he arrived in the Navy Department, Adlai be-
> came a one-man recruiting office for the United States government
> exhibiting an unflagging zeal for helping even casual acquaintances
> find appropriate assignments in the public service. This was not
> merely an expression of his fondness for people, and it was certainly
> not the politician's instinct for patronage. It sprang from his deeply
> held conviction that the government needed and deserved the best
> talents that the nation could produce. [6]

*Carl McGowan, another Chicagoan recruited by Stevenson, served on
Stevenson's own staff. McGowan pointed out that Stevenson was more*

[3] Elizabeth Stevenson Ives and Hildegarde Dolson, *My Brother Adlai* (New York:
Morrow, 1956), p. 203.
[4] These letters are in the MacLeish collection, Library of Congress.
[5] Both letters are in General Records of the Department of the Navy, Record
Group 80, the National Archives.
[6] "Flaming Arrows to the Sky," *Atlantic,* May, 1966, p. 42.

important to the Navy than his title indicated. He was popular with Navy personnel, and the confidence Knox had in Stevenson — and his respect for Stevenson's advice — meant that Stevenson influenced many major political-military decisions.[7]

Archibald MacLeish stated: "Adlai was doing far more responsible war work than was generally recognized. Everyone who had to do with him in Washington in the days when he was assistant to Secretary Knox soon learned that the best way to get action in some places in the Navy Department was through Adlai." [8]

Stevenson's role as expediter in the Navy Department was exemplified in his work for Cargoes, Incorporated. He was a member of the board of directors of this government corporation, which was charged by President Roosevelt with responsibility for developing special types of cargo vessels. When the Navy's Bureau of Ships wished to retain control of certain contracts, Stevenson explained that control belonged to Cargoes, Incorporated. Malcolm S. Langford, secretary of Cargoes, Incorporated, wrote Stevenson on July 29, 1942: "Thanks ever so much for straightening this matter out. Obviously before you came into the picture the Admiral had been laboring under a misapprehension as to the facts. Now everything is lovely." [9]

Stevenson's official letters and memoranda are in the General Records of the Department of the Navy, Record Group 80, the National Archives. We are grateful to Captain F. Kent Loomis, Assistant Director of Naval History, and Robert H. Bahmer, Archivist of the United States, for helping us locate this material.

In Part One we identify only those Stevenson papers not in this collection. We identify those in the Stevenson Collection, Princeton University Library as A.E.S., P.U.L. We have retained Stevenson's own idiosyncrasies of style and spelling in his handwritten letters. Some carbon copies of his personal correspondence and diaries were saved from these years.

Since Stevenson's leave of absence from his law firm was only for three months, Mrs. Stevenson and the three sons remained at Libertyville during the summer of 1941. Cousin Davis Merwin, president of the Pantagraph Company, wrote Stevenson congratulating him on his position and in a joking fashion advised Adlai against leaving his attractive wife behind in Illinois.

[7] Interview with Walter Johnson, May 24, 1966.
[8] Ives and Dolson, *My Brother Adlai*, p. 203.
[9] General Records of the Department of the Navy, Record Group 80, the National Archives.

To Davis Merwin[10]

July 26, 1941

Dear Dave:

Thanks for your letter. As for my old lady, I think you better check up on her while you are in Illinois and report any suspicious behavior. I suspect there is plenty.

I wish I could tell you what my job is, but at the end of the first week I have not found out myself — perhaps legal maid servant to Frank Knox would be accurate. At all events, it is interesting if not important and I don't know whether I am here for my original agreement of three months or for the duration. If it is the latter, it will be damned expensive for your Uncle Adlai — so get out to Bloomington at once and shove a needle into the Pantagraph's earnings!

My sentiments to your lady.

Yours,

To Mrs. Ernest L. Ives[11]

July 27, 1941

Dear Buff —

Lying reflectively on Sunday bed this morning it suddenly came to me that I had not observed your recent birthday by so much as a note. Please forgive me — I was in an awful stew trying to get away.

I've got a grand job tho I confess I don't know yet precisely what my duties are — apparently most anything the Secretary wants to unload. I've played golf with him, been down the river for the evening on his beautiful yacht with a company of distinguished guests, lunched with him in his private dining room at the Dept. most every day and heard all the low down on whats going on & his troubles in the Dept. in a very confidential & disarming way. So I feel I'm in an interesting spot & only hope I'll be able to be of some real service to him.

The Henry Fields[12] are taking me off on an expedition to the country today — for sun & swimming — which will be welcome as I have barely been out doors, except for the rounds of golf with the Sec. — since I came — and you know what an insatiable exercise addict I am!

[10] This letter is in the Adlai E. Stevenson collection, Princeton University Library (A.E.S., P.U.L.).

[11] This letter is in the Elizabeth Stevenson Ives collection, Illinois State Historical Library.

[12] Henry Field, a friend of Stevenson's from Chicago, and a member of the Field family.

I suppose you are off presently for the ranch — if I wasn't here & in the thick of things I would be out there somewhere for a couple of weeks of health and tranquility too! And now I'm beginning to feel sorry for myself & to wish I was somewhere else — when I've really never been so happily exhausted!

I'm thinking of moving into Curtis Munson's[13] house for a few weeks tomorrow — he's going to Martinique on a "secret" mission, his wife's away, etc. Might as well save some dough & live in luxury all at once —

Love   Ad.

The Committee to Defend America by Aiding the Allies supported President Roosevelt's foreign policy and frequently helped prepare public acceptance of policies desired by the White House. New York City's Mayor Fiorello La Guardia was also serving as head of the Office of Civilian Defense.

To Clark M. Eichelberger[14]

August 1, 1941

Dear Clark:

For your personal and confidential information, I enclose a memorandum which is self-explanatory and is following out a suggestion from the President that activity along the speakers' front be increased. This sort of pipe line into the Government is something I know you want, and I hope you will plan to be here in person for a meeting next Wednesday morning at Mayor La Guardia's office to see if we can't get this under way. The man to head this up should be in the Office of Civilian Defense and will be the "spark plug" from the Government end. He should be selected with some care. I believe William Y. Elliott[15] is eager for this assignment on a temporary basis.

I will wire you the hour of the meeting later.

Sincerely yours,

Stevenson's senior law partner Edwin C. Austin wrote August 1, 1941, that he was sorry not to have seen him before he left Chicago. He expressed the "feeling that the lure of public service will be quite strong and you will stay beyond the time now anticipated."

13 A Canadian who married Edith Cummings, a Chicago friend of Stevenson's.
14 This letter is in A.E.S., P.U.L.
15 Professor of Government, Harvard University.

To Edwin C. Austin[16]

August 4, 1941

Dear Ed:

It was good of you to write me — the office letterhead always gives me a slight attack of homesickness! I had hoped for a talk with you before I left about this adventure, and perhaps it is not too late yet. I will be much disappointed if you do not let me know when you are here. I can even offer you very comfortable accommodations — temporarily! a friend who is out of town has turned over his empty house and very competent servant to me, and I am fixed for a while.

The job is quite as represented so far — trouble shooting and special assignments by Knox and Bard, and I am hoping that no administrative routine stuff will develop.

Yours,
ADLAI

On July 29, 1941, Benjamin S. Adamowski sent Stevenson an analysis of Illinois Democratic primary results from 1932 to 1940. Adamowski stated that a strong opponent of the Kelly-Nash Chicago Democratic machine who strongly supported President Roosevelt's foreign policy could win the U.S. Senate seat held by Republican C. Wayland Brooks. In 1942 Brooks was reelected and Adamowski was defeated in his bid for congressman-at-large.

To Benjamin S. Adamowski[17]

August 4, 1941

Dear Ben:

I was delighted to have your letter and your interesting analysis of the recent primary figures. I have no doubt that your anti-machine record would be an asset downstate. Moreover, I am by no means convinced, as I told you, that the name is a serious disadvantage — I just don't know. I agree that the issues, if they are clearly defined on the present basis, a year hence are going to decide the election independently of any name consideration — or machine identification, for that matter. What worries me is that the issue will probably not be as sharp as it is now. Brooks will retreat and will be talking about his patriotism

[16] This letter is in A.E.S., P.U.L.
[17] This letter is in A.E.S., P.U.L.

and war record; the [Chicago] Tribune will be sulking and sharpshooting and the atmosphere will be more Democrat vs. Republican than interventionist vs. isolationist. If the trend is that way we will need all the help, work and luck we can get to beat the Republican draft and win — we will need the machine and all it has in Chicago and the best available candidate for downstate.

As I told you, I think you or T. V. Smith[18] are the best bets — You are doubtless better qualified politically and he may have some name advantage downstate. So an important consideration becomes the enthusiasm and support of the Chicago organization. How this would develop I do not know, but I can see the manifest advantage in avoiding a bitter primary fight. Recognizing these considerations, we need the man who will get the best support from the organization in Cook County and the most support from the machine haters downstate — and that's a tough one!

I have not talked about these things with Colonel Knox but I hope to before long. I know you have his great good will and friendship and I should think he would be disposed your way if he could get Courtney[19] out of his mind. I have seen him only in a meeting since he returned from Chicago. He has not told me about his conference with Courtney, and now he has left for a week. I will let you know when he does tell me what happened.

Sincerely yours,

Adlai

Stevenson's first major assignment for Frank Knox was to draft papers, including an executive order for the President's signature, for the government to take over the Kearny, New Jersey, shipyard of the Federal Shipbuilding and Dry Dock Corporation. On August 7 the union went on strike.[20] When the corporation refused to accept the recommendations of the Federal Mediation Board, it was decided that the President must sign the executive order to place the shipyard under federal operation. But the President was meeting with Prime Minister Winston Churchill aboard ship off Newfoundland, where among other things the Atlantic Charter was proclaimed. On August 16, Roosevelt's ship was to return to Rockland, Maine.

[18] Former state senator and congressman-at-large, 1938–1940.
[19] Thomas J. Courtney, state's attorney for Cook County.
[20] CIO's Industrial Union of Marine and Shipbuilding Workers. For a discussion of this issue, see Joel Seidman, *American Labor from Defense to Reconversion* (Chicago: University of Chicago Press, 1953), pp. 42–43, 62, 63, 97–98, 99–100.

It was decided that Stevenson was to fly to Rockland to brief the President and secure his signature on the executive order. Just before he left, Knox called him into his office and informed him that Admiral Chester Nimitz had a message for him to deliver to the President in person. "You are to deliver this message to the President, and to no one else!" the Admiral stated. "Tell him I have learned today, from a heretofore reliable source, that Stalin has opened negotiations with Hitler."

What took place on his trip to see the President, Stevenson enjoyed telling in immense detail. Since the story is told elsewhere, it is sufficient here to present only a summary.[21] *Weather prevented Stevenson's airplane from taking off. When the plane finally reached Rockland, the President's ship had already docked. Stevenson persuaded the pilot to land in a primitive grass field, then flagged a car down and asked the driver to take him into town. But as Stevenson reached the station, the train was departing. He had the pilot fly him to Portland.*

After several hours watching a motion picture until the President's train reached Portland, Stevenson found the platform blocked by a huge crowd of people. Portland policemen were unimpressed when he told them he had an important message for Roosevelt. Finally Senator Claude Pepper of Florida appeared and Stevenson explained the urgency of his mission. Pepper went aboard the train and after some fifteen minutes a presidential aide, Edwin M. Watson, emerged and asked Stevenson for his papers. After Stevenson refused, Watson returned to the train. Five minutes later, Watson appeared again and said the President would see him.

Roosevelt was at dinner with Mrs. Roosevelt, Harry Hopkins, Grace Tully — the President's personal secretary — and presidential aide Marvin McIntyre as Stevenson entered the car.

"Well, Adlai," said Roosevelt smiling. "I'm glad to see you again. Glad to hear you're working for Frank Knox."

According to Stevenson, he mumbled something incoherent and said he had some emergency papers for him to sign.

"Let's have a look at them," Roosevelt said.

Stevenson's own written account of what occurred follows.[22]

---

[21] See Ives and Dolson, *My Brother Adlai*, pp. 114–119; Kenneth S. Davis, *A Prophet in His Own Country: The Triumphs and Defeats of Adlai E. Stevenson* (New York: Doubleday, 1957), pp. 230–234; Kenneth S. Davis, *The Politics of Honor: A Biography of Adlai E. Stevenson* (New York: Putnam, 1967), pp. 142–145.

[22] Adlai E. Stevenson read Kenneth S. Davis's *A Prophet in His Own Country* in galley proof. Stevenson checked the interviews he had given Davis and made suggestions or corrections in the proofs. Handwritten letter, Stevenson to Davis, March 19, 1957, in the possession of Davis. Unfortunately, the proofs with Stevenson's handwritten comments were destroyed.

I opened up my brief case clumsily and fished out the Kearny shipyard papers. I explained the intricate situation as best I could, as the President's dinner got colder and the others more restive, and pointed out where he was supposed to sign the order. He looked it over for a minute and then said:

"Well now, Adlai, you just leave all these papers in your folder with me, and I'll read them over tonight. We'll have a meeting at the White House in the morning. You fly back to Washington and arrange it. Tell Secretary Knox I'd also like to see him and Myron Taylor and the Attorney General at nine o'clock — and you be there, too."

"But Mr. President," I said, "this executive order is supposed to be signed right now!"

"I think it will work out all right this way," said the President.

"Well," I said, "if you say so I guess it will be O.K.!" I marvel that I could have talked like such a fool but I was so nervous I hardly knew what I was saying — mostly, I suppose, because I hadn't yet said the really important thing — the message — and I didn't know how to deliver it with all those people sitting around. I could see he was waiting for me to leave, and I had to come out with something. The talk went about like this:

"I have something else to tell you, Mr. President."

"Do you, Adlai? What is it?"

"Well, Mr. President, it's a message from Admiral Nimitz. He said to tell you . . . alone."

"Oh, I think you can tell me here, Adlai."

"No sir, I can't." I had a feeling that everyone was doing his best to keep from laughing! I had an idea, just in time. "Can I write it down, sir?"

"Why, certainly."

I took the menu and I wrote on the back of it, "Admiral Nimitz has heard from a heretofore reliable source today that Stalin has started negotiations with Hitler."

Then I gave him back the menu. He read it carefully and then looked up at me.

"Adlai," he said, "do you believe this?"

That was too much! I didn't know what I thought. "Why, I don't know, Mr. President," I stammered.

"I don't believe it," said F.D.R. "I'm not worried at all. Are you worried, Adlai?"

I said I guessed I wasn't so much worried after all. Then, mission completed after a fashion, I took my departure, and in my embarrassed confusion, I wheeled around and crashed right into a closed door, thus bending my crooked nose some more. I flew back to Washington, woke Secretary Knox to tell him about the meeting at the White House, and we all went over there at nine o'clock. My crowning mortification was that the President hadn't even opened the envelope containing my precious Kearny shipyard papers. He pulled them out and settled the whole business in fifteen minutes and signed the Executive Order. As for the negotiations between Stalin and Hitler, the President was, of course, right, and the Admiral's source was unreliable that time.

Stevenson was the alternate for the Secretary of the Navy on the Economic Defense Board headed by Vice President Henry A. Wallace. The board was established by Executive Order 8839, July 30, 1941, "for the purpose of developing and coordinating policies, plans, and programs designed to protect and strengthen the international economic relations of the United States in the interest of national defense." On December 17, 1941, the board's name was changed to the Board of Economic Warfare.

To Frank Knox

August 27, 1941

MEMORANDUM TO THE SECRETARY OF THE NAVY

RE: *Meeting of the Economic Defense Board, August 27, 1941:*

The meeting commenced with a consideration of assistance to the Latin American Republics through sharing of our balance for civilian consumption of certain critical materials.

The State Department presented figures and reported that a promise had been made by Under Secretary Wells[23] some time ago to provide the Latin American Republics which cooperated with us by imposition of export controls. All of the Latin American Republics, except three, have cooperated and meanwhile, are "starving" for want of various materials. The figures presented were not accurate and no final decision was taken. The general policy expressed by the Chairman seemed to be that we would share our surpluses for civilian consumption with Latin America on, roughly, the basis of our relative civilian needs subject to adjustments in special situations.

Mr. Clayton[24] suggested that small bureaus, manned by Americans, could be set up in the various Latin American capitals to talk with importers, explaining the situation and to acquire useful information.

The Chairman requested that the Treasury, Export Control Administration, Federal Loan Agency and the State Department submit reports as to what they were doing, respectively, in the general field of Economic Defense.

[23] Sumner Welles.
[24] Assistant Secretary of Commerce W. L. Clayton.

There was some discussion with relation to this Board to the new Priorities Board, presently to be created by Executive Order.

The proposed organization chart of the Board was approved.

The Chairman announced the appointment of Milo Perkins[25] as Executive Director and also announced that Dr. Winfield Riefler[26] would work in the field of Economic Re-construction on a project basis, spending a couple of days a week in Washington.

To Frank Knox

September 8, 1941

MEMORANDUM TO THE SECRETARY OF THE NAVY

RE: *Meeting of the Economic Defense Board, September 3, 1941.*

The Chairman announced that offices of the Board had been opened at Que Gardens, telephone Republic 5050, extension 1000.

Mr. Ham[27] of the Office of Price Administration submitted a plan for Government control of coffee imports (attachment). The price of coffee has risen rapidly in recent months and any plan for easing the price has important economic and political implications in South America. The Chairman referred the proposal to Representatives of State and Agriculture with instructions to consult the existing Government Coffee Committees and OPM [Office of Production Management] and thereafter to make further recommendations to the Board.

The attached report and recommendation with respect to policy and procedure in connection with export licensing and priorities treatment for Latin America was presented. Note that it restates the policy suggested at the last meeting; ie, equal treatment for the requirements of the other American Republics and United States civilian requirements.

There ensued a long discussion regarding the operation of SPAB's [Supply Priorities and Allocation Board's] authority over priorities and allocations and the administration of its decisions by OPM in so far as they relate to Latin America. The State Department expressed doubt as to whether the plan could operate officially without State Department participation in the decision of SPAB. Concern was expressed over possible dispersion of authority over exports or, alternatively, exercise of final authority by an agency which does not have all the necessary information and foreign policy and diplomatic considerations. The

[25] Milo Randolph Perkins, assistant administrator, Farm Security Administration, 1937–1939; associate administrator, Agricultural Adjustment Administration and president, Federal Surplus Commodities Corporation, 1930–1941; executive director, Board of Economic Warfare, 1941.

[26] Unable to identify.

[27] John E. Hamm, senior deputy administrator of the OPA.

Chairman requested Acheson[28] and [W. L.] Clayton to discuss with Nelson[29] methods of administering allocations of civilian supply for export.

The State Department reported that it was not yet ready to make a recommendation regarding purchase of African vegetable and mineral oils to prevent their reaching Marseilles.

No report was yet available regarding the activities and authority of the various Government Agencies which are presently participating in the field of economic defense.

The Chairman reported that all out economic warfare on Japan had been approved by the President. It was suggested that export control in the Philippines could be further tightened and that further steps could be taken by "preclusive selling" to deprive Japan of her remaining markets in Latin America through export subsidiaries on certain commodities such as cotton goods. As a result of the freezing of Japan's credits, she is now selling little and buying almost nothing in South America and, due to shipping restrictions, Japan is not taking the iron ore from the Philippines which is still available to her.[30]

Mr. Clayton reported that the Federal Loan Agency was negotiating agreements with Chili [Chile] and Argentina similar to the agreement with Mexico which has choked off Japanese access to many raw materials. Practically all Japanese shipping from the east coast of South America has now ceased.

The further de-Germanizing of air lines in Latin America was discussed. Evidently Germany is still receiving platinum, quartz crystals and mica but industrial diamonds have been effectively shut off.

A Chicago acquaintance wrote Stevenson requesting a biographical sketch.

To Newton Rogers[31]

September 11, 1941

Dear Mr. Rogers:

Thank you for your letter. I doubt if there is much to add to the "plain facts" as you so aptly put it, but here goes.

I am the son of Lewis G. Stevenson and Helen Davis Stevenson of

[28] Assistant Secretary of State Dean Acheson.
[29] Donald Nelson, chairman of the War Production Board.
[30] President Roosevelt froze Japanese assets in the United States, July 25, 1941.
[31] This letter is in the possession of Adlai E. Stevenson III.

Bloomington, Illinois. My grandfather Davis was the owner and publisher of the Bloomington Pantagraph, which was founded about 100 years ago by my great-grandfather, Jesse Fell, who migrated to Illinois in 1832. Fell was a close friend of Lincoln; in some biographies is reported to have first suggested him for the Presidency and Lincoln addressed his famous autobiographical sketch to Fell in 1859.

My father was appointed Secretary of State of Illinois by Governor Dunne and my paternal grandfather, for whom I am named, was Vice President with Grover Cleveland in 1893–97; was nominated again for Vice President in 1900 with Bryan and for Governor of Illinois in 1908.

I was born in Los Angeles; my family returned to Illinois to live when I was five or six and I was brought up and educated in the public schools of Bloomington with a year or so of school abroad, until I went to Connecticut to preparatory school in 1916, then to Princeton where I graduated in 1922. For a while I worked on the Pantagraph at Bloomington as Assistant Managing Editor; attended Harvard and Northwestern Law Schools, receiving a degree from the latter in 1926 and was admitted to the Illinois Bar the same year. After six months in central Europe and Russia as a correspondent I commenced law practice in Chicago with the old firm of Cutting, Moore and Sidley, now Sidley, McPherson, Austin and Burgess.

For a year and a half I did legal work for the government here in Washington, mostly in the Agricultural Adjustment Administration, largely because I was much interested in the agricultural problem. I own several farms in the Middle West.

At the end of 1934 I returned to Chicago to the same firm and became a partner a year later. My practice has been fairly general with increasing concentration on corporations and security issues.

I have had a good many outside interests, probably too many. For a long while I have been impressed with the necessity for a more general recognition of the growing economic and political inter-dependence of the world. Hence, I have done some work in the field of international relations and American foreign policy and have traveled a good deal. For many years I have been a Director of the Chicago Council on Foreign Relations and President several terms. I have also been President of the Board of Governors of International House at the University of Chicago and Trustee of the Library of International Relations and World Citizens Association. Among sundry charitable and civic activities, I am Vice President of the Illinois Children's Home and Aid Society; former President of the Legislative Voters League and Princeton Club of Chicago; Director of the Immigrants Protective League and Hull House. I have been much interested in civil rights and their preservation and served as the first Chairman of the Civil Rights Committee of the Chicago Bar Association.

I am a member of the Academy of Political Science, American Judicature Society, the American, Illinois and Chicago Bar Associations; the Chicago, Onwentsia, Attic, Commercial, Commonwealth and Wayfarers Clubs of Chicago and the Metropolitan Club of Washington. I am a Director of the Industrial National Bank of Chicago and the Daily Pantagraph of Bloomington.

Finally, I like to ride, read and rest — mostly rest — but in that respect this job has been a bit disappointing.

Sincerely yours,

p.s. I don't see how you can make a story out of these dull conventional facts but if you do I wish you would send me a copy with which to impress my three boys — not to mention my very insubordinate wife!

To Frank Knox

September 20, 1941

MEMORANDUM TO THE SECRETARY OF THE NAVY

RE: *Meeting of Economic Defense Board, September 19, 1941.*

Secretary Stimson[32] was present for a few minutes and expressed his intention to attend when any important matters of policy were to be considered. He expressed great interest in the program of economic warfare in the far east and his belief in a firm policy, diplomatic, military and economic with Japan.

Vice President Wallace reported that as the Executive Staff is now organized most of the work could be conducted by the Staff and that only infrequent meetings of the Board would be necessary to consider the most important questions. After some discussion the following was decided:

1. That the Board would meet irregularly upon the call of the chairman or upon the request of any Cabinet Officer.

2. That each member should have only one alternate.

3. That unless a Cabinet Officer or his alternate was present, his department would not be considered as represented at a meeting.

4. That the alternates would constitute a working sub-committee to meet at the call of the Executive Secretary and that in connection with matters requiring specific qualifications, alternates could be represented by other qualified representatives of their departments.

The chairman stated that he would send the Board members a letter

---

[32] Secretary of War Henry L. Stimson.

regarding the foregoing plan of operation and that hereafter announcements of Board meetings would be accompanied by a proposed agenda.

I advised the chairman that you wanted personally to attend meetings of the Board when possible and when major matters of policy were to be considered, and that I was confident the new plan of infrequent but important meetings would be agreeable to you.

The memorandum and recommendations of the sub-committee on the coffee situation (attachment) was considered and the recommendations adopted. Mr. Daniels, the American representative on the Inter-American Coffee Board, was present and stated that he did not think the current price too high but that the increase had been too rapid; that he approved the Committee's recommendations; that studies be accelerated to determine proper price objectives which would assure more stability.

There followed a discussion of maintenance of balanced production of critical materials; Federal Loan Agency has made arrangements to keep marginal copper producers going; OPM [Office of Production Management] has requested Federal Loan Agency to import one million tons of scrap iron from Latin America; State is making a survey of scrap supplies and embargo restrictions and efforts are being made to remove export embargos on scrap from Latin America; Cuba has lifted her embargo to December 31 and Cuban scrap should be substantially exhausted by that time; import of scrap from ports lower down the continent presents shipping problems and a choice as to whether we should import more scrap and less chrome, manganese, etc., i.e., the problem of determining what we want most and also what is best for Latin American economy.

The Department of Agriculture reported that it is planning for substantial increases in soy bean and peanut production for next year to insure an adequate supply of vegetable oils. The chairman stated he thought it likely that purchase and storage of many commodities to maintain adequate supplies was probable and that he considered the handling of critical raw materials both for the war effort at home and for economic attack abroad one of the Board's most important functions.

The Executive Secretary stated that he needed more time to work out the treatment of exports to Latin America. State reported that it was being pressed to fulfill our promise to relax exports in exchange for the imposition of export controls by Latin America so that their materials would come to us and not to the Axis. In general, the policy seems to be developing as follows: Materials which are not subject to mandatory priorities will receive general export license, thus giving Latin America equal access to such materials. As to priority materials, SPAB [Supply Priorities and Allocations Board] will, generally speaking, determine the quantity available for export to the trade area still open to us (largely Latin America) and the Economic Defense Board will determine any questions of allocation within the areas.

The Executive Secretary reported that it was intended to "demilitarize" the Office of Export Control whose functions have been transferred to the Economic Defense Board and where possible to release the military personnel for military service, replacing them with civilians.

To James V. Forrestal [33]

September 23, 1941

If you are interested in the Economic Defense Board and the current state of our "Economic Warfare" the attached release and memorandum would give you a fair idea of the state of affairs as the Board begins to get active. Please return them to me for the file.

Last night at dinner I met a classmate of yours from Baltimore, Dr. Martin, who asked me to remember him to you.

George Morgenstern of the Chicago Tribune wrote Stevenson on October 10, 1941, thanking him for lunch in Washington and saying that he had been called back to Chicago suddenly to fill in for an editorial writer. Morgenstern added that Marshall Field had just hired some editors for the new Chicago Sun. "All of us were once Hearst boys together. If Mr. Field is to carry the shining banner of enlightenment, is this the best policy?" he asked.

To George Morgenstern[34]

October 13, 1941

Dear George:

Many thanks for your letter. I presume that the sudden summons means that Chicago is to get no real light on the Washington situation!

I am much interested in what you say about the new paper and I must say that I have found developments a little disquieting myself — as have others. However, I do not dispare [despair] of all Hearst men — including yourself!

My best to Marcia.[35]

Sincerely yours,

[33] Under Secretary of the Navy.
[34] This letter is in A.E.S., P.U.L.
[35] Mrs. Morgenstern.

On October 18, 1941, Stevenson delivered a speech over the National Broadcasting Company's network entitled "Amend the Neutrality Act." [36] On October 9, 1941, President Roosevelt asked Congress to repeal the provisions of the Neutrality Act prohibiting the arming of American merchant ships and forbidding American ships from sailing through combat zones and entering belligerent ports. Congress adopted the President's recommendations and he signed the new bill on November 17, 1941. On November 3, 1941, Chicago's Mayor Edward J. Kelly wrote Stevenson: "I got a lot out of reading your recent radio talk. It does what too many public utterances are failing to do today — bring the message home."

Yesterday *morning* the Navy announced that one of our newest destroyers, the Kearny, had been torpedoed near our defense outpost, Iceland. Yesterday *afternoon* the House of Representatives voted to repeal Section 6 of the Neutrality Act by a majority of almost 2 to 1.

The Kearny is the first American Naval vessel hit since the war commenced, but the attack on the Kearny had nothing to do with the vote in the House to repeal the Section of the Neutrality Act which prevents the arming of American merchantmen. What then is the explanation for this overwhelming vote to arm our ships?

Was it because 8 American owned vessels, some of them under the American flag, have been sunk by the Germans? Was it because at least 5 of these ships have been sunk outside the combat zones?

Perhaps these incidents influenced a few votes but the real reason is that we and our Congress have learned a lot in the 2 years since the present Neutrality Act was adopted. We've got the measure of Hitler and the Nazis now! We've seen what neutrality, perfect, factual neutrality, meant to Norway. We've seen what even *cooperation* with the Nazis meant to Russia. We've seen a conquerer, the mightiest, most merciless and cynical conquerer in history subjugate and enslave a continent in 2 years, but, *most of all*, we have reluctantly come to the realization that there is something curiously inconsistent about a law which *obstructs* the accomplishment of the very thing we are *determined* to do.

More than a year ago, within a week after the invasion of *neutral* Holland, Congress at the request of the President, commenced the enactment of a long series of measures for National defense; the 2 Ocean Navy was authorized, the National Guard was called up, the Conscription Act was passed, destroyers were traded for Atlantic bases and finally the

[36] The text of this speech is based on a carbon copy marked "Extra Copy," bearing the handwritten initials AES.

policy of "All Aid To Britain" culminated in the lease lend act. In all, we have appropriated more than 60 billion dollars — to do what? To defend ourselves and to help others to defend themselves from our common enemy. Our purpose, our policy is clear. In spite of all the discordant voices, in spite of all the confusion of thinking, over the last fateful tragic year and a half we have evolved a positive and unequivocal policy. Hitler must be stopped!

No one thought the Neutrality Act made all these measures unnecessary, but through the long slow process of preparing to arm ourselves and to help Hitler's victims, we have clung to the so-called Neutrality Act — not because there was any real neutrality in American thought but because we wanted to keep out of the war ourselves if we could. And now our mighty America is at work, at work in earnest. We know what's good for us and while Russia's fate, Hitler's last obstacle on the Continent, hangs in the balance, the tools of war are crowding in a growing stream down to the sea. They *must* be delivered to the fighting lines everywhere. And materials *must* come to us from everywhere, if we are going to do the job we *must* do to end this awful episode in history before we too are engulfed.

But the job can't be done if our ships, if the arms we are feverishly building and the materials to build them, are sunk by the Nazis. It is foreign to the American tradition and instinct to make vain sacrifices. We are not beggaring ourselves to ornament the bottom of the Ocean with the wreckage of our toil. The Neutrality Act was adopted for our own protection, not for Hitler's. But now we know we can't have our cake and eat it too — we can't have victory and safety too! The House of Representatives has realistically faced the fact that neutrality is not to be had for the asking; that the Neutrality Act has neither insured our safety nor stopped Hitler; that Hitler and not Congress had the issue of safety in his hands; that he will strike when and where he pleases and that a law which *helps* Hitler is hardly consistent with our determination to *stop* Hitler. *That* is why the House yesterday voted 2 to 1 to arm our merchant ships.

There has been much discussion of this question. Many questions have arisen — honest questions asked by honest Americans. These questions deserve and should have an honest answer.

If our ships are armed — they ask — will that cause incidents which will lead us into war? If our ships are armed — they ask — will it actually give them any real protection? And they ask — some are *still* asking — would we not be better off to take our shipping off the seas entirely, rather than risk involvement? Again they ask — have we got the guns and men needed to arm our merchant ships?

I'd like to try to answer all those questions, beginning with the last one first. On Wednesday of this week the Secretary of the Navy stated emphatically that — it *can* be done, that the guns and men will be ready as soon as the ships are ready to receive them. Without going into detail, it is possible to say that our merchant ships will be armed with guns from 3-inch calibre up. They will also be armed with machine guns and some with anti-aircraft guns. Trained Navy gun crews will be placed on each ship — crews ranging from 10 men to 16 men. The arming of merchant ships has never been prohibited by international law. We have always done it, and now the Nazis have announced that ships, all ships, carrying aid to the Allies will be sunk. So it becomes imperative that American seamen should be allowed to defend themselves wherever defense is necessary. The Navy is ready to supply the means for this defense — the guns, and the men to man the guns.

To return to the first of the questions that are being asked — if our ships are armed, will that cause *"incidents"* leading to War? The answer to that question seems to be clear: American merchant vessels have already been torpedoed and sunk. Some of the ships were not flying the American flag, but in every case they were flying a *neutral* flag. In *no* case were their colors respected, and in some cases ships were sunk without warning, and with crew and passengers left to drown or save themselves as best they could. In short, American-flag vessels, both armed and unarmed, have been attacked, and unarmed merchant vessels have been sunk.

More incidents will follow — more and more. But thoughtful Americans have come to realize that the issue of war or peace for us will be settled by the *one big incident* — that Adolf Hitler has sworn to blot democracy from the face of the earth.

Our chance for peace does not depend on incidents, but on whether his savage bid for world domination can be forever ended by Allied soldiers using American material. And that means the material *must get there.*

The third question is the one which asks: Would it not be better to take our ships off the seas entirely, rather than arm them and risk attack and involvement? This is an old question; its echo is faint now. It springs from the philosophy that peace, even momentary peace, is better than principle; that to escape possible injury our great, proud Nation should meekly, abjectly surrender our rights at sea, rights for which we fought two wars.

In this connection I would like to quote a recent statement by Secretary Knox, pointing out that true neutrality — yes, and even actual aid to Hitler — is no guarantee of security. He said: "I refer to Russia. Here we have a country which not only did not practice interventionism, but which went beyond isolationism and entered into an *agreement* with Germany — an agreement for the purposes of this very war. If any country ever practiced a policy of 'Russia First,' that country was Russia. She carried it so far that she not only ignored the Allies but entered into a friendly and cooperative pact with Germany. She even shared the loot of the Polish war with Germany. Yes [Yet], the policy of 'Russia First' proved disastrous. Russia certainly served as a fearful example of the inability of a nation to remain neutral by just *wishing* to be neutral." [37]

It is of course obvious that the repeal of Section 6 of the Neutrality Act does not mean that this country expects to change its national policy one whit. It means that the crews of our vessels, wherever they may be, shall no longer be denied the means of protecting themselves and their precious cargoes. It means that we can't patrol all the seas and we can't send Naval escorts with all our ships, but we *can* give them guns and gun crews and a chance to protect themselves and fight for their lives and their cargoes — products of your dollars and your toil!

By protecting our ships and cargoes, we help to guarantee, and none too soon, that our defense production will reach the friends of democracy — production that is costing us untold millions in dollars and hours of labor. We as a Nation have signified our willingness to work and pay in the common cause. But the fact still remains — to be effective the products of democracy's arsenal must be safeguarded until they can be used against democracy's enemies. We cannot afford to waste our time and substance. *There is no time and no substance to waste.* We have seen too much of "Too little and too late" — already.

Now I'd like to consider the last question. Can a mere cargo vessel, even if armed, be effective against a modern warplane, a submarine, or a surface raider. The answer is an emphatic "Yes." Already this present war has provided us with some facts and figures to prove it. On Friday, October 10th, a report from London disclosed that since the beginning of the war, British merchant vessels have engaged in 70 successful engagements with U-boats. In some cases the merchant vessels have evaded the U-boats by forcing them to submerge under gunfire. Doubtless many were sunk, or crippled. In that same period, British merchant vessels and fishing boats have shot down more than 80 Nazi planes, some of them giant bombers capable of wrecking whole sections of a city. And one of the brightest acts of heroism of the entire war occurred when an armed British merchantman fought a German pocket battleship

[37] Germany attacked Russia on June 22, 1941.

until its guns were awash — allowing most of a large convoy to escape to England with their cargoes intact.

The greatest menace to shipping, of course, is the submarine. If a ship is unarmed, a submarine can with a few shots from its deck gun send the vessel to the bottom. No submarine would dare risk such an attack, however, if the merchant vessel were armed — a submarine is delicate and very vulnerable. It cannot risk a direct hit by a gun, even a 3-incher. Against an armed ship, the submarine must fire its torpedoes while submerged, sometimes with not even the periscope showing. Handicapped in this way, the U-boat's aim is of course much less effective. It may have to fire several torpedoes and still not effect a direct hit. Submarines can carry only a few torpedoes. When their ammunition is gone, they must return to their home port, often a long trip taking up much time, and lessening the menace on the seas.

The same generally is true of raiders from the air. In the case of an unarmed merchant ship, a bomber or fighter can dive down to within a few feet of a ship's masts. It has nothing to fear. In perfect safety, it can bomb the ship to oblivion or strafe its decks. But if the ship mounts an anti aircraft gun the pilot must bomb from a high altitude. His chances of a hit are infinitely less, and there is always the chance that the gunner on shipboard will get the first hit. Even 50 calibre machine guns can make bombing awkward.

In brief — those are the answers to the questions most often asked about arming merchant vessels. In addition, however, there is another important consideration — the *morale* of the men who man our ships. American seamen are as brave as any in the world. When they are asked to risk their lives, and at the same time are forbidden any means to protect themselves — that is asking for more than bravery. It is asking too much — and the danger is *not* hypothetical for the Nazis have struck us again and again already.

We cannot for[e]tell the shape of things to come. But we do know, we all know, that if the future belongs to the Nazis, the American dream of truth and freedom and justice will perish. We also know that Hitler's time is short. His slaves are revolting and the mighty mechanism of America is whirling faster and faster! Britain is still steadfast and the Russians are selling ground by bloody inches. Hitler is throwing everything into the great gamble for total victory. We cannot afford to hesitate now. We must send more and swifter aid and — it must get there. Our own *laws* must not obstruct our own *purpose,* our own *self interest.*

The Navy and the Merchant Marine are ready for the new assignment!

To James V. Forrestal

October 20, 1941

I would like to talk with you about this Economic Defense Board sometime. [Milo] Perkins wants the alternates to attend regularly without substitutes, so I do not think the idea of your going *occasionally* will work very well. It may be, therefore, that you should be the alternate.

Moreover, if important decisions are required you could make them on the spot for the Navy, though I have not seen anything of that kind yet. I could do any preparatory or follow up work here for you so that the time demand would be little more than the meetings. These take about a morning a week, but may diminish as the work gets better organized. At least Mr. Perkins hopes so.

Possibly you should talk with Judge Patterson[38] sometime and get his view. If you decide to take on this further responsibility, I will arrange the designation with Colonel Knox.

To Frank Knox

November 25, 1941

MEMORANDUM TO THE SECRETARY OF THE NAVY

The recent legislation repealed Sections 2, 3, and 6 of the Neutrality Act. Section 5, which is still in effect, forbids citizens of the United States "to travel" on the vessels of any belligerent state, "except in accordance with such rules and regulations as may be prescribed." It may be that the word "travel" can be construed so as not to cover crew members, but, if not, Section 5, in the absence of applicable regulations, prohibits American sailors from serving on British ships.

Perhaps thought should be given to having the President or the Secretary of State issue regulations permitting American sailors to serve on British and Allied vessels with such restrictions or conditions as are deemed advisable.

I do not know whether the question of American sailors working on British ships has arisen, but I suppose it will and that it might be well to anticipate it now unless the Department has some contrary policy.

To Loring C. Merwin[39]

November 25, 1941

Give my regards and congratulations to Hasbrouck.[40] . . . My earliest

[38] Under Secretary of War Robert P. Patterson.
[39] This telegram is in A.E.S., P.U.L.
[40] Jacob Hasbrouck, a longtime employee of the *Daily Pantagraph*.

recollection of Pantagraph is Jake pecking away at his typewriter & patiently explaining the mysteries of newspaper making. For him there can be no retirement. He will always be a large part of the fine newspaper he helped build. But if he gets restless tell him to join the Navy.

On December 8, 1941, the day after the Japanese attack on Pearl Harbor, Stevenson prepared a statement for Frank Knox and another for Knox and Secretary of War Henry L. Stimson.

SUGGESTED STATEMENT TO NAVY YARDS:

The enemy has struck a savage, treacherous blow. We are at war, all of us! There is no time now for disputes or delay of any kind. We must have ships and more ships, guns and more guns, men and more men — faster and faster. There is no time to lose. The Navy must lead the way. Speed up — it's your Navy and your Nation!

SUGGESTED STATEMENT ON A. F. OF L. WORKMEN
By Adlai E. Stevenson

America will not soon forget the heroism and sacrifice of the defenders of our Pacific Island outposts, Hawaii, Wake, Midway and Guam. And the defenders were not only the fighting men of the fighting service. A bright chapter in our history was written by the craftsmen of the American Federation of Labor who were building our defenses in the far flung Islands — peaceful, patriotic Americans who volunteered for this essential work far from home and family. But when the enemy struck they dropped their tools and joined in the defense with selfless valor and indifference to danger. Some are dead, some are prisoners, some are still fighting and many are safe.

The services will not soon forget the men in overalls who fought side by side with the men in uniforms across the Pacific from Pearl Harbor to Guam on December 7, 1941.

To Frank Knox

December 18, 1941

MEMORANDUM TO THE SECRETARY OF THE NAVY

I would like to suggest that it would be good public policy to have some ships christened by wives of workmen who have actually built them. Perhaps something of the kind could also be done with Navy air planes.

[25]

I am not sure whether it would be appropriate for Navy vessels but many people in the Government concerned with public relations think it should have careful consideration. Perhaps the idea should be brought to Admiral Land's[41] attention also.

For months, Lloyd Lewis of the Chicago Daily News, *and Stevenson's close friend and Libertyville neighbor, had been talking to Illinois Democrats about supporting Stevenson for United States Senator against Republican incumbent C. Wayland Brooks. Stevenson was more than interested. On Sunday morning, December 7, 1941, he discussed it with his old friend Hermon Dunlap Smith, a Republican. Stevenson said: "Well, it probably doesn't make any sense. You might ask around about it, though, and try to find out if there's anything to it. And let me know."*

That afternoon on the train to Chicago, Mr. Smith said to Mrs. Smith: "This political business — it opens up possibilities for him I'd never thought of."

Mrs. Smith, who had been riding in the back seat of the automobile with Mrs. Stevenson, replied that she had not heard the conversation since Ellen Stevenson had been discussing the difficulties of life in Washington and how little time Adlai was able to spend with his family.[42]

Lloyd Lewis wrote Stevenson on December 17, 1941, that there was strong sentiment for Thomas J. Courtney, state's attorney for Cook County, to oppose Senator Brooks. It was also possible that Secretary of State Warren Wright might oppose Brooks in the Republican primary. "Downstate Dems. say, however, that the very thing that works against agitation for your suitability — your absorption with distant war work, preventing not only your campaigning but even discussion of your availability — may, in case of a stalemate before the primaries, rebound strongly to your credit." [43]

To Lloyd Lewis[44]

December 22, 1941

Dear Lloyd:

Your letter gives me the picture perfectly and I am deeply indebted. To be candid — a difficult role for me — I am not disappointed. In the first place I have something to do here that needs doing, secondly, I never fancied myself as a combatant politico and, third, it's just possible that Courtney will at least vote right and follow the leader.

---

[41] Emory S. Land, Administrator of the War Shipping Administration.
[42] See Davis, *A Prophet in His Own Country*, pp. 237–238.
[43] A copy of this letter is in A.E.S., P.U.L.
[44] This letter is in A.E.S., P.U.L.

But I am concerned as much as ever about beating Brooks and all he represents, and I am fearful now that the Roosevelt haters and the "its-not-our-war-riors" will flock to his "patriots" standing in droves. I am glad Wright is developing some following. A good, bitter primary in which Wright calls Brooks by his right name and Brooks describes Wright suitably might make Tom look like a statesman.

Life is stern here now and the froth has subsided! We are hoping you and Catherine[45] will find it convenient to occupy our guest room before long. There is still agreeable conversation on all subjects — without white ties! We were relieved to hear that you were patrolling the Des Plaines — at night I presume!

Sincerely yours,

P.S. I can't thank you for all the trouble you have been to and I am still a touch dizzy that the thing ever occupied the attention of an enlightened adult — at least I never had any doubt about your enlightenment before!

To Frank Knox

January 8, 1942

If you are going to discuss press relations at the staff meeting, I wish you would also say something like this:

"My Assistant, Adlai E. Stevenson, represents the Navy on the War Information Committee of the Office of Facts and Figures which is developing a project in public education as to the Navy's manifold functions, responsibilities and limitations in the global war. The purpose and necessity for this sort of education to forestall public criticism, misunderstanding and impatience and to promote confidence in the Navy is manifest.

Christian Herter,[46] a highly experienced and competent man in public relations, has been designated by the Office of Facts and Figures as its representative in the Navy Department. His job is to help us in this and other public opinion projects relating to the Navy and I hope you will all give him every consideration. Naturally his work will clear through Admiral Hepburn[47] and the Public Relations Section and through Mr. Stevenson, our representative on the War Information Board."

[45] Lewis's wife, Kathryn.

[46] Representative in the Massachusetts legislature, 1931–1943; later a U.S. representative from Massachusetts, governor of Massachusetts, and Secretary of State under President Eisenhower (1959–1961).

[47] Admiral Arthur J. Hepburn, Director of Public Relations in the Navy Department; later senior naval adviser at the UN Conference in San Francisco, 1945.

On January 8, 1942, Professor Paul H. Douglas wrote Stevenson that he wanted to become a private or ordinary seaman but since he was forty-nine it was necessary to get a waiver on his age.

To Commander E. P. Forrestel [48]

January 20, 1942

Professor Paul H. Douglas of the University of Chicago is a very distinguished member of the faculty and a friend of Colonel Knox. He is also an Alderman in Chicago and well known throughout the State.

He will be 50 on March 26 and is desperately eager to get into the service as an ordinary sailor or soldier. Assuming he can pass the physical examination, do you know of anything that can be done with an over-age destroyer like this?

To Paul H. Douglas[49]

January 21, 1942

Dear Mr. Douglas:

Further in regard to your ambition to be a gob, please send me at your convenience a little biographical sketch with particular emphasis on the field of teaching.

I am sure it's not the kind of service you are looking for but I think they can use you anytime as a teacher in one of the training schools.

Sincerely yours

During Stevenson's service with Secretary Knox, he and columnist Walter Lippmann were in frequent communication. Lippmann often passed on, for Stevenson's information, ideas and letters he had received. Lippmann was planning a tour to the West Coast and Stevenson obtained a letter of introduction — a "directive" — from Secretary Knox.

To Walter Lippmann[50]

January 24, 1942

Dear Walter:

The enclosed "directive" presented to the Commandants will get you what you want.

[48] An officer on the staff of Admiral R. A. Spruance. This letter is in A.E.S., P.U.L.
[49] This letter is in A.E.S., P.U.L.
[50] This letter is in the Walter Lippmann collection, Yale University Library.

As to what you *should* see, I confess perplexity, and the people around here seem curiously partial to their own activities! Perhaps the best thing would be to talk to the Commandant at each district and let him suggest what he thinks most significant. Please let me know if you want anything else.

The names of the respective Commandants to which the enclosed is directed are attached.

Sincerely yours

Hermon Dunlap Smith wrote Stevenson on February 5, 1942, wishing him a happy forty-second birthday and enclosing a clipping about the Democratic senatorial primary.

To Hermon Dunlap Smith[51]

February 9, 1942

Dear Dutch:

How come you know my birthday — my wife doesn't! I am flattered and touched. Or were you figuring out my probable expectancy? If so, knock off ten years.

The political pot has been boiling and I have been conferring with a stream of Illinois statesmen. But the organization wouldn't have me — "not well enough known," so they took McKeough[52] who is one of the boys. But there were other reasons against me — most of which I'm proud of!

Love to Ellen[53] — and don't forget my wedding anniversary or Pearl Harbor!

Sincerely yours,

AD

In addition to writing speeches for Secretary Knox, Stevenson was called upon by the Navy to give some speeches of his own. He continued to develop his unique style. "My object has merely been to talk as well as I can — to honor the language and elevate the listeners if I could," he said years later. He aimed for clarity and simplicity but also for eloquence. According to biographer Kenneth S. Davis:

[51] This letter is in A.E.S., P.U.L.

[52] The Kelly–Nash machine picked Congressman Raymond McKeough, who defeated Professor Paul H. Douglas in the primary and was then defeated by Senator C. Wayland Brooks in November.

[53] Mrs. Smith.

It was, he admitted to himself, a thrilling power; it was also a sobering one, counseling humility. One could become addicted to this kind of power. And one could misuse it to disastrously egotistical ends, as Hitler had done, if one let it slip the leash of logical rigor and moral responsibility. He therefore strengthened the leash. He began, more and more, to weave strands of humor into it — a wit which not only leavened his serious message, making it more palatable, but also illumined the points he wanted to make. It was himself he most often laughed at publicly. He presented himself in the role of Everyman, whose individual fate is tragic, certainly, since the grave inevitably awaits him, but who is also a comic character as he fumbles and stumbles along his path, striving to hide his woeful inadequacy behind a thousand ridiculous pomposities.[54]

On February 17, 1942, Stevenson spoke to the Chicago Council on Foreign Relations.[55] *The Chicago* Sun *the next day stated: "The talk which Adlai Stevenson gave . . . was sufficient to make him one of the most celebrated men of the times."*

THE ROLE OF THE NAVY

Because what I have to say here today is not happy, I came prepared to divert you for a moment with an amusing story, only to discover that it has already preceded me to Chicago. I'll never tell a newspaper man a good story again. But its dry, laconic style is so characteristic of my new master, the Navy, and my so-called speech, that I am going to read it to you anyway. It's a letter to the Executive Officer of a ship from a seaman, second class, who was overdue from his leave.

"1. I left the ship on 10 days leave at my brother's farm in Cobblerock, Arkansas. On September 10 my brother's barn burned down, all except the brick silo, which was damaged at the top.

"On September 11 he decided to repair the silo right away, because he had to get his corn in. I rigged a barrel hoist, as I had been taught to do by my division officer, to the top of the silo. Then we hauled up several hundred bricks.

"This later turned out to be too many bricks. After my brother got all the brick work repaired, there was still a lot of bricks at the top of the silo on the working platform which we had built. So I climbed down the ladder and hauled the barrel all the way up. Then I secured the line with sort of a slip knot so I could undo it easier

[54] *A Prophet in His Own Country*, p. 242.
[55] The text is based on a copy prepared by the Lecture Reporting Service, Chicago. The editors have taken the liberty of correcting the spelling of a few words.

later. Then I climbed back up the ladder and piled bricks into the barrel until it was full. Then I climbed back down the ladder. Then I untied the line to let the bricks down.

"However, I found that the barrel of bricks was heavier than I was and when the barrel started down I started up. I thought of letting go, but by that time I was so far up I thought it would be safer to hang on.

"Half way up, the barrel hit me on the shoulder pretty hard, but I still hung on, as my division officer told me always to do when holding a line. I was going pretty fast at the top and bumped my head hard. My finger also got pinched in the pulley block. However, at the same time, the barrel hit the ground and the bottom fell out of it, letting all the bricks out.

"I was then heavier than the barrel and started down again. I got burned on the leg by the other rope as I went down until I met the barrel again, which went by faster than before and took the skin off my shins and hit me on the other shoulder. I guess I landed pretty hard on the pile of bricks, because I completely lost my presence of mind and let go of the line and the barrel came down pretty fast and hit me squarely on top of the head.

"2. The doctor wouldn't let me start back to the ship until September 16, which made me two days overleave."

Certainly you will agree that there is nothing wrong with a Navy that produces seamen as resourceful, shall I say inventive, as that one. And I have already prepared a similar letter to my boss which I expect to mail when I leave here, substituting the Palmer House for the silo.

My subject is "The Role of the Navy." I haven't the slightest doubt that your President and Mr. Utley[56] assigned me that subject maliciously, knowing full well that you have to do time on a destroyer to know anything about the role of the Navy and that I'm lashed to a swivel chair in Washington. But I'm going to get back at them by proposing a resolution at the next annual meeting that the permanent role of Ex-Presidents of the Council is obscurity — and by the time I've finished I know I can count on your unanimous support.

But I do want to talk to you a little bit about the Navy's functions in this war. With no thought of telling you anything you don't know, I am going to begin by reminding you that this is the first really world war in modern history. For this is war everywhere — on all the continents, on all the seas and all the oceans. This is tyranny's — and tyranny is much older than freedom — grandest, mightiest bid for mastery of the world. There are no neutrals. The combatants are all the living and the stakes are all we have and all we are. It is them or us. There are no choices, no

56 Clifton Utley, director of the council.

compromise, no turning back. There is only win or lose. And the weapons are not only guns and airplanes and ships; they are also industry, economics and ideas. The battle ground is not only the land, the sea and the air; it is the factory, the ether waves and the spirit of men. It is a war everywhere for everyone and by everyone; it is world revolution; a convulsive struggle between ancient and irreconcilable ideas — man or state. The first world war was only the warning. This time there is no quarter — and we are *losing* the war for the world which many of us thought America — the richest prize of all — could somehow escape.

I don't mean to be alarmist or sensational — certainly I would never risk it before this audience! But because the battlefields, the wounded, the dying, the awful destruction, are a long way from us here in Chicago I am afraid the reality of the war is still a long way from us — I'm afraid that too many of us groan over the newspapers, the taxes and the shortages, confident that somehow it is going to be all right. So perhaps it's worth a moment to take an inventory of our situation; to make a brief, realistic appraisal of this war which has implications for us, for everyone, implications that we are only now beginning to understand as something more than abstract, intellectual diversions. It has been going on for about 28 years, with interruptions for reorganization and realignment. The sides are now chosen for the final struggle — the Axis against the United States — and history's greatest drama is rapidly moving toward its fearful climax. The issue is in grave doubt, the pattern is spotty, and the shape of things is far from comforting.

Let us look at the four principal stages on which the orthodox, visible war is being fought. First, the North Atlantic — the sea way to Britain is open. The United Kingdom is stronger than she has ever been. Much precious Allied shipping was lost last year, (I can't tell you how much) but in the last half of the year after the occupation of Iceland [57] an enormous quantity of goods was delivered to Britain and after our Navy went to work the losses in the North Atlantic declined to a negligible quantity. But now the enemy is striking again, striking with numerous submarines a few miles off the Atlantic Coast. Since January 12 we have lost almost a ship a day. To sink any ship when the war depends on ships is a victory for the enemy. But if we withdrew escort vessels and patrol planes from Iceland to strengthen the Coast line patrol, the convoys to Britain and Russia become vulnerable and he strikes us there. If they are withdrawn from the Pacific or the Mediterranean the result is the same. And now Germany's great battleships are loose again, augmented by the Von Tirpitz and perhaps other ships.

[57] On June 5, 1941, President Roosevelt ordered American forces to replace the British in Iceland and extended American naval escort of convoys to that point.

The battle of the Atlantic is far from finished. But Britain has been immeasurably strengthened in the last year. Our first expeditionary force is already in Northern Ireland and on balance the situation is not unfavorable. Ultimately the South Irish must resolve their debate too — ultimately they too must realize that politics and hatred must yield to military necessity; that there is no escape and everyone must choose sides in this final struggle for the mastery of tomorrow.

So the battle of the Atlantic is still on and amid the confusion of voices we should keep one thing clearly in mind — Britain, the symbol and the arsenal of the Empire's battle — our battle now — is the only accessible base for operations against the continent we have left. *The preservation of that essential base depends on ships and sea power.*

On the Russian front the news continues good. Perhaps some day history will assign startling weight to the Russian courage and the Russian cold this fateful winter. Perhaps sometime we will discover that had it not been for Russia the war would have been lost while we were still debating. But in the late spring or early summer Hitler will strike East again, probably from lines hundreds of miles closer to his goals than they were last June.

Will the Russians hold? Can they hold? How much material will they have? How much can we send them? Will it be enough? Can we deliver it? How many ships will it take? Can we afford them? How many escort vessels? These are the questions that keep the lights burning in Washington and London — these dreadful questions of distribution of inadequate supplies, inadequate shipping, inadequate forces to all the fronts of this vast war. Years hence we may know how many of these questions were answered right and how many wrong. The margin of error, the area of miscalculation, is terrifying and in the case of Russia the stakes are at once a mighty ally, the Dardanelles, Turkey, the Middle East, oceans of oil and the road to India. Has the master of the West a rendezvous with the master of the East at Delhi to light the funeral pyre of the British raj? I hear he has, but Russia and an avalanche of Russians are still in his way — and last June wise men said they might hold out a month or so!

We must not forget that wherever the fighting is — Pacific, Mediterranean, Atlantic, Europe, Asia — it is all one war and that the enemy has lost more men, more material, and more morale in 8 months between the Baltic and the Black Sea than in 30 months of war everywhere else. The supply problem is terrific; 12,000 miles from the Atlantic seaboard to the Persian gulf and then 3,000 miles across Iran, the Caucasus, the Ukraine to Moscow; 4,600 miles through the North Atlantic, past the German bases in Norway to the Arctic ports of Murmansk and Archangel, transshipment and then 650 more miles by rail to Moscow, 5,000 miles across the Northern Pacific from San Francisco to Vladivostok, transshipment and then another 5,800 miles across the interminable Trans Siberian to Moscow. But that route is not healthy any longer. No, the end is not yet in Russia; and what we can do to help ourselves on that front again depends largely on ships and safe journeys through the long highways of the sea.

In the Mediterranean: the pendulum is swinging back toward Hitler's goal at Suez. Large enemy air forces are concentrated in Italy. Malta is bombed almost daily. Some of Britain's mighty ships are gone. Gibraltar, the west gate, is closed. Can the British afford to deplete their Mediterranean fleet further to send more naval reinforcements to Australia? Will troops and tanks pour over to General Rommel and will what was almost victory become defeat?

If Egypt and Suez fall the enemy can turn West and have his way with the rest of North Africa. We cannot be sure that French ports are not being used against us even now. With the Axis the only power in the Mediterranean can we be sure the great French fleet, all repaired and recommissioned, will be able, or even care to, resist the victor's blandishments? If the Axis overruns North Africa, Gibraltar is outflanked. Moreover, the harbor can be easily destroyed by the big German guns back of Algeciras and across the straits at Ceuta — guns which remind us of that genteel, democratic paralysis known as "non-intervention in the Spanish Revolution." And if Hitler gets across or around the straits even while the British hold out in Egypt our problems increase a thousand fold.

Casablanca and Dakar as enemy naval and air bases challenge our vital communications around the Cape to Suez, to the Persian Gulf, to the back door to Russia, and, if things get too tough in the South Pacific, our last route to the Orient. Finally, the Azores on the north and the Cape Verdes on the south occupied or even dominated by the Nazis through a puppet government, are the *eastern* stepping stones to our hemisphere, just as the myriad islands of the South Pacific are the *western* stepping stones.

I don't think these developments are imminent but they are part of the gigantic unfolding program of world dominion and I can assure you that the problem of North Africa is preoccupying a lot of people. Again, as in the case of Britain and Russia, what we can do to defeat the enemy in Africa depends largely on communications — ships, safe voyages and sea power.[58]

[58] On October 23, 1942, the British Army saved Egypt by attacking General Erwin Rommel's German troops at El Alamein and then started to drive them back to Libya.

In the Pacific, where the Japanese partner paid us the flattering tribute of treachery, the development of their enormous, long-planned offensive can leave even the most myopic of the "this is not our war-riors"
little doubt as to the objective. Briefly stated, it is occupation of all the
United States' territories in the South West Pacific; free access to the Indian Ocean; isolation of the unconquerable China; neutralization or
conquest of British India; ultimate conjunction with the Germans.

Gambling on large numerical superiority on land, on the sea and in
the air, the Japanese attack has developed an all-out offensive fan-wise
along an arc 4,000 miles long from Burma to the Bismarck Archipelago.

At the beginning, the United Nations' territories in this area fell
roughly into two lines: an advanced line constituted by the Malay
Peninsula, Singapore, the major islands of Borneo, Celebes, Amboina
and New Guinea, with the outposts of Hongkong and the Philippines; a
second or main line comprising Burma, the islands of Sumatra, Java and
Timor, the Continent of Australia, the islands of New Caledonia and
New Zealand.

The outposts were quickly taken, except for General MacArthur's gallant and incredible delaying action on the Bataan Peninsula. In only 9
weeks of incessant attack the enemy has not only breached but occupied the whole advance line. The main line was reached first with the
fall of Moulmein and the advance toward Rangoon and the Burma
Road. Immediate, all-out attacks on the Salween River, Sumatra, Java
and the whole main line will follow — and finally, on Australia herself,
because the Japanese High Command has little time to lose. Japan's
army is stretched all the way from the Siberian frontier to Borneo, over
4,000 miles. Her navy is convoying on many lines all over the China Sea
and the South Pacific. She was badly hit in Macassar Strait. And the
Navy's raid on the Marshall Islands (which you will sometime read
about in text books on Naval warfare) cleaned up some dangerous menaces to our supply routes and crippled her flanks badly. Everywhere
they pay an awful price, but still the Japs push on regardless of cost.

In short, the war in this area is revealed as what it always was; a
race between the Japanese blitz and the arrival of large reinforcements.
But if Japan's time is short, so is ours. If Java and Timor fall, Australia
itself is vulnerable. If Rangoon goes, our gallant ally, China, is all but
isolated and Japanese forces move by sea and land on India.

Reinforcement — as in the case of Britain, Russia and Libya — depends on sea borne communications but the naval bases — Hongkong,

On November 8, 1942, United States and British troops landed in North Africa.
Allied forces closed in on Rommel from both sides. On May 7, 1943, German and
Italian troops surrendered and the Allies now had bases for an assault on Italy.

[35]

Cavite, Amboina, Singapore — are gone or useless and Surabaya's days are numbered. The big bombers can get there by themselves and are — by Africa, Arabia and India. But the bombs, the fighter planes, the guns, the men, must go by water, and remember that it takes merchant ships about *two months* to deliver goods to Australia.

Now I have attempted to summarize the war situation as I understand it (and without revealing even the tiniest secret!), for two reasons. First, because everyone must realize, if they don't, that not only *can* we lose this war but at the moment we *are* losing it; that we are on the defensive, fighting desperate rearguard actions, fighting for time until we can catch up with the thieves whose knives were sharpened long ago, while in characteristic democratic manner, we were arguing as to whether they were thieves and whether they really planned to use knives. We must realize, I say, that Japan's new order in Asia is all but a reality, that the thief is in sight of the wealth of the Indies, and that it may take years of heartbreaking war and blood and treasure to drive him slowly back in the Pacific; that there is nothing very reassuring, nothing to support satisfied complacency anywhere in the panorama; that when Manila, Singapore, Java fall to the enemy[59] it is a matter of vital concern to us here in Chicago; tin and rubber and a dozen other commodities are not only essential to civilian life and comfort but to our war effort, and as the enemy cripples *us he* gets stronger materially and strategically.

Oil is the best example. Japan has to import ¾ of her oil. There is much in the Indies that Japan wants — but oil more than tin or rubber or anything else. The East Indies, together with British Borneo and Sarawak, produce about 8½ million tons a year — all the Japanese want to build the Empire of the East on one side of us, while Hitler, with Russian and Iranian oil, is building the Empire of the West on the other side. True, the oil wells, the storage tanks and refineries — a hundred years of thrifty development and hundreds of millions of investment are being destroyed as the sturdy Dutch slowly retreat across their green islands. But new wells can be dug, perhaps long before the Japs are likely to be in desperate need of fuel, thanks in part to *our* flourishing oil business with Japan these last few years.

But that's only half the story. If the Dutch Islands fall — and it is

---

[59] Singapore surrendered on February 15, 1942; by mid-May most of Burma was under Japanese control and the Burma Road to China was sealed off; Manila had fallen by January 2, 1942, Bataan surrendered on April 9, 1942, Corregidor on May 6, 1942; all of the Netherlands East Indies surrendered by March 9, 1942. On May 7–8 U.S. naval and air forces turned back a Japanese invasion fleet in the Coral Sea separating Australia from the Solomon Islands. This was the turning point of Japanese expansion.

well to remember that they are 3,500 miles long with a population of 70,000,000, almost the same as all Japan — where do *we* get oil? Australia has no oil wells; there are no other sources of oil in that part of the world. If Australia becomes the last rampart in the South Pacific, when the reserves are exhausted, oil for the planes and ships and mechanized forces would have to be hauled all the way from the American mainland or the Near East — another long and hazardous supply route. That is, if we have the tankers to do it. The United Nations have none too many and you have observed that the rattlesnakes have been paying marked attention to tankers since December 7.

But the Indies are not yet lost by any means. Sumatra is very vulnerable, but Java will be the main stronghold and the indomitable Dutch had an army of 100,000 in the Indies when the mother country was invaded in May, 1940. No figures have been issued since. Admiral Helfrich had at the start 5 cruisers, 8 destroyers, 20 submarines and a force of torpedo boats and auxiliaries and, as you know, this little fleet has been striking mighty blows.[60] The shortage is planes, tanks and artillery.

The line has become a melancholy cliché. As everywhere, it is a race against time in the Netherland Indies. But reinforcements have arrived and more are on the way. The defense of Singapore saved a few days and sapped much enemy strength. The Japanese tide MAY be halted on the long beaches of Java.

In the second place I attempted to point out in my crude appraisal of the war situation that on every front the problem is supply; first to gain equality in the air and stop the enemies, then superiority and finally overwhelming offensives. In short, victory — ultimate victory everywhere — depends on supply, sea borne supply. Our task is not only to make the bombers and the fighters and the bombs and tanks and artillery, but also the ships to deliver them in, and it's the Navy's job to see that the ships get there — get everywhere. The Navy's task is colossal. In 1917 it was one sea, one direction. This time it is all the seas and all directions at once. The Navy's front is planetary. We have 12,000 miles of coast lines to guard. In 1938 we carried from port to port in this country 338 million tons of cargo. Think what would happen to our already overburdened internal transportation system if it had to shoulder any substantial portion of that burden.

Then there are the far flung bases, built and building, and the Panama

[60] An Allied fleet under Dutch Admiral C. E. L. Helfrich was wiped out between February 27 and March 2, 1942, in the Battle of the Java Sea. For a history of the Navy in World War II see Samuel Eliot Morison, *History of United States Naval Operations in World War II* (15 vols., Boston: Little, Brown, 1947–1962), and his *The Two-Ocean War: A Short History of the United States Navy in the Second World War* (Boston: Little, Brown, 1963).

Canal to protect, and the myriad ships crawling over the oceans of the earth carrying away from our shores the planes, tanks, munitions and all the countless things you are making and the men at the far away fighting fronts are praying for. They have to be protected and their precious cargoes. And there are also myriad ships steaming slowly night and day across the wastes of water bringing to us the numberless things we need. The ships are precious — there are nowhere near enough ships — the cargoes are precious, very precious, in spite of our vaunted self sufficiency about which we once heard so much. They need protection.

It is 9,000 miles from the nearest port of embarkation in India to the nearest port in the United States. During 1940, 1,450,000,000 ton miles of manganese moved to this country. It will be much farther now. From Brazil, 3,000 miles away, came 1,200,000,000 ton miles. From South Africa, about 7,000 miles away, 1,125,000,000 ton miles. Take chromium — 1,500,000,000 ton miles from Mozambique, 900,000,000 ton miles from India and the Philippines and lesser amounts from Egypt, Turkey, New Caledonia and Cuba. Rubber, tin, graphite, copper, wool, mica, lead, bauxite, cork, zinc — the list is long and in ton miles the aggregate figures are astronomical and meaningless, except to demonstrate that supply is a two-way problem and to illustrate the immensity of the Navy's task in this world war.

It amounts to this: There are mines to be laid; mines to be swept; harbors to be patrolled; coasts to be guarded; skies to be guarded; and the endless lines of ships creeping across the world to be protected, and finally there is fighting to be done. The job requires huge merchant tonnage and a huge Navy.

You have not forgotten that in 1922 we turned our backs on the world politically and really went to work to get rich in a big way. We were going to sell and everyone else was going to buy, and the fact that the buyers were broke didn't make any difference. We also inaugurated the new era of political indifference and commercial magic by scrapping 1,000,000 tons of Navy.[61] Ten years later when the mysterious prosperity was overtaken by mysterious poverty our Navy had sunk to levels below Britain and Japan, even France and Italy, in numbers of effective fighting ships. But that man in the White House had another extravagant idea and little by little got the Navy started again. Now Congress gives the Navy anything it wants and, thanks to some foresight you have a great Navy, growing greater every day.

[61] At the Washington Naval Arms Limitation Conference, February 6, 1922, Great Britain, the United States, and Japan agreed to a 5:5:3 ratio in battleship and aircraft tonnage; a ten-year "holiday" on building capital ships; and a restriction on the burden of all battleships to 35,000 tons. The U.S. also renounced strengthening, in a military sense, any bases, including Guam and Manila, west of Pearl Harbor.

I am not going to talk about battleships, cruisers, destroyers, submarines, navy yards, air stations, aircraft, aircraft carriers, laboratories, ordnance, armor plate, torpedoes, tenders, mother ships, radar and all the infinitely complex and intricate equipment and organization of a modern Navy.

But I can tell you that this is an all ocean war and we still have a one-ocean Navy, albeit by far the most powerful in the world. But the job is being done faster and faster. Yesterday the Alabama was launched 9 months ahead of schedule. Destroyers used to take 2 years or more from keel to commission, now they take 10 months. We need more and more destroyers and more and more planes and they're coming now, faster and faster, to escort grubby freighters from the Arctic to the Southern Cross, and to raid the enemies' sea borne lines of communication. Eighty-six navy yards, 140 private yards, countless airplane and ordnance plants are forging the greater Navy, 24 hours a day and seven days a week! We have made enormous strides since Dunkirk and now that we have begun to fight we are building as we've never built before.

You have asked yourself where the Navy is, what it's doing. Perhaps you've been impatient. Perhaps you have heard alarming rumors. Perhaps you've talked to what Commander Brown, the Public Relations Officer for this District, very aptly calls "The December 8 Admirals who are more plentiful than Saturday night quarterbacks." I know a lot of these sea dogs want to know just what the fleet's doing, if anything, and why it doesn't crash through with a blow, as some of them put it to me with some vigor, "right at the heart of Japan," or as another said, "Why don't we destroy the Japanese fleet first, or did they destroy *us* first at Pearl Harbor?" I have tried to give you some idea of the *enormous unsung* job the Navy is doing and, as for assault, you saw something of it in Macassar Strait and in the perfectly synchronized raid on the Marshall Islands at points as much as 1500 miles apart.[62]

And if you suspect the Navy of inactivity because it hasn't bombed Tokyo and destroyed the Japanese fleet, remember that a fleet must be anchored at a base. Its effective operating range is only about 2500 miles and it is 3500 miles from Hawaii to Japan. Moreover, there are undamaged Chinese held air fields that offer the best opportunity for bombing Japan, which means Rangoon and the Burma Road, thousands of miles away, must be saved now. The distances in the Pacific are enormous. At 15 knots it's a 10-day voyage to Yokahama from Hawaii, 14 to Manila,

[62] Between January 23 and 28, 1942, four American destroyers, assisted by units of the Dutch navy, inflicted heavy losses on an enemy convoy in the Macassar Straits. On February 1, 1942, two U.S. carrier task forces attacked Kwajalein and other points in the Marshall Islands.

16 to Singapore. Of course, Naval vessels can steam much faster than 15 knots. But fuel consumption increases at a fantastic rate at higher speed. A destroyer with a cruising range of 6,000 miles at 15 knots would have to refuel [at] about 1,000 miles at 36 knots.

And the speed of a convoy is the speed of the slowest freighter — 10 knots is about the top. The effective range of ships, particularly war ships, is smaller today than in the Naval wars of the Napoleonic era. Fuel, instead of wind, is a tremendously limiting factor. Modern guns consume ammunition at a fearful rate and must be constantly replenished. The bottom of a steel ship must be kept clean to maneuver swiftly. Propelling machinery is delicate and must be constantly maintained and repaired. It's all very unlike the simple problem of canvas, cordage, cannon balls and hardtack. Logistics, the science of supply, preoccupies the Commander today, whether his forces are fighting on land, at sea, or in the air.

Japan has the great advantage of interior lines. The advance bases are gone and we must fall back to Australia and New Zealand. We cannot expect drastic action without air superiority, which is to say until the basic problem of supply is solved. The Navy is cleaning out the pirates, dusting off the stepping stones to Asia to get the bombers and the fighters to the British, Dutch and Australians — to get them the material that wasn't there in Luzon, in Malay and Singapore — that is never there when democracies are attacked. If it was they wouldn't be attacked. Perhaps it's someone's fault it wasn't there. Perhaps there was too much in England and not enough in Asia, or perhaps there just wasn't enough to go around. Take your choice. The job now is to get it there and arrest the Jap tide, stabilize the lines and start to win back, the meanwhile harry him on the flanks, cut his communications[,] pick off his ships and planes and wear him down.

You have heard from your great Navy and you will hear from it again and again where and when strategic and not foolhardy considerations dictate. And when you're hungry for great sea battles, please don't ever forget that victory depends on endless lines of freighters crawling across *all* the seas and that they have to be protected.

One reason there has been so much misunderstanding about the Navy, one reason why the American people feel themselves uninformed, why one hears complaints that it is the "Administration's war," or a "confidential war," coupled with the plea that the people be "let in on it" is because of the delicate balance between aid and comfort to the enemy and aid and comfort to the people, between what the service calls "security" and you call "secrecy." Yesterday I had a letter from a prominent man in Colorado complaining about large scale deception in the government's information policy generally, and specifically in the case of Pearl Harbor. I want to quote a paragraph:

"If the people come to believe that the administration is gagging press, radio and private citizens, in order that the public may be kept in ignorance of facts *which the enemy knows,* and is doing so to escape criticism, great damage will be done to the national solidarity."

So far as I know there has been no deception in the case of Pearl Harbor unless it was the omission of detailed information on the damage to the ships — not specifically named. And you will note that the complaint assumes that the enemy knows all about the damage. That's a very considerable assumption and the experience of intelligence work in all countries has taught us that we can never be sure what our enemies know and what they don't know; popular belief to the contrary notwithstanding. There are too many lives and too much at stake to take anything for granted, and I am reasonably sure that Japanese agents have not gotten aboard and inside the ships to determine the degree of the damage. Moreover, the communication of information — even what you can see — presents some difficulties now that we are at war and have taken censorship measures we couldn't in peace time.

In theory a democratic people is entitled to all the information its government has. But in war it is entitled, obviously, only to what is consistent with national security. The balance between news and security presents infinite and daily problems. It is a constant tug of war between information agencies and security agencies. The enemy wants to know everything. His agents have even been instructed to comb annual reports of corporations for production figures. He is adept and experienced in the war of nerves and the arts of uncertainty. How many of you have asked, "What is Hitler going to do next?" Heretofore he hasn't been troubled with uncertainty about what we were doing. We have a lot to learn about security vs. information and we can't afford many mistakes.

Heretofore the government has given the enemy everything he wants to know in elaborate, detailed and official form about our industrial production. We even published airplane figures until a few months ago. Information is essential to preserve healthy criticism of the conduct of the war. But if they know what kinds of weapons we are producing and in what quantities and where, they can make some shrewd guesses as to our war plans and, of course, direct sabotage to the critical spots. So hereafter public information on the progress of the production effort will be confined to overall dollar expenditure figures and some safe yardstick to measure progress on the President's specific assignments for this year — 60,000 planes, 25,000 tanks, 8,000,000 tons of ships, etc.

I hope and believe the information problem will evolve satisfactorily and in the sombre days ahead patience and understanding will increase and people will come to realize that information is a deadly weapon in this war. At least I am confident that what you get from the government will be the truth in contrast with the Axis strategy of falsehood and terror.

In the dreary days of frustration and doubt that lie ahead, we must never forget that the enemy is ceaselessly attacking the minds and spirit of men and that you and I and everyone of us are on the barricades too. Let's not forget that for several years before Pearl Harbor, Hitler propaganda in this country attempted to paralyze our thinking, to give the impression that the war was none of our business, that America should not prepare to defend herself, that England started the war, that Hitler had no intentions against the United States, that Germany's cause was just, and that England expected the United States to fight her battles. German propaganda was hard to identify; it was widely circulated, often by innocent, loyal Americans. Many rumors, all of them false, were spread throughout the country to demoralize not only the draftees in our camps, but their parents at home. Stories were circulated that epidemics had broken out in army camps, that the food was bad, that desertions were numerous, etc. As in France, postcards were mailed to parents, painting false pictures of conditions in the camps. The British, the Jews, and the administration were unscrupulously accused of driving the country into war.

War has only intensified the barrage of propaganda. Day after day the axis short waves pour falsehoods into the United States. Hitler instructs his agents here, not by code, but by short wave. From the programs, they learn the current "line," and act upon it, spreading rumors that will leave the impression on American minds that Hitler wishes to leave. German stories of losses at Pearl Harbor, for example, are the signal for the Hitler agent to spread wild rumors: that we have lost our fleet, that important facts are being withheld from the American public.

To destroy unity and create unrest, Hitler will try to set capital against labor, white against Negro, Christian against Jew. While reading our newspapers, we must remember that he controls the sources of news in Europe, even in Sweden and Switzerland. We read what he wants us to read. He will try to play upon our fears, raise hopes, confuse and bewilder us. Through statements from so-called "authoritative sources," he will present false pictures, lead us to believe that he is weak when he is strong, napping when he is preparing to spring.

Hitler now wants us to believe that: Democracy is a dying doctrine. Our armed forces are weak. The "New Order" is inevitable. We must concentrate all our strength in the Pacific. The cost of the war will bankrupt us. Civilian sacrifices will be more than we can bear. Stalin is getting too strong. Bolshevism will sweep over Europe. Our real danger is the Jap. We must join Germany to stamp out the "Yellow Peril." American democracy will be lost during the war.

To spread these lies, Hitler will pull every trick in his black bag. But we will not be fooled. Because we know that he is frightened; that his troubles are many and his hours few. He knows that if we have the will to do it we and we alone can beat him. This year, perhaps the next six months, will tell the story. Can we do it? I submit, not in our present frame of mind. Not until we get mad, fighting mad. Not until all thought, all hope of miraculous escape is banished. Not until we have the will to win; a burning, fierce will to save our great ideal for tomorrow. Not until every vestige of complacency is blasted. Not as long as ladies bravely say they've bought their last dress, confident they'll get another when they want it. Not as long as solemn gentlemen gravely assure us that our greater resources will prevail. This dreary old business of matching resources has been a false friend. The bankrupt brigands haven't any oil and they haven't any fats and they're short of this and short of that, but they've got all of Europe and most of Asia and I haven't seen a single resource spring up to smite them!

No, we have been cursed with calm; not grim determination, but the calm that is the cousin of apathy, and apathy is defeat. There has been an idea that because we never lost a war we can't lose this one. But we can and we probably will if we don't perform miracles of production this year. Frankly the production effort is not good enough. We've got to become intolerant and contemptuous of delay, of indecision, of flabbiness. We can't risk any obstruction by labor or management. The big offensive of 1941 [1942] is in the factories of America. The tone, the pitch of the worker and the manager will reflect the community. The thrust, the success of the offensive depends on all of us, on single-minded pityless dedication to the job of forging the weapons. There's no more time for argument. We've got to clear the decks, throw overboard the paraphernalia of peace and hit the ball, for we're in the finals now and it's going to be no game for the faint-hearted.

One last word. We're going to do it because we're awake now. The troubled sleep is over and we're on our feet and getting angry. Hong Kong, Manila, Singapore, our symbols of security, are falling, but so is fat and fun and filibuster. And courage, honor and faith have not fallen!

And when it's over, please remember that if the four freedoms of the doctrine of the Atlantic Charter is to have a chance, peace must be guaranteed and there will be worthy work for your mighty Navy on the long journey to the promised land — in the *American age!*

QUESTION: Can you give us an idea of how much naval assistance we can expect from the South American republics?

MR. STEVENSON: I am not letter perfect on that at all. I believe, however, that it is safe to say that the total amount of assistance we can expect is negligible at best. Brazil has some ships, hardly anywhere enough to patrol her own coastline. The Argentine has some, but the coastline is very long indeed, as you know. Chile has a little navy and likewise an enormous coastline. I think if anything the converse is true, that the South Americans will expect a great deal of help from us.

MRS. EMMONS BLAINE: I would like to ask one question. I feel that the only reason for hearing a dark picture or seeing a dark picture and having it presented to us, is to evoke the question: What is there for us to do, each one of us, in the United States, in the light of this dark picture? I would like to give two answers that I received from Mr. Stevenson, and then I will ask him to pick up from there and go on. One answer is patience; another answer is to have trust. Now I will ask Mr. Stevenson to go on.

MR. STEVENSON: I think perhaps Mrs. Blaine has indicated my answers all right, perhaps more eloquently in their brevity than I can answer them. I don't know what every one of you can do. At the same time I must say that I think there are quantities of things you can do. I think the kernel of our state of mind, that I see reflected here and elsewhere, is an anxiety to participate, and there is a great sense of frustration because there doesn't seem to be enough apparently for participation. Over all, I think it amounts to this: That your joint concern, your apprehension, and what Churchill called your calm, grim determination are the things that create the spirit and the atmosphere in the community that can do the job.

The job at the moment is production and preparation. That means that every man in the country who has to do with production has one job to do, and he ought to be doing it with all the energy and all the resource and all the vitality he has to spend. When I get down to the minutiae of detail with respect to what the ladies might do beyond the joint effort to create the will to win, I should prefer to call upon the Office of Civilian Defense, if it is here represented!

QUESTION: What do you include in the 12,000 mile coastline?

[44]

MR. STEVENSON: Only continental United States.

QUESTION: You said that the Alabama was launched nine months ahead of schedule. By what standard do you say it was launched nine months ahead of schedule?

MR. STEVENSON: My understanding is that when the keel was laid down, a schedule — as is usually the case in ship construction — was prepared, which schedule establishes a measure, a standard, a yardstick against which construction of the vessel shall be tested for progress. The launching of the Alabama was originally set for nine months from now.

QUESTION: Can you divulge why the Normandie was so vulnerable? [63]

MR. STEVENSON: I wish I could divulge it. I wish I knew it myself. I can only say that an acetylene torch is very dangerous. It is a very dangerous implement and it is a nightmare to ship constructors to have these dangerous weapons, if you please, of sabotage or of negligence lying about. As to why it was vulnerable, whether it was inadequate protection, inadequate investigation of the people who were employed to work on the Normandie, the present investigation will disclose.

QUESTION: Would you be willing or in a position to explain why there was a so-long delay to have the 24-hour day and the 7-day week, which was advocated by some well-informed men months ago?

MR. STEVENSON: I must say that I find it somewhat difficult to answer the question, because, unhappily, we haven't even got a 24-hour day yet in many industries. We haven't even a 7-day week in a good many. I can cite you cases of industries where there isn't even Saturday afternoon work going on yet. That is the kind of thing I am talking about. That is why we have to speed up. We have to hit the ball as we have never hit it before. It is why you and everyone in every community in the country cannot countenance, cannot tolerate, any delay, any interference with what has now become a matter of life and death. Are there any further questions?

QUESTION: This is now past but why didn't they have some planes at Singapore?

MR. STEVENSON: I attempted to suggest during my remarks that I didn't know why they weren't there, or, rather, why there weren't enough there. Perhaps it was because there weren't enough to send there. Maybe there were too many in Britain. Maybe there were too many withheld in Libya. Maybe there just weren't enough to go around.

---

[63] The French liner S.S. *Normandie*, which had been commandeered by the U.S., burned and sank while it was being converted to a troopship.

Here is a very good written question. I wish I were competent enough as a propagandist to know all the answers: "You say that the enemy is attacking our minds and our spirits. What are the healthiest means of combatting that kind of attack?"

Of course you must bear in mind that we, too, are attacking the minds and spirits of the enemy, of the occupied territories and of Germany herself. We, too, have continuous short-wave broadcasts, beamed all over the world, and I want to tell you, because it is a matter of great interest to me and I have had occasion to look into it at some length, that it is based on fact. What we are doing in the way of counter-propaganda, counter-intelligence, if you please, is to send them factual reports of what America is doing, what America's state of mind is, of what our determination is. It is propaganda based on the strategy of truth rather than the strategy of falsehood.

As to how to counteract the effect of enemy propaganda within this country, I can only suggest that we closely scrutinize, that we develop a sense of discrimination about everything we hear. We must be sure that we do not lend ourselves to the perpetuation or furtherance of rumor, that we do not become a party to recrimination and unintelligent, unreasoned, confusing criticism and attacks on the leadership or on the commander or on anybody else, that we be as considerate, that we be as patient, and that we be as understanding as we can.

To Frank Knox

February 25, 1942

MEMORANDUM TO THE SECRETARY OF THE NAVY

As you know, the Committee on War Information is an interdepartmental committee advisory to the Office of Facts and Figures. The latter is charged with the responsibility of formulating information policy for the Government and is of great importance and utility to the Navy. The number and variety of questions relating to the Navy which are discussed at meetings of the Committee has increased since the war began.

I have had excellent cooperation from the Office of Public Relations and from the security officers of CNO [Chief of Naval Operations] in connection with various matters which required their assistance. However, as the war develops it becomes more and more apparent that many information problems are becoming closely related to operations and war plans. It would be helpful, therefore, if the Commander in Chief [of the United States Fleet] or the Chief of Naval Operations could designate some officer familiar with operating problems with whom I could confer directly from time to time. My demands would be infrequent at most.

Accordingly I suggest that Public Relations and the Commander in Chief or the Chief of Naval Operations each be requested to designate an officer with whom I can confer when necessary and who can attend CWI or OFF meetings when matters within their fields of special knowledge are being considered.

Stevenson's old Chicago friend Clay Judson, who had presented the America First Committee's position in debates with Stevenson when Stevenson headed the Chicago Committee to Defend America by Aiding the Allies, wrote Stevenson on February 24, 1942, that he agreed with 99 per cent of his February 17 speech. But, he added:

> I have only one minor criticism to make, and you will recognize that it evolves out of my own experience and convictions since September, 1939. In the course of your address you spoke critically of those who, prior to December 7, had been contending that it was the Administration, the British and the Jews who were getting us into this war. I recognize your reference. So far as I am concerned, I was always opposed to any mention of race in this connection, and I do not write from the standpoint of one who thinks the Jews should be blamed in any way whatsoever. Neither do I think now that any good could be accomplished by any reference to the policies pursued by the Administration, or to Mr. Churchill's diplomatic triumph so far as our participation in the war is concerned.
>
> What I do feel very strongly is that any reference of the kind you made can accomplish no good whatsoever. On the contrary it tends to stir up division of opinion and disunity. Every American should now be united on one job, and that is to do everything possible to win this war. Name calling and criticism of positions taken before war was declared, it seems to me, are unwise and unfair. They are unfair because now in time of war no answering argument can be made. They are unwise because they detract from our major objective, which should be to win this war.[64]

To Clay Judson[65]

February 24, 1942

Dear Clay:

Thank you for your letter and your flattering remarks about my "effort." The paragraph to which you refer reads as follows:

[64] This letter is in A.E.S., P.U.L.
[65] This letter is in A.E.S., P.U.L.

"Let's not forget that for several years before Pearl Harbor, Hitler propaganda in this country attempted to paralyze our thinking, to give the impression that the war was none of our business, that America should not prepare to defend herself, that England started the war, that Hitler had no intentions against the United States, that Germany's cause was just, and that England expected the United States to fight her battles. German propaganda was hard to identify; it was widely circulated, often by innocent, loyal Americans. Many rumors, all of them false, were spread throughout the country to demoralize not only the draftees in our camps, but their parents at home. Stories were circulated that epidemics had broken out in army camps, that the food was bad, that desertions were numerous, etc. As in France, postcards were mailed to parents, painting false pictures of conditions in the camps. The British, the Jews, and the Administration were unscrupulously accused of driving the country into war."

I don't see how you can take exception to this statement. Certainly the Axis continually built its propaganda around the British, the Jews and the Administration.

Sincerely yours,

On March 11, 1942, Henry D. Chaplin of the Rumford Press wrote Walter Lippmann that over twenty men he knew had been given definite assignments in the Army, Navy, and various government agencies but that final approval had not been forthcoming for them to go to work. Mr. Lippmann sent the letter to Stevenson.

To Henry D. Chaplin[66]

March 17, 1942

My dear Mr. Chaplin:

My friend, Mr. Walter Lippmann, has been good enough to refer to me your letter of March 11.

I shall not attempt to "explain" the difficulties incident to getting the people into war work but I would very much like to know whether the twenty men of your personal acquaintance who "have been given definite assignments in the Army, the Navy and various government agencies" have been commissioned as officers or what the character of these "assignments" is.

My impression was that there is little delay between commissioning

[66] This letter is in the Walter Lippmann collection, Yale University Library.

and assignment to active duty in the services except in some classifications where there is an abundance of reserve officers. Perhaps I am wrong in this regard and if I am I am sure the matter should have prompt attention.[67]

Sincerely yours,

On April 17, 1942, Professor Paul H. Douglas wired Stevenson asking him to use his influence to have the age limit lifted so that he could enlist as a private in the Marine Corps.

To Paul H. Douglas[68]

April 24, 1942

Dear Paul:

I know you were pleased with the Secretary's letter to General Holcomb[69] and I thought you might like to know what he said about you and your value to the Marine Corps was spontaneous and wholly sincere.

I hope you survive the physical examination and all goes well.[70] Keep me advised.

Best regards!

Sincerely yours,

To Frank Knox

April 25, 1942

MEMORANDUM TO THE SECRETARY OF THE NAVY[71]

The Navy Department and the War Department should have a policy and the same policy with regard to labor relations in private plants, requisitioned or merely operated by the government. Any such policy should have the President's sanction.

I suggest the following outline of a general policy designed to preserve the status quo in labor relations. Of course special circumstances

[67] Mr. Chaplin thanked Stevenson for the openmindedness of the Navy Department to his letter and added that actual assignments had now been made final for a number of those he had written about.

[68] This letter is in A.E.S., P.U.L.

[69] General Thomas Holcomb of the U. S. Marine Corps.

[70] Douglas passed the physical and entered the Marines as a private in May, 1942. He served with the 1st Marine Division at Peleliu and Okinawa, was severely wounded and received the Bronze Star, and was mustered out as a lieutenant colonel in 1946.

[71] This memo is in A.E.S., P.U.L.

in each individual case may require ad hoc departures to insure maximum production.

> 1. *When the government takes possession of and operates the plant* (as at Federal, Air Associates and Brewster).
>> a. *If due to mismanagement or troubles other than a labor dispute:*
>> The government will preserve the status quo and accord labor all existing contract rights — including closed shop, checkoff, union maintenance, etc.
>> b. *If due to a labor dispute* (other than a wage dispute):
>> The government will preserve the existing status quo and accord labor all existing contract rights but no additional ones.
>> c. *If due to a wage dispute:*
>> The government will use its own discretion as to wage changes and will preserve the existing status quo in other respects.
>
> 2. *When the government acquires a plant by requisition, purchase or otherwise and operates it directly.*
>> The plant then becomes part of the government establishment, existing labor agreements will be cancelled and the plant will be operated like an Army Arsenal, a Navy Yard, etc. (Under Civil Service or not, as conditions dictate). The government will fix wages, will not "bargain collectively" in the technical sense or recognize labor organizations as such.

I believe the foregoing summarizes your views and I would be glad to submit the reasoning for each suggestion.

If this seems a reasonable approach, I will discuss it with the War Department. Admiral Fisher[72] concurs and I believe Ralph Bard [73] will also be in agreement.

To Frank Knox

May 21, 1942

MEMORANDUM TO THE SECRETARY OF THE NAVY

Removal of Italians from the classification of enemy aliens has interested me for sometime. It is now being widely discussed in the government.

---

[72] Admiral Charles W. Fisher, Director of Shore Establishments.
[73] Assistant Secretary of the Navy.

I hope you will look through this memorandum and let me have your reactions. The proposal will be debated at the Committee on War Information meeting on Monday.

To Walter Lippmann[74]

June 9, 1942

Dear Walter —

Such a gentle woman merited a better & wiser philosopher. Your note should have gone to her. As for my evening — it was epic, what with a "civilized" lady, an air marshal and Mme. Bruggaman[75] — for whom I've a passion, albeit elevated.

Sometime lets talk about the Navy Dept. My vision is opaque, but I'm tempted to think things are moving apace — and ahead.

Yrs

On June 24, 1942, Stevenson and newspaperman Paul Smith, now a lieutenant commander in the Naval Reserve, left Washington on a tour of inspection of Navy installations in the Caribbean. They returned to Washington, July 8. Stevenson kept a handwritten diary of the trip.[76]

Wed. June 24, 1942

Took off 1 hr late from Wash by EAL [Eastern Air Lines] for Miami. All curtins drawn in and out of town — [illegible], Savanna & Jacksonville. Trip uneventful except for right angle turn off the course below Jacksonville when pilot circled object that looked like submarine periscope about 3–4 miles out to sea. Wonder why commercial planes don't fly off shore course for additional sub. detection where it makes little difference in their course, via Fla east coast. Plane late in Miami — Lieut. Wm Pepper DPRO [Deputy Public Relations Officer] met us in station wagon & drove to McAllister Hotel. Decided to take drive before dark & to check luggage with Pan Am first. Customs & immigration censorship & Naval intelligence inspections very slow — inefficient, inexperienced operators. No special treatment for officers or gov. officials travelling on orders. Must submit to all inspections. Had to get license to take blueprints in my brief case from Naval District Hqs. — customs

74 This handwritten letter is in the Walter Lippmann collection, Yale University Library.

75 Mary Bruggman, wife of the Swiss minister and sister of Vice President Henry A. Wallace.

76 The diary is in A.E.S., P.U.L.

officer said he was forbidden to pass blueprints without license even carried by Gov. official travelling on orders.

Thurs. [*June 25*]

Dinner with Pepper & up at 4:30 AM to airport. Spent from 5 until 6:15 being inspected by Customs, Immigration, Treasury & Pan Am. Fearfully hot and stuffy standing in interminable lines. Whole operation appeared dreadfully inefficient — and I used to curse the Europeans! The numerous Latin Americans didn't like it any better than the Americans. Once thru all the inspections and ticket fumbling we had to wait 1½ hrs to take off — first in a stuffy room without even a fan & then loaded and unloaded onto the plane *twice* because of engine trouble. *Why wasn't plane serviced and baggage loaded the night before or during the 1½ hours of inspections & ticket trouble?* Curtins closed for long time out of Miami; sea surface visibility very poor & altitude high. *Why doesn't Pan Am fly lower on all Caribbean and Gulf flights for observation.* Crossed palm jungle approaching Camaguay [Camagüey], Cuba — tall white trunks and new paler green frond like plume from top of most trees — suppose it is season's new growth. Appeared to be much abandoned land once cleared — boundaries still distinct — now going back to jungle. Refueled at Camaguay — good airport, radio station, no city nearby. Talked with John Clark of CIAA [77] bound for Cali, Santiago, B A etc — month's trip. Clouds lifting, visibility improving, sea blue and rougher. Passed off west end of Jamaica covered with a rough frosting of white cumulus clouds.

Arrived Allbrook Field, Balboa, about 2 hrs late. Quick, efficient customs inspection. Army captain dropped us at 15th N. D. Hqs. in his car. Adm. Van Hook[78] out; Chief of staff, Capt. D. E. Cummings very cordial; presented letter from Col. Knox. Ordered Flag Secretary, Lt. Cmdr. R. N. Gardner to start our tour. Left bags at Cummings quarters — wives & families all evacuated early in Jan. — A & N [Army and Navy] only. Pan. Canal Zone employees families not evacuated. Had drink with Gardner & planned trip. Started about 4 for Flamenco Island via Camp Amador. Passed 14″ railroad rifles; passed thru long tunnel bored into rock and big mortars at inshore base of island; 320 feet up in elevator; barracks in rock near top full of soldiers; mostly young fine looking boys. "Bridge" on top of Flamenco is harbor entrance control post. Lt. Cmdr on duty explained everything — mine fields, sub. detection loops off outlying islands, disposition of Navy batteries, arrangements for ship identification, sub. nets at entrance to canal etc — all

[77] Special assistant to Nelson A. Rockefeller, Coordinator of Inter-American Affairs.
[78] Admiral C. E. Van Hook, Commandant, Fifteenth Naval District.

controlled from "Bridge" & army control post on lower level, evidently good A-N [Army-Navy] coo[r]dination — ships forbidden to enter at night & mine field switched on.

Next crossed canal bridge — new, great improvement in traffic handling over old ferry system — to Corozal, past Army posts and gigantic excavations for 3rd locks, workmens barracks. (Indians with long hair trudging home from work), neat tidy settlements of Canal employees and almost continuous Army construction projects — to New Hour Station, fine new hospital & quarters being constructed; visited Naval Ammunition depot nearby — magazines all painted green, new trees planted (drop a seed and jump back!) will be excellently camaflouged as trees grow. Ex officer — Cmdr Howard — showed us in a 1000 lb. bomb magazine — bombs packed in steel frame cases without [illegible] and fuses. Not very hot — about 85° — but dreadfully humid & very uncomfortable. Began to feel weak. And so back to Balboa & then trip thru Panama City — contrast between spick and span Zone & Republic. New houses of rich on recently developed heights above city very ornate; shabby & ugly. Woodbury Akers' [79] house one of best with magnificent view of sea. Old city very quaint & typically Spanish. Stopped to see ancient ruins of flat arch [?] church probably sacked by Morgan (must check up on this — forgot to ask & Gardner didn't know).[80]

Dinner with Capt. [D. E.] Cummings — passed over, highly responsible, intelligent and valuable officer — compendium of information about C Z [Canal Zone], evidently good strategy and operations man but loaded with administration; stiff & sterile, doesn't drink or smoke. Had a little saki before dinner; gift from some Japanese admirals he whisked thru the Zone before the war. After dinner Paul & I moved our bags next door to Admiral Van Hooks. Splendid man, forceful, strong, simple, businesslike. Told many stories of post Pearl Harbor while he had the [illegible] — plan for attack on the Marshalls to relieve Wake; . . . Much talk of district problems — 1200 mile advance base patrol, anti-sub. operations — suspicious except in Honduras, Army-Navy cooperation — delays in bringing PBYs & patrol craft over to Atlantic from Pacific because of Army reluctance — now eye to eye with Gen. Andrews[81] etc. To bed dead tired after getting up at 4 in Miami.

Friday [June 26]
Caught 7 train for Coco Solo with Gardner for guide — interesting

[79] Unable to identify.
[80] In January, 1671, Sir Henry Morgan, the British pirate, captured and sacked Panama City.
[81] General Frank M. Andrews, Commander, Panama Department; later appointed Commander U.S. Forces, European Theater (1943).

trip, ballo[o]n bar[r]age over Pedro Miguel locks & Gatun locks & spill-way. Passed anti-glare curtains — to reduce lighting of locks if town should burn. Furious inspecting all morning at Coco Solo — Naval air station — much construction — shortage of repair materials — 24 PBYs & only 12 fit to fly. "Flying pants off them." . . . Repair & material Officer very good, only worried about material and hand tools; submarine base & ships — operation & administration combined in same ad. bldg. with air station — 10 subs. two in for overhaul, 1 for torpedoes. Went thru her. . . . Sub crews are tops. Could hardly squeeze my fat body around her. How can men live that way? She was Bonita, S class, 1926 & new ones are better. Examined much new construction & enormous unused married enlisted men's quarters now that families are evacuated . . . Lunch at enlisted men's mess. *Excellent food!* 3 "big" meals a day — men seem to eat intelligently. Went thru quarters — very fine, roomy & airy — "nothing any better anywhere." Dreadful torrential, tropical rain as we were to take off to come back to Balboa in a small flying boat. De-layed 1½ hrs. — kind of storm very common during rainy season. Can't fly over Canal — about 40 air miles across & we flew 80 — across solid wild jungle. . . . Even Gen. Andrews doesn't fly over Canal — danger of anti-aircraft fire — most heavily defended area in the world.

Stevenson and Paul Smith left Balboa on Saturday, June 27 for Port of Spain, Trinidad. There are two pages of notes about the visit to Panama in the diary. They were evidently rough jottings which Steven-son spelled out in his brief report that follows this diary. The same is true for the visit to Trinidad, June 27–28. They flew to San Juan, Puerto Rico, on Monday morning, June 29.

San Juan NAS [Naval Air Station] air field. [June 29]
From Trinidad? Miles — met by Lt. Cmdr. Harwood Hull, P.R.O. sharp 1 PM. Stayed at Condado Hotel. Air station building progress OK — usual lack of material, tools and planes — 2 squadrons of PBYs. About 2000 Navy personnel — up & down as ships come & go. Expect it to double in year. Men eating damn well as usual! Omaha based on San Juan. Lt. Cmdr. [Noah] Adair Off. of NAS showed us around. *Excellent, quiet, serious, intelligent officer.* Did not meet NAS Comdt. Landing field development way behind — enormous job — air field labor ade-quate — common rate about $1.60 per day. Serious civilian gasoline shortage. Admiral Hoover's[82] *very fine new house* at 6:30 for a drink.

[82] Admiral J. H. Hoover, Commandant, Tenth Naval District.

Cocky, self-confident, little bastard, perfunctorily agreeable, no disposition to discuss his problems; knows all the answers. "Too busy" to attend conference with Van Hook & Kauffman.[83] No interest in Van Hook's ship identification project. Says he knows all about habits of submarines — do not fuel in Carib. — men can't stand to stay that long; "must have [actinic?] rays of sun." German seaman landed in Martinique — has scurvy — also injured etc. . . . Hoover recently vice adm. *Why!* Evidently entirely content that all possible is being done on submarine.

Visit to Harbor Entrance Def. Post on top of El Morro — anti aircraft defenses & coast defense guns along beaches and at harbor entrance. Hotel adjoining Condado has machine guns etc on roof. All coastal defense done by Army. Delicious lobster for dinner at excellent old restaurant — Mollar?

San Juan — cont. Wed. 7/1

Finally got a dispatch sent accepting engagement to speak at Convention of Secy's of State on A-N absentee voting problem in Baltimore next week. Communications didn't want to accept it — said it was personal — got plenty mad. Capt. ? Hoover's chief staff finally convinced it should be sent. Long drive along North-east coast to the great Ensenada-Honda development — Roosevelt Roads will hold the entire fleet when completed. Had lunch in officers-contractors mess. Never saw so much food! Attended meeting with contractors — good idea — held daily to discuss all problems. Lt. Com Roy C.O. good, tough, business like officer, shown around by Lieut. Denny — swell Boston Irish contractor — knew his stuff. Huge excavation for dry dock — will start paving concrete soon. Have had a current famine. Cuban ship with cargo for army at St. Thomas just arrived. Quarry almost ready at Vieques — miles of breakwaters to be built to protect the Roads. Why such a gigantic project which can do no good in this war with Guantanamo only 600 miles away. Could not the material be used better elsewhere for the present?

Back to San Juan along the East coast and up thru the interior. Very beautiful country — sugar, sugar, sugar — visited Fortado Centrale. Didn't see any livestock except small herd of dairy cattle near San Juan and many bullocks (Brahmin X American) used for draft animals — little poultry, few vegetable gardens — beautiful roads — . . . petal strewn road — hibiscus hedge — beautiful children everywhere — few old Spanish buildings — fine old church in Humaco. Some 30 000 army in PR — 15 000 native — widening some main roads. Brief swim on hotel beach. Cocktails with Mr. & Mrs. Hull & Lt. Com. Matthews of

[83] Admiral J. L. Kauffman, Commander, Gulf Sea Frontier.

USS Blakeley — bow blown off by torpedo off Martinique in May — false bow being installed in dry dock at S.J. for trip to Charleston for permanent repairs. Story of 40 seamen saved by mess cook and flit gun & miraculous escape of Lt. Owens who somehow emerged from wreckage of bow unhurt. Story of utter indifference of Martinique fishermen who didn't stop fishing for the torpedoing or to investigate life raft that drifted in between them. Matthews quickly got tight & we went to [illegible] for dinner — gay night club full of young naval officers & pretty P R & American girls.

Thursday 7/2 —
To Guantanamo by NATS 600 miles — Capt. [G. L.] Weyler, Cmdt., met us & took us to his house — reception quite a contrast to Hoover's. Had lunch & spent entire day in intensive sightseeing tour personally conducted by Capt. Weyler — very proud of his work — a sturdy, bluff, blue-eyed man. Knew every inch of the stat[i]on . . . & showed us thru everything including great water system — comes from River off reservation — 3 or 4 miles away — 3 chlorination, filtration & softening plants. Much housing vacant because of evacuation — huge low cost housing for married men now empty. Officers quarters will fill up as new ships arrive. Very proud of recreational facilities he has created — golf course, riding, swimming pools, outdoor movies every night. Only accessible town is Chimeneras [Caimanera] — 5–6000 Cubans. Took fine ride in late afternoon up to ridge. . . . Thence to movies beneath the stars.

Friday 7/3 —
Guant. cont. — Boat trip to inspect net defenses — torpedo inside & submarine outside — and Leeward point field — net factory — anti aircraft emplacements. Weyler needs more men; more planes, patrol craft. Believes in hunting submarines — teams of 1 plane & 1 ship operating on 70 mi[le] radius on projection of probable locations — maintains daily patrol of Bahama channel along north coast and area to [illegible] North and Jamaica South. Seems to me if Comdrs. of the 3 areas & their base commanders like Moran and Weyler could get together for conference each familiar with [illegible] & material they could organize the work better.

On July 3 Stevenson arrived back in Miami where he spent two days inspecting installations. Admiral J. L. Kauffman, Commander, Gulf Sea Frontier, he found to be "enthusiastic about his job." Kauffman believed German submarines were refueling in the Caribbean and he agreed with

Admiral Van Hook's plans for ship identification. The submarine school in Miami, Stevenson described as "one of the best operations I have seen."

On July 5, Stevenson visited the Naval Air Operational Training Center at Jacksonville, Florida. He was "much impressed" with the training schools with courses in "everything from sheet metal to aviation machinists." He stopped at the naval installations at Charleston, South Carolina, and Norfolk, Virginia, and reached Washington on July 8.

He wrote the following undated statement about part of his trip.[84]

Panama —

Admiral [C. E.] Van Hook is *first-class*, serious, intelligent, imaginative. Captain D. E. Cummings — good, upright, routine Chief of Staff. Van Hook would have had more anti submarine protection on Atlantic side sooner, but was delayed by General [William E.] Shedd [Jr.], Chief of Staff to General [Frank M.] Andrews. Andrews and Van Hook get along well and Army-Navy cooperation is "perfect." Van Hook is in defacto charge of submarine warfare but technical subordination to Army has inherent weakness. Spent half day with General Andrews and his staff. Atmosphere in service alert and business like everywhere. Inshore and lock defenses good and improving rapidly.

Should have more flying equipment promptly. Pacific advanced patrol never more than 65% effective and now below danger point. Commander Cooper — assembly and repair officer at Coco Solo — *pleading* for more hand tools and repair material to keep the 24 PBYs in the air for anti submarine work. Not more than 50% in flying condition now and only 12 have radar.

Van Hook would like to feel free to go to confer with [Admiral J. L.] Kauffman and [Admiral J. H.] Hoover whenever he wishes. Their jobs and problems are similar and their operations overlap. Occasional discussion meetings would seem desirable.

Van Hook would like authority to proceed with bomb proof operations and communication shelter back of present District Headquarters at Balboa.

Van Hook feels confident that submarines have been making refueling contacts in the Caribbean area; has already uncovered suspicious people in Honduras.

Trinidad —

Progress on base fine. Mr. Sweeney, contractors representative, a

84 This statement is in A.E.S., P.U.L.

dynamo but dying from T.B. Certain buildings, principally power plant, seem unnecessarily exposed. Suggest more discretion for building location alterations on the site as work proceeds.

Captain Thomas Moran, Commandant, enthusiastic, diligent, but new and insecure. Captain [S. P.] Ginder, now Commandant of NAS [Naval Air Station], has done good job. Expects to be transferred now that Moran has arrived. The Headquarters building in Port of Spain — 10 miles from Bay — almost ready. Moran should and plans to live there. He should have an assistant Commandant to handle the Base so he can concentrate on submarines and convoys. (I understand this has already been arranged by transfer of Olendorf from Aruba.)

Commander Penney has done fine job in developing the section base at Teteron Bay.

Captain Moran reports good Army cooperation. The General was away and I did not see him. Large ship concentrations for convoy at Port of Spain. Harbor seems vulnerable and net laying should be accelerated. As everywhere, they need more patrol planes desperately.

Trinidad seems destined to be hot spot for submarine activity and their material requirements should have careful consideration.

San Juan —

Very able officer, Commander [Noah] Adair, Executive of Naval Air Station, reports usual lack of repair materials, tools and planes. Air field enlistment work slow — enormous fill job. Inshore defenses look good.

Admiral [J. H.] Hoover very cocky and self-confident. "Too busy" for conferences with Van Hook and Kauffman. Knows all the answers — sure submarines do not refuel in the Caribbean. Evidently entirely content all possible is being done and not interested in Van Hook's small coastal ship identification plan. I take it he does not believe in aggressive anti submarine activity but rather in protective escort.

Activity at Roosevelt Roads very impressive. Excavation for first dry dock completed and will soon be able to start work on the breakwaters on Vieques Island. This enormous project does not seem to have much present value and I question wisdom of using so much good personnel and material. Why was it started in the first place? I find many officers who question its wisdom.

Guantanamo —

Captain [G. L.] Weyler a fine officer — sturdy, rough and no airs. Knows every inch of his station and very proud of tremendous development. Recreational facilities best I have seen. Everything from swimming to horseback riding.

To Frank Knox

July 13, 1942

Dear Colonel:

I enclose a hasty memorandum noting some miscellaneous things I observed at some of the places you are going to visit.

I intended to get this to you when I heard you were leaving this afternoon, but I was a little late.

Sincerely yours

To Frank Knox

July 13, 1942

MEMORANDUM TO THE SECRETARY OF THE NAVY

Charleston — Admiral [W. A.] Glassford's office is at the District Head-quarters at the Navy Yard. He has a Board room covering all operational activity relating to submarine warfare. In Charleston, several miles away, the District Intelligence Office has a combat intelligence unit where the recording of submarine activity is virtually duplicated. In still a third building the Port Director also duplicates submarine operations in connection with his convoy routing work. The Ft. Sumter Hotel is centrally located at the Battery and these activities could be advantageously consolidated in that building.

Indeed it might be desirable to consolidate all the District activities in this one building which are now scattered through several buildings and at the Yard. I have already discussed this here in the Department.

Some consideration might also be given to designating a Commandant of the Yard and divorcing it from the District Commandant. After all they are largely unrelated activities and Admiral Glassford must necessarily give the Yard but little attention; the more time he has to concentrate on the submarine warfare and the District the better. I suggest you talk to Admiral Glassford about the shrimp boat program.

I hope you will find a moment to talk with Captain Baker and Captain Penn. They have demonstrated what can be done with southern labor in the rapid development of the Yard. You will also find increased employment of women trained in vocational schools at Charleston. There is a housing shortage in the vicinity of the Yard.

Jacksonville — The Port Director in Jacksonville — Commander Kirkland — is familiar with the shrimp boat program and most of the conversion of these boats is being done in the Jacksonville Yards. I believe Kirkland recommended the use of these boats *last year!*

[59]

If you have not seen it I suggest you visit the service training schools at the Air Station. I was much impressed with the school and with Lieutenant Commander Higgins who runs it. The decompression chamber at the dispensary is also interesting. I believe we have only one other altitude testing device of this kind.

The A&R Building is the best equipped I have seen. Possibly some of these tools would be more useful just now at some of the off shore bases where there is a shortage. There are about 45 PBY training planes at the Air Station. Possibly a few of these could be more advantageously used in submarine work for a while.

Miami — By all means visit the Subchaser School. Perhaps more publicity for this would be helpful in our submarine warfare enlightenment program. The CO is Commander McDaniel and one of the best men I met.

Admiral [J. L.] Kauffman has the most efficient physical organization of his operations I have seen and I was impressed with the better-than-average work they are doing in evaluating reports.

To General Frank M. Andrews[85]

July 17, 1942

My dear General:

I returned from my journey in the tropics to find that you and Admiral Van Hook were in Washington. I had a good visit with Van Hook and hoped for a glimpse of you and an opportunity to thank you for your great kindness and consideration to me in the Canal Zone.

I shall not soon forget your personally conducted inspection tour — by land and air! I feel, thanks to you, that I learned as much about the situation in Panama as a man could in the same period of time and still keep his wits!

It was a privilege to meet you and I hope that there will be another opportunity before the war is over and we wretched civilians drift back to our homes.

Cordially yours,

To Malcolm S. Langford [86]

August 4, 1942

Dear Mr. Langford:

I suggest that the first sentence of the paragraph entitled "contract be-

[85] This letter is in A.E.S., P.U.L.
[86] Staff general counsel in the Office of Lend-Lease Administration.

tween the United States (Bureau of Ships) Navy Department and Weaver Associates Corporation" in the minutes of the meeting of the Directors of Ships Incorporated held July 9, 1942 be revised to read as follows:

> "The Secretary presented a copy of a proposed contract with Weaver Associates Corporation and negotiated by the Bureau of Ships with the advice and assistance of counsel for the Lend-Lease Administration covering the work already completed by Weaver Associates of redesigning the "Sea Otter" type of vessel so as to conform to the requirements for the Seamobile."

I would like to get in the thought that you participated in the negotiation of the contract and any revision you wish to accomplish this purpose will be satisfactory.

Sincerely yours,

To Joseph C. Grew[87]

September 9, 1942

Dear Mr. Ambassador:

The Chicago Council on Foreign Relations, of which I was once President, advises me that you have been invited to address the Council on October 3.

I take this means of assuring you that the Chicago Council on Foreign Relations is perhaps the best public forum for the discussion of our foreign affairs in the Mid West. It has a very large and enlightened membership and a distinguished record of activity in this field for the past twenty years. I am sure you will have a most cordial and appreciative reception.

I personally feel very strongly that for reasons which are well known to you the use of middle western forums for public statements by our senior government officials is manifestly desirable and I sincerely hope you will find it possible to accept this engagement. I shall be glad to give you any information you may wish regarding the Council as I have been a member of its Executive Committee for many years and am intimately familiar with its affairs.

Sincerely yours,

---

[87] Special assistant to the Secretary of State; formerly U.S. ambassador to Japan (1932–1941). This letter is in A.E.S., P.U.L.

On May 14, 1942, Stevenson received a telegram from George T. Donoghue, general superintendent of the Chicago Park District, asking if he would accept nomination by the Democratic party to run as a trustee of the University of Illinois. Stevenson wired the next day that he "could not serve actively" but subject to that consideration "I would accept the nomination gladly."

To Arthur Sullivan[88]

September 12, 1942

Dear Mr. Sullivan:

I am in a quandary and am taking the liberty of turning to you as the source of all wisdom on matters political!

I hear that I was nominated at the Democratic Convention for Trustee of the University of Illinois. I am, and have been since July 1941, working for the Navy Department and in this particular job I have a Civil Service status. I had previously given no thought to the candidacy but now it occurs to me that perhaps it is inconsistent with my employment by the government and perhaps even a violation of the Hatch Act. If such is the case I presume I should withdraw promptly in order to enable them to select another candidate.[89]

I hesitate to bother you about this and I will be glad to take it up with someone else if you suggest. I am sure you will appreciate my apprehension and anxiety to do the right thing. Moreover, I suspect before the war is over I will be commissioned as an officer — in the event that makes any difference. At Colonel Knox's request I have continued as a civilian until the present and will probably remain as such for a few more months.

With very best regards and my apologies for imposing on you, I am

Sincerely yours,

To Rear Admiral Richard S. Edwards[90]

October 16, 1942

Please note the attached letter. . . . Drawings, stress analysis, design study, etc., on this boat are on file in the Bureau of Ships and the results

---

[88] Chairman of the Democratic State Central Committee of Illinois. This letter is in A.E.S., P.U.L.

[89] Sullivan replied that the Democratic Convention decided not to nominate him since his candidacy would be a violation of the Hatch Act forbidding civil servants from running for office. His letter is in A.E.S., P.U.L.

[90] Chief of staff under Admiral King.

of tests at Stevens Institute have been presented to Ivan G. Wanless, Chief of the Preliminary Design Section of the Maritime Commission.

As I understand it, the advantages of a catamaran, airscrew boat of this kind are diminished roll and wake and therefore improved operation of sound gear.

The Lend-Lease Administration wants to proceed at once with the construction of an experimental boat of this kind. I have told them that I would attempt to ascertain whether such a boat would be useful to the Navy, assuming it possessed the claimed qualities.

I would like to talk to you about this at your convenience.

To Malcolm S. Langford

October 29, 1942

Dear Malcolm:

I have just looked through the minutes of the last meeting of the Directors of Cargoes, Incorporated, and I am reminded that the Supervisor of Shipbuilding in the Boston area is Rear Admiral Harold T. Smith, Quincy, Massachusetts.

I think he should be interviewed in connection with the placing of any contract for the tugs. I am sure you will find him quite familiar with the shipbuilding facilities and labor situation in that area.

Sincerely yours,

Captain W. D. Puleston, naval historian and on duty with the Board of Economic Warfare, wrote Stevenson, October 30, 1942, that Colonel Knox's speech at the Navy Day dinner "reads better than it sounded and it sounded very good, indeed. . . . Now that I know who wrote it, I will pass along my compliments to the author as well as to the deliverer of the speech."

To Captain W. D. Puleston[91]

October 30, 1942

My dear Captain:

Many thanks for your letter.

Your kind comments are more than the speech deserved and they make me feel very good indeed. You know what little nourishment we poor ghosts get!

Sincerely yours,

[91] This letter is in A.E.S., P.U.L.

On November 10, 1942, Secretary Frank Knox asked Stevenson to prepare a list of members of both the Senate and the House of Representatives "with whom you are on good relations and to whom you could readily go at any time in behalf of a matter in which the Navy might be interested." Stevenson listed the following:

SENATORS	REPRESENTATIVES
Claude Pepper–Florida	Walter G. Andrews–N.Y.
Joseph F. Guffey–Pa.	Leslie C. Arends–Ill.
Scott W. Lucas–Ill.	Harry P. Beam–Ill.
Alben W. Barkley–Ky	C. W. Bishop–Ill.
Styles Bridges–N. H.	Charles S. Dewey–Ill.
Warren R. Austin–Vt.	Everett M. Dirksen–Ill.
Tom Connally–Texas	Christian A. Herter–Mass.
Theodore Francis Green–R.I.	James M. Curley–Mass.
Carter Glass–Va	Lyndon B. Johnson–Tex.
Gerald P. Nye–N.D.	George A. Paddock–Ill.
Raymond S. McKeough–Ill.	Adolph J. Sabath–Ill.
	Samuel A. Weiss–Pa
	Richard B. Wigglesworth–Mass
	Ralph C. Church–Ill.

To Frank Knox[92]

December 9, 1942

MEMORANDUM TO THE SECRETARY

I want to suggest that voluntary appearances before Committees of the House and Senate might be an effective method of:

A. Improving our congressional relations generally.

B. Providing Congressmen in the most advantageous atmosphere with information to which they are legitimately entitled.

C. Heading off in advance undesirable Congressional action.

D. Learning in advance something more of what they are thinking.

Presumably the new Congress will be more inquisitive and independent than the old. I understand that already some five new investigations are incipient. To satisfy curiosity voluntarily would be both flattering and friendly and should create a more wholesome understanding and respect for the Navy's problems and for the Navy and its leadership. Congress' influence on public opinion is conceded. As they think better of us, so will the people.

[92] The original is in the possession of the Department of the Navy, Office of the Chief of Naval Operations.

I have in mind that from time to time any of the Secretaries could suggest to a Committee Chairman that he would like to talk about some Navy matters to the Committee. I suspect that the Chairmen would be glad to invite the Committee members to attend informal meetings for exchange of information and opinion with representatives of the Navy Department.

I can think of various examples from the past of the kind of interesting and non-routine things we could discuss — logistics, security of information, submarine warfare, inherent unbalances in the supply problem, Navy Yards and their peculiar functions, civilian employment, the small business problem, labor relations, etc.

Operational information would, of course, be the most interesting. The gigantic job the Navy has done, for example, in hacking out, manning and holding the supply lines to the South Pacific, plus the fighting, is a story which we have not made much affirmative effort to dramatize. A lot could be done with maps.

I am constantly reminded that, except for a relatively few, most of the members of Congress are as ignorant, unsophisticated and interested as the next layman in matters relating to the war which we are inclined to take for granted.

To Edward D. McDougal, Jr.[93]

December 29, 1942

Dear Ed:

Evidently you are not going to let me forget I am — or was — a lawyer! It looks like an engaging little book and if and when that quiet evening turns up I expect to have some fun with it.[94] Many thanks. It is nice to be remembered when you feel like an exile.

Your largesse overwhelms me! If Ellen and the children ever get back from North Carolina[95] she will thank Kate[96] for the lovely little basket — but I doubt if she finds any biscuits. Thanks again.

Finally, let me say I never enjoyed imposing on anyone as I did on you a week ago tonight. Thanks again and again.

Yours,

AD

[93] The original is in the possession of Mr. McDougal.

[94] Stevenson and his Lake Forest and Libertyville friends customarily passed books around to each other at Christmastime.

[95] Mrs. Stevenson and the three sons spent the Christmas holidays with Mr. and Mrs. Ernest L. Ives at Southern Pines, North Carolina. Stevenson joined them there Christmas day and returned to Washington that night.

[96] Mrs. McDougal.

Apparently as a New Year's resolution, Adlai Stevenson decided to try once more to write a diary. After a few days in Washington, he, Captain Frank E. Beatty, naval aide to the Secretary of the Navy, and Rawleigh Warner, adviser to Colonel Knox, accompanied Secretary Knox on a tour to the Pacific theater of the war. Stevenson's handwritten diary is difficult to decipher. We have retained his own spellings and abbreviations. The ellipses are the editors'. Despite their efforts, the editors were unable to identify many of the persons mentioned by Stevenson. The diary is in the Stevenson collection, Princeton University Library.

Friday, January 1, 1943

Wash — Black, ugly day. New Yrs eve dinner with Harris Wards.[97] "Young party." Lunch with Chas. Denby[98] — now head of a division of Lend Lease — foreign mission, state Dept lia[i]son etc. Thanked Dean Acheson for recommending me to Gov. [Herbert] Lehman. He asked me to let him know when I am "free" to work anywhere else.

. . . David Lawrence[99] said he was going to continue pressing for more [aid?] for Far East; thought he would "take after" British resistence to diverting more material to that area.

Saturday, January 2, 1943

Wash. Routine day at office . . .

Visited Special Devices bldg of Bu Aero [Bureau of Aeronautics]. Important contribution to development of training aids. Gunnery & identification devices particularly good.

Long talk with Capt. [William D.] Puleston this PM. State Dept. has won long fight for more economic pressure on Sweden. [Secretary Cordell] Hull intervened with President. Evidently somewhat governed by reluctance to risk anything there until our situation in Africa improves.[100]

Puleston says we must insist when Russia recovers Estonia, Smolensk, Sevastopol line that she fight Japan & let us into Vlaadavastock [Vladivostok].

Sunday, January 3, 1943

Wash — Ellen & boys returned from Southern Pines. Wonderful to

---

[97] Friends from Chicago.
[98] A Princeton and Harvard Law School classmate.
[99] The columnist.
[100] On October 23, 1942, the British army opened its drive at El Alamein and started to push Axis forces back to Tunis. Allied forces landed in North Africa on November 8, 1942. The two forces finally crushed the Axis in Africa in May, 1943.

have them back. Look well but had bad weather there. Jim Oates[101] for lunch. Sincere and flattering letter to Ellen from Struthers Burt[102] about her poetry. She *must* find time or *organ[i]ze* her time to write more. Her quality is so high but her output so low.

Monday, January 4, 1943
    Wash — Routine day. Lunched with Capt. Puleston & Lt. Cmdr. Keith Merrill, his ass't at BEW [Board of Economic Warfare]. Latter invited me to play squash on his court any time. OWI [Office of War Information] meeting called off & gay dinner with Ellen & the boys. Read an Uncle Remus story aloud to them — rather pleased with my negro accent even if the boys weren't.

Tuesday, January 5, 1943
    Wash — Long talk with Adm. Bowen[103] re a recent talk with Senator Brewster.[104] Afraid Bowen may be a little too forward in promoting his ambitions for Adm. [S. M.] Robinsons job as Chief of OP&M [Office of Procurement and Materiel]. Brewster confirmed his implacable opposition to Adm. [C. A.] Jones for that job. Jack Kellogg[105] for lunch — disquieting comments on ONI [Office of Naval Intelligence] foreign sections & failures to provide adequate information for North Africa expedition. . . .

Wednesday, January 6, 1943
    Wash — Selection Board met — Knox, King,[106] Jacobs,[107] & Frank Beatty was not included on list of 30 captains for Admiral altho they took some who tho senior had less votes than he did. Feels that he has no future as long as King is C in C.
    Puleston sent me brief memo on State Dept's non support of Navy in past decade — annual refusal to permit warship to visit [Japanese] Mandated Islands to check on fortification etc. etc. Showed it to Arthur Krock at Metro[politan]. Club but didnot identify author. Long talk with [Walter] Lippman[n]. Feels we have not done enough to focus [illegible] orrizationally [organizationally?] the importance of anti submarine warfare. Suggested an Asst. Secy. in charge; more civilian

---

101 James F. Oates, Jr., of Stevenson's Chicago law firm.
102 The author.
103 Admiral Harold G. Bowen, director of the Naval Research Laboratory and technical assistant to the Secretary of the Navy.
104 Senator Owen Brewster of Maine.
105 John P. Kellogg, an old friend and Libertyville neighbor of Stevenson.
106 Admiral Ernest J. King, Commander in Chief, U.S. Fleet.
107 Admiral Randall Jacobs, chief of the Bureau of Naval Personnel.

consultation etc. Will ask Sec'y to ask King to give full report on the ASW organization etc. Showed Lippman[n] Puleston memo & he agreed Navy should compile record of our relation with State for last 10 yrs. — not for publication. Knox read Lippman[n] his letter to Stimson of 1/24/42 anticipating areial attack on Hawaii.

Lunch with [John] Kellogg & Maj. Rogers USMC — excellent man — re ONI [Office of Naval Intelligence]. Rogers on N. Africa expid. & states very plausible case on imperative necessity for improvement of foreign intelligence work of ONI.

Office party for dinner — Oates, Balls, Days, McDougals, Starks. Amusing communique to SMA&B from the emigrés.[108]

Thursday, January 7, 1943

Wash — Sat in Mrs. K[nox]'s seat in Executive gallery at opening of Congress, with Herbert Gaston, Asst Secy. of Treas., Mrs. Morgan-thau[109] & Mrs. Robert Sherwood alongside. Mrs. [Franklin D.] Roosevelt and other dignitaries, Mrs. [Henry] Wallace in box. Diplomats all sat on floor of House for first time. President seemed to have difficult time getting up to rostrum. Good speech — used one sentence in almost haec verba from speech I wrote for K[nox] about a month ago. Threats of air bombardment harder & harder evidently for psychological effect abroad. Ham Fish[110] didn't applaud once. Republican applause very light on "birth to death" social security reference. All eyes on Clair Luce[111] below me. Mrs. Morganthau made flattering reference to Mrs. Carpenter's[112] war bond work in Chicago. Agreed emphatically that Woodrow Wilson Foundation should do something aggressive with its money — now.

Lunch with Senator [Harry] Byrd & K[nox]. K. did fine job on him. Byrd very agreeable — "Navy has done best job on controlling unnecessary personnel." Very emphatic about necessity for labor legislation . . .

[James] Oates & Jack Kellogg for dinner. Tom Corcoran[113] and others

---

[108] The guests at the party were from Stevenson's Chicago law firm, Sidley, McPherson, Austin and Burgess, and in 1943 all were engaged in the war effort. They were James F. Oates, Jr., George Ball, J. Edward Day, Edward D. McDougal, Jr., and Franklin C. Stark and their wives. Mr. Stark, now practicing law in California, recalls that the house was cold in spite of numerous fireplaces, because of the fuel shortage, but that the gathering was a very pleasant one. Letter to Carol Evans, February 21, 1969.

[109] Mrs. Henry Morgenthau, wife of the Secretary of the Treasury.

[110] Hamilton Fish, the isolationist Republican congressman from New York.

[111] Clare Boothe Luce, Republican congresswoman from Connecticut and wife of magazine publisher Henry Luce.

[112] Mrs. John Alden Carpenter, Stevenson's mother-in-law.

[113] A White House aide.

called me from Harvard Law School dinner to say "hello" etc. Probably should have gone.

Friday, January 8, 1943

Wash — Oh God these people who want commissions! Will it ever stop. Call from Chris Herter — now in Congress. Dispensary fixed my ear which was stopped up. May I never be deaf! Mr. & Mrs. [John Alden] Carpenter arrived — found Mr. C. in bed with grippe and doctor at the house. . . .

Mrs. C. seemed confident she would "unload" 1020[114] on Wesley Hospital & would take Reids apt. at 1550 N. State at $350 per mo. Not sure there is enough economy to warrant the deal. Mrs. C. full of her national charity concert plans.

Packed for trip — too late to bed. Ellen quite mournful.

Mrs. C's womens Com. in Chicago has sold 90,000,000 war bonds in less than 1 yr. Not bad.

Saturday, January 9, 1943

Wash — Frenzy cleaning up last minute things — and finally off for Anacostia with K[nox], Beatty & Warner at 1. . . . K. delayed for 2 hrs at rubber meeting — insistence . . . that synthetic program get better priorities.

. . . Lunch on plane — Memphis for fueling . . . gave "press" interview for K. Atmosphere — not very good view of Memphis. Arrived Dallas NAS [Naval Air Station]. Dinner with Cmdt — Capt. Meadow[*] — walk in Texas starlight & to bed at 10 — 1406 air miles.

Aboard the plane Stevenson wrote a letter to Walter Lippmann about his January 5, 1943, New York Herald Tribune *column criticizing the Navy's antisubmarine warfare.*

To Walter Lippmann[115]

January 9, 1943

Dear Walter —

I missed you[r] piece on Tuesday. I have just read it and am writing

---

* Notes on talk with Meadow about air field — leased by Army & we can't use it — N. has 5 mil investment! Take up with BuAir [Bureau of Aeronautics]. . . .

114 The Carpenters' home at 1020 Lake Shore Drive, Chicago.
115 This handwritten letter is in the Walter Lippmann collection, Yale University Library.

this on the plane en route west. I am gathering a comprehensive report on the organization of the Navy's A S W (anti sub) work. Perhaps it will interest you. At least I believe you will agree that it can hardly be characterized as "primitive" or "lethargic." And I earnestly hope you will find an opportunity to visit the anti sub. school at Miami and the . . . school at Key West — also an operations center at a sea frontier head-quarters. I'll risk a bet that you'll have a healthier opinion than the piece indicates of our consciousness of submarine power, tactics, strategy etc. and of the personnel assigned to this work. Incidentally I find since our talk the other day, that several insignia for A S personnel are under consideration and one of them may have already been approved.

But what I really started to write this note about is your suggestion that the Navy has been non receptive to "other methods of dealing with subs." I hope when I get back that you will give me some clues on this. Certainly we cannot afford to miss any bets.

In so far as your article relates to submarines — rather than anti-submarine — I suspect you will agree that our Navy need not concede first place to the Germans or the Japs either in quality of material, techniques or personnel. The school at New London would interest you in this connection. As you know — the sub. service has for many years been the biggest paid and has attracted the most daring & imaginative men in the service. It has had for a long time an energetic tradition of its own. The same independent spirit is rapidly developing in the A S W service.

I fully realize that the Navy will have to withstand much critical scrutiny on the anti-sub front in the months ahead until the D. E. [destroyer escort] program catches up, and your views will as always, be most helpful. Meanwhile I want to get you such information as I can about what we are doing and have done lest you have any misconceptions on that score.

And when I get back you will also have to listen to a recount of my adventures in the Pacific!

Yrs

ADLAI

Sunday, January 10, 1943

Dallas — Breakfast at 7:15. Took off at 8. Beautiful sunrise as we passed great Consal. plant on edge of Lake Worth. Endless Texas! Guadalupe pass thru mountains — El Paso — into N.M. & landed at Army Air Field at Tucson for lunch in officers club . . . Calif. champagne for lunch! Beautiful weather. Off at 2:10 and up the valley to Phoenix . . . Phoenix area green and more hospitable than Tucson.

Passed the city to the south . . . West thru arid country to the Salton Sea & Palm Springs, Indio etc. Out of the Desert, over the mountains . . . and over the orange groves of San Bernadino valley — Arrowhead lake. Turned north over Te[ha]chapi Mts., Death Valley up San Joaquin Valley to Alameda. Bay area covered with fog! Thru ugly Oakland to Adm. [J. W.] Greenslade's Home on Goat Island. Drink & talk & on over the Bay Bridge to St. Francis Hotel . . . 'Royal suite' for K[nox] & *adequate* for us . . . Cocktails with manager of Hotel . . . About 1700 miles today. . . .

Monday, January 11, 1943

San F[rancisco] — K. woke us up at 7:15. Pitch dark. No better here than at home. Breakfast in our rooms — shopping for "trading good" — most whiskey & off for Mare Island at 9:30. Out of the fog up the East Bay; Hills green. Shacks, trailers, housing bad at Vallejo . . . Review of San F. crew;[116] little speech by K. Fine looking crew . . . Bridge structure had been all shot away — two big holes in side . . . Electrical wiring hardest & slowest part of repair. Jap. plane fell on after superstructure. Many subs. for overhaul . . . Hospital burns & fracture wards with Doc. Amen. Some harrowing cases. Burn cures good with wax treatment. Mostly Guadalcanal wounded.

Long drive back to Hunters Point — talk about crowding at Treasure Island . . . Hope dry dock will be finished by mid April. Except 16000 workmen by end of year. Repairs should be done on West Coast; bldg. east. Hunters Point has great future. Mare Island should not be farther expanded. Dinner with . . . Gen. [John L.] De Witt etc. (My right shoulder hurts like hell. Whats the matter? Never had this before. Can hardly raise my arm.) Gen. De Witt, Adm. [Raymond] Spear (working hard, seemed happy, but he always did) and others came in to pay respects to K . . . Left at 8 for Pan Am on Treasure Island — up & down other side of Goat Island, across causeway. A World's Fair bldg. — weighing and waiting waiting waiting & — fuel pump out of order. Abo[a]rd great Bo[e]ing Clipper — us 4 — A[d]m. [John S.] McCain & [two others] — Taxied thru the darkness all the way to Oakland. Off about 9:55 over Golden Gate bridge, clear fine view, white moon ½. Bunks for all — very stuffy. Arm hurts — can't lie on it — can't move — no sleep . . . about 85,000 lbs at takeoff — blue flame of exhaust — all asleep but me still reading & wondering. First full night on plane in 8 yrs+.

[116] The cruiser *San Francisco* had been severely damaged in the naval battle of Guadalcanal, November 12–15, 1942.

Tuesday, January 12, 1943

Pearl Harbor. Up about 8 San F. time. Feeling low. Heavy cumulus — occasional sight of sea. Little talking. Picked up Molokai or Maui about 9:30. Recognition circle off Koko head — right over Diamond Head, Dillinghams[117] house, Waikiki beach & perfect landing at Pan Am stage at Pearl City — 14 hrs 50 min — 2100 miles. Worked into dock slowly. Adm. Nimitz,[118] . . . etc to meet K[nox]. Ride thru Pearl City and back of P H to officers quarters . . . Capt. Quinn [Allen G. Quynn] . . . my host — new houses — Adm. Nimitz 2 doors away. Unpacked — lunch with Quinn . . . Dr. Graff . . . took me to hospital. . . . Passed from Dr. to Dr. All very polite and proud of mag. new hospital on heights well back of P.H. Never saw anything so fine as this hosp. anywhere. Had Xray & found a bursar on shoulder. "No wonder it hurts," Dr. Wright gave me an injection of novocaine — Alarm! — Condition! — Handed gas mask with my shirt off! Everyone surprised, non communicative and trying to be blasé. Electrical short circuit. Back CincPac Hqs. Not feeling a bit gay. Sat in intermittent sun & dozed a little. Watched Quinn & . . . play horseshoes. Quinn a shark. To Quinn's for drink — Adm [Howard M.] Good just back Sou Pac — orders to Bu Pers [Bureau of Personnel]. Horrors! Good, tough man. [Cruiser] San Fran could have been repaired as well (?) and quicker at P.H. — sent back to home town for morale etc. Both shave & dinner clothes (this is why I brought them I guess!) & off to Adm Nimitz for dinner feeling much better. Novacaine doing its work now. All the top officers & Walter Dillingham & Alex. Walker[119] (only civilians). Sat between Adm [Raymond A.] Spruance, Nimitz' Ch of Staff, and . . . Spruance stern and righteous; a little humorless. Cundoms to Canton Island! . . . Much talk of So Pac. To bed at 10:30.

Wednesday, January 13, 1943

P.H. Break at 8 — very good too. Feeling much better. Off on inspection tour 3 or 4 auto — . . . Oklahoma salvage operation — [120] *Is it worthwhile?* West Va in drydock. Delicate job on stern repairs . . . Many ship in repair — all battle damage cases — stirring stories. New dry dock excavated & pouring concrete in the water. No evidence of Dec. 7 damage anywhere. Boat shop very congested. Should be relo-

---

[117] Walter F. Dillingham, a wealthy Honolulu businessman, chairman of the board of the Dillingham Corporation and the Bank of Hawaii, and his wife, who was a friend of Stevenson's mother-in-law, Mrs. John Alden Carpenter.

[118] Admiral Chester W. Nimitz, Commander, Pacific Fleet.

[119] H. Alexander Walker, Honolulu businessman; president of American Factors.

[120] The dreadnought *Oklahoma,* hit by bombs and torpedoes on December 7, 1941, rolled over on her side and parts of her bottom faced the sky.

cated . . . Av. work week 6o hrs. Wage rate now 25% above states . . . Attrition among workmen, (23,000) about 300 per mo; No family, amusements, congested living etc. Housing for 7000 workers — 3 or 4 bunks to a room but quite good . . .

Machine gun nests underground at cross roads en route to Ewa and Barbers Point & Marine airfields. Barbed wire along beaches and everywhere else. *Waste of steel.* Concrete shelters for fighters. Won't be large enough to house anything larger. Fine dispersal at Marine Field. Large taxiways . . . Along beautiful sea road to NAD [Naval Air Defense] at Lua Lualai — (raining off and on all the time) — fine waterfalls down mountain sides, NAD like all the rest — much new construction. Clouds low on sides of steep, wild mts, waterfalls out of the clouds against green backdrop of the hills. Over the military road to Schofield Barracks — public forbidden — fine view from top over "Waiewai Pocket" — radio transmitter station & NAD area. Long ride around North shore to Alex. Walkers beach House for lunch.[121] Many officers. Just Mrs. Wal & her married daughter. Attractive — typical. Adm Nimitz, Frank B[eatty] & I took a swim — surrounded with barbed wire!

. . . Along beautiful shore road, past Coopers Ranch where Ellen & I had lunch on our trip around the island in Aug. 1934.[122] Overcast, dark & rainy most of the time. Not the best time for flowers. Seem to see only Japanese [Americans] along the roads. Sense of desertion & isolation about this wild & beautiful place. To Kamahoe [Kaneohe] Bay NAS [Naval Air Station] for presentation ceremony of decorations. Held in hangar that was destroyed 12/7. Now replaced. Very good station. "Refreshments" in officers club — "refres." always whiskey. Presented with Leis — kiss on both cheeks . . . The airmen are the best talkers, salesmen, personality, good looking divil may care boys. (Only Navy Cross was won by a Jew named Rothenburg!) . . . On along the coast past Koko head, Treasure Island, Holmes' place, the blow hole where Ellen & I stopped to gawk, Rabbit Island & into the suburbs back of Diamond Head . . . to Waikiki to see a Navy rest home for submarine officers — former beach club — thru the city — past Moana Seaside where E[llen] & I stayed & back to P.H. Called Mrs. Dillingham. Very hospitable[123]

121 Mrs. Walker's beach home, Muliwai, was closed during the war. When the Knox party, accompanied by General Delos C. Emmons, Hawaiian military governor, and other high-ranking military officers, went on an inspection tour around the island, Mrs. Walker recalls, she was asked to open the house and to serve them lunch.

122 As an attorney for the Federal Alcohol Administration, Stevenson had visited Hawaii in 1934.

123 Mrs. Walter Dillingham entertained visiting notables — a "command performance" in the "plantation psychology" of Hawaii of those days. See Lawrence Fuchs, *Hawaii Pono: A Social History* (New York: Harcourt, Brace, & World, 1961).

. . . To Adm Nimitz for "the Volcano," picture of the eruption on Hawaii last summer. Why doesn't Army release it? Extraordinary.

Thurs, Jan 14

P.H. — Up at 6 — Bad night. Is my *left* arm going bad? Cup of coffee & farewell with Quinn. Break. with the others at Adm. Nimitz'. Adm's barge to Ford Island; just at faintest daylight. Past Okla & Ariz.[124] latter just a flag pole now — dock around her. Adm Towers to bid us farewell. Party in 2 PB2ys. We — K[nox], Adm N[imitz], Adm [John S.] McCain [Jr.], [Captain] Beatty, [Rawleigh] Warner, N's aide & me, off first — long taxi — 2 trips — different course — long taxi — she's on the step — she rocks — long bounces (weight about 63000) — shes up, — 30 ft, 50 ft — I cross to peer out of port window for view of P.H. below, turn back to starbord window, only Beatty in cabin with me. Motors suddenly cut, coming down steep, hit water hard, bad list to Port — look out, wing tip under Oh! Oh! Blue jacket hands me life belt. "stand by" — shouting above — "are we taking water?" Main hatch door opened. Water 1 inch below the edge on port side. Ordered up topside & out on starbord wing . . . we almost fall off! Every one sort of gay, Col. [Frank Knox] enjoying it thoroughly. (. . . pilot, explains that No. 2 engine failed, tried to right, slipped to port, water tore off pontoon.) Much excitement — Sec Nav & Cincpac almost crack up in middle of Pearl H! Small boat takes us in tow. Adm N. very calm; no word of criticism of pilot — tells him to take charge & that we want to get started for Midway as soon as possible. Transferred to other plane; some mail sacks removed to compensate for our extra weight* & off at last about 9:30 — 1½ hrs late! — About 10 passengers & 10 or 12 crew. Beautiful day — Passed "French Frigate" [shoals] — Coral atoll 450 mi. w. of P.H. — circled over airfield on W. edge of reef made out of sand spit — will enable fighters to fuel on the way & thus fly to Midway. Sea calm & sky beautiful. How *could* they beat us? Plane noisy — little talk. Gazed long at blue Pacific thru bombsight part. Read and smoke; inspect plane; wish I could work. Can neither sleep nor work in planes.[125] Sight outer reef about 3:30 — 2 P40's winging out to meet us — sky grey now — fighters graceful — over and under us — now one on each side. Adm. N[imitz]. says "I wish they would go away — dangerous." Hard for them to cut to

* The boys at Midway would rather see that mail than me!

[124] The battleship *Arizona*, sunk on December 7, 1941, is considered by the Navy as still a ship, not a memorial. A structure has been erected over the sunken hulk, which is visited by thousands of people each year.

[125] This certainly was not true later when he could read, write, and sleep aboard planes at any time including takeoffs and landings.

our speed. Eastern island & Sand Island — more of an estab. than I thought. Skeleton of hangar on Sand — beautiful turkoise [turquoise] water inside the reef. We land — and taxi inside breakwater-buoy — whale boat comes along side. Clamber in — about 4:30, 1200 miles . . . transfer to a larger boat. Too rough to bring it alongside plane. Around breakwater to boat haven — Sub. in slip; planes in the sky. Thru tangle of wooden bldgs on inspection tour. Bomproof power house. Hangar, only sign of damage.[126] Goonies everywhere, bowing and dancing, setting on their nests, awkward take offs and landings; always proud and dignified. Black more animated than white. Strange and lovable birds; must be lonesome when they go. Ground covered with moaning bird holes; pure white love terns, yellow Laysan finches, Bosun birds that fly backwards!, little wingless rails; golden plovers in the ironwood grove by the old cable co. bldgs. Norfolk island pines, a few banyans, fine ironwoods and everywhere solemn goonies — wind and sand. Much larger project than I had supposed. 3 huge runways in const. Underground hospitals, Marine gun crews still all live underground by their gun positions. Not wholly underground — mounds — water at 4'. Plane crews live by their planes except officers — at BOQ. Never been in so many tunnels! How did we ever get along without the CBs! [127] Everything but a tailor among them. Vehicles all painted white like the sand. N[imitz]. nicked his scalp on forced landing at PH. Getting dark; absolute blackout. Morton's[128] house for a welcome wash & then Officers Club for party. Crowd — Goodlooking men — all youngish. Goonie Murals in Bar very good. Why hasn't someone taken good movies of these marvellous, friendly birds? Walk in the moonlight on the "snow" with Beatty. Sky whirring with moaning birds — but not much moaning — mating season over. E[e]rie silence figures silouettes of human ants. Up to knee in hole. To bed, dead at 9:30.

Hard to keep fighter pilots on edge with little to do at Midway. Army squadron there 7 mos.

Fri, Jan 15
Midway. Up at 5:30. Pitch dark. Crossed to Eastern Island in gathering day light. Much more primitive; more as I had expected. Girl pic-

---

126 On June 4, 1942, Japanese planes attacked Midway, but U.S. forces repulsed the Japanese invasion fleet.
127 The Navy's Construction Battalions, popularly known as the Seabees, were established in January, 1942. Men of various trades of construction work were recruited. Furer, *Administration of the Navy Department in World War II*, pp. 411, 421–424.
128 Mrs. H. Alexander Walker believes this is Marine Captain H. M. Martin.

tures in the tunnell barracks. Marines looked the best as always. Battery crews cook where they live — or at scattered small messes. Seem to have plenty of everything — except women. "What has Honolulu got that Midway hasn't? Goonies without feathers." Visited Army fighter squadron & Marine ready rooms. Always impressed with communication systems. Adm N[imitz]. constantly concerned with fuel storage — wants a lot more out here. Will never forget explosions of 17 of 32 tanks on June 2 — 2 days before battle began. Were testing their demolition equipment. Farewell to the marines & back to planes to take off for Johnston [Island]. Still fueling. Transferred to smaller boat to make the contact & tossed around waiting word to come alongside. Finally advised that one of the fuel barges had stove in one of the planes. Should we leave in the other alone? Conf. No. Wait for repairs — 2 hrs. Back around the breakwater to the boat dock. Another submarine in, just off patrol. Went aboard. "Porpoise." Capt. showed photo of Jap. merchant sinking. Hit 2 more — 3 misses; out 47 days; crew pale; unhealthy looking. Get a good rest in the PanAm hotel — pleasant bldg. — rest haven for submarines. Sign on men's toilet — "Used Beer Dept." (Another in "officers club" on Eastern Island — "Powder Room." Wishful thinking.) Inspected everything we missed yesterday. Japanese stones at Adm. Bldg. Evidently a memorial. Dug up at airfield. Also "newspaper stone." Word now arrives that a pontoon on the other plane has been damaged & won't be repaired before tomorrow. Capts. house — unpack — game of horseshoes. N. good. Like him more and more. Quiet, modest, steady, not garrulous or arbitrary . . . After lunch — sun gone, getting cold, high wind. More inspection. 40 mm. gun position. How high they bounce off water on flat trajectory. Sand everywhere — hard on men and machines when wind blowing. Other batteries. Bombs strewn around near plane dispersal areas for quick loading on Eastern Island. Not a tree on Eastern Island. Hard to tell Army Navy Marines & CB apart. Certainly seem united here. Fierce red beard on carpenter petting a Goonie by the boat dock in the grey dawn. Magnificent mustaches & beards everywhere. Gas tank shower baths. Everyone cheerful. Radar screen — 30 minute watches — 150 mile search from the big one. Operator had hard time explaining IFF markings on screen. Smaller radar for close in plane search. Franks sidelong glance at enormous sundae at ships service canteen. Walk in the twilight with Frank. White love terns — Hovered in silent protest over this branch. Five times they came back. Barbed wire around the island & obstruction under water. Fine state of readiness. N thinks the Japs will use their 2 AC's [aircraft carriers] to try again. Can't use them in SouPac. Dinner — movies. Dark, raining, no sign of life. Crowd inside. Music. "Attention"! We take our seats. "Carry on"! . . . Something

I saw under the stars in Guantanamo in June. Ah's and oh's! when the girl appeared — men quick on uptake when any joke.

Midway, Sat, Jan 16

We've been gone a week — ½ way to Japan — what a week. Up at 5:30 again. Off in PT boat for the plane. But the rearing [?] boat can't be started. Very rough in mooring area. Baggage boat drops anchor and goes aground! Raining constantly — cold wind. Consultation . . . Can't take PT alongside plane — may smash her side. Back to harbor. Tow out the whale boat. "Condition 1. SNAFU." Transfer to pitching whale boat. Almost lose leg between. All safe. Where is luggage? Still ashore. Condition 2. TARFU. Maneuver whale boat from line to PT — beautiful handling of PT. — drifts alongside plane & somehow we crawl thru forward hatch head first on the anchor gear. A bad pitch and someone would be badly injured. But Col K[nox] made it on the second try. Thought someone would get cut in two on the [illegible] by the sharp edge of the plane hatch and the bouncing boat. We decide to let the other plane bring the luggage. Off at last about an hour late — over the creamy ring of surf around the reef & into the south wind for Johnston Island. Little talking, much reading and snoozing. K has finished another one. His concentration and rapidity with most any book amazes me.[129] Reads almost constantly with no apparent bad effects on his eyes. Heres Johnston — distant white patch on deep blue sea — the same circular reef and inside even more beautiful irridescent blue butterfly water streaked with white sand and mottled with purple patches where the coral pinnacles rise from the white sand bottom. The water in the lagoon looks shallow & the purple patches look like myriad islets — Johnston is two islands — one composed of two tiny sand spots joined by a causeway.

---

[129] Biographer Kenneth S. Davis published the following interview with Stevenson: " 'I loved that man,' he said, long afterward. 'He was brave, and honest. And he made a very great contribution to his country in her hour of greatest need. It cost him a lot. I'm sure it shortened his life. He was no intellectual, God knows, but he was highly intelligent — which a lot of "intellectuals" aren't, you know — and he knew his fellow man from a rough and crowded life. His loyalty to President Roosevelt, his political adversary in 1936, had a defiant quality, and his admiration and respect for his chief seemed to grow as the going got tougher. He had the ability to simplify complex problems. He and I saw eye to eye on foreign policy. On domestic policy we often disagreed pretty radically. But he never held that against me. We belonged to different generations, and I really think he became a lot more tolerant as a result of his Washington experiences. Although he continued to regard himself as violently anti-New Deal, of course, he liked to call me *his* New Dealer. He used to say, "I have to have a New Dealer next to me to protect me from the New Dealers around here." And he'd turn to me and say, "Adlai, you're not letting any of 'em creep in here, are you?" Yet I can't recall that he ever vetoed an appointment I wanted made or ever asked me more than perfunctory questions about it.' " *The Politics of Honor*, pp. 146–147.

840 miles today.

The water is calm & we get abo[a]rd the rearing boat with all baggage easily. Pick up passengers from other plane and head for Eastern Island — also the lesser and marine garrisoned island as at Midway. Very small — guns — hard, sunburned men. Best underground machine gun post and quarters. Built by the marines. Rocks along the causeway black with Frigate birds — soaring high in the warm blue sky. Long hooked beak; sharp sting ray tail they are among the fastest birds known. Seldom move their wings. Some of these marines have been here more than year! Standard tour is 6 mos for enlisted personnel & 9 for officers. Too long. The command car stops in middle of dock just its width! Hushed mirth from the dozen hanging on waiting to hear — the Comd't seized the wheel when all got aboard & said he would drive! It starts. The Capt. is saved. Back to the main island — a few acres & two runways. Tanks in hidden revetments & the crews burrowed into the sand beside them . . . N[imitz], F[rank Beatty] . . . & I go for a swim off the seaplane runway in the soft, warm pale green water. Sunset and we repair to a Quonset hut — the Off. Club — for a drink. Castor bean plants — venerated — only green. Col K arrives in a jeep — it looks like a rocking chair. Introductions — embarrassed silence until every one gets a drink & then the self consciousness disappears. Men look fit — no illness here. Ringworm about all. Dinner in the gen'l mess — officers at one end. Turkey & dehydrated potatoes, peas & carrots & the usual canned juices, but best of all fresh Aleuha — a fine fish caught in the lagoon. Frank & I go fishing with the dentist and the contractors foreman. . . . Bright moon, bright stars, puffs of white cloud. We try the ship channel by a shoal white with booby birds — they protest and fly down to our heads & then relax. No luck — feel our way across lagoon a mile or so to the "garbage dump" — by another shoal covered with black silent frigate birds. They rose, wheeled thru the moonlight against the white clouds & settled down again. — lie fascinated watching the fairy castles thru the bottom glass growing out of the white sand and shallowly illuminated by the moonlight thru the transparent water. The water contracts the vision — 20 feet look like inches — but we don't hit anything. No fish — rain squall & we head for the island with the constant thunder of the surf on the reef like the rumble of a distant train. To bed in darkness — total blackout. Must tell Rawleigh [Warner] my 9 roommates were quieter than he was at Midway.

Sunday, Jan 17 — Johnston Island

Up at 5:30 as usual. Cold water shave — lost my comb in the darkness. Wonderful breakfast — including a real apple. Why do they always have white bread everywhere. Wouldn't men like whole wheat as well? Morning "newspaper" — good war summary — little domestic. Off in the R A boat for the planes just as light is breaking. N[imitz] points out the southern cross. Taxi out to runway — but one motor won't start for a long while — thought I heard someone mumble SNAFU. But she started and we plu[n]ged thru white foam and rose with a hot red sun, circled and said goodbye to those little white dots in their circular white wall of foam. Into the south wind for Canton . . . we relapse into the books and magazines. Cotton for the ears from now on for me. K[nox]. shows no signs of fatigue. Spoke to the men at the movies last night while we were fishing. Will he ever ask for quarter?

We are approaching the equator. I am summoned to the after cabin for my initiation as a pollywog. Its an August moment. N is Neptune, B[eatty] is Queen, R[awleigh Warner] prosecutor & K judge. Wonderful paper bag hats contrived somehow by the cook — N even has a paper beard. R. reads the charges;[130] K finds me guilty as charged and pro-

---

[130] The typewritten "charges," preserved with the diary, read:

CHARGE ONE

CONDUCT TO THE PREJUDICE OF GOOD ORDER AND DISCIPLINE. SPECIFICATION ONE.

IN THAT ADLAI E. STEVENSON, POLLYWOG, WHILE APPROACHING THE DOMAIN OF NEPTUNUS REX, DID, ON OR ABOUT 17 JANUARY, 1943, TREAT HIS MAJESTY WITH CONTEMPT BY SLEEPING WITH HIS SHOES ON A HITHER-TO CLEAN BLANKET.

SPECIFICATION TWO.

IN THAT ADLAI E. STEVENSON, POLLYWOG, DID MAKE DISCOURAGEING REMARKS ABOUT THE LOVE LIFE OF SOME OF HIS MAJESTY'S MOST LOYAL SUBJECTS THE GOONY BIRDS OF MIDWAY ISLAND.

SPECIFICATION THREE.

IN THAT ADLAI E. STEVENSON, POLLYWOG, WHILE ENTERING THE REALM OF HIS MAJESTY NEPTUNUS REX, DID INSULT THE RULER OF THE RAGING MAIN BY WEARING DRESS UNBECOMING TO A CHICAGO LAWYER OR EVEN TO A DOWNSTATE ILLINOIS POLITICIAN AND EDITOR.

SPECIFICATION FOUR.

IN THAT ADLAI E. STEVENSON, POLLYWOG, DID IN GENERAL PERMIT TOO GREAT INDULGENCE OF AN INSATIABLE CURIOSITY, THIS BEING AN INSULT TO THE SUBJECTS OF HIS MAJESTY NEPTUNUS REX.

CHARGE TWO

CONDUCT TO THE PREJUDICE OF GOOD FORM:

SPECIFICATION ONE.

IN THAT ADLAI E. STEVENSON, POLLYWOG, DID ON OCCASIONS TOO NUMEROUS FOR INDIVIDUAL ENUMERATION, PLY HIS KNIFE, FORK AND SPOON ASSIGNED TO HIM TO SUCH AN EXTENT AS TO RESULT IN A PERMANENT DISTORTION OF HIS FIGURE BELOW AND BEHIND THE WAIST, THIS BEING AN INSULT IN FORM TO THE RULER OF THE RAGING MAIN.

nounces the sentence while I am beat about the head with a sock filled with too fragrant talcum powder and about the bottom with a spiked paddle. Sentence: drink a toast to Neptune. What a drink — I can barely get it down. My guess is crank case oil, paprika, alcohol & Wo[r]cestershire sauce boiling. Cruel mirth — I do it and then am ordered to the forward gun turret to report the crossing of the line thru my binoculars; 2 roles of toilet paper on a string made of strips from a seaman's shirt. I'm led out with a rope around my neck. But the view from the gun turret was wonderful & I'm a shellback at last with a certificate signed by N & K!

Canton Island — Phoenix group [British possessions] — the roughly circular edges of a crater — 26 miles around and 500 yds wide at the widest place. Treeless except for a little vegetation around the Pan Am bldgs — now used for transient NATS [Naval Air Transport Service] & Ferry Command parties, officers club etc. — and one lone palm tree used for observation post. This is an Army post; . . . The lagoon is beautiful from the air. Same irridescent water; white sand bottom and long sinuous streaks of deep purple coral; coral heads and pinnacles scattered about. A small boat passes under us as we circle for a landing — its wake is lavender. Pres Taylor on the rocks at entrance to Channel — looks as tho she was standing in. Everywhere army tents, huts, shelters, guns, planes. Messy, disorderly looking place. Life is hard here. Officers call it Isle of Atonement; you are not assigned to Canton, you are condemned. Plane crews lying under wings for shade. Back from the inspection tour and McCloud [131] reports that one engine has gone bad on our plane. Can't get one down from Hawaii in time. Shall we double up & go on in one. Yes. Horray. Feel as tho I ought to drop out & lighten the load on the one plane. Rubber steak for dinner. PBM just in "from the South" with sick nurse & some officers . . . on way back to get another destroyer. Many greetings — everyone in Navy seem to know each other. Miss Morrow — only woman on an island of 3000+ men — is quite an attraction. We all gather in one room of "Pan Am Hotel" for drinks. After dinner the inevitable movies. Have 4 on island. To bed much too late and . . .

Monday, Jan 18 — Canton Island
Up at 5:30 as usual. All clamber aboard one plane (13 P–6) and off for Suva shortly after light. She struggles up while we — I — hold my breath. We cross Hull Island in an hour. Also one of Phoenix group — same circular crater edge, but part at least is covered with cultivated

---

[131] Lieutenant Commander Bowen F. McLeod, the pilot.

coconut palms. Why didn't we develop this one instead of Canton? Suppose because Pan Am facilities were already there. But why did they go there — more equal hop distance? Dust along runways bad; have to water and roll constantly. Col. Ferrin refers to my trousers "What an issue." Rash of photography and short-snorter signing at Canton. Christmas trees with trimmings in an Off. Club shack underground. Plenty of beer — but Coca Cola is gold!

Circled twice over Wallis Is. Large — lush green vegetation — palms — Several settlements — 3 churches — 1 large one looks like cathedral — red roofed white French plantation & adm. bldgs. Native thatched huts along the shore line — surrounded by reef. Passed over perfect circular hole in the volcanic rock filled with brown water. Was the mouth of a later eruption? Wallis is the best looking island we have seen. So far the goonies are the best thing I've seen.

At 2:30 we pick up Nggele Levu [Island], the first [of] the "foothills" of Fiji. I'm in the pilot room. Ask one of the pilots — crisp young man from N.Y. if he doesn't get tired. "Its so monotonous — I should have taken fighters." Off to starbo[a]rd green circular streaks in the water and reefs of all sizes; in the distance can barely discern the mountainous outline of Vani Levu [Vanua Levu Island], the northernmost of the two main islands. Rugged — huge palm plantation on flatter land at so. end. Jump a broad stretch of blue sea & some small islands and below are the red roofs of Suva & the large Adm. Bldg. [British] Gov's Residence, parade ground with its inevitable little judges stand for racing. Beautiful setting, huge bay surrounded by jungle covered, rough, volcanic mountains and a circle of surf on the reef to seaward. Gen. [Charles F.] Thompson, Vice Adm. [Herbert F.] Leary, Comdr. F. S. Holms, N. Z. [New Zealand] air officer and others meet us. Some of us are dispatched to the Gov. Res. — H. E. Brig-Gen. Sir Philip Marshall. Solid military man recently from Africa. Spacious, solid, cool and ugly cream colored bldg. in beautiful park; vast variety of flowers. Sentries, blue tunics, crimson sash, silver buttons & white saw tooth knee length skirts. Great bushy heads & never a hat. N.Z. soldiers, Am soldiers, native soldiers, sailors. Natives make fine jungle fighters, quiet, can see in the dark. N[imitz]'s story about negro soldier first saw a Fiji bushy head & skirt & chased her into the bushes. So startled to find she was a man that he almost let him go! Great view over the bay from the wide Lanai at the Residence. Welcome bath & first civilian clothes since we left Pearl H. Drive thru clean and typical little colonial town; reminded me of Port of Spain but smaller cleaner and setting very beautiful. Many Hindus (with colored turbans) about as many Indians as Fijians. Don't mingle. Indian servants on residence — bare foot, white linen, blue sash & great silver SRI buckles. Soldiers along the road, Indians, bushy Fijis — what these boys of ours will have seen when the[y] go home again from all over the world! (As co-pilot said — The more I see the better I like Grammercy Park!) Step out of car at army tent hosp. back of Suva & shake hands with Col. Geo. Finney, Princeton 1921 & old friend, the commanding officer. Many malaria and battle damage cases from Guadalcanal. These boys lying staring at the ceiling in tents and flimsy shelters dreaming of home — some for months. I'll never forget the old Marine bandsman — 62 — 40 yrs in the service — tottering along with a soldier supporting him — green with potassium permanganate. His skin had died [dyed] from iodine to kill poison ivy he got at Cactus; motionless, swollen hands turned inward to his stomach & half shut eyes in an ivory green face. Geo. says Ridge Trimble[132] is at Brisbane. Geo. has done a fine job building up this hospital out of a boys school. Will soon have 500 beds under cover.

Tried to do some shopping on way back to residence — mostly tawdry Indian stuff. Passed big troop ship teeming with soldiers bound for some place. Dinner at Residence. Napkins, maiden hair ferns and beautiful lavendar flowers. "Indian servants love to decorate" Brig. Wales, commanding NZ's. Thinks climate has lot to do with Aust[ralian]. deficiencies. Ev[idently?]. NZ's feel themselves much superior to Australians. Magnificent sunset into the sea as we drove to the residence along the quayside.

New ADC just arrived today from N.Z. Lost arm in Egypt. Submarine "sighted" report just before dinner. Patrol out. Dropped charges. Nothing found. Easy, graceful way English entertain. No fuss, no apologies. All in white dinner jackets & K[nox]. W[arner]. & I feeling comfortable and a little overdressed in our civilian clothes after a week in the same k[h]aki shirt & pants. Talked with the financial secretary after dinner with much & good wine. Seemed to feel that we had not made most of depot potential at Suva. Didn't make much sense. Talked about how much had to be done by hand at Button etc. To bed at 10:30 after a long look at the almost full moon & the bay & tropical park. Mosquito netting.

Tuesday, Jan 19 — Suva — Fiji
Awakened at 5 — dawn — by a solid wall of noise — birds chattering raucously. N[imitz]'s story about Minas flying into take piece of thread from Mrs. N's sewing machine in Hawaii. Tea & pap[a]ya & then a few minutes perched on the lanai wall in the warm fresh early morning &

132 Dr. I. Ridgeway Trimble, Jr., a Princeton classmate of Stevenson's, on General Douglas MacArthur's staff as chief surgical consultant for the Pacific Area.

the breath taking view. "Oahu bombed — alert over in 7 minutes." Dispatch — everyone confused & not very communicative. Suspect a false alarm. Breakfast on trays on lanai & off after farewells to Gov & his staff & signing "the book." Fly along the rugged coast to Nandi our base — ships & airfields. Fiji changes from lush dark jungle around Suva to paler green, thinner vegetation — less rain. Shore and little valley mouths dotted with clusters of bures ("Buays") native thatched huts. Fish snares here, project from shore line like giant leis. Constant miracle of water colors with changing cloud and sky. Rainbows all about — water as green as a lime. Word before we left that our relief plane had also broken down at Canton. Esp. [Espiritu Santo] Harbor a beautiful channel of deep water between Esp. and Aori islands [New Hebrides]. Full of ships — little evidence of the shore activity from the air except the airfields — coconut plantation all around the settlement of Lunaville, palms and jungle make fine camouflage. We go aboard Curtiss — seaplane tender — splendid ship — new . . . I bunk with Cmdr. John F. Greenslade, son of Adm. [J. W.] Greenslade; serious, conscientious, hard working staff officer. . . . Big lunch party. They do eat well!! Go ashore for inspection trip — caravan of 4 or 5 command cars. Worst dust I've ever seen. All roads built since we arrived last May; and largely since . . . early August at time of Solomon's invasion.[133] No dock for ships yet. Unloading all by landing boats. This is certainly major service of the 50′ tank lighter! Truck[s] back wheels in water and landing boats run up to them. All hard work. Fantastic accomplishment.

First along shore then settlement of a few small warehouses and Burns & Phelps store then shady coconut grove — passed male natives coming into town — Micronesians — lowest form — small black bushy haired, g-string & longflap, shell or head necklaces, bow & arrows, hearts of boar tusks. Not very dangerous looking. This is most civilized of New Hebrides; most plantation; missionaries. To Col Evans Carlson's Second Marine Raiders Batallion encampment.[134] Big [illegible] head sign at entrance with MAKIN, ——— GUADALCANAL. 4 or 5 Cos' drawn up in a clearing — all dressed in grey green coveralls — fine looking lot of youngsters. A little shrine where the names of the casualties are pa[i]nted. Bandstand, amplifier. Carlson introduces Sec & Sec. gives them the works. Carlson leads in singing

---

[133] Allied forces invaded the Solomon Islands on August 7, 1942. After months of bitter fighting, the Japanese evacuated Guadalcanal early in February, 1943.

[134] Carlson's Raiders staged commando-style raids on enemy-held territory. On August 25, 1942, for instance, they made a hit-and-run raid on Makin Island. Robert Lechie, *Strong Men Armed: The United States Marines Against Japan* (New York: Random House, 1962), pp. 117–120.

> *Oh, we'll hang the Old Mikado to the cherry*
> *blossom tree —*
> *Glo[r]y, Glory we are Raiders*
> " " " " "
>
> *As we go marching on!*
> *Oh, we'll take the Rising Sun & we'll set it*
> *in the West etc.*
> *Oh, we'll take the little corporal for a one*
> *way Ride etc.*
> *Oh, we'll bury Mussolini in a big brick tomb*
> *etc.*

Then it was to the tune of "Around her head she wore a yellow ribbon" —

> *Around her thigh she wore a purple garter;*
> *And if you asked her why she wore it —*
> *She wore it for her Raider who was far, far*
> *away*
> *Far away, Far away etc*
>
> *Every day she pushed a baby buggy;*
> *And if you asked why she pushed it —*
> *She pushed it for her Raider who was far,*
> *far away*
> *Far away, far away etc*
>
> *Behind the door her father kept a shotgun;*
> *And if you asked him why he kept it —*
> *He kept it for her Raider who was far, far*
> *away etc.*

It ended with some lively verses about the exploits of the Raiders to the tune [of] Abdul de Bull Bull Ameer.

Carl[s]on is a tall, lean, thin lipped and hawked nose fighting man and the collegiate atmosphere about the performance seemed a little incongruous in view of the stories about the blood thirsty raiders and the necklaces of Japanese ears.

We drove back to the boat dock by the seaplane base along the coconut shaded beach past the little French Catholic mission. Soldiers & sailors — all look alike & dress alike — along the way bargaining with the diminutive natives with their front tuft of bus[h]y hair dyed a reddish tinge with lime. Then on along the dusty roads that the CB's have hacked thru the groves and the tangled jungle to the airplane strips. We crossed the ———— river on a narrow pontoon bridge. The water was deep green and cool and fresh and liberty parties were swimming from the steep jungle banks — swinging out on rope ladders & diving from the great trees overhanging the water. A swimming [illegible] in paradise. We drove on thru an endless procession of camps over roads that only jeeps could negotiate. New dock out to deep water filled in between piling laced with coconut trees and faced with flattened gas drums. Air strips; taxiways, dispersal. Areas, camp sites, storage etc. hacked out of jungle that looks like a solid wall. Our driver was a colored Captain, probably a chaplain attached to the negro AA army unit. Men mostly in tents. The dust was suffocating and when it rains the roads are a quagmire. When the work started in Aug. in earnest there were no roads — only trails between the plantations & to the native villages. Our guide was Lt. Col. J. W. Hart USMC . . . a swell guy. He's given me copies of the new verses for the Marine song "From the Halls of Montezuma" evidently written by J. Bowen, Lt. Comdr. USN (I met him in the Curtiss & suggested he keep notes on his conversations with the coast watchers. I prophesy that their exploits will be among the best reading of the war) and ending with this morsel:

> "Now when Gabriel toots his mighty flute,
>   calling old campaigners home,
> * And Tojo's balls hang on the walls, of
>   Valhalla's golden dome,
> Then the Lord will wink at Vandergrift,
> While he's eating spam and beans,
> Saying "God on high sees eye to eye,
> With the United States Marines."

* Or if you prefer delicacy —
"And Tojo's ears have hung for years, from Valhalla's golden dome."

We ended up at Gen. [Roy S.] Geiger's Quarters for beer — God it was good! Much talk as always when this caravan comes to a moment's stop about Guadalcanal. I asked Adm. [Forrest] Sherman what his guess for Jap. casualties was to date on "the island of death." Didn't think it could be less than 20 000 including losses at sea. Halsey[135] . . . told about the massacre by tanks at the [illegible] River etc; difficulty of rooting them out etc. More inspecting & back to the Curtiss for dinner . . . Talked . . . about photography and photographic interpretation. Sequence of photos of Munda airfield — built under the trees between

[135] Admiral William F. Halsey, Commander, South Pacific Force.

Nov 24 & Dec 15. Can clearly trace development in spite of the camou-flage by careful study of the photos. This work seems very good & of enormous value. Our men think we have developed it better than the Japanese. We have followed the English.

To bed early — on deck — suffocating inside. Ships blinking at each other but blacked out. Shadowy figures creeping all around with bed clothes to escape heat inside. Its beautiful moonlight & one could ha[r]dly believe the turmoil behind those peaceful, graceful silent palms along the moonlit beach. Everything is still on deck — I'd like to watch the dark forms of the ships in the moonlight's path — but I can't keep awake — a typewriter is still chattering slowly in the communications room on the deck just above and behind us. It happened all of a sudden. I don't believe I was awake but I distinctly heard a series of 5 or 6 rapid and distant thuds. I thought I could feel the concussion a little. Someone stirred on a cot nearby and mumbled "whats up." No one answered — I said — "sounds like AA fire." Then silence & back to sleep. Can't understand why I was so indifferent — perhaps I was trying to behave like a sophisticate . . .

Wednesday, Jan 19 — Espiritu Santo — New Hebrides
Got up with the first streak of light about 4:15 & pretty soon I heard the muffled voices in the Capt's cabin behind us saying we'd been bombed. The sunrise was magnificent — I heard the PBY's taking off & the patrol planes — there's thunder with the dawn in this war. With all the excitement of the bombing over by the airfields a mile or more away I felt a little compensated for being left behind. After a good breakfast with Capt. W. P. Cogswell he showed us over the Curtiss. Its a whole community of trades and services. We spent a long time down in a swe[a]t box way below where some young boys were preparing torpedoes. The ship is fearfully crowded. Men all catching a little rest in every odd corner. In the bunking spaces night crews were sleeping with lights on. The planning and the fittings that go into a tender ship like this that must be ready for anything. I don't see how any other peo-ple could do it better than we do. At 10:30 we attended the daily in-formation review — Barry Wall P[rinceton] — 1924 was conducting it! A B17 had shot down a P-40 near the Shortlands! More reports from the Coast watchers. Those guys fascinate me! I went below with a couple of young officers to get some ice cream at the soda fountain — just out so we had Coca Cola. . . . Long talk with Capt. C. S. Defoney — head medical officer on Adm. Halsey's staff — about necessity for more ma-larial fighting equipment. Gave me list of things he is asking . . . for. Natives all have it; many troops on Guadalcanal; scourge of these islands.

After lunch went ashore & by Jeep* out to Capt Joel D. White's adv. base hospital. Always humble in the presence of the Army & Navy doctors; what they can & have done, cheerful & enthusiastic, mostly reserves. Vis[i]ted his improved laundry, drier; storehouse, xray, lab. etc. The M C corpsmen deserve more recognition! Anopheles mosquito, malaria carrier, bites only at night. Flies bad during the day in all these places. Almost passed out from heat, smell and horror in one surgical hut. All the boys with fixed glazed eyes staring at the ceiling, half naked; brave smiles; no complaints. Boy wounded in neck, breathing into his tissue, inflated scrotum as big as a grapefruit. His body creeks to the touch as tho his bones were all smashed. He'll recover. Amputated leg on another; 36 shrapnel wounds. Intake of about 2000 per mo. here and only lost 7 so far! Blood plasma, sulfa drugs and rapid evacuation from the front by air before the gas gangrene sets in is the explanation . . . I reeled out into the sunlight. But I didn't fool the doctors — they sat me down just in time, pushed my head between my knees and spirits of ammonia under my nose. Visited enclosure for Jap medical cases. Small emaciated men — 9 or 10 of them — 1 psychotic, 1 flyer with compound fracture; others mostly malarial. This was their rest period. Some struggled to make a bow. Visited site of new hospital CB's are building — 1000 beds. Higher ground. Need 100 man Quonset huts — laundry machinery. Place them end to end. Fine layout prepared by the doctors. Why shouldn't this be a major base hospital instead of sending them all the way to N Z & Fiji? Clear up malaria in vicinity first.

Dr. White . . . took me back to the boat dock to meet Harris, the Burns and Phelps, South Seas Co., representative. They saved his life last summer from [heart?] disease. In Espiritu Santo 19 yrs & So. Seas 30. Australian — fat, browned, heavy drinker I guess, mild spoken, very intelligent, anti French . . . We drank Australian beer in his bare, dirty shack; old Tonkinese paddled around in background. Electric ice box; bare table, one electric light, fly specked empire poster or so, kerosene stove, nothing else. Caracture of a south seas trader. Gave me a huge conch shell horn and a boar's tusk. Much info. about natives; debauched by French traders; flat head gin; importation of Tonkinese; brought syphilis; "yaws" very prevalent. Catholic, Methodist and 7th Day Adventist Missionaries — latter called Kiki grass-vegetarians. Low form of native — Micronesian — Negroid. (Still cannibals on Malekula island.) Live off of taro, yams, fruit, wild boar, some fish. Only about 2 or 3000 natives on Espiritu Santo. Ship of his Co. used to come in about once a

* Jeep driver from Miss — welder in CB Cub unit — could make $150 per mo. more at home — wife — 2 children.

month. Seemed genuinely fond of the natives; disliked the French planters & their predatory colonial policy contrasted with English paternalism . . . He was apprehensive lest we overpay the French for damage to their coconut groves.

Took Harris bouncing back with us over the dusty roads to Dr. Smith's quarters — tidy tent house — for a wash up & then to very festive mint julep part[y] at Med. officers "Club" — a Quonset hut as usual . . . Everyone got very high and after all my good resolves I finally became a "Short Snorter" — ! To mess with the doctors — duck again! and after many farewells back to the ship in the launch with Harris; a little wistful by this time — had been here too long — wanted to get out — in Aust[ralia]. only once in 19 yrs; all changed now, would never be the same again. Usual note of distrust and dislike for the English that you so often detect among the Australians. The black forms of the ships in the moonlight on the beautiful harbor and to bed on the cool deck with the white full moon in my eyes. You can't write about a day like this one when everything from heroism stories on Guadl. [Guadalcanal] to laundry machinery to cannibalism has tumbled into your head like the topsy, turvy cargoes in the merchant ships you hear so much about. I watched them loading candy bars! in the forward cargo hatch and then fell into another exhausted sleep alone on the deck with Rawleigh [Warner].

Thursday Jan 20, Espiritu Santo
The thunder of the planes taking off came with the first streaks of the flaming dawn. (I wonder if Lt. Comdr. Crowley got off for Cactus at 2 alright — he was mighty raucous when he walked out of the mess last night reminding me again to remember him to Congressman Woodrum[136] and that he had not seen his little daughter for 2 yrs).

Marines in remote spots like Cape Cumberland buy native wines for $5!

Up early; swell French toast for breakfast with Capt. Cogswell. Very hot sun today. What should we do — take off for Efate [Island] where we are going to meet the others coming back from Cactus or wait until we get a departure report? Long talk with Ike Couch[137] — This war is going to do wonders for a lot of privileged Americans of every generation — but can we count on more political maturity as a result of these experiences . . . Wanted to visit coast watcher signal center with Lt. Comdr Bowen. Harris knew all these fellows . . . & told me much about their methods of operation with the friendly natives, surrounded by

[136] Representative Clifton Woodrum.
[137] Unable to identify.

Japs. Torture of a native police sergt. who was also a chief on Guad[alcanal]. by bayonet stabs to surrender one of the watchers. (Surrender cards — dropped over Jap lines — telling just how to surrender — promising good food — with picture of a naked lady on the reverse side) But we didn't have time so after farewells and messages back home (I left a bottle of whiskey for Capt. Cogswell on his bunk — I hope the stewards don't get it first) R[awleigh]. & I take off in the big plane for Efati. Malekula very wild and rugged; deep gorges; heavy jungle, few plantations along the shore line — few visible native villages. The home of the cannibals! Ambrym Is[land, New Hebrides]. — great coal black valleys in the green jungle where the lava has flowed down to the sea. Must be young island. The crater is filled with cloud — perhaps its smoking a little. Long stretches of jet black beach and creamy white surf — What was the name of the beach on Hawaii Ellen and I saw in 34 — the black sands of Kalepona [Kalapana]? We approach a perfect cone island rising out of the sea — but the side view spoils it! And in a moment we're circling another great concentration of ships in a strip of sea between two islands — Havannah Harbor — Efate. We land off a seaplane "base" — the usual small boat dock, mooring kuays [quays], gasoline drums, small barges, k[h]aki tents peeping thru the jungle and all the symptoms of feverish activity behind the curtain of palms. An officer . . . comes along side and finds R & S instead of SecNav, CinC and Com So Pac! [138] He takes us to the Wichita — Adm [R. C.] Giffen, large, bluff, jolly and clear blue eyed man surprised to see us. Has had no arrival report. Summons communication officer etc. Lunch is over but the quiet ine[vi]table Filipino mess attendants get going & in a few minutes we have filet mignon . . . This is a taut ship; a marine in the detachment tells me it was called the luxury liner of the Atlantic Fleet. Adm. Giffen, at sea for more than 2 yrs now, and long director of athletics at Annapolis talks of Iceland convoy duty, his battle with the French in Casablanca, his farm in Maryland, and sports with equal emphasis and vigor and humor. Here's a good one. We talk of French policy in No. Africa. Wish I could enlighten him more. The French fought well; good shooting. Much applause for the reservists. They constitute about 75% of the officer personnel on most of the ships now. We go over the ship and marvel again at the miracle of Radar. A junior engineer . . . shows me the boiler and engine rooms. The heart [heat] is intolerable and my admiration for the men below decks bubbles over. In the superheat boiler room at full speed the temperature is 160°

[138] Secretary Knox, Admiral Nimitz, Admiral Halsey, Admiral McCain, and Captain Beatty had flown to Guadalcanal and left Stevenson and Rawleigh Warner behind.

and the men have to stand watch and watch. About 4:30 the Secy's party arrives; they are piped over the side with side boys, marine detachment and all formalities. The men groan a little at these extra trimmings in war time, but it helps keep the ship taut I suppose. Captains from the other ships arrive to greet the party. I'm quartered on the Suwanee — One of the tankers converted into carriers — with Adm McCain & Comdr. Anderson. A lau[n]ch takes us over and Capt. McMahon who took command yesterday greets us. A shower and a shave and a look at the roster. Lieut. Irving Peck is assistant operations officer. Looks fine and takes me over the ship. Full of enthusiasm and interest. Has been aboard after duty in Atlantic Sea Frontier office since October. Asked no questions about home and his friends. They all seem to have adapted themselves to the new life with little nostalgia — its like amnesia. A destroyer is fueling alongside. These converted tankers carry a lot of fuel oil. Pilots ready room is air conditioned and comfortable. The heat is awful below decks as usual. Back to the Wichata for a big dinner party. The chef produces a highly ornamental cake in honor of the Sec. [Knox] which he reluctantly cuts. Everyone seems tired; the conversation is not very sprightly. Perhaps its too much rank. (N[imitz]. tells me he doesn't think we could turn Negro units into service units) Much talk about Guad[alcanal]. — they were bombed repeatedly during the night — Took to the shelters the first time and then didn't bother. Sec. didn't even wake up. All news from there is good. Wished I dared write all I've heard about operations in the last few days. But one still wonders how island by island we can ever do the enormous job ahead out here. But of course I don't know the grand strategy of the Pac[ific]. I wish I did. I wish someone would tell me what it is. Or even assure me that we have a grand strategy. Could we [win] without Russia? Certainly the destruction, even gradu[a]l of Jap Navy & shipping is a comprehensible strategy, but must we just hold, hold, hold in this infinity of islands? After dinner Adm Mc[Cain] & I pass the movies and cross the beautiful moon bathed harbor to our home on the Suwanee — I'm still perspiring from my visit to the engine room & go up on the flight deck to cool off. A knot of men amidships are watching the movies below in the hangar well from the vantage point. Others are scattered about asleep — the early comers under the wings of the TB in case of rain. I lie down forward. Beside me on the gun gallery the watch occasionally mumbles something over their ear phones. In a few minutes I'm asleep on the hard deck wondering if I'll have gobs of grease or tar or something on my good pants the tailor let down for me on the Curtiss — they're almost to the ankles now! Should I go below & sleep in the fine bed the Ex officer has given me? Yes — and a good night it was too.

Friday, Jan 21 — Efati

Up at 6 — its always a struggle — breakfast with Adm Mc[Cain].
. . . & Capt. McMahon & off to the seaplane landing. We're in the air
& over the proud ships in Havannah harbor on schedule. In a couple of
hours we pick up the N E tip of New Caledonia — rugged, red soil;
sparser vegetation than we've seen before. The shore line is rugged —
bays, small islands & reefs. We circle the harbor and Noumea and Isle
Nou. This is the first real town we have seen since P.H. — ships, red
roofs. Its a town of some 10 or 12 thousand, largely native. We land at
the seaplane dock on Isle Nou; Adm. [M. A.] Mitscher meets us and the
usual tour follows. It reminds me of Arizona, cactus and flowers and
rough, arid hills. Building everywhere, natives, marines & Tonkinese.
Old French women's prison with high stone walls. Marine salvage yard
"You Report 'em — We go get 'em" full of damaged planes. They're a
spare part supply base. We cross over to Noumea in launches and tour
about the town, docks, nickle plant, confusion of command headquarters
what with Army, Navy, Marine Corps. Thin air forces and supply.
Typical French town. So this is the secret "White Poppy"! An officer tells
me it was a shipping address for 1 year & they even printed it on the
money orders — and then made it secret. Trenches in the Park — recreation center going up. Ships along the inadequate dock and everything
from canned pineapple juice to bombs piled about. Dusty, hot, hardened
troops embarking with full equipment "going north." Native workmen
with garlands of green leaves in their hair — for sunshade or ornament!
And always their hair died [dyed] a henna color in front. It teems with
activity; trucks, tractors, jeeps, command cars, sailors on liberty from the
warships (1 day in 20), C B's building, building, building, MPs, SPs,
white women & children — something we haven't seen before. Tonkinese
in peaked wide straw hats and colored skirts; babies locked to their
backs.

Its something like a frontier town and if you set anything down you
better keep your eye on it — most every one you see is looking for something from a ship, a comp. an office & God helps him who helps himself!
Adm. Halsey's for lunch — a comfortable, ugly red brick house set on a
hill with a fine view of the bay. It was the Jap. counsels [consul's] house!
And we admire cheep Japanese decorations, furniture and eat off of
Japanese dishes. On the way we passed many concrete pill boxes built
during the "revolution" last April — a confused business between a new
Free French Governor and the old one[139] whom the natives liked. The
new one somehow treacherously lured him onto a ship & then sailed
away!

[139] Of the Vichy government.

In the afternoon we drive all over the nearby countryside, but don't get to the marine amphib. camp & all my efforts to reach [Congressman] Maury Maverick's boy by telephone were in vain. Beyond the nickle plant we're bldg. a new dock — and the CB have even made their own nails! One hears stories about French non cooperation — haven't offered to turn over Gov's offices; barracks, demands for rent for little narrow guage Ry. for dock, for road maintenance etc. — but no one is giving much away at home either! One wonders about this enormous development in Noumea and all about it. Its a long journey to see even a little of it. Should we slow down here and build up Button for the major base. With Guadalcanal ours, Noumea falls still further back and Espiritu Santo becomes more secure (tho they did bomb it unsuccessfully again last night). Is our logistics as audacious as our tactics? Recreation situation not very good but most of the men you meet or see seem happy. Problem of promotions in Army units which are at full strength and held here or in Suva for months and months is bad; particular in Air Force where promotions for less experienced people at home are more rapid. We visit the NAD and an adjoining CB camp — orderly and efficient as usual — cameras appear magically out of the dust also as usual. Beer cuts the dust!

I am quartered with Gen. [E. N.] Harmon — Com Gen Sou Pac — a quiet, wiry, tough and sick looking little Maj. Gen. (Air) who should and will be promoted. His song is skip bombing on the Tokyo Express. Gen. Barnet acts as host — Gen. H. to A[d]m H[alsey]'s for dinner with the big shots — and we have Turkey & wine! I've seen no sign of short rations anywhere & the C.O.'s do very nicely. Before dinner the Sec. [Knox] had a press conf. at Adm Halsey's — their sqwak [squawk] is no longer allowed trans[port]. by air which limits their [illegible] and flexibility. (Adm Nimitz doesn't give me much help on this — "there's never a vacant place anywhere — there's always mail.") Halsey's optimistic statement about Japan being beaten this yr. comes up, of course. (Rawleigh [Warner] tells me Halsey said it to provoke the Japs — to bring them out to strike him — he's public enemy No. 1. I wonder.) Talk about aviation mostly — (the "black cats" deserve a hand) — and I'm reminded that there are a lot of suspicious aviation enthusiasts at home that would have been comforted by the concentration on aviation I've seen on this trip! Gen. H. returns & tops off the day with ping pong with Gen Barnet & so to bed.

Saturday, Jan 22 — Noumea

Up at 6 or worse — after a losing battle with the mosquito net around my narrow cot — farewells and we're off in the lau[n]ch for

Isle Nou and the plane in the sharp early morning heat I've learned to dread at home. We swelter and trickle in our life belts in the sealed cabin while the engines are warmed and the plane makes her peculiar maneuvers before the take off. Farewell to New Caledonia — will I ever be this close to Australia again?

Beautiful Suva harbor again — I've seen nothing better and the Governor's Res. & beautiful park look very fine down below after our adventures up front — tho I confess I've had little discomfort to complain about. We go to the Res where the Gov & the nice one armed NZ [New Zealand] ADC welcome us cordially again & into the great cool drawing room with the life size portraits of Geo V and Queen Mary long ago and full of wonderful flowers. Gen [Charles F.] Thompson invites us all to dinner at the Grand Pacific Hotel. Adm. [Charles P.] Mason is over from Nandi. N[imitz], . . . Mason & Thompson take a walk while F[rank Beatty] & I wait around for another tennis racket in the beautiful park — an egg fruit tree, begonias, spider lilys around the base of great trees, many kinds of mangoes and myriads of things I've never seen before. Evidently all the subtropical, tropical & temperate things grow in this warm but kindly climate. The tennis racket doesn't arrive & we play squash on a court built, H.E. [His Excellency] says, for the Prince of Wales. At 5:30 there is a Navy Cross and White star presentation with a blue jacket in whites & a marine detachment & officers on the residence lawn. The recipients are Murphy, a Marine private and Comdr. Sullivan, supply officer on the Hornet. Its a fine show in a beautiful setting and the officers are invited in for drinks afterward by H.E. I talked with a fine figure of a man — a native chief and head of the Fiji troops. He speaks perfect Oxonian English — the Residence guards with their enormous bushy heads, blue tunics and white saw tooth lava lavas are Fiji constabulary in dress uniform. The natives have an extraordinary sense of smell; know how to live off the jungle & the troops are intensely eager to get battle duty. Murphy is a mick from So Boston; "wanted adventure & to see the world & now all I want is to get back to Boston and get married." He's not yet 21 & disappointed that there isn't more to drink in Suva! "I've had a belly full & when everything was hitting us I really prayed mister — they're no heathens in a fox hole."

Dinner at the Hotel was gala — all the ranking officers. 3 wines. I sat between Capt. Robertson, the 6'6" bespectacled Colonial Financial Sec'y and Mr. Crompton, an arthritic who came to Suva for his health 40 yrs ago and is now one of the patriarchs and leading barrister of the colony. He regaled me in a barely audible voice & thru clicking false teeth with tales of the cannibal islands before the cession to Britain in 1874. I told H E that Crompton should write a history of Fiji & he agreed. There is no good one. Talked with a Gen & a Colonel after dinner. Promotion problem for their division — unfair — men here too long and getting dull. Army may reap sad harvest from its rapid promotion practices! The sunset was glorious and retreat and the lowering of the flag at the residence in tune to the bugle by the native guards was something I wont forget. "They love to play soldier." To bed after a couple of stories by N. . . .

Sunday, Jan 23, Suva

Up in hot bright sunshine and another luxurious breakfast on the verandah outside the bedrooms with a tray. Damn these egg cups. Adm McC[ain] got a glass out of the bathroom. Farewell to the beautiful park — along the sea coast road — horses galloping on the coral beach at low tide — stories about Gen Mac A [Douglas MacArthur] by Adm [Herbert F.] Leary who was with him for 9 mos in Australia. Good soldier 20 yrs ago; egotism, "afraid of me," law unto himself. Knows little of ships & Navy. Doesn't consult. Gen. [Robert C.] Richardson wouldn't take post with him. Gen. [George C.] Kenney good man. Off for Upolu — western Samoa on time. Crossed Niaufoo — island like a great green doughnut in the deep blue sea. Volcano crater, no reefs, black lava flows. Crater a dark, green lake in perpendicular walls. 3 little green islands and one has a little pale green lake in it! 2 more lakes on the doughnut, one cream colored, one yellow & a little red roofed village in a coconut grove — no beach. This is without doubt the most remarkable island I've seen.

At Faleolo Airport, Upolu, Gen Price[140] and all the off[ic]ers, including the N.Z. [New Zealand] administrator, met us. The tropical paradise at last! Inspection. Beautiful air strip along the coast in palm grove bordered on the rocky beech by native huts called fales — woven matting on the sides hung like clapboards — Samoan venetian blinds. No nails; held together by cords of fiber — beautiful workmanship — and the roofs are thatched with cane leaves which will last several years. But they have run out of cane! These are officers quarters with palms overhead, flowers about them, the beautiful sea in front & the airstrip behind! The installation is on "the largest plantation in the south seas" — belonged to the Kaiser. The place was a ju[m]ble of poles, quonset huts, tents & wooden shacks and all about the lush green jungle and the coconut groves. Somehow here the jungle seemed more hospitable and less forbidding, solid and [illegible] than Espiritu Santo [New Hebrides]. This is the rainy season. We arrived in a rain squall but it was soon bright again. They had 50" in 30 days — but it has been an exceptionally

140 General Charles F. B. Price, Commanding General, Samoan Defense Force.

dry winter! The native Polynesians are husky looking, men naked except for a lava lava but the women are well covered. They are very heavily constructed from the waist down, huge calfs & knees. There is considerable mild elephantiasis & some of our men get swelling in the scrotum after 6–9 months. They are promptly sent home and recover with [no?] ill effects. No malaria.

All aboard 2 PBYs for Tutuila — engine won't start on one and at last K[nox] & N[imitz] et al dismount and we all pile in the other. SNAFU! McLeod is grinning! We fly along the coast — it is more populous than anything we've seen. Many native villages — clean, orderly [illegible] built on mounds of black lava rock and always a large white red roofed church. The small humble villages and the large proud churches remind me of Mexico and Spain. The missionaries have been very active in Samoa for a long while and the Samoans are very generous people! We pass over Apia; a tiny little red roofed town and the only harbor in Western Samoa — and a poor one at that. The pilot circled low over Robert Louis Stevenson spacious, white, green roofed home back of the city at the foot of the hill on which he is buried. The place is evidently well cared for [by] the N Z authorities and reminds one that Apia is no war boom town like most everything else we have seen. In 50 minutes, thru a rain squall & across more of the bottomless blue Pacific, we are over the rugged shore of American Samoa — Tutuila — more neat little villages, but the churches seem smaller. The interior looks too rugged to support any population. We land on a fine white coral built on largely made land projecting into the sea. The flashlights pop, greetings with the officers; Frank [Beatty] has a reunion with Capt. [William] Wallace, an old friend from his days in China[141] and we drive off with him along the new coast road 7½ miles into the storied harbor of Pago Pago — its a deep green walled fjord. Enroute the same neat native villages, crawling with Marines. They have been here a year now and the friendly, happy Samoans have been very kind to them. The crop of half breeds is ripening. K coins a new word. The next generation will be Marinesians instead of Polynesians. . . .

Large whiskey & soda party at Gen [Charles F. B.] Price quarters. Good conversation with Lieut Henry A. Zuberano USNR, formerly clerk of the court & resident of Samoa for 15 yrs. Knows & loves the natives. They like litigation! What lawyer wouldn't like them. At Capt. Wallace's suggestion he agrees to arrange a Siva dance for us. Tropical downpour. Mess with the officers in one of the old marine quarters — large comfortable cool family houses in a row along the bay, but now the dock has been enlarged and liberty ships are unloaded 24 hrs a day just off

[141] Captain Beatty had served aboard a United States ship on the China station.

the porch! Col K. & Adm McC & N don't join the Siva expedition. Its in a large chief's fale [house] on the edge of the little town — lit by 2 undisguised electric bulbs hanging from ceiling! Its open on the sides, supported by huge hardwood beams and posts. At one end is large tapa cloth curtain — chief's. Fine patterns & subdued coloring — woven out of bark fiber of a tree something like our mulberry the chief tells me. High chief Tufele greets us with his talking chief and another elderly chief. Our host is a huge smiling man with a calf bigger than your head, intelligent face and a bright green cloth lava lava. No 2 chief wears black and all the male singers and dancers wear white denoting no particular rank. Tufele is variously reported as weighing from 300 to 350 — he has brought 150 of his people from Manua — group of small islands 60 miles east — to work as stevedores on the dock. They work 3 mos & then go back to tend the crops & another group comes over. There are perhaps 20 of us guests and we sit cross legged on the mats in front of a muslin curtain at one end of the fale (behind it I soon discover are dogs children and women) and along the sides. It all starts with long speeches by the talking chief at the other end in a loud voice accompanied by approving shouts of emphasis from a group in a row by the Kava bowl. I seem to be the guest of honor, the c[h]ief, in the absence of Col. K. First I am presented, for him, a kava root — a very fine one I am told. It looks like a medieval bludgeon. When the speeches of welcome, assurances of loyalty, anxiety to help with the war, I make a little speech of ack. which the chief translates — evidently also enlarges! — for the approving shouts of his people. Then the Kava ceremony begins. Its a large wooden bowl a couple of feet in diameter sitting on many legs and ca[r]ved from a single piece. Water is poured on the shredded kava root. The long white Fan-fiber "fly switch" strainer — is energetically bathed and stirred around in the bowl, sque[e]zed and flung backward out of the tent by the Kava mixed [mixer] with never so much as a glance behind him! Someone in the dark seizes it and snaps it violently back and forth to shake out the larger particles and then hands it back in — this goes on 8 or 10 times until the Kava is ready. Amid much shouting — the talking chief is now introducing the distinguished guests — a fine big samoan with a fine flourish on bended knee and lowered head hands me the Kava cup. I spill a little on the mat as a gesture of something and then in a panic drink the least bit of the tasteless dishwater that they prize so highly and will give you utter relaxation, even paralysis of the legs. So it goes all around the guests and some of the hardened, experienced officers do the traditional bottoms up.

The chief comes over and joins R[awleigh Warner] — with me in the center — at the end of the room and after some more speeches and thanks for their courtesy and hospitality and loyalty the singing and dancing begins. Some 30 great muscular Samoans with garlands of green leaves in their hair come in and sit in a circular group at the far end in front of the chief's beautiful tapa cloth curtain. Their chorus singing of historical songs is very fine — rythmic and melodious. They sing better than the Hawaiians I'm told. Tufele was educated in Hawaii, is very intelligent and informative and passionately fond of Camels. Women bring us conch shell ash trays and the singing gets wilder. They have no drums, just pat the mats with their hands and keep perfect r[h]ythm in some songs with a loud & soft hand clap. A man dances. They commence tatooing at the waist at puberty and as one's deeds warrant continue until many of the men are tatooed solidly from the waist to & including the always large overdeveloped and ungainly knee. Then a long procession of women dance — two of them are young and their breasts are bare, — a special compliment! They shine with coconut oil, have beautiful but stiff looking tapa cloth skirts and much of the dancing is in a semi stooping position with movement of the feet, hands and arms but not much body. No hula hula torsal contortions to speak of. It all had a symbolism I suppose. Two little girls, 7 & 9 danced very well. They all, boys & girls, learn from the time they can walk. The last bare breasted girl to dance was very pretty — they all have perfect white teeth — and the chief proudly announced to me that she was his eldest daughter — 16. After she finished her dance to the male chorus — the women don't sing — he ordered her over to shake hands with me. The last "number" included his wife, his elected successor as chief, and the middle aged daughter of a high chief in Western Samoa. It was a wild, noisy climax with one of the women occasionally kicking the fale posts. The chiefs wife in spite of 9 children could still handle her bulky body with grace and extra[ordinary]. agility. When it was over Tufele insisted on presenting me with the Kava bowl, cup and pan. I asked him to come to Ks house in the morning to receive his personal thanks and that evening became an everlasting memory.

Monday, Jan 24 — Pago Pago
Up at 6; breakfast in the officers mess; a short drive about to see some more of the development (Sadie Thompson's Hotel — a shabby 2 story house) and we drive along the fine shore road for the airport — past the extraordin[ar]y "flower pot" — a pinnacle of hard volcanic rock topped with palms, standing out of the sea — and the water side latrines

on stilts. At the airfield K[nox] appropriately thanks Tufele & the "vice chief" and we're off again for Upolu in Western Samoa. We switch to our plane and at 10 we're in the air bound for Canton [Island].

Canton is bare & desolate as ever. Col. [William W.] Jenna reports mysterious shelling a few nights before. Much speculation as to what it could be — sub[marine]. or imagination. No shells landed on the beach. F[rank Beatty], N[imitz] & I took a swim. High Eastern trade wind — and a sunbath. Whisky with the office[r]s and at last a copy of the Honolulu Advertiser & a list of the officers lost on the Martin Clipper between Hawaii & the mainland last Friday in addition to Adm. [Robert H.] English. Capt. Thomas who came out with us from San Fran. & Miss Morrow, the Navy Nurse we met here last week — poor girl! Adm N told them about encouraging progress "down south," as they say, the usual wretched dinner at Canton, movies & bed. Why don't they get a better mess here? I've seen nothing in any naval estab[lishment]. as bad. Col. [Charles S.] Ferrin reports good progress since we were here last in other respects — gas tanks covered, better camouflage, more barbed wire etc — and after he gets thru I daresay something will even happen to the mess!

Tuesday, Jan 25 — Canton

Up and off in 2 planes without incident except that an unidentified object and lights appeared off the island again last night. Palmyra [Island] is next stop. N[imitz] says its a fine place compared to Canton — I hope so. Comdr. [William M.] Nation, commanding the PB2Y squadron has brought a relief ship so we divide up again. He is skipper of the squadron & things look OK again! Off about 7:30 & at 10:30 we get a message from him "Slow down 5 knots; I am on 3 engines too high oil temperature on No 3 engine." Whats going to happen next? We cross a typical Atoll with its ring of white surf, coral shelf, rough circle of sand and palms and green lagoon. How did the coconut palms spread to all these widely separated and myriad islands? Sea birds could bring small seeds in their craws but hardly a coconut. The ans[wer]. must be that they have floated from island to island & still germinated.

Palmyra is as beautiful as advertised. What a happy contrast to desolate Canton. A string of some 53 islands and most all connected now by our military road . . . we have quarters in a dormitory in the little officers club. Inspection trip around the defenses and a walk along a coast patrol path around one point thru a fairy land tropical grove of Pisonia trees — great greenish trunked monsters with bulwarked bases. The beautiful white love terns hovering about our heads; setting on their large brown speckled eggs perched precariously on branches without nests; babies of all kinds peering out of puffs of down and the sky above the trees overhead teeming with sea birds of all kinds. Frigates way up in the blue sky, boobie birds, bosun birds that can fly backwards, sooty terns, Hawaiian terns, curlews, etc., all chattering and screaming with the coming evening. We can't find a coconut crab — the marines have, I fear, all but extinguished them. They live in the tops of the coconut trees and break the nuts with their great claws. But there are countless reddish land crabs scurrying into their holes along the shaded path. This little walk in the forest twilight with the friendly birds all about, the bright blue sky overhead and the pounding surf on the reef thru the trees to seeward [seaward] comes close to the tropical paradise of fiction, in spite of the communication wires, observation posts, barbed wire and sand bag rifle shelters!

There are "swimming holes" in the lagoons all about the place. R[awleigh Warner], F[rank Beatty] & I take one in back of the officers club — being warned to wash our ears with fresh water to guard against fungus infection — There's always something! Lieut H. W. Meers of Chicago introduces himself as an old acquaintance and with his friends is very hospitable and informative. Everywhere in the quarters all the same dogeared collection of old magazines and the same pictures of lovely ladies most from Esquire. For the first few weeks fellows talk about the job, the war & are filled with enthusiasm, but before long women is about the only topic of conversation among these men, many of whom have been isolated for a year or more — and feminine art of the procreative kind is about all you see on the walls of the living quarters, flyers ready rooms, clubs, etc.

Dinner in the mess — hearts of palm salad & turkey & coconut tart with ice cream! A special for the Secretary & what a contrast to the horrible food at Canton. The movie was the Great Victor Herbert — and very good too. I've been to the movies more on this trip than I have in the last 10 years and most of them have been lousy, but this was splendid. Out into the pitch dark night, thru the baffling blackout baffles and to bed in utter darkness in a strange room — enlivened by wise cracks and the gropings of Adm. [Theodore S.] Wilkinson who came in late after a conf. with N. & is bound for Noum[e]a as deputy Comdr. Sou-Pac. The trade wind was cool & it would have been a good night except for the pool table, the radio and the chatter in the clubroom on the other side of the plywood partition.

Wednesday, Jan 26 — Palmyra T.H.

Up with the help of a little moonlight and a flash light; shaved after the cruel fashion in cold water; stuffed things in the suitcase, breakfast;

farewells and off to the planes at 7. Half hour, ¾, but *both* are out of order — long repairs are necessary. TARFU again! Unload and back to the island for a big game of kelly pool in the deserted officers club while a boat is prepared for a fishing expedition ordered by Adm N[imitz]. Its a beautiful big rescue boat with a PT. hull and we dash out the channel and onto the blue Pacific and into the giant swells. Between rain squalls I sunbath[e] & in about half an hour N tells me to put my shirt and pants on — thank God. Another half hour and I would have been in the hospital! We have fine deep sea trolling tackle. St[r]ike! Ten minutes later a sand shark is along side and [Frank] Beatty's arms are numb. They shoot him, unhook with pliers and throw him back. Four good sized Barracuda — one mine — with their vicious teeth, one blue marlin — or is it a wahoo? — and a beautiful irridescent Ono. For me its great fishing but the Adm says its not much good and we go back to the island at 28 knots thru the great swells about 3. The sun is intense and a "souwester" tops my burning head. 40 MM anti aircraft practice on a sleave target with a green gun crew. Red tracers soar up into the blue sky all around the flying target and between firings I pick up a myriad of shells and corals. R[awleigh Warner], F[rank Beatty] & I borrow one of the command cars that are all painted white to match the sand and drive around the island again for a liesurely walk thru the fairyland we visited yesterday. A descending coconut crashed down and gives me a start. I could spend a long time in this tranquil spot watching the sea birds, drowsing in the shade and marvelling how the coconut palms' sinuous tru[n]ks curve around to find a place in the sun for their tuft of plumes. The usual talk with the officers and drinks before dinner and then our fish — and it was very good; Barracuda which is almost inedible in Fla. To bed again in the utter blackout.

Thursday, Jan 27 — Palmyra

A good night — tho bar rooms are not the best bedrooms. My sunburn isn't so bad except around the wrists. Off in darkness on schedule . . . Party divided in two planes — its dawn now and light enough to see that Comdr. Nation can't get one of his engines started as we cruise about the lagoon waiting for him to take off. And then [Lieutenant Commander Bowen F.] McLeod arrives to inform us that he has magneto trouble — the same as yesterday — but on another one of our engines! So everything is unpacked, clothes, luggage, food, and we pick up the rest of the party and all their gear, parachutes & lifebelts — Mae Wests — and all pile in a third plane that arrived yesterday with additional parts for us. After an anxious run somehow she gets into the air in spite of the weight and we are off for P.H. at last and only about 1–¾ hrs late. I've been reading Capt. Pulestons book[142] on the Armed Forces in the Pacific and ran across this Imperial precept to the Japanese Army & Navy — "Bear in mind that duty is weightier than a mountain, while death is light as a feather."

Its a long hop to PH [Pearl Harbor] — about 8 hrs — with the trade winds against us and the ship crowded. But the air is smooth & we have steak for lunch instead of the corned beef hash and canned asparagus.

I watched Oahu emerge from clouds on the horizon from the Co pilots cockpit — first a faint white strip of beach and then the grey green outlines of the hills — and in a moment were coming in over Barbers point and circling back of P.H. after a couple of fighters have charged up menacingly on our flanks, had a look and darted away. A boat takes us to Ford Island where Adm. [J. H.] Towers, Adm. [D. W.] Bagley et al meet us and we transfer to CinC's smart barge. In a few moments the bulk of the Oklahoma — (will the enormous hoists turn her over on Ford Island?) — and the grave of the Arizona are behind us and we're back in the quarters we left 2 weeks ago. A shave, hot shower for the first time since Suva & civilian clothes again & I'm off to a cocktail party* for my host, Capt. [Allen G.] Quinn, evidently one of the more popular of the "Monks of Makalapa" as the bachelor residents of Makalapa Drive call themselves. Quinn has his orders back to Cominche's[143] staff after 3 years without of [a] glimpse of his wife & 4 children. Dinner in the officers mess — much talk about our trip & then a special movie by command of Adm N[imitz] that he thinks very amusing called Star Spangled Rhythm — and it is!

Friday, Jan 28 — P.H.

Talked with Waldo Drake, public relations officer, at some length; prepared suggested answers to some written questions the press are going to ask K[nox]. at the conference, but of course he won't use them. Press people full of complaints about cutting off air transportation. I'll try to do something about this. K. makes fine report on the trip to a large conference — and of course doesn't use the answers I so diligently prepared. Buffet lunch for the press at Adm N[imitz]'s quarters & good conversation with B. J. Mcquaid of Chi Daily News and sundry other gentlemen

---

* The first white women I've seen in 2 weeks.

142 W. D. Puleston, *The Armed Forces of the Pacific: A Comparison of the Military and Naval Power of the United States and Japan* (New Haven: Yale University Press, 1941).

143 The Commander in Chief, United States Fleet (Admiral Ernest J. King).

of the Press.* After the guests depart — so do we in 2 cars for the
Damon beach house at Waikula which the Navy has rented for the
relief of overworked officers! Thru Honolulu and up the beautiful Nuana
[Nuuanu] valley past the fine old gardens & houses & the country club
where Ellen & I went to lunch with the brewers and distillers in our
honor in 1934! Adm N., almost loquacious and tells me more about the
technical st[r]ategic problems in the Pacific than I've hea[r]d on the
whole trip. Since all the warnings I've had about not putting anything
of importance in this diary (N[aval]. officers are not even permitted to
bring diaries into the country unless they bear a censurs stamp) I'm beginning to wonder why I've kept it at all. Its hard to write an interesting
or useful account of an inspection of the war in the Pacific and not say
anything about the war! So N's info. must die on my finger tips.

The beautiful ride up the mountains thru the forest of some larch like
conifer to the Pali past the waterfall that is reversed by the wind is
grander than I remembered it. And the view from the summit, which is
only about 1500 feet above sea level, at the perpendicular green palisades on the N side of the mountains and down into the green valley below and out to the blue sea beyond is magnificent — I'm glad I didnot
miss this trip. When they came over here on the way out I was in the
hospital with my bad shoulder. I wonder if Ellen's memory of this scene
is better than mine was. I hope so — one should never forget the Pali on
Oahu.

The beach house is attractive; the sun hot & the beach white and long.
R[awleigh Warner], F[rank Beatty], Adm N., Adm Shafroth & I walk
along it for miles. Its almost deserted. I got blisters on both heels from
the friction of the hard fine sand, but the swimming was superb. The
chauffeurs had a pitcher of fresh coconut milk for us and we drove back
over the breath taking Pali feeling gay and [illegible]. Dinner with
Adm. N., Adm Spruance and Dr. Jandreau & then the inevitable movie
which I'm too weak to resist. It was prefaced by some pictures of P. H.
after the attack which we had not previously seen. Mrs. [Walter] Dillingham returned my call to bid her goodbye and express regrets that I had
not been able to get to see her. She invited us all for lunch tomorrow &
we accepted. She reports she hasn't seen Robt Allerton[144] for a long time
but that he has asked them over to Kauai to visit him and they are go-

* Word comes that weather conditions on the coast are bad and that
we cannot take off at 3 as planned. We're getting hardened to these misfortunes and there is plenty to do with another day here.

[144] A former Chicago businessman, who became one of Hawaii's leading philan-
thropists.

ing soon — that she is writing Mrs. C,[145] well and busy with her OCD [Office of Civil Defense] work etc; distressed that she had not heard from me sooner so that we could have come for dinner tonight. To bed early and I remembered to put up the black out window!

Saturday, Jan 29 — P. H.
    . . . The weather report is O.K. for San Diego & we plan to leave by Clipper at 3. Had a good talk with Comdr. Libbens Curtis, the salvage expert, who did so much to refloat the ships after the [December 7, 1941] attack and is now in charge of salvage operations for the SouPac area. For days after the attack he and Capt. [James M.] Steele were fired at from the shore while working in the harbor in small boats by the overwrought guards. The transformation of Oahu; the order that has come out of chaos, the alert calm that has followed the frightened confusion is one of the great transformations wrought by the war. Hawaii is ready now and knows it — and so do the Japs I suspect. Comd. Curtis told me about the salvage of the "Thomas A. Edison" on a reef in the southern Fijis with a 14 million dollar cargo, mostly torpedoes for which they were crying in SouPac & Australia — They were at the bottom of the cargo and he got them off in barges just before a hurricane struck. The aerometer registered 125 miles and couldn't go any higher. When the wind subsided and he got back there from Suva a few days later all but the stern of the ship had vanished and that was hardly recognizable. I inspected one of the huge transient personnel cantonements with Capt Quinn & Curtis — built in the last few months as a receiving ship extension and accomodating 7500 men. The barber gave me a fine haircut. He was an old sailorman and his son is an air gunners mate on Guadalcanal. You encounter that sort of thing all the time. . . .
    Next we go down to the Navy Yard and weave in around the docks and all the confusion of ships undergoing repair — each of which has a long dramatic story to tell — to the just arrived heavy cruiser Pensacola who got a torpedo in the after engine room in the wild melee south of Guadalcanal on the night of Nov 30–Dec. 1, when the Northampton went down. The damage one torpedo can do is staggering — 125 men killed and 4 to 6 mos for repairs. Her after end in the port compartments was still flooded and you could see daylight thru the water from the torpedo hole in her side. I'm often reminded when I see these damaged ships from the Pacific war of my wide eyed, horror stricken wonder of a year ago last September when I saw the British light cruiser Delphic or Dido[?] battle damaged in Crete at the New York Navy Yard. It looked

[145] Mrs. John Alden Carpenter.

pretty bad then, but those bomb damages are nothing to torpedo damage and how the Pensacola survived at all is a miracle and is due solely to the heroic efforts of the damage control crew a modest, pallid, weary officer assured me. As we were crawling around her charred carcass a blue jacket arrived with a message that we were leaving at 1 instead of 3. So I hurried by to get packed, stopping at District Hqs long enough to see Ensign Robert Crown, son of a client[146] of Henry Blum in Chicago who's in trouble with his eyes. They will transfer him to some non combatant duty now and perhaps his anxious father will now stop worrying! [Frank] Beatty has notified Mrs. Dillingham that her luncheon party for Knox, Nimitz et all is called off at the last moment because we have to leave a couple of hours earlier than planned to take advantage of some promising weather on the coast.

After many farewells — and I forget to pay my mess bill to my kind hosts! — we leave in a cavalcade of cars for the Pan American terminal in Pearl City. More farewells and we are off on the same Boeing Clipper with the same crew that brought us out. Pearl H., Honolulu, Diamond Head, Koko Head, and the beautiful, jagged sky line of Ohau [Oahu] quickly fade into the clouds. Adm. McCain has his luggage and all is well! We have a sumptuous dinner of squab; long talk with McCain & Reilly about Gen. Arnold,[147] his distaste for the Navy, neglect of the Pac; inadequate training program for sea operations etc. McCains suggestion is to give him 4 stars and put him in charge of our forces in hell! One by one we drift off to bed — My God it is a quarter of 12 coast time — in our folding bunks. McCain's teeth are out and he suddenly looks like a little old man instead of a little fighting rebel from Mississippi. Our pilot has gone north and found a tail wind and what promised to be an 18 hr flight looks more like 15 hrs and we are heading for San F. instead of San Diego because the soup has closed in down there. So we are awakened early.

Sunday — Jan 30 — El Paso

The sky ahead is a thin flat layer of pink over the black sea and just above the wing between the pale blue plumes of the starboard motors' exhaust is a bright crescent moon and one star. It doesn't seem possible but there it all is and the black wall ahead is not the eternal fog bank over San F. bay but land. We pass over a large liner blacked out and crawling slowly toward the golden gate. Just as the orange dawn fades in the light we cross between the two arches of the Gate bridge. The

[146] Henry Crown, chairman of the board of Material Service.
[147] General H. H. Arnold, chief of the Army Air Forces.

city is a pale grey carpet flung over the sprawling hills on the right and as we swing around to the south over the bay bridge lights come on along the waterfront and the city takes shape. In a moment we have swept over the edge of Oakland circled north and west and swooped down onto the still waters of the Bay and landed like a feather; and here we are at the Pan Am Terminal with Adm. [J. W.] Greenslade waiting for us — just as tho we hadn't been to the So Seas & back since last night when he said goodbye to us — but it wasn't last night. It was 18 nights and a life time of adventure. Greetings and farewell to Adm [R. A.] Theobald* and we are off again to Alameda thru hideous O[a]kland where Col K's & Adm McCain's planes are to meet us. But they haven't arrived from San Diego where they were expecting us until the route was changed sometime last night so we have a large breakfast and I called Mrs. White in Pasadena to report that Dr. White on Espiritu Santo is well and lonesome. The poor woman is so happy it is even worth $4.30! The planes arrive, gassed and we are off again, but not east, south to San Diego where the weather may be better to turn east. Down the bay, over San Jose, Palo Alto and down the beautiful Calif coast, over Monterey penninsula, Pebble Beach where we had that lyric day last May, Carmel, San Simeon's pile of transcient glory, Santa Barbara and Los Angeles that stretches as far as you can see in all directions even at 7500 feet. Below LA the coast line is less interesting and the mountains on your left less wild. La Jolla looks nice and then over Point Loma and we circle the city and Coronado and land on North Island. The camouflage of the airplane plants and test fields around LA & San Diego is something to remember, the bldg roofs are painted to blend into the surroundings — bldgs on hills; the runways have house tops painted on them. You have to look sharp to pick them out.

All the officers turn out; it is cold and overcast; McCain's plane comes in; Bud Easton shows up; conference among the pilots and aerologists and — must we stay all night — no, will push on to El Paso & have dinner in Mexico and be 1000 miles on our way by nightfall. Hooray. I'm wild to get home now that the great adventure is over. Whats happened in 3 weeks — will all be well? . . .

We're in the clouds and the desert almost at once and then the endless arid wastes of Southern Ariz & N M and the grandeur of the mountains and the infinite variety of coloring of land and sky. Flying is al-

* Delivered all the press stories of Col Ks. interview in P.H. to our public relations officer for immediate release. Wire to Ellen. Does she know yet?

ways beautiful. At 5:30 we're in El Paso — but what time is it in El Paso? I've moved my watch back and forth over a range of 8 or 9 hours and crossing the [international] date line rattled me so I never knew what day it was. Moreover I've lost a whole day somewhere — this should be Jan 31 instead of Jan 30.

Major Lockwood, Executive officer of Biggs Field, Army, met us and quartered us in individual cubicles in a new officers barracks that was only half finished and we had a communal head on the floor above. Drinks and dinner at the officers mess & to bed early in our little iron cots in the barren and paint perfumed barracks. I even resisted the tempting proposal of some of the young Navy officers in the plane crews to accompany them to Juarez for a look see.

Monday, Feb 1, El Paso.

Up at 6 — and its really cold for the first time since we left Wash — fine breakfast and we are on the "line" before the first faint sign of dawn. We take off in darkness and are 100 miles on our route home, with uncertain weather ahead, before sun up. We cross Guadalupe pass east of El Paso at 10 000 feet and never see the ground.

To H. Hamilton Hackney[148]

February 4, 1943

Dear Hacker:

I returned yesterday after a long trip through the South Pacific. Picture my lovely face lit with joy when I stepped forth from an automobile at a base hospital far, far away for an inspection and into the arms of your fellow townsman, Colonel George Finney.

I told him that I would report his good health and magnificent service to all and sundry. To that end I am using you as the best mouth piece I know. It's too bad you haven't some other qualifications, by the way!

I will tell you more about George and what he is doing sometime if we have the misfortune to meet. And I hope you will communicate my report of his good health and fine work to his family or anyone else in interest because my news is very fresh!

Yours,

[148] Judge of the Juvenile Court of Baltimore and a Princeton classmate of Stevenson's. This letter is in A.E.S., P.U.L.

To Frank Knox[149]

February 23, 1943

MEMORANDUM TO THE SECRETARY

Since the publication of the White Paper by the State Department,[150] I have been thinking that it might be profitable to assemble an historical outline of the Navy Department's relations to the Congress and the Executive Departments since the last war. Such a study would, I think, point up the fact that the services, and peculiarly the Navy charged in the first instance with the defense of the country, have not enjoyed the voice and influence in the conduct of our foreign policy to which their ultimate responsibilities entitled them.

For example, I understand that the Navy made repeated requests commencing about 1934 for permission to send ships to the Japanese mandated islands. The State Department demurred with the result that official information on the fortification and the violation of the mandate was never obtained.

The failure of Congress to implement the Hepburn report[151] and other illustrations could be cited, which sustain, I believe, the proposition that the Navy was not accorded a consideration consistent with its mission.

I know little or nothing of the Navy's relations with the State Department preceeding Pearl Harbor, but it may be, as many have suggested, that we did not receive an adequate and continuous evaluation of the situation during the months of critical deterioration prior to the attack.

What has happened before is important, perhaps more with relationship to what benefit the Navy can derive from it in the future. I have in mind commitments incident to the peace and the inevitable intragovernmental conflicts in connection therewith. To know where mistakes were made in the past might be helpful in establishing the Navy's position in the future.

I am by no means certain that this project would be useful, but it *might* be. That alone, in view of the Navy's future responsibilities, would seem to justify it. Moreover, it should not be a difficult or prolonged piece of work. . . .

---

[149] This memorandum is in A.E.S., P.U.L.

[150] This probably refers to Department of State, *Peace and War* (Washington: Government Printing Office, 1943), which discussed relations with Japan.

[151] Admiral Arthur J. Hepburn headed a special board in 1938 which recommended the building of a fully equipped fleet and air base at Guam to help defend the Philippines. Congress rejected this.

To Henry W. Capen[152]

March 1, 1943

Dear Heinie:

I am mortified that I have not written you before this. I only heard about your father's death yesterday. You know all about his long, loyal and valued friendship to me and my parents. In turn I know something of what you have been through — having had the unhappy experience myself.

I wish I could have been there. I shall never forget his thoughtfulness and kindness to me at the time of father's death when mother was abroad. His passing will leave another great hole in Bloomington for me.

Please give your dear mother my affectionate regards. And my very best to you and Mary.[153]

Sincerely yours,

On March 11, 1943, Stevenson drafted a possible press statement by Secretary Knox on antisubmarine warfare. American, British, and Canadian officers were conferring in Washington on this question. The conference is discussed in Ernest J. King and Walter Muir Whitehill, Fleet Admiral King: A Naval Record *(New York: Norton, 1952), pp. 460–461.*

SUGGESTED RELEASE ON ANTI-SUBMARINE ACTIVITIES

Plans to perfect the effectiveness of the combined Anglo-American activities to check the submarine menace were completed today with the formation of the (???) Combined Staff for Anti-Submarine Activities (??? — Check on correct designation of this unit), it was announced in Washington by the Secretary of the Navy. The head of the Combined Anti-Submarine Staff is ———. The British members are ———, ———. The other American members are ———.

"For eighteen months the American and British Navies have been in constant touch on matters relating to anti-submarine activities," Secretary Knox explained today. "Since America's entry into the war this cooperation has become steadily closer. The two Navies exchange information about the techniques of anti-submarine activity and have developed

[152] An old friend from Bloomington, Illinois. This letter is in A.E.S., P.U.L.
[153] Mrs. Capen.

efficient methods of joint cooperation in protecting convoys and in curtailing the activities of enemy submarines. The new committee has been formed in the knowledge that the German high command will do everything in its power to intensify submarine activities in the next few months in a last desperate effort to prevent the United Nations from bringing the full strength of their material and manpower to bear in effecting the unconditional surrender of the Axis powers."

With the large increase in shipping and the coming of better weather in the North Atlantic in the spring and early summer, it was explained today in Navy Department circles, German submarines will have better hunting. This fact, coupled with the obvious need of the Germans to pour their last reserve strength into submarine warfare in the next few months, suggests that sinkings may increase before combative measures can put an end to the submarine menace.

The American Navy has been devoting the closest attention to all possible devices for combating submarines. In conjunction with the British Navy it has perfected a convoy system through which ———— men have already been transported overseas at a loss of less than 1,000 soldiers. The Navy escort vessels, which are now beginning to be launched in increasing numbers, are expected to expedite the task of driving the "wolf packs" off the seas.

(Add brief biographical material about members of the staff.)

C. Daggett Harvey, formerly in the same Chicago law firm as Stevenson, wrote expressing his desire to be transferred to more active duty.

To Lieutenant C. Daggett Harvey[154]

March 17, 1943

Dear Butch:

I haven't forgotten your deplorable predicament and I have a suggestion to offer. Why don't you make another request for transfer? This time to the Advanced Intelligence Training School at New York with a view toward being assigned ultimately to Naval Intelligence duties in some theatre of operation.

Understand there are no guarantees, as usual, but things seem to be opening up a little and I have found a friendly spirit who might be of some help to you in the Office of Naval Intelligence.

Should you do anything about this, be sure to send me informally a

[154] The original is in the possession of Mr. Harvey.

copy of your request, together with endorsements from your Commanding Officer.

Yours,

*Stevenson's Washington friend John Monroe wrote him on March 19,
1943, that he had just read the speech that Stevenson had written for
Secretary Knox to deliver on St. Patrick's Day. "I always had a feeling
that you were good," Monroe wrote, "but I did not realize that you were
a maestro. . . . All I can say is that Frank Knox is about the luckiest
man I know — and the richest man that I know — to possess the devotion and ability which you give him."*

To John Monroe[155]

March 22, 1943

Dear John:

I have your letter and I don't know whether to say "thanks" or "horse
feathers." Perhaps "thanks for the horse feathers" is best!

Sincerely yours

*Stevenson delivered the following speech to the Daughters of the
American Revolution on March 30, 1943. It was transcribed in 1959
from the original handwritten copy, which is in the possession of Adlai
E. Stevenson III.*

I might as well admit that my recollections of my grandmother are
very remote. She died when I was about 13, but her gentleness, her dignity and modulated voice I can remember well. She was a gentlewoman
with that rare quality of serenity, competence and cultivation which I
am told are frequently found among southern women of that generation, in spite of the hardships, or what seem to us hardships now, which
they endured.

She was a descendant of Augustin Warner of Warner Hall, Glouces-
ter County, Virginia. Augustin Warner, you will remember, was the father of Mildred Warner, the mother of George Washington,[156] and you

---

[155] This letter is in A.E.S., P.U.L.

[156] George Washington's mother was Mary Ball, not Mildred Warner. Mrs.
Ernest L. Ives drafted this speech for her brother, and in her haste made this error,
which she believes may have been a confusion with the name of her cousin, Lady
Bailey, the former Mildred Warner Washington Bromwell. Letter to Carol Evans,
November 18, 1971.

can see his tomb today in a little family graveyard enclosed in an iron fence at Warner Hall down on the end of the peninsula. Two wings, fragments of the original house built in the 17th century, are still standing and by some antiquarians are said to be the oldest dwellings still extant in Virginia.

She was related to many of the early distinguished colonial figures in Virginia, and I heard much in my childhood of her ancestor General Joshua Fry of Viewmont, near what is now Charlottesville. General Fry, you may recall, was commander of the Virginia militia in the French Indian War and died at Mills Creek on the way to Fort Duquesne. He turned over his command to his lieutenant and kinsman, a boy of 22 named George Washington.

Grandmother's father was Dr. Lewis Warner Green, a severe Presbyterian divine who had enjoyed the rare privilege for three times [terms?] of study abroad in Germany and Edinburgh. He was successively president of several of the little denominational colleges that were springing up in the wake of the westering pioneers and ended up as President of Center [Centre] College in Danville, Kentucky, which was then, before the Civil war, the foremost seat of higher learning in the west. Those of you that have seen the beautiful old buildings at Center, surrounded by a countryside rich and populous and dotted with fine estates, can imagine the comfortable and cultivated society that flourished out there in the early days. It was there in Danville that she grew up and there she met my grandfather when he was a student. He moved with his family to central Illinois in 1858, and not long after she married him and moved to Illinois too, where her sister, Mrs. Matthew T. Scott, who, I believe, was twice President General of the Daughters of the American Revolution, had preceded her.

Evidently she was equally at home on the frontier prairie of Illinois and in the drawing rooms of Washington and Europe. She and grandfather were very formal with one another. They always addressed each other as Mrs. S. or Mr. S., and I am told that it was only in anger, which was very rare, that grandfather ever addressed her as "Letitia!"

We went there for Sunday dinner as a routine. Grandfather sat at one end of the table in a Prince Albert coat and white tie, and grandmother at the other end in a black silk dress. I used to think how uncomfortable they must be on hot days. There was always grace — I felt unreasonably long. Frequently my cousins — three very rowdy boys, and sons of a Presbyterian minister — were visiting there, and grace invariably ended with a disturbance of some kind, a glass of water upset, silver fell on the floor and not infrequently, as if by magic, a butter ball struck the ceiling and hung precariously. My cousins were always guilty but they sat like impassive innocent angels while I squirmed with laughter and pro-fessions of innocence. The grandparents discussed juvenile dereliction briefly, making me almost feel guilty for my cousins' misdeeds, and then turned to a discussion of the sermon of the morning. Invariably the discussion of the sermon slipped into stories by grandfather and mother and the dinner became so lively that even small boys could sit still until the inevitable vanilla ice cream arrived.

I have wished a thousand times that more of grandfather's stories had been recorded. Some of them are in a book he wrote toward the end of his life called "Something Of Men I Have Known." [157] Since I have grown up many people of his generation have told me that he was one of the great raconteurs of his period. Indeed, his political enemies said that that was his only qualification for public office. If so he must have been good, because he was nominated once for Governor of Illinois and twice for Vice-President, and elected with Cleveland.

I am quite sure I have bored you with this bit of self indulgence — there is little time for talking of yesterday in this world of tomorrow. My grandmother's serenity, dignity and charm was constant. Senators or servants found her always the same. She was, I think, a great lady.

And I am more than happy that my grandfather's grand niece, Ileen Bullis Campbell, is carrying on with such vigor and competence the good work in the D.A.R. in which Letitia Stevenson and my great aunt, Julia Scott, were so long engaged.

On April 5, 1943, Princeton classmate Robert Buechner wrote Steven-son thanking him for speaking to their class dinner in New York and saying how much his talk was enjoyed.

To Robert Buechner[158]

April 7, 1943

Dear Bob:

Ho — hum! Will I ever learn to follow wise example — and go to bed on time? And if you ever see me on the streets of New York after mid-night again, please remind me of the foregoing sober reflection.

I enjoyed the evening and I only hope my desolatory [desultory] con-versation wasn't too dreary. After the heroic effort you had been to to round up those wretches, I felt you and they deserved a better fate.

Yours,

[157] Chicago: A. C. McClurg & Co., 1909.
[158] This letter is in A.E.S., P.U.L.

C. Daggett Harvey replied to Stevenson's letter of March 17, 1943, that his unit was now to see active duty and he no longer wanted to be transferred.

To Lieutenant C. Daggett Harvey[159]

April 12, 1943

Dear Butch:

I have just read your good letter and am much relieved to hear that you are now reconciled and moving in the right direction.

I quite agree that it would be a little foolish now to jump out and into something else and I have no doubt that your squadron will move on in due course and you will get your heart's desire — and how!

Should it be otherwise, let me know, as opportunities seem to be improving for active service for experienced people. Meanwhile I will tell the people who were going to arrange your transfer to lay off for the present.

I was in Chicago last weekend and spent Saturday morning in the office. I need hardly tell you that it made me all the more content with my lot here. And a Saturday evening in the old Lake Forest routine was only a little less enervating — but don't quote me!

My love to Jean.[160]

Yours,
STEVE

On June 7, 1943, Charles N. Wheeler, political reporter for the Chicago Daily News, *discussed in his column the possibility of Stevenson or John E. Cassidy of Peoria as a candidate for governor of Illinois in 1944.*

To John E. Cassidy[161]

June 9, 1943

Dear John:

A friend in Chicago has sent me Charlie Wheeler's story from yesterday's News.

I report in haste that I am highly flattered to share a column with you. You should keep better company!

Yours,

159 The original is in the possession of Mr. Harvey.
160 Mrs. Harvey.
161 This letter is in A.E.S., P.U.L.

[113]

To Charles N. Wheeler[162]

June 9, 1943

My dear Mr. Wheeler:

I have just seen your story about John Cassidy and myself in the News. You were very kind to me and it made me feel like a statesman — almost! Some day you must tell me all about those big shots in the hinterland who think I look like a possibility. I suspect Lloyd Lewis is all of them!

Many thanks and warm regards.

Sincerely yours,

P.S. It is not the "Scripps" biography — it's the first one, 1859, I think, and it was addressed to Jesse Fell who used it to try to interest people in the East.[163]

To Richard S. Folsom[164]

June 9, 1943

My dear Mr. Folsom:

You were more than kind to send me the clipping from yesterday's News. I had not seen it. I suspect Charlie Wheeler's reports on my availability from downstate were largely imaginary which your listening posts will confirm. But anyway it was flattering and nice to feel that after almost two years here I am not altogether forgotten in Illinois.

I admire John Cassidy very much and I should think he would make a splendid candidate. I suppose you are concerned with the Catholic angle. Some day we must talk about these things — but not about me!

Many thanks and warm regards.

Sincerely yours,

Stevenson addressed the sixtieth anniversary dinner of the Chicago Real Estate Board, June 11, 1943.

[162] This letter is in A.E.S., P.U.L.

[163] J. L. Scripps, editor of the Chicago *Tribune*, wrote one of the earliest campaign biographies of Lincoln, which was based on his reading of the autobiography that Lincoln had prepared at the request of Jesse Fell. The Scripps biography was published in both the Chicago *Tribune* and the New York *Tribune* in 1860. Letter, Ralph G. Newman, Abraham Lincoln Book Shop, Chicago, to Carol Evans, January 12, 1972.

[164] Of the law department of the Chicago Board of Education. This letter is in A.E.S., P.U.L.

The subject assigned me this evening is "The War and Beyond." It was expressly designed by your former President, Lieutenant [Ronald] Chinnock (whose exceptional gifts are well known to you) to meet my suggestion that there be no title at all! To those of you who know that I am really only an indifferent La Salle Street lawyer, if it seems a bit presumptuous for me to talk about the war and the future merely because I've spent a couple of years with Colonel Knox in the Navy, let me promptly say that I'm shameless; the present and the future is not enough for me and I propose to start with the past!

I propose to start with a reminder that this week is one of the great anniversaries of history. Just three years ago France fell; most of Europe was overrun; by a miracle the shattered British Army had escaped at Dunkirk but lost all its equipment. Italy shouted "me too" and, as the President said, stabbed the prostrate French in the back. Mussolini was in Ethiopia and Libya and in between was Egypt and Suez almost defenseless. In South America there was no defense. In Asia dismembered China was slowly bleeding to death. Russia was apart and silent. In Britain there was scarcely one fully trained and equipped division to meet invasion. The channel ports that summer were alive with barges and invasion boats and in the sky clouds of Nazi planes hovered for the kill. The conquerors were singing "We Are Sailing Against England."

In this country we were unprepared, confused and divided. I am proud that with the help of others of like mind I organized here in Chicago in those dark days of June, 1940, a group to agitate for aid to England and to advertise our own peril. I think it did some good — at least it made a lot of people angry and set some to thinking!

A year later, in June, 1941, the Lend-Lease Act had been passed after six weeks of debate;[165] Britain still stood firm among her ruins, but Greece and Crete were gone and hope for the Mediterranean was not bright. Then came the inevitable attack on Russia and the wiseacres said it would be all over in a few weeks. Our country was still reverberating with controversy as to whether all this was any of our business and, if so, how we could win it without fighting.

By last June it was different. Japan had made some things clear to all of us, which our own leaders couldn't. We had witnessed the conquest of an Asiatic Empire of fantastic magnitude and wealth in the space of six short months. Meanwhile, our ships were sinking in sight of our coast, while we struggled to establish and maintain supply lines thru

[165] The Lend-Lease Act passed Congress in March, 1941. The bill authorized the President to "sell, transfer title to, exchange, lease, lend or otherwise dispose of . . . any defense article" to any nation whose defense he found vital to the security of the United States.

hostile waters thousands and thousands of miles long; to improvise and build bases, depots, ports and airfields in every continent and in every climate; to build and train a great Navy and a great Army; to build ships to transport them; to build weapons and equipment for them and for our Allies.

Then came the battle of Midway in June. That was the turning point in the Pacific. The Russians withstood the second great offensive at Stalingrad. That was the turning point in Europe.

And now June has come again. Three years have passed and we have witnessed an historical miracle. The Axis has been erased from Africa. The Japs have been arrested and turned back on the frontiers of their stolen empire. The cities of Germany are crumbling. Our fighting forces have proved themselves in combat on land, at sea and in the air from the Arctic to the steaming jungles. Our ships, our aircraft, our guns and tanks have all been tried. We don't have to worry about our fighting men or their weapons and equipment any more. We are getting stronger and stronger while Germany gets weaker and weaker. The day of invasion draws near. No longer does the German radio play "We Are Sailing Against England." Today their theme song is "The Watch on the Rhine."

Yes, we have come a long, long way since those dark hours just three years ago when the British Commonwealth and China stood alone and we argued whether this was our war, with comforting reminders that the Atlantic was still three thousand miles wide and, besides, Germany would soon run out of oil and fats.

We can, indeed, be of good heart in this June of 1943. Our industrial production is soaring. In this year alone the tonnage of combatant ships in the Navy will increase by two-thirds and in numbers will double; combat Navy planes will treble, fighters will multiply by five times the number in service at the beginning of the year. So it is with everything.

Latterly the submarine menace has also been declining. Probably the good news is only temporary. But the shipping losses suffered by the United Nations since Pearl Harbor have now been replaced by new construction, and with the destroyer escort building and training program now in full swing, with our air coverage of the sea lanes fanning out wider and wider, with auxiliary aircraft carriers joining the convoys, with various new secret devices and methods coming into operation, with continual bombing of German production, overhaul and operational centers, it seems likely that this formidable foe cannot stop us and that the slave drivers have sentenced thousands of U-boat sailors to horrible deaths in the dark depths of the sea.

However, it would be foolhardy to suggest that the submarine is under control. It will never be licked as long as the war lasts. Nor is it the only enemy of our vital shipping. Let me remind you that since the war commenced in 1939, submarines have accounted for only something more than one half the total shipping losses, both Allied and enemy. Aircraft, mines, marine disasters, storms, all the perils of the sea, also take their toll. We are pushing forward into hazardous, ill charted, unfamiliar waters and in the South Pacific I have seen fine ships pounded to pieces on hidden reefs.

Let me also say in connection with the submarine problem, which has been for more than two years a principal preoccupation of the high command of our Navy, that I deplore the surrounding secrecy. I know, and the Navy does too, that there is no substitute for the whole truth; that in times past, and perhaps to come, full disclosure of losses, the enemy's and ours, of methods and counter measures, would have made for a sympathetic understanding of the magnitude and complexity of this problem and might, indeed, have saved us much criticism, misunderstanding and abuse. I can tell you too that your distinguished fellow townsman, the Secretary of the Navy, as both a great newspaper man and a great public servant, has understood and wrestled diligently with this vexatious problem of Navy news from the start.

The facts are that the British have strong convictions on the subject, as do many of our people. There can be no doubt that accurate confirmation of losses periodically would be of enormous advantage to the enemy in evaluating his own information and attack techniques. Anything we disclose about our methods, it must also be remembered, would be promptly copied by the Japanese, for in the Pacific the submarine is our weapon — and a very successful one too. There are also important considerations of domestic psychology in Germany. Unreported and overdue submarines had a damaging effect on morale in Germany during the last war.

It's a complicated story. I am by no means satisfied that it has been handled properly, but I want to make it emphatically clear that the policy of secrecy is neither captious nor arrogant. If and as the situation improves, more can and will be told. But there have been many, many reasons heretofore why the responsible officials, military and civilian, both here and in England, have felt that it was in our best interest not to disclose all the information everyone would like.

Another word about production. For the first three years of the war program the estimated value of construction and facilities within the continental United States was almost as much as the estimated output of munitions; in other words, we have devoted almost 90% as much effort to construction and facilities as we have to the production of end items that can be used against the enemy. But now the end of the preparatory effort is almost in sight; the construction facility curve is sharply down and production of end items sharply up. Indeed we are turning out almost as much goods for war now, measured in terms of dollars, as we ever produced for peace, and still there is enough productive capacity left over to maintain the civilian economy at a level few thought possible.

Moreover, the goods are reaching their destinations. In the first six months of the operation more than 11,000,000 gross tons of shipping arrived in North African ports from this country and the United Kingdom. What goes over must come back, so that the American and British Navies escorted twenty-two million tons in that period — and the losses amounted to 2.16 per cent! At the same time offensive operations of the British in the Mediterranean took a very large toll of Axis shipping. What the reopening of the Mediterranean means is well known to you. With the fall of Tunisia the route to the Middle East has been cut by thousands of miles. Around the Cape of Good Hope ships between England and Egypt have been able to make only about three and a half round trips a year.

I should like to stop after this reassuring resume of the last three historic years. I should like to conclude on this happy, optimistic note and tell you about some of the interesting and exhilirating things I have seen and some of the places I have been. I would like to tell you about some ships, the destroyer escort for example, some weapons and some men I have met. I would like to tell you about the laughing spirit, the resolution, the almost irreverent courage of American boys on desolate, lonely islands, in boiler rooms, in airplanes, and also in little iron cots, row on row, dazed with malaria, wounded and wan, struggling to grin and whisper gallant little stories that make you wince and feel very humble and proud of your breed. I would like to tell you about legions of artisans with no threat of the draft who have given up families and four times the pay to join the CB's and build camps, airfields, docks and everything else in paralyzing cold and crawling heat, in snow and desert and jungle.

But I'm not. I'm going to first remind you that the note of optimism and satisfaction with our progress and our prospects which I have struck is the stuff of which the poison of complacency is concocted. The news is not by any means all good. The Nazis have not yet shown their hand in the summer campaign in Russia. We have great confidence in the Soviet power, but we also know that the Germans still have a mighty sledge hammer. China is near exhaustion. There is little cause for rejoicing from that direction. The reconquest of Burma and the opening of any kind of a supply line to China is a gigantic undertaking. The submarines still lie across the shipping lanes in wolf packs and more are coming. We have not yet invaded the continent of Europe, altho some people can't seem to understand why we didn't do so a year ago.

Moreover, I have detected, as all of you have, especially since the Tunisian success,[166] a disquieting degree of self-confidence. Many people talk and act as though it was all over but the shouting. There are still work stoppages and strikes; there are black markets all over the country and, what's more, people who profess patriotism frequent them. Perhaps it isn't complacency; perhaps it isn't even overconfidence. But certainly it's undisciplined; certainly there is not that sense of urgency which befits the testing that confronts us. Every day this war is prolonged means the lives of your neighbors' sons; means millions of your dollars and untold destruction, waste, suffering and heartbreak throughout the world.

Yes, we've come a long way since those apocalyptic June days of 1940. We have averted disaster by a narrow margin and by the indomitable courage and bloodshed of peoples who know no price for their freedom. But the worst is still to come. There are long weary months and years of waste and pain ahead of us — between us and the certain victory. We can't afford to be diverted for an instant from the job in hand. That's why one hesitates to talk of peace and the problems beyond the war, particularly one attached to the armed forces.

On the other hand, we *must* profit from our past mistakes. We were unprepared for war, both physically and intellectually. But war and the problem[s] of war with all their complexity are relatively simple, for the objectives are clear — to destroy the enemy and provide the wherewithal to do it. But the problems of war are dwarfed by the problems of peace. We cannot afford to be as unprepared for peace as we were for war.

Hence, I want to suggest some very obvious considerations.

First: This is a democracy. Our decisions are made by the processes of public debate. By that process we must evolve a broad domestic policy and a broad foreign policy for after the war. I submit that we have neither now. When the fever of war subsides there will be imperative demands for prompt and simultaneous action in a multitude of directions, domestic and foreign.

Can we safely defer formulation, consideration and popular acceptance of major policy until then? Can sound policy be established in haste amid a babel of voices, a confusion of tongues and a deluge of pressures? Is it likely that unless we are prepared for peace our course will depend,

---

[166] On May 7, 1943, Tunis fell to the Allies and in the days following a quarter of a million German and Italian soldiers surrendered. Now the Allies had bases for an assault in Italy.

in Alexander Hamilton's words, "not on reflection and choice but on accident and force"?

In short, I suggest that it is *possible* to win the battles but lose the war; it is *probable* if we are unprepared for peace; it is *certain* if, being unprepared, we improvise badly. So my argument is that it is imperative that the outlines of our broad policies at home and abroad be determined by popular reflection and choice in advance. The details can wait the unfolding conditions.

Second: Employment is the simple, central theme of our post-war domestic problem. There will be about 12 million in the armed forces and 20 million in war industry. Not all of them, but most of them, will want work. When peace breaks out we will have a plant capacity, much of it belonging to the government, capable of producing perhaps double the volume of durable goods Americans have ever been able to buy. We will have the instruments of an undreamed of standard of living for everyone. People are beginning to understand that it can be done. What will happen if it isn't?

Fortunately we will have an enormous accumulated demand for goods of all kinds and at the same time a gigantic flood of dammed up purchasing power to cushion the impact when war expenditures of 80 billion dollars a year are abruptly slashed. Inflation is an enemy as sinister as the Axis. There will be a clamor for abandonment of all inflation controls, but with the best and boldest leadership in private enterprise the job can be done without a violent boom and a ruinous depression. And it's a job, we'll all agree, for private enterprise with government's help.

Idleness, be it of men, money or machines, will be the one unforgivable sin. Unless we can eliminate mass unemployment we had better anticipate some guy on a white horse who says he knows how to do it — and he may be very popular!

Third: We must form a national foreign policy. We dare not emerge from this war without some simple national convictions which will lift fundamental foreign policy out of the arena of party politics. We have had no national foreign policy; we have had only epithets and bitter, misleading and unending domestic controversy. During the last election we did not discuss "our" foreign policy; we called it "Roosevelt's foreign policy." From the enunciation of the Monroe Doctrine to the Spanish American War we have been committed to defend about a third of the world — from Greenland to the tip of South America and from Alaska to the Philippines. At no time, as Walter Lippmann has pointed out very recently, have we had the means to fulfill our commitments.[167] We have

[167] Walter Lippmann, U.S. *Foreign Policy: Shield of the Republic* (Boston: Little, Brown, 1943).

unconsciously relied on friends to help us — the British Fleet in the Atlantic — and we very nearly overslept when our friends were attacked.

The conduct of our economic relations has been no better. As a creditor we insisted on selling and not buying. We even preferred to export dollars rather than import goods. We furnished Japan our raw war materials at a price and then loaned China money to buy our finished war materials.

We fought the last world war to preserve our security and about all we preserved was the absurd illusion of our invulnerability. We'll have to do better this time all along the line. Our manpower and resources are limited; our position exposed; our commitments large; the world is shrinking and is full of people who are just as smart as we are.

The purpose of a foreign policy, I take it, is peace and security. But they are not equal partners. Independence and security are more important than peace.

I suggest that there are two simple propositions underlying a foreign policy so defined:

First, our power must match our commitments. Let's not sink the Navy this time. It will be expensive, but it will be much less expensive than a frenzied last minute preparation like this one. And who can be sure that we won't be too late another time? A Naval officer said after the last war: "If the world is to have peace, the power to wage war must be lodged in the hands of the nations who hate war."

The second proposition underlying peace and security is friends, or cooperation, if you please. I don't know what the post-war settlement will be. I hope it will be flexible and deliberate. Relief, rehabilitation, disarmament of the enemy, federation, a world court, an international police are all means to an end. The end is the advancement of the common welfare by cooperation. There are a lot of families living in this crowded house. They must all be healthy and contented or in time there will be trouble. The economic well-being and progress of the other peoples of the world is in our own manifest self-interest. That's not "soggy sentimentality" or "sappy idealism." It is the best possible guarantee of enduring world peace.

If our people are convinced of these simple fundamentals of foreign policy — power commensurate with responsibility and enlightened cooperation — *before* the war ends, we should have, I think, a very good chance of at last establishing a rational foreign policy calculated to insure security and preserve peace. But if these convictions have not already been formed, the complicated details may obliterate the simple principles in controversy, discord and reaction.

I am embarrassed to have brought you such a lot of familiar, shopworn talk. What I have said this evening reminds me of Holmes' apostrophe to the woodpecker — "Thou sayest such undisputed things in such a solemn way." My purpose is to suggest that while saving freedom for tomorrow by *fighting* now, we must prepare to save it for day after tomorrow by *thinking* now. If the people know just what they want from this war, and want it badly enough, they can get it.

On June 15, 1943, Frank Smothers of the Chicago Sun *sent Stevenson a copy of an editorial from that day's paper praising U.S. Supreme Court Justice Owen J. Roberts for supporting a United Nations federation. The editorial also pointed out that Adlai E. Stevenson said the week before in Chicago that the United States needed a bold foreign policy of "international co-operation."*

To Frank Smothers[168]

June 17, 1943

Dear Frank:

Many thanks for the clipping. This is most exalted company for a common war monger, but I am trying to keep a straight face! I'll bet you don't dare send one to Justice Roberts!

A thousand thanks.

Yours,

William H. Avery, of Stevenson's law firm, wrote on June 7, 1943, asking if he was still a resident of Cook County and thus liable for a personal property tax.

To William H. Avery[169]

June 17, 1943

Dear Bill:

Many thanks for your letter. My domicile — or is it residence? — is equally fascinating to me. I seem to have all the residence attributes of a deep sea sailor — but I haven't even a uniform!

Since my mother-in-law moved from 1020 Lake Shore Drive and our things have been removed to the country or to Washington, I guess I have taken up residence, at last, on St. Mary's Road, Libertyville —

[168] This letter is in A.E.S., P.U.L.
[169] This letter is in A.E.S., P.U.L.

while I continue to live, or exist, in Washington. Moreover, I have been paying personal property taxes there for several years. So with my body in Washington, my heart in Libertyville and a few securities in Chicago I guess I'll follow my heart and move to Libertyville. Hence, please don't file a personal property tax for me for 1943. But should I file something taking me off their records?

Yours,

On August 2, 1943, Hermon Dunlap Smith, in his role as a director of the Illinois State Historical Society, invited Stevenson to speak at its annual meeting. He also told his old friend that he was "scouting around among the grass roots" to test support for Stevenson to run for governor in 1944.

To Hermon D. Smith[170]

August 4, 1943

Dear Dutch:

Many thanks for your letter. What would I talk to the Illinois State Historical Society about — the Life and Times of Baby Bliss — Fat Boy of Bloomington?

Anyway I am flattered in the extreme that you ever associated me with a learned society, and I can see that you are developing all the instincts of a good press agent and a politician!

Anyway, the facts are that I have just a couple of days ago accepted an invitation to speak before the Council on Foreign Relations on October 28 [171] and to prepare two speeches in one month and win the war is even more than I can do!

Many thanks. I'll be seeing you soon and will be much interested in any information you have uncovered.

Yours,

Stevenson's friend Struthers Burt wrote from Jackson Hole, Wyoming, on July 3, 1943, describing the speech to the Chicago Real Estate Board as "magnificent." He expressed the desire that President Roosevelt speak out more to the people on domestic problems and the peace to come. He mentioned that he was writing articles for Esquire *and that the editors had spoken of Senator Scott Lucas as a possible vice presidential nomi-*

[170] The original is in the possession of Mr. Smith.
[171] Stevenson actually delivered the speech on October 8.

nee in 1944 and were of the opinion that Colonel Robert R. McCormick and his Chicago Tribune were losing ground in Chicago. Burt also told Stevenson that he had written a similar letter to Jonathan Daniels of the Raleigh News and Observer.

To Struthers Burt [172]

August 5, 1943

Dear Struthers:

Your fine, instructive letter is a month old! I have been in and out of town and I've even had a week's leave. The last weeks of Congress were hell for me! I fell heir to the Elk Hills–Standard Oil contract and the shameless anxiety of people — both in the Administration and on the Hill — to get into the newspapers is a constant disillusion.[173]

. . . I was much flattered by your approval of the speech and my secretary says she sent you some more copies. Your eloquent piece in the Charlotte News and the coincidence of our views is reassuring.

I agree that there is uniform approval of the President's "foreign policy" among informed people. But I cannot overlook the growing feeling among the wise guys that a change of Administration marches step by step with victory in the field. There are always the usual qualifications about "if Roosevelt runs" and "if the Republicans nominate a reactionary," but the underlying tone is an increasing apprehension that change is the natural release of the American people once the pressure is lifted. I have little doubt, however, that the President can be elected easily. But a Republican House — perhaps a Republican Senate — seems very likely to me.

This confusing situation has personal implications for me. I have been beset of late to run for Governor of Illinois next spring and you would

[172] This letter is in A.E.S., P.U.L.

[173] In May, 1943, Knox handed a sensitive problem to Stevenson. Ever since the Teapot Dome scandals of the Harding administration, the question of naval oil reserves contained potential political dynamite. At the reserve at Elk Hills, California, Standard Oil of California owned some 9,000 acres and the government owned nearly four times that amount. Standard had to fill huge war orders for oil. But if it operated its acres independent of government control, it would drain off oil Congress had reserved under the Naval Reserve Act as amended in 1938. In November, 1942, Secretary Knox signed an agreement with Standard for the company to operate the pool under Navy supervision. Soon there were rumors the contract was illegal and there was graft and corruption involved.

Stevenson worked for weeks drafting a temporary operating agreement with Standard while the Navy prepared amendments to the 1938 Act for congressional consideration. President Roosevelt and Attorney General Francis Biddle approved the temporary agreement.

not blame me for eschewing certain defeat — not in the primaries, but in the election next November.

Roosevelt's position is surprisingly strong even now and he has a happy faculty for permitting his popularity to reach the bottom when it makes no difference and hit the top at election time. This consideration fills me with humility and I sometimes find it difficult to join in the emphatic assertions about what the President "must do" and "must not do." It seems to me he does pretty well and for timing, most of these people around here are students, not teachers. At all events, I agree with you on the direct reports to the people, of which the first has already transpired. I understand more will follow; when, I don't know.

Meanwhile, I am more than a little upset by the policy that seems to prevail in high places against education for the peace. I presume with the war in still delicate shape, it is not for the President to talk about it too much but certainly it seems to me that others should. Yet the conventional comment is still "put out the fire first and talk about rebuilding the house later." Perhaps the answer is that it is impossible to take the people into confidence until we can see more clearly what we *can* do after the war vis a vis Russia, for example. I would feel better about it if I was confident that we were even sure what we *wanted* to do, let alone what we had agreed with Britain to try to do.

I have a warm regard for Esquire — and it's not limited to barber shops! It's a grand sheet, and the sailor boys think so the world around. I've seen it in foxholes and ward rooms, dog-eared and overworked. I am delighted you are going to do some pieces and I wish I could give you a good thumb nail on Scott Lucas. I have known him a long while but never intimately. I am not sure he has the farm vote. I think it's a mistake to assume that individuals have or don't have strength with the farmer just now. They'll be for or against Roosevelt, and Lucas incidentally, largely on the basis of their position in the scheme of things next year. And their position ought to be pretty good if the government buys essential food commodities at fair ceilings and resells to distributors at a loss to make price controls work. Also you will remember Scott's courageous fight against the farm block on price control last winter. He has the looks and the manners and the agility, but there is certainly something wanting in profundity and that odd thing called "leadership." Confidentially, he's been very apprehensive about Illinois going Republican next year, but I understand that he's feeling better now and will run again for the Senate, unless, of course, the Vice Presidential lightning should strike him — a possibility he has been actively promoting.

Scott is a small town boy (Havana, Illinois, — educated at Wesleyan in Bloomington) who has made good in a big way without any real distinction any where along the route, which, if I recall correctly, has been conventional — local lawyer, American Legion, local politics, state tax commission and Governor [Henry] Horner's good will. Lloyd Lewis could tell you a lot of personal stuff about him. Scott is tall and stoops. At the Bermuda Conference he had a stomach ache one day and told the distinguished British diplomats that he was trying to stand up straight and put on his Senatorial dignity, but it hurt his stomach. He's human, unaffected and his head isn't swollen — at least not much. In short, he seems to me a good, steady, well-balanced guy who'll never set the world on fire — but can and has done a workmanlike, conscientious and enlightened job in public life. I realize that this is not exhilarating material for a sketch and I wish I could do better, but I really don't know him very well and I think Lloyd Lewis would be your best bet if you could stop off and see him at the Chicago Daily News on your way back.

I was interested in what the Esquire people had to say about McCormick. The other day he said that all the responsible posts in Washington were manned by "nude dancers and other deranged sadists." Certainly that kind of intemperance ought to finish him, but it has been going on for years. If you are not familiar with the Col. McCosmic cartoons in the Daily News you should be. Hereafter they are going to put a crack in his tin helmet! [174]

I agree with you about Johnnie Daniels and have the good fortune to see him occasionally hereabouts. That Southern tranquility and his everlasting good humor are tonic to me.

I hope you will not forget to send me the Ladies Home Journal pieces. God knows there never was a time when we needed more cogent, pointed writing in popular periodicals. As for the liberal sheets, I'm getting thoroughly fed up on them and their constant sniping at this and that. But more of that another time; I must catch a plane for another trip.

Many, many thanks again for your splendid letter. I hope there will be more!

Yours,

P.S. Dictated last week and signed this week! I am indebted to you for that superb phrase — "rides with the long rhythm of destiny." My best to Mrs. Burt. The above address fills me with envy. What I wouldn't give for a week on a horse in Wyoming!

[174] Cecil Jensen satirized Robert R. McCormick's pretensions to being a military expert in "Colonel McCosmic" cartoons in the Chicago Daily News throughout the war.

Mrs. Robert Biggert of Winnetka, Illinois, who was active in many Chicago civic groups, described to Stevenson a forthcoming meeting at the Chicago Stadium — it seated approximately 20,000 people — at which Vice President Henry A. Wallace was to speak on postwar policy. She mentioned that Wallace's assistant, Harold Young, had just been to Chicago to enlist the help of Mayor Edward J. Kelly and Corporation Counsel Barnet Hodes in filling the stadium.

Mrs. Biggert also described the work of supporters of Wendell L. Willkie for the 1944 Republican nomination, and she mentioned some activities by Willkie's right-wing Republican opponents including Colonel R. R. McCormick. She expressed the opinion that the Chicago Sun was "just another paper" and that until publisher Marshall Field removed executive editor Silliman Evans the paper would not improve.

To Mrs. Robert Biggert[175]

August 23, 1943

Dear Bee:

I have your letter of the 19th and am going to talk with Harold Young. . . . I am practically non compos mentis with my own affairs and bedevilments and I hardly know what to suggest or what to do to relieve your predicament. The latter I can well imagine. It reminds me of some awful nightmares in the past. Why did they ever make that stadium so large!

I suspect Kelly and Hodes may have to do one of their jobs to get it filled. It would be interesting as an experiment to see what could be done without them. I have always suspected that there might be a little myth in the assumption that it can't be done. The V. P. would be a good place to experiment. But one hesitates to risk a failure in those circumstances and I would play it safe. If I develop any thoughts with Young I will act accordingly and let you know. . . .

I was much interested in the little appraisal of the Chicago scene. You omitted nothing except the crop prospects! I think you are right on your appraisal of the Willkie sentiment and that some of the dop[e]sters who have counted him out may have another guess. The local scene interests me a good deal as I have been undergoing one of my periodical political flirtations — this time relating to the Governorship. Frankly, I don't know what's developing, if anything, but I believe some exploratory talks are being held with Kelly. I am as apprehensive as you are about "independent — nonpartisan" support. But, as usual, the gestures seem to come largely from that direction. Marshall Field purports to be inter-

175 This letter is in A.E.S., P.U.L.

ested, also Sam Levin,[176] Lloyd Lewis, et al. As for Stevenson, he is not sure whether he is interested or not and certainly doesn't seem to have any time to do much about it.

I think you are 100% right on the Sun, though I had felt that it was looking up a bit and I am told that there has been a marked circulation improvement, taking into consideration the usual summer seasonal loss, etc. I am afraid he [Marshall Field] is reluctant to play it alone until he gets his bearings and learns a little more about the business. But I can't believe he is wedded to Evans. Evidently Chicago is destined to be the capitol of all the erratic lunatics, thanks to Colonel McCormick. Los Angeles and Detroit better look out. They will, undoubtedly, contribute confusion and division in the political scene next year and McCormick will use them for all they are worth. But on the other side will be Mrs. Beatrice Biggert!

Yours,

On August 24, 1943, Richard Jacobson, editor of Standard Opinion, *a Chicago political weekly newspaper, sent Stevenson a clipping from John Dreiske's column in the Chicago* Times *of that date, stating that the Secretary of the Navy was pushing Stevenson for governor as were downstate Democrats. In July, 1943, when Stevenson mentioned the talk about his running for governor to his sister, Mrs. Ernest L. Ives, she replied: "That you should be considered as material for Gov. of your state is of course a very high honor & would fill the hearts of our departed dear ones with the greatest pride. . . . Naturally I will be terribly proud of you & in fact am already a bit overcome that you are so important except of course I've felt & seen & heard what an extraordinary position you have made for yourself for a long time."*

To Richard Jacobson[177]

August 27, 1943

Dear Mr. Jacobson:

Many thanks for your letter of August 24 and the enclosed clipping from the Chicago Times. It was all very interesting and I am much indebted to these anonymous Democrats who are interested in my candidacy. I suspect it will be something of a surprise to Colonel Knox as I doubt if he has heard about it before!

With renewed thanks for your courtesy, I am

Sincerely yours,

[176] A Chicago labor leader.
[177] This letter is in A.E.S., P.U.L.

On August 25, 1943, Richard S. Folsom of the Chicago Board of Education also sent Stevenson a copy of the Dreiske column in the Chicago Times.

To Richard S. Folsom[178]

August 27, 1943

My dear Mr. Folsom:

I have your letter of August 25 and the enclosed clipping and appreciate very much your thoughtfulness.

I am much flattered and indebted to these anonymous Democrats. But I suspect it will be a great surprise to Colonel Knox to hear that he is pushing me! I doubt if he has ever heard of the idea.

I look forward eagerly to an opportunity to talk with you about the political situation but I have no immediate prospects for coming to Chicago, although I have no doubt I will be out there sometime in September and I will look forward to a visit with you. I will try to let you know as far in advance as I can when I am going to be there.

With warmest regards, I am

Sincerely yours,

To Edward D. McDougal, Jr.[179]

September 1, 1943

Dear Ed:

I have an inquiry about Karl Malcolm Gibbon, a partner in the Poppenhusen firm.[180] If someone in the office knows him and can give me a brief and candid report on him I would appreciate it very much.

He does not seem to have had much corporate practice, but evidently has had some tax experience which might be useful to the Judge Advocate's office. As you will understand, he is an applicant for a commission and I occasionally get inquiries about Chicago lawyers. I have no recollection of Gibbon and am sure I did not know him personally.

I had expected a visit from you in the course of the summer and must serve notice herewith that the lodging facilities at 1904 R Street terminate as of September 15. Ellen and the children are going to stay in Libertyville this winter for a multitude of reasons and I am going to take

[178] This letter is in A.E.S., P.U.L.
[179] The original is in the possession of Mr. McDougal.
[180] The Chicago law firm of Johnson, Thompson, Poppenhusen & Raymond (now Raymond, Mayer, Jenner & Block).

a small apartment with Frannie Comstock[181] over in Georgetown.[182] A corner of the living-room rug will always be available for you!

Hastily yours,

AD

Struthers Burt wrote Stevenson on August 27, 1943, saying that Senator Gerald Nye had just been to Jackson Hole, Wyoming. The Senator had with him a copy of John Roy Carlson's Under Cover: My Four Years in the Nazi Underworld of America — The Amazing Revelation of How Axis Agents and Our Enemies Within Are Now Plotting to Destroy the United States *(New York: Dutton, 1943). The book was highly critical of Nye, and Burt added that the Senator was most cordial although Burt had praised the book on the dust jacket. Burt also urged Stevenson to run for governor.*

To Struthers Burt[183]

September 7, 1943

Dear Struthers:

I have been chortling quite a bit about your encounter with Senator Nye. I have not yet seen "Under Cover" but I have heard liberal quotations and hope for a chance to read it. Certainly your pal Nye's performance in the last few years entitles him to an honored position under that cover. These auspices never cease to confound me — they are, for the most part, such genial, attractive guys socially. I have played golf with Nye once or twice in the last couple of years out at the Burning Tree Club in the Sunday morning shuffle and found him very agreeable. As for Burt Wheeler,[184] they say there is no better companion. I am always irritated to find myself responding cordially to people whose views I detest. . . .

I suspect the Governorship business will take care of itself by the

[181] An old Princeton friend.

[182] Mrs. Stevenson's unhappiness over Washington and her husband's absorption in his work was one reason for her return to Libertyville. Stevenson's sister, Mrs. Ernest L. Ives wrote him in September, 1943: "I feel very deeply that more, almost than anything, you need Ellen's loving cooperation in all you undertake & that, at the moment, you do not have. . . . If you give up 'public life' & settle down to what she wants would you be insuring peace & a beautiful productive living pattern? If you would then that is doubtless what you should do. . . . I suppose you realize that all your friends know from Ellen about the possibilities of your running for the Senate or for Gov. . . . I fear your affairs & her relationship to you are too freely discussed."

[183] This letter is in A.E.S., P.U.L.

[184] Democratic Senator Burton K. Wheeler of Montana.

gradual elimination of everyone, including me, except the present Secretary of State,[185] who is a very successful vote getter, even if he is identified with the Kelly-Nash machine and a little lazy. But more of this when I see you.

Sincerely yours,

Secretary of the Navy Frank Knox was soon to visit the United Kingdom. Stevenson prepared the following memorandum on September 14, 1943, as background material for any talks the Secretary might make.

The British people have been at war for 4 years. Frome June 1940, when France fell, to June 1941, when Hitler attacked Russia, they stood virtually alone. One house in every 5 in the United Kingdom has been destroyed or damaged; about 50,000 civilians have been killed in air raids about 60,000 seriously wounded. Their Navy has lost some 250 warships; their people have lived in blackedout cities with short rations and immense dislocations of daily life. They are tired from this long strain, abnormally sensitive and more emotional than usual.

The British people have an intense admiration for Russia. It is a mixture of amazement at Russia's military and industrial achievements and gratitude for Russia's help in weakening the common enemy. It is an emotion shared by all economic and social groups in Britain. As in this country Russia elicits more applause and admiration than Britain, so in Britain America can't compete with Russia, I understand. This may be changing in our favor now that masses of American troops are going into action alongside the British on the Continent of Europe.[186]

The American troops and airmen stationed in the U. K. are better fed, better clothed, and far better paid than the British. In spite of these and other handicaps, our men are, on the whole, well liked and arouse unprecedented interest in the country and the communities from which they come. It surprises the British to find so many of the Americans with Polish, Italian, Greek, and other non-Anglo-Saxon names, perhaps because the British know so little of our history and our national development, and forget that they themselves are a melting-pot which has had a thousand years to simmer instead of a hundred.

There is still, I understand, widespread suspicion about our willingness to cooperate with them after the war and some sensitiveness about

[185] Edward J. Hughes.

[186] On July 10, 1943, Allied forces landed in Sicily and the island was conquered by August 17. On September 3, Field Marshal Montgomery's men landed on the toe of the Italian boot and General Mark Clark's troops landed at Salerno six days later.

the threat of American "imperialism." OWI [Office of War Information] thinks this distrust springs from (a) bitter memories of 1919, (b) the preoccupation of British commentators and correspondents with the news of domestic politics in Washington, and (c) the cynicism and defeatism about America which is openly expressed by many unofficial Americans — commentators and newspaper correspondents especially — who have lived in London for a long time and have lost touch with home.

If the British people have their doubts about us as a post-war partner, they also are not quite sure that we are in this war heart and soul. This is the product, partly, of our immunity to bombing and other war horrors, but partly also of our past tendency to "glamorize" the war in our war communiques, speeches, news dispatches, radio broadcasts, and above all, in our war films. We have said a good deal, and with ample reason, about the heroism of our fighting men; we have flooded the British with statistics about our production and our power, which no one ever doubted; we have not said or shown nearly enough of the conditions our men are enduring in lonely posts of danger from Iceland to the Southwest Pacific.

In particular the British are ignorant of the Pacific war. In the last 6 months they have caught some realistic awareness of the nature of our job in the Pacific. But they do not yet fully realize the burden of our Pacific supply route or the demands made upon our men and ships in those areas. They should realize that our men not only can "take it" but do "take it"; that this is not a Rover Boys' war for us in the Pacific any more than it is in the Mediterranean.

I should think you could well tell the ordinary people, as SecNav and from personal observations, something of the war on the other side of the world and its toughness; the gigantic job of, first, building a supply line 8–10,000 miles long and then supplying countless bases and fighting fronts on land and sea with men, food, munitions, gasoline, everything; the terrific conditions — the heat, the rain, the jungles, the malaria. There seems to be little enough understanding of the Pacific theatre and of our job out there. They have heard plenty of hero stories — ours as well as theirs. The Public Relations officers of the Army Air Force have evidently been particularly busy and respect is very high for our fighting men, although they may not have heard as much about our sailors as our flyers and soldiers. What seems to be wanting is a consciousness of the magnitude of our mass fighting. Our participation in the Mediterranean war is now well known, but, due to the concentration of public attention on Europe, there is little vividness about the grim, bloody, enormity of the Pacific war; what we have done out there, what we are doing, and what remains to be done to bring the Jap to his knees.

The time is past when we need to talk in terms of production promises; what they will want to hear now is of our ships, etc., actually delivered and in action.

I am told that without trying to compare the impact of the war on Britons with the impact on Americans, the degree of sacrifice and the amount of dislocation here is little appreciated — overcrowded houses, migration of labor, workers living in trailors, etc. We lived on rubber tires; now the highways are empty. Our houses were overheated; now they are cold. Our food was varied and abundant; now it is rationed. The food we send abroad no longer comes out of our plenty; our plenty is gone and America is deliberately tightening its belt. Millions of our men are overseas — in Britain, in Africa and also in numberless lonely barren islands and posts in distant oceans. Our taxes, like the British, are heavy and getting heavier, consumers' goods in [are] running low; you can no longer buy anything you want, be it goods or services. The factories are full of working wives and mothers, while our men in arms approach ten million. And women are waiting by thousands in our port cities for men who will never come back, just as they do in Portsmouth and Plymouth.

The amazing and heartening thing is that all this has been done in less than two years by people who have known little of regimentation in the past and have felt no real threat of direct attack upon their homes.

Even as here, concern about post-war commercial plans is becoming widespread in Britain and already dwarfs the fear that we will return to ostrich isolationism.

The people of Britain are particularly disturbed, for example, over the alleged post-war advantage which our shipping program as well as our aircraft construction program gives to the United States. Two obvious answers to fears of this sort are (a) they are not always well grounded in fact, and the masses of American people have shown no signs of sub-scribing to the extreme form of trade imperialism; (b) there need be no such fears in Great Britain if through international collaboration world trade is really promoted instead of restricted. The American Government for 10 years has promoted a program of reciprocal trade treaties, low tariffs, and the avoidance of cut-throat competition for foreign markets, and all indications are that a majority of Congress and of the American people support such a program. In each country a minority want to turn the clock back. But we know — and they should realize that we know — that the alternative to cooperation is disastrous competition, and that cooperation is, therefore, the wiser course if a recurrence of the present worldwide tragedy is to be averted.

As to America's part in the post-war world, I suppose the most heartening and honest thing is the advance our people have made since 1919, through experience and education, in understanding their place in the world; the decency and generosity which they have in common with the ordinary people of all countries. Finally, in spite of violent disagreements over domestic policies, there is an overwhelming determination among political leaders and the partisans of both parties to win a lasting victory, and there will be an understanding and realization of what "durable peace" means this time as never before.

To Frank Knox

September 29, 1943

MEMORANDUM TO THE SECRETARY OF THE NAVY

I feel very emphatically that we should commission a few negroes. We now have more than 60,000 already in the Navy and are accepting 12,000 per month. Obviously this cannot go on indefinitely without making some officers or trying to explain why we don't. Moreover, there are 12 negroes in the V–12 program[187] and the first will be eligible for a commission in March, 1944.

Ultimately there will be negro officers in the Navy. It seems to me wise to do something about it now. After all, the training program has been in effect for a year and a half and one reason we have not had the best of the race is the suspicion of discrimination in the Navy. In addition, the pressure will mount both among the negroes and in the Government as well. The Coast Guard has already commissioned two who qualified in all respects for their commissions.

I specifically recommend the following:

(1) Commission 10 or 12 negroes selected from top notch civilians just as we procure white officers, and a few from the ranks. They should probably be assigned to training and administrative duties with the negro program.

(2) Review the rating groups from which negroes are excluded. Perhaps additional classes of service could profitably be made available to them.

---

[187] Because of the severe disruption of the country's educational institutions many college buildings and facilities were idle. President Roosevelt asked the Secretaries of the Navy and Army to develop programs so these facilities could be used. By the end of 1943 the Navy's V–12 program and the Army's Specialized Training Program were using many of them to provide war training for thousands of men.

I don't believe we can or should postpone commissioning some negroes much longer. If and when it is done it should not be accompanied by any special publicity but rather treated as a matter of course. The news will get out soon enough.

Stevenson spoke before the Chicago Council on Foreign Relations on October 8, 1943.

Before coming here today I read what I had said when I spoke to you in February, 1942. Although many people did not realize it, our military fortunes were at a low ebb and it was a gloomy speech. I want to quote something I said at that time — 20 months ago:

"Everyone must realize that not only *can* we lose this war but at the moment we *are* losing it!; that we are on the defensive, fighting desperate rear guard actions, fighting for the time until we can catch up with the thieves whose knives were sharpened long ago, while in characteristic democratic manner, we were arguing as to whether they *were* thieves and whether they really planned to use knives. We must realize that Japan's new order in Asia is all but a reality, that the thief has the wealth of the Indies almost in his grasp, and that it may take years of heartbreaking war and oceans of blood and treasure to drive him slowly back in the Pacific."

I told you then, when our losses in the Atlantic were mounting with alarming rapidity, that Britain was the only accessible base for operations against the continent we had left, and that its preservation depended on ships and sea power; that the same was true of aid to Russia; that, likewise, what we could do to destroy the enemy in Africa and save the Mediterranean depended on communications — ships, safe voyages and sea power. I tried to tell you in some detail about the enormity of the task that confronted us in establishing and securing a supply line to the Southwest Pacific — the difficulties and the distances — and the danger that the Japanese blitz would win the race before we could pave the long road to Australia and bring up the reinforcements.

I suggested that the grand strategy of the Axis was to effect a junction — the Germans pushing east and the Japanese pushing west — and that our fortunes and our future rested on shipping and sea power the world around.

That was 20 months ago. The dreadful danger that beset us then has passed. Hitler and Tojo will not dine together in the marble palace at New Delhi and divide the world. The route to Australia and the myriad islands is now a great highway dotted with service stations. The Japanese have been driven back 300 miles in the Solomons; eastern New Guinea is cleared and the vise is slowly tightening on Rabaul. The Aleutians have been fumigated and our planes are reconnecting the Kurils. Not we, but the Japs are on the defensive now. About three billion dollars worth of food and war material has been shipped to Russia in those 20 months. The Germans have been driven back 650 miles from Stalingrad to Kiev and they too are on the defensive now — very much so! In the Atlantic more than 4000 United Nations' ships crossed safely from May through August and the losses from submarines were less than one half of one per cent. (But the U-boats are coming back again with new weapons and we have by no means heard the last of them.) Finally, the Mediterranean has been liberated, the Sicilian narrows are opening and in Italy we begin to see the shape of things to come on the blood walls of Hitler's fortress.

All these miracles of salvation have come to pass in the last year and a half. Why? Because sea power, or more properly, what is now called sea-air power made them possible.

In Sir Francis Bacon's aphorism, "He that commands the sea is at great liberty, and may take as much or as little of the war as he will." It's all one war and we had to take all of it or none of it. What has always been true is still true. The seas are highways and to wage intercontinental war control of the highways — the lines of communication — is essential. Unless you control the highway you can't control the destination. You can't control a distant land or the skies above it unless you control the seas in between. Ships alone can no longer do it. To resort to Bacon again: "He that will not adopt new remedies must expect new evils," and all the actions of this war to date have demonstrated that modern sea power is an air-sea team. One without the other is inadequate. The plane is of little value in bad visibility or in bad weather or at night and the ship is slow and vulnerable without aircraft protection. The team is indivisible.

Although, it may interest you to know, there is still less total merchant shipping in the world than there was on September 1, 1939, when the war commenced, it has been the miracle of Allied ship and plane production, largely in this country, that has turned defeat into victory. Sea power has been the very basis of our strategy; it has been at once the limiting factor in our operations and the means of our operations against the enemy by land and by air. Each month as our merchant shipping has grown and the power of our air-sea combat teams has increased, the area dominated by the enemy has contracted, and the area in which we can strike him has enlarged. This mobility, this rapid development of our ability to use the sea lanes for supply and reinforcement and to pick and choose the place of attack, has saved us from disaster, has given us the strategic initiative and has proved again the validity of sea power.

Air and sea power cannot be evaluated independently and it is well to bear in mind that air power cannot supply air power, let alone ground forces and civilian populations. Air power can strike the enemy where it hurts most, but to do so with any effectiveness it is dependent on ships for gasoline, bombs, ground personnel, repair and maintenance facilities, supplies and, of course, first of all, upon ship-borne men and machinery to build the distant airfields. Only recently General Marshall, commenting on the great tactical mobility of air power, pointed out that it is dependent for strategic mobility upon surface transport. The 300 mile-an-hour bomber is still tied strategically to the 10 knot ship. That is our difficulty in China where there is no ship-borne supply route and air combat operations hang on a long, fragile — and gallant — thread of transport planes clear across hostile Northern Burma and the huge hump of mountains and bad weather into India.

The influence of sea power in this war can be illustrated in many ways. Let me cite some of the more obvious examples. First, the Atlantic blockade of Germany and the counter blockade of the United Kingdom. For a time German sea forces threatened our ability to take the war to the enemy. The U-boats not only sank many ships but also diverted many aircraft from combat service. It is said that until a few months ago there were as many bombers in the British Coastal Command as in the RAF Bomber Command. In the same manner American submarines are crippling Japanese sea communications in the Western Pacific. The submarine has been at once our deadly foe and our deadly friend.

Another case in point is the somewhat passive Italian fleet. But for more than three years its very existence has required the concentration of large naval and air forces in the Mediterra[n]ean which were desperately needed in the North Atlantic, the South Atlantic, the Indian Ocean and the Western Pacific.

Again, had the German Navy been any match for the British, Hitler would very likely be ruling the United Kingdom today instead of chewing his fingernails in Be[r]chtesgaden.

Sea power made possible and supported the invasions of North Africa, Sicily and Italy. Naval gunfire played a large part in stopping the German tanks and saving the beachhead at Gela in Sicily and in turning the tide of battle in the first bloody hours at Salerno.

The ability of ships to transport troops around the enemy and outflank him by sea has already been demonstrated and is an incalculable tactical advantage. Where the enemy can only be reached by sea, direct assault must be preceded by amphibious operations. Already we have spent more than a billion dollars on landing craft alone. Invasion in terms of modern requirements is a complex innovation in warfare. First there must be the ships specially built to transport and land quickly the men and weapons of land warfare — ships for personnel, for tanks and mechanized artillery and equipment — ships that can drive right up to the beaches and disembark their combat freight under fire. There are many varieties and sizes of these ships, most of them designed in the Navy Department in Washington. Then come the transports and the supply ships. No invaders could exist on hostile territory very long without rapid reinforcement of men and supply. Bear in mind that there are no docks and all of the men and material of invasion have to be unloaded over the side into little motor-driven lighters. They have to be brought along too. Then there is the naval force covering the landing against enemy submarines, surface forces and airplanes. Finally, the air forces, land-based if possible because land is unsinkable, to soften up the defenses by bombing and strafing and to cover the landing against enemy air attack. The whole has to be perfectly synchronized and there must be enough ships, enough men, enough tanks, enough of everything at the right place and the right time. A failure anywhere along the line may mean disaster.

The Mediterranean is a dramatic case in point. In 1940 it looked as though Italian air power had bested British sea power and severed the life line of the Empire. In 1941 land-based German aircraft wrote a new chapter in warfare with the successful invasion of Crete. Soon the Luftwaffe based on Sicily was subjecting Malta to merciless bombardment and taking a heavy toll of British convoys in the narrow waters between Sicily and Tunisia. Not long after Pearl Harbor the British Battle Fleet in the Eastern Mediterranean had been reduced to only three cruisers which faced an Italian Fleet of six battleships, 19 cruisers and many smaller vessels. But the Axis didn't know it. Malta was daringly reinforced by carriers and miraculously survived. British submarines sank 1,335,000 tons of Axis shipping with a loss of 41 submarines. The fleet air arm, operating from carriers, from Malta and from the western desert, accounted for another 410,000 tons. The Axis didn't have the ships to pay the tribute and to reinforce Rommel too. Then came the Allied invasions of North Africa, Sicily, Italy, Sardinia, Corsica — and more are coming.

Sea power spoiled Napoleon's African adventure and it spoiled Hitler's. With it vanished Hitler's gra[n]diose hope of closing the Mediterranean, driving through the Near East to cut the Russian supply line on the Persian Gulf and thence triumphantly on to his rendezvous with the Japanese conquerors in India.

Instead of that, this: Germany and Japan will not make a junction; the invasion of the Nazi continent has begun; the Balkans are accessible through the Adriatic and the Aegean; India is thousands of miles closer, which means that millions of tons have been added to the Allied shipping pool; the Italian Fleet is no longer a menace but an asset;[188] powerful British Naval units are now released to support the reconquest of Burma and to press from the east while we press from the west. Japan is between two fires.

Future historians may write that World War II was won, not in Europe or Asia, but in Africa. In any event, it's all one war and the housecleaning in the Mediterranean is a victory in the Indian Ocean and a victory in the western Pacific. Japan will get no naval aid from her partner now. She stands alone.

The real meaning of sea power becomes clearer as the offensive develops. Without dominion on the seas the war at best would be a stalemate; at worst a defeat. Sea power has saved us from defeat and it is the key to victory.

At the risk of telling you more and more of what you already know, I want to say something about Japan and the sea power implications of that front. The territory under Japanese dominion is composed of an inner and an outer zone. Japan proper, Manchuria, Korea, North China and Formosa comprise, roughly, the inner zone. The outer zone is the gigantic area conquered in the last two years, including South China, Indo-China, the Philippines and stretching 6000 miles from Burma through Malaya and the Dutch East Indies to the Gilbert Islands. Japan's economic potential is concentrated in the inner zone. The outer zone furnishes raw materials. The heart of this vast empire is Japan and the arteries are ships. Her logistic situation is not dissimilar from ours. She is fighting on the fringes at the ends of extended communication lines, but her war potential is a fraction of ours.

For more than 12 years Japan has accumulated stock piles of combat armament. Though constantly increasing, total wastage thus far has probably not been serious, and Japan has on hand the equipment to support vigorous military activity for a long period. But her capacity to exploit her vast resources in raw materials and expand industrial production to keep pace with the growing strength of the United Nations is limited by shipping and processing capacity. The extent to which military and naval interference is exercised against Japan will determine whether she can continue to build up armament reserves and organize basic in-

188 On July 25, 1943, the King of Italy removed Mussolini and made Marshal Pietro Badoglio premier. On September 3, Badoglio surrendered and the Italian fleet was turned over to the Allies.

dustrial capacity for large scale expansion. To date the greatest single retarding factor has been the loss of merchant shipping by our action.

Because of the lack of industrial capacity, the deteriorating shipping position, the expanding power of the Allies and the probability of German defeat, it seems clear that Japan is putting aside large scale development of the newly conquered areas and is concentrating on intensive development of the inner zone. This means stock piling of strategic materials from the outer zone to strengthen the inner zone and the development of those industrial facilities and those raw materials which will provide the highest possible measure of self-sufficiency within the inner zone. Loss of the outer zone would deprive Japan of a major source of war materials, but if this loss were postponed long enough the stock piling program, combined with industrial expansion in the inner zone would still leave Japan with a war potential capable of prolonging hostilities for a long period.

You will say that concentration in the inner zone, particularly in Japan proper, is a weakness in itself because of its vulnerability to air attack. Sustained, long-range bombing, at least from China, even after the Burma Road is opened, is still a long way off due to the enormous transport difficulties and, moreover, the Japs have been busily engaged in decentralizing certain strategic industries to reduce this hazard.

So Japan will fight at the outposts of her stolen empire to hold what she can and will retreat inch by inch to gain time to fortify the heartland. To fight she needs warships, to maintain and supply the garrisons all around the great circle she needs merchant ships, to develop the inner zone she needs merchant ships, to protect them she needs warships. It's a race with time. We must relieve the pressure on China. We must batter down the outposts, sink ships, cut the arteries and enfeeble the heart lest it get too strong. We've torn off some of the fringe territory at great cost and with great exertion. We've made a good start on the long journey to Tokyo and she is bleeding where it hurts most. We have sunk 180 Japanese warships and more than 2,500,000 tons of precious Japanese shipping. That is about a third of the estimated total shipping available to Japan since the war began, and 77 per cent of it was sunk by American submarines, those unsung heroes of this war whose story has been only half told. I've seen them come into Pacific bases from their long solitary patrols in Japanese waters. I know how they live, how their ships look, and how they look and I've heard some of their stories and seen some periscope photographs I won't soon forget. No service, in my opinion, deserves more thanks than the submariners who are slowly draining the life blood of the Japanese Empire.

The map is the best evidence of the role that sea power must play in crushing the Japs, in smashing forever in Japanese minds the myth that they are invincible, that the gods chose Japan as the center of the universe and sent the God-Emperor to rule the human race.

I have dwelt at some length on the role of sea power in this war, not in the hope of bringing you anything fresh, but because it is a reaffirmation in modern terms of sea power's influence on history, and it also points up the vital significance of the gigantic development of our Navy in the last three years.

The figures are familiar, but some of them are worth repeating — they have a significance that reaches way beyond surrender day.

In July, 1940, the Navy received five newly-completed vessels; in June, 1943, almost 1200. I can't give you the later figures.

In July, 1940, the Navy received 25 new airplanes; in June, 1943, almost 2000.

Between those dates the Navy built 2,200,000 tons of ships; added to its air arm 23,000 planes and completed $6,500,000,000 of shore facilities.

Three years ago the Navy had 1076 vessels; it now has well over 14,000.

Three years ago the Navy had 383 fighting ships; today it has well over 600, after all losses, transfers to other nations and conversions to non-combat types.

In July, 1940, the Navy air arm consisted of 1744 planes; today it is way over 18,000, after transferring to other agencies and writing off for obsolescence more than 9000 planes.

Navy fighter planes today fire in one minute five times the weight of projectiles their 1940 predecessors fired. A battleship's antiaircraft fire power is 100 times what it was three years ago. Torpedo production last month alone equaled the torpedo production during all of World War I.

By the end of this year we will have more than fourteen first line aircraft carriers; double the number we had on the date of Pearl Harbor, and you can guess where most of them will be working. I don't include the numerous smaller auxiliary and escort carriers.

By the end of next year the Navy will reach a total of five million tons, or 3-½ times its strength in mid-1940.

I have tried to show how sea power in this transoceanic war is the foundation of strategy. In the midst of war, the United States has built its Navy into the greatest sea-air power on earth. The ability to build — and rebuild — on this scale is the basic advantage of the American Navy. Its size and power is matched only by the task that confronts it.

Whether it is the functioning of the channels of supply which one rarely hears of unless they fail, whether it is the invasion of the Balkans through the Adriatic and the Aegean, whether it is the invasion of

Burma from the Bay of Bengal, whether it is the seizure of the Kurils from which to bomb the heart of Japan, or whether it is working northward past Rabaul and Truk toward the inner zone, success will be dependent on sea-borne forces and sea-borne communications for supply and reinforcement. Whatever it is, sea power, control of the seas, is obviously an indispensable factor in the future of this war as it has been in the past.

Captain William D. Puleston, a distinguished naval historian, recently said of Japan that "the first insular nation in modern history which dared to challenge superior sea power will pay for its temerity, first with the loss of its temporary overseas conquests and, second with the surrender of the homeland."

But let me add, the greatest battles and the saddest losses are still ahead of us. We have averted disaster by a narrow margin and by the sacrifice and indomitable courage of peoples who know no price for their freedom. But for us — in spite of our gallant victories and heavy losses — the worst of the waste and pain and heartache is still between us and the last victory. That's why one hesitates a little to talk of peace and the problems beyond the war. But we must profit from our past mistakes. We cannot afford many more, and in that connection I think the Navy deserves some attention.

Perhaps a little reflection on our historical behavior would be germane to consideration of our future policy.

In 1812 we built up our Navy and then neglected it for 30 years.

In 1845 we started again, but the war was soon over and with it the naval expansion.

In 1861 most of our ships were in foreign stations and it took a year to bring them back to make the blockade of the Confederacy effective. But happily we had a large merchant marine and we rapidly built up a respectable blockade force by conversion and new construction, including monitors for service in the rivers and inland waters.

From 1865 to 1883 there were no appropriations for building, only for repair, and when the Navy built a new ship on the keel of an old one Congress, properly enough, passed a law limiting expenditures for repairs to a percentage of original cost.

Commencing about 1883 the Federal Government was so prosperous, due to the tariff which Congress did not care to reduce, that some money was spent on the Navy. An incidental by-product of this period was the improvement in metallurgical processes in this country, due in large measure to more exacting steel specifications laid down by the Navy.

By 1898 we had about five battleships designed for coastal defense. It is interesting to recall that by the time Cevera's[189] fleet reached the Azores there was a terrific clamor to use the Navy for the defense of our Atlantic seaports and Congress insisted on building three useless new monitors for harbor protection.

But the Navy enjoyed a great impetus from the Spanish War and in the succeeding administration of its champion, Theodore Roosevelt.

Then when war spread over Europe the Navy found another friend in Woodrow Wilson.

But after the World War came the Washington Disarmament Conference in 1922 and we sank and scrapped about a million tons, including two brand new battleships, and seven battleships and six battle cruisers which were on the ways and building. These 15 capital ships averaged 35 per cent complete and it cost us some $75,000,000 to scrap them.

During the next ten or twelve years the Navy was neglected again, until Franklin Roosevelt started to build it up with relief funds.

It is a spotty, erratic history — a history of indecision and confused perception of our responsibility as a nation with vast overseas commitments and of the requirements of our national security.

A distinguished physician once remarked to me that his only explanation for the survival of the human race was that women seemed to forget about childbirth so easily. It seems to be the same with war — people forget about it so easily.

After this war the United States will for the first time be the greatest sea power in the world — a circumstance of profound historical significance — just as our new found creditor position was after the last war, which we promptly overlooked. But tomorrow is not yesterday. And this time, when our enemies are crushed, defeated and disarmed, perhaps we will remember and go on remembering that in sea power lies our security, that the great Navy we have wrought with such travail and expense is a mighty instrument of peace as well as war, and that it will continue to be until new methods of war and commerce are devised or until man, the rational animal, with God's help, fashions the machinery of rational living and enduring peace.

I want to read you something: "It does not seem safe to entrust the preservation of peace for several years after this war is ended to international bodies proposed in this tentative plan for the organization of the world to prevent war. Until the world has constructive evidence that Germany has abandoned her theory of State and her policy of domination, and has abolished her military class, I think the peace of the world

[189] Spanish Admiral Pascual Cervera led an abortive attempt to break the American blockade of Cuba in July, 1898.

should be kept by a combination for offensive and defensive purposes of the Allies and the United States, and that this combination should organize and maintain the military and naval forces necessary to prevent a breach of peace. No reduction of armaments will be possible until it is made completely visible to all nations that the peace of the world is going to be preserved by just that combination of powers competent and ready for that job. In my judgment, it is highly desirable to make that combination forthwith."

Charles W. Eliot[190] wrote that 25 years ago. Amen, you say. But what happened? For 20 years after the last war we tried practically every peace prescription in the catalogue. We, and the other like-minded nations, tried limitation of armaments seriously, conscientiously and almost disastrously. We tried self-denying ord[i]nances like the Nine-Power Treaty regarding China.[191] We tried the high-minded and soul-stirring Kellogg-Briand renunciation.[192] Less charitable people have called it an "incantation" and "yogi." We even tried something approaching suicide with the neutrality laws. And all the while there was the League of Nations, "the greatest experiment and the greatest effort that mankind has ever made to assure the peace of the world." Fearful at last that all these efforts would not work, we tried cajolery of the aggressors; then lecturing them and finally appeasing them. And after 20 years we were in the most dreadful war in history!

All the public opinion polls these days show approval of a post-war policy of international collaboration and the preservation of force for the preservation of peace. Although we didn't have polls, the same was true during the last war. But look what happened. Collective security and force don't seem to occasion any alarm during wartime when we are enjoying the benefits of the collective force of our Allies on the battlefield. But in peacetime the acceptance of precise formulas to implement such a policy seems to be a horse of a different color. We can foresee with certainty that with our enemies defeated and helpless, concentrated as we will be on manifold domestic questions, tired and irritable, magnifying minor disagreements with our Allies and in an atmosphere of general intellectual softening, it will seem cheaper, easier and even safer to a lot of people to go it alone. And the oversized Navy will be an easy

[190] Former president of Harvard University, and author of numerous publications on the problems of post-World War I peace.

[191] In the Nine Power Treaty, February 1, 1922, the United States, Great Britain, France, Japan, Italy, Portugal, Belgium, and the Netherlands pledged "to respect the sovereignty, the independence, and the territorial and administrative integrity of China."

[192] Under the Kellogg-Briand Pact, 1928, the contracting nations renounced war as an instrument of policy and promised to settle all disputes by peaceful means.

mark for the economy shouters and pacifists — even if we have bases scattered all over the Pacific and Western Atlantic to maintain and protect.

What we are fighting for in essence is peace — a better world in which there are no wars or, at least, fewer wars. To stop wars people must hate wars. But all people won't hate war as much as the conditions that breed war. The elimination of the causes of war will be, as it always has been, man's greatest challenge. It has not been done in the past; it won't be done in the future unless this country takes a large part in the doing, and it certainly won't be done overnight. We won't even have a chance to do it unless, in the meantime, there is force in the world prepared and determined to crush a peace breaker. Until there is collective force to police the road to the better world, there must be individual force ready and determined to keep order until the community is organized.

The first step is to organize the strong men in the community. They dare not compete; hence they must merge their strength for common purposes. When the war is over the United States and Britain will have unchallenged mastery of the seas and Russia will be the most powerful land force in the world. Together we can do everything. Apart — well, it's unthinkable.

But we won't be apart. Together with the enormous potential of an industrialized China, our collective force can and must insure the peace of the world while we strive to create the atmosphere, promote the conditions and fashion, experimentally, slowly but surely, the institutions of law and order on a world-wide basis. How long will all this take? No one knows. But blue prints, plans and specifications will not be enough. The house must be built and the numerous families must live in it for a while before the strong men dare neglect their arms.

This is one war — we are all in it. It must be one indivisible peace — and we must all be in it. The key, of course, is Russia. The papers are reverberating these days with speculation about Russia's intentions. Some counsel courtship, some counsel reserve; some are suspicious of Russia, some are equally suspicious of ourselves; some want "alliances," others "understandings"; others want "collaboration," and most everyone wants "friendly relations" with Russia. The same is true in Britain. The approaching conferences[193] will be held in an auspicious atmosphere as far as we are concerned. But what do the Russians want?

My guess is that they want friendly relations just as much as we do.

[193] The Moscow Conference, October, 1943, and the Teheran Conference, December, 1943. At the latter conference Churchill, Roosevelt, and Stalin met together for the first time.

Prejudice and distaste have cursed and confused our thinking about Russia. We have come to accept anything mischievous about Russia. But prejudice and national self-interest must not be confused.

The Russians have been suspicious too. For a generation they have lived in apprehension of invasion and counter revolution, building up the war machine that has saved the Eurasian Continent and more than a billion people from domination by the tyrants of Tokyo and Berlin.

The Czars didn't like democracy and the infant, revolutionary American Republic. Russia was the last major power to recognize our national existence. But we did not like the Czars either. Nor did we like Bolshevism any better, and the conservative United States was the last major power to recognize the revolutionary Soviet Union. We have never liked one another's government, but over this span of 150 years Russia is about the only major power with whom we have never had any trouble.

It is well to remember that we don't have to have the same form of government to have the same interests. Policy based on prejudice is the antithesis of realism. The Russians don't work that way and neither must we.

To be sure, there are many difficult and delicate obstacles between us and the understandings on which the future peace of the world depends. There will be disagreements, conflicts and compromise inevitably.

But the fundamental fact is that Russia and the United States have always been useful to each other in the past, but never more so than now. Russia needs peace for reconstruction and rehabilitation of the vast and populous areas which have been devastated by the Nazi hordes; she will need our help. She must have peace to evolve her economy — a frugal structure on a rich foundation; she will need our help for that. And she must have peace to work out to its conclusions her experimental political system.

Russia wants and needs a stable world more, if anything, than we do. Britain and America will have all the sea power and most of the air power. They will be a great comfort to us. And the Russian realist knows they are prerequisites of a stable world, until we can create something better. What he does not know is whether we in the United States will keep and use this stupendous power, whether we will play our part. And that's up to you and me!

Stevenson's Uncle Louis B. Merwin of Bloomington wrote him October 15, 1943, praising his speech in Chicago. He expressed the hope that his nephew would occupy the governorship if he desired it.

To Louis B. Merwin[194]

October 18, 1943

Dear Uncle Lou:

Thanks for your note. I am glad you liked the speech, which was intended as a plug for preserving the Navy after the war but got a little confused with post-war political planning.

If my occupancy of the Governor's chair is a matter of personal inclination, it will be cold as far as I am concerned. Moreover, I do not think there is much realism in this agitation and I am not worrying about it.

I look forward to a glimpse of you in Bloomington next week. It is unfortunate that the day falls in the middle of the week as I should like to stay for a day or so. I've only been in Bloomington one day in more than two years.

Yours,

To Robert E. Sherwood [195]

October 20, 1943

Dear Bob:

It was the best evening I have had since your party for Brendon Bracken.[196]

My evenings with you are becoming the lampposts on my journey through Washington!

A thousand thanks.

Sincerely yours,

Paul H. Douglas wrote Stevenson from the Pacific theater of the war expressing his desire to get into combat and asking if it was proper for Stevenson to help. He also urged Stevenson to run for office.

To Captain Paul H. Douglas[197]

October 29, 1943

Dear Paul:

I was delighted to have your letter and, after some discreet consulta-

[194] This letter is in A.E.S., P.U.L.
[195] Overseas director of the Office of War Information. This letter is in A.E.S., P.U.L.
[196] British Minister of Information.
[197] This letter is in A.E.S., P.U.L.

tion, I feel I can safely say that it would not be improper for you to put in a request for duty as a regimental adjutant. I have no doubt that you are fully qualified but, of course, I cannot be sure as to what the attitude of the Headquarters will be, altho I can't see why the Commandant should object. You might let me have a copy of any request you put through and I will see what I can do to further it. I suppose it has to have an endorsement by your Commanding Officer out there, altho I am not wholly familiar with the Marine Corps routines.

I appreciate your flattering comments regarding politics. I am still in a very indecisive state of mind and look forward to the possibility of being chosen as the candidate for Governor with grave misgivings and, unhappily, active disinterest. I feel that what I am doing here is wholly satisfying and the prospect of undertaking an ordeal like that is not attractive to me, particularly in war time. However, I have decided to coast along without saying anything definitely and see what transpires.

Ed Hughes[198] is ill and apprehensive. There are other candidates, of course, but there seem to be objections on one ground or another to each of them. And to me on the ground that I am little known. Perhaps it will all blow over and if it does I won't be disappointed.

I saw your charming wife in Chicago a couple of weeks ago when I was out there to speak to the Council on Foreign Relations. I wish I had had an opportunity for more of a visit with her.

Best wishes!

Sincerely yours,

David Bazelon, a Chicago lawyer, wrote Stevenson on October 29, 1943, speculating that a voluntary and spontaneous committee should be organized to support him for governor.

To David L. Bazelon[199]

November 1, 1943

Dear Dave:

Many thanks for your letter. . . .

I have done nothing about encouraging any voluntary, spontaneous committee organization and I really don't know whether I should or not. Consistent with my attitude that I am not seeking anything and entirely content where I am, I had thought that it was inappropriate to do anything of this kind. Nor do I know if anyone else has it in mind tho sun-

[198] Illinois Secretary of State Edward J. Hughes.
[199] This letter is in A.E.S., P.U.L.

dary people have suggested something of the kind. I would be glad to have your views.

I had a fine talk with Judge Igoe.[200] He indicated that, although the Mayor[201] was not too favorable, he was going to make some other inquiries and bring it to his attention by other indirect methods again.

For my part, I am still in a quandary as to what I should do should the opportunity arise. I wish I had a little more enthusiasm!

Sincerely yours,

To Edward D. McDougal, Jr.[202]

November 22, 1943

Dear Ed:

My sister and I as tenants in common own a farm situated near Perrysville in Vermillion County, Indiana, which is not far from Danville, Illinois. I am making arrangements to sell this farm and have accepted an offer. The purchaser has engaged an attorney named M. C. Wiggins of Newport, Indiana and he is revising a sale contract submitted to him by the people who have been managing this farm for me for many years — The Decatur Farm Management, Inc., 420 South Franklin Street, Decatur, Illinois. I am apprehensive that there may be some title troubles and I also, confidentially, have little confidence in the purchaser.

I would appreciate it ever so much if you could select an attorney to represent me in Danville. I assume the [Illinois Bell] Telephone Company has someone there or that the firm has had some experience with someone there. I believe my father, many years ago, used a Mr. James Meeks, now deceased, who had a partner named Louis Lowenstein but I know nothing about him.

In any event, if you would be good enough to pick out someone and send the name to Walter W. McLaughlin at the Decatur Farm Management, Inc., sending me a copy of your letter for my information, I would appreciate it immensely.

I have missed you on my last several visits to the office and I suspect you have been as busy as I. I hope for better luck next time, which may be soon.

Sincerely yours,

AD.

[200] Federal Judge Michael Igoe.
[201] Chicago Mayor Edward J. Kelly.
[202] The original is in the possession of Mr. McDougal.

To Marshall Field [203]

November 30, 1943

Dear Mr. Field:

Walter Lippmann just told me that he was going to be in Chicago on Sunday of this week at the Union League Club, evidently with nothing to do. I did not mention it to him but it occurred to me that if by any chance you were in town and interested in seeing him this would be a good opportunity. He will be at the Union League Club, arriving early Sunday morning.

Please do not bother to acknowledge this letter and forgive me for imposing this bit of gratuitous information upon you.

Sincerely yours,

Between December 7, 1943, and January 17, 1944, Adlai E. Stevenson was head of a mission to Sicily and Italy for the Foreign Economic Administration. His papers about that mission appear in Part Two of this volume. When Stevenson returned to Washington, he resumed his post as Special Assistant to Secretary of the Navy Frank Knox. Before he had left on his mission, his relative Mrs. Carl Vrooman of Bloomington wrote him wishing him "Godspeed" on his trip and added, "I hope you won't mind if I end on a serious note, for that 'soul' of yours which you jestingly reported as being rather neglected and down at the heels, is still very much on my mind and heart."

To Mrs. Carl Vrooman [204]

January 19, 1944

Dear Cousin Julia:

I returned this morning from my adventures abroad and find your good letter of December 15. It was sweet of you to write me and I am delighted that my soul is on your mind and heart! I hope you will keep it there and do anything you can about it. I am sure it needs a lot of attention, that is if it hasn't atrophied from neglect and malnutrition already!

I look forward to seeing you and to a good dose of your fine medicine. Meanwhile best love and many thanks for thinking of me.

Affectionately,

ADLAI

[203] This letter is in A.E.S., P.U.L.
[204] The original is in the possession of Mrs. Vrooman.

On January 27, 1944, Leo T. Crowley, administrator of the Foreign Economic Administration, wrote Secretary Frank Knox stating that Adlai E. Stevenson was needed to head relief and rehabilitation operations overseas. "Adlai Stevenson is uniquely qualified for the work," Crowley said. "His report on his findings in Italy and his general observations on the subject of relief and rehabilitation clearly demonstrate that he has a thorough understanding of the problems involved." [205]

To Frank Knox[206]

January 28, 1944

Dear Colonel:

John Dillon[207] has shown me the letter from Mr. Crowley requesting my services in FEA. He told me he would not bother you until you returned to the office and I did not realize he was going to write you.

He is right that there is an immense job to be done there and I am flattered that he thinks me qualified. However, I doubt if I care to go there at this time unless you think I should. There are a lot of things about the organization and its jurisdiction which confuse and worry me. Moreover, while you and Jim Forrestal are both away I think it would be well for me to be here. So I suggest you write him a note at least delaying any decision until you have returned and we have a chance to talk it over.[208]

Hastily yours,

ADLAI

On February 25, 1944, Bruno Foa, on assignment to the Federal Reserve System, wrote Stevenson complimenting him for the "masterful survey" of the situation in Italy.

To Bruno Foa[209]

February 26, 1944

Dear Mr. Foa:

Many thanks for your note and your very flattering remarks about the

[205] This letter is in A.E.S., P.U.L.
[206] A copy of this letter is in A.E.S., P.U.L.
[207] Confidential assistant to Knox.
[208] Knox wrote Crowley on January 29, 1944, that because of a bad cold he had to leave Washington and recuperate for several weeks and needed Stevenson to stay in his post during that time. A copy of this letter is in A.E.S., P.U.L.
[209] This letter is in A.E.S., P.U.L.

report on Italy. Coming from you it is more than a little gratifying and I am sure my associates will be delighted to hear that you approve of their work.

With kindest regards, I am

Sincerely yours,

Walther Thayer, of the Mission for Economic Affairs at the American embassy in London, wrote Stevenson on March 29, 1944, that he began reading his report on Italy "at 11.0 o'clock last night and finished it sometime around 3.0 this morning. I think it is by far the best job of this kind that has been done since the words 'liberated areas' were coined. . . . I congratulate you on a very superlative job."

To Walter Thayer[210]

March 29, 1944

Dear Walter:

Your flattering and charitable comments on the Italy report have perceptibly brightened this dismal, rainy day.

I am not a little impressed that you found the time and energy to read such a ponderous tome, and I hope you realize that much of it on the organizational aspects is long since obsolete.

I continually hear nice things about you and I also hear that you are not going to be carrying a gun for at least a few more months.

With every good wish and my warm thanks, I am

Sincerely yours,

Secretary of the Navy Frank Knox, a "Rough Rider" with Theodore Roosevelt in Cuba in 1898, was a firm advocate of Roosevelt's strenuous life. But in 1944 he was seventy and refused advice to slacken his pace. On April 23, he suffered a heart attack. Two days later he went to his office but became so ill he had to return to bed. He died on April 28. Ellen Stevenson and Mr. and Mrs. Ernest L. Ives were visiting Stevenson when he heard of Colonel Knox's death. "None of them would forget how profoundly the news affected him," Kenneth S. Davis wrote.[211]

---

[210] This letter is in A.E.S., P.U.L.
[211] *The Politics of Honor*, p. 156.

To Edward D. McDougal, Jr.[212]

May 1, 1944

Dear Ed:

Thanks for your notes. The Colonel's death is a severe blow and my future plans are uncertain, but I shall doubtless stay here in any event for sometime and have not forgotten my commitment about the bed.[213]

I have done a little negotiating about giving up my present apartment and joining up with you and Jack Kellogg and perhaps another officer in a house.[214] It would be no more expensive and perhaps more agreeable. However, you can count on me to take care of you — as usual!

Sincerely yours,

The War Production Board asked Stevenson to draft a resolution about Frank Knox for the board to issue. Stevenson drafted the following statement on May 1, 1944.[215]

RESOLUTION

Whereas, the Honorable Frank Knox, Secretary of the Navy, was a member of the War Production Board from its inception and of its predecessor organizations, the Supply Priorities and Allocation Board and the Office of Production Management; and

Whereas, his life and his public career have ever served as an inspiration to high accomplishment in the nation's service; and

Whereas, his good judgment, wise counsel, warm heart, courage and vigorous determination were ever at the command of the members of this body, and through them at the command of the entire nation; and

Whereas, his contributions to the war effort as Secretary of the Navy, including his service to the War Production Board and its predecessor organizations, have earned him an enduring and exalted place in the annals of our troubled times; and

Whereas, his qualities as an American in our noblest tradition, commanded the profound respect and admiration of all who knew him, and

[212] The original is in the possession of Mr. McDougal.
[213] Mr. McDougal had just accepted a position in Washington.
[214] The scheme to rent a house fell through, and Stevenson, Kellogg and McDougal went to live with their mutual friend and Lake Forest neighbor Colonel James Douglas, who with his wife had rented a large house in Georgetown. Letter, McDougal to Carol Evans, November 15, 1971.
[215] This resolution is in A.E.S., P.U.L.

his sincerety and genial warmth as a companion and associate won the affectionate friendship of us his fellow members of the War Production Board;

NOW, THEREFORE, BE IT RESOLVED that we, the members of the War Production Board, extend our heartfelt sympathy to Mrs. Knox, pledge our devotion to the memory of a beloved leader, and dedicate ourselves anew to the successful realization of the high ideals and aims which Frank Knox so nobly espoused.

Stevenson's old friend Charles P. Megan, a Chicago lawyer, wrote him on April 26, 1944, that "high-class" people in Chicago who opposed the policies of the Chicago Tribune *were afraid to speak out strongly for fear that it might help President Roosevelt.*

To Charles P. Megan[216]

May 2, 1944

Dear Charlie:

I was delighted with your letter. It's about as lucid a picture of the eternal morass of half rights and half wrongs that seem to be our lot in Chicago as I have seen. But what does one do? And now with the lusty voice of the Colonel [217] stilled, I cannot feel any happier about it. And I suspect that, war or no war, the campaign will bring out all the bitterness, obscurantism and impotent confusion of our best people. Certainly the spectacle of a leader of American business resisting the orderly processes of law and government until he has to be removed bodily from his office by soldiers is more calculated to promote heat than understanding of much of anything.[218]

I'm sometimes glad I'm not in Chicago! Which isn't to say that I'm too happy about staying here year after year. I look forward to a glimpse of you here or there sometime. And it was good of you to write me. I hope you'll feel like doing so again sometime.

Yours,

[216] This letter is in A.E.S., P.U.L.
[217] Frank Knox.
[218] Sewell Avery, chairman of the board of Montgomery Ward and Company, refused an order of the War Labor Board to extend an expired contract with the union. On April 6, 1944, President Roosevelt directed the federal government to take over the company's Chicago plants. Mr. Avery refused to leave his office and was carried out by soldiers.

To Edward D. McDougal, Jr.[219]

May 5, 1944

Dear Ed:

I am just advised that your commission as Lieutenant Commander is being issued and you will be notified in the course of the next ten days.

I do not yet know my plans nor am I clear on my summer living program, but various alternatives are available and I wish you would let me know promptly what your maximum expenditure for food and rent would be. We could go in with some other agreeable gents but I don't know just how to negotiate on your behalf on the expense division.

Hastily yours,

To Cyril H. Jones[220]

May 11, 1944

My dear Mr. Jones:

Somehow I misplaced the catalogue and application you were good enough to give Mrs. Stevenson and me when we visited the school a couple of weeks ago.

I will appreciate it immensely if you will forward an application to Mrs. Stevenson at St. Mary's Road, Libertyville, Illinois. We are still somewhat undecided, in a measure due to my own uncertainties on account of Colonel Knox's death.

It was good of you to take such an interest in our boy[221] and I appreciated immensely your cordiality at Milton.

Sincerely yours,

To Cyril H. Jones[222]

May 16, 1944

My dear Mr. Jones:

Many thanks for your good letter which I am passing along to Mrs. Stevenson in Illinois.

We have made arrangements for Adlai to take the required examinations for admission to Exeter in accordance with our original program

[219] The original is in the possession of Mr. McDougal.
[220] Headmaster of Milton Academy. The original is in the possession of Milton Academy.
[221] Adlai Stevenson III.
[222] The original is in the possession of Milton Academy.

and I presume the results of these would be suitable for your purposes should she decide to reconsider.

I know how awkward parental uncertainty of this kind is for you and I hope we can arrive at some conclusion without delay. It has been impossible for me to get out there for a talk with Mrs. Stevenson but I am hoping to do so very soon now.

With warm regards and many thanks, I am

Sincerely yours,

On May 16, 1944, Herbert Bayard Swope wrote Stevenson, "I hope the new line-up in the Navy Department will bring you something important. There isn't a job you can't do — and do damn well!"

Undersecretary of the Navy James Forrestal was made secretary by President Roosevelt. Assistant Secretary Ralph Bard was raised to undersecretary. President Roosevelt favored Stevenson for assistant secretary since he knew how influential Stevenson had been on major decisions made by Secretary Knox. But Forrestal objected. Stevenson had heard that Forrestal had said of him that he was "too diffuse." Stevenson reported this to Carl McGowan, who was on Stevenson's staff, and remarked: "Whatever that means." [223]

To James V. Forrestal [224]

May 19, 1944

Dear Jim:

With the probability of an early conclusion of the Elk Hills phase of our oil problems, the most pressing of my responsibilities under Colonel Knox will be concluded. [225]

Assuming that you will want to reorganize your office in due course, I am, accordingly, submitting my resignation as Special Assistant to the Secretary to you herewith to take effect at your pleasure. I need not add that I have enjoyed and benefited from my association with you and I have comforting confidence that you will more than measure up to the enormous responsibilities you have been called upon to assume.

With sincerest best wishes, I am

Faithfully yours,

[223] Carl McGowan, interview with Walter Johnson, April 24, 1966.
[224] This letter is in A.E.S., P.U.L.
[225] The contract for Standard Oil of California to operate the Elk Hills reserve under naval supervision, which had been prepared by Stevenson, was soon to be signed by President Roosevelt. See note 173, above, for a fuller discussion of this question.

To James Forrestal

May 29, 1944

MEMORANDUM TO THE SECRETARY

The Japanese Mandated Islands have a special juridical status. Whether sovereignty rests with the Allied and Associated Powers, to whom they were ceded by Germany, or with the League of Nations which was entrusted with the supervision of the mandate is immaterial at the moment; the substantive point is that they constitute a special type of juridical situation and obligation involving the Allied and Associated Powers of the last war, the League of Nations and a treaty approved by the United States Senate. It would seem in the interest of the United States and consistent with its general policy of observance of all treaties that due account be taken of this special situation. If the United States scrupulously observes all the forms it will be both consistent with our traditions and helpful toward getting other governments to exercise the same scrupulousness; if it does not, it may weaken its own position and provide an historical excuse for other governments not to observe all the obligations and formalities of treaties.

Thus far President Roosevelt has said that the Mandated Islands would never be returned to the administration of Japan. Similarly, the Cairo Declaration stated something to the effect that Japan would be stripped of all her conquests, including these islands.[226] Many have shared the view, including Secretary Knox, I believe, that these islands should be transferred to the United States as part of its defenses.

Whatever solution is finally reached after the war, it would seem desirable for the United States to take official cognizance of the special status of these islands in order to keep the record clear and beyond question.

Accordingly, I take the liberty of suggesting that the State Department consider an announcement — possibly following the conquest of Truk — that in taking military possession of these islands, the United States had fully in mind their special status and their relation to the League and treaties concerning them. Such an announcement presumably would also state that inspection, which had never been permitted by the Japanese, had confirmed Japanese violation of the terms of the mandate by fortification, etc. Perhaps the announcement could properly

---

[226] President Roosevelt, Prime Minister Churchill, and President Chiang Kai-shek issued the Cairo Declaration, December 1, 1943, stating that Japan would be stripped of the Pacific islands and the territories Japan had taken "such as Manchuria, Formosa, and the Pescadores" would be restored to China.

include a statement that this government would follow the same policy here as well as elsewhere in not attempting to make any territorial decisions or settlements during the war and that both the territorial and juridical disposition would be held in suspense during hostilities.[227]

Something like this would seem to me a wise precedent and calculated to hold other nations to observance of their treaty obligations and the formalities.

The question arises as to whom such a communication might be addressed. Possibly the easiest and regular method would be to make the text public in Washington and address the communication to the Acting Secretary General of the League in Geneva.

Adlai E. Stevenson left Washington for his home at Libertyville, Illinois, on June 13, 1944. The night before he left Washington Mr. and Mrs. R. Keith Kane — Mr. Kane had served as chief of the Bureau of Intelligence of the Office of War Information — held a party in his honor.

Mrs. Kane wrote the following poem:

> Though you refuse to stay afloat
> Perhaps you'll keep your Navy throat
> So here's some grog — (a little drink
> Will even mix with printer's ink!)
> To vary Greel[e]y's old refrain —
> "Come East, young man,
> Come East again!

Mrs. Kane's views were shared by many people. Benjamin V. Cohen, of the Office of War Mobilization, wrote Stevenson on June 13, 1944: "You must not stay away from Washington too long. You are needed here."

Julius H. Amberg, special assistant to the Secretary of War, wrote on June 13, 1944: "You have done a grand job here and there are many people who know it."

Walter Lippmann wrote on June 13, 1944: "We shall miss you in Washington, but I fully expect to see you back in the not distant future."

Byron Price, director of the Office of Censorship, wrote on June 13, 1944: "I am very sorry to see you leaving the Navy Department. Aside from all of the notable service you have rendered there, I have a selfish

[227] The United Nations Security Council placed the islands herein discussed under a United States trusteeship, April 2, 1947.

interest because of the great help you have been to Censorship from the very beginning."

Harvey H. Bundy, special assistant to the Secretary of War, wrote on June 14, 1944: "You will find plenty of people waiting in line to get you another war job before you come back this way. I congratulate you on the splendid work you did for Mr. Knox and I know whereof I speak."

Undersecretary of State Edward R. Stettinius, Jr., wrote on June 14, 1944: "I am terribly sorry to hear that you are leaving the Navy, but I do hope that sometime, somehow, we may have the pleasure of an association."

Oscar Cox, of the Foreign Economic Administration, wrote on June 14, 1944: "As soon as you are at all ready for one of those new, good jobs, let me know — and we will really go to work!"

Assistant Secretary of War John J. McCloy wrote on June 15, 1944: "It was always a pleasure to go to meetings at which you were across the table, and I do hope that we see something of each other in the future."

Admiral Emory Land, chairman of the U.S. Maritime Commission, wrote on June 15, 1944: "I deeply regret that you are leaving the Navy Department and sincerely trust that you will be called back to Washington for some other job as I firmly believe you are the type of man that should be in Washington under present conditions."

Nelson A. Rockefeller, Coordinator of Inter-American Affairs, wrote on June 15, 1944: "Few people have served this country with as much loyalty and devotion. I know the high regard and warm affection Secretary Knox had for you, and the degree to which he depended on you."

J. M. Juran, who had served with Stevenson on the board of directors of Cargoes, Inc., wrote on June 17, 1944: "Your judicial approach, your high sense of fair dealing, and your balance as a person — one does not relish being cut off from association with such a combination."

U.S. Supreme Court Justice Stanley Reed wrote on June 19, 1944: "Do not loose [sic] sight of another return. . . . I have always felt that you would enjoy [Department of] Justice and its purely legal work."

Archibald MacLeish, Librarian of Congress, wrote on June 26, 1944: "I don't think I have ever had an opportunity to tell you what a tower of strength you were — you and Jack McCloy — in those very tough days of the beginning of OFF [Office of Facts and Figures]. You and Jack certainly gave more to the Committee on War Information then any of the rest of us. And if credit is ever given — which it never will be — to the work done by OFF in the first six months of the war, a large part will go to you two."

Henry P. Chandler, director of the administrative office of the U.S. Courts, wrote on July 15, 1944: "In your quiet, self-effacing manner I *know that you rendered a great service to him [Frank Knox] and to the country in the difficult task of building up the Navy in a race against time."*

The day after Stevenson left Washington, Secretary of the Navy Forrestal wrote him: "I have a feeling that no one could properly thank you for your service in the Navy Department except the Colonel himself. I am sure you know how much he appreciated your loyalty and counsel. Nothing I can say could add materially to the satisfaction you deserve to feel because of the reliance he placed in you." [228]

To James Forrestal [229]

June 19, 1944

Dear Jim:

Your letter greeted me at my old office this morning. It was good of you to write me and I appreciate your generous remarks more than I can tell you.

I was more than a little disappointed not to see you to say good-bye, and to tell you a little about some of the unfinished work I left. However, I believe I have discussed it sufficiently with some of the others so that you need not be concerned.

You may be sure that I will take the liberty of calling on you if and when I return to Washington. Meanwhile, my warmest regards and with very best wishes,

Sincerely yours,
ADLAI

P.S. I am sure you will let me know if there is ANYTHING I can do for you out here.

---

[228] All the above letters and Mrs. Kane's poem are in A.E.S., P.U.L.
[229] This letter is in the James Forrestal papers, Princeton University Library.

Part Two

Mission to Italy
December 1943–January 1944

On July 10, 1943, Allied forces landed on Sicily. Thirty-nine days later all opposition ceased and the Allies were ready for the assault on Italy. While the fighting was taking place on Sicily, King Victor Emmanuel III deposed Benito Mussolini on July 25. During the next five weeks the new Italian government led by Marshal Pietro Badoglio negotiated with the Allies. On September 3, Italy surrendered. The Germans, however, were firmly entrenched and the struggle for Italy was a long-drawn-out affair from September, 1943, to May, 1945.

On September 3, 1943, British and Canadian troops established beachheads on the toe of the Italian boot. Six days later, the U.S. Fifth Army under General Mark W. Clark stormed ashore near Salerno, forty-five miles southeast of the Bay of Naples.

On October 1, Allied forces entered Naples. They found the city in ruins, its harbor blocked with wrecks, its people starving and suffering from typhus. During the rest of 1943, Allied forces pushed north slowly. By the end of the year, Allied forces were just south of Cassino, less than a third of the way up the Italian boot.

In November, President Roosevelt authorized the Foreign Economic Administration, headed by Leo T. Crowley, to send a mission to Sicily and that part of Italy under Allied control to study what role the FEA should play in relief and rehabilitation. On November 22, 1943, Mr. Crowley wrote Secretary of the Navy Frank Knox: "The man we should very much like to head this mission is Mr. Adlai Stevenson, if you felt you could spare his services to us for a period of about six weeks. . . . We would all place a good deal of confidence in any report made by Mr. Stevenson and I also have full confidence that he would handle himself with tact and discretion while overseas." Knox agreed with the request, provided his special assistant "takes the necessary innoculations [sic]. I do not want him to go without taking them." [1]

[1] Both letters are in General Records of the Department of the Navy, Record Group 80, the National Archives.

[163]

In addition to Adlai E. Stevenson the mission included David D. Lloyd, lawyer from the Office of Price Administration; Hugh G. Calkins, from the Department of Agriculture; and Nils K. G. Tholand, an industrial engineer. Stevenson's Princeton classmate William E. Stevenson was in Naples in charge of Red Cross operations when the mission arrived there. Years later William Stevenson wrote:

> In no better way did Adlai Stevenson demonstrate the value of a Princeton education than through his constantly increasing intellectual curiosity and growth through the years after his graduation. This came to my attention in Naples in 1943 when we were both there on war service. . . . I was impressed with how Adlai, in only a few weeks, put his finger on the principal economic and political problems and needs of that war-torn country. He took back to Washington a report that was comprehensive and astute.[2]

The report that Stevenson submitted to the Foreign Economic Administration on February 5, 1944, increased his status within the Roosevelt Administration and, according to Professor Stuart Gerry Brown, "became a model that was studied in connection with reconstruction and foreign aid for many nations."[3]

Lauchlin Currie, Deputy Administrator of the Foreign Economic Administration, wrote Stevenson on May 24, 1944: "I . . . think you can take considerable personal pride in having written a report that has been given such careful consideration and that has received such general praise. It is quite clear that your mission has been responsible for considerable soul-searching on the part of the ACC [Allied Control Commission] and I am sure has had considerable influence on their forward planning."[4]

During the 1952 presidential campaign Senator Joseph McCarthy charged that Stevenson had "connived" to bring Communists into the

[2] "Two Stevensons of Princeton," in *As We Knew Adlai: The Stevenson Story by Twenty-two Friends*, edited and with preface by Edward P. Doyle, foreword by Adlai E. Stevenson III (New York: Harper & Row, 1966), p. 20.

[3] *Adlai E. Stevenson: The Conscience of the Country* (Woodbury, N.Y.: Barron's Woodbury Press, 1965), p. 44. Stevenson told Brown that during his service on the American delegation to the United Nations, 1946–1947, many delegates mentioned to him how useful the report was. Brown, interview with Walter Johnson, July 8, 1968.

[4] This letter is in the Adlai E. Stevenson papers, Princeton University Library (A.E.S., P.U.L.). Harlan Cleveland, who in 1943–1944 was working on Italian reoccupation plans in the FEA, later wrote: "My recollection is that the Stevenson report was a useful input to the staff work in Washington supporting appropriations for the economic side of the ACC's program i.e., the bulk of the funds available to Allied Military Government." Letter to Walter Johnson, July 31, 1968.

Italian government. The report was declassified at this point, and Professor John Norman of Fairfield University, who had studied postwar Italy, pointed out the absurdity of the charge. Norman wrote: "The Stevenson report presented a masterly summary of the disruption in the collection, distribution, and marketing of food and other farm products. It listed the deficiencies and shortages. But it did more! It analyzed the cause of all these pressing problems so that immediate corrective action could be taken." Norman concluded that many serious problems "were corrected, at least in part because of the Stevenson report." [5]

The trip to Italy also increased Stevenson's determination to be in public life. "It happened," he later told Joe Alex Morris, "that while I was in Italy I saw a public-opinion poll in which seven out of ten American parents said they didn't want their boys to enter public life. Think of it! Boys could die in battle, but parents didn't want their children to give their living efforts toward a better America and a better world. I decided then that if I ever had a chance I'd go into public life." [6]

Stevenson kept a diary during part of his trip. The diary is in the Stevenson papers, Princeton University Library. The ellipses are the editors'. We print Stevenson's spelling of certain words as he wrote them, but no sic has been added. Despite the efforts of the editors, it has been impossible to identify many of the persons mentioned by Stevenson.

Armed with letters of introduction to generals and admirals (including one to Dwight D. Eisenhower), Stevenson and his three companions departed from Washington on December 7, 1943.

FEA Mission to Italy

Tuesday, December 7, 1943, Pearl Harbor Day
No alarm clock — up at 6 by keeping awake from 4 on! Breakfast with a lamb chop — cleaned up the ice box & left apt in some kind of order. . . .[7]

Tholand & wife called for me at 7 — all the wives at airport for farewells from 7:30 to 9:30. Just as glad Ellen didn't stay over. Herded into bucket seats in luggage compartment of old converted TWA stratoliner.

[5] *Herald Magazine*, supplement to the Bridgeport, Connecticut, *Sunday Herald*, September 9, 1956.
[6] "Rebel In Illinois," *Saturday Evening Post*, April 2, 1949, p. 112. See also Adlai E. Stevenson, *Major Campaign Speeches of Adlai E. Stevenson: 1952* (New York: Random House, 1953), p. xviii.
[7] Mrs. Stevenson and the three sons were living at Libertyville. Stevenson shared his "bachelor" apartment with several other men.

The passengers cabin and good seats reserved for "officers" apparently. Even 3 women in the "steerage" with us while the lieutenants take it easy & reflect on their weighty problems. Miami at 3:30 — 6 hrs. Interminal [interminable] business of inspections — supper — & off at 6:30 in same plane. Horrible night sitting up. Stopped to refuel at midnight . . . in S. W. Cuba. Beautiful warm, moonlight night. Back into our sardine can.

Wed. 12/8.

Arrived Georgetown, British Guiana, about 8. Breakfast at officers club at field. The town is 28 miles away. Swampy, uninhabited jungle everywhere. Getting hot by the time we took off at 9:15 for Belem. Everlasting jungle — flat — broken by patches of open country. Hardly any evidence of inhabitation. God, what vast areas of unused & useless land I've seen in the last couple of years! Crossed the series of great rivers and swampy jungle that are the delta of the mighty Amazon, over brown, buff sun-baked Belem perched on the low lying bank of the huge cafe au lait Para river and into the brisk efficient Army airfield about 3 P.M. Tried for something to drink at the airfield canteen. Little Brazilian girl waitresses made it gradually known that there was literally nothing to drink except water — a light brown liquid. I couldn't face another sandwich or fried egg & settled for one green orange. Hugh Calkins met an old friend . . . on his way home after 2 yrs in China. . . . This is the wild rubber collection place — we didn't get into the town. Very malarial.

More horrors of discomfort, sleepless contortions in the steerage of the crowded plane and into Natal about midnight. Full moon, gorgeous night, soft wind from the sea, enormous, accommodations for 800 transients. Comfortable, bunked in barracks, supper, shower & bed at last.

12/9 —

Slept late — very tired — called on Commandant of the Naval facility who with some difficulty provided us a car & passes to go into Natal which is out of bounds . . . spent several hours examining the hideous little town. Nothing much of any interest — all Latin American places look alike. Tholand says this is a fair sample of the Brazilian towns except for Rio & Sao Paulo. Brazilians all very small.

A beer at the officers club, outdoor movie standing up and off at 11 in a modified Liberator for Dakar across the moonlit sea. Mr. Guerin, Asst. Commissioner for Colonies of French Com[mittee]. of Liberation, en route to Algiers had seat opposite me. I was reminded of all my earlier experiences with travelling Frenchmen & their horror of cold. First he took off his elegant shoes & put on slippers, then his coat & put on a heavy wool sweater, then a sheep skin lined jacket, then a camels hair great coat, then a knitted contrivance over his head & ears, then a ski cap emerged from somewhere, finally a muffler around his neck and another one was wound around his legs — I've omitted the Mae West life belt we all had to wear! All this went on in a blacked out plane that was as crowded beyond description. I watched him emerge in the morning with wonder.

12/10

We hit Dakar right on the button about noon their time & followed the coast line out to the airport of Rufisque 20 miles away. After being quart[er]ed & lunch at the officers mess I called Admiral Glassford [8] & he sent a car out for us at 3. Passed thru Rufisque — natives blue black, even lips are jet black. Colorful in their white, blue & yellow [illegible]. Women all unveiled with pretty ornamental head[d]resses. Had long talk with Glassford — Pres. party sailed off yesterday evening and everyone exhausted.[9] Also talked at length with Maynard Barnes, Consul. Very emphatic in his criticism of disorganization in Wash. and difficulty of doing anything satisfactorily on economic programs. Spoke well of Brunson MacChesney and his work.[10] Glassford said French suspicious of him & what he's there for. Has a considerable staff. Drove about the beautifully situated, clean, orderly town, cocktails with the ebullient Dody Glassford & back to base for early bed. (Dakar is capital of the region and also of 8 provinces comprising gigantic French West Africa.) Mosquito precautions!

12/11

Up at 5 — off at 7:30 over sparse arid Senegal & then the endless rubble sand & rocky deserts of Mauritania to the oasis of Attar where we stopped to fuel. Garrisoned by a camel corps and inhabited by a pure bred Arab. Ancient caravan route from Morocco south. All gas & oil & supplies must be hauled by truck convoy 450 miles across the desert from Dakar. Off our course over Rio de Oro (Spanish) to look for a B–24 reported lost. The desert seems endless — hour after hour without sign of a living thing. Gets cold 40° & lower at night. As we approach the

---

[8] Admiral William A. Glassford, personal representative of President Roosevelt to French West Africa with the rank of minister.

[9] President Roosevelt was returning to Washington from the Teheran Conference with Stalin and Churchill.

[10] Professor MacChesney of the Northwestern University Law School went to Dakar in May, 1943, as chief of the mission of the Board of Economic Warfare to French West Africa. While he was there the Board of Economic Warfare became the Foreign Economic Administration.

haut Atlas the little, circular Arab villages & patches of palms begin to appear. We climb to 12,000 into the rugged snow mountains — now there's water shining in the streams and fertile little valleys with terraced fields up the hillsides and many villages hanging precariously. They must be thrifty farmers these Moors. Over the pass with snow an arms length off each wing and down onto the fertile valley of Marrakech — surrounded with fine citrus groves and gardens and the innumerable curious pock-marked irrigation ditches which everyone notes . . .

Tunis & Algiers were white when Ellen and I were there 15 years ago this month, but Marrakech is pink. The fine hotel is teeming with soldiery. I met David Rockefeller in the lobby.[11] At sunset we were in the bazaar at famous Place Jimalfa teeming with thousands of Arabs. We saw the sun set in fire over the pink city behind the minaret on the great mosque from the roof of a building overlooking the bazaar and wandered thru the crooked narrow side streets canopied with matting and lined with stalls & shops. It was a wondrous sight and the least spoiled spot they say in N.Af. I hope we can have a longer look on the way back.

12/12

Up & off in darkness. The weather is thick and we can see little of the ground. Long talk with Rockefeller. He's in the Joint Intelligence Collecting Center in Algiers. As we approach Oran and the sea the weather gets worse — bumpy, high wind, white fog rolling in from the sea. All of a sudden we're over the water & then there followed the worst hour I've ever had. The pilot was lost. The coast is dangerous flying — mountains & valleys. He had to pull her nose up sharp several times and almost turned me inside out & all the while the big plane was shaking like a leaf & the wind was howling as I've never heard it. It was raining torrents and the ceiling was O. They put up a smoke screen on the ground that finally gave the pilot a fix & at last we landed on instruments. There was no going on and we were quart[er]ed in a nearby French air force barracks but a kind Mr. Hill of OSS [Office of Strategic Services] rescued us and thanks to Col. Shears of Gen. Wilson's staff we were handsomely quart[er]ed in a villa in the town. Sightseeing trip with Hill thru Oran and Mers-el-Kebir. Dinner at the villa & our first experience with the smiling cheerful Italian prisoners for waiters and servants. To bed — dead!

12/13

A wild windy rainy dark day again. Foolishly I decide to motor to

---

[11] Stevenson had come to know Rockefeller when Rockefeller lived at International House, the University of Chicago, while studying for a Ph.D.

Algiers in a station wagon & what a trip! 300 miles — first we break a fan belt — repairs at a French Army Camp thanks to my French. Thousands of French, British and Am. army trucks on the road. Thru the mountains just before dark — then a flat tire & repairs by a french soldier under a street lamp in Blida again thanks to my French! I wish Ellen could have heard me giving technical directions. Finally reached Algiers after 10½ hrs of beating & a gay dinner at Cercle Interallié with Capt. Edson and Lt. Cmdr. [Charles W.] Folds (Chicago) who were still waiting patiently. To bed at last in Rockefeller's bed who was still stuck in Oran.

12/14

Will the others get thru from Oran today? Presented myself at the palpitating AFHQ at the Hotel St. George to see Gen. Eisenhower and present my letters from Pres., Sec. War and Sec. Nav. Ushered into General [Walter Bedell] Smith, the Chief of Staff instead. Long talk, very cordial, much about the Italian political situation & plans to force the king's abdication, military gov. etc. & then to Brig. Gen. Julius [C.] Holmes, the Civil Affairs Officer. Very cordial, suave, self-confident, state dept. type. OK (?) To billeting officer & sent to 4th rate Hotel Feminine! No sheets, no hot water, tiny cell, dirty. What kind of reception is this for Pres. emissary! Lunch down town a[t] L'Hurlevant, only good restaurant, with Wesly Surges[12] . . . Much info. Communism inevitable in Italy whatever we do economically — how much or how little — says Sturges. Back to talk with Holmes' staff and there are my lost colleagues! Much talk re Italy supply problem; stumbling around the darkened city looking for a mess where wretched civilians would be admitted. To dinner with Holmes & Murphy[13] in their fine villa opposite St. George. Turned out to be villa Buffy had for a year! [14] Harry Hopkins boy is there with tales of the Pres. trip to Teheran. . . . Murphy big, ungainly, agreeable & only moderately impressive . . . Holmes much disturbed when he heard I was poorly quartered — somebody had slipped, please forgive, all would be corrected tomorrow, etc.

[12] Wesley A. Sturges, Professor of Law, Yale University, on leave. Chief representative of Office of Economic Warfare for French North and West Africa and principal representative of U.S. Commercial Company in Algiers, 1943–1944; sub-area economic coordinator for Sicily, 1943–1944.

[13] Robert Murphy, State Department expert on France.

[14] Stevenson's brother-in-law, Ernest L. Ives, had been U.S. consul general at Algiers. Stevenson sent the Iveses a postcard on December 16, 1943: "I wish you were here to show me about a bit! So far so good. Well if a touch tired. Off tomorrow at 5 A.M. for the hard part with a bedding roll and a knapsack for luggage." Elizabeth Stevenson Ives papers, Illinois State Historical Library.

12/15

No trouble sleeping in my army blankets & up in a cool, clear, blue sunny day to resume the endless conferences and planning. More talk with Sturges, Sundelson, Southard (excellent man from Treasury) Col. Claybaugh, No. 2 man on Gen. Hilldring's staff. Shall we join forces thru Italy? Visit with Adm. [S. S.] Lewis & Capt. Old in Navy H.Q. Feel more at home with Navy where I have exalted status. Give my letters etc. Holmes aide insists on taking us to new quarters — the others to the Aletta — best hotel & me to beautiful Villa Bel Air — reserved only for generals, admirals and the most distinguished guests of Gen. Eisenhower. Bath tub, even hot water! and its own private mess. All is forgiven! Dinner at the Aletta (down town) mess for colonels and up with Col. Claybaugh's & talk of our trip. Walked most of the 4 or 5 miles home thru the blackened streets alone — with a flash light — soldiers, sailors, girls and trucks! To bed in my elegant quarters after the first decent bath since the barracks shower bath in Natal almost a week ago.

12/16

Breakfast with one armed British Admiral. Visit with Henri Bonnet, Minister of Information in the French Committee of Liberation, at his office. Like all ministers of public enlightenment he has had his troubles, tired but still as loquacious as ever. Assured me that the conservative assembly was truly representative of all the old parties. Recognizes Anglo Am. dislike for [General Charles] de Gaulle — He's had his troubles too I gathered.

Conf[erence]. with . . . the OEW [Office of Economic Warfare] enemy intelligence officer. Excellent man & much of interest about his job of gathering info. re enemy materials & weapons — except aircraft. Also articulate story of mistakes and misfortunes of the economic agencies in N.A. Leaving soon for Italy with a staff he has gathered together & without permission from Wash. Enterprize! Conferences with State Dept. people & long talk with Grady who has just arrived. Sound man with no fancy ideas and quite bewildered if not distracted or confused. Gathered up our laundry, lire, etc. etc. & Bonnet called to take me to dinner in his nice little flat thru the darkened ghostly streets. Bad auto shortage for the French. Nice supper & good talk — air raid practice alert seemed like nonsense. Imagine doing it in Kansas City! Detected some disillusion and a little bitterness particularly about the British, "We must be united when we enter France." Home & to bed after a long wrestle with my blanket roll.

12/17.

Breakfast at 5:30 and off to the airport & new adventures in a British car. Ugly grey day — long delay — off at last for Tunis. Billeted in filthy "hotel" two in a bed. Saw Tunis and utter destruction of port. . . . Visited Bey's old palace — not used for 100 years & spent a rainy afternoon in Souks[?]. Some of the stalls open. Troops British & American everywhere. Supper in an Am. officer's mess — dropped in a British Forces recreation center & drank beer & talked to Scotch soldier from Perth — 4 yrs in army — wounded at Dunkirk — 21 weeks in hospital and yearning for his farm and black cattle. I couldn't remember where Ellen and I stayed 15 yrs ago but I'm sure it wasn't this place. Do we dare sleep on the sheets?

12/18.

Up in the cold darkness — no water! — hasty breakfast at the mess a couple of blocks down the street & off in a welter of assorted officers, men and baggage for La Marsa airfield jammed with military going in all directions — off at last for Palermo, many wrecked planes around the field — large German transport planes. Poor visibility — passed large convoy west bound & passed by Trapani. Sicily very rugged. Into Palermo airport thru the mountains by back door. Capt. [Leonard] Doughty . . . sent his car for us.[15] Italian prisoners waiting at airport and Italian soldiers guarding the entrance! 40% of houses in P. destroyed & large section of most of the public bldgs. out of commission, mostly from the [two words illegible] plane raid of May 7. Doughty quartered us in his beautiful Villa Sofia — vast place in beautiful old park built by Englishman named Whitaker — "King of Sicily" — The man who introduced Marsala wine to England, also hawking & publishing family. Very comfortable — even hot water. Put car at our disposal. Spent afternoon in conferences at AM G [Allied Military Government] regional and local headquarters. Col. [Arthur N.] Hancock, British, selected to succeed Poletti[16] who is to be on Interior division of ACC [Allied Control Commission]. Dined with Major [Archibald S.] Alexander at an officers mess & Col. Hancock. As was to be expected the problem is food. Much

---

[15] Stevenson's position as special assistant to the Secretary of the Navy greatly facilitated his mission. The naval commander at Palermo placed a car with two sailors at his disposal. For the next six weeks Stevenson's group drove around Sicily and southern Italy gathering information for a report.

[16] Colonel Charles Poletti, formerly lieutenant governor and governor of New York, head of Allied Military Government for Sicily. Colonel Poletti was not "to be on Interior division of ACC," as Stevenson thought, but was to take over command, in January, 1944, of AMG for Naples and southern Italy, with headquarters in Naples. Letter, Poletti to Carol Evans, January 26, 1972.

organizational confusion due to ACC — their foreward group has just left for Naples in convoy of 90 cars! Movies at the Villa & a dance at officers club. We declined & talked too late to Lieuts. Tilelo (Sardinia) and Brusia, intelligence officers on Doughty's staff. To bed, deader than usual!

12/19

Sunday is no day of rest. Into town to attend meeting of Provincial Senior Civil Affairs Officers. Reports on all subjects. Fair average group of English & Am. officers — a few outstanding. Trying to increase ration of bread for Christmas from 150 to 250 grains [grams]. Hoarding, inadequacy of police, black market etc. Expect trouble when Badoglio gov. takes over. Consensus against use of troops to force grain in. Workmen from country bring in "lunch" in two large "suitcases." Sicily has 3 things it doesn't want — "Badoglio, House of Savoy and British." "Respected and disliked the Germans; like the Americans, but don't respect them." 25000 public officials in Sicily — reason all Facists have not been eliminated. "To work is to starve — to not work is to live" — philosophy of black market. Much theft — congenital with Sicilians. No evidence of starvation — but people pinched and hungry for anything. Salutation of children — "Hello, Joe, give me cigarette." More & more talk with more & more officers.

Lunch at casual officers mess with Col. Cla[y]baugh and Capt. Nordon [?] and out to see the magnificent Cathedral . . . built by William the Good of Normandy in late 12th century . . . Perched on side of steep hill. Drove on a few miles — many pill boxes & wreckage of war. Back to Villa for big dinner party — some Italian and 3 Red Cross girls. Drinks and much talk with Comdr. Revell, Doughty's Ex. officer, afterward & to bed too late.

12/20

Inspected damage in harbor. Fine salvage work & bridging over immovable wrecks by Army Engineers. Tremendous job of cleaning up the water front. Fine ship repair yard & much material left by Italians but 90 Ry [railroad] carloads were removed & got across the straits of Messina to mainland before we came in.

Conf. with Col. [Charles] Poletti. Quite confident of no trouble & important to turn over [Government?] to Italians. No oath of allegiance to King will be required of Sicilians. (Navy very loyal to King — "never Fa[s]cist") Poletti critical of ACC [Allied Control Commission] organization set up: Usual solution of economic situation — import more food. Dynamic but not very tough. Constant trouble getting any help from

Army. Lunch with "Mayor of Palermo" — Major Haley — good man — calm. Pretty much same story — food shortage makes black market — like to get out. But Sicilians don't want us to go. Communists strong; indep[endent]. Sicily movement. Called on Charly Darlington in hospital with sciatica. Doing fine job as chief of Industry & Commerce sec. of ACC. Will move on to Naples. Thinks expert civilian trade & technical people should come in right away. Getting out first ship of lemons, nuts, wine, pumice etc 3314 Tons. More political chatter after dinner — Capt. Doughty out — and to bed early thank God.

12/21

Off at 9:30 — 1½ hrs late, in command car with trailer for luggage — our blanket rolls, cans of gas, musette bags and a couple of boxes of Army K rations. To the map depot for maps of Italy & Sicily — thru golden groves of lemons & the incomparable jumbled & beautifully cultivated gardens of Sicily. Cauliflower season. Thousands of tons of lemons that Sicily needs to sell and England is crying for will go [to] waste this year for want of ships — Only one cargo has been shipped out since the invasion & that sat on the docks at Palermo for 3 weeks. Also shortage of packing materials and the everlasting problem of transport to the city. Along the northeast thru the incomparably beautiful and rugged landscape of Sicily to Termini and thence on to Cefalu and a glimpse of its beautiful and neglected old Cathedral built by one of the Norman kings toward the end of the 12th century. Hill top castle crowned towns from whence they've climbed up and down to cultivate every square inch of their little valleys for time out of mind. The Germans retreated along this road — pill boxes at every strategic point — cunningly placed, every bridge on road and parallel railway blown up. The work of the engineers in building temporary spans or fording the stream beds and preparing the approaches for the endless procession of motorized equipment that constitutes the modern army is as impressive as anything I've seen. But it will still be a long time before the Ry can be in operation all the way between Messina & Palermo. The road side as we roll along on a lovely, rare for this season, sunny day, is strewn with the wreckage of war — mostly wrecked or burned out trucks and vehicles of all kinds — German and American — occasional tanks and landing craft along the beaches. It was along here that we made the serious [series] of flanking amphibious landings that rolled the enemy back to Messina. The towns as always are crowded, dirty and uniform in their soiled, dilapidated colorless pale grey stucco sandstone. Occasionally a blue or pink villa. Long zig zag climb from teeming, endless, ugly Barcellona into the mountains on the N E corner where there was severe G[erman]. resistence and down the other side in the late afternoon into Messina. Dreadfully damaged — little intact — across the narrow straits looms the mountainous mainland. I had not expected it to be so high. Lt. Col. Stephen Story, [illegible] Civil Affairs Officer greets us cordially and we find Lt. Comdr. Malcolm McLean with him. He rigs up cots for us in the public bldg. he is using for AMG [Allied Military Government] Provincial HQ. and my blanket roll about which I was a bit casual in Palermo goes into service the first night out. Some bread shortage, black market stories here. Story, excellent officer, former city mgr. of Rochester [New York] & his senior Ass't Major Deutsch very bitter about no promotions for their officers. Wonderful story about carabin[i]eri guarding flour truck at night & getting tail slashed by knife — man trying to slit a bag from underneath. Also story of establishing cordial relations with Bishop — exchanging visits — very accom[m]odating & helpful & then word from G–2 to jail him at once as dangerous Facist.

12/22

Spent morning scrounging gasoline, cans, funnel etc. Big British salvage dump — refuse of war collected to go back to England. Scenes at dock where LCI's land trucks, troops and weary, ragged, half starved Italian soldiers, being returned to Sicily. The war they never wanted is over for them. We join a train of British Ammo. trucks & board an LCI for the mainland along with Capt. Hank Young, Princeton 1922, AMG [Allied Military Government] officer inspecting Italian prisons & finding his way around borrowing transportation as best he can. Great Fascist inscriptions on the walls of bldgs — "Daggers in your teeth, bombs in your hands and a sovereign disdain for danger in your heart" "To die for Italy is to live forever." Incongruous in this setting of devestation and destruction and utter defeat. Sense of isolation here among AMG officers — communications bad even with Palermo. Apprehension of Sicily returned to King — don't like even Badoglio. Enormous "DUX" on Cathedral foundations crowning city and visible half across straits where we pass long convoy of the familiar indispensable LSTs south bound. We land on the beach & churn up rocky path thru a fishing village to main road where a British MP orders us south to Reggio Calabria to be checked in at the traffic control post and then we start the long journey N[orth] to Naples full of good spirits, K rations and expectations. The road rises and falls along the rocky coast amid terraced vin[e]yards past Scilla where we bid farewell to Charybdis and the straits of Messina — the funnel of Greco-Roman history. The road & the views are incredibly beautiful — in the distance across the blue sea Stromboli lifts his conical, smoking head out of the sea as he has always done and one thinks a little sadly of all the wars and all the legions that have passed before him along these shores. Everywhere the ragged smiling urchins beg for cocomillas or anything to eat & the boys of any age shout "Hello Joe, give me cigarette." We careen thru the villages & with their accustomed reluctance the sea of humanity tumbles away from the car at the last moment like the cut water of a boat. The days are short — darkness comes early and swiftly. We stop at Nicastro — the crowd gathers around the car & the sailors take up their accustomed positions on each side of the car with side arms and joke with the crowd & the inevitable repatriated Italian who used to live in Brooklyn, while we go in search of the Civil Affairs Officer at the Municipio where as usual the British & American flags are flying. He's away visiting another commune but we find a B[ritish]. NCO [noncommissioned officer] from "Claims and Hearings" dickering with some "Guineas" and he directs us to the best Hotel — Albergo Central . . . four of us share a room and the sailors another over the protests of a reluctant proprietor. Dinner is a kind of spinach soup, beans and a piece of black market meat and plenty of vino. The proprietor's father, an old man deafened in the last war, who used to live in U.S. talks with us for a long while — too many facists still in office, damaged his hotel with a bomb within 2 weeks etc. Nice old fellow & his hotel was the one bright spot in Nicastro — except the movies which we worked into for 2 cigarettes a piece. The audience were Italian soldiers and the movie Italian of a quality of 20 yrs ago. So to bed by flashlight in our single room for four, but there were sheets & I think that was where the trouble started tho I didn't notice the bites the next morning. I noticed hardly anything else for 10 days! [17]

12/23

Our luck couldn't hold & we were off without breakfast in a cold grey dawn. K rations on a deserted road in the country but somehow the children showed up accompanied by a cheerful young philosopher driving a donkey who pointed to our car and said "American Car" & to his donkey — "Italian car," to our shoes, "Am shoes" to his bare feet — "Italian shoes" — to our K rations — "Am. food," to a small crust of black bread in his shirt — "Italian food" — and then laughed merrily. He got his reward & I some phrases that summarized my whole experience in Italy — and also an uneasy feeling that such contrasts won't endure forever. But how is the Am. taxpayer to be persuaded that to help Italy at his expense is to help himself & perhaps his grand children. Soon the

[17] This sentence suggests that Stevenson wrote his diary entries days later from extensive notes or that he added this sentence to the diary days after the original entry was made.

rain came & we drove up & down in breathtaking beauty thru all kinds of country full of surprizes — and soaked, I expected pneumonia by dark which overtook us at Vallo de Lucania. We found our way in the torrent to a girls convent school & crisp, sweet, quiet nuns took us — sailors and all, into their spotless building. On the top was a dormitory. They brought mat[t]resses & sheets & made the beds but there was no supper and they accepted the boxes of K rations and can of pineapple juice we gave them hurriedly.

Stevenson's last diary entry was on December 23, 1943. Shortly after he returned to Washington to resume his position of special assistant to the Secretary of the Navy, however, he delivered a speech before the Beacon Society of Boston on March 27, 1944, describing his visit to Sicily and Italy.[18]

Perhaps in these days of preoccupation with the war it is worth while to reflect for a few minutes on what lies in wait for us behind the bloody walls of Hitler's fortress. We have a long, sad and painful road yet to travel before we get to the ruins of Berlin and Tokyo, but we will get there sometime and when we do we are going to confront some appalling problems. What the Allied governments can do about them and how soon may have a considerable influence on the shape of the new world which will emerge from this global holocaust. We can win the battles and lose the war. History has too many such precedents, and our diabolical enemy can rise from the ashes of his armed might and snatch from us the victory for which we will have paid such a fearful price.

The job that confronts the Allied armies, the governments in exile, the United Nations Relief and Rehabilitation Administration, the Foreign Economic Administration, and all the similar agencies of the Allied Governments, as our armies plow thru the morass of desolation, disease and misery that may be large sections of Europe, has an importance for the future that imperatively demands attention and understanding. The first peek we've had under Europe's shroud was in Italy. It was not a happy sight, but it may be only a preview of what's to come.

My mission consisted of an economist, an agricultural expert, an industrial engineer and myself. Just how they classified me, if at all, I never discovered! We started at Palermo and travelled across Sicily by military car and all the way up the peninsula to Naples, which afforded

[18] The manuscript is in General Records of the Department of the Navy, Record Group 80, the National Archives.

us an excellent opportunity to see first hand the condition of the country and the people and to talk with the military government officers along the way. At the outset I want to say that I do not mean in anything I say any direct or implied criticism of the performance of Allied Military Government. On the contrary, they have, in my opinion, done admirable, and in many cases, heroic work under the most difficult circumstances of inadequate food supply, ineffective local government, inadequate personnel and inadequate transportation in an overpopulated, rugged, impoverished and backward portion of the country. Our failures were rather in organizational confusion due in large measure to the unexpected bitterness and slowness of the military campaign, and in the planning and execution of the civilian supply program. And that in turn was due in part to the prolongation of the fighting and the consequent demand on our shipping for military supply. Moreover, our mistakes and our misfortunes in Italy have been valuable lessons for the even greater economic problems that will confront us in the rest of Europe.

But to return to my travelogue. Palermo was about 40% damaged, mostly by our aerial bombardment preceding the invasion. The fabulous cathedral of Monte Reale outside the city, which was built by the Norman Kings in the 12th Century, is intact but the reverent tourists today are American and British soldiers. Down by the bay the Villa Aegia, which you will recall as one of the most luxurious winter hotels in Europe, is the somewhat battered barracks of the Navy's enlisted men who emphatically believe in joining the Navy and seeing the world — de luxe! The port area was completely demolished but the port is operating and very busy. Many sunken ships have been raised and moved by the Navy and large ones that sank along side the docks and could not be moved have been ingeniously bridged over by the Army engineers. Incoming ships tie up along side the sunken ships and unload on to these improvised wooden platforms. We have a fine little naval base and repair yard there with some excellent facilities and equipment left by the Italians.

The craters in the streets have been filled but throughout the city are gaping holes and piles of rubble where bombs exploded. A large part of the population fled during the invasion and the bombings, but most of them have returned now and one has the impression of fearful overcrowding. But that was always true in Sicily where only the palaces have even chimneys, let alone running water and where most of the people live in conditions that we find it hard to adjust to.

Food was very short and the black market flourished everywhere. There was even a black market in ration cards. The legal price of bread is 3½ cents a kilo, and the black market price is 80 cents to $1.30. The daily ration of legal bread in January was about 150 grams, or about four slices of an American loaf. For a time in the autumn it was half that. Olive oil is very scarce and there is virtually no macaroni. There are vegetables in season but the price is high in the cities due to the shortage of transport facilities. There are plenty of oranges, tangerines and lemons and many, many thousands of tons of lemons will rot on the ground in Sicily this winter for want of transportation to carry them to the ports, packing materials to pack them and ships to move them. But the export of citrus, sulphur, nuts and miscellaneous products of Sicily, mostly to the United Kingdom, is slowly being organized at Palermo, Catania, Messina and Siracusa. Fishing is slowly getting started again as boats are repaired, mines are swept, etc.

Shops are open, but there is little consumers goods like clothes or shoes to be had, and then only at fantastic prices. Children are barefoot and women wear wooden shoes throughout Italy. The evidences of alarming inflation are every where. Studies by the Allied Military Government in Sicily indicate that the cost of living had increased 150% from September '42 to September '43 and had risen to 200% by the first of November. It is now probably over 300%. Currency circulation in the liberated portion of Italy has probably doubled since the invasion.

The serious food shortage is in large measure due to the fact that in Sicily not more than a third of the local wheat crop found its way to the legitimate market following the invasion. There are doubtless several reasons for this; the collapse of transport inhibited normal marketing; wealthy people bought direct from the farmers for their own supply and for speculation; much was hoarded by the producers themselves; the shortage of consumers goods left the producer little inducement to convert grain into money; there was a general lack of faith in the currency and finally a growing fear of famine. All of these factors contributed, with the result that in January when the official price of wheat was 360 lire a quintal, the black market price was over 3000 lire and rising. Military government had counted on the availability of about 2,000,000 quintals of wheat. When that didn't come to market voluntarily and could not be collected by force and we could not supply the deficiency, the shortage in the cities became acute.

The enforcement situation was complicated by the unreliability of the Italian police. Their prestige among the people had fallen very low anyway and in addition many of them, like most everyone else who wasn't a food producer, in spite of their larger rations, patronized the black market for extra food for their families or took bribes from black market operators. And, of course, the Allied Military Government did not have sufficient personnel to enforce the law itself when practically everyone was a violator. Among a people who have never been passionately fond of work, many soon found that they could do better in the black market than they could working.

Finally, the demoralization of transport and distribution all over Italy has presented unsurmountable obstacles. There are few trucks or motor vehicles of any kind in working condition. There has been insufficient maintenance, spare parts, tires, etc., for years. To see people hanging on the sides and top of any vehicle is not the exception but the rule.

Bridges have been blown out everywhere on roads and railroads and their restoration is a slow process by the cut stone method without cement or steel. It should be remembered that there is not even any native lumber in Sicily. But progress is being made on the restoration of cement plants, and bridges are slowly being rebuilt in the vicinity of Palermo. The railroad along the north coast is in operation for a total of about 30 miles of the 100 or more miles between Palermo and Messina.

Elimination of the Fascist officials has presented other perplexing difficulties. There were a total of 25,000 public officials in Sicily. In order to hold a job they had to be at least nominal Fascists. Separating the sheep from the goats was no easy business with all sorts of conflicting information from the citizenry. In some cases AMG [Allied Military Government] found it necessary to retain undesirable Fascists in office until suitable experienced and competent replacements could be found, and they have not been easy to find.

Schools are slowly reopening in Sicily as buildings are repaired or evacuated by the military, but there are hordes of ragged, dirty, hungry, smiling children in the streets everywhere throughout Italy.

As far as I could see, no Fascist program had been as successful as Mussolini's campaign for more babies! The children call all Americans "Joe" and the formula is always the same — "Hi Joe, cigarette, caramella" — and if you have a cigarette or an Army gum drop or lump of sugar, they're apt to get it, always accompanied by the bland assurance that the cigarette is for "me papa."

We left Palermo for Messina in a Navy command car with two armed bluejackets, — blanket rolls, cans of gasoline and boxes of K rations. A Captain in the Navy saw us off in the early morning. He noticed that the leather was neatly slashed out of the whole front seat and asked one of the sailors, a little briskly, how that had happened, explaining what we already knew that there was hardly an Army car in Sicily with its leather intact but that such things never happened to Navy cars! The sailor, quaking with apprehension, replied: "Captain I can't explain it. I haven't been off this seat for the two months the car has been here!" That's the way it is in Sicily — things disappear while you sit on them!

We drove along the rugged north coast across little valleys yellow with ripe lemon groves and green with cabbages, cauliflower and artichokes, past castle crowned mountain tops, thru numberless towns suffering from various degrees of damage. The coast is scalloped with countless rivers coming down from the mountains and everywhere one or more spans of the old masonry bridges had been blown out by the retreating Germans. The same was true of the steel bridges along the adjoining railway line. We had to ford all the rivers, creeping down the sides of the steep gorges and across wooden bridges improvised by the engineers.

The roadside was strewn in places with burned out German, American, British and Italian trucks, cars, mobile guns and tanks, and at every strategic spot concrete pill boxes frowned on us from the cliffs and hills. We caught occasional glimpses of landing boats and amphibious equipment smashed up on the little beaches by the river mouths where last summer our forces fought their way ashore in that series of amphibious flanking attacks that helped so much to roll the Germans back to the straits of Messina.

Messina we found worse damaged than Palermo. The civilian supply situation presented roughly the same picture as Palermo — shortage of food, inadequate transport and demoralized local administration. The senior Civil Affairs officer told me a revealing story about a reliable and faithful Italian policeman who was taking a small truck load of flour to a nearby commune a day or so before. The truck broke down and he burrowed down among the sacks to spend the night and guard the precious flour. During the night the peasants sneaked up under the truck to slit the sacks with their long knives and draw off the flour, but, mistaking the rear end of the policeman for a sack in the darkness, they punctured him instead.

Standing on the ruined quays in Messina harbor waiting our turn to cross the straits to the mainland on an American landing craft, I watched a hundred Italian soldiers come ashore, repatriated at last to their native Sicily. They were the raggedest, weariest, most wretched white men I've ever seen. Some couldn't walk and had to be supported by others; some were very sick men. There was no welcoming crowd; just the usual myriad of half clothed, shivering children begging cigarettes and caramellas or anything else from the British and American truck crews waiting to board. There was no band, no families, nothing but a dock full of crater holes and a city square surrounded by the scarred shells of buildings and up on the hill overlooking the harbor and the city the great cathedral with one word painted on the wall in black letters 40 feet high so that mariners sailing the straits between Scylla and Charybdis could see it miles away — "DUX" — a name that had long since lost its magic for those miserable soldiers. As they stumbled down the ramp, some fell prostrate and unashamed kissed the ground of Sicily, some cried and few spoke. An officer formed them up and they straggled off across the square just beneath a shattered wall of a once fine warehouse. They didn't look up, but I did and there in great stone letters on the wall was engraved these words: "With a dagger in your teeth, a bomb in your hand and a sovereign disdain for danger in your heart — Il Duce." It was an incongruous spectacle — Caesar's hungry, peasant legions staggering home silhouetted against the ruins of mad Caesar's vanished dreams.

We crossed the straits to Reggio Calabria and drove north thru rain soaked mountainous Southern Italy, fording streams, foraging for a place to sleep in the dirty villages and talking along the way with military government officers and Italians about agriculture, industry, food, transportation and the consequences of war, invasion and political upheaval. In one place where kindly nuns put us up for the night in a closed school there had been no legal bread for 8 or 10 days and the nuns found even our K rations very good indeed.

In Naples the port area was completely destroyed and there was much damage to the Royal Palace and the great hotels and fine buildings along the bay, with miscellaneous damage here and there throughout the business section. But the higher parts of the city are almost intact. In the industrial suburbs, however, the demolition by the Germans was methodical. They probably had some 4–6000 sappers and engineers at work for more than 3 weeks destroying anything of possible advantage to the Allies. . . . The senior civil affairs officer showed me a great ancient hand wrought spike — all that remains of the library of the University of Naples, one of the oldest and greatest repositories of learning in the world.

The port was a shambles when our forces arrived and the work that was done by the Navy in restoring that port which is so essential to the supply of the 8th and 5th armies is now an almost legendary achievement. What ships had not been sunk by our bombing, the Germans sank in order to block all the docks and then they systematically ruined all the unloading equipment and the dock sheds and warehouses lining the long waterfront. The great port of Naples is the largest area of concentrated devastation it has been my misfortune to see, but in spite of it all we were very soon handling an enormous volume of tonnage thru there — I wish I could tell you how much. Truck convoys come in, load and depart for the front, in an almost uninterrupted procession and the harbor is so full of ships you lie in wait for an air raid every night, until you decide it isn't worthwhile, which is usually about the second night.

The German industrial demolition was done very systematically and thriftily. They concentrated on public utilities and the larger industrial plants, not overlooking food processing plants like canneries. The great Ilva steel works, the Ansaldo chemical works and the Breda locomotive plant are acres of scrap iron. But their technique was mostly selective demolition — don't waste explosives blowing up heavy concrete walls; put little charges in transformers, electric motor housings, gear boxes, switchboards; crack all weight carrying structural members so that operation will be impossible without complete rebuilding; crack and topple over transportation machinery, overhead cranes, etc; crack the foundations of ponderous things like heavy presses, furnaces and leave a few time bombs and booby traps about to make salvage unhealthy. I'm told they floated time charges on cork or wooden rafts down the sewers so they would explode in inaccessible places.

Naples was an experimental laboratory for the Germans. Much of the industrial establishment cannot be rehabilitated at all and will have to be rebuilt from the ground up. It will be a long, long time before anything like pre-war production can be restored. Demolition is far more effective than bombing, and the not unreasonable assumption that they will follow and further perfect the industrial scorched earth policy in the rest of Europe presents an appalling prospect of prolonged recovery.

As for the food supply situation in Naples, it's much the same story except the bread ration was lower — about 125 grams a day. It has been raised now, I understand, to about 200 grams, but is still far from adequate. The black market is undisguised and there is some leakage of American flour thru the Italian distribution system into the black market. Olive oil, a staple of the Italian diet and their only fat, is almost never available for official distribution, and the black market price is now about $2.80 a litre. Virtually all staple foods except the daily bread ration have to be obtained at black market prices.

Again the problem is importation of more flour, and transportation. The Allied Military Government gathered together some 690 Italian trucks in Naples and vicinity, and it is all they can do to keep 125 of them in operation.

Unless prices are stabilized and an adequate supply of basic food insured, it is hard to see how the poor are going to survive. A stenographer in the AMG office made up a typical budget showing a cost of 175 lira per day to feed a family of 5 one meal, and that a limited one. And 300 lira a week was fairly average pay for a stenographer.

I spent a day at the front and came away with a healthy respect for that war along the muddy, bloody, mountainous road to Rome. I wish I could describe that mud that has to be shovelled off the roads like snow and the cold penetrating rain, the stench of those ruined towns with their unburied dead in the rubble, the conditions in which the dough-feet — as they call them — live and fight, up and down those stony rugged mountains, supplied by donkeys, with the Germans and their machine guns and screaming mortars always above them on the next hilltop.

Ernie Pyle, the newspaper correspondent, put it very well. I saw him in Naples a few evenings later and asked him what the soldiers were thinking about up there in the Liri Valley. "They are thinking of only one thing," he said, "and that's a dry place to sit on so they can wring out their socks."

On the valley floor the olive groves have been shaved off close to the ground and the shell holes merge into one another. It looks like the western front in the last war. I stood on the rubble of what was San Pietro, only a few miles south of Cassino to watch our shell bursts. Cassino is just about half way from Salerno to Rome — and we landed at Salerno 6½ months ago. I would like to talk about the Italian campaign, which has proved so desperately difficult, but perhaps I had better stick to the economics which are also desperately difficult.

However, I do want to tell you about a scene I witnessed that has been repeated many times along that front. The Italian peasant lives in villages in those limestone mountains and most of them hide out in caves until the shelling subsides. Then they come back — women, children and all — to erase the scars of war on their precious little fields of winter wheat. After a month or more in the caves, you can picture for yourselves their condition of malnutrition and filth. They burrow into the rubble of their village to find a cellar for some shelter. Then comes the AMG officer and rounds up the priest and doctor. If the mayor has disappeared, the officer selects a new one from the group and appoints him on the spot. His first instruction is in equitable distribution of some sacks of flour that are unloaded from his car; then there is a discussion about the water supply, about sanitary regulations and finally the officer unloads a huge can of delousing powder — for lice carry typhus — and translates the instructions on the label from English to Italian. He orders the mayor and doctor, if there is one, to repeat the instructions. If they have it right, he orders them personally to delouse every one in the village before he returns for inspection and with more flour in a day or so. And off he goes with the wretched, half dead peasants beaming and eloquent with thanks. I tell you it was a very impressive and efficient performance.

I want to say something more about Naples. I want to remind you that when our forces entered the city on October 1st there was no water, no electricity, no kerosene, no candles, no light, (cables attached to the generators of Italian submarines in the harbor supplied the first electric power), there was no gas, no fuel, no telephones, the sewers were blocked, the streets were blocked with rubble, the port was useless, there were no buses, no trolleys, no taxis, no communication, the telephone exchange had been blown up, the banks were closed, the stores were closed; 400 bodies lay in the streets, the mayor had fled, the chief of police had fled, the courts were closed, there was no government — and greater Naples is almost as large as greater Boston! Within a few days water was restored. Within a few weeks all of the essentials of civilized existence, on at least a minimum basis, had been restored to that populous community by the Army engineers, the Navy salvage organization and Allied Military Government. I think it was a redoubtable achievement. And so was the decisive way the Army Medical Corps took hold of the alarming typhus epidemic this winter. They deloused literally hundreds of thousands of Italians, and that serious menace is now over. But then Vesuvius erupted and now Military Government has another immense burden on its sagging shoulders in that sad city where bread is everyone's preoccupation and there are no street singers anymore.

To summarize: The Italian distribution system is in a state of extreme disorganization; transportation by truck, rail and ship is totally inadequate and the collection of local foodstuffs is impeded by hoarding and speculation, resulting in a huge black market operating at exorbitant prices.

The cost of living is rising rapidly and wages have had to be increased. There is little confidence in the lira. The Italian budget, already heavily supported by Allied Military currency, will be subjected to increased burdens, and tax collections are way behind. Currency circulation, already largely inflated, has probably doubled since the invasion and is being constantly increased by heavy Allied military expenditures for troops, labor, services and goods. And the currency is exposed to complete devaluation by the Germans if they choose to dump lira in the North as a weapon of economic warfare, for all the printing presses are in their possession. It is hard to see how and when the inflationary spiral can be arrested.

Agricultural production has suffered from several years of deficiencies of farm equipment, fertilizer, insecticides and fungicides. Destruction of irrigation and drainage works has been serious and may be more serious further north. What with war devastation, the shortage of fertilizer, draft animals and transport, crops may be still shorter this year and conditions may get worse before they get better.

Much industrial plant cannot be rehabilitated at all and will have to be reconstructed. Allowing for possible greater war damage as the intensity of the conflict increases, it is not unlikely that the industrial scene will further deteriorate, as, if and when we push further north and more millions are liberated. And then, as military activity diminishes, unemployment will increase.

The present government of the King is neither popular nor strong.

Finally, there is no starvation, but malnutrition is commonplace and with it susceptibility to disease.

In short, Italy imposes a far great burden on Allied resources and shipping for civilian relief and rehabilitation than had been expected. And this burden has coincided with increasingly heavy demands for military supply.

But there are some improvements in the Italian situation. The Army is making more and more trucks available to relieve the food collection and distribution difficulties. And the Army supply program of food, mostly flour, has recently been largely increased. The schedule is calculated on a basis of less than subsistence, but local resources of olive oil, vegetables, wine, fruit and nuts will add to the caloric value, and, of course, an assured supply of imported food, even if meager, will in time do much toward restoring confidence, breaking the black market and drawing the local food out of hiding.

In conclusion, Italy has been a headache. The magnitude of the food supply program alone leaves no uncertainty that the United Nations will be hard put to it to supply the minimum requirements of liberated Europe over any extended period. Prompt selective rehabilitation of industry and agriculture to increase self-support in food and essential consumer goods seems to be the only answer. Every day of delay in tackling this problem will aggravate economic disintegration, increase the burden on our food supply and shipping and pile up problems for the future. It may well be that if shipping limitations preclude both food and rehabilitation, then less food and more seed and rehabilitation goods would serve us and them better in the long run. For example, 1500 tons of soap making equipment would produce about 30,000 tons of soap per year in Italy.

Prompt delivery of adequate civilian supply following the invasion is not merely a notion of altruists; it is basic to our military and political objectives. Italy has left no doubt on that score and if Italy has been a headache it is well to remember that it is only a prelude to what we may find when we batter down the walls of Hitler's ghastly fortress.

The only safe assumption is that the factors of devastation, hunger, inflation, confusion and demoralization of economy and government which have characterized Italy will be found in varying degrees behind the Nazi's armies throughout Europe. Food, sanitation and civil order will be the first requirement. But beyond this limited objective are other goals. Delay in planning and initiating essential rehabilitation will only injure local morale, multiply our burdens, prolong the period during which we must feed the populations, and impair our larger interest in laying the foundations of enduring peace.

After delivery of this long and tiresome reminder of another obstacle on the treacherous trail to peace, I should sit down. But I am sure you realize that as an official of the Navy it requires more restraint than I possess to talk about economics and the European Theatre when the greatest naval campaign in history is just gathering momentum in the Pacific. So I am compelled to add just a word about the Navy.

You are not unmindful of the fact that the Navy's destination is Japan and that some considerable progress has been made in that direction of late, thanks in large part to you — to American industry, American labor and American inventive genius. Production figures are tiresome, but perhaps a brief, up-to-date inventory of what the Navy has will explain what the Navy has done and why we know where we are going.

Since July 1, 1940, the Navy has increased the number of warships in the fleet by 130 percent; it has built the greatest fleet of supporting vessels and landing craft the world has ever seen; the firepower of our fleet has been trebled; the air force has been multiplied by fourteen; personnel has been expanded almost fifteen times — the greatest marshalling of men and materials in American naval history. During the past three and a half years the Navy has spent 45 billions and entered into commitments totaling almost 75 billion dollars.

Last year alone the number of warships in the fleet was more than doubled. Last year we completed two new 45,000-ton battleships, six aircraft carriers of the 27,000-ton class; nine aircraft carriers of the 11,000-ton class; 50 escort carriers; 11 cruisers; 128 destroyers; 306 destroyer escorts, and 56 submarines. And the 1944 schedule calls for completion of substantially more combatant ships than last year!

At the end of 1943 the Navy had, after all losses and transfers to other nations, over 800 combatant vessels and about 20,000 other craft — the largest naval force in the world. By the end of this year, our Navy will equal in strength and ships the combined navies of all the other nations on earth — including the Axis fleets.

As you know, a vast landing craft production program is underway. It will cost more than five billion dollars. One out of every four dollars the Navy will expend during the next ten months will go into that program. Upon its successful completion depends in great measure the success of forthcoming operations, for this year, as never before, the Navy's mission will be a match for its fighting strength.

And as soon as Germany's defeat becomes imminent, the British and American Combined Chiefs of Staff have definite plans for implementing the transfer of the Allied fighting power from the European to the Pacific Theatre. When that transfer begins to take effect it will be the signal for full speed ahead in the Pacific and you will hear more and more from your mighty Navy.

Stevenson's mission returned to Washington on January 15, 1944. He delivered his report on February 5, 1944, to Leo Crowley, Administrator, and Lauchlin Currie, Deputy Administrator of the Foreign Economic Administration. The report, including illustrations and charts, consisted of 122 single-spaced pages. A copy of it is in the Stevenson papers, Princeton University Library. All that we reproduce here is Stevenson's letter of transmittal, the Table of Contents to indicate the detailed nature of the report, and the Conclusions and Recommendations.

REPORT OF FEA SURVEY MISSION TO ITALY

The purpose of the mission was to explore in general the nature and extent of the civilian economic needs of Italy with particular reference to rehabilitation and reconstruction, and also to suggest what the role of FEA should be in meeting those problems and when it should undertake to operate in this field.

In addition to myself, the Mission included David D. Lloyd, Hugh G. Calkins and Nils K. G. Tholand. In general, Mr. Lloyd concentrated on the general economic and inflationary situation, Mr. Calkins on agriculture, Mr. Tholand on industry and I on organizational relationships.

My colleagues worked with the utmost diligence and, I believe, discrimination under trying circumstances. The Mission left Washington December 7, 1943 and returned January 15, 1944. We were in North Africa a week going and returning and in Italy and Sicily about three weeks. We interviewed a large number of British and American civil affairs officers and tactical officers at all levels and also had informative conferences with Italian business, agriculture, labor and political leaders, including some of the prominent members of the Naples Committee of Liberation. We proceeded by car from Palermo to Messina and thence to Naples which afforded the Mission an opportunity to survey conditions in the country at close range.

We attempted, in this limited time, investigation over a broad area, and our conclusions, though checked as thoroughly as circumstances permitted, are subject to all the frailties of breadth and haste.

I am mindful of the responsibility and the importance of this Mission and I am appreciative of the confidence displayed by you in selecting me as its chief.

Respectfully submitted,

REPORT OF
FEA SURVEY MISSION TO ITALY

Table of Contents

CONCLUSIONS AND RECOMMENDATIONS

REPORT

CONCLUSIONS AND RECOMMENDATIONS

A. *The Economic Situation in Italy*

The following summary of economic conditions as the Mission found them should be prefaced by the reminder that when our forces landed in Italy, the country was in a state of economic and administrative disorganization as a result of the Fascist regime and the war, and that the military situation has confined Allied economic activity to an area which has always been impoverished and industrially undeveloped.

1. DISTRIBUTION

The Italian distributive system is in a state of extreme disorganization; transportation of civilian supplies is difficult and totally inadequate to the needs of the country, the collection of locally produced supplies is impeded by hoarding and speculation resulting from the black market. Distribution through the rationing system is unsatisfactory. Large quantities of food are sold through extra-legal channels at exorbitant prices. Price control is practically non-existent except with respect to the quantities of bread, pasta, olive oil and a few other basic foods and fuels that pass through legal channels.

2. FOOD SUPPLIES

As a result of these factors, Italy presents a far greater burden upon Allied resources for relief and sustenance than had been expected. Allied Forces Headquarters recommends the importation of 700,000 tons of flour alone in the first six months of the year, with monthly shipments thereafter depending on future developments. In addition to flour, the importation of 257,353 tons of other foods is assumed to be necessary for the first six months of 1944. Even these vast quantities are not calculated to provide an adequate daily calorie ration for the bulk of the population.

3. EMPLOYMENT

The Allied armies are now the largest employers of manual and industrial labor. A substantial degree of industrial employment in Italian plants cannot be expected until Italian industry is rebuilt. As military activity diminishes the unemployment problem will increase.

Present estimates of unemployment are little more than guesses. Unemployed workers entitled to unemployment compensation under Italian law receive benefits at the pre-invasion rates. As our armies withdraw, the need of relief and compensation for the unemployed will constitute a heavy drain on the Italian budget.

4. HEALTH OF THE POPULATION

The shortage of food in the cities is having an adverse effect on health. In Naples responsible officials estimate that from 40% to 80% of the people are suffering from malnutrition. This lack of food weakens resistance to disease. There is serious typhus in Naples. Medical supplies are apparently being provided in sufficient quantity.

5. INFLATION

The cost of living is increasing at an accelerated rate. In the twelve months from September, 1942 to September, 1943, it is believed to have increased 150%. In the two months from September 1 to November 1, 1943 it rose to 200% of the September, 1942 level. Wages have had to be increased. There is little confidence in the lira both because of the low value placed on it by Allies and because of the constant increase in the currency circulation resulting from the war and the occupation. The Italian budget, already supported by AMG [Allied Military Government] with AM lire, will be subjected to increased burdens in the future. The currency, in addition to being increased, is exposed to complete demoralization by the Germans if they choose to operate the printing presses and dump lire in the North as an instrument of economic warfare.

6. AGRICULTURE

Italy is primarily an agricultural nation and the collection, distribution and marketing of food crops and other agricultural commodities has been severely disrupted. Production has suffered from several years' cumulative deficiencies of farm equipment, fertilizers, insecticides and fungicides and in some regions has suffered considerably from war damage. In some regions the destruction of irrigation and drainage works has been serious and may be much more serious in central and northern Italy. The crippling of processing plants closes an outlet for important farm products, complicates food conservation and will contribute to unemployment. Export of crop surpluses is at a standstill. What with the collapse of the Italian governmental mechanism for agriculture, war devastation, the shortage of fertilizer, draft animals, and transportation, crops may be still shorter this year and conditions may get worse before they get better.

7. INDUSTRY

Complete and methodical destruction by the Germans of almost all industry in those areas in which they have had an opportunity to apply their "scorched earth" policy before evacuation presents formidable problems of reconstruction and restoration of balance to the economy. Much of the industry in the Naples area cannot be rehabilitated and will have to be reconstructed from the ground up. But the very extent of the destruction presents an opportunity for selective restoration calculated to meet the demands of a sound Italian economy without the unsound creations of Fascism. Industrial destruction will contribute to unemployment which will increase as the employment provided by military operations diminishes. Assuming the Germans will continue to follow the same scorched earth policy as they withdraw, and making allowance for possible greater bombing and war damage in the industrialized North, it is not unlikely that the over-all scene of industrial destitution will further deteriorate.

8. ITALIAN ADMINISTRATION

The Italian administrative mechanism is feeble as a result of years of Fascist corruption, low civilian morale and the want of a central government commanding general popular support.

9. IMPORTS AND EXPORTS

In the future, the Italian government is to be charged with the landed cost of imports for civilian consumption, as a future rather than immediate claim. Against this charge the Allied Control Commission (ACC) will receive lire at prevailing internal prices. Such receipts will, in the aggregate, be well below the amounts charged to the Italian government.

Producers of exports will be paid by ACC in lire, and proceeds from the sale of exports will be held in the currency of the purchasing country to the credit of the Italian government. In the foreseeable future, the proceeds from exports cannot possibly balance the amounts that will be charged to the Italian government. There is little prospect of balancing Italian trade so long as Italy must look abroad not only for a large proportion of its food, but also for basic consumer goods and reconstruction supplies.

B. *Economic Operations of Military Government*

1. RESPONSIBILITY OF AMG

These problems of civilian economy are the responsibility of the Theatre Commander and as far as our Mission could determine, it is the policy of the Theatre Commander to retain such control until the military and shipping situations ease.

To date these problems have been handled through Allied Military Government (AMG), but in the near future Sicily, Sardinia and Italy south of Salerno-Barletta will be restored to Italian government which will be supervised by the Allied Control Commission, an organization responsible to the Theatre Commander.

2. LIMITED OBJECTIVES OF THE MILITARY

Military government has a limited objective — maintenance of civil order in the rear and prevention of disease among the civilian population. The military are primarily concerned with the supply of food, fuel and medicine and only the necessary minimum of economic restoration to prevent starvation, disease and revolt. Military government makes no provision for the importation of supplies for the restoration of agriculture, industry and employment.

The restoration of Italian agriculture is an urgent necessity and much can be done through the coordination and stimulation of local effort without severe taxation of shipping facilities to import supplies. To this problem ACC should bring a staff adequate in numbers, skills and training.

With respect to the restoration of essential public services, public health and law and order, AMG, the Army and the Navy have done a remarkable job in Italy. It is not the intention of this report to criticize, but only to call attention to the limited objectives of the military.

3. FUTURE TRENDS IN THE ECONOMIC SITUATION

The net effect of this policy has been to defer the major economic questions for future handling. Failure to bring in necessary rehabilitation goods at this time must necessarily aggravate the Italian economic situation. On the agricultural side, inadequate crops next year will increase the demand on our supplies and may intensify the panic sense of shortage in Italy which has already contributed to hoarding and speculation. As military operations diminish, employment will also. Prolonged shortage of consumer goods will intensify the inflationary spiral. As inflation increases, the demand made upon the governmental budget by the unemployed and those with fixed salaries will also increase. Bad as the Italian economic situation is now, it may be expected to be worse six months or a year from now, subject only to the moderating effect of reasonably adequate food imports.

C. *Responsibility for Future Economic Operations in Italy*

1. CONTINUING NEED FOR ALLIED HELP

After the cessation of hostilities the Italian economic problem will continue to require Allied supervision, control and assistance. Rehabilitation will, we presume, become the chief objective in order to mitigate the burden of support as rapidly as possible.

Destruction of utilities and industry will demand highly selective rehabilitation since it will be impossible to satisfy all the pressing needs at once. This may mean continued governmental screening of requirements and governmental procurement for some time. The unsettled internal condition of the country, inflation and the probable weakness of the Italian administrative organization will require supervision of the distribution of imported supplies and equipment by a governmental agency in Italy. Furthermore, by the time hostilities cease, the Allied Governments will have made heavy commitments or expenditures on Italian account. The problem of transferring these obligations to the Italian government, and indeed the whole problem of the postwar financial settlement, will probably require the supervision of a governmental mission in the field. Closely related to this is the problem of encouraging exports and working out a sound basis for Italian trade.

2. JOINT ACTION OF THE ALLIES IS DICTATED BY THEIR INTERESTS

The Mediterranean Theatre is becoming, to an increasing extent, the responsibility of the British. Both in the military organizations and in the ACC, the top positions are being assigned to British officers. In the postwar future Britain has certain obvious strategic objectives to preserve in the Mediterranean. Furthermore, the principal exports of Italy are of more importance to the United Kingdom than they are to the United States. It is, therefore, probable that after the war considerations of British foreign policy will be dominant with respect to the future role of Italy.

But the United States has obvious long-range interests in developing the climate of enduring peace in Europe, eradicating Fascism and in democratic evolution in Italy on a sound economic foundation. Moreover there are short-range considerations which cannot be overlooked. The food supplies which are now so essential are coming predominantly from the United States. It is probable that much of the rehabilitation supplies which will be required in Italy will come from U.S. sources. Remittances from Italians in this country [U.S.A.] from U.S. citizens of

Italian descent constitute an important factor in the economy of Italy, and the Italian population in this country will take an active interest in the economic and political future of Italy.

Russia has already evidenced an interest in the policy of the United States and Great Britain toward Italy. This may increase if, as a result of the progress of the war, Russian influence is extended in the Balkans and in the Eastern Mediterranean.

It follows that consultation and cooperation among the Allies must be continued with respect to Italy after the war, and that a mechanism must be maintained for the formulation and execution of a combined policy.

It is contemplated, we understand, that after termination of hostilities the existing Advisory Council for Italy will constitute the "Board of Directors" for the Italian economic operation.

D. *The Instrument for Allied Economic Policy*

1. THE MAJOR QUESTIONS ARE A CIVILIAN RESPONSIBILITY

From what has been said above concerning the nature of the economic problem in Italy, it is clear that the economic operations of the Allies in Italy, even now, present questions which are necessarily the concern of the civilian policy-making agencies of government. Even the initial steps of rehabilitation of agriculture and transportation to relieve the burden on us raise problems with respect to Italy's fiscal future, its foreign trade, its industrial and commercial redevelopment and its relations to other nations, which are no concern of the military.

2. SEVERAL U.S. CIVILIAN AGENCIES WILL BE CONCERNED WITH ECONOMIC OPERATIONS IN ITALY

It is clear that no single agency of the United States Government can assume sole responsibility for economic operations in Italy. At the present time the Army must postpone or disregard certain vital problems. The State Department is concerned primarily with policies and not the conduct of economic operations. The Foreign Economic Administration cannot handle the operating problem alone even in the economic field, because one of the overwhelming considerations in the Italian scene is the currency and the government budget. In these fiscal matters the facilities of the Treasury are and will continue to be required. Even after the termination of hostilities it is probable that assistance will be necessary in policing the internal economic system. This is a function that may require services which are not normally offered by either the FEA or the Treasury.

It seems apparent that personnel from more than one agency of our government will be required. Moreover, it must be constantly remembered that the operation will also have to be a combined Allied responsibility, at least until something resembling normal commercial relations can be resumed. Combined operation by individuals from different governments is difficult enough; combined operation by individual agencies from different governments would be far more so.

For sometime to come, therefore, the Allies must maintain in Italy a combined supervisory administrative body as comprehensive in its scope as the ACC, covering almost all aspects of the Italian economy and administration responsible, first, to the Combined Chiefs of Staff and, after hostilities, to some other combined agency. Its composition should be individuals selected for specific competence from private life or the several departments of the Allied governments involved.

3. THE ALLIED CONTROL COMMISSION AS THE AGENCY FOR ALLIED ECONOMIC OPERATIONS

The Allied Control Commission has been established as a mechanism for the transition from the period of Allied military government to Allied supervision of the Italian government. This organization was established by the Theatre Commander to enforce and execute the instrument of surrender of the Italian government, to insure that the conduct of the Italian government conforms to the requirements of an Allied base of operations, and to be the organ through which the policy of the United Nations toward the Italian government is conducted. The Commission is responsible to the Theatre Commander, who is ex-officio president of the Commission. It operates under Allied Force Headquarters and all communications between the Commission and the governments of the United Nations are transmitted through Allied Force Headquarters.

The scope of the activities of the Allied Control Commission is indicated by its table of organization and its directive. It has four major sections; namely, a Military Section, a Political Section, an Economic and Administrative Section, and a Communications Section. Each of these sections has a number of subcommissions. For example, under the Economic and Administrative Section are subcommissions on finance, industry, commerce, public works and mines, agriculture, forest and fisheries, labor, interior, legal, public safety, public health, education, fine arts and property control. Under the Communications Section there are subcommissions on shipping, internal transportation and posts and telecommunications. There is also an industrial planning staff. Suggestions, extraneous to this report, could be made on modifications of the organizational structure, such as the division of the Economic and Administrative Section into two parts.

The Commission is directed to operate through and upon the Italian government in all its branches.

The directive establishing the Commission does not indicate what is to happen if and when the armistice is superseded by another arrangement between the Allies and the Italian government. Neither is it clear what effect the termination of hostilities in the Italian area will have on the Commission. But, as indicated above, it has been suggested that the Italian Advisory Council for Italy might replace the Theatre Commander as "president" of ACC.

The Commission is directed to engage in long-term planning to attain "objectives ultimately desired" and "for the early furtherance of the United Nations' war against Germany and Japan."

While the Allied Control Commission is now staffed predominantly by AMG officers, civilians, of course, dominate the Political Section and Mr. Grady* has with him now a staff of six U.S. civilians in the Economic and Administrative Section.

It is obvious that many of the questions with which the Allied Control Commission is entrusted by its directive are a concern of the civilian agencies of the Allied governments and have only a remote connection with the military. The introduction of civilian administrative and technical personnel into the ranks of the Commission is consistent with its objectives and there is no doubt that, in addition to assisting the officers with current operations, they could do much essential forward planning looking beyond the military period without any interference with the current military responsibilities. Indeed, we believe that gradual demilitarization of ACC is not only inevitable but quite consistent with the military view.

It may seem anomalous that a civilian or partly civilian agency concerned with non-military problems should continue to be responsible to military command. And it is true that during the period of military control at least, agencies of the government who should be responsible for the long-term questions with which the Commission is dealing would have no contact with the civilian members of the Commission other than through Allied Force Headquarters. These considerations, however, may be more apparent than real. In any event, as long as economic supervision of Italy is a combined operation, formal communication between

* The Theatre Commander and President of the Commission, General Sir Maitland Wilson, is British; his Deputy President of the Commission, Lieut. Gen. Mason MacFarlane, is British; the Vice-President in charge of the Economic and Administrative Section, Lord Stansgate, is British; his Deputy Vice-President, Henry W. Grady, is American.

the Commission and the departments and ministries of the several governments will be thru a coordinating body of some kind, be it military or civilian. Moreover, it should not be impossible to evolve practical means for direct informal communication.

Much of the organizational confusion of the past period resulting from the unexpected prolongation of the war in Italy and the multiplicity of headquarters can and will be eliminated; exclusive responsibility for Allied economic operations in liberated Italy can and should be reposed in ACC. Not only is it a potentially adequate instrument to do the job during the present period of military operations, but it is a convenient vehicle for future planning and present training of personnel, British and American, to execute those plans and policies after responsibility for the Italian economy has been transferred from the military to the civilian agencies of government. If combined economic activities are continued thereafter, it could easily be converted from an Allied armistice control commission under the theatre commander and the Combined Chiefs of Staff to an Allied economic commission under some other agency created by the Allies to coordinate its activities and the activities of such similar bodies as may be created to conduct such post military combined economic operations in other countries.

Aside from the considerations that dictate the continuity of ACC's exclusive responsibility in Italy during the period of primary military responsibility and perhaps thereafter under civilian direction, it is more than probable that the Theatre Commander would view with disfavor the advent of any governmental agency independent of ACC and not wholly responsible to him. This is not to say, however, that even during the transitional phase from military to civilian direction there may not be specific assignments which ACC may find it convenient to delegate to FEA, MEW [Ministry of Economic Warfare] or some other agency to perform in the field. That such agencies will be called upon from time to time to furnish individual specialists on a temporary basis seems certain. And it seems certain that the services of such FEA corporations as the Export-Import Bank and the U.S. Commercial Company will be required later on as our economic policy and objectives in Italy are better defined and the transactions become more complex.

4. THE NEED FOR POLICY DEFINITION

Forward planning in a vacuum is uneconomic and embarrassing. Time and energy are wasted; hopes are aroused and frustrated; and uncertainty, indecision and confusion in the field are the result. We recognize that it is impossible to lay down with any precision our long-term economic policies for Italy at this time. But it should be possible to define at least our short-range policy. At present the ACC directives for supervision of the Italian government are wanting in clear-cut economic objectives.

Presumably we want to transfer to the Italians as rapidly as possible the burden of feeding, clothing and keeping the people reasonably healthy. Presumably Congress and public opinion would support measures of reconstruction and rehabilitation to that end.

If this is the present limit of policy decision, it should be made clear. And then the subsidiary questions should be clarified. Is this primarily a British sphere of interest and responsibility? If it is, are we going to continue to participate actively and energetically in the direction and operations of ACC? If so, how far are we going to go in rehabilitation? Are we going to supply just seeds, tools and services to rehabilitate agriculture? Are we going further and help with the restoration of the fertilizer, power and transportation industries, bearing in mind that they have a value to Italian economy beyond food production and distribution? What about the food processing and clothing industries? What funds are to be used? etc., etc.[19]

Beyond these simple, preliminary decisions which should be made to guide ACC, there arises a host of more intricate economic policy questions which will clamor for attention, along with related questions all over Europe.

5. NEED OF AN EFFECTIVE ITALIAN GOVERNMENT

The Allied Control Commission or any other Allied agency in the economic field in Italy will have to rely on the Italian government to administer in detail whatever it attempts to do with respect to Italian economic affairs. It is the Mission's observation that the present Italian government of the King and General Badoglio commands little respect or support among the people. The anti-Fascist elements in the south of Italy have refused to cooperate as long as the King or his son remains. While the Mission was not directly concerned with political questions, it cannot fail to point out that, in its opinion, the present unhappy political situation will constitute a formidable obstacle to orderly and effective realization of our economic aims and operations.[20]

---

[19] Some of these questions were already answered in a letter from the Secretary of State to the Secretaries of War and Navy, dated January 1, 1944, which, however, had not come to the knowledge of Stevenson's mission at the time its report was being prepared.

[20] In June, 1946, a popular referendum abolished the monarchy and established a republic.

E. *Recommendations*

There follow some specific recommendations deemed within the scope of the Mission's inquiry and some general observations which seem worth mentioning.

1. ORGANIZATION

(a) The Allied Control Commission (ACC) should be the exclusive and continuing mechanism for executing Allied policies in Italy during the period of military responsibility; and thereafter it could be readily adapted to discharge whatever longer term policies the Allied governments evolve for combined economic supervision and assistance in Italy.

(b) No civilian agency, British or American, independent of the military should be established in Italy at this time.

(c) The ACC should be gradually demilitarized and its military personnel replaced by administrative and technical civilians against the day when military funds and responsibility for the civilian economy will terminate and exclusive civilian responsibility will commence. The ACC affords a convenient vehicle to effect a smooth transition from military to civilian staff and direction.

(d) The ACC should be rapidly staffed not only to perform its present economic mission under the military, but also to plan and execute now, so far as possible, our broader economic objectives. It would seem prudent to initiate promptly the necessary adjustments in ACC planning and personnel.

(e) The FEA should act as the United States clearing house or agency for the recruitment of personnel with the specialized skills required from time to time by ACC. Such personnel may be found in private life, in the various agencies of our government or in FEA itself.

(f) ACC should be officially informed that FEA is prepared to cooperate in supplying U.S. personnel required by ACC. Various alternative methods of starting could be suggested: FEA could send men to understudy the chiefs of certain of the subcommissions of ACC — Commerce, Industry and Agriculture, for example; or send men to act as assistants to Mr. Grady,* selected with particular reference to their ability to plan and coordinate groups of related activities, such as food and agricultural supplies, industry and industrial supplies, price control and distribution.

(g) The Mission is impressed with the lack of information about the Italian situation in Washington. The civilian agencies will be ultimately

---

* Lord Stansgate (British) is the Vice President of ACC in charge of the Economic and Administrative Section and Mr. Henry W. Grady (American) is his Deputy Vice President.

responsible for the economic operation in Italy. For FEA to function effectively now or in the future vis-a-vis the ACC it should be represented on the Combined Civil Affairs Committee as to all matters relating to Italy, both to insure full information and an opportunity to exercise its influence at the policy level.

(h) Thought should be given to the establishment of an Allied co-ordinating group to perform the present functions of CCAC and CCS [Combined Chiefs of Staff] after responsibility for Italian civil affairs has been transferred from the military. The successor of ACC will have to be directed by such a combined civilian affairs group and the machinery should be at hand to redefine the task of ACC and to coordinate its direction. Presumably such a combined group would be representative of the Anglo-American government agencies directly concerned and would similarly direct whatever other combined economic field operations we jointly undertake.

(i) Consideration should be given to the designation, as soon as the need arises, of someone in ACC as an official representative of FEA to enable him legally to perform the functions of the FEA commercial corporations, such as the Export-Import Bank and the U.S. Commercial Company. Ultimately it may become desirable to have such corporations directly represented in Italy to provide the financial services which ACC or its post-military successor may require.

(j) The attention of ACC should be invited to the availability of individuals or groups of U.S. personnel to undertake spot assignments, investigations, etc., on behalf of ACC. The FEA should be prepared to provide the facilities to perform any such specific services.

2. SUBSTANTIVE

(a) Economic policy objectives with respect to Italy should be defined progressively, sharply and as far in advance as possible. There should be enunciated now the feasible objectives, however limited, to which ACC should direct its planning and operations.

(b) We suggest that present policy should include not only the military objective of food, fuel and medicine, but also at least a minimum of selective rehabilitation of industry and agriculture to increase self-support in food and essential consumer goods. Every day of delay in tackling this problem aggravates the economic disintegration, increases the burden on our food supply and shipping, and piles up problems for the future. If shipping in excess of the Army supply program is not and will not be available, it may well be that less food and more seed, rehabilitation goods, etc., in the next few months would better serve ourselves and the Italians in the long run.

(c) In furtherance of such a policy the following appear to be the most pressing requirements:

Agriculture and Food

(1) A well-balanced staff in the ACC representing all the essential techniques, at the national, regional and provincial levels.

(2) Aid in the prompt reorganization and direction of the Italian agricultural and food supply agencies.

(3) Expediting procurement and distribution of supplies and equipment to stimulate production and for processing of agricultural products.

Industry

(1) Prompt measures to salvage and "cannibalize" damaged industrial equipment.

(2) Repair and rehabilitation of power and transport industries essential to resumption of fundamental distribution services.

(3) Renewal of fertilizer production, soap production, food processing and sundry other essential manufactures.

(4) Expediting planning and procurement to minimize the long lag between requirements and delivery of industrial goods.

Finance

While it is beyond the Mission's scope or competence, the inflationary situation is so threatening to all economic operations that we are constrained to suggest that continuous attention both here and abroad be given to more vigorous steps to arrest the trend. Various possible steps have been suggested and considered and the Mission is aware that the uncertainties of the currency situation in the northern area now held by the Germans present imponderable obstacles to present measures.

3. GENERAL OBSERVATIONS

The only safe assumption is that the factors of devastation, hunger, inflation, confusion and demoralization of economy and administration which have characterized Italy will be found in varying degrees behind the retreating German armies throughout Europe. Food and civil order will be the first requirement, but beyond this limited military objective are other goals. Delay in planning and initiating essential rehabilitation will only injure local morale, multiply our burdens, prolong the period during which we must feed the populations, and impair our larger interest in laying the foundations of enduring peace.

(a) Delivery of adequate civilian supply on schedule in our future military operations is not merely a notion of altruists; it is basic to our military and political objectives. If local supplies are larger than anticipated, shipments can be reduced or diverted more readily than deficiencies supplied.

(b) Requirements for resumption of essential production should be ascertained at the earliest possible moment and the procurement machinery set in motion. To this end clear definition of policy will make both for prompt, orderly planning and also for confidence and morale among the people.

(c) The importance of the time factor in attacking rehabilitation requirements suggests that the non-military agencies of the Allied governments must not only be accurately informed of the scope of the economic responsibility they will inherit in liberated areas, but should contribute from the outset to the military planning.

(d) As soon as possible after the early stages of invasion and combat, military requisitions of productive property by tactical forces must be supervised carefully. Damage to the local economy must be scrupulously avoided where possible. What we do in indiscriminate haste to serve momentary convenience may occasion lasting difficulties and burdens later.

(e) The magnitude of the economic problem in Italy as a preface to what's ahead makes it imperative that concerted action shall not be obstructed by jurisdictional confusion and dissension in Washington or in the field.

Part Three

Chicago, Europe, Washington, and San Francisco

1944–1945

W hen Adlai E. Stevenson joined his wife and sons at Libertyville on June 14, 1944, his motivation was not solely — or even primarily — that with the death of Secretary Frank Knox he no longer had the same important responsibilities in the Navy Department. In addition, there was the possibility that he could become the publisher of Knox's Chicago Daily News.

After Colonel Knox's funeral, several Daily News employees including Stevenson's close friends Lloyd Lewis, managing editor, and Paul Scott Mowrer, editor, urged him to form a syndicate to purchase Knox's controlling stock from the estate. The opportunity rekindled Stevenson's desire for a career in journalism. Moreover, it was an opportunity to combat through the paper the isolationist views of Colonel R. R. McCormick's Tribune.

When the Daily News was sold to a higher bidder, however, Stevenson returned to government service. His old friend and law associate George Ball, who was with the Foreign Economic Administration in Washington, wrote him on June 14, 1944: "If, however, your Chicago project doesn't materialize, I certainly hope you will return to Washington. I know about some of the spots which are being offered to you both in Washington and abroad, and I feel strongly that it would be a tragedy for your services to be lost to the Government at this time, unless you can be in a position really to influence the Chicago situation." [1]

During November and December, 1944, Stevenson traveled to England and France with George Ball and others to study the effects of allied bombing on the German war effort. Shortly after Stevenson returned to Libertyville, Assistant Secretary of State Archibald MacLeish prevailed upon him to join the Department of State as special assistant to the Secretary. He worked with MacLeish in Washington and then in May, 1945, joined the American delegation at the San Francisco Conference to handle relations with American newspapermen.

[1] This letter is in the Adlai E. Stevenson collection, Princeton University Library.

The papers used in Part Three are in the Adlai E. Stevenson collection at the Princeton University Library unless otherwise indicated. We have retained Stevenson's spellings and abbreviations.

On June 27, 1944, Stevenson received a letter from Abbot Low Moffat, Department of State adviser in the Liberated Areas Division. He asked Stevenson if he would accept the post of adviser on economic matters to the U.S. embassy in China.

To Abbot Low Moffat

June 30, 1944

My dear Mr. Moffat:

Thanks for your letter.

I needed no reminders about you and your work in the Liberated Areas Division, and was much flattered by your consideration of me for the China job. I know it is an assignment of the first magnitude and it has great attraction for me.

Unhappily, I have some work on hand here that cannot be deferred and which made it necessary for me to leave Washington — at least for the present.

In the current state of affairs I cannot foretell whether I will be at large again to do some other government work for the balance of the war, but in any event I will be tied up for at least a couple of months. Should I then be free again, you can be sure I will let you know against the possibility that there may be some billet you would risk entrusting to me.

It was good of you to think of me — I appreciate it.

With warmest regards, I am

Faithfully yours,

To Lieutenant Commander Edward D. McDougal, Jr.[2]

July 6, 1944

Dear Ed:

Many thanks for your good letter and the enclosure, which gave me an entertaining moment, together with your highly appropriate and penetrating comments thereon.[3]

---

[2] The original is in the possession of Mr. McDougal.

[3] Mr. McDougal had sent Stevenson a humorous suggestion for a column in the *Daily News* should he become the publisher.

I am delighted to hear that all goes well and that the job still consumes all of your attention and enthusiasm.[4] I confess moments of acute nostalgia for Washington myself.

Things hereabouts seem normal, and I am making a little indistinct progress, I think, on my project. The employees are still enthusiastic, but the competition is keen and the money is not too conspicuous.

I shall be coming down that way one day and will look forward to a chatter with you.

Yours,
Ad

To Lieutenant Commander Edward D. McDougal, Jr.[5]

July 11, 1944

Dear Ed —

Early in June I ordered some clothes from Brooks Bros. and I believe I asked them to deliver them to Jim's house.[6] I have the bill but have never received the clothes! If there is a box of Brooks Bros. around there addressed to me, would you please forward it to St. Mary's Road, Libertyville? If it is not there, please advise me and I will look for it elsewhere.

I cannot yet report any actual progress but things are beginning to shape up and I should know what the prospects are before long. I hope all goes well with you — and thanks for having your Panama hat cleaned! I have found it a very useful substitute for my own which is undergoing similar reconditioning. But you won't need one again for a long while anyway!

Yours,
Ad

To Cyril H. Jones[7]

July 11, 1944

My dear Mr. Jones:

My own situation continues uncertain. I may stay here — depending on some developments in connection with Col. Knox's interest in the Chicago Daily News — or return to the government for the balance of

[4] Mr. McDougal was a legal assistance officer.

[5] The original is in the possession of Mr. McDougal.

[6] Stevenson and McDougal had rooms in the Georgetown house of Air Force Colonel James H. Douglas.

[7] Headmaster of Milton Academy. The original is in the possession of Milton Academy.

the war. But, meanwhile, we have about decided to send Adlai away to school in any event. Happily, he seems to be keen to go; I suspect he finds the family uncertainty quite as disconcerting as we do!

Against the remote possibility that he can still get into Milton, I am enclosing the Exeter report on his examinations. He is going to Canada with a couple of other boys from the Bell School to stay for six weeks with Mr. Bell, Jr.[8] who will tutor him in Latin, which they say (and the examination confirms it) is his worst subject. I am afraid it is hereditary!

If you could let me know whether you can accept him, the dates, etc., I promise faithfully that Mrs. Stevenson and I will not emerge from executive session until the matter is settled.

With renewed apologies and many, many thanks for your patience, I am

Sincerely yours,

To Cyril H. Jones[9]

July 24, 1944

My dear Mr. Jones:

The Stevensons and the Democrats[10] convened concurrently — but not collectively — and Milton was nominated on the first ballot.

I hope you will not regret accepting Adlai sight unseen. I am sure he will be diligent and law-abiding and that he will try hard, but I have some misgivings about his preparation after attending three different schools in the last three critical years.

If there are any additional forms or information which you, or we, should have in order to complete the arrangements and make him ready, please send them along. We will see to it that he is at the school September 18 with his loins properly girded and his lamps lighted — I hope!

You have been very considerate of our uncertainties, and we appreciate it very much.

Cordially yours,

The Democratic convention rejected the renomination of Vice President Henry A. Wallace and nominated Senator Harry S. Truman. The Republicans nominated Governor Thomas E. Dewey and Governor John Bricker. Stevenson's friend Struthers Burt, who had visited with him just

[8] Alexander C. Bell, Jr. of the Bell School in Lake Forest, Illinois (now merged with the Lake Forest Country Day School).
[9] The original is in the possession of Milton Academy.
[10] The 1944 Democratic convention.

before Truman defeated Wallace for the vice presidential nomination, expressed the hope that Wallace could be more valuable for the cause of liberalism out of that office than in it.

To Struthers Burt

August 24, 1944

Dear Struthers:

We have read and reread your wise, eloquent, and philosophical letter. I cannot take issue with you on the prospects for Wallace in the future, or his mistakes of heart and mind in the past. I don't even feel badly about his defeat in Chicago. It just seemed to me that in a way he was what this interval of history has all been about.

As for strength or weakness to the ticket, I wonder if it really made much difference. As things are turning out, for my part, I can see little more now to encourage the Republicans than I could before the convention. And Wallace or Truman have nothing to do with it!

I have little doubt that Roosevelt will have important uses for Wallace after the election and, as you say, his future utility may, if anything, be the greater.

It doesn't look like much of a show this time. Dewey will try too hard to be elected, and touch few hearts in the process, open no vistas, and comfort few but the regulars. Albert Lasker, who directed national Republican publicity for the last three or four campaigns, has withdrawn and told his friends hereabouts that he is obliged to vote for Roosevelt. It is not important, but it is significant. And I hear tell of others!

I have nothing to report on the News yet. I hope to be able to put in a bid in September but I doubt if any decision is reached before October. If I am out of it, I shall probably go back to Washington for the winter.

Ellen and the children are going East for a couple of weeks after Labor Day, and I will be in Washington for a few days. Let us know if you can stop off on your way East, and many, many thanks for your letter — and your visit. It was all profit for us.

Ellen joins me in salutations to you both.

Yours,

To Merritt A. Hewett[11]

September 6, 1944

Dear Mr. Hewett:

My wife has just given me the enclosed letter and I am replying hastily

[11] Registrar of Milton Academy. The original is in the possession of Milton Academy.

that Adlai is a conscientious, diligent boy, quite self-reliant I think but perhaps a little immature.

He is somewhat reserved and finds his own company not uncongenial. He is by no means an athlete but enjoys games and is healthy and reasonably strong, but he has grown very rapidly in the last year and a half and he seems to be awkward at this stage.

He is much interested in shooting and a fine shot for his age. His habits are normal, with a taste for reading which has not been well organized, and, as I have indicated, some tendency toward solitude. I think he is something of an introvert, but there is nothing solemn about him and he has a very lively sense of humor and comedy. I suspect he will conform to the rules and be entirely orderly without much effort.

I am afraid the foregoing is a very inadequate essay, but I hope it will serve your purpose.

With kindest regards and many thanks for all your courtesies, I am

Faithfully yours,

Edward D. McDougal, Jr. wrote Stevenson on September 25, 1944, suggesting some people who might join his syndicate to purchase the Chicago *Daily News.*

To Lieutenant Commander Edward D. McDougal, Jr.[12]

September 25, 1944

Dear Ed:

Many thanks for your letter!

I have made good progress on the money but I suspect I will not care to bid as high as some of the others and the matter is rapidly reaching a crisis, with all the bidders in town pleading their cases. I will let you know how it turns out and if it is adverse I shall probably come down there looking for something to do for the balance of the war. . . .

Best regards!

Sincerely yours,

AD

Colonel Knox's will left his entire estate to Mrs. Knox. She; H. D. Pettibone, president of the Chicago Title and Trust Company; and Laird Bell, Knox's attorney, were the three executors. The will gave

[12] The original is in the possession of Mr. McDougal.

them the discretion to sell the newspaper to anyone at whatever price they desired. The will, however, asked them to do everything possible to perpetuate the personnel and policies of the paper.

After professional appraisals, Stevenson felt justified in bidding $12 a share for the 149,941 shares of common stock. This bid was considerably lower than several others. After consulting with his investors Stevenson raised the bid to $13 per share. His old friend Hermon D. Smith, who was an investor, urged him to bid higher.

His friend Marshall Field III, publisher of the morning Chicago Sun, *offered to make up whatever balance he needed for a fair, acceptable bid. Stevenson could have outbid his rivals with this offer, but he was uneasy about having a publishing competitor, no matter how friendly to him personally, with a large stock interest.[13]*

To Hermon D. Smith[14]

October 19, 1944

Dear Dutch:

I am sending this letter to each of the people who agreed to participate in the group which I organized, at the behest of the senior employees, to acquire the Knox stock in the Daily News.

I am, of course, disappointed that the project you so generously helped finance did not succeed. As you know, it was conceived with a view to insuring the preservation of the integrity, character and traditions of the News in accordance with Col. Knox's will and not to compete on price with all other bidders.

I believe it served its purpose. It provided the executors an offer at a fair price, local ownership, earnest support from the staff and machinery for insuring continuity of the controlling interest. Other bids were substantially higher and as long as the executors found at least one of them satisfactory as far as the future of the paper was concerned, I didn't feel that I could properly ask you and the other participants to increase our offer merely to take possession of the paper by force of money alone.

As proposed publisher and using your money, you will also understand my personal reluctance to urge payment of a competitive price which I could not conscientiously recommend.

Both on my own behalf and on behalf of the members of the staff whose support encouraged me to undertake this project, I want to thank you most heartily for the confidence which your generous participation

---

[13] Kenneth S. Davis, *The Politics of Honor: A Biography of Adlai E. Stevenson* (New York: Putnam, 1967), pp. 157–158.
[14] The original is in the possession of Mr. Smith.

disclosed. I am returning your signed subscription agreement herewith and I hope to have an opportunity soon to thank you in person.

Sincerely yours,

On September 21, 1944, President Roosevelt by executive order created the Office of Foreign Economic Settlement within the Foreign Economic Administration. This new office was to "assure the proper disposition of surplus property abroad and the settlement of claims in other countries." After securing the approval of President Roosevelt, Leo Crowley, Administrator of the Foreign Economic Administration, offered the post of director of the new office to Stevenson. The Office of War Information at approximately the same time asked him to head all its overseas operations.

To Oscar S. Cox[15]

October 27, 1944

Dear Oscar:

I have given the job a lot of thought and taken altogether too much advice about my future plans! The result is that I have decided not to take on any long-term government work and to rejoin my firm some time around the first of the year. Meanwhile I am going to get my own affairs in shape and take a vacation and do a lot of those things we always plan to do and never do — I hope!

The prospect of getting back to the old routine during the war and the tumult and the shouting is not exactly exhilarating, but there are a lot of considerations and they are not wholly caution and security. I am sure you will be understanding and forgive me for all your precious time I have taken. I really wanted to try this job for a year or so. It is closer to my interests than anything I can imagine and to work with you and Mr. Crowley is not the least of its charms. Besides, I was more than a little flattered that you both thought I could do it! I will probably fall for some short-term assignment for a few weeks before the first of the year.

If I get to Washington I will hope for a moment to apologize and thank you in person, and I am writing a note to Mr. Crowley.

Yours,

On September 9, 1944, President Roosevelt signed a directive creating the U.S. Strategic Bombing Survey (USSBS). It was to measure the

[15] General counsel of the Foreign Economic Administration.

achievements of air power in the European theater of the war. Before the USSBS was created the Army Air Forces had evaluation boards to appraise the effectiveness of the air offensive.

After the September 9 directive, these evaluation boards were subordinated to the USSBS and were made responsible for the study of tactical rather than strategic bombing. Stevenson's old friend George Ball was a civilian member of the evaluation board established in Paris after the French capital was liberated in August, 1944.

In October, Ball was made a director of the USSBS to be headquartered at 20 Grosvenor Square, London. Franklin D'Olier, president of the Prudential Insurance Company, was chairman of the USSBS. While Ball served in London for the USSBS, he needed "an alter ego" for an interim period to take over his duties on the evaluation board in Paris.[16]

He phoned Adlai E. Stevenson in Libertyville and Stevenson agreed to take the assignment. Ball wrote: "Adlai tackled the more limited assignment with curiosity and resourcefulness. As always when he faced a new problem, he talked to everyone who might have information on the subject and filled dozens of yellow pages with his carefully handwritten notes. . . . His notes, gathered during his work in Paris and amplified and confirmed by the expert advice and eyewitness accounts he collected at the front, provided an invaluable addition to the store of information needed for the work of the Evaluation Board." [17]

Stevenson kept a brief diary of his mission. We have retained his own spellings and abbreviations. The ellipses are the editors'. Despite their efforts, the editors have been unable to identify a number of persons mentioned by Stevenson. The original of the diary is in the Adlai E. Stevenson collection, Princeton University Library.

---

[16] For a discussion of the USSBS see *The Army Air Forces in World War II*, Vol. II, *Europe: Torch to Pointblank, August 1942 to December 1943* (Chicago: University of Chicago Press, 1949) and Vol. III, *Europe: Argument to V–E Day, January 1944 to May 1945* (Chicago: University of Chicago Press, 1951), particularly pp. 789–792. Both volumes were prepared under the editorship of Wesley Frank Craven and James Lea Cate. George W. Ball wrote: "I had invited Adlai to help me because I was in a difficult spot. In becoming a Director of the Bombing Survey, which would be based in London, it was understood that I would continue to remain a member of the Air Force Evaluation Board, which would be based in Paris. . . . With two geographically separated jobs, I needed someone who could protect my interests in Paris while I helped organize the Bombing Survey in London." Letter to Walter Johnson, September 4, 1968.

[17] "With AES in War and Politics," in *As We Knew Adlai: The Stevenson Story by Twenty-two Friends*, edited and with preface by Edward P. Doyle, foreword by Adlai E. Stevenson III (New York: Harper & Row, 1966), p. 141.

U.S. STRATEGIC BOMBING SURVEY HQRS.
20 Grosvenor Square — London

11/2 —

Telephone from Geo. Ball to Libertyville — must be in D. C. tomorrow to leave. Dreadful last minute scramble to get off. Ellen took me to Lake Forest. Hard to say good-bye in spite of all the practice I've had. Children at school.

11/3 —

Arr. War Dept. Trip postponed until tomorrow. Physical exam . . . "Indoctrination" on job . . . talked with Ellen by phone . . . Visit with the Edgar Mowrers about [Chicago Daily] News affair; night with Ed McDougals.

11/4 —

Visit with Mr. Burling[18] to thank him for support in News venture; visit with friends in FEA; lunch with Harvey Bundy in General Staff mess at War Dept. and off to ATC [Air Transport Command] terminal with Mr. D'Olier and [Harry L.] Bowman at 2. Paper checking, weighing in, elaborate "ditching" lecture on use of life rafts etc. and off at 3:50 in C–54 Skymaster for Stephenville, Newfoundland. Our party: Franklin D'Olier, Henry Clay Alexander, Col. Guido Perara [Perera], Col. Donaho [Donahue], Geo. Ball, Fred Searls, Paul Nitze, Mr. Bowman (Pres. of Drexel Institute), Mr. Lickert, psychologist, myself and sergeant-secretary.[19] Over N.Y. in twilight, Boston in faint light — Beverly — could see beach by Carpenter's[20] house. Must have passed close to Milton and the beloved Bear.[21] Arr. Stephenville 9:15. Greeted by C.O., drinks in fine new "hotel" on field. We are advance noticed as VIPs — very important personages. Supper and off for the Azores at 10:10.

11/5 —

Couldn't get to sleep until after 3. Moonlight on the sea. Arrived

---

[18] Probably Edward E. Burling, of the Washington law firm of Covington & Burling.

[19] Mr. D'Olier was chairman of the U.S. Strategic Bombing Survey and Mr. Alexander, of the Morgan Bank, was vice chairman. The other members of the USSBS on the flight were George Ball; Fred Searls, Jr., a mining engineer; Paul Nitze, director of the U.S. Strategic Bombing Survey; Harry L. Bowman, president of Drexel Institute and director of the Physical Damage Division of the Bombing Survey; and Rensis Likert from the University of Michigan.

[20] Mrs. John Alden Carpenter, Ellen Stevenson's mother.

[21] Adlai Stevenson III was a student at Milton Academy.

Lagens airfield, Terce[i]ra (3rd) Island, about 7:15 Washington time. Breakfast but no shave. This is "bastard" field, British, U.S. Army and U.S. Navy — about 150 miles east of Horta on Fayal Island. Came in over small seaport town of Praia. Cultivated — mostly corn — right over the rough volcanic hills. Corn neatly stacked in husks in cone shaped stacks. U.S. developing large field on another island — San Miguel — military personnel must wear civilian clothes when visiting but not here because of 400 year old treaty of mutual aid between Portugal & England . . . Held up here 4¼ hrs. by magneto trouble. Off at 12 (4 PM local time) for Prestwick, Scotland, big Air Transport terminal.

Arrived Prestwick 8:15 EWT; 1:15 Greenwich time. Customs, security control etc & off in a bus for transient officers hotel along shadowy, unlighted roads. How pilot ever found the field with so few lights! To bed at 2:45 AM in a Victorian manor house converted into officers hotel.

11/6 —

Called at 5:45 — 3 hrs, in a good bed too! First war time English breakfast, Tomato juice, pancakes, bacon & coffee & off to field at 6:30. Ordered out to plane for Bovingdon field, London, at 7:30 in violent rain and wind. Drenched. Still dark. Off at 7:50. The visibility will be bad. . . . South over the Irish sea, then inland as the clouds opened. Beautiful rolling country, great manor houses, close cultivation & into Bovingdon field — 28 miles west of London at 10 . . . Drove into London; airplane traps to prevent planes from landing on broad highway as we approached city. Occasional bomb damage — much worse on east side. Billeted at Cumberland Room with Searls. Took cab to Simpson's for lunch with Searls & Nitze — the home of roast beef; had choice of curried mutton, potted hare or 'ake! Called on some Navy friends. All American military & Navy activities centered around Grosvenor square. Passed dingy looking old Connaught Hotel in nearby Carlos Place where Ellen & I stayed in May 1939. Bomb damage in Berkeley square. Hyde Park full of barracks. Meeting of mission in our room — all very tired after 2 hrs sleep. . . .

11/7 —

Election day! Busy with meetings at our offices at 20 Grosvenor Sq. Officers Club for lunch in Sir Philip Sassoon's house in Park Lane. Ran into Bud Merwin[22] on street & dined with him in his room on Upper Brook — fine lunch, fine dinner, beef both times & always potatoes, cabbage or brussel sprouts. He is just back from the landing on Walcheren Island — mouth of Schelde — awful losses on east side. Took over party

---

[22] Stevenson's cousin Loring C. Merwin, of the Bloomington *Daily Pantagraph,* was a lieutenant in the Navy.

of correspondents & went into Flushing from South. (Will take longer than expected to dredge & sweep Schelde & open Antwerp which we need so desperately to supply armies in the west). Bud didn't look too well but is interested in his work & has received commendation decoration! Must get citation and write Panta[graph].

11/8 —

Roosevelt wins! Breakfast at a Red Cross place on invitation of Mrs. Tony Biddle[23] produced by Searls. No excitement. Out to . . . hqs. at Hampton Court for conference with General Fickle.[24] Fine gent & took Ball & me back to town for a drink at his room at [Hotel] Dorchester. Dinner at Officers Club with Bill Stone and Survey people to loosen up our areas to Economic Warfare Division (Embassy) personnel, records etc. (Lunch at Senior Officer's mess in Grosvenor House. Huge junior mess known as "Willow Run.")

11/9 —

Office — struggles with organization chart etc. . . . Lunched with Lester Armour, now head of OSS [Office of Strategic Services] here while David Bruce is in France — at Buck's Club. Very old English — no smoking in dining room — saw Brendan Bracken.[25]

11/10 —

Office. Must merge AAF Evaluation Board and Survey . . . To drinks across Hyde Park in dark to Wallace Deuel's[26] house — man from Embassy, [Lieutenant Colonel] John Whitaker, Deuel, Hamilton Fish Armstrong[27] & lady. Line on Harold Nicholson's biography of Lord Curzon — "married two of the most beautiful women of his time — and richest — owned great estates, walked across all the best lawns of England etc etc, but never became Prime Minister or won the Derby and all his

[23] Margaret Thompson Biddle, wife of Anthony Joseph Drexel Biddle of Philadelphia, who ran the American Red Cross in London.

[24] Major General J. E. Fickel, the head of the Air Force evaluation board for the European Theater.

[25] The British Minister of Information.

[26] Foreign correspondent for the Chicago *Daily News* and a friend of Stevenson's from the 1930's. Deuel was in London on loan to the Department of State from the Office of Strategic Services. Mr. Deuel wrote: "With characteristic kindness, he [Stevenson] had got in touch with my wife in Westport, Conn., told her he hoped to see me in London and had ascertained how she was feeling, so that he could give me a first hand report about her and the boys and bring me any message she might wish to send. He phoned her from New York when he got back to this country, moreover, and gave *her* a report on *me*." Letter to Carol Evans, May 3, 1967. Stevenson phoned the wives of many of the people he met on his trip to London and the Continent. The list is in the Stevenson collection, Princeton University Library.

[27] Editor of *Foreign Affairs*.

victories were only proof of the injustice of his defeats." Dined with [George] Ball and Col. Beatty, Gen. Fickle's man over from France to conspire with us.

11/11 —

Lunch at Claridge's — Whitaker's party. I brough[t] Jan Masaryk.[28] Others — Deuel and Armstrong who is an advisor at Embassy. Good conversation. Masaryk is showing his age a bit and slowing up, not well, must take rest. His story about silk stockings he brought from U. S. — promptly stolen from his apt. — "has had to live in celebacy ever since." . . .

11/12 —

Sunday. Went out to Guildford to see Mildred Bailey.[29] Drove past parliament en route to Waterloo station. Little evidence of damage around Whitehall — altho Commons was destroyed and Westminster Hall hit. Much damage around station full of soldiers — Br, US, Canadian coming & going — some in full field equipment.

Milly's house at Guil[d]ford in the rain — modest old brick cottage farmstead belonging to Sir Bede Clifford whom I met in Trinidad in July 1942 — He is Governor of the colony. Guests — Lady Mida Hawkins, daughter of the Duke of Buccleugh & wife of Capt. of the cruiser Kent which just intercepted and sank many ships in German convoy off Norway. Rita Curzon-Howe, widow of former Naval attache at Washington and Lieut Patrick Best, young beau of Patricia stationed on a P.T. boat at Portsmouth. Jolly visit to a neighborhood pub. for a drink before dinner. One bottle of gin every 6 weeks is ration. Off early in morning for London.

11/13 —

Worked at Survey Office at 20 Grosvenor Sq. and saw many people until Sunday at 6 AM 11/19 when Geo. Ball and I loaded our baggage & ourselves in an overfilled truck in the darkness that seems to always accompany my military air travel. Took off from North Holt after some delay and indecision for Paris where we arrived at shattered Le Bourget at about 11. Bus into town — no damage, bread and vegetables in evidence. Constant uncomfortable feeling that "only yesterday" the Germans were everywhere as the Americans are today but Paris showed no change visibly after four years of their occupation. We found the Communications Zone Hq. in the Place de L'Opera teeming with life that seemed

[28] Son of the late president of Czechoslovakia who became Foreign Minister after the German surrender.
[29] Lady Mildred Bailey was the daughter of Colonel and Mrs. Charles Bromwell. Mrs. Letty Bromwell was a first cousin of Lewis G. Stevenson, Adlai's father.

as much the same as it did in memory — except for the fantastic hats & hair dos on the otherwise [drably?] dressed women. Lunch at the casual officer's mess in the splendid Cercle Militaire Bldg. on P. St. Augustin &, after rapid negotiation with a passerbye of exchange of chocolate bars for bottle of champagne for Gen. Fickle, we set off for St. Germain.

Quartered with Gen. Fickel in a good, tasteless house, in St. Germain. No coal, very damp & cold at 32 Rue Ann Barantin.[30] Indeed sleeping in that house was the worst discomfort I had on the whole duty. Officers in old orphans school alongside the Ecole Normale which housed the Hq. of USSTAF. Messed with latter. Very poor mess.

11/14 —

A week's work and many trips to Paris & Versailles to Shaef Hq. and others and then off early Wed. 11/23 with Gen. Fickel, helmet, gas mask, bedding roll in his car with Cpl Rosanski driving for Luxembourg. See notes on this trip in brown backed notebook.[31]

11/26 —

Saturday returned to St. Germain & went to Vice Adm. Allen Kirk's for dinner. Fine chateau. Had been used by Germans. (Maid at our house long employed by family said when I asked her how she liked the Germans who also lived there: "Ils sont gentile aussi."

11/28 —

Worked in Paris and went to cocktail party Edith Munson gave in Adm. Flanagan's[32] rooms at George V Hotel. Afterward to dinner in Allen Kirk's[33] apt. in the Navy's Hotel — Royal Marceau — with him, Gen. Salbert, Edith and Mrs. Sloane Colt. Afterward Arrabella, accordionist entertainer for GIs came up to play for us. Also Beatrice Eden, Anthony's wife, and a British lady. Very gay and home to St. Germain very late.

11/28 to 12/9 —

Saturday. More work and interviews with Army people. Must have been in most every Army office in Paris and climbed 1000 stairs. Saw Henri Bonnet — just designated Ambassador to U.S. Lunched and dined

---

[30] A few weeks before, the German generals commanding the veterinary corps were housed here — and, Stevenson strongly suspected, "their horses and other patients as well." George Ball, "With AES in War and Politics," in *As We Knew Adlai*, p. 141.

[31] He kept five pages of handwritten notes, but they were so fragmentary that the editors used none of the material.

[32] Edith (Cummings) Munson, of Chicago, was the wife of Curtis Munson, in whose house Stevenson lived in Washington, D.C. Admiral "Flanagan" may be Rear Admiral Howard Flanigan, who served as director of Naval Transport Service during the war.

[33] Vice Admiral Alan G. Kirk, Commander, U.S. Naval Forces, France.

on snails with Stoneman and Kirkpatrick.[34] Lunch with 2 caraffs of wine at Maison Inter Alleé for 3 cost them $60. Paris dreadfully expensive on the arbitrary rate of exchange of 50 frs. to $1. Went to some theatres. With no coal and frigid interiors incidence of pneumonia among chorus must be terrific! Fine performance of Faust at Opera with Gen. Fickel and Margaret was slim and pretty. I thought of Edith Mason at home — as wide as high — in the same role. Marvellous scenery & filled with soldiers of all grades.

Walking to our garret rooms in Regina Hotel from Montmartre one night with Ball and Villard [35] about 2:30 A.M. came across an MP raid on a bldg. off limits and out emerged fine assortment of Am. officers all very angry and irritable and one Britisher, quite philosophical and good humored about it all. Very entertaining performance.[36] Hope I can persuade Foreign Service to stand by the Chicago Daily News, at least for present.[37]

12/9 —

Set off with [General] Fickel, Capt. Hewitt, fighter pilot, in the Gen's Car for Spa, via Reims, Sedan and the Ardennes Forest in a snowstorm. Like fairyland. Will never forget that lovely winter scene — with the lines only a few miles east. Went first to Maj. Gen. [Elwood] Quesada's Hq. at Verniers — 9th Tactical Airforce. Found the well known flyer and gallant, dynamic, cordial, good looking and full of ideas expressed with difficulty on tactical support of ground forces. Back to Spa and fine din-

---

[34] William Stoneman and Helen Kirkpatrick, foreign correspondents for the Chicago *Daily News*.

[35] Unable to identify.

[36] George Ball described the scene: "We were walking in the vicinity of the Place Vendôme — appropriately enough, as Adlai observed, on the rue Casanova — when we encountered American military police raiding an off-limits house. Field- and company-grade officers were debouching into the street in maximum disarray, protesting with spleen and outraged innocence at the affront to their dignity.

"Adlai and I, although civilians, were in uniform (we each had the assimilated rank of colonel) and hence were indistinguishable from the culprits. This created a situation of some hazard, for Adlai was enchanted with the spectacle of so many chagrined and choleric officers 'whose expectations and consummations,' as he said, had been abruptly interrupted. He insisted on seeing the show, and at least twice his curiosity led him so far into the crowd that he found himself shoved into a paddy wagon. It took all the advocacy my colleague and I could muster to establish Stevenson as a noncombatant and save him from the indiscriminate sanctions of military justice.

"It was the kind of absurd situation he thoroughly enjoyed. Thereafter in my presence on several occasions he repeated the story with imaginative embellishment — generously substituting me for himself as the epic figure rescued from incarceration." "With AES in War and Politics," in *As We Knew Adlai*, p. 142.

[37] Actually, a number of the foreign correspondents for the Chicago *Daily News*, as well as such editors as Paul Scott Mowrer and Lloyd Lewis, left the paper under publisher John Knight, who bought it over Stevenson's bid.

ner in his very fine house which belonged to the collaborationist proprietor of the Casino. Whitney Bourne, Red Cross & daughter of Mrs. Nancy Gibson, also there.

(12/1 Message to Ellen about our anniversary. No assurances when it will arrive!)

12/10 —

Attended briefing of Gen. [Courtney H.] Hodges at First Army Hq. in Hotel Brittanique. Very impressive. Off to front with Col. Morgan, Quesada's air support officer as guide, thru Eupen past "You are entering Germany!" sign, thru the dragons teeth of the Si[e]gfried line to Karnelimunster and Hq. of 7th Corps — Gen. [J. Lawton] Collins — for lunch. The big push is on and he is out at Division CPs. Much sup[p]ressed excitement and nervousness. The town was a rest camp and selective breeding place for the super race. Listened to talk between planes in the air over Germany and fighter controller. On to Aachen and thru the utter ruins of that ancient city of 150 000 and out on the bloody broad autobahn to Eischweiler past woods shattered with shell fire and thru shell pocked sodden ground. Every foxhole & every crater level with water. Eischwe[i]ler wrecked — conf. with Gen. Terry Allen of 104th Inf. attacking Duren in his forward CO in the basement of a "bank." Artillery banging away on all sides. Lines several miles further east. No inhabitants about altho they say some 6–12 000 are in back in the cellers of Aachen. Souvenir hunt thru adjoin[in]g little shops and houses. Nothing of interest except the quantities of home preserves. Flight evidently very quick.

Back to Verviers and Spa via Statberg. Had dinner as guest of proprietor of Hotel Cardinal and her son whom [William] Stoneman got released from jail as suspected collaborator. This is their farewell thanks to him. He is leaving for Paris, London & home to consult [John] Knight on future of [Chicago Daily] News foreign Service in accordance with my advice. . . . Such a dinner — 3 wines, meats, pheasant and Perderau, coffee, cigars. "Belgians are the technicists of occupation." Didn't sell their precious olive oil etc etc to the hated Germans at double the price. Stories of the German occupation and 24 hr. service of the German Army girls here in Spa where troops come to rest. If girl had VD *she* was punished. All part of Army and paid by Army etc.

12/11 —

Briefing at Gen. Hodges with Gen. [Omar] Bradley of 12th Army Group and Gen. [William H.] Simpson of 9th Army also present. Very, very impressive. Then on tour of radar installations for controlling our own planes and tracking enemy. Witnessed experiment in blind bombing by automatic radar release of bombs. Not too successful; controller a little nervous and leaders plane evidently didnot have automatic release.

On to Liege after lunch and farewells at Verviers . . .

Considerable damage in Liege from recent heavy fly[?] bomb attack. Along densely populated and heavily industrialized Meuse to Namur which we reached at last light. Comfortable night in officers of Ad Sec [Administrative Section] — Com Z. Hotel.

12/12 —

Spent morning talking with Ad Sec. people about engineering and transport problems in battle of France and subsequent. Lunch at their Hq. in Belgian West Point and on to Brussels via Waterloo. Taken in nicely by fast talking old Belgian woman souvenir salesman. Studied the great panorama with the old guide long and well. Said he refused to show the Germans and had had a 4 year vacation!

On to Brussels and conf. with Gen. [George] Erskine . . . of the Shaef mission to Belgium. Quiet dinner & HOT bath in the old Astoria Hotel in the quiet and refined atmosphere of senior English officers. Was to[o] tired to take a walk after dinner in the blackout.

12/13 —

Morning with the Shaef Mission people re Survey and Board work in Belgium. Difficulty finding . . . airport to get plane to London. Persuaded the Gen. to go with me — those 2 stars are so useful! — passed huge concentrations of M T in the parks. I guess Gen. [Bernard] Montgomery is gathering together his insurance of success as usual. Story of Churchill's comment on the unhappy plight of the German Gen. . . . taken prisoner in Africa after El Alamein — "Poor, wretched man had lost his battle, his division, his honor etc — and then had the melancholy missfortune to have to dine with Monty."

At airport advised no plane to London — fogged in. Agreed to go to Broadwell near Swinden [Swindon], 90 miles from London. Finally off in an RAF litter C47 with a Canadian crew at 2:45 from a nearby field. Belgium and France mostly clear. Beaches near Calais most intensive bombing effects I've yet seen — not craters — but one intermingled crater for miles along coast. England utterly fogbound — Later told "by far worst fog in 1944." Couldn't get into North Holt, ordered to Bradwell, just as bad, ordered to Adium (!); no beam equip. on our plane. Sun low, only 35 minutes of gas left. To get to South Coast would take 25 — then what if we couldn't find a field and lost our day light? Pilot spotted fragment of runway thru aperature in fog and sat her down quickly & without accident miraculously. It was Harwell an RAF training station.

Tea! No customs or immigration formalities & then a 5 mile bus ride to Didcot thru the fog. Took 50 minutes. Train to Reading; changed & stood up all the way to Paddington. No cabs because of fog. Struggled with our luggage thru the metro to Marble Arch & collapsed in the Cumberland Hotel — after a sandwich and a beer — about 12:30. Fickle said the flying experience was his worst, and as the senior general of the Air Corps, he ought to know!

And this is as far as this little diary got!

On December 16, 1944, a quarter of a million of Germany's best troops struck in the Ardennes. Over the next few days a great bulge, forty-five miles long and sixty-five miles deep, was being cut into the Allied lines. It was not until the middle of January that the Ardennes salient was reduced, and Allied forces could once again plan their assault on Germany.

In a speech in 1947, Adlai E. Stevenson mentioned that he had heard no word about any German attack in any of the briefings he had had at the front. But back in London:

> It was hard to do any work and hard to get any information the next few days. [General] Hodges had moved his whole headquarters, thousands of men, convoys of equipment out of Spa overnight. Even the press officers were carrying rifles and side arms. A German tank column had reached Roquefort in the heart of the forest — it had been so beautiful and still, with a soft snow on the trees, and I knew how thin our line was from Luxembourg north to Malmedy.
>
> But I reached Chicago Christmas eve, after a little involuntary rest in Iceland, and heard the Battle of the Bulge on WGN.[38] Perhaps if it hadn't been for that narrow escape and for that last look see at the war from Holland to Metz, I would have said no and kept on saying it when Stettinius[39] asked me to come to the State Department in February. I did say no a few times, but Archie MacLeish was too much for me.[40]

On January 16, 1945, Archibald MacLeish, former Librarian of Congress and by now Assistant Secretary of State for Public and Cultural

[38] The Chicago *Tribune*'s radio station.
[39] Secretary of State Edward R. Stettinius, Jr.
[40] Speech to the Commonwealth Club of Chicago, January 22, 1947.

Relations, wrote Stevenson, "I have felt since the days of the Committee on War Information that you were one of the most valuable men in this Government. . . . In that difficult, confused, and rather desperate first year of the war, there were about a dozen men in Washington who seemed to me to be irreplaceable. You were one of them." MacLeish then added: "I felt at the time your resignation from the Government was a disaster. I feel the same thing now."

MacLeish explained that President Roosevelt and Edward R. Stettinius, Jr., who had become Secretary of State on December 1, 1944, were determined to improve the relations of the Department of State with the American people. The post that MacLeish wanted Stevenson to fill "is a job tailored to measure for you. The job is, first, to give the people of this country the information about public affairs they need to have in order to form a foreign policy which will produce the peace which alone will justify this war — and which alone will preserve us from another war to follow; second, to create, in a world in which communication has been interrupted and suppressed and blanketed by the war and by the conquests of our enemies, the kind of communication between peoples which is essential to the understanding on which, and on which alone, a true peace can be built."

In order to carry out his responsibilities, MacLeish told Stevenson, "I need far more assistance than I have, and, above all, I need the assistance and the counsel and the collaboration and the advice of a man who believes what you believe, who sees the problems as you see them, and who has had your experience, both of this country and of this Government."

A week later the Secretary of State wrote Stevenson, "If there is any possible way in which you can arrange your affairs to join us in the Department, move Heaven and earth to do so."

To Archibald MacLeish

January 25, 1945

Dear Archie:

This is the hardest letter I've ever written! The answer is no. You are altogether too good and too persuasive and perhaps I'm just trying to fortify myself by resisting the greatest temptation so that my small vices won't seem worth resisting. But then there is my decision to come home and discharge some of my obligations to my family — and, incidentally, make a living again.

I'm struggling languidly to get long neglected personal affairs in order. Then I suppose some day I'll rejoin my old law firm. And with this nice, orderly program barely launched you haul off and write me that letter. It ain't fair — it ain't even humane. Kamerad! It's hard enough to dedicate one's overvalued life to corporate sterilities in this tormented world without estimable people weaving distracting spells; even poking at a torpid conscience!

Besides, who knows, maybe some time the young will wander off and then the weaver and I, sound and sober if slightly aged, can wander back to those lowland pastures where the great foregather and find a small place again near the circle's edge. Don't say, "It will be too late — now is the time!" because you might be right and I would rather not think of that just now.

You have my thanks and top place among my many creditors. And don't think I underestimate the job you have or the opportunity you have offered me. . . .

Yours,

P.S. Reading this over leaves me as confused as you will be. In short, I want to come but I don't feel I should.

To Mrs. Ernest L. Ives[41]

January 31, 1945

Dear Buff —

Please ask Ernest to send me all the information for deductions for your 1944 income tax return as soon as he can and also Form 1040F for Paint Hill.[42] If you should receive from the First National Bank their income tax information report for 1944 please send it along to me promptly. It is due about this time. I am very anxious to get this income tax job done up as far in advance this year as possible.

Your letter was most informative and I was glad to have all the news. I had not heard of Lydiard's death[43] until I read about it in the Panta-[graph]. I knew you had great affection for him and losses like that that look back so many years and reawake so many nostalgic memories are hard to take, but there will be more and more of them as we get older and one certainly has to be philosophic — or in tears all the while!

I don't know what to say about this wretched smoking habit. I think it's diabolical and wish to hell I had had the character to resist the temptation to start when I went off to college in the Navy and everyone was doing it. I've come to admire my friends who don't smoke more and

41 This handwritten letter is in the Elizabeth Stevenson Ives collection, Illinois State Historical Library.
42 The Iveses' farm in Southern Pines, North Carolina.
43 Lydiard Horton, a family friend who had lived for a time in Bloomington.

more — it reveals to me a degree of self possession and strength that seems wholly admirable and I am sure that for normally nervous people, who seldom can do it in moderation, it is a curse — by moderation I mean as a social thing rather than a habit. Ellen has promised each of our boys $1000 when they are 21 if they don't smoke. I don't think that bribery idea is too good, but I don't know a better alternative, except example, and constant deprecation — which isn't very persuasive if you do it yourself. But if he is self conscious about it and feels he has to know how because the others do, rather than be different and not do it, then I think Tim [Ives] certainly did it the manly way. So much of what seems sissy and unconventional as a boy — be it not smoking, hard work, intellectual precociousness etc — quickly become assets as a man.

I am glad you had a good trip to N. Y. It must have been a great lark for Tim. Ad.[44] has a long week-end after exams this week and is going to N.Y. with Betty.[45] We had hoped to show him N.Y. for the first time ourselves. You're lucky to have some solution at least of the servant problem. Ellen is still doing all the cooking, beds, cleaning (?) etc. and we haven't yet anyone regular to help her. But getting up at 7 and working to 10 each night seems to give her a lot of satisfaction and I hope and pray that she can stand the pace until something turns up.

I don't like to see you spend any more money on that place — I doubt if you ever get it out. But perhaps after the war the community will look up a bit and be a more agreeable place to live.

I didn't have time to talk to the real estate people about the house while I was in Bloom[ington]. and if you prefer to postpone final sale until you get back there this summer and can investigate it a little more, its OK with me. You should keep a file of some kind in which you keep all data about expenses of repair and improvement of the place. I don't mean operating expenses, but some data to show how much it represents in added investment since you inherited it. That information will be essential and perhaps worth considerable money some day when you sell the place or die. Also I think you should begin to give up to $5000 annually to Tim to keep your estate down. Series E War bonds are a good way to do it for the present — or any gov. bonds. I'll suggest to [Stephen] Hord the next time I see him that you transfer $5000 of bonds to him out of your account for this year if you approve. I think Tim already has some securities. What are they and where are they? Do I have them among your papers in my box?

As for myself I don't yet know what I'm going to do. I thought I would come back here & practice law, but there is not much incentive to make

[44] Adlai Stevenson III.
[45] Mrs. Robert Pirie, Stevenson's sister-in-law.

more money under the present tax rates and it would preclude any activity if not any interest in public affairs — at least in this office under the present management. Meanwhile I'm bedevilled with propositions from Wash. and latterly Ed Stettinius and Archie Mac Leish have put the heat on to come to the State Dept. to help with the information program — or at least temporarily until the Senate ratifies Dumbarton Oaks.[46] It's a temptation to do some more of the things I believe in, but meanwhile procrastination about getting back in the groove here is doing me no good professionally. I dread the thought of moving back to Washington for an indefinite period — the present difficulties and the uncertainty of what lies beyond. I don't know what to do and I feel like a fool to be so indecisive. I'm going down to Wash. next [week?] to talk things over with people and I'm not sure whether I hope I'll fall for something or hope I won't! . . .

We're making a little progress at long last on the radio station in Bloom[ington]. Its too tentative yet to have any confidence that something might be worked out to enable us to buy at least a half interest, but at least their disposition to talk and talk in reasonable figures is encouraging.

Best love,

AD

After Adlai E. Stevenson talked to Archibald MacLeish in Washington — the Secretary of State was with President Roosevelt at the Yalta Conference — MacLeish wired Stevenson on February 12, 1945, that he was writing the latter's senior law partner about the need for Stevenson in the Department of State. MacLeish added: "Will you let me know what reaction you hear from Mr. [William Pratt] Sidley."

Stevenson wired back: "Will report next Tuesday I hope. You'll be sorry! Regards."

On February 23, 1945, Acting Secretary of State Joseph C. Grew announced that Stevenson had joined the department as a special assistant to the Secretary of State to work with Assistant Secretary Archibald MacLeish "in matters relating to postwar international organization."

---

[46] On January 29, 1945, MacLeish had sent Stevenson a telegram: "Please wire me that you are coming and soon." At Dumbarton Oaks, a private estate in Washington, D.C., representatives of the United States, the United Kingdom, and the Soviet Union met during August and September, 1944, to draft proposals for a constitution of a world organization. The proposals were formally approved by Roosevelt, Churchill, and Stalin at the Yalta Conference, February 4–11, 1945, and became the basis for the discussions at the San Francisco Conference which opened April 25, 1945.

And, at this point, Adlai E. Stevenson commenced his "most intensive postgraduate education." [47]

MacLeish and Stevenson launched a public relations campaign to rally support from the public for the Dumbarton Oaks proposals. They distributed a documentary film; produced a radio discussion series, "Building the Peace"; and arranged for the publication of four pamphlets which were widely distributed by private voluntary organizations.

They did so well that by May, Senator Robert A. Taft charged the Administration with "superpropaganda . . . aimed at Congress." By late April letters to the Department of State on international organization had jumped from five hundred a day to over five thousand. Edwin A. Lahey wrote in the Chicago Daily News, *April 12, 1945: "MacLeish, with the valuable assistance of Adlai Stevenson of Chicago, is making the people of this country State Department conscious. . . . This kind of mail certainly indicates an awakened public interest in the function of the State Department, which is to wage peace. It is no small tribute to the performance of MacLeish and Stevenson."*

Stevenson said in a speech two years later: "I don't know how successful it was but without spending any money, because we didn't have any, we put out so much stuff on the air, in the press and motion pictures and lecture platforms that we got roundly attacked in Congress by an assortment of ostriches — so I guess we did pretty well in two months." [48]

To Walter Lippmann[49]

February 26, 1945

Dear Walter:

I was "in conference" with some State Department people until later Sunday afternoon — and too late to get to your house.

I am more than disappointed and look forward to seeing you soon. Perhaps you will let me know when you are free for lunch some day.

Yours,

ADLAI

---

[47] *Major Campaign Speeches of Adlai E. Stevenson, 1952,* with an introduction by the author (New York: Random House, 1953), p. xx.

[48] Speech to the Commonwealth Club of Chicago, January 22, 1947. See Robert A. Divine, *Second Chance: The Triumph of Internationalism in America During World War II* (New York: Atheneum, 1967), p. 283.

[49] The original is in the Walter Lippmann papers, Yale University Library.

To Archibald MacLeish[50]

February 26, 1945

We *must* get organized so that you will have to spend *no* time on administrative details of San Francisco, both before and during the Conference.

1) You are responsible for the formulation and approval of the policy generally.

2) McDermott's[51] office should, in my cpinion, be responsible for detailed execution of that policy.

3) As he is not adequately staffed and no preparations have been made, I suggest you start the ball rolling by laying the whole problem before a meeting of —

Elmer Davis[52]
Jonathan Daniels[53]
Representative of McDermott —

with a view to finding someone to buttress McDermott on planning and execution. Paul Porter[54] could be consulted.

The United Nations Conference on International Organization convened in San Francisco on April 25, 1945, with nearly three hundred delegates representing fifty nations. In addition to the technical staffs and secretariat, an enormous press and radio corps — over twenty-five hundred — reported the proceedings.[55]

Secretary of State Edward R. Stettinius, Jr., was head of the United States delegation. His position at San Francisco was difficult. He was aware — as were others — that President Harry S. Truman had decided to appoint James F. Byrnes as Secretary of State after the close of the conference.

To Mrs. Ernest L. Ives

April 19, 1945

Dear Buffy:

It has been a hectic week. I have no certainty of the future here, but

[50] The original is in the Archibald MacLeish papers, Library of Congress.
[51] Michael J. McDermott, State Department press officer.
[52] Director of the Office of War Information.
[53] Administrative assistant to President Roosevelt.
[54] Chairman of the Federal Communications Commission.
[55] Ruth B. Russell and Jeannette E. Muther, *A History of the United Nations Charter: The Role of the United States 1940–1945* (Washington: Brookings Institution, 1958), p. 625.

it has little effect on me in view of my plans. I had lunch with Ed Austin[56] on Saturday, and I think it may be possible now to work out an entirely satisfactory arrangement with the firm which would give me more freedom than I previously thought was possible. Ellen's visit was a great success,[57] but we are as far as ever from definitive summer plans in view of my uncertainties.

Archie [MacLeish] left yesterday for the West Coast and will probably be there the first week of the Conference, and when he returns, I will go out. I'll try to keep you advised of my plans when I know what they are more definitely. . . .

I will let you hear further about the tax bills when the receipts are returned for the '44 tax. I think there is something wrong, and maybe we have been paying the personal property tax twice.

I had a visit from Ernest's devoted friend, Louis Dreyfus, one day this week. He is our Minister in Iceland and was on his way back after a brief visit with his sick mother in California.

Love,

P.S. I've paid the 1944 personal property tax bill from our joint farm account, i.e. 50–50.

P.S.S. *Very confidentially* I think Ed. Stet[tinius]. will have to go sometime later this summer. The politicians don't like to have an heir apparent to the Presidency who is not a regular democrat & Ed. of course has no democratic political background. But its imperative to hush this talk about his going now so as not to undermine his leadership with the foreigners. I suppose Byrnes will succeed ultimately — but I don't know. I still want to get home this summer if I can.

To Lieutenant Loring C. Merwin

April 23, 1945

Dear Bud:

. . . a lot of people have heard about the *Pantagraph* for the first time, and with a few of the more literate, I have lived of late in Art's reflected glory. His book, as you know, has received very flattering reviews (New York *Times* enclosed).[58]

I am working on sort of a temporary deal with Archie MacLeish and doing chores for Stettinius. They are old friends, and I agreed to help if

---

[56] Senior partner in Stevenson's law firm in Chicago.
[57] Mrs. Stevenson and the boys were living in Libertyville.
[58] While Mr. Merwin was in the Navy, Arthur Moore ran the *Daily Pantagraph*. He had just published *The Farmer and the Rest of Us* (Boston: Little, Brown, 1945).

I could for a few months. It has been interesting, and I hope, useful, but I expect to get home for keeps this summer — it has been four years now and it's high time. I'll be going to San Francisco for the Conference, but I am afraid it is going to be accompanied with a distasteful amount of work. My allergy for work is getting progressively worse as this long drill in Washington gets longer. I hope all is well on Little Brook Street [London], and I daresay you will not be too disappointed if you miss the streets of Guam, but don't count too much on the rapidity of the clean-up out there.

Yours,

At the San Francisco Conference, Secretary of State Edward R. Stettinius, Jr., was in a nearly impossible position. Not only was he aware that James F. Byrnes was to replace him, but he had difficulties with the American delegation — Senator Tom Connally, Senator Arthur H. Vandenberg, Congressman Sol Bloom, Congressman Charles A. Eaton, former Governor Harold E. Stassen, and Virginia C. Gildersleeve, dean of Barnard College. They were individualists with no experience in delegation teamwork. Two of the members were possible presidential candidates. While the delegation supported Stettinius at public sessions of the conference, in private several members disparaged him. And Senator Vandenberg and others refused to authorize Stettinius to speak to newspapermen on behalf of the delegation. Moreover, in the early days of the conference, the delegation, after each morning's session, could not agree on a statement to issue to the press. As a result, American correspondents went to the British and French delegations to find out the American position on a number of questions. And the American newspapermen became increasingly critical of Stettinius.

Arthur Krock told Stettinius that someone had to be appointed to brief the reporters, even if it was only an unofficial spokesman whom the delegation might repudiate. Krock insisted that the spokesman had to be a person trusted by the correspondents. He suggested Adlai E. Stevenson and Thomas K. Finletter. On May 10, 1945, Stettinius assigned Stevenson the task. Before he arrived in San Francisco, Finletter and Edward Miller — representing private groups affiliated with the American delegation as consultants — got the "leak" office working.[59] It was called Op-

[59] Arthur Krock, interview with Walter Johnson, November 20, 1966; Thomas K. Finletter, interview with Walter Johnson, April 14, 1967. See also Walter Johnson, "Edward R. Stettinius, Jr., 1944–1945," in *An Uncertain Tradition: American Secretaries of State in the Twentieth Century*, edited by Norman A. Graebner (New York: McGraw-Hill, 1961), pp. 220–221. Adlai E. Stevenson read a draft of this chapter in November, 1959, and added useful material on Stettinius at the conference.

eration Titanic. Stevenson attended the delegation meetings and also meetings of Stettinius with the heads of the British, Russian, French, and Chinese delegations. He then used his own judgment about what to say to the reporters who were admitted to the "leak" office. He later wrote: "My job was to disclose what information about the American position to the press I felt could be and should be disclosed each day, in view of the impossibility of getting agreement . . . on any formal communique." [60]

To Archibald MacLeish [61]

May 16, 1945

Dear Archie:

. . . "Operation Titanic" is operating like hell! It's a good thing you got out of town before you got smeared with any responsibility for this thing. [62]

Yours,

AES

P.S. Your wire just received. The press conf. on human rights was O K — a little lame on the questions — but quite satisfactory method and the published statement was very good. Ed's talk with the consultants in the afternoon was also very good if not enlightening. I've talked with several of them & I think his status is O K — if not enthusiastic. The conference is pressing hard on the heels of the U. S. Deleg. which is behind the procession but catching up now that regionalism is out of the way (?), with the help of morning and evening meetings of the delegation. We've really put in some effective lids on the press but, what with the customers dropping in all day, its becoming increasingly difficult to keep abreast of developments all across the front. Ed. was much disturbed by the N.Y. Times story implying that Truman was entitled to the credit on regionalism. I've corrected that here and there. Stassen did a beautiful job on trusteeship at the Press conf. yesterday and for the consultants in the P M. The contrast on substantive knowledge is too apparent, but there's growing realization that E. S. has a "lot to do," what

---

[60] Letter to Cornelia Meigs, May 30, 1958. Stevenson made longhand notes of the various meetings he attended. There are approximately two hundred pages of these notes. They explain the stand on specific questions of various delegates. But they throw no light on his own thinking and we therefore have not reproduced them.

[61] The original is in the Archibald MacLeish papers, Library of Congress.

[62] Thomas K. Finletter has remarked that Stevenson "did not like the surreptitious nature" of the operation. "It wasn't his dish of tea." Interview with Walter Johnson, April 14, 1967.

with all the negotiations and the incessant meetings in the Pent House.

I understand you approve our Monday broadcast report to the nation combined with plug for trade agreements. God knows how we're going to get the thing written properly. I'd like to give a hand to it but its impossible to do that and Titanic too.

Call any time. I'm usually in after the delegation meeting adjourns at 10:30 for the rest of the day.

Hastily
AES

To Edward R. Stettinius, Jr.

May 21, 1945

MEMORANDUM TO THE SECRETARY OF STATE

In view of some misapprehension expressed in the Delegation with reference to "verbatim" reports of Committee meetings which have appeared in the papers in the last day or so, I want to report the results of a hasty investigation:

1. The [John H.] Crider story appearing in Sunday's New York *Times* on the proceedings in Committee III/1 on voting procedure was reported by Evatt[63] in full detail to the *Times* immediately after the Committee meeting Friday night.

2. After the meeting of the Trusteeships Committee on Thursday, at which Mr. Fraser[64] complained of news leakage from committees, the *Call Bulletin,* within three hours, carried a full account of the proceedings with quoted ex[c]erpts from the debate. The *Call Bulletin* has never asked or received any information from the American Delegation about Committee or other meetings.

3. Crider of the *Times* wrote a story on Sunday on "full employment" from which he read ex[c]erpts to Finletter and myself. It was tantamount to a report of implacable United States opposition to full employment as an objective. I told him that the American Delegation was *not* opposed to the objective of full employment, but that it was concerned with the implication in the language of Chapter IX, Section A, Paragraph 1 that the world organization could promote full employment by interference in our domestic affairs, and that the Delegation wished, if possible, to rearrange the language to eliminate any such implication. I also suggested that "full employment" in itself was a meaningless phrase in that it gave no indication of wage levels, etc.

63 Australian Foreign Minister Herbert V. Evatt.
64 New Zealand Foreign Minister Peter Fraser.

Archie —

For your information — I sent this to Ed. as an excuse for sending copies to the other members of the delegation —

AES

In 1947, Adlai E. Stevenson described his work at the San Francisco Conference:

My job was to act as spokesman for the United States Delegation and sub rosa to conduct an underground news leakage office for the U. S. press. It was all a little ridiculous — me interpreting developments play by play in a secret room in the Fairmont Hotel, whose number was known to not less than 50–75 U. S. correspondents, when I had only a primary education in the charter. But the newspapermen didn't know much either and besides they couldn't get into the meetings and I had a whole staff of observers telephoning in synopses of what was going on. Anyway, it worked and the American position began to get out in more accurate form and the American press didn't have to get their news from British, French and Chinese sources any longer.

We slipped as the newsmen slipped a few times. Once the American position was published in the N. Y. Times wire photo edition in S. F. before the Delegation had even acted! On these occasions there was always hell to pay in the Delegation meeting.[65] The Secretary and the senators would get apople[c]tic with rage and make speeches about the flannel mouthed staff or look at one another suspiciously or threaten to call the President, while I cowered in my corner in abject terror, timidly proclaiming my innocence. But as they filed out of the room after the meeting I always had an approving wink from [Arthur] Vandenberg and [Harold] Stassen. And it became S O P [standard operating procedure] for Stettinius once a week to read me a burning lecture somewhere on the essential importance of absolute secrecy about delegation and Big 5 meetings in the famous penthouse on top of the Fairmont. But these admonitions were always reserved for the presence of certain U. S. delegates and afterward we went into his bedroom for a drink and a review of "Operation Titanic" as it was called — whether I needed more help, what such and such a section of the press was saying and could I get out a little more in this direction or that.[66]

[65] For the proceedings of these delegation meetings see *Foreign Relations of the United States, Diplomatic Papers 1945*, Vol. I, *General: The United Nations* (Washington: Government Printing Office, 1967). For references to Stevenson see pp. 797, 804, 830–831, 906, 977, 1054, 1092, 1106, 1117, 1129, 1145, 1266, 1279, 1365, 1391.

[66] Speech to the Commonwealth Club of Chicago, January 22, 1947.

Occasionally the rather complete diary that Secretary of State Stettinius kept during the San Francisco Conference reflects some of the difficulties Adlai E. Stevenson had in his role between the U.S. delegation and the newspapermen. On June 3, 1945, when the heads of the Big Five could not reach an agreement and reporters were pressing for information about these private discussions, Stettinius wrote: "Meanwhile Mr. Stevenson had been looking askance at the differences of opinion and the prospects that no statement whatsoever would be forthcoming. Lord Halifax pointed out sympathetically, 'We are asking Mr. Stevenson to make bricks without straw, you know.'" [67]

On June 4, 1945, when the Big Five could not agree, Stettinius wrote: "As the meeting closed, Mr. Adlai Stevenson, who was denied permission to make a formal press release on deliberations of the American Delegation, complained that anything that happened in the Big Five meetings 'leak[s] out of that room quicker than I can get out.'" On June 23, 1945, as the conference neared its close, Stettinius gave Stevenson a present and wrote: "Your keen understanding of the goals and aims of the Conference has fitted you well for the task of helping to keep the press informed and advised of our deliberations. On numerous occasions my staff has informed me of the high value which many individual members of the press have placed upon your assistance and counsel." [68]

To Edward R. Stettinius, Jr.[69]

June 29, 1945

Dear Ed:

I want to thank you from the bottom of my heart for the beautiful bowl — not only the bowl, but the extravagant recognition of my small services. I will cherish it always, and I should really be sending you a symbol of my gratitude for the opportunity you gave me. I hope it won't be the last opportunity you give me to be of any possible assistance to you at any time — and I almost added, *anywhere!*

Faithfully yours,

En route from San Francisco to Washington, Stevenson visited in Chicago and spoke to the annual meeting of the Chicago Bar Association on June 28, 1945.[70]

[67] The Stettinius diary is in the University of Virginia Library.
[68] These letters are in the Stettinius papers, University of Virginia Library.
[69] The original is in the Stettinius papers, University of Virginia Library.
[70] The last four pages of this speech were published in the Bloomington *Daily Pantagraph*, July 15, 1945.

Mr. Chairman:

I had the good fortune to be invited to sit with the American representatives at the Big Five meetings in San Francisco where I heard for the first time Lord Halifax's familiar figure of speech — he said one day, "Mr. Chairman, I am more than a little impressed with what just fell from Monsieur Paul-Boncour."

And I, Mr. Chairman, am more than a little impressed with what just fell from you. Perhaps "depressed" would be better, because I have neither the talents and qualifications which you have suggested, nor have I the thoughtful, well-prepared speech which this historic Conference and this distinguished and discriminating gathering of my fellows at the Chicago Bar deserve.

Rather I have recorded hastily some desultory thoughts which I hope may be of some slight interest to you as background, if you please, for the Senate's consideration of the Charter of the United Nations which commenced with Senator [Tom] Connally's speech this afternoon, and which will continue with hearings before the Senate Foreign Relations Committee next week, and thence to debate on the floor, without interruption we hope.

Speaking of the Senate Foreign Relations Committee, you will be amused by a fragment of conversation I heard at a party one night when a French delegate asked Sol Bloom a member of our delegation and chairman of the House Foreign Affairs Committee, why in the Senate it was called the Foreign Relations Committee and in the House it was called the Foreign Affairs Committee. Congressman Bloom replied that it was because the Senate was too old to have affairs. I'll admit it's an old joke, but I'm not sure whether the Frenchman laughed or marvelled at the sophisticated delicacy of our parliamentary practices.

My primary job was to try to keep the American working press assigned to cover the American delegation informed accurately, promptly, and as fully as possible consistent with the best interests of our negotiations and the conduct of the business of the Conference. I was, of course, in constant trouble with complaints of indiscretion on the one hand and too much discretion on the other. I don't know yet whether my office was a positive menace or not — I suspect there is substantial reliable opinion on both sides — but certainly when I arrived a couple of weeks after the Conference started, the situation was deplorable both for the press and for the delegates. The delegates were heavily outnumbred and the newspaper men, without other sources of information, pursued them like a cloud of mosquitos. . . .

There were, as you know, 50 nations represented at San Francisco by 285 delegates and some 1,450 advisors and technical staff. The accredited representatives of the press, radio, and newsreels numbered 2,600. The office of the Secretary General included more than 1,000. In all, almost 10,000 people were involved on a full-time basis. The average daily output of printed or mimeographed material by the International Secretariat was 500,000 pages — with a high for any one day of 1,700,000. The press filed an average of 150,000 words a day. The New York Post printed and sold a daily San Francisco edition, and the New York Times published a wire-photo edition, and distributed *gratis* 3,000 copies daily at a cost to the Times of about 50¢ a copy. It was a remarkable demonstration of future possibilities in newspaper-making.

The Conference was divided into four commissions: one on General Provisions; one on the General Assembly; one on the Security Council; and one on Judicial Organization. The commissions, in turn, were divided into committees. For example, Commission III on the Security Council had committees on

> Structure and Procedures,
> Peaceful Settlement,
> Enforcement Arrangements, and
> Regional Arrangements —

and, of course, there were many subcommittees of the various committees.

The Conference in Plenary Session was the top body, and the Conference was managed by a Steering Committee comprising the heads of each delegation, of which the Secretary of State was chairman. He was also chairman of the Executive Committee of the Steering Committee, which included the chiefs of 14 delegations and was the working managing body.

The work of debate and drafting was done in the committees and their subcommittees. They reported their work to the Commissions for approval, and from the Commissions the approved articles went to a Coordinating Committee to coordinate the document as a whole, and thence to the Plenary Session for final approval.

There were interminable debates about procedure and the jurisdiction of various committees, and, if you are impressed with the ponderous magnitude of the whole thing, let me ask you also to reflect on the fact that every word spoken in a meeting had to be translated into at least one other language, and frequently two — every English word into French, and every French word into English; and every Spanish or Russian word into both English and French. But translation has its compensations and I suspect many a hot word cooled while the interpreter droned on. . . .

This, then, was the setting in which 50 nations of different colors, creeds, and cultures met to write a charter for a world organization. The *reason* they met was because in a period of 30 years some forty million human beings have been killed by the oldest and worst plague we know. The *purpose* for which they met was to write a constitution for an organization through which the nations of the world might work together in their common hope for peace.

Amid the confusion, the babel of tongues, and the complexity of it all, a cynic could well say that the remarkable thing was not that they wrote a better charter than anyone had a right to expect, but that they succeeded in writing a charter at all! They succeeded because it was the common and equal determination of all those who participated in its labors that the Conference *must* reach agreement; that a charter *must* be written — not *a* charter, but the best possible charter on which all could agree.

There was no cynicism, no complacency, and no resignation. The principal delegates knew too well the temper of their peoples, they knew too well the horrors of war, and they knew the meaning for every one of them of that endless, stately procession of ships in an[d] out the Golden Gate. The atmosphere was urgent — patient, but urgent. But they didn't look at the clock at San Francisco, and they *did* look, and looked hard at every clause and every word. They brought in over 100 amendments to the Dumbarton Oaks proposals, and they discussed, debated, revised, and compromised — and slowly, painfully wrote a document which is at once a declaration of peace by the United Nations and an instrument by which that declaration can take practical effect. They didn't merely ratify what the Big Powers proposed; they performed a great task of creation, and produced a document immeasurably better than the Dumbarton Oaks proposals.

It was an achievement about which history will have much to say, and perhaps it could only have been done in the course of a great war by a generation which has suffered frightfully, and by nations many of whom have lost the best of two succeeding generations.

As a *declaration*, it constitutes a binding agreement by the signatory nations to work together for peaceful ends and to adhere to certain standards of international morality. As a *constitution*, it creates four principal social instruments by which these ends may be achieved in practice and these standards maintained.

What are these instruments?

— a police force continually in operation and continually vigilant;

— a forum in which to discuss, to let the light in, to ventilate;

— a court whose decisions are binding on the parties and all member states;

— and an institute to apply to social and economic problems the knowledge and experience of the world.

These are the fundamental instruments to which free men are accustomed — instruments in the use of which we have become experienced over many generations — instruments which have behind them the impetus and momentum of the long history of democratic institutions.

The preamble, the statement of purposes, and principles of the organization are, I think, clear and as strong as they can be made. But what about these tools to effectuate the purposes, to give them life, vitality, and endurance? Are they adequate? You can say with reason, and it is going to be said in the next few weeks by people who really want a better charter, and, in part, by people who really don't want any charter, that the purposes and principles are fine, but that these instruments, these tools, are incomplete and inadequate and can't do the job. It is going to be said that the Security Council has no weapons of its own; that it can use only what forces the member nations agree to give it. It is going to be said that the General Assembly is only a debating society which can't legislate. It will be said that the World Court can't compel member states to accept its jurisdiction. It may even be said that the Trusteeship system is a fraud because no state is compelled to place any territory under the system.

And all of these things are true! But, before anyone writes it off as a futility, let him always think, first, whether he would have it any other way as to his own country; second, even if he would, what would he think of the chances of ratification; and, finally, whether he would rather not make a start by transplanting into the international world instruments of proven social value, subject to *whatever* limitations, which have behind them a demonstrated usefulness and an historical momentum which mean far more than the precise legal terms by which they are established in their new position.

Take the Economic and Social Council — what can it do? It can initiate studies, make reports and recommendations with respect to international economic, social, cultural, educational, health, and related matters. It can make recommendations for the purpose of promoting respect for and observance of human rights and fundamental freedoms for all, and it can draft conventions and call international conferences. I submit that, if you have an agency operating in a field as close to the lives and direct interests of human beings throughout the world as these fields of interest are and you authorize that agency to make reports and recommendations, call conferences, and draft conventions, you can come out at the far end with a whole body of world opinion and you have created something that can roll right up a mountain.

Much was said about the veto — about the necessity for unanimity among the five big powers in taking enforcement action. Many felt that the unanimity requirement should be modified; but, *beyond the point of discussion of disputes,* it was recognized that decisions and actions by the Security Council could well lead to major political consequences. In view of their primary responsibility, the permanent members felt they could not be expected, in the present condition of the world, to assume the obligation to act in so serious a matter as the maintenance of international peace and security in consequence of a decision in which they had not concurred.

But even the requirement of unanimity among the permanent members for enforcement action does not invest them with any new rights, and the formula proposed for taking action in the Security Council by a majority of seven, including the permanent members, makes the operation of the Council *less* subject to obstruction than under the League of Nations Council which required complete unanimity of all its members, whether permanent or not.

The League broke up because the great powers were not united, and history may say that the attention directed to the veto at San Francisco was less important than the unanimity of the large powers. Like the great medieval Pope who declared that he was the servant of the servants of God, so the Major Powers must be the first servants of the common society, for San Francisco was a great effort to tie up the shattered bits of international order under the leadership of the *major* powers in an association of *all* powers.

In other respects the new Charter marks a long advance from the League:

1. When ratified, it will command the support of all the powers which the League did not.

2. It successfully marries regional arrangements with world organization. The Pan American security system and the Act of Chapultepec, for example, finds its proper place, not as a substitute but as a buttress of the main edifice.[71]

---

[71] The Act of Chapultepec, signed by the inter-American nations on March 8, 1945, stated that an act or threat of aggression against one American state by any country was a threat to all the American states. Article 51 of the Charter of the United Nations stated: "Nothing in the present Charter shall impair the inherent right of individual or collective self-defense if an armed attack occurs against a Member of the United Nations, until the Security Council has taken the measures necessary to maintain international peace and security."

3. The arrangements for military contingents and for strategic planning and the disposition of forces are an important advance over the League.

4. The Trusteeship chapter is a landmark in the treatment of dependent territories. They are a sacred trust and the members are bound to protect the peoples from exploitation and to develop self-government and free political institutions.

5. Likewise, the Social and Economic Council sets up a great target and at the same time protects us from interference in our domestic affairs.

But the San Francisco Charter is not only a long advance from the League of Nations, it is also a much more flexible and democratic document than the Dumbarton Oaks proposals — thanks in large measure to the leadership of the American delegation and the very aggressive participation of some of the smaller states, — and most of all to the fact that the Big Five were able to compromise and reach agreement on *all major issues*.[72]

I don't have the time, nor have you the patience to listen to a detailed discussion of some of the major problems on which we had to work out laboriously a common position, like the question of the veto on discussion and consideration of disputes in the Security Council, on which the Soviet Union finally acquiesced in the interest of harmony after a prolonged deadlock.[73] But I do want to point out what I am sure you all know — that the *disagreements* made the news, not the much wider area of *agreement*.

The Great Powers did not spend their time during these past two months discussing the things on which they *agreed* (like the Dumbarton Oaks proposals, themselves, or the twenty odd four-power amendments which they proposed at the outset). They spent the time discussing the area of *disagreement*, and most of the news reports dealt with the negotiations on these disagreements, thereby creating the impression of endless contention. The result — in spite of the fact that agreement was

[72] The Dumbarton Oaks proposals and the Charter of the United Nations are reprinted in Department of State Publication 2490, *The United Nations Conference on International Organization: Selected Documents* (Washington: Government Printing Office, 1946).

[73] The San Francisco Conference nearly broke up when the Soviet delegation rejected the agreement concerning voting in the Security Council that had been reached at the Yalta Conference. Secretary of State Stettinius dispatched a cable on June 2 to Ambassador Averell Harriman and Harry Hopkins in Moscow, which instructed them to warn Stalin of the gravity of the situation and to explain the necessity of adjourning the conference unless the Russians supported the Yalta agreement. Four days later Stalin agreed to abide by the Yalta agreement.

reached over a vast area and on most everything of importance, in spite of the fact that the Russians and ourselves agreed far, far more often than we disagreed — the result seems to be, in some quarters at least, dark forebodings, fear, and a widespread feeling that the conference has merely proved how difficult it is going to be for the United States, Great Britain, and France to work with Russia.

It *is* difficult to work with the Russians. I am told it always has been — back to the days of Nicholas I, 100 years ago. Their representatives do not have the same latitude ours do. Negotiations have to be interrupted constantly for them to consult their government. You can argue for hours and they don't budge, (more often than not because they can't). They are suspicious of the western states which intervened during the revolution, which haven't been so cordial until recently, which did little to save the League [of Nations] or stop German rearmament or Mussolini's aggressions, and which have detested and feared their political philosophy. And there are doubtless Russians who dislike and fear capitalism just as we dislike and fear communism; perhaps they even fear the great American democratic tradition which has now emerged from a successful war as the most powerful moral and intellectual force of our time.

And let us not forget that, after a few tentative unsuccessful probings between the wars, it is only now that Russia is emerging from a long isolation, because they, like we, know that in the modern world isolation is not strength but weakness.

Russia (and these are personal opinions) will attempt to surround her borders with friendly governments as a defense against the world of capitalism whose motives and power still worries and frightens her. They made it quite clear at San Francisco that they are not going to abandon or weaken these primary alliances, and they want a minimum of outside interference in this zone. But beyond lies the world and, like ourselves, they see in this new organization an instrument through which they can watch and take part in world policies and decisions which might adversely affect their interests. This can be the great information center, the assay office of world opinion. Here they can watch trends, help impede anti-Soviet developments, and work with the rest of the world toward conditions that will help them restore and develop their shattered, backward country, *for which peace and our cooperation is the first essential.*

I don't think it requires any blind, slap-happy optimism to conclude that the earnestness with which the Russians approached Dumbarton Oaks and San Francisco is the measure of their sincerity and self-interest in creating and supporting the United Nations Organization. But I have no illusions that there will be many years of difficulties, misgivings, and contentions, which only patience, firmness, and organized reason in the forum of the world can resolve.

Meanwhile, the Charter has been written — a better, more liberal and flexible charter than seemed possible a few months ago — but it is only paper and no better and no worse than the will and intentions of its five major members. Everything depends on the active participation, pacific intentions, and good faith of the Big Five, and particularly the United States, Russia, and Britain. Everything we hope for depends on their collaboration in peace as in war; and I risk the estimate that in the United Nations Organization that collaboration is based on the most solid of all foundations — national self-interest.

Part Four

The United Nations Organization

1945–1947

During an interview in 1942, Adlai E. Stevenson told a reporter: "I believe that in the agony of Pearl Harbor a golden age was born, the American age, an age in which America will assume the responsibility that destiny has assigned her, the responsibility for intelligent leadership among the peoples of the world, a responsibility which people of small understanding evaded after the last war." [1]

After the San Francisco Conference ended on June 26, 1945, he returned to Washington to work on Senate ratification of the Charter of the United Nations. In the autumn, he went to London to be the deputy to Edward R. Stettinius, Jr., head of the United States delegation to the Preparatory Commission of the United Nations.

On June 26, 1945, when the delegates at San Francisco signed the United Nations Charter, they also signed "interim arrangements," which provided for the establishment of a preparatory commission to meet in London. Among other things, the commission was to plan the convoking of the General Assembly; prepare a provisional agenda; and formulate recommendations concerning the transfer of League of Nations assets to the United Nations, the organization of the Secretariat, relationships with the specialized agencies, and the location of the permanent headquarters.

When Stettinius became ill, Stevenson became head of the delegation. "It was the most exacting, interesting and in many ways the most important interval of my life," he wrote later. "After almost four years of preoccupation with war, the satisfaction of having a part in the organized search for the conditions and mechanics of peace completed my circle." [2]

[1] Washington *Times-Herald*, April 14, 1942.
[2] *Major Campaign Speeches Of Adlai E. Stevenson, 1952*, with an introduction by the author (New York: Random House, 1953), p. xx. Historian H. G. Nicholas wrote: "Conspicuous amongst the other national delegations was the American deputy delegate, a Chicago lawyer and temporary civil servant, Mr. Adlai Stevenson." *The United Nations as a Political Institution* (London: Oxford University Press, 1959), p. 41.

At the completion of the work of the Preparatory Commission, Stevenson remained in London to serve as a senior adviser to the American delegation to the first meeting of the United Nations Assembly. He returned to Chicago in March, 1946, to resume the practice of law, but that fall he was an alternate delegate on the American delegation to the United Nations Assembly meeting in New York. The following year President Harry S. Truman appointed him again to the American delegation as an alternate delegate and for another three months he worked in New York to strengthen the world organization.

The papers used in Part Four are in the Adlai E. Stevenson collection, Princeton University Library, unless otherwise indicated. We are grateful to Mrs. Anne Gustave, librarian of the United States Mission to the United Nations, for her assistance.

Speeches at the plenary sessions of the United Nations are available at the Library of the United Nations. The library has only summaries of speeches made in committee sessions. All these meetings were recorded, however, on disks. Pierre Furst, of the Communications, Archives and Records Service, located for us the only disk of a statement by Stevenson that has been preserved. Mr. Jack Banks, of Archives at the United Nations, found three other items which had been transcribed. We are grateful for their assistance. When we have been unable to locate a text of a Stevenson speech as he actually delivered it, we have had to use a press release of the speech. The United States Mission to the United Nations has copies of the press releases.

We were able to locate some handwritten letters for these years. We are particularly indebted to Mrs. Edison Dick for her assistance. Mrs. Dick submitted extracts to the editors from handwritten letters she received from Stevenson. She has indicated with ellipses material that was deleted by her. The originals of all the handwritten letters are in her possession.

To Ralph A. Bard

July 2, 1945

Dear Ralph:

I reached the fetid banks of the Potomac Friday afternoon at 5 and my oven in the State Department at 5:30 — in time to be advised that you had left for Chicago that very day, after devoting at least some of your precious last minutes to planning the presentation of something to me.[3]

---

[3] Mr. Bard had just resigned as Under Secretary of the Navy. On July 7 the Navy Department was to present Stevenson with a Distinguished Civilian Service Award

It was thoughtful, it was typical, and it reminded me afresh of all the many kind, comforting and helpful things you've done for me and said to me over these past four frenzied years — things for which I've never thanked you and never could.

I'll miss you mightily, hereabouts, but not for long, because I expect to be done with this detail in a few more weeks and then back to Chicago to pick up the threads of workaday living again. It won't be easy I know, but if misery loves company, I should find a little comfort in old man Bard!

Affectionate regards to your child wife.

Yours,

At the close of the San Francisco Conference, President Harry S. Truman appointed James F. Byrnes as Secretary of State. Byrnes replied to the following letter by asking Stevenson to continue in the Department of State until he returned from the Potsdam Conference.

To James F. Byrnes

July 3, 1945

My dear Mr. Secretary:

With all the things you have to attend to and the limited time at your disposal, I will not ask for an appointment to congratulate you and explain my position in the Department.

I returned to Chicago January last expecting to resume my law practice after an absence of almost four years. In February, Archie MacLeish and Ed Stettinius prevailed on me to come to the Department for a limited period to help with the information work on the Dumbarton Oaks Proposals and with the Conference.

I am now engaged in the preparation and briefing of our witnesses before the Foreign Relations Committee. With ratification or even before, I will have fulfilled my commitment to Ed and Archie and plan to return to Chicago. As you may still be away at that time, I should like to feel free to resign when my utility is at an end, and perhaps the Acting Secretary could merely announce that I have concluded the work for which I had joined the Department a few months ago. I trust this will be satisfactory to you.

Let me add my confident belief that under your firm direction and experienced leadership, this Department will nobly meet the demands of

---

for "exceptional performance of outstanding service to the United States Navy as special assistant to the Secretary of the Navy from June 30, 1941, to June 13, 1944."

the future which are weighted with such importance for us all. I am delighted to have had a few months here and a minor participation in this great undertaking.

Faithfully yours,

On July 8, 1945, the Washington Post *published the story of Stevenson receiving the Navy's Distinguished Civilian Service Award and illustrated its story by printing a picture of former Vice President Adlai E. Stevenson, Stevenson's grandfather.*

Paul Miller, assistant general manager of the Associated Press, wrote Stevenson July 9, 1945, congratulating him on the award and adding: "Now, if they will just do two things, I, for one will be satisfied: (1) Give you a similar award for what you did for the Press at San Francisco; (2) Use your own photograph when they want to print any accompanying picture!!"

To Wayne Coy

July 9, 1945

Dear Wayne:

The attached is from yesterday's *Post*. Ho hum, I've a white mustache and a wing collar and I'm 70, and all the time I thought I was a young man and in the very mold of fashion. But then perhaps it's just as well we see ourselves as "ithers see us," and the resemblance would be very surprising to grandfather, dead these 35 years. But no more surprising than the news that I was born in Libertyville!

Yours,

When Edward R. Stettinius, Jr., resigned as Secretary of State, President Harry S. Truman made him ambassador to the United Nations and head of the U.S. delegation to the UN Preparatory Commission. On July 3, 1945, Stettinius wrote Stevenson: "My association with you has been of the happiest of my life and I shall never forget it. I appreciate with all my heart the confidence you have had in me and the support you have given me. Your advice and assistance have been invaluable."

To Edward R. Stettinius, Jr.[4]

July 19, 1945

Dear Ed:

Mr. Byrnes wrote me on July 6 that he wanted me to carry on until he

[4] The original is in the Stettinius papers, University of Virginia Library.

returned from Europe. I have concluded the work for which I came in February and am planning to go home the middle of next week. I will not separate from the Department and will be available to come back here to talk with him if and when he wants to see me before I resign officially.

Before I leave next week, I hope to have a talk with you. If you can find a few minutes, please let me know.

Sincerely yours,
ADLAI

After writing the following letter, Stevenson went to Libertyville to be with his family. Mr. MacLeish replied on July 30, 1945: "Your description of AES makes me think of one of those travel books about America written by distinguished British men of letters which enlivened the literary history of the last century. The features of the landscape were always recognizable and the natives were always picturesquely presented. The only trouble was that the distinguished authors had never seen the things they looked at. I suspect your acquaintance with AES is of the same character. You make him a charming and lovable figure, which indeed he is, but you have never really penetrated the depth or the height of his soul. Some day I shall enlighten you."

To Archibald MacLeish

July 26, 1945

Dear Archie:

I've been thinking about what you said yesterday. What I meant was that I don't think I "rate" your job[5] should the Secretary accept your resignation — that is, I have no distinction and little experience in the field of information, cultural relations, etc. I'm just a low order of country lawyer with a congenital taste for public service, politics, politicians and the public trough where my family have been nibbling, frugally, albeit, for several generations. My only other attributes are acquaintance around Washington, agreeable, inoffensive manner untarnished with aggressive ideas (in spite of my Navy citation!), and a long, if superficial, familiarity with foreign relations — with a slight predisposition for the economic.

Add to the foregoing, restlessness, ambition (wholly undirected) and a strong feeling that after four years here I should get back to the prairies and act like a responsible husband, father and breadwinner instead

[5] Mr. MacLeish was Assistant Secretary of State.

of a piecework man in Washington. Having no other talents or opportunities, I suspect I'll have to do my winning at the law — ho hum! But then maybe after several years being a good citizen and a *good* Democrat in a town not over endowed with either, perhaps I'll get another chance when the boys are grown and off to school. (But I hope the Secretary doesn't press me — I can resist anything but temptation, as you know.)

Meanwhile, I hope the Department will keep me in mind as an "expert" on most anything, should there be opportunities to serve on missions, commissions, conferences, etc., for private citizens for limited periods. Maybe it would help to fool the clients and the politicians — and it would make life on La Salle Street tolerable!

Since you have nothing to do this afternoon except baffle the Japs, I'm taking leave this way. I've had a wonderful time — its been the best detail I've had yet, and if I wasn't much help, my only defense is that I warned you in advance. And if you need a good character as a boss, please send any doubtfuls to me!

Devotedly,

P.S. I think I'm prouder of having had a part in the information job on Dumbarton Oaks than anything in these four eventful years. If there's room on your epitaph, that job mustn't be overlooked.

To J. C. Folger[6]

August 30, 1945

Dear Cliff:

Commander Edward D. McDougal, a member of the Naval Price Adjustment Board is being proposed for resident membership in the Metropolitan Club and I have sent a letter of endorsement. He doesn't know any of the Directors except Ben Thoron and I have taken the liberty of suggesting that he add your name and that he call on you and make good that representation. He is as dear a friend as I have and a great guy. To which I should add, he was a partner of mine in Chicago for many years and that I am an entirely prejudiced witness. I hope you will forgive me for suggesting that he use your name. I am sure you will like him enormously.

Yours,

While Stevenson was on leave without pay from the Department of State, Secretary of State Byrnes and Ambassador Stettinius phoned him

[6] Carbon copy is in the possession of Edward D. McDougal, Jr.

and persuaded him to be Stettinius's deputy with rank of minister to the Preparatory Commission in London. Before accepting the post, Stevenson insisted that he must bring his family with him. Mrs. Stevenson, Adlai III and Borden followed him to England a little later. John Fell remained at Libertyville with Mr. and Mrs. Ernest L. Ives.

The two following letters to the senior partner in his law firm and to his contemporary in the firm were written from Washington, D.C.

To Edwin C. Austin

September 4, 1945

Dear Ed:

A little more reluctantly than I care to admit, in view of my proclaimed respect for public service, I have succumbed to considerable pressure to go to London for the organization work of the United Nations. There is great anxiety to get organized and started as promptly as possible. My title is Deputy United States Delegate to the Preparatory Commission of the United Nations Organization. I will have the personal rank of Minister and some thirty-five to fifty people on the United States staff to direct. It will not be an easy assignment, but everyone seems confident that the preparation work can be completed by Christmas.

I am flattered, of course. I suppose I was selected because of my previous work on the charter, and I confess I will get some personal satisfaction out of seeing the organization on which I have spent so much time and toil come into existence.

I hope then to come home and pick up where I left off. Meanwhile, in view of my prolonged absence and indecision, I feel that I must say to you and through you to the firm that I consider you no longer in any way obligated to me as a former partner; that I am full of gratitude for all the consideration and genuine friendship you have shown me. And I mean that as sincerely as I have ever meant anything, but I know what you are up against there in planning for the future, and that my eccentric behavior has not made it any easier. Moreover, I am a little embarrassed by all the special consideration I have asked for. So I have concluded that the firm must be in a position to make its plans without further reference to me.

You can be sure that when I return to Chicago for keeps, the office will be the first place I will go. If there is then no position for me, I will be neither surprised nor hurt and as full of gratitude for all you have done for me in the past and during the war as I am now. I know you will believe me.

[255]

So please consider this a "mutual release" and with it my heartfelt thanks and abundant affection for you all.[7]

Yours always,

To James F. Oates, Jr.

September 4, 1945

Dear Jim:

Well, I've done it again! And I am beginning to feel a little psychopathic about my irresolute behavior. I had hoped to see you while I was in Chicago over the weekend, but you were fishing — I was glad to hear! Yesterday they sent a plane out for me and I flew back this morning so that I could get off for England with Byrnes and his party tonight. I had hoped to stay until Wednesday to clear some things and to see you.

I have just written Ed, copy enclosed. I hope you agree that in the circumstances I could no longer in fairness ask for further consideration. What with my suggestions for special treatment, coupled with Ed's sympathetic patience and good will, and my inability to return now when they need me, I feel that they have more than discharged any obligation to me — if there ever was any.

This will be a tough job in a new field for me — international negotiations — but I will have competent technical support. Also, the division in the State Department which backstops the work is first rate. We will operate like a diplomatic mission in the field, taking our general instructions from the Department and doing the best we can with them on the spot. Perhaps I'll learn something about the position the Russians were in at San Francisco!

There is now so much anxiety — at least among the Big Five — to get the organization set up and functioning promptly, I am hopeful that the original work program of the Preparatory Commission can be cut and the whole process accelerated. But it will be slow and tedious at best and I'm destined to learn something about patience in three languages!

Taking Ellen and a couple of the boys will be a comfort for me. That I wasn't going to be separated from my family any longer with the war over was the one resolution on which I never wavered. But I guess they expected that one and they were all ready for it. They are paying me at

---

[7] Mr. Austin wrote him in reply: "I certainly congratulate you most heartily on your present appointment. I think you have a little tendency to deprecate the significance of your achievements in public life. I really feel very proud of what you have accomplished, and of what you are doing at this moment." He added that as a friend he would like to see him wholeheartedly either in public service or in their law firm. "I am skeptical as to how you will come out if you try to 'play in both leagues.'" He then stated that he would be delighted if the outcome was a return to the firm on a "really fulltime basis."

the rate of $10,000, plus $25.00 per diem, so taking the family won't be too disastrous and it should be a good experience for them even if living conditions are a little rugged.

I wish we had had our good bicker. Your confidence and judgment about things is my best hitching post, but it won't be long before I present you with some new quandarys. Meanwhile I feel better, having absolved the office of further responsibility and full of gratitude, affection and good will, coupled with a sense of mutual freedom, if you can understand these clumsy words.

My love to the family and many, many thanks for all your help. You'll be seeing me along with the Christmas trees.

Yours,

P.S. My address is care American Embassy, Grosvenor Square, London.

On September 4, 1945, Adlai E. Stevenson sailed from New York City with Secretary of State Byrnes, who was to attend a meeting of the Council of Foreign Ministers. Among those accompanying Byrnes as aides were James C. Dunn, Ralph Bunche, Dorothy Fosdick, Charles Bohlen, Benjamin V. Cohen, and John Foster Dulles. Stevenson kept the following diary of the early days of his mission.[8]

September 4th, 1945

State Department sent plane out to bring me back so I could catch the boat for England tonight with Secretary Byrnes. Left Glenview Naval Air Station in Army C–47 alone — Major Barron, pilot — for Washington at 8:30 A.M. Busy afternoon with conferences and last minute preparations. Major Barron flew me to La Guardia Field at New York, leaving Washington at 8 P.M. Ed McDougall accompanied me to airport to say goodbye and flew on to New York for the ride. Army car met me at La Guardia to take me to the Queen Elizabeth at pier 90, where I met Secretary Byrnes and party just going aboard. Shared a cabin with Dr. Norman Padelford of Massachusetts Institute of Technology and [an] expert on waterways, attached to the State Department Delegation headed by Secretary Byrnes, and destined for the Meeting of the Council of Foreign Ministers in London to work out the peace treaties for the satellites and Italy.

Found Anne O'Hare McCormick of the New York Times and her husband and Carl McCardle of the Philadelphia Bulletin on board. The lat-

[8] The editors used a typescript of the diary. It probably was dictated from handwritten notes, but we were unable to locate them.

ter had covered the San Francisco Conference where I had seen much of him. Encountered Bob Kintner, now Vice President of the American Broadcasting Company and wife, Jean, who had come to see Ben Cohen off. They induced us to go ashore for a little festivity at the Stork Club as the ship did not sail until 5:30 A.M. Much trouble about getting off the boat due to Army security regulations, as she is still a transport in military service. Turner Catledge, destined to be Managing Editor of the New York Times,[9] Mrs. McCormick, McCardle and sundry others joined us for a sandwich and champagne at the Stork — the only food I had had since breakfast in Illinois with the family early in the morning.

The Queen Elizabeth (84,000 tons) and her sister Queen Mary are still transports. The "Liz" delivered 15,000 American soldiers at this pier only three days ago. There are twelve little iron bunks in our cabin for Padelford and me to sleep in!

September 5th, 1945 — September 10th, 1945

Pleasant crossing. McCormick and McCardle much concerned about news facilities at the Council of Foreign Ministers. Secretary Byrnes unwilling to talk with them on the boat. Not much impressed with his assistant, Walter Brown, who is evidently to have much to say about information policies during Byrnes' tenure as Secretary. Had some interesting talks with Sir Ashley Sparks, American Director of the Cunard White Star Line, much hilarity in evenings at cocktails in the Dunns' cabin and playing checkers with Ben Cohen late into the night. Only one conference alone at lunch with Secretary Byrnes about our work on the Preparatory Commission of the United Nations Organization. He felt I had been wise not to commit myself beyond the preparatory period, and probably should return to Chicago when that was over if I was going to do anything politically. Told me that Mayor [Edward J.] Kelly had been to see the President and himself about locating the headquarters of the [United Nations] Organization in Chicago and seemed much impressed with Kelly's arguments. His attitude with respect to Russia at the Council of Foreign Ministers seemed emphatic and firm. Hopeful that all of the major issues could at least be aired before he returned to the U.S. in late September. Insisted that discussions on financial aid to Britain must be coupled with the elimination of restrictions on post-war trade, and that Assistant Secretary [Will] Clayton et al had been instructed not to talk with Lord Keynes, [Lord] Halifax and the British experts except on that basis at the forthcoming discussions in Washington.

Our fellow passengers are some 2,000 assorted Europeans, going home

[9] Mr. Catledge did not become managing editor until 1951. Whenever Stevenson dictated from his notes, he must have added material like this.

after the long refuge, Red Cross girls, British soldiers, sailors and flyers and U.S. Army people — soldiers and civilians — going to Germany.

Chip Bohlen, Russian expert from the Department, joined us in our cabin en route but we were quite comfortable, scattered amongst the forest of tiny bunks. . . .

Arrived Southampton September 10 at 2:30 P.M. Met by Stettinius' representative and a car and drove up to London bringing Bohlen and Phil Moseley, Assistant to Mr. Winant,[10] who is going to act as Jimmy Dunn's[11] assistant at the Foreign Ministers Meeting. Quartered at Claridge's. Dinner with Stettinius and Virginia and Teddy[12] and their brother-in-law Colonel John Marsh of the Control Commission in Germany.

September 11th, 1945

Conference with Stettinius and staff before the Executive Committee meeting of the Preparatory Commission.[13] Attended the meeting at Church House where I found the facilities superb and met many of the delegates and their deputies and staffs. It seemed apparent that from the discussion of timing the conclusion of the work of the Executive Committee and the convening of meetings of the Preparatory Commission and General Assembly, that the British Chief Delegate, Philip Noel-Baker, Minister of State in the Labor Government, would like to proceed deliberately and postpone the first meeting of the General Assembly until January, after the holidays; also would like to have the scope of the meeting broader than the organizational functions which we had envisioned. The Canadians and Australians likewise felt that the meeting should be open to discussion of substantive matters as well as organizational matters. The Russians represented by [Andrei] Gromyko, Ambassador at Washington, and the Chinese, equally emphatic that the work should proceed as rapidly as possible and that the first meeting should be essentially organizational.

In the afternoon I attended, as our representative, a meeting of Committee 10, to discuss the selection of site. It served to whittle away a lot of underbrush about the qualifications of the site and whether the principle should be centralization of the organization or decentralization.

---

[10] John Gilbert Winant, U.S. ambassador to Great Britain.
[11] James C. Dunn, Assistant Secretary of State.
[12] Mrs. Stettinius and their son.
[13] The members of the Preparatory Commission at a meeting on June 27, 1945, at San Francisco left to a fourteen-member Executive Committee the task of preparing a detailed report for its consideration. The Executive Committee started to work in London on August 16. After three months of work, their report served as the basis for discussion by the full Preparatory Commission which held its first meeting on November 24, 1945.

The view was unanimous that the principle should be centralization but exceptions must be contemplated, World Court at the Hague, etc.

Dined with Bill Stoneman and Nat Barrows of the Chicago Daily News foreign staff. Found them reasonably content with the treatment their copy was receiving at home.

September 12th

Committee Meetings. Conference with Stettinius on the program for expediting the work. Bad news about finding a place to live, diluted by comforting reassurances from Mrs. Laing, my British secretary.

September 13th

Long meeting of the Executive Committee to discuss dates for completion of the Executive Committee work, and for convening the Preparatory Commission and the General Assembly. Our view that the first meeting of the General Assembly should be organizational only met with approval. The British seem to be opposed to holding the first meeting in London following the Preparatory Commission, and it is apparent that Noel[-]Baker was hoping to get it to Geneva in January. Attended a meeting of a Committee to consider the qualifications of the site of the permanent headquarters. Interminable talk — am constantly amazed by the prolixity of international discussions.[14]

Dined as Mr. Noel Baker's guest at the Ritz with Stettinius, Gil Winant, our Ambassador to the Court of St. James, Gladwin Jebb, Executive Secretary of the Preparatory Commission and Professor [Charles] Webster of the British Delegation. Good food, wine and talk, and notable progress with Noel Baker on the desirability of bringing the Organization to birth before the end of this year, which clearly means an Organization Meeting of the General Assembly in London early in December, so that we can conclude and all go home by Christmas — I hope! Winant was very helpful on this score, but not too helpful in locating the permanent site in the United States, being an old Geneva man himself.

September 14th

Attended sub-committee meeting on drafting a resolution for the Executive Committee and found it very easy to suggest language which would meet the Russian's apprehension that committees appointed by

[14] Wilder Foote, assistant to Ambassador Stettinius, wrote to his wife on September 13, 1945: "Adlai is discouraged at the amount of talking that seems to be necessary before anything gets done in the committees. It is certainly a slow process. The least point is discussed and since every speech has to be translated from English to French or French to English, the time drags horribly." Letter in the possession of Mr. Foote.

the first General Assembly might duplicate the work of the organs themselves in the interval before the full dress meeting of the Assembly next April.

More committee meetings, and mounting terror about the prospect of housing the family, and a tent in Hyde Park. The hotels are all stuffed and the good ones very expensive.

Dined with Tom Blake of the Division of Current Information at the State Department, who is on his way back from Nuremberg, where he has been arranging press facilities for the war criminals trial. He indicated that he would be glad to be invited to come back to assist us with press arrangements for the Preparatory Commission and Assembly Meetings. At dinner I ran into Frances McFadden[15] and Patrick Hill.[16] Afterward we all went up to Sir Arthur Salter's[17] apartment and drank copiously in farewell celebration for Frances, who was leaving the following morning, after fifteen months in the OWI [Office of War Information] in London. Pat Hill when I told him about the advent of Ellen and the children, seemed seriously disposed to send for Jinny. I hope I have not started an influx of American wives!

September 15th

Caught up with a small portion of a huge mass of accumulated papers, and spent the afternoon walking in Kew Gardens in a cool wind and fleeting sunshine — a memorable afternoon.

September 16th

Interviewed hotels and worked. Went to impressive service at Westminster Abbey, commemorating the Battle of Britain, five years before, and the Sunday engagement in which 185 German aircraft were knocked down and the tide of invasion stemmed. The orderliness of the British crowds. Dined at the officers mess with Dulles, Byrnes et al, and talked at length about the progress of the Foreign Ministers Meeting. Had a feeling that we present our real position sometimes too soon with embarrassing results, and that the Russians are using the technique of increasing their demands continuously. Our Delegation is now pressing for United Nations' trusteeship of the Italian colonies, which I had advocated on the boat, after abandoning their first proposal of Italian trusteeship under United Nations' supervision.

---

15 Miss McFadden, an old friend of Stevenson's from Chicago, was with the magazine division of the Office of War Information.

16 Husband of John Alden Carpenter's daughter Genevieve.

17 Member of Parliament, Oxford professor, and former Senior Deputy Director General of UNRRA (1943–1944).

September 17th

Executive Committee Meeting adopted our draft resolution on target dates for completing the work, almost without modification, but it took four meetings.

Met with the Big Five, Gromyko, Massigli,[18] Noel Baker and Victor Hoo.[19] Found Noel Baker hostile to any Big Five agreements, but the others pleased with the prospect of getting together again to discuss the more important matters of mutual concern. Gromyko seems to be getting more cordial and agreeable. Little progress towards any final decisions, but we presented them with nine questions, and discussed several of them usefully.

Dined with Mr. and Mrs. Ned Russell (New York Herald Tribune London correspondent) and Wilder Foote. Mrs. Russell . . . seemed very nice and interested herself in my housing problem. I think he has a story in the Herald Tribune which discloses the whole case in the Italian colonies, but I have no indication of his source. Mrs. Russell felt that housekeeping was not out of the question at all, and the food situation was not too bad if one dined out occasionally. She seemed a bright jolly girl and talked with great candor about her father who has been in Spain during the war, and I gather is suspected of strong pro-Franco sympathies. She said her brother, who is about 25, has married a widow of 39, and other lively gossip about her family. The candor was either deliberate or most engaging. . . .

September 18th

More interminable meetings. Lunch with Shirley Swann[20] who was on his way back from a mission in Germany, to study industrial chemistry developments. He said that in research and development they were very good, but in production methods way behind us, and that the great volume of information they have accumulated will in due course be made available to the public, and will perhaps be of value to similar industry in Britain and the United States.

Dined with [P. H.] Gore-Booth of the British Delegation at the Royal Automobile Club. An agreeable thoroughbred who neither drinks nor smokes. How diplomats can lead an aesthetic [ascetic] life I cannot understand.

[18] René Massigli, chief of the French delegation.
[19] Deputy to Chinese Ambassador Wellington Koo.
[20] Sherlock Swann, Jr., a Princeton classmate of Stevenson's and research professor of chemical engineering at the University of Illinois; with the Office of Production Research and Development (1944).

September 19th

Long meeting of the Committee on permanent site, at which I was happy to be able to contribute a few simple sentences here and there that somewhat perceptibly seemed to speed up the procedure. Drafting some fourteen people in two languages was not easy.

Househunting and there are some prospects, all expensive and not too good, but I am reconciled to most anything now.

Dinner with!

Stevenson's diary ended at this point. Shortly after he arrived in London he received letters from James F. Oates, Jr., and Kenneth F. Burgess of his law firm concerning his letter of September 4 to their partner Edwin C. Austin. Mr. Oates wrote: "You will make a lasting contribution to the welfare of the whole world in a way that is offered very few men. No one could be better qualified for the task you are now undertaking — qualified, that is, in the right spirit and a sense of prudent compassion and charity for the welfare of others." He added, "However, I will never again be fully happy and at home until you are once more in the next room as my partner." Mr. Burgess wrote: "The future of our country and of the world is in a way in your keeping. . . . Don't worry about the future. When you come back you will be a much more valuable partner in our firm than you were when you left." Mr. Burgess added that he had recommended him as a member of the Chicago Transit Commission.

To James F. Oates, Jr.

September 13, 1945

Dear Jim,

Your letter of the 6th refreshed me not a little when I walked in this afternoon after several hours of wrangling in two languages in the middle of this mare's nest of long distance talkers. I have always thought you were pretty good at words, but you could not pass the primary grades in this international carnival of language.

Things are not too disorderly hereabouts, and I am still hopeful that we can conclude the preparatory portion of this work by December. But meanwhile I am appalled at the prospect of the advent of Ellen and the colts. Living conditions are no better than they were a year ago — indeed my secretary assures me that they are worse. Rest assured that I will keep you advised of important developments from time to time, and meanwhile, I too, look forward to that happy professional relationship which you keep dangling before my bloodshot eyes.

My love to Rosalind.[21]

Yours,

p.s. I had a very comforting letter from Kenneth [Burgess]. In the process of congratulating me on being here, he makes me wish all the more that I was there!

To Kenneth F. Burgess

September 24, 1945

Dear Kenneth,

Your letter welcomed me when I arrived here — and it was a very welcome welcome! You were good to write me and I was much pleased that you felt I did the right thing to accept this assignment, and I was sorry I did not have the opportunity to talk with you about it, but I had to make my decision very hurriedly.

I have had a feeling for a long time that everything I do is temporary, and I am getting tired of "piece work," but I agree that it is of first importance to get this organization established as quickly and as well as we can, and it is going to be largely for us to produce the leadership and drive to do it. While the Council of Foreign Ministers meetings have been going very badly, as the press is now disclosing, our meetings are going very well, and there is a fair chance that our work may be completed on schedule by the end of December. But of course the bad news blankets the good, and at the moment things are pretty blue here — with the guns hardly silenced!

You were good to recommend me for the Transit Commission — if I had known that I might not be here.

Please remember me to Geraldine and Ken[22] when you write him. I am anxious to hear what he plans to do, and I hope he won't be diverted from Law School.

Many thanks again — and let me know if any of your myriad interests need part time attention in London.

Yours always,

[21] Mrs. Oates.
[22] Mrs. Burgess and his son, Kenneth, Jr.

To Mrs. Ernest L. Ives[23]

October 10, 1945

Dear Buffy,

There is evidently something bib[l]ical about the airmail. Your report No. 1 arrived a few days after report No. 2 but the two together have lifted our spirits very high and Ellen is purring with contentment with the news that all is well with John Fell and you. . . . I am so glad to hear that you are finding some opportunities to visit around with your friends but the weather sounds dismal. This is usually our best season and I hope you get a break before the cold weather sets in.

I am very enthusiastic about your idea of a history of the Pantagraph. I think it would be a splendid promotional stunt and should coincide with the centenary. . . . The suggestion of Sinclair[24] sounds good to me. I don't know the other man whom you referred to — Jay Monaghan.[25] Who is he? Did you have an opportunity to discuss the matter at all with Sinclair? In a way it is a pity this thought did not occur to some of us before because Jake Hasbrouck[26] knew more about it and more about the source material than anyone else. Lloyd Lewis might have some ideas on possible writers. It is the sort of thing I would love to do myself but I don't see any prospect of finding the time to do it properly. My recollection is that 1946 is the centenary year. Is that correct? Have you written to Buddy[27] about it? If not, I suggest you do so and tell him it seems to me a great idea and something we should get started on promptly.

The little house is working out very well at last.[28] It was dirty beyond description and Ellen is still at work on the cleaning but it is most attractive and habitable. We have a good cook who works from early morning until midnight and a charwoman who comes in for half a day and does nothing at all! Ellen is piecing out the food situation by borrowing ration books and dexterous shopping. After much soul searching and debate we have started the boys[29] in school at Harrow. They leave in the morning at a quarter of eight and get back three afternoons a week at 7:30 and the other days in the early afternoon. It is a hard routine but I

---

[23] The original is in the Elizabeth Stevenson Ives collection, Illinois State Historical Library (E.S.I., I.S.H.L.).

[24] Harold Sinclair of Bloomington.

[25] A Lincoln scholar and close friend of Lloyd Lewis.

[26] A longtime employee of the *Daily Pantagraph*, by this time deceased.

[27] Their cousin Loring Merwin.

[28] The Stevensons had found a house at 2 Mount Row, just off Grosvenor Square.

[29] Adlai III and Borden.

am sure it is better to keep them busy than loafing around the house with too little to do. You can imagine that they confronted the prospect of a new school in a strange country with many misgivings, but I think it will work out and it should be an experience of enduring value.

I can't be definite yet, but there is still a very good prospect that the first organizing meeting of the General Assembly will be held here in London in December and concluded before the Holidays. At all events, our schedule still looks forward to Ellen and the children being home for Christmas even if I get hung up for a little while longer. Ed Stettinius is returning next week for some consultation in Washington and will be back here early in November.

We have not seen Mildred Bailey[30] but I suspect she will be in London before long. I wish she would write Sir Basil Brooke in Belfast and tell him if he should be in London while we are here it would be a great privilege to see him or his wife. My office telephone number is Mayfair 9222, Extension 410.

Jan Masaryk[31] left for Prague the day I got here and I understand now will not return before the General Assembly meeting in December. I suspect things are not going too well and probably he does not enjoy the full confidence of the Russians.

Ellen has been trying to write you ever since she arrived but what with the ordeal of getting settled I am afraid she has done nothing about it but will soon.

> Best Love,
> AD.

On October 16, 1945, Edward R. Stettinius, Jr., had to fly to New York for an operation. Stevenson assumed the chairmanship of the U.S. delegation. On October 18 the Chicago Tribune *referred to him as "the boy orator of Bloomington" while the Chicago* Daily News *wrote: "This step brings an able man to a bigger job than he has previously held." On October 21 the* Tribune *denounced him as being "all for England and nothing for America."*

To Hermon D. Smith[32]

October 30, 1945

Dear Dutch,

You were good to write me and enclose the clippings which I had not

---

[30] Their cousin.
[31] Foreign Minister of Czechoslovakia.
[32] The original is in the possession of Mr. Smith.

seen. I am even indebted for the Tribune editorial, which left me no doubt that the Chicago scene remains undisturbed. Sometimes I share the incredulity of people I meet and talk to about that newspaper around the world. What I mean is that I sometimes wonder if I am really telling them the truth when they look so incredulous. If I have had any doubts of late, your enclosure fortified me.

The going has been tough here for the last few weeks, but now we are in a little lull between the Executive Meeting of 14 nations and the Preparatory Commission of 51, which will convene the latter part of next month.

We are comfortably settled in a little house and the boys are going to Harrow as day scholars. I do not think they are going to be advertising the fact when they return, but I am sure it will be a worthwhile experience for them.

I have not seen Graham Hutton[33] or really had an opportunity to call him up but I hope to do so soon. Meanwhile I have received a letter from your friend Gerald Russell and I hope we will meet him soon.

My love to Ellen.[34] I can assure you that the longer I am away from home the more of an exile I feel, and I would even like to attend a board meeting of Hull House again!

Yours,
AD.

P.S. Ellen sends her best and the boys a big cheer for Lake Forest!

Wilder Foote, who remained in London to assist Stevenson after Ambassador Stettinius had to return to the United States, wrote Mrs. Foote on October 18, 1945: "Adlai presided today and did a good job. He gave the Russians every opportunity to present any counterproposals, and when they plainly indicated they had none, he let the report [on UN Trusteeship Council] come to a vote, making clear that all recommendations of the Executive Committee are preliminary and subject to reexamination in the Preparatory Commission."

Two days later Mr. Foote wrote his wife that at the executive committee meeting the day before, Ambassador Andrei Gromyko had stated that he was willing for discussions to proceed on various reports but hoped the committee would not vote since he did not have experts on his delegation and had to send the reports to such experts. "In other words," Mr. Foote wrote, "he had had to send them to Moscow for in-

---

[33] Of the British Information Service.
[34] Mrs. Smith.

structions and had not yet heard. Adlai, who was presiding, rightly decided not to press for a vote." [35] Mr. Foote pointed out that the newspapers thought the Russians were stalling. While this might be true, he added, the Soviet method at conferences was entirely different from that of the Americans. In the subcommittee stage, the Americans fought out the points at issue. The Russians did not, since they viewed that stage as technical and subject to political review. As a result, when a subcommittee approved a report without apparent objection and then an objection was raised in the final stages, Americans tended to look upon this as evidence of Russian bad faith. Mr. Foote observed: "It's just their way of doing business. . . . We go through this experience at every conference, yet we never seem to remember to make allowances for it. Our minds are trained to work one way, the Russian's another."

Then he remarked, "Adlai is following the right approach, I think. He is talking frankly with Gromyko." [36]

The executive committee completed its report on October 27. The Sunday Times of London reported the next day: "Before the Executive Committee adjourned last night the chairman, Mr. A. Stevenson (United States) said they had passed another important milestone in the history of the United Nations. Though they had had their disagreements, what was more important was that the area of agreement had been broadened."

To Mrs. Ernest L. Ives[37]

October 31, 1945

Dear Buffie,

I have just emerged from a couple of weeks of day and night toil and hence I have neglected your letters. Ed Stettinius fell ill and had to return suddenly to the United States two weeks ago just as it was our country's turn to act as chairman of the Executive Committee and just as the work was concluding and the sessions were becoming daily instead of weekly. The result has been that I have had to preside during this concluding period and it has been quite an ordeal, but I enjoyed it immensely and feel reasonably sure that the United States is suffering no disasters! Now we will have a little respite in the intensity until the Preparatory Commission convenes on the 23rd of November. I am hopeful that I can get things in the office in order and perhaps Ellen and I

---

[35] The verbatim minutes of the meetings of the executive committee are in the United Nations Archives, Dag Hammarskjöld Library, the United Nations.

[36] These letters are in the possession of Mr. Foote.

[37] The original is in E.S.I., I.S.H.L.

can go to Paris for a couple of days to visit the [Edgar Ansel] Mowrer's. The boys, as you know, are at Harrow as day scholars and, though not wildly enthusiastic, I think it will prove a most valuable experience. Adlai is always apprehensive that he is not learning anything and will be retarded when he gets back. But Borden, as usual, is oblivious of the work and turns the charm off and on to serve his purpose. We took them for a weekend to Ronnie Tree's fabulous place[38] up north of Oxford and they had a delirious time.

Your trip down state made me envious and I am literally *delighted* that John Fell finally got to Bloomington. I feel so miserable that with these long years of absence I have had no opportunity to give the boys any education in Illinois. Ellen was so pleased to hear that he seemed to be stuttering less and that everything was running smoothly at the house. She has us well organized here now with an excellent cook and plenty of food within the narrow limits of the rationing and we couldn't be more comfortable. Meanwhile, she is having an opportunity to meet some of these people and, on the whole, I think she is well content, in spite of her moments of longing for John Fell. We had our first glimpse of Mildred [Bailey] today. She came up from the country to lunch with us. . . . She has promised to come back and take the boys out to the Naval College at Greenwich where there are famous Christopher Wren buildings and the great Maritime Museum which the boys have been so eager to see.

. . . As you may have read, the Preparatory Commission has been postponed until the 23rd of November and the General Assembly until January. The result may be that I will not get home until the end of January or early February. However, I am still planning to send the family the middle of December in time for Christmas. I suspect they will have to go by boat and it will be dreary here alone without them. I should have realized that no international conference ever ended on time.

I have been paying a lot of household bills for the month of September and will continue to do so as they arrive, so be sure that we don't pay any of the same ones and also forward any that you have incurred which need prompt attention, or pay them for me and keep a record of them so I can take care of them when I return.

I hope if you encounter Mr. [William P.] Sidley or any of the partners in my firm you will tell them with what misgivings I have gone on doing these government jobs and how restless I am to get back to Chicago and practice law again somewhere. I have not, as you know, committed my-

[38] Ronald Tree, Parliamentary Secretary of the Ministry of Town and Country Planning, and his wife Nancy, niece of Lady Astor, lived at Ditchley Park, Oxfordshire.

self to go back to that firm, but I want to keep the opportunity available in case I decided that that is the best thing to do.

I hope the throat trouble you mention in your letter of the 13th has cleared up and that you are well. I miss the fall days there on the farm more than I can tell you. Give my love to John Fell. I have neglected him dreadfully, but the opportunities to write suitable letters have been few up until now. I will do so soon.

Love
Ad.

p.s. Ellen was so hopeful that the cook would stay on after she returned but your letter sounds as tho she is determined to leave.

To Kenneth F. Burgess

October 31, 1945

Dear Ken,

Our conversation on the 'phone the other night gave me a nostalgic reminder of home and my long exile.

I am delighted that you are interested in the Association of Commerce presentation of the case for Chicago.[39] It will need all the persuasion you've got. Up to now Chicago has received literally no attention or serious consideration. As you will understand, in my official capacity as United States Delegate, I cannot express any preference, under strict instructions from the President, and the sentiment seems to be preponderantly in favor of the East coast, at least among those who favor the United States at all. But I have little doubt that the latter will be an overwheming majority when the Preparatory Commission convenes on November 23rd. So many of the European states are still outside awaiting the conclusion of the peace treaties or as neutrals.

But, although I can take no active part of course in the selection of the site, I can and will take every opportunity to explain what Chicago has to offer and I have already done so discreetly from time to time. Meanwhile, Philadelphia* arouses no wild enthusiasm and nothing else on the East coast has been presented emphatically or effectively. So, the delegates are pretty much up in the air and I think the decision is still wide open. Moreover, as I have indicated, I have little doubt that the United States will be selected and the Preparatory Commission will attempt to recommend a specific city. In this connection, I am enclosing a copy of

---

* But has made an excellent presentation.

[39] As permanent headquarters for the United Nations.

the recommendation adopted last Saturday night at the last session of the Executive Committee. Incidentally, Ed Stettinius fell ill and was obliged to return to the States just as it became our turn to preside as chairman of the Executive Committee. Upon his withdrawal I was elected just as the Executive Committee commenced meeting daily instead of weekly as it had theretofore. It was an ordeal but a fine experience and I really enjoyed it. And I think the United States emerged without any serious disasters. Certainly the work that has been accomplished here in less than two months is formidable and we have created the organizational structure and rules and regulations for the General Assembly and all the organs. The report is a monstrosity of some 200 pages but I think it has sharpened up the issues neatly for a decision by the Preparatory Commission and finally the General Assembly. Although we had many disagreements and some bad hours with the Russians and a few of the other delegations, on the whole, the area of agreement was very large and perhaps 90% of the report represents unanimous agreement. I feel that on the evidence to date the Russians are entirely sincere about the United Nations, but it's a slow and tedious process to educate them in western ways and methods, and the negotiation becomes dreadfully trying at times.

To return to Chicago — I rather doubt if the Preparatory Commission will attempt to send a mission to the United States to make on-the-ground investigations. It seems to me more likely that they will take the material available here and try to arrive at an agreement on some site, once the selection of the United States has been ratified. I anticipate that the Preparatory Commission will be in session for about a month and, accordingly, I would suggest that, if you plan to send anyone over here, they should arrive by the first week in December. I am loath to make any predictions as to a time or the situation they will encounter, as the whole program on the selection of site is fluid and somewhat ambiguous. Of course the final decision must be made by the General Assembly which will probably convene about the 7th of January. But the recommendation of the Preparatory Commission may have considerable influence on the Assembly's decision, particularly as the United States delegation at the Assembly will officially keep hands off. I cannot, therefore, be certain that it would be profitable to send anyone but, if the Association [of Commerce] is disposed to do so, I should think it would be well for them to be here, as I say, during the Preparatory Commission period. The living and housing conditions in London are frightful and hence, it should not be more than one or two people in any event. I have no information as to whether other cities are sending delegations to the Pre-

paratory Commission, but perhaps you can find out what Philadelphia*
is doing.

What I seem to encounter most generally is the feeling that Chicago
has an abominable climate. I would be particularly prepared on this
score — and also the fact that the additional distance for travel from
Europe is inconsequential. San Francisco has deposited a most formidable presentation of its case, but I think there is little prospect of reaching agreement on the West coast, due to the determined position of the
European states on distance. Further thoughts will occur to me after the
fog of the last few weeks has swept away and I will write you again. I
understand from a letter from Leverett Lyon[40] that the formal Chicago
presentation is enroute and you should have no hesitancy in asking my
advice about anything, bearing in mind the limitations on what I can do
positively. For your convenience, I am sending a copy of this letter to
Mr. Lyon and the Mayor.

With best wishes to you all, I am,

Sincerely,

* There is a rumor that Phila is sending a delegation & that the Black
Hills intends to send one if Phila does.

*After the Executive Committee had completed its work, Philip Noel-
Baker wrote Stevenson: "Taken all around, I think the results are very
good and the business of the whole Commission and its Committees will
be very well conducted. If that is so, it is certainly due to you. . . . The
full onslaught of the Soviet campaign fell on you, and I wish we had
been able to share it better. But at least it makes it easier for me to
congratulate you on the fair and public-spirited work you did, and on
the amazing patience and skill you showed. None could have done it
better."*

*On November 13, 1945, Stevenson, in a speech to British servicemen
at Nuffield House, described some of the work of the Executive Committee of the Preparatory Commission.*

Let me say at the outset how happy I am to have this opportunity to
spend an evening with you gentlemen. For I might as well confess at the
outset that I am here under false pretenses. I am only masquerading as
a diplomat. I feel it wise to make that confession before you discover it
for yourselves. I am or was until almost five years ago a common or
garden variety of corporation lawyer in Chicago and then my dear friend,

[40] Executive officer of the Chicago Association of Commerce.

the late Frank Knox, the Secretary of the Navy, persuaded me to come to Washington as his personal assistant and I worked and traveled with him during those dramatic years of the creation of the modern United States Navy until his death — years that saw defeat and misfortune transformed into victory in the Pacific and the preparations for the landing in Normandy all but completed. They were the three happiest and most satisfying years of my life and now that I have been impressed into service as a diplomat and seem destined to spend my days, at least for awhile, with diplomats, those years and life in the service look all the better to me.

I feel like the boy from my home town — Chicago — who served with General Allenby in Palestine during the last war. Story.[41]

But much as I would prefer to talk about the Navy and the war, I am afraid there is nothing I could say which would be of any interest to this audience. So perhaps it's just as well for me that I have to resume my disguise as a diplomat and tell you something about what is to me, now that the war is won, the most important thing in the world today and perhaps for years to come. I mean the United Nations, the most recent attempt at international organization for peace.

I need not trace for you the evolution step by step — the United Nations Declaration of January 1, 1942, the Moscow Declaration of November 1, 1943, calling for the establishment at the earliest possible date of a general international organization for the maintenance of peace and security, the Dumbarton Oaks proposals of the United States, the United Kingdom, Russia and China which were published October 7, 1944, and finally the Charter of San Francisco of June 26th last — a Charter written by 50 nations in two months of travail while the war was still being fought. And now today only three months after the end of hostilities the Charter has become effective under its terms and some 38 nations have deposited their ratifications in the State Department in Washington.

Meanwhile to prepare all the elaborate machinery to get the organization into motion as soon as the Charter became effective, the signatories of the Charter at San Francisco also signed an interim agreement which was not a treaty and required no ratification creating the Preparatory Commission of the United Nations on which all 51 signatory states are represented. To this Preparatory Commission is assigned the very formidable task of preparing the agenda, rules of procedure and organizational structure of the GA [General Assembly], the secretariat and all the organs of the UN — the SC [Security Council], ECOSOC [Economic and Social Council], TC [Trusteeship Council] so that the United Nations can organize and commence to function at the earliest possible date.

41 Not included with the manuscript.

For better or for worse I have been designated since Mr. Stettinius fell ill and was obliged to return home as the U.S. Delegate to the Preparatory Commission which will meet here in London on November 23. My opposite number for the British is the Honorable Philip Noel-Baker, Minister of State, for the Russians, Gromyko, Soviet Ambassador to the U. S.; for the Chinese, Dr. Wellington Koo, Chinese Ambassador to the UK and for the French, Rene Massigli, Ambassador of France to the U. K. Let me hastily and parenthetically say that I join in your prayers that perhaps the very competent staff of experts which our government has provided me may save us from disaster.

But the Preparatory Commission will not start with a blank sheet of paper, because at San Francisco it elected an Executive Committee of 14 nations, including the Big Five, and this Executive Committee has been working here in London since the last of August. After 8 weeks of literally day and night work its report of some 200 pages was completed on October 27th and it adjourned — to my great relief as its chairman.[42]

The Executive Committee of the Preco worked out slowly and painfully with many compromises provisional agenda for the first meetings of the GA, the SC and ECOSOC; drafted rules of procedure for each of the organs of UN; worked out organizational structures for each of them and for the international secretariat. In short it put the flesh on the bare bones of the San Francisco Charter.

And now this report of the Executive Committee will go to all the 52 nations when they convene as the Preco on November 23. I anticipate that it will take Preco about a month to review and work over all this material, reconcile the unsettled disputes and prepare the final recommendations. And then the GA will meet the first week in January, elect the members of the SC, ECOSOC and the TC, elect a Secretary General, select a permanent site for the headquarters of the organization, adopt its rules of procedure and perform a myriad of other tasks and — I hope — then adjourn to meet again in the spring or early summer at the permanent site. The anniversary of San Francisco — April 25th — has been suggested. In short, it is the hope and purpose of our government that the GA can meet and the organization commence to function with the

[42] *Report by the Executive Committee to the Preparatory Commission of the United Nations.* November 12, 1945. PC/EX/113/Rev. 1. Published by the Preparatory Commission, United Nations Archives. On November 1, 1945, Stevenson sent a memorandum to the Secretary of State entitled "Synopsis of principal issues developed during Executive Committee of the Preparatory Commission." It is published in *Foreign Relations of the United States: Diplomatic Papers, 1945,* Volume I, *General: The United Nations.* Department of State Publication 8294. (Washington: Government Printing Office, 1967), pp. 1463–1474.

active participation of more than 50 nations, including all the great powers, in the first month of the first year of peace. It is also our hope that this first meeting of the GA can be exclusively organizational in character — it is our hope that it will set up the organs so that they can promptly meet and commence the attack on the myriad of problems — political, economic and social — that are vexing this distracted world and after adequate preparation make their reports and recommendations to the later meeting of the General Assembly. We think this a much more orderly way to proceed then to discuss substantive problems at the January meeting before the UN are really organized and ready to function.

In Europe and in Asia there is untold disorder and suffering and there will be more this winter. Everywhere there are millions who look with despair upon the ruins of homes and factories. Their hearts will not be lifted upwards, nor their hopes, by boundaries drawn upon a map. They need emergency relief, but they need more than that. They need, and if we are to have any stability in the world, they must have, action that will open the way to a future of productive work, of decent living conditions and of security. They need proof that the nations of the world can work together to build as well as destroy. That action UN must provide and our government feels that its best chance of prompt, effective action would be two meetings of the Assembly — the first just to organize, then a period of work and preparation by the various councils and technical committees, and then an action meeting — "a town hall of the world" as Senator Vandenburg[43] calls it — later on. This U.S. proposal was adopted by the Executive Committee and we trust it will prevail in the Preco and GA meeting in January, but of course with the world in torment it will be a temptation to many to inject discussion of substantive problems into this first meeting.

From this tiresome little review of what has happened to date you will see that in just a little more than a year from the very preliminary vision of Dumbarton Oaks the UN has emerged as a living organism and by January will be standing on its own feet (story about Ed Stettinius and Gromyko and the baby).[44]

Altho the work of the Executive Committee during the past 8 or 9 weeks has probably in large measure fashioned the form of UN for many years to come, its work was so dry and technical and undramatic — ex-

[43] Senator Arthur H. Vandenberg of Michigan, senior Republican member of the Foreign Relations Committee; member of the U.S. delegation to the UN conference at San Francisco and later member of the delegation to the first General Assembly.
[44] Not included with the manuscript.

cept for occasional lively moments that you can always count on the Russians to provide when Moscow calls some new signals — that it had little attention from the press.

I was amused by a bit I saw in the London Economist[45] last week in this connection: "International committees, though attended by many blessings, are saddled with one curse. Their proceedings are dull to the eye and ear. They lack pageantry and symbolism. Drably clad delegates sidle into place. Interpreters drone on. Spectators try to puzzle out which is Gromyko and which Mexico. Public interest is almost impossible to sustain."

. . . The news emphasis was, as usual, more on disagreements than the really much more significant aspect of the work of the Executive Committee which was the very broad area of agreement. I venture to say that 90% of the recommendations were adopted unanimously and considering the wide disparity of viewpoint, tradition and experience in procedure and government organization among the governments represented, it was almost spectacular. But the disagreements, the hot words and the Russian stubbornness always made the news and will always do so, I suppose, not only through Preco and the GA but on and on into the future which will not make it any easier to enlist the enlightened public opinion of the world.

The emphasis on the unimportant recalls the old story about the milk-wagon horse — story.[46]

I dwell on this matter of balanced news reporting because no scheme for peace can succeed unless it is supported by the informed public opinion of the world, for "public opinion is the sovereign of us all," as someone has said.

In this connection with the rapid accumulation of unsolved problems around the world I detect a growing cynicism; mistrust of Russia is becoming almost a phobia; the perfectionists are saying that we must organize for peace but the United Nations isn't good enough, only a world government will do; the isolationists who don't know they are vestigial remnants of the pre-atomic age are emerging in new clothes; many at home are saying why help Britain financially, haven't we helped her enough already, let's help ourselves first. And beneath it all runs a current of impatience — you see it here in England — a current of cynical impatience; that we must get all the problems settled at once and settled according to our liking or we can't get them settled at all.

But why do we get so impatient?

45 November 3, 1945.
46 Not included with the manuscript.

What do we expect, after a war like this, coming so soon and so hard after another war?

It was certainly bad to become indifferent to what was going on in the world, as so many of us did in the late 20's and early 30's. It led to the most unpleasant surprises. But is it not equally bad to expect too much too quickly?

After all, there was trouble aplenty after the last war. Civil war in Finland; German free corps fighting along the Baltic; Poles and Russians fighting; Lithuanians rowing with Poles, and Poles with Ruthenians; Czechs and Poles squabbling; Serbs and Croats; Croats and Austrians; Italians and Yugoslavs; Serbs and Bulgars; Albanians and Italians; Albanians and Greeks; Greeks and Turks — the list seems endless. The Japs getting cocky. The Russians paralysed by revolution and defeat. The French bled white. The Americans dropping out in impatient disgust, and the French and British endlessly quarreling. German putsches, German ill will, Bolshevism in Hungary. The French occupying the Ruhr in defiance of Britain's wishes. And the Big Three of those days — the United States, France and Britain — what authority did they have, when they couldn't even agree among themselves?

Disagreement! It made a holiday then for the leaders of every just cause, but also for every agitator, every ambitious adventurer. Among them all, they reopened every old sore in the world of politics.

And now once more we have trouble, after a war, in every old sore spot, and a lot more besides.

Yet in spite of all discord and disunity of view, the world did settle down somewhat. And if ever there was a completely unnecessary war, a preventible war, it was this one.

We must give time a chance to do its work. In history, there is no other healer.

Much that is happening now is the kind of thing that has always happened in similar circumstances. What we have to concentrate on are the new things — the faiths and forces that are making the United Nations possible, and a dozen other accords of one sort and another which, for being unsensational, are nonetheless dedicated to the healing of war's deep wounds and the weaving of peace.

The trouble is that there isn't as much time as there used to be. Gibbons[47] remarked that the greatest theological controversy which rocked the Roman Empire and affected the peace of millions turned on the question whether a certain word should be spelled with one diphthong or another.

[47] Edward Gibbon, *The Decline and Fall of the Roman Empire.*

But today we have suddenly been projected into a situation where no controversies that affect peace can be tolerated, whether they related to diphthongs or anything else. The age old emotions of hatred, jealousy, suspicion and intolerance have at last been armed with weapons by which man can achieve his own complete destruction in one burst of universal fury.

This is the point in human destiny to which all the glories and toils of the past have led us. These are the gifts which science has suddenly dumped on our trembling knees. Man's mastery of science and the physical world has far outrun man's mastery of himself. Is man to be the master of the energies he has created or is he to be their victim?

We must come to terms with our atomic bombs. "We must choose to live together or we must choose, quite literally, not to live."

That is why it is the policy of the U. S. to get the U. N. organized and functioning as rapidly as possible; it is only a spade as Lord Robert Cecil has said. And like a spade it will not work by itself. It will take the faith, confidence and energy of all of us all the time to make it work. But it is the only practicable alternative and, fortunately and thanks to the vision and determination of many people, it is almost ready to take up its mighty burdens, just in time!

And that is also the policy of the British Government and of many governments, who know that it is not machinery but people who will determine the accuracy or inaccuracy of [Immanuel] Kant's grim prophecy that the world will be "the graveyard of the human race," but who also know that without the machinery, without the spade, there could be no organized concentration of human aim and effort, of human will.

You may be asking if the Soviet policy with regard to U. N. is the same.

I think it is, with a different emphasis — a preoccupation with power and the supremacy of the SC in which Russia has a veto; a realistic rejection in international politics of the democratic idea of one man one vote whatever his station — that the Soviet Union and El Salvador have any basis of equality; constant concentration on what this or that means to the Soviet Union irrespective of what it means to others. They reject the idea that a man can serve the U. N. first and his country second. They are most difficult and trying in negotiation. First of all they have little latitude of authority and must sit rigidly and sometimes painfully on their orders however unreasonable and however isolated and even ludicrous the position may be. And then they often have suddenly [suddenly] to reverse themselves — without a smile! (Technical people) They have no ease, no self-confidence, no language facility, move slowly, awkwardly. They are suspicious, stubborn, blunt, often almost discourteous and always determined and conscientious. And always improving!

I don't presume to know what's going on in Moscow. Struggle between isolationists and internationalists. Rigidities of a bureaucracy disciplined by fear. Many of you know far more than I. But one can detect a pattern beneath the confusion and contradictions of the surface if you look at the thing as a whole — to be as difficult as possible and get as many political concessions as possible, but never to lose sight of the fact that internal reconstruction and development, improved living standards, is the first objective — and the condition for that is peace!

Molotov[48] last week pointed out the differences between Russia and her Allies as they appear in Russian eyes — the control of Japan,[49] slowness over German reparations to which she believes herself entitled by the enormity of her injuries, fears of Western blocs, differences between Soviet and Western views of what constitutes "democracy." But the spirit of the 28th anniversary[50] and the slogans advanced for it disclose a preoccupation with the great tasks of internal reconstruction and development and her need for peace after this most ghastly of all struggles.

By no means [should we be] discouraged about Russia but what we must never lose sight of is that she is the key to the peace and prosperity of the future and little by little, year by year, we must make progress in the difficult art of getting along with her, of reassuring her that our motives are not sinister and disingenuous. For the worst thing that could happen to us all would be for her to take the veil, to withdraw behind her walls of secrecy, to go it alone in isolation. That's the road to disaster.

I'm afraid I've gotten a little out of character. The temptation has been too great for me. I'm not a statesman or a prophet. I'm just a machinist helping to build the complicated machinery of the United Nations for all of us to operate and when that's done I expect to return to Chicago and see if there are any corporations without more lawyers than vice presidents.

And when the machinery is constructed then the peoples must force their governments to make it work. For peace is not merely the absence of war. It is not a static thing, it is dynamic. It is something that has to be fought for all the time — now and in the future — something that we'll all have to fight for all the time with high courage and fanatical patience.

Before I sit down and release us both from this agony may I say one

[48] Vyacheslav M. Molotov, Russian Minister of Foreign Affairs and delegate to the first UN General Assembly.

[49] The Soviet Union was excluded from any influence in the postwar occupation of Japan.

[50] Of the Russian Revolution.

personal word from the bottom of my heart to you British soldiers and sailors. I have been here before when the buzz bombs and rockets were rumbling across London, and since the days when you and your country-men stood fast and saved for us both the hope of ultimate victory I came to know a few of the men in and out of the services who led you through the war.

And I too want to make my acknowledgement of the greatness of your nation — which is your people. And I too want to express my confidence that such a nation can and will face the future with pride and confidence — and help to save it again and again.

With victory won we must somehow stagger wearily through the days of discouragement and inevitable letdown. There are strikes in America and rations are tighter than ever here. What's worse we are going to have to listen to discordant voices of little men on both sides of the Atlantic sniping at each other. But I know, as Ed Stettinius said here at Albert Hall a month ago, that the real people in America believe in you, just as I hope and believe the real people in England believe in us.

We have come a long way together — we have a longer way to go — together. This has been the bloodiest century in history. But together we can show the world the way to retrieve it. We are in the mud now but we are on the threshold of great events. "We have," as Tom Paine said 150 years ago — "we have it within our power to begin the world over again." To that I would like to add one word — "together."

The Preparatory Commission met on November 24, 1945, and referred the report of the Executive Committee to eight technical committees for study. The Preparatory Commission concluded its work on December 23, 1945.

In a speech on January 22, 1947, Adlai E. Stevenson said:

Periodically I asked the State Department to send over the Under-Secretary and let me go to Chicago or Libertyville or Bloomington and hide, but they always said no, no, you're doing fine, and will send you some more help, and pretty soon a new contingent of professors and secretaries would arrive, when there wasn't even a spare lamp post to lean against in shattered, overcrowded London — and most of the time Grosvenor Square below my windows was a bedlam of G.I. brides carrying babies, inside or out, and demanding transportation to the U.S. I felt like joining them.[51]

[51] Speech to the Commonwealth Club of Chicago.

Edward R. Stettinius, Jr. wrote Stevenson on November 28, 1945: "I appreciate the fine manner in which you have picked up and carried on the important work in London. I hear nothing but praise for the way in which you have not only completed the work of the Executive Committee, but also the way in which you have taken hold in the Preparatory Commission itself."

Many years later Donald C. Stone, who was a member of the U.S. delegation, wrote Stevenson that recently while in London he had passed the house Stevenson had lived in, "and recalled the very pleasant visits I had there. I have often looked back on the days I worked with you in London as among the most enjoyable in my life. This is because the team was such a harmonious one and the top man provided the best leadership I have ever enjoyed." [52]

It is possible for Stevenson's role from November 24 to December 23 to be revealed by publishing his statements at the meetings of the commission and its subcommittees and his reports to the Department of State. [53] *Although the editors have made selections from these sources, they rely more heavily on the few extant letters he wrote during this period and on an off-the-record speech he made in Chicago on March 9, 1947, which is in reality an* aide-mémoire *of the Preparatory Commission and the first UN General Assembly meetings. This particular document is a careful description and a perceptive analysis of an important stage in the building of the United Nations.*

To Mrs. Ernest L. Ives[54]

December 12, 1945

Dear Buffy,

. . . This afternoon is the first tranquil spot I have found in the turbulent stream for the last several weeks. I am remorseful that I have not written you long before and I have neglected John Fell shamefully but there has been literally no time. I hope the change of plans and Ellen's

[52] This letter is in the Adlai E. Stevenson collection, Illinois State Historical Library.

[53] Verbatim minutes of the meetings of the Preparatory Commission are in the United Nations Archives, Dag Hammarskjöld Library, United Nations. See also *Report of the Preparatory Commission of the United Nations*, December 23, 1945. Document PC/20. A number of the reports Stevenson sent to the Department of State on the work of the Preparatory Commission are published in *Foreign Relations of the United States: Diplomatic Papers, 1945*, Volume I, *General: The United Nations*, pp. 1479–1509. Included is Stevenson's summary of the main changes by the Preparatory Commission in the Executive Committee report.

[54] The original is in E.S.I., I.S.H.L.

decision to stay on until after Christmas and then send Adlai direct to Boston from New York was not too inconvenient for you. It was difficult for her to make up her mind, due to my indecision and the uncertainty about the dates of the Preparatory Commission beginning and ending and the General Assembly and my participation therein. As to the latter, I still have no information but I suppose the Department will want me to stay on here during the Assembly which may last into the middle or end of February. In that event I suppose I will capitulate and Ellen is giving some thought to returning in January with John Fell although I am afraid it is asking too much of her.

It has been an interesting experience and I have genuinely enjoyed it but it has been disappointing as far as seeing much of the boys is concerned due to the pressure on my time. Your reporting of events at home has been marvelous and a source of almost daily comfort. Ellen has had no worries about things there which would have been the natural accompaniment of no news.

I am delighted with the progress on the book project[55] and I think if it works you will have done the paper and all of us a great service. I wish I could be there to participate in these discussions with [Harold] Sinclair.

Please assure John Fell that his father hasn't forgotten him and that it's going to be a dismal Christmas without him. I have no doubt you will make his a happy one but I am a little appalled at the prospect of another electric train! I think the basement is already full of the wreckage of old ones. I suspect you have been extravagant again.

Please give my best to Ernest and know how everlastingly indebted we all are to you for holding the fort.

Love,
AD.

P.S. I see a notation on the Nov. 11 telephone bill of $108.35 (!) which I have just paid that you will pay the toll service item of $36.39. Thanks! But are you sure its all yours? If so send me a check at your leisure.

The location of the permanent headquarters of the United Nations received widespread attention in the press as the question was discussed by Committee 8 of the Preparatory Commission. Twenty-two U.S. cities had representatives seeking the site for their respective municipalities. Stevenson, following policy set in Washington, emphasized

[55] A history of the *Daily Pantagraph.*

that these delegations were private citizens whose arguments should be considered on their merits and not as an expression of the official U.S. position.

On December 7, 1945, at the beginning of discussions in Committee 8, Stevenson stated:

> In order that there may be no misunderstanding, it may be helpful to the Committee if I state again the position of my Government on the location of the permanent headquarters of the United Nations.
>
> Our position remains exactly as it was when the Executive Committee voted on this recommendation: my Government wishes the members of the United Nations to come to their decision, whatever it may be, free from any influence or pressure and after the different points of view have been fully and fairly presented. If they decide to confirm the recommendation of the Executive Committee to come to the United States we want that decision to be made solely in the best interests both now and in the future of the United Nations Organization as a whole and for no other reason whatever. My Government has not sought and is not seeking the headquarters, should you decide to locate the permanent headquarters in the United States, my Government, and indeed the American people will welcome that decision and will gladly undertake the very great responsibilities which that honour entails. (Applause).[56]

In the debate that followed, a Philippine delegate stated that "the best way to keep the United States in the United Nations is to put UNO's feet in the United States." He warned that the danger of U.S. isolation was "as great today as ever." The U.S., he added, "behaved like an elderly excited lady about to become a grandmother at San Francisco when she observed the birth pangs of the UNO. She threw out her arms in hysterical hospitality to the delegates."

Stevenson replied that he was "shocked" to hear his country referred to as an excited grandmother. The U.S. position, he believed, was more comparable to that of "an agitated, blushing debutante." As the delegates roared with laughter, he added: "But the young lady is not sensitive and she wishes you to converse as freely as possible about her, in connection with the UN site — and not only about her, but about all the other ladies in the block."

Stevenson cabled Washington, however, that Erwin D. Canham, edi-

[56] Verbatim minutes, United Nations Archives and Records Retirement, PC/ Microfilm Roll 13N. *Foreign Relations of the United States: Diplomatic Papers, 1945,* Volume I, *General: The United Nations,* p. 1486, has a slightly different version of Stevenson's statement. Apparently the editors of *Foreign Relations* used a press release rather than the verbatim record.

tor of the Christian Science Monitor, *had warned that the U.S. official position of not seeking but welcoming the permanent headquarters might enable the British to win sufficient votes for a European site. The Observer (London) on December 9, 1945, published an article by Canham with the headline "UNO H.Q. in Europe Would Shock America." Such a decision, he stated, would be a rebuff to the Truman Administration.*

On December 15, after days of discussion, a proposal to hold a secret ballot on the question of a permanent headquarters was defeated. Stevenson voted against the secret ballot and after the proposal was defeated he told Committee 8:

> At the outset of our meetings a couple of weeks ago, I explained the position of the US on the question of the location of the permanent headquarters. I said that I would abstain from voting on the location lest there be any misunderstanding about what the position of the United States was. I must take this perhaps tardy opportunity to explain that at the outset of our meetings in Committee 8 I made as clear as I could the position of my Government on the question of the location of the site of the permanent headquarters of the United Nations. I also said at that time that I would abstain from voting inconsistent with the policy of my Government on the location; but I said that I would participate in matters of procedure, and I voted against the secret ballot not on any legal grounds and not, I beg you to believe, to serve any ulterior motive; I voted against it because I feel — and so does my delegation and my Government — that secrecy is a bad precedent for the United Nations; because we felt that our decisions, in so far as they could, consistent with the rules, should be arrived at openly, after the fullest, freest and frankest discussion. Both now and hereafter, as Mr. Noel-Baker so eloquently said the other day, we have spoken — frankly on this issue, and for my part my delegation rejoices that the debate has been candid and free; and we felt that we should vote freely and frankly in the same spirit. I am happy that in its infancy the United Nations has not adopted the methods of secrecy.[57]

Later in that meeting after an amendment to place the headquarters in Europe was defeated by a vote of 25 to 23 with 2 abstentions (two-thirds was required), the recommendation to place the UN in the United States was adopted 30 to 14 with 6 abstentions. A motion to make the

[57] Verbatim Minutes, United Nations Archives and Records Retirement, PC/Microfilm Roll 13N. *Foreign Relations of the United States: Diplomatic Papers, 1945,* Volume I, *General: The United Nations,* pp. 1488–1489, has a slightly different version of Stevenson's statement. Apparently the editors of *Foreign Relations* used a press release rather than the verbatim record.

vote unanimous was supported strongly by British delegate Philip Noel-Baker and it carried with acclamation.

On December 18, 1945, the British Broadcasting Corporation interviewed Stevenson.[58]

LINDSAY: Hello, Radio News Reel. This is Vera Lindsay speaking from Church House, Westminster, and I have the good fortune to inveigle Mr. Stevenson, United States delegate, from his work in the Preparatory Commission, to speak to us.

I've been watching and listening to Mr. Stevenson during Committee 8 — the Committee that decided on the permanent site. If I may say so, manoeuvred through stormy discussions to the decision and choice of the United States as a permanent home.

Mr. Stevenson, I consider it a great success. How do you feel about it?

STEVENSON: Well, I hardly think manoeuvring is the word, Miss Lindsay. The United States never sought the permanent headquarters. We wanted the United Nations to make the decision without pressure or influence from us, and after the fullest, freest discussion of the relative merits of the United States [and] Europe. We had that kind of a discussion, I think, in Committee 8, and it was most gratifying to my delegation and to my Government. I'm sure the decision to come to the United States is equally gratifying to the American people as a whole. Public opinion as someone said — I think it was an Englishman — is the sovereign of us all. It is America's destiny to take a leading part in the world of tomorrow and I hope and believe that the permanent headquarters in the United States will serve to increase the understanding of the American people in the objectives and problems of the United Nations. And with that understanding will come, I believe, a better informed public opinion, which will mean so much to the support of the Organization in the future.

LINDSAY: Do tell me, Mr. Stevenson, will there be much greater interest in the United States now?

STEVENSON: I can't but believe that the presence of the United Nations in the coming and going of all the statesmen and diplomats to the United States will serve to increase constantly the public understanding of the objectives and the work of the United Nations, and with that understanding a greater sympathy and support, I trust and believe.

LINDSAY: Now do tell me, Mr. Stevenson, when the actual place is de-

---

[58] The text is a transcription made from a telediphone recording. The original is in the possession of the BBC, London.

cided, what would you think of workmen from other lands coming to help to build the actual site?

STEVENSON: Well it's been my good fortune and the good fortune of many others to see much of the beauty of the world as a whole, and I can only hope that the United Nations buildings, when they're finally erected, will reflect much of the beauties of Europe — the architectures, the fabrics, the furniture; the beauties of Asia and all the continents of the seas. It would seem to me that it would be most fitting and appropriate that we should have materials, that we should have craftsmanship, that we should have architecture reflecting some of these magnificent cultural traditions of the peoples who comprise the peoples of the world, and accordingly I can only hope that as these buildings are erected that we have the participation of other governments and other peoples and other cultures in their final composition.

LINDSAY: Mr. Stevenson, when did you take up politics?

STEVENSON: Well, I shouldn't — I didn't realise that I'd ever taken up politics, Miss Lindsay, to be quite accurate about it. I, like many of my countrymen, saw the war coming and early in 1941 I left my law business in Chicago and went to Washington as assistant to the late Frank Knox when he was Secretary of the Navy. I served with him during that interval in which we were creating the new great modern American Navy, up until the time of his death in the early summer of 1944. Then I left, expecting to go back to my law business in Chicago, and instead I was diverted and went along the battlefronts on a tour of duty for the War Department. I then resigned again from the Government and returned to Chicago and again I returned somewhat reluctantly but I'm happy that I did now to the State Department, where I've served with Mr. Stettinius and the present Secretary of State Mr. Byrnes; and it was due to them that I found myself in this not wholly comfortable position, but very responsible opportunity here, as the United States delegate to the Preparatory Commission in London.

LINDSAY: Mr. Stevenson, do you plan to continue this work or to go back to law in the future?

STEVENSON: Well I've always planned to go back to law; on the other hand I would like to make my small contribution to the peace as I attempted to do to the war. Just when I can return to my home in Chicago I can't now foresee, but I fully expect to some time and I hope it's not in the too far distant future.

LINDSAY: Well thank you, Mr. Stevenson, very much indeed. If I may say so, I think the United States is very lucky in its delegate.

On December 11, 1945, Undersecretary of State Dean G. Acheson wrote Stevenson: "I want you to know how much all of us in the Department appreciate the magnificent job that you have been doing in London on the Preparatory Commission. We are most fortunate to have had you there throughout the work of the Executive Committee and the Preparatory Commission, and we would have been in bad shape without you. I am delighted to see Noel Baker's letter to you, and I have heard from many other sources nothing but the highest praise for the tact and effectiveness with which you have directed the work of the United States during these last few weeks."

To Dean G. Acheson

December 29, 1945

Dear Dean,

Your letter gave me more comfort than anything that has happened since I have been here. It was more than decent of you to write me and I feel rewarded for what has been, at least industrious if not brilliant service. I felt, as you know, that after I inherited, unwillingly, the responsibilities of the job here during the Preparatory period that I should also have inherited the "titles and estates" and that they would have fortified my position.[59] But no harm has been done, I think, and things have gone rather better than I had any right to expect.

We continue to raise periodical cheers for Acheson and I have some idea of the frightfully difficult days you have weathered in these last few months. I don't envy you but I am thankful that you have been there.

My warmest regards to Alice[60] and Eddie Miller[61] and all power to your good right arm and your frontal lobes.

Faithfully yours,

---

[59] Stevenson's opposite numbers among the Big Five held the rank of ambassador while his rank was minister. In an interview with Walter Johnson, November 30, 1955, when Stevenson read the draft of an article on Edward R. Stettinius, Jr., by Johnson, Stevenson expressed his displeasure since he believed the rank of ambassador would have increased his effectiveness.

[60] Mrs. Acheson.

[61] Edward G. Miller, Jr., a New York lawyer and special assistant to the Undersecretary of State.

To Captain Edward D. McDougal, Jr.[62]

December 29, 1945

Dear Ed,

Many thanks for your Christmas card which arrived just in time. I too look forward to a talk with you eagerly and I hope the opportunity will come on my way back in Washington after the General Assembly which should conclude its labors early in February.

The future has me as confounded as ever but I still yearn for home and normal life again, subject, as always, to all the misgivings there that you are familiar with.

I am curious to know about your present plans and prospects for getting out of the Navy. Do send me a line some day. My love to Kate.[63]

Yours,

AES

On November 12, 1945, William P. Sidley wrote Stevenson that he concurred with Edwin C. Austin's letter of September 19. He then wrote: "Much as I would like to have you return here for a full time partnership, I am even more interested in your making the right decision in your own interest. You have a wealth of ability, character and intelligence which I wish to see put to the fullest possible use, and if the diplomatic or public field is likely to bring you greater distinction and happiness, then I am for it. However, I can't help you make your decision. . . . You will always find a warm welcome in this office, whether you come as a permanent resident or a transient guest." Mr. Sidley concluded by describing Leverett S. Lyon of the Chicago Association of Commerce, who was to present Chicago's request to be the permanent home of the United Nations.

To William P. Sidley

December 29, 1945

Dear Mr. Sidley,

I have just emerged from weeks of frenzy and I am reminded again that I have never properly acknowledged your kind, thoughtful and encouraging letter of November 12.

It was good to have a glimpse of Leverett Lyon over here and he was

[62] The original is in the possession of Mr. McDougal.
[63] Mrs. McDougal.

as dignified and enlightened a representative of an American city as the United Nations were privileged to see. I wish you would remember me to him most cordially when you next encounter.

As you know, by this time, the selection of the city seems to be narrowed down to the eastern seaboard and more specifically, the neighborhood of Boston and New York in the broadest sense. I am not surprised at this development in view of the anxiety of the countries that supported the United States to propitiate the Europeans, but I feel it may be a mistake in the long view of things not to go to the Middle West where the education would be most useful. I did what I could, consistent with my official position, to keep at least a few of the principal delegates aware of some of our domestic problems in this connection, but you will understand that it was impossible for me to respond to the innumerable whispered inquiries as to "what we really wanted" in any emphatic terms.

As to my future, I am in the usual state of confusion with a mind so full of the current pressing problems here that I have had little time for deliberate, intelligent reflection. I had expected to be home by the first of the year and really completed my responsibilities with the completion of my service as Chief Delegate to the Preparatory Commission. But then, of course, the Secretary asked me to continue during the General Assembly as the Senior Adviser because the delegation is political in composition and only a few of them have much background. So I will be here through the General Assembly which will probably last until the middle of February. Then I plan to return to Washington, clean up my work, and then to Chicago for keeps, I hope. And my first objective will be a vacation in the sunshine somewhere! If you have spent many months in the London fog, you will understand that uncontrollable desire.

Please give my love to Mrs. Sidley and my affectionate regards to everyone at the office. I miss you all more than I can tell you.

Yours,

The first session of the General Assembly met in London on January 10, 1946. The United States delegates were Secretary of State James F. Byrnes; Edward R. Stettinius, Jr., U.S. representative to the UN; Senator Tom Connally; Senator Arthur H. Vandenberg; and Mrs. Franklin D. Roosevelt.

Foreign correspondent William H. Stoneman wrote: "Foreign diplomats were slightly surprised when Stevenson was made senior adviser to the American delegation to the assembly, instead of being made a full delegate or an alternate. Americans who had watched his work during earlier meetings were not only surprised they were slightly disgusted." Stoneman observed that the forty-six-year-old lawyer from Chicago "has become conspicuous for his skill and tact in getting the big boys to agree." While diplomats and politicians made speeches, Stevenson was the one "who actually does much of the leg work and no small part of the brainwork. . . . He burns the midnight oil in the late conversational pieces presenting our position, listening to arguments of others and suggesting compromises. When we reach agreement, he is generally largely responsible for it." Stoneman added that during the Preparatory Commission meetings, "time and again he broke impasses between the powers when agreement seemed impossible. In the process he earned the full respect of large and small powers alike, including that of the Russians, who are particular about their friends." [64]

Edward R. Stettinius, Jr., noted in his diary that on January 14, 1945, he had told the Secretary of State that "some recognition should be given Adlai Stevenson for his fine work." He recommended that Stevenson be considered for the post of alternate delegate if one of them did not attend the Assembly meetings. Byrnes replied: "Well, you are right, Stevenson will be given consideration and I will work the matter out somehow."

Stettinius also wrote that Stevenson had told him that he should get back to Chicago as soon as possible, "saying that he might not be needed here after another week or so. I told him that this was unthinkable and would be misunderstood and that he should stay on until all the work was completed, and that from his own selfish standpoint it would be a great mistake to leave before the end of the Conference." [65]

Byrnes left Stevenson in charge of the political negotiations for the United States with the other delegations on the selection of the president of the General Assembly, the vice presidents, the chairmen of various committees, and the representatives on the UN agencies. On January 13, 1946, for instance, Stettinius wrote in his diary that Stevenson phoned Byrnes to report he had been working with the British to try to persuade them to decide between New Zealand and Yugoslavia for the remaining position on the Economic and Social Council.

The following day Saville R. Davis wrote in the Christian Science Monitor that the important posts had been filled. "Taken as a whole, it was a remarkable achievement." The "hero of the elections," he stated,

---

[64] Chicago *Daily News*, January 14, 1946.

[65] This diary is in the Edward R. Stettinius collection, University of Virginia Library. Wilder Foote in a letter to Mrs. Foote wrote on January 30, 1946, "Adlai worries about his status and future." Letter in the possession of Mr. Foote.

"is Mr. Adlai Stevenson." Davis remarked that when Stevenson was be-
ing congratulated, he said with a laugh, "I guess I'm just a ward politi-
cian at heart." "This modesty wholly misrepresented his talents," Davis
observed. ". . . He drafted with great patience and skill a list which
represented not what the United States wanted but, nearly as possible,
what all delegations and groups wanted. The result was a phenomenal
electoral success."

To Loring C. Merwin

February 6, 1946

Dear Bud,

I am now planning to return about the end of this month and I will
telephone you when I get to Chicago. I am eager to hear what your investigation of the radio situation has disclosed.[66] I assume that the alternative options were executed and that we will have to exercise by the
middle of March.

We have about reached the end of this formative phase of the life of
the United Nations — and the end of my nervous equilibrium in the
process! See you soon.

Yours,

To James F. Oates, Jr.

February 7, 1946

Dear Jim,

The end is in sight. We expect to leave here on the 21st of February
on the Queen Mary after the conclusion of the General Assembly, and
— I hope — a short trip to Germany and a few days here to clean things
up. I plan to return with Ellen[67] to Chicago and then, God willing, to go
off on a holiday somewhere for a while.

On Sunday we had the news about Bobbie Pirie,[68] and of course we
are desolate and anxious to get back as soon as possible for that further
unhappy reason.

I look forward to talking with you and hearing all the news about developments at the office before I go away on the holiday. I think this is

[66] The *Daily Pantagraph* was negotiating for a radio station in Bloomington.

[67] Mrs. Stevenson had taken Adlai III and Borden back to Libertyville in January
and then rejoined her husband in London. (The original of this letter is in the
possession of Mr. Oates.)

[68] On January 31, 1946, a plane crash killed Robert S. Pirie, husband of Mrs.
Stevenson's younger sister Betty.

the "end" of my Government service but, as you know, I have said that before and of course the old familiar pressures are commencing again, but this time I have felt more confident than ever before.

Ellen joins me in love to you both.

Yours,
STEVE

To Mrs. Ernest L. Ives[69]

February 9, 1946

Dearest Buffy,

I have been in such a "flap" — as the British say — for the last month that I have utterly neglected to write you and to thank you for taking care of John Fell. Ellen reported that he was flourishing and all was well at the house when she returned but that she had missed seeing you.

I have just had your letter from Bloomington and I am delighted that you have had some talks with [Harold] Sinclair. I do hope some progress can be made on the history of the paper as it seems to me a most desirable project. I wrote Buddy[70] about it a long time ago, giving it my ardent blessing.

The news about Bobby Pirie has left us desolate. He was a stalwart and a dear friend as well. I am a little appalled at the multitude of petticoats over which I will have to preside in the family henceforth!

. . . We are now planning to leave here definitely on February 21 on the Queen Mary and will go right out to Chicago after a glimpse of Betty Pirie in New York. I will then have to do some income tax work,* etc., and then I hope we can get off for a holiday. I had hoped we could go down to Florida with the Carpenters[71] but it may be too late by the time I am ready to go.

As for future plans, I am still of a mind to go back to the law business in Chicago and get out of the Government, at least for the present. But I have a great reluctance about going back to the old firm and there may be a good prospect of organizing a new one with Glen Lloyd [72] and Ed McDougall. Please say nothing whatever about this for the present.

I hear tell that you made an ardent defense of Leo Crowley[73] somewhere in Chicago while you were there. It amuses me a good deal as I have always felt he was a first rate dope.

[69] This handwritten letter is in E.S.I., I.S.H.L.
[70] Loring C. Merwin.
[71] Mr. and Mrs. John Alden Carpenter.
[72] Stevenson's next-door neighbor in Libertyville.
[73] Administrator of the Foreign Economic Administration.

Our work here in the General Assembly should conclude next week and then I am hoping to go with Ellen on a quick sightseeing tour to Germany to see the trials at Nuremberg with Mrs. Roosevelt and Senator Connally and his wife; then back to London to close up things here and get off on the 21st.

We had some letters from Mademoiselle, John Fell and Borden yesterday and they were all in fine spirits and health, I gathered, so Ellen is reassured, but she was disappointed that she was unable to reach John Fell by telephone on his birthday.

I hope all is well with you and Ernest and you are keeping cheerful and your sense of humor intact. I am convinced that the latter is perhaps more important than anything else and if we can avoid taking ourselves too seriously there may be some hope of keeping our sanity!

Best love,
Ad.

P.S. — I have not written a line to Tim [Ives] since I have been here and I am mortified. It seems to have been peculiarly difficult for me to find time to do what Ellen calls the "essential things," but I have certainly spent a lot of time on the non-essentials!

* Be sure that Ernest has all your information for me at Libertyville when I get back — unless he is preparing your return —

REMARKS BY MR. ADLAI STEVENSON, UNITED STATES REPRESENTATIVE ON THE PERMANENT HEADQUARTERS COMMITTEE, AT MEETING OF THE COMMITTEE, FEBRUARY 12, 1946 [74]

I appreciate the courteous remarks that some Delegates have made about the neutrality of the United States Delegation in this Committee. But, as many of you know, it is a role in which I have had considerable practice and I hope I have profited from long and painful experience in the Executive Committee and the Preparatory Commission.

This Committee, on which all the United Nations are represented, has now recommended a specific area for the permanent headquarters as a basis for further examination and final decision.

The United States Delegation will continue to refrain from injecting itself into the decision on the site, but lest there be any question as to whether the United States Government is prepared to cooperate under the resolution you adopted last night, let me say that my Government is prepared to cooperate in further exploration of the Westchester-Fairfield

[74] The original is in the possession of the U.S. Mission to the United Nations.

area, *or any other site,* and feels that the formula, the method you have adopted, for investigation of sites of various sizes for development is sound and will produce the full information, including costs, which the General Assembly will need to make an intelligent decision and selection.

On February 15, 1946, Stevenson recorded the following statement for a radio broadcast.[75]

Late last night the first General Assembly of the United Nations chose the United States as its permanent headquarters. It was the very last item of business on the agenda of this first meeting of the United Nations organization, which is the hope of so many millions for the future peace of the world.

This last formal decision of the historic first Assembly was the culmination of a long debate which commenced early in October in the preliminary meetings. As the United States representative to the Preparatory Commission of the United Nations I stated before the debate commenced in that body that the United States had not sought and was not seeking the headquarters. After a long and lively controversy over the relative merits of Europe and the United States as a permanent home for the organization the Preparatory Commission finally voted to recommend the United States to the General Assembly. At that time, December 15, I said to the Preparatory Commission: "You have not only conferred a great honor upon the United States, but have entrusted to our government and people a heavy responsibility for the success of the United Nations. Your decision will require from the government and people of the United States an extra measure of that loyalty and devotion to the purposes of the United Nations Charter which is an obligation that rests upon us all.

"With your help — with God's help — my country will not fail to meet the challenge. As Tom Paine said one hundred and fifty years ago, when speaking of the small and weak Republic that was then the United States of America: 'We have it in our power to commence the world again.' It is in that pioneering spirit that all the peoples of the United Nations must now seek out together the way to lasting peace."

Now the decision is final and the temporary headquarters will be in New York pending determination of the permanent site which may be chosen at the next Assembly in September.

[75] The original is in the possession of the U.S. Mission to the United Nations.

What I said in December I could say now. The United States did not seek the great honor and the great responsibility of the world's capital. But we are grateful for the confidence that a majority of the United Nations has reposed in us and we are deeply sensible of the solemn responsibility which is ours. Destiny has assigned the United States a place of power and influence in this modern world — but power and influence are also the measure of responsibility. And our responsibility is all the greater as the host of this organization which is man's hope for peace and order in a world wrecked by war.

After Stevenson said goodbye on February 21 to the staff in London, Bert Tracey, who had served as his "English office boy" — to use Stevenson's own description — wrote him: "Guys like you should be left over here (pardon the American term) to add to the magnificent impressions you have already created among us. Finally, I am deeply honoured to have done my humble little in your service. I saw the glad light in your wife's eyes one day when she saw you. I now know the reason. I hope to live long enough to hear of your sons, following your footsteps."

Professor Charles Webster, a member of the British delegation, wrote on February 28, 1946: "We have come through some big things together and I shall always look back on our co-operation in so many delicate and difficult things with the warmest feelings toward yourself. You had a very great responsibility placed upon you at the most critical period of the negotiations and, if I may say so, I very much admired the way in which you faced up to it."

Ambassador Stettinius wrote Stevenson on February 17, 1946: "You have reason to be very proud of the part you played in bringing the United Nations into actual being, and I hope some day I will be in a position to see that you are properly rewarded for the great contribution you have made."

While Stevenson was aboard ship, Secretary of State Byrnes wrote on March 6, 1946, thanking him "on behalf of the President and myself for the distinguished services you have rendered in London. . . . You have helped greatly to get the United Nations started as a going concern." He added that he understood Stevenson's desire to return home, but "I am sure that in case of need I may always call upon you and have the benefit of your wise and disinterested judgment and your experienced and devoted service."

To Captain Edward D. McDougal, Jr.[76]

February 21, 1946

Dear Ed,

I am sailing on Sunday on the Queen Mary and plan to come to Washington for two or three days en route to Chicago. I will probably reach there on March 1 and look forward to a good talk with you. I hope you will be in town.

I would appreciate it very much if you will be good enough to call Ambrose Cremer.[77] I have a cable from him advising me that they have rented Henry Field's house on Dumbarton Place and have asked me to stay with them while I am in Washington. If you would be good enough to tell him that I would be delighted to do so, I would appreciate it. I do not have his address but I suspect you can reach him through the State Department or the telephone book at his previous address which was also on Dumbarton Place.

Hastily yours,

AES

On March 9, 1946, shortly after his return to Chicago, Stevenson described his recent experiences to his fellow members of the Commercial Club.[78]

Milord Chairman, Excellencies, Lords, and gentlemen: I think I have heard that ponderous formula not less than a hundred times in the last six months, and usually it masks a wise and frequently a witty and enlightening speech.

I have about concluded that the British as after-dinner speakers are better than we are. So it makes me the more unhappy to come back to see you again after being gone for so long — without a properly prepared speech for you.

With your Chairman's permission, however, I have agreed to talk informally, and I have written down some notes hastily, and then perhaps at the conclusion of my uninteresting remarks you would be good enough

[76] The original is in the possession of Mr. McDougal.

[77] Chicago architect Ambrose Cramer.

[78] The speech was published in the Commercial Club's *Sixty-eighth Year Book, 1945–1946* (Chicago: Lakeside Press, 1946) pp. 128–153. He repeated much of this speech with some change in phraseology to the Chicago Council on Foreign Relations on March 22, 1946.

to ask me some questions — which I will not attempt to answer but which I shall very gladly respond to!

I have been gone . . . almost five years from Chicago. The last year I have been in the State Department, and latterly, for the last six months, in London, as United States Minister and representative on what was called the Preparatory Commission of the United Nations. And then most recently as Senior Adviser to the American Delegation to the first General Assembly. That should at once disqualify me from talking to you here today, because I have been obviously too close to this thing. I am like a Surgeon, perhaps. I know more about the insides of the patient than I do about the patient.

I suspect, as I have tried to reflect over what I should say here today, that I have been lost in the trees. My perspective is confused. However, I shall attempt to tell you something about my adventures in London.

It was a dull business, a very hard business, ruthless and relentless sort of business. You recall the origins of the United Nations; the period of gestation of this infant which has now been born.

It started with the Atlantic Charter in December of 1941, between Roosevelt and Churchill. Then there followed, in January of 1942, the United Nations Declaration, whereby 26 countries agreed to join in war, and join in the preservation of peace after the war.

There followed, in November of 1943, the Moscow Declaration, calling for the establishment at the earliest possible opportunity of an organization for the maintenance of international peace and security.

And then there followed the Dumbarton Oaks proposals, proposals which were largely evolved by the United States, with the active cooperation at that long Conference of the British, the Russians and the Chinese.

Then the San Francisco Conference, which at long last wrote a charter in two months of travail in San Francisco last summer. The San Francisco Conference established an interim organization called the Preparatory Commission which was charged with the duty of creating the machinery — of hanging the flesh on the bare bones of the Charter.

That Preparatory Commission of all 51 nations, in turn, elected an Executive Committee of 14 nations which commenced meeting in London in the latter part of August and continued in constant session, until the latter part of October. I was the United States representative after Mr. Stettinius fell ill and was obliged to return to this country, and continued during the meeting in November and December of the Preparatory Commission of the 50 nations. Costa Rica was absent.

These were the bare pre-natal facts. And during this interval there were created a number of special organizations to deal with special aspects of the post-war world: the United Nations Relief and Rehabilitation Administration; the Food and Agricultural Organization; an International Bank and Monetary Fund; the Civil Aviation Conference; and the United Nations Educational, Social and Cultural Organization.

And then, finally, there came in January and February of this year the First Assembly of the new United Nations.

This organization, in short, was conceived in the din of the battle for survival, and born amid all the stresses and strains which succeeded this elemental struggle. It was no more than born, carefully and tenderly clothed, and washed, when they hit it over the head with everything they could find.

But much to the surprise of some of the more apprehensive midwives, it trudged off the stage in London without even a limp, and mumbling something, as someone said, that sounded like "Wait until I grow up."

I do not know, frankly, whether it is going to grow up, or not. That, I think is the business of all of us. But I am exceedingly proud of the initiative of the United States throughout this whole organizational period. Each of these steps were taken largely at the initiative of the United States and under its leadership. I think when the history of the evolution of the United Nations is written, whether it succeeds or fails, that we will have more than expiated any sins of failure to support the organized effort for peace after the last war.

What the Executive Committee and Preparatory Commission did in four months of day-and-night work in London was largely prosaic stuff. It was preparation of the rules and regulations for each of the organs of the United Nations; for its General Assembly; for the Economic and Social Council; the Trusteeship Council; and the Security Council. It was the creation of the vast, complicated structure of this new adventure in international organization. And at the conclusion of the work its reports numbered more than 300 printed pages.

I can say without any misgiving whatever, that the cooperation, the diligence, the enthusiasm with which the 14 nations that comprised the Executive Committee dedicated themselves to that tedious labor, was almost 100% perfect. The same was true during the interval of the Preparatory Commission. There was substantial unanimity, curiously enough, in the results of that long effort.

You have read, of course, in the papers about the disagreements. The disagreements always make the headlines. I suspect they always will — perhaps they should.

I was, unhappily, elected to preside over the deliberations of the last two weeks of the Executive Committee, and it was a difficult ordeal. We met every day for fourteen consecutive days, morning, afternoon and evening, and seldom adjourned, to my recollection, until 10:30 or midnight. It was at that interval that we fought out most of the basic problems which perplexed our work on the organization, and which probably fixed for many years to come the basic structure of the United Nations.

When this meeting finally adjourned about the 1st of November I said that we had reached agreement on more than 90% of our work, and the Soviet Union was a most active participant in the work of the Executive Committee and each of its ten subcommittees.

However, as I have indicated, the points of disagreement were the points that attracted the major attention, and there were a good many. We disagreed violently on dates! That is the sort of thing that seems to preoccupy international conferences — dates of meetings; when the Executive Committee should try to complete its work, when the Preparatory Commission should be called into session, etc. The Australians, for example, being a long way off, felt there should be a long interval in between. Others felt it should be a very short interval so the Assembly could be called sooner.

The composition of the General Committee — the steering committee of the Assembly — for example, was a substantive matter on which there was lively disagreement by the Russians and we had bitter debates about that. And there were several other serious fundamental conflicts.

Then the question of the permanent site of the United Nations provoked interminable, sometimes bitter, controversy. The Executive Committee had to make a recommendation on this and the Preparatory Commission had to make a recommendation. It was a subject of prolonged and angry debate in both.

The problem of a Nominations Committee, was another controversial issue, for example; whether members of the Councils, Chairmen and Vice Chairmen of the committees, etc. should be nominated by a committee or whether they should be elected without previous nomination. A thing like that, to us, seems of very little import, and hardly worth wasting lots of time about. But things like that took hours and hours of debate and negotiation.

I recall, with regard to the Nominations Committee, that the Russians led the opposition and when the resolution was finally beaten — when we were beaten — somebody said, "The proposal of the United States for a Nominating Committee has been drowned in a sea of words," and someone added, "No, not in a sea of words. In the Red Sea!"

We spent a great deal of time arguing about the agenda of the Security Council. The Russians were persistent in their anxiety to keep the Security Council sacrosanct and not to permit the smaller countries to have much to say about its organization or agenda.

We spent a lot of time on the matter of Trusteeship. There was an interesting illustration of difficulty with the Russians. We had proposed a Trusteeship Committee which was to act in the interim until trusteeship agreements could be worked out, and until the Trusteeship Council provided for by the Charter could come into existence.

There was general agreement on a temporary committee whose job it would be to review proposed agreements between the mandatory powers for the creation of permanent trusteeships. The Russians interposed no objection until just before the end of the Executive Committee. In fact, they participated very vigorously in the subcommittee which was charged with the business of making recommendations for the proper disposition of the Trusteeship problem.

Gromyko had left for Washington. He was to be gone for sometime to discharge business at his Embassy. But he returned to London after a day in Washington. I suppose Moscow had reviewed this situation and concluded that the proposed Trusteeship Committee was a means or device, if you please, to postpone the creation of trusteeships and to leave the mandatory powers in possession of their territories.

So, reversing everything that had been done in the committee, he came back to London in a hurry and fought the thing tooth and toenail.

Their instructions on important matters are rigid and they sometimes get a change of signals, and have to alter their position almost over night and keep a straight face while doing it.

We had a lot of trouble with the Specialized Agencies, the International Labor Organization, in particular. It was quite apparent that the Soviets were anxious to see the International Labor Organization discredited if they could. They are sceptical about some of these international agencies in which they have not participated in the past and intend to scrutinize each one deliberately from the point of view of the Soviet Union before it has their blessing.

Then we struggled over the organization of the Secretariat, the Secretary General and his Assistant Secretaries General, and the division of their responsibility. It will be a rather large organization, and a controversy with the Russians developed as to whether the secretariat should be organized on a functional basis to serve the whole organization of the United Nations or should be rigidly compartmentalized to correspond with the organs.

We struggled over many other things — including the meaning of words. But they made many concessions on the whole. They are always stubborn. They are always prepared to debate any issue, no matter how small and inconsequential it seems to us, and to debate it indefinitely. They negotiate in an entirely different manner from us. They seldom project their proposal. They let someone else lead. They very seldom come in with a draft document. They don't originate much of the paper work. They pick to pieces someone else's proposals. They never look at the clock, never! They are as good at 4:00 o'clock in the morning as they are at 4:00 o'clock in the afternoon. They are prepared to sit it out and argue it out as long as human endurance can withstand the pressure.[79]

I think that we have much to learn from the United Nations' negotiations. We can't persist in the practice, of always watching the clock. We are always in a hurry to get something buttoned up, to get something finished and to get on with the next item of business. The Russians don't play it that way.

I do not know whether it will interest you, but before luncheon Kenneth Burgess suggested I discuss some of the personalities there, tell you something about those with whom I worked most closely.

My opposite number, was, on behalf of the Russians, Andrei Gromyko, who is the Soviet Ambassador to the United States, and he was fortified by a rather small but highly competent staff. The Russians suffer acutely from a shortage of personnel. As you can imagine, since the Revolution, there is virtually only one generation of people who have had any education in diplomacy or in international affairs.

There was little communication between Russia and the Occident between the wars, with the result that most of these men have no background of occidental culture or amenities. They have come from the Proletariat. They have been educated in Russia. And there are only a few they can call on that had much pre-war, pre-1914 war, contact with Western culture, education and methods. Their manners sometimes seem a little crude. They are blunt.[80] They are very forthright, and in some ways they are very endearing. By that I mean to say that when one of these men likes you and trusts you, you are apt to know it. They never let down their reserve, or almost never. But vodka helps!

I reached a personal rapport with Gromyko which was very agreeable to me, due to the fact that we had seen each other, worked together, for a long time both in this country, at San Francisco, and then in London. But you have a feeling that they are constantly apprehensive that if they become too intimate with any foreigner it may not be good for their career.

[79] Fred Charles Ikle, *How Nations Negotiate* (New York: Harper & Row, 1964), has a discussion of the Soviet technique of negotiations similar to this.

[80] Stevenson erred here in assuming that only since the Russian Revolution had Soviet diplomats become "a little crude" and "blunt." This had been a practice of Russian diplomats since Peter the Great. For a discussion of this see Gordon Craig, "Techniques of Negotiation," in *Russian Foreign Policy: Essays in Historical Perspective* (New Haven: Yale University Press, 1962), pp. 351–373.

Publicly they are always formal. They are stubborn. They are persistent, very industrious and very disciplined. Each one has a mission and, I suspect, rigid orders. He often has little latitude in negotiation. He is seldom in the happy position of the rest of us being able to go out and make the best deal we can. They go out to make *a* deal, and if they can't make *that* deal then they probably have to get a change of instructions.

(Mr. Stevenson then discussed political relationships between various nations and groups of nations "off the record.")

Mr. Ernest Bevin, as you know, enjoys the enthusiastic support not only of the Labor Party, but of the Conservative Party quite as much. His selection as Foreign Minister was acclaimed by the Conservatives, if anything, more than it was by the Labor Party. The reason, of course, was that the Conservatives had such a load of suspected anti-Russianism to carry that it was felt that Eden would not be able to maintain his position in public life and at the same time stand up to the Russians as well as a labor man like Bevin, with a fine record of Russian cooperation, would be able to do. That has all been true. Bevin stood up to them, as you well know, very vigorously, indeed.

But the trouble is that the Russians, if anything, are more suspicious of the British labor movement than they are of the British conservatives. They see in the Socialists a competition, philosophically, with communism. Perhaps they are reminded historically of the struggle between the Mensheviks and the Bolsheviks, between the second Internationale, and the third Internationale.

That is an interesting thing that perhaps we are inclined to overlook: Socialism in Great Britain or Western Europe as the ideological enemy of the Communist state in Russia.

(Mr. Stevenson spoke off the record.)

On the United Kingdom side my opposite number was the Minister of State, the Honorable Philip Noel-Baker; perhaps as busy a man as there was in the British Cabinet, who, nevertheless, could always find time to attend the critical UNO meetings, and a good many others that seemed to me hardly worth the time of a cabinet minister. He is a brilliant man, a forceful, graceful speaker with a profound knowledge and experience in international affairs. As Lord Robert Cecil's personal secretary, and one of the few living "insiders" at the Paris Peace Conference and the League of Nations' birth, his interest in and devotion to UNO was only matched by his loyalty to the League and he is quick to challenge any reflections on the League. He is a man of uncompromising principle, but I felt, not always the best judgment.

The United Kingdom had a very strong delegation. I would say that with the exception of the United Kingdom the United States contributed more draftsmanship, more documentary draftsmanship and creative thinking, than all of the other nations in the Preparatory Commission, all 49 of them put together.

(Mr. Stevenson then read from a confidential document.)

My opposite number for the Chinese was Dr. Wellington Koo, the Chinese Ambassador to Great Britain, a distinguished man of very large international experience, who was a sort of elder statesman.

The Chinese delegation was strong and able. They were always cooperative and diligent and made many important contributions to the work. On many occasions Dr. Wellington Koo helped the situation materially by his happy interventions as a conciliator.

His first assistant was a remarkable man named Victor Hoo. Victor Hoo speaks, reads and writes Russian, French and English equally well. He was born in Russia. He understands the Russians perhaps as well as anyone I know in the international field. He has now been made Assistant Secretary General of the United Nations in charge of the Trusteeship affairs.

Our relations with the Chinese were exceedingly cordial and Dr. Koo was very helpful to me personally as a wise adviser on many occasions. Their dexterity in steering a middle course without being ineffective was something I shall not soon forget.

The French Ambassador to Great Britain, Rene Massigli, was chief of the French delegation to the Preparatory Commission. He was a member of DeGaulle's original committee of Liberation in North Africa and a distinguished man in pre-war France.

The French attitude changed perceptibly since San Francisco. In San Francisco they were playing close to the Russians following the Franco-Russian Pact. But in view of DeGaulle's strained relations with the Communist Party in France this summer and fall their attitude seemed to change as they drew closer to the British. On the whole, their participation was vigorous in some aspects but not over the entire picture.

The United States pressed incessantly to keep the work moving as rapidly as possible. We were anxious to see the thing set up and functioning as early as we possibly could. We anticipated some of the troubles that eventuated, and we felt that the organization must be constructed and prepared as soon as possible to deal with them.

We had hoped that the first General Assembly would not deal with substantive matters; that it would be confined exclusively to organization and that the urgent world problems could be better dealt with after careful preparation at the second assembly. We believed that when the Economic and Social Council and the Security Council, and so on, were all elected and organized and the Secretariat established and settled in their permanent home — as they were strengthened and their operating machinery was tried and proven — they could better prepare and deal with these vexatious problems as they came along.

Unhappily, that was not the case. There were too many urgent problems pressing for immediate attention and it put a dreadful load on the machinery before it was even completed.

I would like to say a word about the General Assembly. Much has been written about it. Everyone has reported on it and perhaps you know as much about it as I do.

The President of the General Assembly was Paul Henri Spaak of Belgium, a remarkable man; one of the most accomplished, one of the most gifted, presiding officers I have ever seen. He is Foreign Minister of Belgium. He would have been Prime Minister of Belgium had his party won in the recent elections. It did not. But he will continue as Foreign Minister in the new cabinet I have no doubt. He had, I think, the unanimous regard, respect and admiration of the General Assembly. He presided with decision and brilliance in some of the most difficult procedural tangles.

International conferences are just a series of procedural difficulties. I would say that at least 50% of all the time of an international conference, any that I have attended, has been devoted to procedural matters rather than substantive matters.

The elections by the General Assembly of the Security Council, and the Economic and Social Council, and the World Court, in addition to Chairmen and Vice Chairmen of the standing committees and the Secretary General took up a great deal of time in negotiation. The United States took the initiative in trying to work out slates that would provide adequate geographical distribution of these posts.

We had to negotiate on most of these matters commencing as early as September. It was exceedingly difficult to reach any agreement among all five of the great powers. Little by little we wore them down, and I am modestly prepared to report that we elected five out of six of our slate on the Security Council; seventeen out of eighteen on the Economic and Social Council; and twelve out of fifteen members of the International Court of Justice.

The negotiations among the "Big Five" for the selection of a Secretary General covered a period of many months. We had supported Pierson [Lester B. Pearson] of Canada, along with the British and French and Chinese. The Russians had a candidate of their own, Ambassador Simitch [Stanoje Simic] of Yugoslavia.

We could not reach an agreement, and we finally compromised on

Secretary of the Navy Frank Knox at his press conference at the Navy Department, Washington, D.C., April, 1942

Admiral Chester W. Nimitz with the Secretary of the Navy's party at Pearl Harbor, Hawaii, before their visit to the South Pacific in January, 1943. Standing, left to right: Rawleigh Warner, Secretary of the Navy Frank Knox, Admiral Nimitz, Rear Admiral John S. McCain, Adlai E. Stevenson. Squatting, left to right: Captain Frank Bean, Lieutenant H. A. Lamar, Captain E. G. Small

DEPARTMENT OF THE NAVY
OFFICE OF THE SECRETARY
WASHINGTON

Dear Walter –

Such a gentle woman merited a better & wiser philosopher. Your note should have gone to her. As for my evening – it was epic, what with a "civilized" lady, an air marshal and more. Brueggeman – for whom I've a passion, albeit elevated.

Sometime let's talk about the Navy Dept. My vision is opaque, but I'm tempted to think things are moving apace – and ahead.

yrs

 AES

6/9 [1942]

Letter from Adlai Stevenson to newspaper columnist Walter Lippmann,
June 9, 1942

*Adlai E. Stevenson, Special Assistant to the Secretary of the Navy,
October 22, 1943*

Meeting of the U.S. Delegation to the United Nations, San Francisco,
June, 1945. Left to right around table: Dean Virginia Gildersleeve;
Congressman Sol Bloom; Senator Tom Connally; Edward R. Stettinius,
Jr., Secretary of State; Senator Arthur H. Vandenberg; Congressman
Charles A. Eaton; Commander Harold N. Stassen, USNR; Donald Stone;
Nelson Rockefeller; Adlai E. Stevenson; Green Hackworth; John Foster
Dulles; Harley Notter. Dr. Joseph Johnson is in back of Senator
Vandenberg. Next to Johnson is a representative from the FBI.
The man in back of Congressman Bloom is Robert V. Shirley

January, 1946 — Meeting of the General Assembly in London.
Adlai E. Stevenson is talking to Secretary of State James F. Byrnes.
At right is Senator Tom Connally. Behind him is
Postmaster General Frank C. Walker

December 11, 1946, Flushing Meadow, New York. Adlai E. Stevenson,
member of the U.S. Delegation to the second part of the first General
Assembly of the UN, addresses a plenary session

1947

Jan 1   Party at Oates' with children. Jim told some amusing stories well as always. Quartet by McDougal family very impressive.

Jan 2   Dr Nansen to discuss freedom of emigration. Lunch with John Cassidy. Asked me to speak at annual Lincoln Birthday Banquet of Peoria Bar Assn. for Supreme Court Judges.   Kribbens for dinner.

Jan 3   Lunch with Raddie Oates. Serious girl. Determined to have foreign experience. She'll get what she goes after and do everything well — but she won't have enough fun in process.

Jan 4.   Talked with Katharine Watson about Stettinius' new activities.   Donald Stone & Bill Stoneman telephoned again from N.Y. about accepting job as deputy to Trygve Lie, Sec. Gen.; U.N. Agreed to go to N.Y. to help Lie find someone else.

Jan 5   Left for N.Y. 2 hrs late.

Jan 6   Arrived 4½ hrs late. Lie offered me $24300 tax exempt and the "great house" at Lake Success. Long interview followed by talks with Stoneman and Owen. Lie trying to get off for Central Am. on Friday. Can't make decision so quick.

Jan 6–7 Contacted a lot of people & arranged for Wilson Wyatt, Julius Holmes & Milton Eisenhower to see Lie. Tempted myself, but I must stay at home now & get family situation straightened out. Also might as well try out political situation there.

Jan 9   Benton at Council. Sat next him and Bob Hutchins. Marshall's appointment as Sec State just announced. Met Paul Hoffman for first time at Speakers table.   Dinner at Commercial Club for Stoddard, new Pres. of Ill. Unaffected, serious. I like him.

*September 16, 1947, Flushing Meadow, New York. Delegates' Lounge
before the opening meeting of the Second Regular Session of the UN
General Assembly. Left to right: Charles E. Bohlen, U.S. Adviser;
Andrei A. Gromyko, U.S.S.R. Permanent Representative to the UN;
Adlai E. Stevenson, U.S. Adviser*

*September 27, 1947, Lake Success, New York. Members of the General
Assembly's Fifth Committee: A. A. Roschin, right, U.S.S.R.; Kenneth G.
Younger, center, United Kingdom; and Adlai E. Stevenson, United States,
before the fourth meeting, at which a general debate on the budget
estimates for 1948 was continued*

December 30, 1947, Chicago. Adlai Stevenson during his acceptance speech before the Democratic Slate Committee

Official campaign photo for the 1948 campaign

Adlai Stevenson at his farm in Libertyville, Illinois, during the 1948 campaign

Stevenson with "Artie" walking down a path of his Libertyville farm during the 1948 campaign

*Adlai E. Stevenson, Democratic candidate for governor of Illinois,
addressing a crowd during a regular ward organization meeting,
44th Ward Democratic Headquarters*

Stevenson with son Adlai E. Stevenson III, Vice President Alben Barkley
and nephew Timothy R. Ives at Bloomington, Illinois,
during the 1948 campaign

Stevenson and wife, Ellen, with sons John Fell and Borden,
at Libertyville farm, during the 1948 campaign

1116 EAST WASHINGTON STREET
BLOOMINGTON, ILLINOIS

Sunday

Dear Sherwood –

I'm stopping off here for one comfortable night on my endless quest and its the first opportunity I've had to write you since I heard about your mother's death in Shelbyville yesterday.

I am so distressed to hear of your misfortune and my thoughts are with you. I wish there was something I could do — but I'll content myself for the moment with adding your speech to mine!

With deep sympathy and my warmest regards to you and your wife —

Sincerely,

Adlai S. [signature]

ORIGINAL IN POSSE
Sherwood

Letter from Adlai Stevenson to Sherwood Dixon, Stevenson's running mate for lieutenant governor, September 5, 1948

*September 16, 1948 — Adlai E. Stevenson on train platform as he arrives
in Bloomington, Illinois*

*October 8, 1948 — Adlai E. Stevenson speaks to the League of Women
Voters of Illinois at a luncheon meeting in the Stevens Hotel, Chicago.
Governor Dwight H. Green listens at right*

*November 2, 1948 — Adlai E. Stevenson, Democratic candidate for governor
of Illinois, after voting in Half Day, Illinois*

*November 3, 1948 — Governor-elect Adlai E. Stevenson with
Mrs. Stevenson and son John Fell, after defeat of Dwight H. Green
for the governorship of Illinois*

Trygve Lie of Norway. He is a big, sturdy man and the Foreign Minister of Norway. I believe he will do a good job.

The General Assembly also did a vast amount of complicated organizational work which the Executive Committee of the Preparatory Commission had laid out.

I quote here from something that I read in Senator Vandenburg's speech, after he returned to the United States, which impressed me. He said:

> When we look at London and the first General Assembly of the UNO, let's remember that its organizational phase was a phenomenal success and a vigorous omen of hope for the tolerant cooperations which are the lifeblood of this adventure in behalf of the collective security for which men and women pray, in a hundred different tongues, at the war-scarred hearthstones of the world."

We did a lot of other things there that you know about. The Atomic Energy Commission was established. The world's attention was brought to the great unfinished task of UNNRA [United Nations Relief and Rehabilitation Administration]. The devilish difficult problem of refugees was fought out, and an effort by the Russians and their satel[l]ites to permit involuntary repatriation of political refugees was decisively defeated by a vote of 31 to 10 under the leadership of Mrs. Roosevelt who represented the United States on that committee.

The General Assembly used its gigantic resonance to bring to a single dramatic focus the gravity of the world food shortage; a problem that we are aware of here but perhaps we do not see as vividly as they do abroad.

We also got through a proposal for an International Conference on Trade and Employment, for the latter part of this year; a project dear to the State Department; also a Conference on Health Organization; also a resolution regarding extradition of war criminals.

And then there was the dispute which started the day the General Assembly convened, and lasted until its very end, about the admission of the World Federation of Trade Unions. Speaking for 60,000,000 organized workmen the world around, they demanded immediate admission with special privileges to the General Assembly and Economic and Social Council.

Sponsored by the Russians and supported by the Belgians, French and others, Senator Connally, speaking for the United States, led the opposition. After weeks of debate and argument he got the resolution watered down so that in its last form it was unobjectionable and included the

American Federation of Labor, which, of course, is really not international in character. The expenditure of time and passion on this issue was eloquent evidence of the importance the Soviet attaches to this organization.

One thing amused me a good deal. The Russians had been, as I have said, very vigorous in their anxiety during the preparatory work to do something about the trusteeship business. I had a feeling that they wanted to strike a strong propaganda blow against Britain and France and the Colonial powers. But, as it happened, at the very opening of the General Assembly each one of the mandatory powers, with the exception of South Africa, in its formal address declared its willingness, its readiness, its anxiety, indeed, to put its mandates under the trusteeship system of the United Nations. This may have been a surprising development to the Russians, even if it was not to us, and perhaps rather disappointed them. I think they had hoped to find the Colonial powers reluctant to let go of their mandates.

As to the United States Delegation to the Assembly, you know all about it and I shall not dwell on it. It does present a problem for the future; whether the delegation should be political in character or comprised of people technically expert in the various aspects of the work, or both. It is a difficult problem. The British made no attempt to resolve it on a bi-partisan basis the way we did. Their delegation was composed of cabinet members representing the Socialist government only.

The atmosphere of the General Assembly interested me. It was one of sobriety, of relentless realism, in marked contrast with the boundless optimism of feeling that prevailed after the last war, at the time of the League's birth. That was proclaimed, as you recall, as the omnipotent organ of universal and perpetual peace. There was no Woodrow Wilson here who reached a height rarely reached before by mortal man at Paris. There was no generation of great Frenchmen; no Briands, Clemenceaus, Poincares — none of those outstanding individuals. It was an extraordinary contrast, and, rightly read, a heartening one. There were no illusions; no slap-happy optimism. There was just sober restraint, not melancholy pessimism, but sober restraint and prayerful anxiety to build well and wisely and enduringly.

There was also an undertone of terrible urgency. The men of London were not carefree, happy men. They had seen too much, and they knew too much. They represented, many of them, devastated, unhappy, miserable countries whose economies had been destroyed and whose futures were obscure. They knew that the machinery they were constructing was not self-operating. They knew that it was the peoples of the world who would determine the accuracy of Kant's grim prophecy that the world would be the "graveyard of the human race," but they also knew that without the machinery there could be no organized concentration of human aim and effort, of human will.

Now, Mr. Chairman, I have not attempted to speak about a thing that no doubt interests you, relations with Russia. I will be very glad to do what I can in response to questions.

Meanwhile, I would like to bring to your attention just one further item.

There was a lot of discussion as a result of the Security Council meetings, which I have not mentioned, and the four political issues that were presented there, as to whether or not the open free discussion was a wise thing, a wholesome thing, or an unwise and dangerous thing.

The almost brutal forthrightness that existed there was a little startling. There were conflicting judgments about that. I do not know whether you here in Chicago felt that there was any question about its wisdom, or not. But there were grave questions in London. I can illustrate it by pointing out what Spaak himself said when he left London:

> "The debates in the Security Council have created an entirely new technique and atmosphere of diplomacy. The completely frank public debate of international issues, followed by a vote, followed by general acceptance of the majority decision — nothing like this has ever happened before; certainly not at Geneva. It sets an entirely new precedent. I think it is to the good. The public exposition of their theses by great nations implies the admission that they need the approval of public world opinion. To take recourse to public opinion in diplomacy introduces a new factor that makes for peace."

The converse of that is an editorial from the London Times, of which I would like to quote you a paragraph:

> "The trouble lies in the fact that both parties, while sincerely desiring friendship, indulge in words and action which excite the suspicions of the other and are treated by the other as provocative. The only remedy immediately available would be to reduce the occasions of public controversy and to multiply those of direct confidential discussion between leaders of both countries.
>
> There is everything to be said for vigorous action, political and economic, where this is required to uphold British interests. There is considerably less to be said on either side for public utterances designed to put the policies or actions of the other in an unfavorable light to score debating points at his expense in verbal or written controversy."

On balance, I think it was generally agreed, however, that the startling candor and vigor of the debates in the Security Council, was wholesome; that a new era of open diplomacy has commenced; that the prestige of the United Nations as the town meeting of the world has been established sooner, and also more violently, perhaps, than anyone expected.

I think also that one of the most wholesome developments throughout this whole series of International Conferences was the general recognition, including Russia, of the imperative importance of public opinion — of informed and understanding peoples around the world. It was on the initiative of the United States that we secured the inclusion in the rules of each of the organizations of the United Nations of a guaranty that the meetings would always be open to the public and the press, except in exceptional circumstances. In other words, the emphasis now is always on open meetings rather than on closed meetings.

I should be delighted to talk to you further about the political issues that developed there, but I do not know how much interested you would be in them. I do not know how much I can add to the information you already have.

Thank you. (Applause.)

VICE PRESIDENT FORGAN: Well, Adlai, the attention of the audience gives you some idea of the real interest that your remarks have been to this group.

Now, we would like to have any questions that anyone has to ask.

QUESTION: I would like to ask a question, Mr. Chairman.

Would you care to comment on the exchange of notes that are going on between this country and Russia, in contrast to the method of the Security Council?

MR. STEVENSON: I do not know that I understand that question, Tom.

We have, as I understand it, in the last two days sent a note protesting a unilateral breach of the Treaty of 1942 with Iran. We have also complained about what appears to be a unilateral withdrawal of industrial equipment from Manchuria. The former is clearly a breach of agreement — the latter is a little more obscure.

I should say with respect to the latter that there should be no doubt on anyone's part any longer that the Russians are going to get everything they can as quick as they can everywhere; that they are going to capitalize this opportunity, this moment of confusion, of fluidity, before the peace treaties are adopted, and before the general political situation is stabilized, to accomplish as much of their objectives as they possibly can, externally.

Related to that is their internal problem. If you read carefully Stalin's speech on the eve of the election a couple of weeks ago when he announced a series of three new 5-year plans, you saw the enormous figures he has established as goals — and they should not be treated unrealistically either — for capital goods production in Russia, and you should be able to envision something of the enormous capital equipment requirements.

It can be said perhaps that Russia has two problems: One, her external security problem; and the other one, her internal security problem.

With respect to the internal one, the more she can get in the way of industrial goods by reparations from Germany, and from Japan in Manchuria, the easier it is going to be for her to further develop her economy; that is just so much goods she won't have to buy with exports at the expense of the living standard in Russia. That living standard is appallingly low. There may be some concern in Russia about the returning soldiers who have seen living standards in Central and Eastern and Northern Europe, the like of which they never realized existed.

That realization may have developed a backlog of complaint, or perhaps dissatisfaction and impatience with the government and the Communist party, which the leaders anticipate. So they are taking anything they can wherever they can as reparations.

With respect to Iran, the situation is more difficult. There they are engaging in oil imperialism with the West for the first time in a long while.

Iran is also, as you know, the territory through which runs the railroad that nourished the Russian war machine in its most desperate hour, and which could also nourish the war machine of an invader.

Also closely adjoing Iran is Irak [Iraq], and in Irak and Iran is the largest oil empire of the United Kingdom in the world. Russia, a young, vigorous, aggressive state of enormous prestige and power, does not propose to sit idly by and see the oil reserves of the world divided between the United States and Great Britain. What underlies the Iranian problem in large measure is, in short, the security of that frontier, influence on Persian domestic politics and an equal position in the oil empire of the Middle East.

Their methods are quite different. She uses the presence of her troops, which I think she will attempt to keep there until she can negotiate a satisfactory agreement or point to the precedent of the Greek case and say, "The troops are there at the request of the Iranian government," if that can be brought about by negotiation and pressure on

Iran. Whether it will be brought about we shall know very soon. If it cannot, I think she will withdraw.[81]

But there is also the apparent fact that she is there to stay in one form or another for a long time. Her method of imperialism is dissimilar from the traditional, and it is well we should take note of it. It is an imperialism of ideas to generate internal discontent. She holds out to wretched, miserable, unhappy, impoverished people the hope for better flocks, for land, for bread, for an improvement in their living conditions.

More than once historically even more advanced people have been ready and willing to trade their freedom for bread.

I have little doubt that the masses of unhappy and miserable peoples in this war-shattered world are going to be very responsive indeed to this hope for improvement in their conditions.

I think I have wandered a little bit from your question.

QUESTION: Well, that is very interesting.

What I have more particularly in mind is the question of procedure: Whether the Iranian question and the Manchurian question can be taken up through the United Nations, or whether it has to be handled unilaterally and bi-laterally.

MR. STEVENSON: The Security Council will convene in New York the 21st of March and there is no doubt but what the Iranian question, unless it has been resolved in the interim, will be presented again.

After the Iranian case was disposed of in London, it was left on the agenda of the Security Council, and the parties are obliged to report the progress of their negotiations from time to time. So that will be handled in the Security Council.

The withdrawal of industrial goods from North Manchuria is a matter that relates to the peace treaties and will be handled at the Peace Conference, or in direct negotiations between our government and the Russians. I do not think that question will get into the United Nations.

QUESTION: Is there any inclination on the part of the nations to believe that since we initiated and backed out of the League of Nations we are likely to initiate and soon back out of the United Nations?

MR. STEVENSON: No. I think on the contrary the world is convinced that the United States is in this for keeps.

Our vigorous leadership in the conception and organization of the United Nations over such a long period has been asserted so many times that there is little apprehension about the United States pulling

[81] He was correct. The Soviets withdrew their troops.

out. There is, however, grave apprehension about public opinion in the United States. It came out in connection with the debate as to the location of the site of the permanent headquarters; whether it was to be in Europe or in the United States.

The argument was advanced, more frequently in those debates than any other, that the presence of the organization in the United States would contribute to understanding of the problems of international concern which are going to confront the next generation, and that without wholesome United States' opinion the United Nations had no chance of success.

The almost desperate anxiety of most of the smaller countries of the world for the United States to exert its leadership is transparent and impressive. It gives you pause and makes you feel a little humble.

There is hardly a country in the world — there is hardly a country in the world — I measure those words — that is not in a state of nervous apprehension, expectancy, and hope that the United States will be able to resolve the conflicts that it knows cannot be resolved by anyone else, only by the strength of our leadership; only if we will remain strong, just, fair and positive in policy.

People came almost in a procession from morning to night to ask, directly or indirectly, "What does the United States want? What can we do to help? What is your attitude about these things?"

I do not mean to say that there has not been a great deal of flirtation with the Russians also. There has. Most of the smaller powers, except for the Russian bloc in Eastern Europe, seemed to be trying to find an alignment on issues which would reconcile differences between the major powers. No state so far as I could detect ever tried to divide the great powers because they all know better perhaps than we that peace and progress and the very existence of the United Nations rests on the unity of the "Big Three."

In the case of the Latin-American bloc, for example, they went along with us on Western Hemisphere matters, generally speaking, and on any very broad major principle, but when it comes to electing officers, when it comes to getting positions, the sort of thing they can capitalize to serve their own ends, they will go out and trade with the Russian bloc or anywhere else that they can get votes.

QUESTION: With respect to the internal situation in Russia, is it your opinion that they are in any position to go the limit in backing up any demands which they make?

MR. STEVENSON: I haven't any opinion on that, Ralph. I think they will go to what looks to us beyond the limit. I think they will press stubbornly and relentlessly to gain their national objectives, most of them ancient objectives of the Czars.

What we must remember is, I think that we must be patient; we must keep calm and steady, striving always to understand them and to eliminate patiently step by step, their basic mistrust and suspicion of us. It is not an easy role and at the same time we dare not forget our obligations to the rest of the world and the smaller states who look to us for steadfast moral leadership.

As to Soviet withdrawal from the United Nations and war, I would say that there are no two countries more anxious to preserve the peace of the world than Britain and the United States, and that they can be counted upon to make every contribution and reasonable concession to that end.

On the other hand, there is no country in the world, presently or historically, which is in more desperate need of a long period of recuperative peace than Russia.

QUESTION: I am rather ignorant about the duties of the Atomic Bomb Commission and its status.

Would you enlighten us upon that?

MR. STEVENSON: The thing has not, as you know, been set up.

The members of the Atomic Commission have not yet been appointed by the member states.

The issue that developed in London, largely within our own delegation there, was whether or not measures for the security of Atomic energy information, international security, would first be established before the information was disclosed. That was the interpretation that was agreed to.

When the Commission is established, I mean to say when the members are appointed which I suspect will be within the next few weeks, they will meet to map out a plan for dealing with Atomic energy in accordance with the draft resolution adopted by the General Assembly. Our government is working on proposals for that plan and I presume the other governments are too.[82]

Whether you will internationalize ownership of all deposits of uranium, or not; whether the experience in the release and control of atomic energy will be internationalized, or whether development will be left to the several states under some system of inspection, all those

[82] For a discussion of the conflict in the U.S. over civilian or military control of atomic energy and of various proposals, which were not adopted, for international control of atomic energy see Richard G. Hewlett and Oscar E. Anderson, Jr., *The New World, 1939/1946* (University Park: Pennsylvania State University Press, 1962), chapters 13, 14, 15, 16.

questions have yet to be worked out by the Commission with a view to the establishment of the effective safeguards on the exchange of information called for by the resolution.

QUESTION: The members have not been selected as yet?

MR. STEVENSON: No. They have not.

QUESTION: Do they have to be voted on?

MR. STEVENSON: No. They are appointed by the member states, the members of the Security Council plus Canada. Each one will designate an individual member of the Commission and he, of course, will have a staff.

QUESTION: With further reference to that question, it seems to me that there are two things about Atomic energy that are fortunate.

One is that a peace-loving nation does have the secret; and the second, that there is a strong organization coming into the picture that might conceivably be able to deal with the problem.

But I wonder whether we visualize the type of thing that is likely to happen.

I understand that our suggestion regarding inspection and other means of control has been accepted if and when the secret is eliminated.

The thing which has always given me concern is that we have no international inspection setup for the internationalization of sources of energy, and if we finally take the tremendously dangerous step of revealing all we know about it to all countries, and then Russia, as she has so often done in the past, decides that there are good reasons why this Commission should not be allowed to go in certain places, and all that, will the United States or will the United Nations ever take a firm and vigorous action in that event, such as is necessary if we are not going to be sitting on a dynamite keg from then on.

MR. STEVENSON: Well, your guess is as good as mine about that.

I would suspect that there is little doubt but that if Russia makes commitments for inspection in the Soviet Union that she will fulfill them. That does not mean to say that secret operations won't go on. Perhaps they will. Perhaps they will go on in other countries — that is one of the serious difficulties with the inspection system.

I do not presume to know anything about the atomic energy problems. The discussion has all taken place since I left the country six months ago. It does little good to speculate, but one of the scientists who made some major contributions to this problem, told me in London that there were seven ways of releasing atomic energy, and the Russians knew at least seven of them! [83]

As to whether or not the industrial equipment which we have developed in this country is known to them, I of course don't know.

I can't foresee at all what this appalling problem will bring forth in the future; whether if we share this information with them, they will take advantage of it, or not.

I think that is one of the things that we have to take on faith, secured by such control machinery as the United Nations Commission can work out. I am sure if the positions were reversed we would expect the Soviet to trust us and our sincerity and honesty.

If the inspection system is adopted and they do refuse to afford access to inspection groups, then there will develop what to me, in the last analysis, is the only hope for this organization anyway, and that is the organized marshalling of the public opinion of the world, conscious of the fact that there is a menace to peace and security, and prepared, I trust and hope, to do something about it. For public opinion is the sovereign of us all. . . .

Secretary of State James F. Byrnes offered Stevenson the ambassadorship to either Argentina or Brazil. Stevenson declined and returned to Chicago. Before joining his old law firm, he discussed the possibility of founding his own firm.

To Captain Edward D. McDougal, Jr.[84]

March 12, 1946

Dear Ed:

Thanks for your note. I hope you will be discreet about the Secretary's proposals as I don't want to advertise them and make it any more difficult for him to get someone else.

I have not yet had an opportunity to pursue the conversations but will do so soon and will keep you advised. Everything seems in order here, and the weather is bewitching!

Love to Kate.[85]

Yours,
AD.

[83] He may have been quoting atomic scientist Leo Szilard, who visited him in London with a letter of introduction from Professor Charles E. Merriam of the University of Chicago.
[84] The original is in the possession of Mr. McDougal.
[85] Mrs. McDougal.

To Arthur B. Perry[86]

March 12, 1946

Dear Mr. Perry:

I enjoyed so much our visit the other day, and I am contrite that I imposed my monologue on you for so long. Adlai's progress and the comforting words about him were most reassuring.

I am a little at a loss about a bill I have, dated February 1st, for $711.18. Perhaps improperly I assumed that the tuition charge of $700 which I paid for the first half year on August 29 would cover the second half year. If I had any misunderstanding about this please do not hesitate to let me know. But if any abatement of the charge for the period while he was not there is proper, I would be delighted. As you know, we get no richer fast in the Government!

With warmest regards to you and Emily,[87] I am

Sincerely yours,

To James F. Byrnes

March 13, 1946

Dear Mr. Secretary:

. . . I appreciated your kind and flattering letter accepting my resignation. I am going to spend a month here getting my affairs in shape and then I propose to take a long postponed holiday before making any final commitments about resuming the practice of law.

If you still have in mind positions where you think I could be of real service I will gladly come down to see you at the end of April, but I have a strong personal inclination to settle down here now and pick up the scattered threads of private life again; which is not to say, as I told you, that I would not welcome opportunities for temporary service. I particularly hope that I can be of some use at the [UN] General Assembly in September.

Faithfully yours,

On May 1, 1946, Franklyn B. Snyder, president of Northwestern University, invited Stevenson to the annual commencement to receive the honorary degree of Doctor of Laws.

[86] Headmaster of Milton Academy. The original is in the possession of Milton Academy, Milton, Massachusetts.
[87] Mrs. Perry.

To Franklyn B. Snyder

May 18, 1946

Dear Dr. Snyder:

I apologize for my failure to acknowledge your letter of May 1 before this. I have been traveling in the East and South for the last several weeks and found it only this morning on my return.

Of course I am bewildered and suspect some error of identification, so I am hastily accepting before a correction is made!

I hope I can find suitable words of thanks to you, and through you to the Trustees and Senate when I see you.

Faithfully yours,

P.S. I have been conspiring with [Dean] Leon Green to arrange a series of lectures at the Law School on the United Nations. As a result of my recent explorations in the East I think it can be done and that the State Department, the Secretariat of the United Nations and others will cooperate. I will present a memorandum to him next week, I hope.

To Andrei A. Gromyko

May 29, 1946

Dear Mr. Ambassador:

I have been asked to invite you to speak before the Chicago Council on Foreign Relations on any day in June that would be convenient for you except Saturdays.

The Council is a large organization of people interested in foreign affairs and roughly corresponds to the Foreign Policy Association in New York. The speech would follow a lunch commencing at 12:15. About 45 minutes is the usual length, but that is entirely flexible.

I hope very much that you will find it convenient to come out here for many reasons. You will know best what to talk about. Something general about the Soviet Union's interest and earnest, hopeful cooperation in all the work of the United Nations and frank recognition of the importance to each other and to the world of Soviet–U.S. collaboration would be appropriate I should think. It seems to me it is clearly time to draw some distinctions between the United Nations and the peace treaty negotiations and that some authoritative, candid statement of the Soviet position toward the United Nations could not but be helpful.

Besides I would like to show you Chicago — and my wife's latest poetry!

With every good wish — and my sincere hopes that you will give this sympathetic consideration, I am[88]

Faithfully yours,

While Stevenson was back at Libertyville with his family, a number of opportunities for public service were offered him. He rejected the chairmanship of the Securities and Exchange Commission. He turned down the presidency of the Foreign Policy Association, and the presidency of the Carnegie Endowment for International Peace. John Foster Dulles, with whom he had worked at the San Francisco Conference and the UN General Assembly in London, was chairman of the committee selecting the new president for the Endowment. Alger Hiss accepted the post.

To John Foster Dulles

May 31, 1946

Dear Foster:

I am glad you called me. I was having difficulty summ[on]ing up the courage to say No!

I suppose that the information aspect of the new program of the Endowment — whatever it is — will be important. To that end you might bear in mind Bill Stone, formerly with the Foreign Policy Association, in New York, then Board of Economic Warfare, and now head of the Overseas Information Office under Benton[89] in the Department. There is also Francis Russell, who has been directing the public liaison work with private groups and organizations in the Department for the last several years. He is rather pedestrian, but tireless and full of intelligent purpose. Ferdinand Kuhn would be entitled to careful consideration if he was available. I believe he has determined to go back to the [New York] Times. William H. Stoneman, Chief of the Chicago Daily News Foreign Service, has resigned, and is now acting as personal assistant to his good friend, Trygve Lie. He has many of the qualifications you want, I think, but no experience in running things. I think he might be available within a reasonable time.

It seems a pity to take any first rate people from the hard-pressed Department [of State] unless they are planning to leave anyway. In the latter connection, in addition to Alger [Hiss], I believe that Joe Johnson[90]

[88] Ambassador Gromyko declined the invitation.
[89] Assistant Secretary of State William Benton.
[90] Joseph E. Johnson, assistant professor of history at Williams College; adviser

is planning to return to Williams College sometime. I have been impressed with his mentality and mature judgment.

I need not say again how much I have enjoyed thinking about this job. It comes close to the perfect prescription for me. I hope you will get the right man, and I shall always feel flattered and thankful to have been considered. Let me know if there is anything I can do to help.

Sincerely yours,

To Arthur Ballantine[91]

May 31, 1946

Dear Mr. Ballantine:

Foster Dulles broke the spell by a telephone call the other night! Perhaps he has told you that after prayerful consideration I decided that I had better not be considered. I suspect I will live to regret it — after I get back into active practice! I have, as you know, an absorbing interest in that field and I felt that the opportunity opened for me, together with the prospect of working with men of like interest and wider experience, could be very rewarding, but I guess the inertia of five exhausting years in the Government and the prospect of uprooting my family again was a little more than I could face.

You were good to consider me and I was very much flattered. I hope there will be opportunities to collaborate and that I can be of some use to the Foundation in the future.

With warmest thanks and best wishes, I am

Sincerely yours,

P.S. It is a comfort that busy people like you can find some time to make important resources count to the full. Surely the times have imposed large responsibilities on the foundations.

Harold Sinclair of Bloomington wrote a history of the Daily Pantagraph. *Mrs. Ernest L. Ives sent a chapter of it to her brother for comment.*

To Harold Sinclair

June 6, 1946

Dear Harold:

Buffy tells me she thinks you might like to move to New York and

---

to the U.S. delegation to the UN General Assembly and to the U.S. representative in the Security Council. He became president of the Carnegie Endowment in 1950.

[91] New York lawyer and trustee of the Carnegie Endowment for International Peace.

work for the United Nations. My information is not up to date, but a colossal number of Americans have applied for the Secretariat at all levels and they can only use a few hundred at most. While in New York a few weeks ago several people close to the Secretary General advised me that he would make no more American appointments for the present until the Secretariat got into better international balance. It is already overwhelmingly American. But they do need bilingual stenographers, interpreters and translators for any nationality.

You might let me know what sort of work you have in mind and I will explore it further, in so far as I can from here and subject to my obsolescence which increases day by day.

At Buffy's suggestion I have read the enclosed copy of chapter 13 and have taken the liberty of making some comments on the margins. I question the wisdom of including the editorial comment on the present importance of the tariff question on page 13–2.

The letter on page 13–4 was *not* from W. O. Davis but from H. O. Davis to his sister Helen, my mother, who was then in Europe and engaged to my father, Lewis G. Stevenson. The story in the St. Louis Chronicle, I think in that respect is quite correct, although the engagement was not announced until she returned from Europe in the spring of 1893. They had been sweethearts for years and I . . . [think] there are still some of their childhood love letters.

My father at the time of the letter was 22 and in very delicate health. If you have run across anything about him "managing" his father's campaign it must have been some courtesy title, and I am sure the reference to "managing" on page 13–5 is inaccurate. He did have much to do with Grandfather's campaign for Governor in 1908 and was active in some capacity in his campaign for Vice President with Bryan in 1900. At least I have a picture of him at his desk in the headquarters in Chicago taken during that campaign!

The letter from Bert Davis, then a young man, does not add anything to the picture of W. O.'s difficulties which you have already described. I would leave out the letter but I would, if you please, add that another complication was a long standing romance between Davis' daughter and Stevenson's son, which did not simplify Davis' predicament.

I have asked Lloyd Lewis to give the book a boost at the Chicago University Press. If they are not interested he would like to try Henry Holt. [Joseph] Brandt, who was formerly with the Press, has now joined Henry Holt and has some interest in this sort of thing.

I will be in Bloomington later in the month and will look forward to seeing you.

Sincerely yours,

On June 24, 1946, Stevenson gave the commencement day speech at Illinois Wesleyan University at Bloomington and he received an honorary degree. When he accepted the invitation on April 12, 1946, he wrote to President W. E. Shaw: "I suggest 'Epilogue and Prologue' for a title. If you think of something better, I am sure I would be delighted for you to substitute anything else. Having the abominable habit of preparing these things all too late, I always find myself confronted with the necessity of suggesting a title before I have a speech — and now it has happened again!"

Are commencement speakers necessary? I haven't any doubt how you feel on that question. I felt the same way on the day I sat in your place and listened to a distinguished man talk sagely about important things that were good for me to hear. But I can't remember who he was or what he said. And the only thing I say today with complete assurance is that you won't remember me or what I say either!

I think I've made an important discovery: All commencement speeches evolve the same way, and always have and probably always will. The speaker says to himself, "I'm not going to tell them how fortunate they are and what they should do with their hard won educational disciplines; I'm not going to tell them that the old order is changing, that the sky is overcast, visibility low, and that in their still soft hands lies the making of a better morrow. I'm not going to repeat *any* of those old platitudes. I'm going to be different!" So he starts off brightly with a quip like: "School is a great thing because children go off just as they begin to ask too many questions," and finally ends up with a ringing quotation like: "Civilization's a race between education and catastrophe." And in between he has contrived to use each of those old platitudes with solemn innocence. And so will I!

Of course the old order is changing. It always is. Of course the future is obscure and full of forebodings. It always is, especially on Commencement Day! Change is the order of life. Change is disturbing. It always seems to be for the worse. We talk of the *good old* days. (When someone sighed that Punch wasn't as good as it used to be, a wiser man replied that it never was!)

I graduated from college and you were born in another hour of change, and a much happier hour than this one. A savage war to make the world safe for democracy had just ended victoriously. A noble concept, the League of Nations, had taken form and substance in the chaotic aftermath of that elemental struggle. It was the twilight of kings and the dawn of world wide democracy. Optimism was boundless and people proclaimed that we were on the threshold of the new era of universal and perpetual peace and prosperity.

It didn't turn out that way. It wasn't a threshold after all. A bitter young man, Lawrence of Arabia, wrote:

> "It felt like morning, and the freshness of the world-to-be intoxicated us. We were wrought up with ideas inexpressible and vaporous, but to be fought for. We lived many lives in those whirling campaigns, never sparing ourselves any good or evil; yet when we achieved and the new world dawned, the old men came out again and took from us our victory, and remade it in the likeness of the former world they knew. Youth could win but had not learned to keep, and was pitiably weak against age. We stammered that we had worked for a new heaven and a new earth and they thanked us kindly and made their peace."

No, there really wasn't much change. It wasn't the dawn after all — those twenty odd years between the wars since you were born. By the time you could add and subtract, the bountiful earth was paralyzed with unemployment and poverty stalked thru fields of plenty. And by the time you were ready for college, they handed you a gun and told you to fight for your life.

Surely there *is* something fateful about a generation that was born in the get-rich-quick era of flappers, Freud, gangsters, bath-tub gin and ostrich politics; that was raised in economic agony, and then had to fight its way out. Had to fight its way out — to what? To mountainous debt, strikes, inflation, quarreling, and politics as usual at home; to hunger, fear and political unrest abroad; and to atomic bombs! Surely this is a doubtful inheritance; surely we are a long way from the four freedoms; surely these graduates are not to be envied, the orators are saying.

No, those twenty odd years between the wars were not an entrance to the new, but they *were* an exit from the old. And you are going to live and work and play, I hope, in a new dimensional world. Call it One World; call it the age of the common man; call it the air age; call it the atomic age. — Call it what you please, great, restless forces are at work — spiritual, philosophical, scientific, economic and political. The remotest corners of the earth feel the ferment.

Yes, granting that in historical perspective the proclamation of a new era after the last war was a little premature, *this* looks like the real thing.

Canning[92] said he called the New World into existence to replace the balance of the Old. The Jinns of Science and the Four Horsemen of the Apocalypse have called the new dimensional world into existence not to replace the balance of the old, but to replace the old.

[92] British Foreign Secretary George Canning (1770–1827).

Electronics, jet propulsion, atomic energy, social security, political security, collectivism, spiritual reawakening, and a hundred other products of the thinking and anguish of our times urgently beseech us to find the discrimination to develop what's *good* in the new and to keep what's *better* in the old.

It is all a little confusing to your elders, even if it isn't to you who are young and unafraid, and see things better because you don't see so much. You know that the world is a tenement with many families. Some are jealous, some ignorant, some ambitious, and so on. They have different ideas about how to keep peace in the house and how to promote their welfare and the welfare of the other tenants. There has been everlasting trouble in this house. Cooperative management is the only hope, and with a great leap forward they have all signed the Charter of the United Nations.

But some believe in capitalism, some in communism, some in socialism. In the American family we believe in tolerance — live and let live. Others, just as eager for peace as we are, may not. They may feel that discord and distrust will always poison the house until everyone thinks alike. The tension will be acute for a long time. We live in one house, but not in one time. Anne O'Hare McCormick put it this way:

> "The primeval tomtom still beats while the atom bomb ticks. Russia is straddling the centuries, in victory more than ever pounding backward to Peter the Great and racing to overtake Henry Ford and Henry Kaiser before she has caught up with Thomas Jefferson. The clocks of Europe are turning back and the clocks of Asia are turning forward. And there are places where time stands still because the night does not lift and there is no tomorrow."

Now you are about to come in from the yard and take an active place in this house. You will live in the best apartment. You will have the best food, the best furniture, the best plumbing, the best of everything. The others will envy you, which doesn't make it any easier for you. But you can't escape. The house is too small. There is no place to go. We've found that out at the price of two wars. You will live with your family, but you will also live with all the other people in this crowded house.

Some of you may be a little confused by the complexity of it all, by the discord, by the conflicts of opinion that pull you this way and that, by the clocks that are out of time and the voices that are out of tune with the bright new world you fought for yesterday. Perhaps some of you don't see just where you fit. Perhaps you're saying, "the world is so big and I am so small, I don't like it, at all, at all."

Let me recall some familiar words that John Donne wrote 300 years ago:

"No man is an Iland, intire of it selfe; every man is a peece of the Continent, a part of the maine; . . . any man's death diminishes me, because I am involved in Mankinde."

You are involved in Mankind; you are a part of your time. What you think, what you say, what you do, influences what others think and say and do, just as they influence you. Whatever your station, humble or great, you will mould the shape of things to come in your home, in your community, in your country, in the world. Whether more or less, is up to you. The church knows this, the educator knows it, and democracy rests upon it. I hope it is more rather than less, because you have the responsibility of an American, and the advantage of some education. (In Iran three out of four of the one out of five who survive infancy never learn to read or write.)

Here at Wesleyan you have learned that knowledge is freedom and ignorance is tyranny. You have also learned how hard it is really to think, to think straight and without prejudice. Voltaire said that "prejudice is opinion without judgment," and that throughout the world "children are inspired with opinion before they can judge." We all dilute our thinking with a large proportion of prejudice. Some of us don't think at all, we just rearrange our prejudices, and some of us reason backward from opinions instead of forward from facts. As the lawyer said to the jury, "And these, gentlemen, are the conclusions on which I base my facts!"

I hope you've decided to do some hard, straight thinking about your world, along with earning a living, getting married and raising a family. There has never been any oppressive surplus of that kind of thinking in our country, even about the simpler, older worlds behind us.

In a free society there is *no* substitute for a conscientious and responsible citizenry. We are going to need that kind of citizenry as never before. There are many who feel that our star is setting; that the United States is a dying relic of 18th Century nonsense about economic and political freedom — to exploit and starve; that your generation will be indifferent to the public interest; that wealth or power or a good time is the measure of an American's ambition; that capitalism is sick unto death and won't survive another severe economic depression.

We dare not let such ideas gain headway. We dare not disappoint the hopes of the myriads of miserable spectators across the earth who share our devout faith in the vitality of the great liberal humane tradition, and who hope and pray that *we* will lead resolutely and wisely into a new era where no one rattles a sabre and no one drags a chain. We dare not default, we who have so much. We dare not encourage others to think that we are apathetic and senile, that the time is at hand to mould the world into a new form in which the individual counts for little and to which we too in time must conform. Because that's the road to war!

We know that there is room in the world for the American way and the Russian way to exist peacefully side by side. But do the *Russians* know it? *They* know that our ideas of democracy and free enterprise after 150 years of ascendency are on trial everywhere, but do *we* know it? *They* know that we can't stand still; that we have to go forward or backward. Do *we* know it?

I hope you *do* decide to do some hard thinking. I hope you *do* decide not to be just a complaining spectator, not to surrender to the corruptions of the easiest life there is anywhere. I hope you decide that it is a part of your job as a *privileged* citizen to live like a *responsible* citizen.

If you *do* decide to take part in the everlasting battle for a better world you will, I daresay, conclude that we can't lead from weakness; that we must practice what we preach; that unless we can make our system work and work well, it won't attract many followers. To make it work, we can't have our cake and eat it too; we may have to decide some of our conflicts of opinion the hard way, the unpopular way. We can't mobilize world opinion behind injustice and inconsistency, behind a policy of heads I win, tails you lose.

You may conclude that as a very, very free people as things go, we too often put our private interests ahead of the public interest; we assert rights vigorously but accept responsibilities reluctantly; we are more intent on getting than giving. Instead of closing our ranks as Americans, we tend to divide them as workers, managers, farmers, business men and so on. And the rights of the public are smothered in the clamor.

You may conclude that we demand too *much* of government and too *little* of ourselves; that government is more than the sum of all the interests, it is the paramount interest, the public interest. If we are going to compete successfully for the allegiance of men everywhere, our government must be the efficient, effective agent of a responsible citizenry; it must not be a wailing wall and a whipping post; it must be the positive business of all of us, and beneath the dignity of none of us. It must be the honorable calling the founders of a government by the governed meant it to be.

Beware of the demagogues with all the answers you want to hear; of the reactionaries who think the 19th Century is ahead of us; of the pre-atomic prophets of the status quo; of the ostriches who damn everyone else indiscriminately. Beware of the dread tyrant — ignorance!

And remember the words of Pascal: "Justice without force is impotent. Force without justice is tyrannical. We must, therefore, combine justice with force." Beware of soft counsels. The time is not yet for naked righteousness. Sometimes the wise have to correct the errors of the good. Strength is still respected in the world. Force is still the instrument of justice and order. With your mind you can find truth and justice; with discipline, strength.

A war is not won until the last battle, and peace is never won. But it can be lost in a single battle. If this is a prologue, if this is to be a new era of enduring peace, you'll have to think hard, you'll have to fight for it, you'll have to wage peace with all the zeal and moral courage you waged war. You can't fight lying down. You can't say "Let the United Nations do it." For the United Nations is only a spade; it won't work by itself. It is only the start. It can't grow ever and ever better, it can't even live, by itself. The weeds that smothered the League will smother it if the garden is neglected. You are the gardners. We are all the gardners, we who know that science has outdistanced philosophy, that there will be no victors in another war, that jealousy, suspicion and intolerance are at last armed with weapons which in one burst of universal fury can fulfill Kant's grim prophecy that "the world will be the graveyard of the human race."

This is a time for thinking, for discipline self-imposed by free men, for vision, for purpose, for example. It's a threshold — a threshold to something very bright or very dark. It's morning. It's exciting. It's a good time to be alive — and awake!

It's your time and you can say with Emerson:

> "If there is any period one would desire to be born in, — is it not the age of Revolution; when the old and the new stand side by side, and admit of being compared; when the energies of all men are searched by fear and hope; when the historic glories of the old can be compensated by the rich possibilities of the new era? This time, like all times, is a very good one, if we but know what to do with it."

To W. E. Shaw

July 2, 1946

Dear Dr. Shaw:

Many thanks for your letter, and the citation was most flattering; also for your generous comments about the commencement talk. I have had some requests for copies, and I am having it mimeographed. I am sending you a copy under separate cover.

I appreciate the honorarium, which I had not anticipated, although I do look forward to treasuring the hood with all its reminders of a happy day and a great honor.

May I donate the enclosed check to whatever purposes of the University that you think best? If it could be added to the Gertrude Bohrer Gift which you mentioned at commencement I would be very happy. But please feel free to do anything with it you please.

With warm regards and many thanks for all your courtesies, I am

Sincerely yours,

In July Mr. and Mrs. Stevenson and their youngest son vacationed in the Pacific Northwest with Mr. and Mrs. Richard L. Neuberger, both later to be U.S. senators. Mr. Neuberger wrote an article about Stevenson in 1952 describing the trip. Neuberger recalled that his most vivid impression of the man whom the Democrats had nominated for President was: "We were looking down a steep white apron of icy snow on the ramparts of Mount St. Helens. At the bottom of this chute, ugly boulders waited with sabre-toothed fangs. The forest ranger and I hesitated so that we could get our bearings. Was there some safer way around the shoulder of the 10,000 foot mountain? Adlai Stevenson plodded out onto the slippery gables of St. Helens and began kicking out footsteps for his wavering companions. 'Come on, Neuberger,' he scoffed. 'Do you want to live forever?' " [93]

Stevenson with Neuberger's assistance wrote a guest editorial for the Portland Journal, *August 2, 1946.*

In the East, much is said of the grandeur of the Pacific Northwest. Seeing is believing. After two weeks here and in British Columbia, I have joined the cheering section.

I do not think you people fully appreciate the outdoor magnificence that is yours. To you, the great snowfields and thick stands of timber seem commonplace. To my family and me, they are almost unbelievable. My work with the late Secretary Knox and Secretary Stettinius took me around the world, but never to places that could match in grandeur Yosemite falls or Mt. St. Helens mirrored in Spirit lake.

As a resident of the United States, I feel that I have a certain proprietary interest in such public lands as the Columbia National forest. I hope that this heritage will be protected. The sight of hideous burned areas was a shock. So, too, were jungles of stumps left by indiscriminate logging operations which clear-cut the land and left no seed trees. I pray

[93] "Stevenson the Man," *Frontier*, September, 1952, p. 11.

that the glorious Pacific Northwest will never suffer the fate that wanton lumbering foisted on the forests of Wisconsin and Northern Michigan. I have found something tranquil, real and very comforting in the unsung forest service. What the men of that service are quietly doing to conserve our precious and majestic forests gives me an humble and grateful feeling.

I made my trip to Spirit Lake near the summit of the Columbia National forest with a new friend and an old one, John C. Kuhns, assistant regional forester, and Richard L. Neuberger, Portland journalist, who served with me in San Francisco as aide-de-camp to Edward R. Stettinius Jr. I have been associated with many nooks and crannies of the government, but I have met few public servants who appeared to me more devoted to their work or more sincerely interested in the public good than John Kuhns. I could not help wondering how he feels whenever you people of the Northwest, who must love your scenic beauties, carelessly toss cigarettes into the woods or heedlessly deface the magnificent camp sites.

I was reminded while in the inspiring shadow of Mount St. Helens of a similar experience during the hectic days of the San Francisco conference when I spent a memorable week-end in Yosemite National park with Archibald MacLeish, assistant secretary of state, and Marshall N. Dana, editor of the editorial page of The Journal. The inspiration of my trip to the Pacific Northwest will remain with me for many years to come. I hope to return soon again. And I hope, also, that many of my fellow delegates to the United Nations will have opportunity to experience the scenic majesty which awaits any visitor to this Pacific seaboard region.

On July 18, 1946, President Harry S Truman appointed Stevenson as an alternate delegate to the second part of the first session of the General Assembly of the United Nations. John Foster Dulles, also an alternate delegate, wrote Stevenson decribing the appointment as "well deserved."

To John Foster Dulles

August 5, 1946

Dear Foster:

Thanks for your note. I look forward eagerly to the Assembly and this further opportunity to work with you. I must say we seem to have come a long way down hill since San Francisco.

Sincerely yours,

Carol Evans, who had been a secretary in the law firm of Sidley, Austin, Burgess and Harper, wrote Stevenson asking if he needed a secretary for the UN General Assembly.

To Carol Evans[94]

August 5, 1946

Dear Miss Evans

Thanks for your letter. We had a lovely trip and I hope you are too. I am starting back to work here at the firm — and I suspect all memories of my period of idleness will soon vanish.

The government furnishes us secretaries for the General Assembly which will last from the middle of Sept. to the first of Nov., or a little longer, I suspect. I had not thought of bringing my own, but if you are going to be in this part of the country and would like to go to New York for that interval perhaps I could arrange it. Let me know your plans and I'll look into it.

Sincerely yours,

To Christian A. Herter[95]

August 12, 1946

Dear Chris:

In June I gave the commencement address at a small, old, honorable university in the Corn Belt — Illinois Wesleyan. Aside from a degree, my only dividend for this effort so far is a visit from a young man, Roy V. Palmer, 1922 East Jackson Street, Bloomington, Illinois, who is determined to make a career in the international field. He was in the Air Forces in the Pacific for three years and is graduating from Illinois Wesleyan this month. I believe he said he was 24 or perhaps 25. His background includes almost no qualifications for this sort of career — except the background itself!

He comes from the heart of the Corn Belt, which as you may have heard, is not fertile soil for the international mind; he has no languages, modest means, I gather, only a fair liberal arts education, I would assume — and a passionate determination since infancy to cross the horizon of the prairies and make his career in a foreign field! His father, manager in a Montgomery Ward store, after a period of bewilderment is anxious to help him accomplish his heart's desire somehow. The young man amazed me with a naive recitation of the investigations he had

---

[94] The handwritten original is in the possession of Miss Evans.
[95] Congressman from Massachusetts.

made of educational opportunities in the field & of foreign relief agencies to which he had applied for positions until he could get into a school. The result of this research, conducted while at college and evidently working very hard, is a burning desire to get into the School of Advanced International Studies as soon as he can. Evidently the School has informed him that there are no vacancies and he is downhearted, but his determination is as strong as ever.

I volunteered to write you as the father of the School to inquire if there were any possibility of his getting in and when. I am bold enough to impose on you only because this is an unfamiliar experience for me — after long residence on the prairies — and a guess that you are not averse to encouraging boys from the rural Midwest who feel a sense of mission which has all the ear marks of permanent obsession.

I have been at home since early March and have resumed law practice after some five years of that engaging turmoil in the Government and a long holiday. To say that my heart and mind have divorced the past would be untrue, but I am struggling with the adjustment and so far, so good. I will be in New York for the General Assembly and look forward to a glimpse of you — but I won't be able to reproduce the London setting of our last encounter, I am afraid!

Ellen joins me in affectionate regards to you both.

Sincerely yours,

On September 15, 1946, Stevenson discussed "One or Two Worlds? The Dilemma of American Foreign Policy" on The University of Chicago Round Table *with Professor Hans J. Morgenthau and foreign correspondent Frederick Kuh. Stevenson said of the deterioration in Russian-American relations:*

The present conflicts with Russia were unthinkable to most of us a year or so ago. People were declaiming about the bright new world of peace and light. They have been quickly disillusioned, and now, with the same intemperance, speculation about war fills the press and the air.

I think we are too impatient, too volatile. Making peace is harder than making war. We seem to have forgotten about the chaos and the turmoil that followed the last war and the last peace.

Russia was not present then. There was no fundamental underlying conflict between the East and the West the way there is now. This is the most elemental struggle the world has ever suffered. Making peace this time will be harder than ever before.

The Paris Conference is just the beginning. Germany and Japan and a host of questions are still a long way ahead. Even then peace will not be documents. It will be secured only by the patient, slow development of mutual confidence and self-discipline for years to come.

Perhaps an optimist would say that it is a good thing that documentary peacemaking is so hard. If it were quick and simple, perhaps a people so easily diverted as we are would forget about it too soon.

When the question was raised as to whether Europe should be divided into eastern and western blocs, Stevenson observed:

Perhaps we have some disagreement here as to whether or not our policy should be the frank, cynical recognition of spheres of exclusive political and economic interest in the world.

For my part I think that we have to go much further than that if we are going to attempt to bring out of this war some of the hopes and aspirations of mankind which we have enunciated so often.

. . . for my part I must say that I still feel that rigid exclusive blocs can only aggravate the fear and suspicion that already trouble the world.

If our peace is to be more than an uneasy and precarious one, we must try to do something better than divide Europe into exclusive eastern and western political and economic blocs.

But I am sure that there is one thing we can all agree upon here. I do not want to overlook the opportunity to say something about how important the health of our democratic capitalism is in all this. I do not think our performance in the first year of peace — our strikes, the merchant marine tied up, steel and rail strikes, skyrocketing prices if you please, black markets, inflation, stock-market crash, and all the irresponsible political shouting — has been very encouraging to our myriad friends around the world for whom the American domestic scene is the barometer of hopes and fears.

Some say that if there is another severe economic depression in the United States, the Soviets are convinced that capitalism will try to fight its way out of it at their expense, and all agree that in the shattering world-wide consequences of an American economic collapse lies the prospect for the expansion of communism.[96]

Just before going to New York City to attend the meeting of the General Assembly of the United Nations, Stevenson made campaign speeches for several downstate Illinois Democrats. The state chairman of the Women's Division wrote him on October 21, 1946: "Downstate Democrats are still talking about the fine address you made . . . in Spring-

[96] *University of Chicago Round Table Transcript*, pp. 1–2, 16, 18.

field. It was a real inspiration to hear a new voice and a new subject."

Warren R. Austin was head of the U.S. delegation at the General Assembly. Other members were Senator Tom Connally, Senator Arthur H. Vandenberg, Mrs. Franklin D. Roosevelt, and Representative Sol Bloom. The alternates were Representative Charles A. Eaton, Representative Helen Gahagan Douglas, John Foster Dulles, and Stevenson.

Correspondent Nat A. Barrows wrote in the Chicago Daily News, *January 3, 1947:*

> Mrs. Eleanor Roosevelt and the Chicago lawyer, Adlai Stevenson measured up to their jobs excellently.
>
> They worked hard, thought clearly, tried to make some sense out of muddled directives and inter-delegation confusion and addressed their respective committees with ideas instead of oratory.
>
> They merit return to the 1947 delegation, with increased responsibilities.

Mrs. Roosevelt when she spoke to the Chicago Council on Foreign Relations on March 3, 1947, said:

> I was very glad when I saw Mr. Stevenson again at the second meeting of the First Assembly in New York. Mr. Stevenson was an alternate, but in all but name he was a full delegate, and certainly carried not only the work of the alternate, but all the work of a delegate. So we became accustomed, I think to feel that he carries his full share of all the burdens whenever he is around, and that was very comforting to other members of the delegation.

John M. Allison, a Foreign Service officer who advised the delegation on Far Eastern policy, remarked that the Department of State staff respected both Stevenson and Congresswoman Helen Gahagan Douglas and could talk and work better with them than with other members of the delegation.[97]

Mrs. Ronald Tree recalled that Stevenson often dined at their home that fall. "He talked about the issues and political problems of the General Assembly and rather reluctantly entered into the ridiculous acting games we occasionally played after dinner. Then, as always, the first impression was his extra dimension of personality. When he entered a room people were aware of him. He had an abundance of those overused words charisma, charm — he was a life-enhancer."[98]

[97] Interview with Walter Johnson, May 12, 1967.
[98] Marietta Tree, "Memories of Stevenson," speech to the Foreign Correspondents Association, Tokyo, Japan, May, 1966. This speech is in the possession of Mrs. Tree.

Stevenson kept a diary for the first two weeks of his service on the delegation.[99] We have interspersed the diary with letters and speeches.

Oct. 17, 1946

Arrived Pennsylvania Hotel 10:00 A.M. Delegation has entire fifth floor. Very efficient layout with all technical staffs and services and Delegates together. I have a suite with adjoining office for secretary.

First meeting of the U. S. Delegation. All present except [John Foster] Dulles, who was ill, and Senators Vandenburg [Arthur H. Vandenberg] and [Tom] Connally and Secretary [James F.] Byrnes, who have not yet returned from Paris.

Senator Austin emphasized time, patience and diligence to get UN going on working basis. But have many projects on which we can agree — health, obstacles to trade, enlargement of access to raw materials through works and deeds that we can help one another and develop mutual trust in larger area of collaboration. As peoples get larger share of good things of earth, everyone profits — including Russians.

Importance of General Assembly for these purposes and contrast to Security Council; felt too much emphasis on veto. U. S. has duty to get across to world that importance of GA — not only a recommending body without power as advocates of immediate administration say. There is no veto in GA. Questions like Headquarters, on which success depends to great extent, decided in GA. Military agreements must be ratified by GA. Quality of smaller states important. Preponderance of smaller states means that great powers must be good, wise, responsible and must deal on basis of equality and respect for interests of smaller powers. Such responsibility of great powers is deterrent to war.

"This General Assembly of supreme importance to future peace." Must show world that we recognize responsibility and are going to live up to it because we have greatest stake in peace. Doing away with causes of war by making all peoples most prosperous is job of GA.

To undertake to amend Charter would be grave mistake before it has had a chance. Great objectives are not obtained in a moment. Must not let people think U. S. is impatient.

Senator Austin announced Committee assignments.

Position papers and background material distributed. Very comprehensive preparation. Best in our experience.

Discussion of press policy. I proposed that the Chairman act as spokesman with respect to Delegation Meetings.

. . . Evidently in addition to serving on the Headquarters Committee,

[99] The diary is in the possession of Adlai E. Stevenson III.

my principal responsibility will be the coordination of the activities of the political liaison officers, of whom there are eight, headed by Ambassador [Samuel J.] Dawson (Uruguay) and trouble shooting for Austin generally. Problem of delegations and staffs and with meetings at Lake Success is very difficult and unsatisfactory. Meeting of Delegation to consider agenda items assigned to Committee 3. Sol Bloom indicated that there would be some difficulty in securing appropriation to International Refugee Organization if Russia and the Satellite countries refuse to contribute.

At 4:00 I left with Mrs. Douglas[100] to speak to the gathering of the representatives of many national organizations in the Fisk Building. The discussion lasted almost two hours.

Dined with Beatrice Pitney Lamb[101] at Cosmopolitan Club to talk about United Nations news and Woodrow Wilson Foundation.

October 18

Delegation discussed sites for permanent headquarters for U.N. Dulles present for first time. [Charles] Fahy, Legal Advisor to the State Department, initiated discussion of site of permanent headquarters of U.N. . . . Sentiment of Delegation was that the U.S. no longer be neutral on specific site; that U.S. rather than U.N. should assume the burden of the irate citizens and cushion U.N. from further displays of public indifference and hostility.

Discussed ways and means of inconspicuously altering U.S. position; discussion of the five sites, various phases, studied by Headquarters Commission in Westchester County. Mrs. Roosevelt indicated her continued interest in consideration of areas further up Hudson. General discussion of how far U.S. should go and if question was reopened to permit consideration of San Francisco.

Had lunch at Barbarry Room, Barbizon Hotel, with Thomas Jefferson Hamilton of New York Times. Met Silliman Evans[102] there entertaining his mother-in-law and aunt from Abilene, Texas, on first trip to New York!

Had long debate in the afternoon with Fahy . . . et al about American position and site matters generally and agreed to make motor trip on Sunday to inspect the Westchester County sites so I would have better understanding of the infinitely complicated problems.

Spent evening on papers, particularly draft speech on veto question

---

[100] Helen Gahagan Douglas, U.S. delegate to the UN General Assembly.
[101] Editor of *United Nations News*, published by the Woodrow Wilson Foundation.
[102] Of the Chicago *Sun*.

which is to be raised by Australia and/or Cuba. This obviously will be most vexatious question in the Assembly. I wish we could take a more positive position in favor of reconsideration of veto on peaceful settlements under Chapter VI of Charter but policy of Department seems fixed that we must not take initiative or ascent [assent] at this time to any modification of veto in view of emphatic Russian feeling.

October 19

Prepared short speech for U.N. radio program over American Broadcasting Company and had talk with Allen Grover[103] about [Archibald] MacLeish, [Robert M.] Hutchins, Time, Life & Fortune etc.

Spoke on radio at 1:20 after a mad scramble to get to the broadcasting station. . . .

AMERICAN BROADCASTING COMPANY
New York — October 19, 1946

There are two or three things which I hope the American people will try to keep in mind during the meeting of the General Assembly of the United Nations.

In the first place the General Assembly must not be confused with the Peace Conference or the Council of Foreign Ministers. Their roles are entirely distinct. It is the function of the Foreign Ministers of the great powers who have been meeting for more than a year to work out peace treaties for Italy and the smaller enemy states. The Peace Conference just concluded in Paris afforded the other allied nations who contributed to the defeat of Germany, and also the enemy states themselves, an opportunity to express their views on these draft treaties.

In short, the function of the Council of Foreign Ministers is to liquidate the terrible legacy the war has left us. Their function is to end the war by formal treaties of peace. Their function is to *make* peace.

But the role of the United Nations is quite different. The purpose of the United Nations is to *maintain* peace. The whole complex structure of the United Nations is painstakingly designed to serve that purpose — through the Security Council which deals directly with situations which endanger or might endanger the peace, through the Economic and Social Council which seeks to eliminate the basic causes of war, and through the General Assembly which is the supreme deliberative body for all the United Nations — the world community.

So when the General Assembly is meeting during the coming weeks, its deliberations must *not* be confused with the news from the Council of

[103] Vice president of Time, Inc.

Foreign Ministers which will also meet here in New York to resume consideration of the peace treaties.

The United States attaches the greatest importance to the General Assembly which has been called the town meeting of the world. I have said that it is the supreme deliberative body of the world community. It can discuss anything, anything relating to the maintenance of peace. It can discuss anything, anything within the vast scope of the purposes and principles of the United Nations. It can make recommendations to the Governments of the world on anything, anything except questions within the jurisdiction and under active consideration by the Security Council.

It does not legislate; it does not order. It discusses and recommends; it expresses the opinion of the world on any subject. It is the will and the voice of the world, the conscience, if you please. And as Sir Hartley[104] suggested there is no more powerful sovereign than the organized articulate opinion of the world. And there is no veto in the General Assembly!

The General Assembly met for the first time in London last winter to organize the United Nations and all of its organs. That intricate and enormous task is now largely completed and the agenda for this meeting of the Assembly is crowded with questions, political and security questions, economic and financial questions, social, humanitarian and cultural questions, questions of trusteeship of non-independent areas, administrative and budgetary questions, legal questions. It must decide on the permanent headquarters of the United Nations; it must decide on the admission of new members of the United Nations; it must elect new members of the Security Council and of the Economic and Social Council, etc.

It will take a long time and you will get impatient with the everlasting talk, and you will get confused — perhaps skeptical about any solid achievement. But there is no other way; no other way peacefully to arrange the affairs of a people, except by *dictatorship*, and no other way peacefully to arrange the affairs of *all* peoples, except by the *domination* of a single people. And we Americans will reject dictatorship in our own country and domination in the world.

So be patient, and try to see this General Assembly in the long perspective of a new and better world struggling for birth amid the ashes of the old. And, finally, try to remember that the spectacular — the quarrels and disagreements, as Dr. Chang[105] said — will be the big news in the papers while the agreements will attract little attention.

[104] Sir Hartley Shawcross, M.P., British Attorney General and delegate to the UN General Assembly.

[105] Dr. P. C. Chang, member of the Chinese delegation to the UN General Assembly and representative of China at the first session of the Economic and Social Council.

It is a great milestone in history — this town meeting of the world — and it will be conducted in a gold fish bowl.

As Secretary Byrnes said last night: "The peoples of this world who long for peace will not be able to make their influence felt if they do not know the conflicts in ideas and in interest that give rise to war, and if they do not know how the statesmen and the peoples of other countries view these conflicts.

"It is better that the world should witness and learn to appraise *clashes* of ideas rather than *clashes* of arms."

[*Diary*]

. . . and then had lunch with Zuleta Angel of Colombia and his assistant, Robaldo, old friends from London, at Voisin. Zuleta had much to talk about regarding tactics on veto, permanent site and other questions in the General Assembly indicating his usual anxiety to cooperate with U.S. A very foxy man and trustworthy only when it serves his own interest; sometimes I suspect even more than his country's interest! Instead of being Chief Delegate this time, he will be ranked by Ex-President [Alfonso] Lopez and two ex-foreign ministers.

Went shopping at Brooks Brothers and back in time to have long talk and dinner with Bill Fowler about economic work of General Assembly and to hear excellent broadcast by Vandenburg from Detroit. I am convinced again that he is the ablest man in the Senate and certainly in our Delegation, if only he wasn't so acid and partisan.

October 20

Left at 8:45 . . . [to visit] the Westchester sites. Lovely mild day. Crossed George Washington Bridge and up the Palisades to look at a site in the Palisade Interstate Park opposite Yonkers. This would be spectacular and seems feasable but has never been considered. On up the Hudson through the Bear Mountain Reservation. Coloring gorgeous and maples even better than at home. Crossed the Bear Mountain Bridge and drove around through the area east of Peekskill which is one of the sites under consideration. Very rugged, many lovely lakes. Had lunch at Otto Koegel's in Somers. He is a partner in Hughes, Dwight, Sherman, etc., and General Counsel of Twentieth Century Fox. Has more than 1200 acres and raises hunters, etc. Beautiful place and a very pleasant man. It was a party for U.N. people interested in the site question to make it clear that he and his committee, although large property owners, were delighted to have U.N. come to that section and would surrender their property without protest. Fritz Dashiell, old friend from college and now Managing

Editor of Readers Digest, was there. My luncheon partner was Mrs. Wendell Willkie, who talked incessantly of Wendell and her boy, Philip, who was also there and not too impressive. Drove on down through Westchester to inspect the site around Purchase, including vast Whitelaw Reed [Reid] Estate which has been boarded up for many years. Stopped at Wilder Foote's at East Chester for supper on the way into the city. Have a pleasant little house in an acre of ground with old apple trees and seem well situated, but Marcia [Foote] is obviously harassed with household work and children.

My conclusion is that the site around Harrison — Purchase — is by far the best in Westchester County although expensive and will cause dislocation of some inhabitants and many complications. Palisades site should be investigated. . . . Relating to site torn from reluctant land owners, was reminded of Russian proverb: "The quality of my shoe leather is not impaired by the fact that the calf yielded his skin reluctantly."

Monday, October 21

Delegation meeting in the morning. Vandenberg said he came back from Paris with one inescapable conviction: "effective success of the United Nations is the success of the world."

Discussion of Trusteeship and strategy as to how to avoid defining "states directly concerned." Discussion of anti-monopoly provisions, etc. This ultimately arose as to our policy with respect to the Japanese Mandates in the Pacific and it was agreed that Byrnes be requested to try to bring this issue between the Army and the Navy and the State Department to some final decision so that we will not be embarrassed by asking for more in our own case than we are willing to grant in the case of others. Evidently Navy is still holding out for annexation.

Delegation meeting all afternoon. Vandenberg worried by probability that many nations would not be able to pay their share of the budget, which in some cases is as low as $12,500 per year, and that U.N. might become "rich man's club" while "its life depends on its universality." Discussion of budget for International Refugee Organization with same objections from Van.

Called on Mrs. [John Alden] Carpenter and Betty [Pirie] in the late afternoon. Our conversation was soon interrupted by the arrival of Louise Dillingham and I returned to the hotel in time for another Delegation meeting at 8:00. To bed exhausted.

Tuesday, October 22

Delegation discussed political and security questions in the morning, and Herschel Johnson[106] defended no action position on Spain on ground that discussion in Security Council in the summer had only strengthened Franco's position as "interference"; also that any economic sanctions would only result in further deterioration of plight of the Spanish people.[107]

I marvelled again at the splendid background and paper work done by the State Department in preparation for this Assembly. In all aspects of the work it is superb and evidently . . . Dorothy Fosdick,[108] et al are entitled to the major share of the credit.

The afternoon session discussed the veto. Connally indicated his sympathy for modification and at instigation of Ross[109] I moved adjournment as Austin had made preliminary statement to enable everyone to read long memorandum and to enable Austin to get final position cleared with President and Byrnes before discussion was resumed.

While out of the room for a few minutes to talk with someone in my office, Vandenberg asked to be relieved of first responsibility for Committee 2 (Economic and Financial) and suggested that I take his place on that Committee. When I returned, I protested but Austin insisted and I am stuck!

It is apparent that they have cut out more work — Committee 2, Headquarters, and political liaison — than I can properly handle.

Dined with Ty Wood [110] . . . and Helen Douglas to discuss Committee 2 work and broadcast in the evening on CBS program with Sir Hartley Shawcross, Attorney General of the UK and number 2 delegate. . . .

To bed more exhausted than ever. Difficult sleeping with so much noise on Seventh Avenue.

Wednesday, October 23

This is the day the Assembly opens! All Delegates to assemble at Waldorf. Drove up with Dulles. Big crowd and saw many old friends. Automobile cavalcade from Waldorf to City Hall for the city reception cere-

[106] Deputy U.S. representative to the UN Security Council with rank of ambassador.

[107] As a result of Franco Spain's sympathy for Hitler during World War II, Spain was refused admission to the United Nations until 1955.

[108] Member of the U.S. delegation to the UN in San Francisco and special assistant to Alger Hiss, secretary-general of the United Nations Conference.

[109] John C. Ross, deputy director of the Office of Special Political Affairs (later renamed United Nations Affairs) in the Department of State. He served as Stevenson's deputy at the meetings of the Preparatory Commission and later as an adviser with the U.S. delegation to the UN Assembly in New York.

[110] C. Tyler Wood, Princeton Class of 1921; special assistant to the Assistant Secretary of State for Economic Affairs and alternate U.S. member of the UNRRA Council.

monies. Drove down with Dulles. Crowds scattered along the route curious but apathetic. At speaking ceremonies at City Hall, found myself seated next to [Andrei] Vyshinsky with [Andrei] Gromyko behind me. Spaak[111] made his usual magnificent extempore speech.

Rode back to Waldorf with Dulles and two members of the Ethiopian Delegation!

Splendid luncheon at Waldorf given by Reception Committee of New York City. Found myself at a table with unfamiliar Latin Delegates and flanked by two officers of Macy's! B. Davis[112] was at adjoining table and invited me for weekend. First time I had seen him for years.

After luncheon drove to Flushing Meadows in automobile cavalcade with police escort. Diverted enroute through the worst part of Brooklyn because of the President's arrival at La Guardia Airport. Assembly Hall at Flushing very impressive; the work, I believe, of Nat Owings and Lewis Skidmore.

President's arrival, accompanied by surprisingly little dramatics. Wilder Foote wrote his speech and one of the best he ever wrote but Truman's delivery was atrocious. He looked tired and sick.

I met Mrs. [John Alden] Carpenter and Betty [Pirie] afterward and drove back . . . to the Waldorf for the President's Reception. Took Mrs. Carpenter and Betty down the line to meet the President. Introduced them to Byrnes, Molotov, Vyshinsky, Gromyko, Manuilsky[113] and assorted Delegates and Americans. They had a big time and Mrs. Carpenter went right to work on Vyshinsky and Manuilsky about some Russian music project. Very fine reception, beautifully done. Dined with Mrs. Carpenter and Betty afterward at Passy Restaurant on 63rd Street. Then to bed . . .

Thursday, October 24

Delegation meeting in the morning. Left at 10:30 with Dulles for Flushing for Plenary session and commencement of general debate. Saw a lot of newspaper friends. Lunched in very elegant and too-expensive Delegates Restaurant in the building with Connally, [Francis] Wilcox and [Dorothy] Fosdick. Listened to speeches all afternoon while all the other Delegates except Mrs. Roosevelt — whose fidelity, as at London, is a marvel — drifted away. Drove back with her afterward and she explained that she felt it was only polite to stay and listen to the speeches of other countries and "moreover I have been doing nothing while our other Delegates have been so busy all summer." Told me about Christ-

[111] Paul Henri Spaak of Belgium, president of the General Assembly.
[112] Norman P. Davis, a Harvard Law School roommate of Stevenson's.
[113] Dmitri Z. Manvilsky, chairman of the Ukraine S.S.R. delegation.

mas parties at Hyde Park for the soldier guards stationed there. Discussed politics, languages, and education. Everything confirms conviction that she is one of the few really great people I have known.

Went to Allan Grover's for dinner about an hour late . . .

Friday, October 25

Delegation meeting. Report by Austin on long meeting of General Committee and "domestic question" raised by India's complaint about the treatment of Indians in South Africa . . .

Met with Helen Douglas and my advisors on Committee 2 in the morning and for most of afternoon. Mrs. Carpenter came to lunch with me in my rooms. Was returning to Boston in the afternoon.

Made good progress on consideration of problems in Committee 2. Helen Douglas very emotional but most interested and diligent. Principal problem relates to whether post UNRRA [United Nations Relief and Rehabilitation Administration] relief contribution by U.S. should be direct or through an international organization to replace UNRRA. Department's policy is for direct but seems to be opposed by Bloom and I suspect we are going to have trouble. May also have trouble on degree of our support for proposed economic support for Europe. Vandenberg seems opposed on ground it will only interfere with occupation authorities in Germany.

Went to Waldorf for banquet of American Association for United Nations and sat at speakers table next to General [Carlos] Romulo of Philippines. A sharp little man and famous orator. Met Mr. and Mrs. John D. Rockefeller at the cocktail party beforehand and also David [Rockefeller]. Nelson Rockefeller presided at dinner and Spaak again made superb extempore speech.

On October 22, 1946, Walter Lippmann wrote Stevenson expressing his pleasure at Stevenson's appointment to the U.S. delegation.

To Walter Lippmann[114]

October 25, 1946

Dear Walter:

Thanks for your letter. It is flattering and comforting, but you are going to be disappointed in my performance. They have given me more to do than I can and — with the usual result — I will do none of it well. Vandenburg [Vandenberg] and Connally will have to divert a good deal

[114] The original is in the Walter Lippmann papers, Yale University Library.

of their time to the Foreign Ministers when their meetings commence. As for Eaton and Bloom, you know the situation. Mrs. Douglas is willing and strong but without background. We are really shorthanded, despite appearances. I hope to see you sometime. My regards to Helen.[115]

Yours,

ADLAI

Saturday, October 26 [1946]

Wakened up by telephone call from Ellen. First I have heard from her. All well at home, thank God. But ten cases of polio in Lake Forrest and Bell School closed. Recommended children go on as usual but avoid sports and getting tired.

Also telephone call from old friend, Nan Tucker of San Francisco Chronicle, now working on Herald Tribune for experience.

Slept better and worked on radio address and papers this morning. Saw [Sol] Bloom and asked him where he was last night when he was supposed to be at the speakers table. He said he passed it up because he was never quite sure when he was getting hooked by a crack pot organization!

Drove out to Pocantico Hills with Mrs. Connally and Vera Bloom[116] to Nelson [Rockefeller]'s gigantic luncheon for 300–400 assorted guests. We finally got seated under huge marquee about half past three! It was too big and in spite of masterful efforts of organization, too clumsy to handle well.

Broadcast on CBS at 10:45. Fifteen minute speech. It was not too good. Had wanted to say something positive about our attitude on veto but Wilder Foote censured [censored] it on ground that Austin would want to make first formal disclosure of our position.

Sunday, October 27

Worked on papers and conferred with Ross and others all morning. Had champagne and lunch following service at the Cathedral for U.N., which I did not attend, with the [Nion?] Tuckers at the Plaza. To Norman Davis' at Chappaqua by automobile after lunch for the afternoon and evening . . . Back by train in the evening . . .

Worked late on the veto portions of Austin's speech to the General Assembly.

Monday, October 28

Delegation meeting in the morning — Vandenberg taking emphatic

115 Mrs. Lippmann.
116 Daughter of New York Congressman Sol Bloom.

position on a ceiling on U.S. contribution to U.N. budget of 25% with addition to 33⅓% as emergency, although experts have computed U.S. share at 50%. Makes a good case on taxation without representation and danger of influence measured by contribution creating disproportionate U.S. control.

Discussed Indians in South Africa and ticklish problem of domestic jurisdiction. If no international agreement is involved, could U.N. discuss lynchings in Georgia on same theory?

Vandenberg expressed view that we should not condone by silence the challenge of the small powers on the veto and should not condone abuse in Security Council by the Russians.

Lunched with group on permanent headquarters and reached tentative agreement on reopening question to consider Flushing Meadows, San Francisco and other free land.

Tuesday, October 29

Delegation meeting. Much discussion of conditions of attendance by specialized agencies and disagreement with Spaak's interpretation of General Committee's action that representatives of specialized agencies can attend and speak on their own initiative. Dulles pointed out that "consult" under Article 71 has definite meanings to some Europeans.

Discussed attendance at Latin American caucus and find general sentiment for my position that we should not participate in regional bloc activities but difficult to avoid offense by refusing to send Ambassador Dawson at least to observe. Vandenberg rather in favor of participating on full scale on ground that we can't risk advantages of hemispherical solidarity for uncertain one world.

Postponed further talk of proposed amendment calling on Russians to disclose their forces in ex-enemy territories pending consultation with Byrnes who seems to be commited to Bevin[117] not to raise the question until Bevin arrives in New York on November 2 as dead line on new matters has expired.

Lunched with Huntington Gilchrist,[118] Sir Angus Fletcher, head of sub-Commission on Permanent Headquarters, which has made exhaustive study of Westchester County sites, and Dutchman named DeRanitz[119] and Dana Wilgress, Canadian Ambassador to Moscow. Much impressed with Fletcher. Was quite candid that U.N. should never have come to New York and equally candid that suitable sites were available in Westchester. His preference seemed to be for about ten square miles, partially

---

[117] British Foreign Secretary Ernest Bevin.
[118] Australian representative on the UN Economic and Social Council.
[119] Unable to identify.

owned and balance controlled, around the Mohanset Park East of Peak-skill.

Drove out to Flushing with Fletcher and Wilgress in time for Molotov's speech.[120] His intemperate propaganda against the U.S. reminds me again that Russians must be either utterly inept or so concerned with the domestic affects [effects] of their propaganda that they are willing to risk alienating the rest of the world. It was a memorable hour in the Delegates' lounge after the speech during the French translation with everybody looking a little incredulous and stupified. I got an inspiration partly in conversation with Edgar Mowrer about the changes that should be made in Austin's speech for the next day. Drove back with [Warren] Austin, [Jack] Ross and [Wilder] Foote and found Austin surprisingly calm and almost happy about the Russian disarmament proposal and the constructive aspects of Molotov's speech. He dismissed the recrimination and invective as the tactics of a trial lawyer with a poor case.

Excused myself from Louis Hyde's dinner party, already an hour late; had long talk with Vandenberg and Dulles later on in the evening. Vandenberg more indignant than I had ever seen him and he drafted a proposed change for Austin's speech, ending with quotation from Vandenberg at the last session of the Paris Peace Conference: "The United States will not plead as a defender among allies to whom it has given every ounce of cooperation in blood, sweat and toil, of which a great and unselfish nation is capable." Finally got started on my draft about midnight and finished at 2:00, after digging up Litvinov's proposal for international inspection in 1929 Disarmament Conference.

To bed exhausted while poor Wilder, Jack, et al started to work to redraft my draft. Dreadful problem of clearance with Department on changes in time for Austin to speak tomorrow; also how to get him on at 4:00 so as not to lose impact of his reply to Molotov.

Wednesday, October 30

Morning started with amusing incident in Austin's room when Vandenberg went in to congratulate him on what he thought was the agreed text, which was my first draft and not a revision. Van insisted on putting in some of my stuff and Austin accepted in good grace and the patched quilt was then cleared by phone with Byrnes.

. . . At Plenary Session Austin made good delivery of the speech and evoked much applause in the early parts replying to Molotov and partic-

[120] Ambassador Molotov delivered a blistering attack against the United States for its "monopolistic possession of the Atomic Bomb." In an effort to convince the Security Council to accept the Russian disarmament plan Molotov chided the United States as the "worshippers of the Atomic Bomb." New York *Times,* October 30, 1946.

ularly at his statement that U.S. made a mistake to disarm unilaterally after the last war and would not do so again.

Dined with Charlie Fahy and some friends of his from Santa Fe . . . Home at 11:00 very tired to find Hayden Raynor[121] waiting for me for another midnight session.

Reminded of jingle by Stephen Duggan which Victor Elting told me about U.N.: "I live in a sea of words where the nouns and the adjectives flow, where the verbs speak of actions that never take place and the sentences come and go."

Thursday, October 31

Breakfast with Charlie Fahy about Mrs. Douglas' pet project of declaration of international crime of genocide-mass murder vis Poles, Jews, Armenians, etc.

Long visit from Walter Lippmann . . . Had many flattering things to say about Austin's speech.

. . . To Flushing for the Plenary session in the afternoon and then to Eddie Miller's for dinner with Marshall McDuffy[122] as other guest. Good conversation. Both Miller and McDuffy very sarcastic about Dulles. McDuffy, old Sullivan and Cromwell man, said something to effect that Dulles did not go for Federal Council of Churches and christianity in such a big way until he had taken public opinion poll on present status of religion and other sharp criticisms. . . .

Friday, November 1

Delegation meeting. Van[denberg] authorized to state position on ceiling on U.S. budget contribution. Discussion of Greece and decision that we would not support her for one of the Councils. Much discussion of India and decision to stick to Syria for Security Council.

Lunched with Headquarters group and decision to ask for reopening to include only New York area and San Francisco on Byrnes' instructions.

First session of Committee 2 at Lake Success. Got into big tangle at the outset when Gromyko asked me to have a Pole elected as temporary chairman until the indisposed regular chairman . . . could get there. I declined on ground that Vice Chairman should preside and then [Philip] Noel-Baker intervened to say that [Oscar] Lange of Poland would be a much better Chairman than the Filipino. So I arranged it with the Filipino to nominate Lange, which he did, and there ensued an hour of

---

[121] Special assistant to the Secretary of State.

[122] Marshall W. MacDuffie, associated with the law firm of Sullivan and Cromwell, New York City.

outraged oratory with result that Vice Chairman took Chairman's place as I had foreseen.

Am told Gromyko does not want this Committee assignment and has been displaced on Committee 1 and will be surly.

Dinner with Jebb [123] and Escott Reid [124] at Betty [Pirie]'s apartment. Jebb obviously very tired and discouraged. Sees little hope for peace treaties and suspects this will be the last Council of Foreign Ministers and we will end up with separate treaties for Italy and the Satellites or at least for Italy, thus perpetuating uneasy situations at Trieste. Suggestion that Russians will file complaint in Security Council against those two menaces to international peace and security — Churchill and [Bernard] Baruch!

Saturday, November 2

. . . Lunched with Aglion[125] at very good French restaurant called Brussels at 56th and Park. Discussed Committee 2 and distress in Secretariat about New York living. Says 30 to 40% of his secretarial staff is out of commission most of the time due to exhaustion from interminable travel to Lake Success.

November 2 was the last entry in his diary. On November 14, 1946, Stevenson appeared on the radio discussion program Town Meeting of the Air *on the subject "Should the Veto Be Abolished in the United Nations?" Ambassador Norman J. O. Makin of Australia upheld the affirmative, Stevenson the negative side of the question.*

I'm not sure we are so far apart. Ambassador Makin has intimated that the United Nations cannot function effectively until the veto is abolished.

I hold that the United Nations cannot function effectively if it *is* abolished.

Our disagreement on this point reminds me of the old saw about married men and their wives: that, if they can't get along *with* their mates, neither can they get along *without* them.

Instead of going to the divorce court and engaging in a legal battle which will never produce a solution of our veto problem, I suggest we sit down around the table and try to work out a way to permit the use, but not the abuse, of the veto in the United Nations.

[123] Sir Gladwyn Jebb, acting Secretary-General of the UN in February, 1946, later British Undersecretary of State.
[124] Adviser to the Canadian delegation to the UN General Assembly.
[125] Raoul Aglion, a member of Secretary-General Trygve Lie's personal staff.

First, let us make one thing absolutely clear. The veto problem itself is not the basic cause of our difficulties. It is only a reflection of the unfortunate and deep-seated differences with the Russians. If we are to escape from the atmosphere of crisis that surrounds our international relations, we must settle these differences. Merely changing a voting formula will never be enough.

In discussing this subject, it will help us to recall that there are three types of situations in which the so-called veto may possibly be used. It may be used, first, in a case where the Security Council is about to take action to maintain peace by the use of force. Second, it may be used when the Council is trying to settle a dispute by peaceful means. Third, it may be used in voting on what is really only a question of procedure — of how to do business. It will be helpful if, while I am speaking, these distinctions may be borne in mind.

The whole issue of the veto — the rule of unanimity, which I suggest is the more proper term — was thoroughly threshed out at the San Francisco Conference a year and a half ago. At that time the smaller states participating in the Conference, including Australia, argued the case against the unanimity rule with great force and cogency.

The unanimity rule grew out of the *facts* of international political life. It is a *fact* that effective military and economic power in the world today is largely concentrated in the hands of five great states. They must carry the burden of enforcing measures to keep the peace. If those states are in agreement, there will be no major war; and an Organization designed to keep the peace will be able to do so because of the preponderant power which can be mobilized to support its decisions. But if the Big Five disagree on a matter involving their vital interests, the application of force against any of them, or for that matter against any state over the determined opposition of any one of them, *will* produce a major war. That is the very thing the United Nations was created to prevent.

Thus, under present circumstances, an effective world organization could not exist and grow unless it was founded on the agreement of the Great Powers. At San Francisco, these powers were not prepared to agree to support on [an] Organization which could take, without their consent, important decisions on matters affecting their vital interests — for example, an Organization that could order American troops into action without our consent. The unanimity rule is the price we have to pay for *any* effective organization.

But please bear this in mind. The existence of the rule does not put any member of the United Nations, large or small, above the law, as people sometimes say. All the members are bound equally by the provisions of the Charter, including the provisions requiring member states to settle their disputes by peaceful means and to refrain from the threat or use of force.

Every one blames the Russians for the difficulties which have arisen in the Security Council in connection with the unanimity rule and certainly I don't condone abuse of the veto. But let us not forget that we, no less than the Russians, insisted on putting it in the Charter. It definitely helped to secure approval of the Charter of the United Nations in the United States Senate by the overwhelmingly favorable vote of 89 to 2.

The argument over the veto is so intense that we sometimes distort its extent and significance. It does not paralyze the United Nations or make effective action impossible. There is no veto in the United Nations General Assembly, the Economic and Social Council, the Trusteeship Council, or any other United Nations instrumentality. In these organs decisions are taken by majorities of various types. It is only in the Security Council, and then principally in connection with decisions directly related to the maintenance of international peace and security — decisions which may either immediately or in the long run involve the use of the armed forces of the Powers to counteract threats or acts of aggression — that the unanimity of the Great Powers is required by the Charter. Compared with the League of Nations, where as a rule *every* member had the right of veto in such cases, this represents real progress toward the organization of a true international community.

We should also remember that issues are sometimes settled not only by what goes on in the Security Council, but by what happens after a case has been brought before it. For example, the French and British speedily agreed with Syria and Lebanon to withdraw their troops from those countries even though a veto prevented a decision by the Council. And Russia withdrew her forces from Iran even though Mr. Gromyko walked out on the Council discussions on the matter.

There has been a good deal of criticism of the use of the veto in the Security Council, in matters which do not directly involve the use of enforcement measures. Under the Charter, the Members of the United Nations confer on the Security Council primary responsibility for the maintenance of international peace and security. Once the Council has embarked on this task, in any particular case, it is always possible that a chain of events will be initiated which will lead, in the last analysis, to enforcement action. As soon as the Council agrees to take any action on a case, beyond mere discussion, it must be prepared for enforcement action when the chips are down.

Nevertheless, the United States hopes that the five permanent members of the Security Council may some day agree upon modification of the unanimity rule so that it is easier to settle disputes peacefully. We feel that necessary action by the Security Council for the peaceful settlement of a dispute should *never* be prevented by the votes of any *one* or any number of its members. The permanent members should exercise self-restraint so that necessary action is never blocked in this way.

But the Organization has been under way for less than a year. The Charter should not be amended until a backlog of experience and — even more important — a backlog of *confidence* has been built up which will make possible substantial changes with the unanimous consent of the five major powers.

We do not pretend that we have been satisfied with the operation of the unanimity rule in the Security Council to date. We do not think it has always been used sparingly, with restraint and self-discipline and in the true spirit of the Charter, as the San Francisco declaration of the great powers indicated it should be used. We condemn the attempt to use it to circumvent the provisions of the Charter.

But to argue from this premise that the rule should therefore be abolished would be, as the French say, to throw out the baby with the bath. Under present circumstances, abolishing the veto would probably mean abolishing the Organization. Instead of running that risk, it would be wise for the Security Council itself to clarify the practices surrounding the operation of the unanimity rule. This could be done, for example, by writing into the Security Council's Rules of Procedure definite statements as to which matters are not subject to the unanimity rule. It could be done by establishing precedents in the Security Council which would tend to set up a limit to the kinds of matters to which the unanimity rule would apply.

Such a course may seem intolerably slow. But it is better to move slowly — it is better to seek unanimity of the Great Powers through methods of persuasion — than it is to break that unanimity with a shock, that would probably shatter the Organization itself.

Stevenson's neighbor on St. Mary's Road, Libertyville, wrote him praising his Town Meeting *speech on the veto.*

To Mrs. Alfred MacArthur

November 26, 1946

Dear Mary:

You were good to write me about that broadcast. I am glad you did as the Town Meeting people have asked me for a report on my "fan mail" and it is so meagre that your letter is even statistically precious!

I look forward to seeing you and Alfred when I get back to the tranquility of St. Mary's Road in December.

Cordially yours,

Mrs. Martin D. Hardin, sister of Stevenson's father, wrote her nephew thanking him for his contribution to a better world.

To Mrs. Martin D. Hardin

November 26, 1946

Dear Aunt Julia:

You were, as always, ever so good to write me that lovely letter. And the quotation from Macauley is something I shall not forget. That it was a favorite of Grandfather's makes it the more valuable.

But at the moment I am more disposed to quote Aunt Julia than Macauley! You've inflated my ego, not alone with this letter but the lovely one which you wrote Buffy which she has forwarded and which I have put away to impress my children some day!

I had as pleasant an evening as I can recall with Ad and Carol [126] in the country after the Yale-Princeton Game. Their children enchanted me and Adlai's sculpture fills me with awe. I am hoping to take Ellen out there for a night some time before we leave if it were only possible to escape the pressures in the U.N.

I have not yet seen Aunt Letitia [Stevenson] but the day will come soon I hope when I will have an opportunity — and then I suspect I will find her engaged.

Devotedly,

To Quincy Wright[127]

November 26, 1946

Dear Quincy:

Somehow I have only now gotten down to your letter of November 15. I am passing it along to Charlie Fahy and I am sure the draft resolution will be helpful.

It was good to see you out there and I am still a little self-conscious

[126] Mrs. Hardin's son Adlai and his wife.
[127] Professor of international law at the University of Chicago. The original is in the possession of Mr. Wright.

about the speech.[128] Meanwhile the accumulation of horrors here persuades me never to leave town again during one of these agonies!

Sincerely yours,

ADLAI

David H. McAlpin wrote Stevenson on November 28, 1946, asking for the names of distinguished leaders in government service and international affairs, under the age of sixty, to be recommended to Princeton University for honorary degrees.

To David H. McAlpin

December 2, 1946

Dear Dave:

You flatter me! If you are assuming that I know something about the standards for academic honor you are wrong. I don't. And having received a couple of LL.D.'s myself I am all the more confused as to what it takes!

Nor, on such short notice, have I any careful considered suggestions in the government or international fields. But some fairly obvious names occur to me. I have felt for a long time that in government few deserve recognition more than Harold Smith, former Director of the Bureau of the Budget and now in his early 50's, I think.

John Lord O'Brian's[129] service deserves recognition, I think, but he is too old for your age bracket.

I could think of others whose work impressed me during my years of war and pace in the government, Charlie Fahy,* for example. But so could many other more competent judges than I.

If Gil Winant[130] has not had a degree from Princeton, he should. Paul Henri Spaak, President of the General Assembly and Foreign Minister of Belgium, is rather obvious in the international field and I believe he is not more than 50 yet. Then there is Ben Cohen who has served his country long and well, lately as counselor of the State Department with a tireless patience and real wisdom. Also Dean Acheson has, in my judg-

---

[128] On November 21, 1946, Stevenson delivered a speech at the University of Chicago on "Civil-Military Relations in the United Nations." It is reprinted in Jerome G. Kerwin, editor, *Civil-Military Relationships in American Life* (Chicago: University of Chicago Press, 1948).

[129] Judge O'Brian, of Buffalo, had served during World War II as general counsel of the Office of Production Management, and also served on the Supply Priorities and Allocation Board and the War Production Board.

[130] John Gilbert Winant, U.S. ambassador to Great Britain.

ment, made a noteworthy sacrifice and positive contribution. Both Ben and Dean, as you know, are well within your age limitation.

Perhaps Leo Pasvolsky[131] is over 60 but I doubt it. And if it had not been for his early preparatory work I doubt if the U.N. would look much like it does. But he was never a public figure, in case that is one of the conditions.

There are many more, but without knowing more about the standards I am afraid I am wasting your time! I hope I catch a glimpse of you before the last translation fades into silence and I take off for Chicago and the law office.

Yours,

* You will recall that Charlie Fahy has been successively General Counsel of the National Labor Relations Board, Solicitor General, Legal Adviser to the Commanding General in Germany and now Legal Adviser to the State Department.

The administration of international relief was a highly controversial issue before the General Assembly. The United Nations Relief and Rehabilitation Administration was soon to go out of existence. The former mayor of New York City, Fiorello LaGuardia, head of UNRRA, insisted that a new international organization was needed. The United States Government opposed this, and it fell to Stevenson to defend the U.S. position at meetings of Committee 2. At one point LaGuardia charged that the United States and the United Kingdom were making a "political football out of food." Stevenson made the following reply on December 6, 1946.[132]

Mr. Chairman, before I proceed, I should like to make one correction in something that the representative from Poland said. I believe he said that I had informed him in the Subcommittee that the United States had already procured grain to meet the relief needs next year. I am afraid he misunderstood me. What I believe I said, or meant to say in any event, was that the grain was procurable, that it was not a problem, that the only limitation with respect to the availability of grain in so far as this country was concerned, was the problem of transportation.

[131] Author and economist, special assistant to the Secretary of State, president of the first session of the UN Preparatory Commission, and member of the U.S. delegations to the General Assembly and the Security Council.
[132] United Nations Department of Information, Press Release #98, December 6, 1946. See also Press Release PM/96, November 14, 1946, and Press Release #112, December 11, 1946, for additional statements by Stevenson on this subject.

Now, Mr. Chairman, I should like for a moment to turn to the proposal advanced by Mayor LaGuardia. My delegation appreciates the spirit of compromise with the views of my government and of others, in which this resolution was advanced, and I regret that we cannot support it. By its terms, his resolution creates an International Board to review needs, to make recommendations as to what these needs for financial assistance are and, to make recommendations as to allocations. I am afraid that this proposal is susceptible to conflicting interpretations by those who want an international organization to establish requirements and to make allocations and by those, on the other hand, who want to coordinate their relief plans by consultation with each other.

I think we must avoid at all costs any ambiguity in this matter. What we want to do, Mr. Chairman, is to resolve differences, not to perpetuate them. We want to avoid arguments in the execution of our relief program, not to encourage bad feelings or suspicions of bad faith. That there is evidently more than a possibility of conflicting interpretation of the meaning of this resolution seems to me quite apparent, if indirectly, from a quotation by Mayor LaGuardia which appeared in yesterday's New York Times. He said, Mr. Chairman, that this plan, referring to *his* plan, would eliminate any suspicion or charge of favoritism and remove any opportunity of retaliation against any nation.

In the light of his pronouncements on this subject during the past months, it is apparent that he interprets his plan as taking away ultimate control over the funds and supplies provided by any nation and vesting control in the Board he suggests. It makes no difference whether he visualizes whether this control will be exercised by direct vote or by moral suasion or by pressure or by any other means. The fact remains that such control is implicit and, as I have often repeated in this debate, the United States cannot participate in any plan based upon this principle of mandatory — be it moral or expressed — international allocation.

No, gentlemen, this is the real issue here which is not bridged by equivocal words, by such a resolution and we had best face this issue now and squarely or else we will only be borrowing trouble for the future.

Mr. Chairman, I am now going to refer, if I may, to the joint resolution proposed by my country, by the United Kingdom and by Brazil. I am not going to make a long speech in reply to some of the things that were said here yesterday. I think that is your good fortune because, had I been permitted to speak yesterday, had time permitted, I might have been obliged to impose upon you at length. Perhaps, for the record, I should do so today. But instead, I am going only to ask for your indulgence long enough to permit me to make a few general observations which, I hope, will serve to unite and not further divide our thinking on this question which, I earnestly hope, will shed more light and less heat on the American position.

The question as we see it, Mr. Chairman, has, in the last analysis, two aspects. The first aspect is the psychological one. It relates to the effect on peoples and governments of the disinclination of my country and others to agree to an international organization to administer relief in 1947. The other aspect relates to the merits of the two methods of accomplishing this task. It relates to the relative effectiveness of the direct method of consultation, each nation controlling the distribution of its own relief needs and the determination and allocation of relief by an international board.

As to this first consideration, we want the Members of the General Assembly to know that the United States understands your concern. It understands the concern of peoples everywhere and, we too, are fearful of any misapprehension about our motives and our policy which may be caused by our declining to participate in an international organization to administer the residual relief needs of 1947 — misapprehension which we fear has only been aggravated, and aggravated out of all proportion by this debate. But, I would ask you to believe that there is no government at this table more anxious to support the principle of international ends than the United States. I would ask you to believe that no government in the world is more anxious to maintain its faith and the faith of its people in the United Nations, its principles, its purposes and its machinery as the last best hope for peace on earth.

The President of the United States has said, "We will support the United Nations with all the resources we possess." I would ask you also to look at the record of my country in international cooperation during the war in the initiation and support of the specialized agencies, some of which were established before the United Nations and in the United Nations itself from Dumbarton Oaks to this present day.

I would ask you to believe and to tell your delegations and your peoples to believe us when we say with all sincerity that we want to cooperate in this humanitarian task, that we want to do our part in the relief of human suffering, as we have in the past, and we want to do it generously, efficiently, fairly and in good time. I repeat, we want to cooperate. We do not want to be obstinate, stubborn or arbitrary — all of these words have been used — we want relief to be available when and where it is needed, without discrimination because of race, creed or political belief. We thought these things were clear. If they are not, then, of course, we will agree to make them entirely clear in the resolution we are considering.

I have tried to say here with more sincerity than eloquence that our position in this matter springs not from the fact that we respect the principle of international organization the less, but because we want to fulfill the hopes of the hungry, the poor. To enable us to do so, to enable us to discharge our responsibility, which is greater than others' because our situation is more fortunate than others', we have proposed an approach which, in the considered judgment of my Government, is best calculated to enable us to do so. As we see it, the issue is not international cooperation versus no international cooperation; it is between two different methods of cooperation among nations. I said, and I repeat, that we seek the fullest cooperation and coordination by consultation directly and through the Secretary-General with all nations in developing our plans and programs for meeting the relief needs of next year, which will be acute all too soon. If your patience permit it, I should like to analyze this resolution. I should like to demonstrate the extent to which it involves cooperation. But what we cannot accept is control of the assessment of needs and the allocation of our share of the relief burden by the decisions or recommendations of international bodies, because we think it will seriously inhibit [congressional] appropriation at home and delay relief abroad, and that it might work serious inequity in the distribution of relief in accordance with relative needs.

In this short-term program we cannot afford the time, we cannot afford the risks involved in any unnecessary difficulties or delaying factors. Discussions of relief needs between the receiving and the supplying Governments have been regular and frequent occurrences throughout the entire life of UNRRA. For our part, we trust and we assume that they will continue as long as needs exist and that they will continue without any such degrading spectacles as Mayor LaGuardia portrayed here yesterday, of bowing beggars, hat in hand, asking a rich, hard-hearted big country, "Please Mister, give me a hand-out so that I may not perish."

Now, I have detected, Mr. Chairman, no bowing whatever around this table. On the contrary, I have detected the most vigorous, the most healthy advocacy of a point of view in sharp conflict with ours. I have detected, and it required no detective work, some vigorous, direct, unequivocal criticism of our position, and I pay my profound respects to the representative of Poland and to others who have given me as thorough a cross-examination in the Sub-Committee as I ever gave a witness in a lawsuit. But, Mr. Chairman, that is what we like, and I am happy to say that I, in this respect at least, can shake hands with my esteemed friend, Mayor LaGuardia. This is the spirit of my country, as he has demonstrated with his customary eloquence. That is our tradition in public affairs, and we commend it by the way, to all of you. I am not disturbed that we have been criticized. I am not disturbed that we have disagreed. On the contrary, quite to the contrary, this debate has illustrated what in our judgment is one of the most wholesome and encouraging developments in the United Nations — honest, fearless debate. We are happy indeed that the posture we have seen hereabouts does not resemble an insincere bow as much as it resembles an honest kick in the pants. But I would be much disturbed if we were misunderstood, if our motives were impugned, if the impression got abroad in the world that the United States was turning its back on international cooperation, that the issue in this little sector of our great work in the General Assembly was international organization for starvation, when the real issue before us is how best to prevent starvation.

This brings me, Mr. Chairman, to our joint resolution. I want first to thank Mr. [Ole B.] Kraft of Denmark for withdrawing his resolution with a view to enabling us to consider ours. The spirit and the devotion to our common cause, of seeking a solution of international problems by international means, which prompted his resolution — I say again, we respect, and we only regret that prudence and judgment have made it impossible for us to embrace his proposal.

Yesterday Mayor LaGuardia suggested some amendments to our resolution. He suggested that the words "free from political consideration" should be inserted in the last paragraph of the preamble of our resolution. I have sought to make clear here and on other occasions that my Government has never used food as a political weapon and does not intend to do so now. There is no disagreement on that point, and if it is deemed a wise precaution to put into this resolution such words, then let us put it in. Let us go all the way and put in the words adopted by the UNRRA Council itself in Atlantic City in November 1943. Let us put in an additional paragraph. I suggest that it be inserted, as the document that has now been circulated to you has indicated, at the end of the preamble and let it read as follows, as the UNRRA language reads: "reaffirming the principle that at no time should relief supplies be used as a political weapon, and that no discrimination should be made in the distribution of relief supplies because of race, creed or political belief."

I submit such language as an amendment to our resolution. Such language will, I am confident, meet with the approval of Mayor LaGuardia. I hope it will meet with the approval of everyone because we all agree that food should never be withheld from hungry people with a view of influencing them to conform with anybody's economic or political ideology. We all agree that relief should be distributed without discrimination of race, creed, or political belief. And underlying this principle, underlying the paragraph I have suggested, and the whole resolution, for that matter, is a basic principle that, I am sure, we also all agree upon, and that is that no country is entitled to seek free relief supplies from other countries unless it has taken and is taking all reasonable measures to help itself to provide the basic essentials of life from its own resources.

Mayor LaGuardia made a second suggestion yesterday. He suggested that we insert after the word "relief," in the second line of paragraph 2 of our resolution, the words "when needed and where needed."

Now, Mr. Chairman, if the Committee thinks that it would be desirable to add these words, I would have no objection. Indeed, I am flattered that the Mayor, whose literary style I respect and admire, should have paid me the flattering tribute of asking that these words be included in our resolution.

Finally, he suggested that the wording of the last paragraph of our resolution, paragraph 4 (b), be changed by deleting the words "facilitate informal" and substituting the words "call from time to time." But I am sure the Director-General of UNRRA will forgive me if I suggest that "to call consultation" is not the best English, to say the least. Moreover, why substitute this for the Secretary-General's duty to facilitate informal consultations? Why limit his usefulness? Why not add it? Why not add what he has proposed so that the Secretary-General can both facilitate informal consultations and can also arrange for such consultations among Governments, arrange such consultations either on his own initiative or at the request of Governments whenever, in his opinion, the purpose of the resolution would be promoted thereby? That, you will note, is what we proposed in this paper that has now been circulated, in paragraph 4 (b), on the second page. You will find such language there, and I must only add that we would wish to insert the word "such" before "consultation" in the third line of paragraph (b), so that there can be no misunderstanding whatever about the informal character of such consultations.

Now, before I conclude, sir, I should like to advert briefly to a suggestion that was made yesterday, I believe, by the representative of Norway,[133] who has had such a wealth of experience in this field and has taken such a leading and useful part in our deliberations.

He has suggested that important additions to the available funds for relief next year might be forthcoming from worldwide contributions of the value of one day's work. I confess we have not reflected on this at length but we are impressed with the potential value of this suggestion. We think something should be included in the resolution to implement this idea. How, I do not know. Possibly the best way to do it would be for a small drafting committee to consider and report back appropriate

[133] Dr. Aake Ording.

language to be added to our resolution or to whatever resolution we adopt. I would hope, Mr. Chairman, in that connection, that it would be the revised joint resolution of the United Kingdom, Brazil and the United States, which we have circulated here this afternoon. I would hope, Mr. Chairman, that this resolution will meet with the approval of the Committee, if not the enthusiastic approval of all the Governments here represented.

I apologize for having kept you so long. I will subside, and as far as this subject is concerned, I hope I shall be able to subside forevermore. I hope, perhaps with a prayer, that a year hence the hungry will have been fed and that the feelings and the misgivings that this discussion has engendered will have subsided too.

Amen. This time I add the amen.

To Eloise ReQua[134]

December 21, 1946

Dear Eloise —

I have taken the liberty of sending you some miscellaneous papers from the General Assembly in New York. It was not a conscious selection but just an alternative to the waste basket when my files were being cleaned up in New York. If you don't want them throw them away —

Yrs

On December 28, 1946, the Woodrow Wilson Foundation sponsored a radio program entitled "From the League of Nations to the United Nations," to commemorate Woodrow Wilson's ninetieth birthday anniversary. Stevenson, in his portion of the program, summarized the work of the General Assembly.[135]

Borrowing much from the men and the memories of the League of Nations, Woodrow Wilson's ill-fated dream of organized peace, borrowing much from the storehouse of his thinking and experience, our country took the lead again toward the creation of this last, best hope for peace on earth — the United Nations. And this time, the best of teachers, time, had done its work and the people and the politicians eagerly followed the path Wilson had pointed out in vain a generation before.

[134] Secretary of the board of trustees and director of the Library of International Relations, Chicago. This handwritten letter is in the possession of Miss ReQua.
[135] All the speeches were published in a pamphlet by the Woodrow Wilson Foundation.

Just a year ago I was in London. We had the Charter of San Francisco and we had a paper organization of the United Nations. Now, a year later, the first great General Assembly is over and we have conclusive proof that the United Nations works! I could say that in 1946 Wilson's vision was vindicated. But that would be melodramatic and premature, and I will only say that the United Nations not only works, but can even succeed.

And the test in New York was a severe one. The Assembly started in a mood of sober hope, followed by shock and pessimism when Mr. Molotov attacked the "atom" and "dollar" diplomacy of the United States. It ended seven weary weeks later in a cordial atmosphere with a record of solid achievement.

If the delegates, a little incredulous and a little surprised, left for their homes all over the world in a state of temperate optimism it was no wonder.

Two significant things happened during those two months in New York which few would have predicted beforehand with any confidence. First, the General Assembly emerged as the organized conscience of the community of nations, an instrument of enormous power in the structure of the United Nations. And, second, those weeks were marked by improvement in cooperative spirit between Russia and the Western Powers.

Questions, scores of them, were debated with no holds barred, without fear or favor, debated in the open, in the presence of each other, in the presence of the press and radio. In the words of Dr. Spaak, the Foreign Minister of Belgium and the accomplished President of the General Assembly, "we dwelt under the sign of open diplomacy." And when the votes were counted, the Assembly, the organized public opinion of the world, had spoken and neither the Soviet Union nor the United States nor any other country rejected the verdict, however adverse.

We have the Soviet Union to thank for raising the question of disarmament and the resolution adopted is an historic first step on the long and tortuous road to reduction and regulation of armaments with adequate safeguards against the hazards of evasion. Had nothing but this one resolution been adopted the meeting would have been worthwhile and established the resonance and authority of the Assembly in the world.[136]

Although none of the great powers were prepared to modify the re-

[136] In an effort to control the production and use of both atomic and major weapons of the world, the General Assembly of the United Nations adopted its first disarmament resolution on December 14, 1946. As a result of banning the use of atomic weapons and agreeing to international inspection, the session began calling itself the "disarmament assembly." But Ambassador Martin of Canada quickly pointed out that the task of implementing the resolution would be "full of setbacks and heartbreaks." New York *Times*, December 16, 1946.

quirement of unanimity in the Security Council on which the very survival of the United Nations depends, the vigorous attack on the veto by some of the smaller powers served an educational purpose about the veto, and its use and abuse.

Again, the ventilation of conflicting views about Franco's Spain and his abhorrent Fascist regime served to clear the atmosphere and narrow the area of disagreement on this sad, perplexing problem.[137]

Trusteeship agreements for eight dependent areas were approved and the Trusteeship Council, provided for in the Charter, was established.

A constitution for the International Refugee Organization was adopted at long last, and, if the money is forthcoming, hundreds of thousands of wretched, homeless people can be cared for after UNRRA ends and repatriated to their homelands, or, if they do not wish to return, resettled elsewhere.

A plan was adopted for handling relief after the expiration of UNRRA next spring when starvation will again threaten some of the devastated areas. A budget of $27,000,000 for next year, the cost of a few minutes of total war, was adopted; economic commissions for Europe and Asia to help tie together the economy of interdependent areas were recommended. And many, many other significant measures were adopted attacking the sore spots in the world, and the political, economic and social obstacles to peace and prosperity.

Such was the record — 33,000 pages, 5,000 documents, 20 million words — of two months of a town meeting of the world where the rich and the poor, the large and the small, the strong and the weak, sat down together around a table, each with one vote, and argued, conceded, and compromised in a common effort to save their people from a more awful recurrence of the fate which Wilson foretold a quarter century ago in these words: "I can predict with absolute certainty that within another generation there will be another world war if the nations of the world do not concert the method by which to prevent it."

As we look into 1947 there is no room for maudlin optimism. But we end the fateful year of 1946 in better heart than we entered it. Day by day, bit by bit, in the Council of Foreign Ministers, in the vast machinery of the United Nations, they are getting the habit of working together, getting to know each other better. As they do, suspicion and mistrust diminish, accord and accommodation become easier about the new prob-

---

[137] The resolution passed by the General Assembly of the United Nations called for the banning of the Madrid regime. Stevenson told the General Assembly: "In the interest of harmony and unanimity this country would vote for the resolution." Many felt that this resolution by the United Nations proved that it meant business. New York *Times*, December 13, 1946.

lems and new frictions which growth and development of international living will surely bring.

Wilson said that permanent peace can grow in only one soil — the soil of actual good will and understanding. He was fond of a story about Charles Lamb who said he hated a certain man. Someone said, "Why, Charles, I didn't know you knew him." "Ah," he said, "I don't. I can't hate a man I know."

Stevenson started the New Year by resuming his diary. Since the daily entries are brief, the editors have decided to publish them without interspersing letters and speeches. These will follow the diary.

Nov. 2–Jan. 1

Like all my other starts at a diary this one failed in 2 weeks and my 2 months in N.Y. at the Gen. Ass. of UN will have no chronicle!

Now I'll start again!

1947

Jan. 1

Party at [James] Oates' with children. Jim told some amusing stories well as always. Quartet by [Edward D.] McDougal family very impressive.

Jan. 2

. . . Lunch with John Cassidy.[138] Asked me to speak at annual Lincoln Birthday Banquet of Peoria Bar Assoc. for Supreme Court Judges. [Earl] Kribbens[139] for dinner.

Jan. 3

Lunch with Roddie Oates. Intense girl. Determined to have foreign experience. She'll get what she goes after and do everything well — but she won't have enough fun in the process.

Jan. 4

. . . Donald Stone & Bill Stoneman telephoned again from N.Y. about accepting job as Deputy to Trygve Lie, Sec. Gen. of U.N. Agreed to go to N.Y. to help Lie find someone else.

---

[138] A lawyer in Peoria and attorney general of Illinois, 1938–1941.
[139] Treasurer of Marshall Field and Company.

Jan. 5

Left for N.Y. 2 hrs late.

Jan. 6

Arrived 4½ hrs late. Lie offered me $24,300 tax exempt and the "guest house" at Lake Success. Long interview followed by talks with Stoneman and Owen.[140] Lie trying to get off for Central Am. on Friday. Can't make decision so quick.

Jan. 6–7

Contacted a lot of people & arranged for Wilson Wyatt,[141] Julius Holmes[142] & Milton Eisenhower[143] to see Lie. Tempted myself, but I must stay at home now & get family situation straightened out. Also might as well try out political situation there.

Jan. 9

[William] Benton at Council.[144] Sat next [to] him and Bob Hutchins.[145] [General George C.] Marshall's appointment as Sec. State just announced. Met Paul Hoffman[146] for first time at Speakers table. Dinner at Commercial Club for Stoddard,[147] new Pres. of Ill. Unaffected, serious. I like him.

Jan. 10

Lunch with Glen & Ed re new firm.[148] Little progress as usual. I'm getting skeptical about ever doing this.

Jan. 13

Lunch with Louis Kohn — my most ardent backer for Senate.[149] Still has hope for me in 1948.

---

[140] A. D. K. Owen, Assistant Secretary-General of the UN.

[141] Lawyer and mayor of Louisville, Kentucky, 1941–1945; later managed Stevenson's 1952 campaign.

[142] Political adviser to Dwight D. Eisenhower in World War II.

[143] President of Kansas State University.

[144] The Chicago Council on Foreign Relations.

[145] President of the University of Chicago.

[146] President of the Studebaker Corporation and chairman of the Committee for Economic Development.

[147] George Stoddard, president of the University of Illinois.

[148] For months Glen Lloyd, Edward D. McDougal, Jr., and Stevenson had been trying to organize a new law firm. They abandoned the idea.

[149] Chicago lawyer Louis A. Kohn, when he returned from military service in 1946, set out to defeat incumbent U.S. Senator C. Wayland Brooks. As Kohn heard Stevenson's public speeches, he became determined to make him the Democratic candidate.

Jan. 14

Lunch with N U [Northwestern University] Law School Faculty . . . Conducted seminar for int. law students with Tommy & Brunson Mac-Chesney.[150] Dined alone with Marshall Field. He seemed in better spirits & more self confident about [the Chicago] Sun. Spent night there.

Jan. 16

Dined with Ellen at Council of State Govt's banquet at Edgewater Beach to hear Austins[151] speech. Wilder Foote with him & we had a drink all together alone in bar afterward. Austin's modesty, humility one of best features. Called in late afternoon on Dutch [Herman D.] Smith, recovering from serious eye operation at Passavant.

Jan. 18

Cancelled date to make brief speech at Council for Democracy dinner & went with Ellen to dinner for Gen. [Dwight] Eisenhower at Casino [Club]. She wanted so much to meet him, but we were late as usual & he left immediately after very brisk, short speech . . .

Jan. 20

Have been worrying about declining that job at UN — equivalent to $75,000 salary before taxes. Why don't I do what I want to do and like to do and is worthwhile doing? The questions others ask sometimes hard to answer.

Lunch with Geo. Richardson.[152] Leaving for Cal[ifornia]. Still wants to get me into Field picture thru [the Chicago] Sun. Thinks I can help with editorial policy. Little hope of any law business.

Delegation of 3 excellent students from N U Law School. Want to work in foreign field somehow. Should they stay in law school? etc?

Jan. 21

Conf. with Hodes[153] re a law case. Much talk of politics. "Kennelly wouldn't have been possible if I hadn't kept gates open by backing Douglas." [154] Not a word about me. Think he's for Douglas for Senate. Wayfarer's [Club] dinner. Dull.

[150] Professor of law at Northwestern University.
[151] Senator Warren R. Austin of Vermont, head of the U.S. delegation to the UN General Assembly.
[152] Assistant to Marshall Field and vice president and director of Field Enterprises, Inc.
[153] Barnet Hodes, Democratic committeeman of the 5th Ward in Chicago and also corporation counsel of the city.
[154] The Cook County Democratic Central Committee refused to support Mayor

Jan. 22

Spoke at Commonwealth Club lunch — personal reminiscences of last 2 yrs. Took so long I never got on serious subjects, except for few who stayed for questions. Afraid I sounded egotistical, but [William P.] Sidley reported a[n] "enthralled" listener he met on street.

Jan. 23

Lunch with Steve Hurley,[155] Tap Gregory[156] & Dr. Manley Hudson[157] passing thru to make speech in Omaha. Hard man to like — so pushy and omniscient . . .

Good talk with Maxwell [158] at the Day School about Borden. Should he go away next fall?

Jan. 24

Lunch with Les Jones[159] — swell, straight forward guy, utterly unspoiled by time & some success.

Interviewed at 3 by Barbara Wendell Kerr[160] & Arthur Schlesinger[161] about Mrs. Roosevelt — story he's doing for Life. No chance to talk to her alone about her domestic situation as Mrs. [Barrett] Wendell has been asking me to do. She doesn't understand Barbara & never will. Awkward position for me, but she says Barbara has great respect for me & will be influenced. Baloney!

Big tea or cocktail party at apt. before Emerson House benefit dinner dance. Too old & tired for these people — or something! Couldn't wait to leave.

Jan. 27

Another wonderful, quiet week end at home. But find it very hard to do creative writing there. Too many diversions. Much talk with Ellen

---

Edward J. Kelly for reelection. Professor Paul H. Douglas, formerly alderman from the 5th Ward, had made a bid for the nomination, but the committee nominated businessman Martin J. Kennelly instead. Stevenson wrote Jacob M. Arvey on December 20, 1946, congratulating him on the key role he played in replacing Kelly with a man who was independent of machine control.

[155] Stephen E. Hurley, lawyer and Civil Service commissioner of the City of Chicago.

[156] Tappan Gregory, Chicago lawyer; consultant to the U.S. delegation to the UN Conference on International Organization in San Francisco in 1945.

[157] Professor of international law at Harvard University.

[158] G. McCall Maxwell, headmaster of the Lake Forest Country Day School.

[159] Leslie N. Jones, special counsel for the Illinois Bell Telephone Company.

[160] Editorial writer for the Boston *Traveler*.

[161] Associate professor of history at Harvard University.

about replacing Frank and Beatrice.[162] We disagree, but she will have her way about how the place is to be run.

Extravagantly flattering story about Gen. [George] Marshall and me! in Inter-Ocean[163] — a political sheet of doubtful reliability I judge. Must thank the editor — Leo Hartford. Good and accurate advance story in Peoria paper about my speech there.

Spoke at meeting — luncheon — by Council on For. Relations for Chicago press and radio commentators with Geo. Stoddard, new Pres. of Univ. of Ill.

Jan. 29

To Alfred Hamills[164] in worst blizzard in my recollection for dinner with Phil[ip] Hofer, curator of Houghton Library at Harvard. Reminded me that we had ushered together at "B." [Norman P.] Davis' wedding in Nashville long ago . . .

Jan. 30

Visit from Carl McGowan, doing part time work for Atomic Energy Commission.

Lunched with that strange and interesting man — Urban Lavery.[165] "Should dismiss thought of political office in 1948"; should be in different firm.

Jan. 31

Visit from Herbert Emmerich;[166] would like the UN Assistant Sec'y Gen'l job. Luncheon . . . for Geo. Weller[167] at Chi[cago] Club. Weller talked about his travels during war. Not very good balance in his choice of emphasis. Hostile about our support of Greek "facist" gov[ernment]. No Russian influence — just rebellious honest Greeks. Mostly a travelogue.

[John] Kellogg's for dinner — some old friends — pleasant, easy, relaxed feeling. Sad how little most of them have lived; done for their generation. Left early.

Feb. 1 & 2

Worked all week-end on contract between Pullman [Company] and French Gov[ernment]. for freight cars which French say are defective.

---

162 The couple who ran the Stevensons' farm.
163 A Chicago political journal that mainly supported the Democrats.
164 A partner in Goldman, Sachs and Company who lived in Lake Forest.
165 A Chicago lawyer.
166 Director of the Public Administration Clearing House.
167 Foreign correspondent of the Chicago *Daily News*.

Sunday supper — cocktail party at . . . the implacable entertainers. Left early.

Ride in cutter in afternoon with John Fell on tobog[g]an. Beautiful winter day.

Feb. 3

Firm meeting at lunch. Talk of dangers of accepting directorships by partners.

To Doc Kinney's[168] for tea to hear . . . talk about Groton School. Rather poor presentation by attractive young man.

Feb. 4

With [Glen] Lloyd & [Edward D.] McDougal to Manager of Field Bldg. regarding space for our "firm." Nothing in prospect. Discouraged about ever getting our project started due to failure to find suitable tax man and office space. . . .

Met Betty [Pirie] at apt. in late afternoon . . . She wanted to talk about my situation with Ellen; told her all was well.

Stayed at apt. to work on speech for Springfield.

Feb. 5

Am 47 today — still restless; dissatisfied with myself. What's the matter? Have everything. Wife, children, money, success — but not in law profession. Too much ambition for public recognition; too scattered in interests; how can I reconcile life in Chicago as lawyer with consuming interest in foreign affairs — public affairs and desire for recognition and position in that field? Prospect of Senate nomination sustains & at same time troubles, even frightens me. Wish I could at least get tranquil & make Ellen happy & do go[od] humble job at law.

Lunch with Princeton 1922 people . . . to talk about reunion plans. John Fell spanked me *very* HARD!

Feb. 6

Lunch with Bob Lasch — editorial writer of [Chicago] Sun. No one runs it [the newspaper]; no spark; sense of mission in staff drying up. Discouraging picture of inside. Evidently no great admirer of Dimitman[169] — the Mgr. editor whose formula is lot of little, insubstantial stories.

---

168 Unable to identify.
169 E. Z. Dimitman, executive editor of the Chicago *Sun*.

Feb. 7

John Fell's birthday — and he was so late at breakfast I drove away without him! Now I'm miserable. After talking about his birthday for days & all Ellen's planning for the big party tomorrow, I even forgot to congratulate him this morning!

Ellen Wilkinson dead — the "beloved rebel" of the [British] Labor Party. I've met a lot of the significant people of this generation.

Max Gardner also dead — just as he was to sail to London as Ambassador. Wonder if [James] Forrestal will get the job this time. How I wish it was me and I had the money to do it. I *know* I could & its one of the few things I do *know* I could do. Maybe the time will come when Ellen would like to do something like that on a scale we could afford. But will I ever get the opportunities again — the way I have in the last year? Is it political stature I need or professional?

The diary ended at this point. During the period that he kept the diary he did considerable public speaking, and he tried to help the Secretary-General of the United Nations find a new Assistant Secretary-General.

To Trygve Lie

January 8, 1947

Dear Mr. Lie:

I have considered a large number of possibilities for the position we discussed in your office. Most of them I have eliminated for various reasons. I list below those who seemed best qualified to me.

Wilson Wyatt — Former mayor of Louisville and Chief of the National Housing Administration. *Heart and soul in the UN.* Much interested in this job but has reestablished some connections in Louisville which make it difficult to leave. Will come to see you Thursday.

Chester Bowles — Was out of town when I called, Tuesday, January 7, and could not be reached. I expect to see him in Chicago, Thursday. I doubt if he will be available.

Harold Smith — Executive Vice President of International Bank. Former Director of Bureau of the Budget. Will call on you Wednesday.

Herbert Emmerich — Chicago. Director of School of Public Administration. Former Executive Secretary of the War Production Board. Will call on you Wednesday.

Julius Holmes — Former career Foreign Service Officer. Former Deputy Chief of Staff for Civil Affairs for General Eisenhower in Mediterranean and European Theaters. Former Assistant Secretary of State for Administrative Affairs. Now with TACA and TWA airlines. Will call on you Thursday.

Milton Eisenhower — President of Kansas State Agriculture College, Manhattan, Kansas. Brother of General Eisenhower. Seems interested, but cannot come East now. Will be in Washington January 17th and could come up to New York to talk to David Owen or someone. He will call on Donald Stone while in Washington.

Milo Perkins — Washington. Long government experience. Organized and directed Board of Economic Warfare during the war. Now in private business as economic consultant on foreign business to several large US corporations. Interested and anxious to help informally at any time but not available for this post.

Herman Wells — President of University of Indiana, Bloomington, Indiana. Did excellent organizing and executive job in State Department for a year during the war. Profound interest in UN. I have not succeeded in contacting him.

Paul Porter — Washington. Former OPA administrator etc. Now Chief of U.S. Economic Mission to Greece. I have not contacted him and he would not be available for a couple of months I assume.

For possible future reference I enclose a list of additional people who have at least some of the required qualifications.

May I add a personal word of thanks for your courtesy to me. It was very flattering and I only wish my personal circumstances made it possible for me to accept — in spite of misgivings about my capacity!

As I am confident that a first rate man must and can be found for this position, I hope it will not be necessary to make a final decision until at least the foregoing have been carefully canvassed.

With every good wish and my profound respect, I am

Faithfully yours,

ADDITIONAL

R. Keith Kane — New York Lawyer. Age 46. Formerly with the Department of Justice, Office of War Information and special assistant to the Secretary of the Navy, where he did much work in connection with trusteeships. Excellent man and am confident would be much interested in this job.

Thomas K. Finletter — Lawyer, New York. Student of world government. Well-known writer. Was assistant to Secretary Hull for several years. Knows US government thoroughly. Profound knowledge of international affairs and wide acquaintance.

Paul V. Harper — Chicago lawyer. Age 58. Trustee of the University of Chicago. Brother of Sam Harper, deceased, well-known Russian scholar. Good linguist. Profound interest in international affairs and much experience in big business.

Francis T. P. Plimpton — New York lawyer. Age 46. Active in international affairs. Excellent reputation. Some government experience in Reconstruction Finance Corporation.

Barry Bingham — Editor and Publisher of the Louisville Courier-Journal. Son of former Ambassador to United Kingdom. Wide experience abroad. About 40 years old. Profound interest in UN.

William Reitzel — State Department. Former teacher Haverford College. Did excellent administrative work during the war with Commodore Sullivan and Admirals Stark and Glassford in European and Mediterranean Theaters.

John Small — Washington. Former Chief of Civilian Production Administration. Age 52 (?) Successful businessman. Some national prominence. Excellent executive. Can be reached through Navy Department.

Arthur Hill — Washington, President Eastern Greyhound Bus Lines and President National Association of Motor Busses organization. Very successful businessman and widely known as an organizer and executive. Handled transportation matters for Navy during the war. Age 53, about.

Edward Young — age 35. Now with New York Port Authority. Remarkable administrative ability and excellent intellect for his age.

Vice Admiral [Arthur] Radford — Deputy Chief of Naval Operations for Air.

Rear Admiral Lawrence Richardson — former Assistant Chief, Bureau of Aeronautics now with Curtis Wright Corporation, Rockefeller Center, New York.

Rear Admiral N. L. Rawlings — Bureau of Ships.

These admirals are undoubtedly among the best administrators in the naval service and they are in their early fifties.

Robert McCormick — New York lawyer. Partner of Alexander and Green. Wide international legal experience. Age early forties. Very mature, calm and competent executive.

Wayne Coy — Washington Post. Former Assistant Director of the Bureau of the Budget and Assistant to the High Commissioner of the Philippines. One of the best administrators formerly in government. Broad experience and interest in UN.

Wayne Chatfield-Taylor — Formerly Under-Secretary of Commerce, Assistant Secretary of the Treasury, President of the Export-Import

Bank. Wide US Government and international experience; particular interest in economic matters. Rather inarticulate and slow but good administrator and profound interest in UN.

Lawrence Duggan — Formerly in important position in Division of Latin American Affairs in State Department. Has succeeded his father, Stephan Duggan, as head of international exchange of students organization.[170] Well-known scholar with a background of long government experience.

John Blandford — Now in China as adviser to Chinese Government on organization. Formerly administrator of National Housing Administration; assistant in Bureau of the Budget and assistant manager of TVA. Very experienced administrator.

Arthur Altmeyer — Washington. Chairman of the Social Security Board. Reported to be excellent administrator. Much interested in UN, particularly economic and social work.

On January 10, 1947, Stevenson received a telegram from Leon Henderson and Wilson Wyatt asking him to become a charter member of Americans for Democratic Action.

To Leon Henderson[171]

[no date]

Dear Leon,

I would like to say yes but I have been so pre-occupied with other things and am so ignorant I think you better leave me out . . . of charter group. Regards.

Stevenson spoke to the Lincoln Library Forum, Springfield, Illinois, on January 10, 1947. (The text is based on a reading copy of the speech. Stevenson inserted a few sentences by hand.)

Just about 30 years ago I was a student in this school,[172] although I am sorry to say, not in this splendid modern building. That old red brick building, which as I recall, incorporated most of the monstrosities of the General Grant architectural period, should have made an historian out of

---

[170] The Institute of International Education.

[171] This reply is handwritten and probably was sent as a telegram.

[172] He attended school in Springfield in 1915 while his father was secretary of state.

me. But it didn't. I hope none of my old teachers are here to testify how little it did make out of me! I recall that in contrast to the school I had gone to, the classes were very large and my classmates looked very large too. I was a *new* boy and I was so frightened that when they called on me to recite one of two disasters always overtook me — either I was paralyzed with fright and couldn't speak at all, or I talked nervously without the slightest idea what I was saying. Unhappily paralysis usually overtook me when I knew the answer and a torrent of words ushered forth when I didn't!

I've thought of that agony subsequently — sometimes laterally when I suddenly discovered myself in the middle of a vigorous speech at one of these international conferences without any very clear idea of what I was talking about or where I was going.

I'm afraid I'm like the old lady from Vermont who said she didn't know what she thought until she heard what she said! . . .[173]

But I'm wandering. I came here to give a lecture. I'm an amateur, but I'm reliably informed that lecturers must start by expressing their appreciation and pleasure. That's easy for me because Springfield has been my home — and who doesn't like to come home — particularly if you are paid for it!

Anyway I am very glad and honored to be here — as a lecturer and not a student, and you can now settle down to a dreary address that will have only one certain conclusion — that you won't invite me again!

Just 18 months ago the bombs fell on Hiroshima and Nagasaki. Just a year and a half ago we awoke from the greatest celebration of the greatest victory over the greatest menace in history. And we awoke with the uneasy realization that our troubles had just begun — that what was finished was just an episode, albeit a critical episode, in the headlong history of our generation. We awoke to discover that the world was restive, that there was a ferment of new ideas all about us, that the delicate balances of the old world had been consumed in the fire, and that a startling new apparition had taken a prominent place at the table. And we don't yet know whether atomic energy is friend or foe. We awoke to discover that our war-born honeymoon with the Soviet Union had unceremoniously ended, and she had become surprisingly aggressive, truculent and suspicious.

We awoke to discover, as many had foretold, that making peace was harder than making war, and the obstacles and hazards infinitely more difficult to understand and evaluate.

---

[173] At this point he told several stories but he used only incomplete phrases to remind himself, not complete sentences.

There was no war leader with resonance to give us all a text; no one to say "With malice toward none; with charity for all; with firmness in the right, as God gives us to see the right." Roosevelt was dead; Churchill was out of office, and Stalin doesn't talk that way.

At San Francisco in May and June, then in London in the fall and winter of that first year of peace I became increasingly conscious that people were troubled about the United States. There were many here and more abroad who were apprehensive that we couldn't take it — that after a few frustrated efforts to mold the world according to our liking we would withdraw, mumbling "to Hell with it," slam the door and pull down the shades. There may have been those who hoped the United States would do just that.

But we haven't! We've *stuck* to the distasteful job of binding up the ugly wounds of a mutilated world, along with a lot of other doctors with very different ideas. We have stuck to it with patience and perseverance — I think with malice toward none, with charity for all, but time will have to pronounce that judgment. And we have been at it for 18 months now — months in which we have, as usual traversed the whole spectrum of emotion. In 1862 Joseph Medill of the Chicago Tribu[n]e wrote that the Union cause was all but hopeless. And I recall vividly from my own experience in the Navy Department the excesses of pessimism and optimism in the early days of this war.

It has been the same in the months of peace. The illusion that the United Nations was a substitute for power politics and a guarantee of automatic peace gave way to black despair, to talk of another war. Now, happily, these violent fluctuations of opinion seem to be levelling off; we are beginning to realize that a cooperative organization of sovereign states can only function thru the instrumentality of international politics, and that the U.N. as such cannot coerce any great power into the path of peace. Our people are coming to realize, I think, that this generation of Americans can never relax; that world peace on an equitable and permanent basis cannot be built in 18 months, or 18 years; that the *price* of permanent peace is permanent *effort* to develop an imperfect instrument into a more perfect union of the peoples of the world.

How would an inventory, a trial balance on the 18 months since hostilities ceased, look? On the positive side I'll mention a few important achievements.

First of all the United States, as I have said, has given unmistakable evidence that, politically at least, it is in the world to stay. The concept of security through isolation is dead, and unmourned. We paid a ghastly price to learn that peace is indivisible, but we learned it for keeps. Instead of refusing even to follow, as we did 25 years ago, we are now leading in the strengthening of international concepts. From my own observation and experience I can say that I very much doubt if there would be a UN at all if it had not been for the American initiative first at Dumbarton Oaks, then at Yalta, then at S.F., then at London with the cooperative participation of other nations growing in intensity with each successive step. Our conversion proves that facts and reason and time can revise a nation's approach to world problems. And that is something to remember when you feel that your patience with the Soviet Union is about to snap.

In the next place — thanks to UNRRA [United Nations Relief and Rehabilitation Administration] — we have hurdled the first great barrier to a healthy, peaceful world — mass starvation. By international organization the lives of fifteen million people have been saved. Five and one-half million displaced persons have been repatriated. The work of reconstruction has commenced; hope has been rekindled. Agricultural production is climbing up in spite of the shortages of fertilizer and machinery; industry and commerce are struggling out of the rubble. I confess that the revival, with all its distressing shortcomings, has been far better than I foresaw from my own observations among just liberated people in Italy, Europe and England during the war.

But the crisis is not past. Starvation will stalk thru Europe again this spring before the next harvest unless we and other countries send more *free* relief, particularly to Austria, Italy, Greece and Poland. And I was delighted to see that Secretary Marshall has asked Congress for $250,-000,000 and has placed relief at the top of his list of legislative "musts."

But the worst is over and where the needs just for survival were universal, now they are scattered. (The cold that has paralysed long suffering Britain and all of Europe gives me an all too vivid impression of human suffering and lost production, because I have shivered and shaken thru the unheated horrors of a normal winter in Naples, Paris and London these last few years.)

Some political danger spots have been erased during these first months of peace. The British and the French promptly withdrew their forces from Syria and Lebanon after the latter complained to the Security Council of the UN. The Russians finally pulled out of Iran after firm persistent goading by the Security Council.

After months of deadlock and exhausting negotiation, patience and compromise have produced peace treaties for Italy and the Axis satel[l]ites, Finland, Rumania, Bulgaria, and Hungary. The Italian-Jugoslav frontier has been settled, a statute for the internationalization of Trieste has been agreed upon, and the principle of equality of economic opportunity in the Balkans and freedom of navigation on the Danube has at least been solemnly recognized.

The liquidation of the awful legacy of war is well under way, and Secretary Byrnes has earned the everlasting gratitude of his countrymen, and in my estimation an imperishable monument for patience and resourcefulness.

Finally, the UN, which was but paper when the bombs fell on Hiroshima and Nagasaki, is functioning with a vigor and enthusiasm that a cynical segment of the press discounted too soon. The General Assembly, sooner than many expected, has become a center where the collective opinion of the world community can powerfully influence the course of events. The Security Council is an open forum for the discussion of any question affecting peace and security, and is about to attack the control of atomic energy and the regulation of armaments under a system of international inspection. The acceptance of the principle of international inspection *alone* is as promising for future peace as anything that has happened since the war. The Economic and Social Council and its commissions are working across the whole front from an international bill of rights to the economic integration of continents. The Trusteeship Council has been established and a new day has dawned for the many millions of dependent and non-self-governing peoples. The new International Court of Justice has been established. Fifteen years ago we would not join the World Court. Today we have even accepted its compulsory jurisdiction!

Subsidiary organizations have been established. UNESCO [United Nations Education, Scientific, and Cultural Organization] is now beginning to function to repair the ravages of the war and extend education, science and culture in a world more than half illiterate, where science knows no frontiers and wars begin in the minds of men. We are in sight of the day when, for the first time, there will be enough to eat in the world, and the FAO [Food and Agricultural Organization] is attacking the basic problems of hunger and malnutrition. The Internation[al] *Civil* Aviation Organization, the International *Labor* Office, the International *Health* Organization are operating. The International *Bank* is about to make large reconstruction and development loans. The International Monetary *Fund* is in operation to stabilize currencies. The General Assembly created an International Refugee Organization to take over the care, repatriation or resettlement of some 850,000 refugees who constitute one of the saddest chapters in the epilogue of the war.

Last and perhaps most important is the development of an International Trade Organization to which our government attaches such importance and such hope, because we know that prosperity, like peace, is *indivisible,* and that barriers to the expansion of international trade are barriers to peace.

It is an impressive record. We have come a long way in a short while. The weapons of peace have been forged under the urgency of the terrible memory of two world wars in a quarter century, and in the shadow of a still more perilous future. They have been forged by men who dared not contemplate failure.

Best of all, men — men of all colors, creeds and cultures; sober, serious, responsible men — are learning to work together, learning more and more about one another. The nations of the world are sitting around a table together — not one table but many tables — day after day.

It reminds me of a story Woodrow Wilson was fond of telling — a story about Charles Lamb, who said he hated a certain man. Someone said, "But Charles, I didn't know you even knew him." "I don't," said Lamb, "I can't hate a man I know." I can testify that it is an encouraging spectacle to see men, not trained diplomats, but politicians, the people's leaders, from all the corners of the earth, from large nations and small, from regions which differ so widely in their attitudes and degrees of development, arguing their points of view for all to hear — fighting for their interests in a goldfish bowl, sometimes heatedly — and then going out to lunch together — or more often to the bar — to talk it over.

I recall so well the day that Ernest Bevin and Vychinsky [Andrei Vyshinsky] exchanged verbal blows and insults in London for several violent hours, and then when Vychinsky had the last word, as he always did, he reached across the table, still apoplectic with anger, to shake Bevin's hand.

We, the United States, are very conspicuous at those tables — and we are at all of them — because we are the richest and most powerful nation on earth, and therefore have the most to lose if the great experiment fails.

So much for the credit side of our trial balance. How about the debit side?

First, in the Western Hemisphere, our backyard, all is not well. The Act of Chapultepec is almost two years old, and the Argentine has not yet fulfilled her commitments. The other republics don't like it, but they don't like our relentless insistence on strict compliance either. And none of us like the long delay in calling the Rio conference and the implementation of our regional defense.[174] There have been revolutions in South America, bloody and bloodless, and there is widespread political instabil-

---

[174] The Inter-American Conference for the Maintenance of Continental Peace and Security met in Rio de Janeiro, August 15 to September 2, 1947. It was agreed that an armed attack upon one American state was considered an attack on all.

ity. Communist party strength has increased rapidly. A short while ago they claimed a victory in the Governorship election in Sao Paulo, the richest state in Brazil.

At one end of the Mediterranean a Fa[s]cist tyrant who actively aided our enemies still rules long suffering Spain with bayonets. Argentina has just sent an Ambassador to Madrid in defiance of the United Nations Assembly decision on Franco.[175] At the other end of the Mediterranean a weak Greek government is confronted with almost unsurmountable obstacles to the rescue of that unhappy, impoverished, divided country. *China*, which we have backed so heavily — in population the largest nation in the world, one of the "Big 5" powers and our hope for stability in the Orient — is still floundering in the morass of civil war and impotence. For *Palestine* no solution has yet been found acceptable to the Zionists that won't arouse the Arab world which occupies such a strategic section of the globe. Political reconciliation of the Hindus and Moslems in turbulent India seems to be making little progress.

Poland has a Communist President and Foreign Minister. The elections were a cynical mockery of the Yalta and Potsdam pledges of representative government through free and fair elections.

Worst of all Europe, which is so interdependent economically, is sharply and dangerously divided politically between East and West. Two world wars have sharply diminished Britain's power and increased her political, economic and military vulnerability.

I could mention the slow progress toward providing the UN with military forces; irregularities (to use a diplomatic word) in the collection of reparations, and many other things you might choose to put on the liability side of our 18-month balance sheet. But one thing I do want to mention. It has little to do with the balance sheet, but its murmuring fills the air and for the future it dwarfs the details of our accounting.

Asia, the most densely populated area of the world — more than half mankind — is struggling to rid itself of its European masters. China, India, Indonesia, Indo-China — the dark colonial peoples — are in revolt at the moment of Europe's greatest weakness. It is the twilight of Empire as we've known it. The French and American liberation movements have reached the older civilizations of the Orient. And as our revolutions sparked the industrial transformation of the west, the decline of colonialism will accelerate the greater industrial revolution of the east.

Here are markets for our vast surplus production — markets on which our prosperity will some day depend. And here are millions and millions

---

[175] Among the decisions dealing with Franco Spain adopted by the General Assembly on December 12, 1946, was the recommendation that member states withdraw their chiefs of mission from Madrid.

who know but little of the blessings of democracy and private enterprise; millions who will be our friends if we, who freed the Philippines, behave like their friends, and don't forget our own revolutionary childhood. Rebellion and insurrection are seed beds of war. While we deplore disorder, we must not be the complacent champion of status quo or injustice either. We must not find ourselves on the defensive, resisting the same natural, normal aspirations that brought our republic to birth. As the oldest revolutionary democracy we have a great opportunity and a great responsibility to moderate an evolution in Asia which will have much to do with our future security and prosperity.

On balance perhaps the progress of the last 18 months is surprisingly good. But I hope I've said enough to leave no complacency. And I haven't even mentioned Germany and Austria, about which you will hear so much for months to come while the victorious powers are engaged in their longest, hardest and most decisive negotiations. They may take two years, and somewhere beyond the German and Austrian peace treaties — if we get over that hurdle — lies Japan, where similar conflicting plans and interests will arise before a treaty is signed. Meanwhile, the future of the Italian colonies in Africa has not been settled and we can rely on Russia to press stubbornly her claim to a trusteeship on the shores of the Mediterranean. Nor have we seen the end of pressure on Iran, and on Turkey for control of the Dardanelles, a strategic Russian ambition that long pre-dates the Bolshevik revolution.[176]

All these differences and tensions — some old and some begotten by war and change which is the order of life — will have to be met one by one. Some can be compromised and settled, some may not be; new ones will arise, and we will be busy for a long, long time to come forging the links in the chain that binds the world together. We must keep the whole in perspective and not lose sight of the chain because of our preoccupation or irritation with the links. We have chosen the path of international organization instead of international anarchy, and thru the Council of Foreign Ministers and the United Nations and all its agencies better machinery and a better workshop is at hand than ever before. And everyone is using it, night and day, impelled by the terrible urgency that sobered our celebration the morning after Hiroshima and Nagasaki.

Whether and how soon the war can be liquidated, how soon the present acute tensions will be relaxed, will depend in large measure — as everyone tells you and as you will quickly discover in an international conference — on the United States of America — on the health, wealth and wisdom of the United States.

[176] In March, 1947, President Truman announced the Truman Doctrine for economic and military aid to Greece and Turkey.

But the liquidation of the war, like the war itself, is only an episode. When it's finished what a moment ago I called the paramount objective of our generation — the establishment of world peace on an equitable and permanent basis — will still stretch out before us as far as we can see. We must not be lulled to sleep because a few links in the chain have been forged. Even they may not hold. First solutions are not always final solutions. The evolution of the United Nations and the rule of law, like all human institutions, must be progressive and perpetual.

But, of course, international cooperation is not the only way to secure the peace. The Romans did it by dominating the known world — for a while. Others have tried that method, but they have all failed disastrously. There may be another way — universal intellectual conformity. Maybe the Russians think that's the only sure road to security. Maybe they propose, if they can, to carry the doctrine of one world still fa[r]ther to one Communist, one Soviet, world by gradually eliminating all philosophical dissent. I don't know. But I do know that thus far they have shown no indifference to the United Nations as "a center," in the words of the Charter, "for harmonizing the actions of nations in the attainment of their common ends" of peace, security and human welfare. On the contrary, their participation has been vigorous and positive and, of course, self-interested.

The prestige of the Soviet Union has reached a level few could foresee before the war. Overnight Soviet influence has been extended from the Baltic to the Adriatic, and into Korea, Manchuria and North China — how far we don't know. Greece and France are political battlegrounds. Scandinavia is uneasy. The Middle East and all of Asia feel the ferment. South America is not untouched. The Red Army occupies half of Germany.

There are those — many of them in Europe — who say with despair that Communism is the wave of the future.

But all these familiar facts don't prove that Communism *is* the wave of the future. It made little progress beyond the borders of Russia between the wars. It has made little since, except by force. Love and fear may produce the same apparent results, but they must not be confused. These facts don't prove that the human spirit's thirst for freedom has been quenched. They dont prove that we have surrendered the citadel of the spirit. At Edwardsville in 1858 Lincoln said — "Our defense is in the spirit which prizes liberty as the heritage of all men, in all lands everywhere. Destroy this spirit and you have planted the seeds of despotism at your own door." They dont prove that this spirit has been destroyed. They don't even prove the adequacy of the Soviet system for other peoples. But they may reveal disillusionment about democracy. And they do prove that the Soviet Union is going to compete for the allegiance of men everywhere with all the power and influence it possesses, and with an idea that may have a lot of validity for the myriads of the wretched around the world who are groping for material betterment. We may despise communist cruelty, repression and subordination of human values, but we recognize and respect everyone's right to believe as he pleases. Obviously, we Americans would like to see the whole world free and democratic in our image. Why wouldn't the Russians, who believe in this [their] system, we must assume, as devoutly as we believe in ours, want to see the world conform to their idealogy? But we are not afraid of competition. We have not lost faith in our way of life — in the sacredness of the individual. All we ask, all we insist upon, is fair competition, live and let live, tolerance.

Whether the Russian objective is world Communism, Imperialist expansion, just its own security, or all of them, it's a contest between ways of life which will last for a long time. I have called it "the 30 years war" — a war not with weapons but with ideas — socialist, communist and capitalist ideas.

The outcome, the hope for enduring peace, depends on you and me, because we are Americans. It depends on the health, wealth and wisdom of the United States.

Health, because if we can't revalidate our system — if we can't make it work at home it will make few converts abroad.

Wealth, because we have most of it, and freedom-loving peoples everywhere are turning to us for assistance.

Wisdom, because we must resolutely lead the perilous way to accomodation between basic differences.

First, as to our health. How can we expect to enlist the masses of mankind under freedom's shining banner when it is stained with bigotry, intolerance and discrimination? It's time we stopped compromising convictions, democratic ideals and, yes, constitutional guarantees. Racial and religious discrimination, double standards of citizenship and oppression are not democratic. They are not Christian. And don't think we are fooling anyone, particularly the Asiatics. You can be sure that they are hearing all about the fire hazards in our basement.

No form of government calls for such intelligence, public spirit and civic virtue as a free democracy. Forty years ago James Bryce said that the greatest obstacles to the success of our democracy were private self interest, excessive partisanship and the sin of indolence. That's still true, and the worst of these, in my opinion, is indolence. He said it consisted of a neglect to inform oneself on public issues and to vote, and in an unwillingness to serve in public office. Indolence contradicts the basic assumption of classical democracy that the average man must be an active, instructed and intelligent ruler of his country. As in the physical body, indolence is a symptom of disease in the body politic.

Somebody once said that "your public servants serve you right." The competence and courage of the people who make and execute American policy is up to you. And the best won't be any too good if our costly, cumbersome, contentious governmental system is going to compete successfully. In the foreign field the best won't be good enough if the people behind them can be diverted by demagogues and newspapers preaching fear and malice toward all.

It would be a wholesome sign if we clamored a little less about our rights as American citizens and reflected a little more about our responsibilities as free men.

And how about our economic health? Our free enterprise system has *not* demonstrated that it can insure steady production and employment and equitable distribution. Another severe economic depression will drag the economies of our friends down into chaos with ours, just when they are hoping, praying, that with our help and example they can recover their economic equilibrium.

I have no doubt that the Soviet leaders confidently expect severe economic disorder in this country, and with it the extinction of capitalism. Perhaps they view the prospect with mingled feelings. On the one hand the collapse and the disintegration of our economic power would leave little obstacle to Russian expansion in the ensuing chaos. On the other, they may fear that capitalism will try to fight its way out in one last convulsive struggle. The Russians are not alone; many, many people, wise people, democratic people, look upon us as a dangerously unstable giant in the china closet of the world.

If the freest society on earth can't solve its social and economic problems, will the ideals of democracy and liberty become meaningless to the masses of shoeless spectators around the world? I might even ask you if they will become meaningless to us?

Our political achievements in foreign policy have been impressive. But foreign policy is both economic and political and the halves are no more effective than the whole. "We cannot," as Secretary Byrnes said in his farewell speech, "abandon the policy of political isolation unless we abandon the policy of economic isolation." We still have to see how this Republican Congress will interpret the bi-partisan foreign policy which it has endorsed in terms of tariff, relief, rehabilitation and reconstruction.[177] There have been some disquieting signs. Senator [Robert A.] Taft's position is not clear. The tariff lobbyists are gathering in Washing-

[177] In the 1946 elections the Republicans won control of both houses of Congress.

ton. Senator [Hugh] Butler calls the reciprocal Trade Agreement Act "a gigantic hoax on the American people." Congressman [Chauncey W.] Reed of Illinois has threatened to introduce a bill to wipe off the books an act which has brought a reduction of 31% in average import duties from the Smoot-Hawley Act level of 1930.

Such moves would erase the hopes aroused by our political diplomacy that the United States is going to use its power and prestige for positive leadership to economic security and sanity. And in helping to put economic relations on a healthier basis by wise lending and by active stimulation of foreign trade we are not playing Santa Claus. We are helping ourselves, because no nation in these times can long enjoy a rising standard of living without increasing foreign trade; particularly our country with its vast productive potential, threatened with the spectre of mass unemployment. And we can't sell if we don't buy. Everyone's prosperity is our prosperity. America's bread is buttered on the same side as the rest of the world's.

A full belly is a better obstacle to communism than a bayonet. But words alone won't fill many bellies, especially words that have already lost most of their meaning. The easy and eloquent self confidence with which we Americans still prescribe capitalist free enterprise, which made this country great, as the remedy for the world's economic anguish is a dangerous symptom of ignorance. We dare not confuse myths with facts. We dare not disregard the unhappy fact that capitalist free enterprise is almost extinct except in this country, and even here it is no longer very free. The world has gone socialist. The choice most peoples face is not so much between the capitalist way of life and the communist; rather it is a choice between *socialism* and communism. And it is *socialism* that doctrinaire communism detests and fears most of all, because the socialists promise economic and social security in a planned economy, and also protection of the fundamental personal freedoms. That's a promise the communists can't better, because communism is the negation of freedom.

Yes, our frie[n]ds are socialists; governments of the non-communist left. To protect our way of life we must help them. Paradoxically the survival of socialism seems to depend on American capitalism!

We can't lead from ignorance, and there are some other myths we can ill afford. One is that we can somehow purchase passive acquiescence from the Russians. But when we talk of overcoming the Soviet idealogical concept we are talking of overcoming not only a social — a polit[ic]al concept but also the most basic and deepest elements of traditional Russian thought. We are not dealing with individuals, whims or personalities, but on the one hand with deep-seated habits of thought, conceptions and ways of looking at the world formed over the space of centuries, and on the other with the magic of a great idea.

Diplomatic dispatches from the American Ambassadors to Czar Nicholas II regarding the suspicion of foreigners, spying, the difficulty of obtaining information, etc., written in the eighteen fifties, another period of intense Russian Nationalism, almost 100 years ago could be written today to the slightest detail. Nor is there anything new in the messianic quality. From early times a thread of superstition runs thru this people, who have never known friendly neighbors, that they were destined to conquer the world. Witness the old idea of Mother Russia. The concept of Holy Russia extended as far as Orthodoxy. In the days of Czar Ivan the Terrible they spoke of Moscow as "the third Rome."

Like all those who hold beliefs with fanatic conviction the Soviets will seek to propogate theirs, without dilution or compromise. The idea that we can somehow buy out Soviet evangelism is foolish and insulting. We can't convert them with honey any more than they can convert us with vinegar.

But a *worse* myth is that conflict is inevitable. It is not inevitable. In his speech in the General Assembly Molotov laid emphasis on the concept of the "peaceful competition" of divergent systems. If we can contain the dynamic, centrifugal force of Soviet power and the Soviet idea long enough it will slow down and evolve peacefully — and we can save the friendly Russian people and ourselves from catastrophe. If we are afraid we will fail; if we are impatient and arrogant we will fail; if we are weak and insecure we will fail; if we are unjust we deserve to fail.

I have said more than enough to express my views.

The paramount objective of this generation everywhere is peace on an equitable and permanent basis.

The United Nations is the organized conscience and will of the community of nations. It is an arena, a forum of incalculable influence for peace and progress.

But the work of making and keeping peace has just begun and the end is distant, the perils many.

Failure is death, and success depends on the United States most of all.

It depends on our *political* health. We can't lead if our own free way of life doesn't work and work well. If we can't solve our problems at home we won't solve many abroad.

Success depends on our *economic* health. Prosperity like peace is indivisible. The best assurance of peace and human freedom is the economic stability of this country and the progressive improvement of the condition of the common people everywhere.

Success depends on the wisdom, vision and the courage of our statesmanship, and the moral and physical strength behind it. If we have the
statesmanship — labor, management, agriculture, as well as government
— tomorrow will be the golden age.

There is nothing to fear save our own cupidity, short-sightedness and
weakness. With malice toward none, with faith and tolerance, there is
nothing to fear but our own default.

To A. D. K. Owen

January 21, 1947

Dear David:

Thanks for your letter. I hope if and when I can be of any service you
and the Secretary-General will call upon me. I have had many moments
of misgiving about my own decision and I need not tell you how eager I
am to help — or try to help — at any time on any problem.

Herbert Emmerich tells me that he is much interested and feels that
his interview with Mr. Lie was not very satisfactory in view of the time
limitations. I have little doubt that he is available if you want him. I saw
General Eisenhower here on Saturday but, unhappily, had no satisfactory opportunity to enlist his help with Milton. But I shall write Milton
and ask him to stop off here for a talk if he can do so conveniently before
he makes a final decision.

. . . I suppose you got some other possibilities I passed along to Bill
[Stoneman], including Paul Porter, whom I believe would be very good
if and when available.

Sincerely yours,

P.S. The people at Northwestern University want to know if they have
your permission to publish your talk here in February in the Illinois Law
Review?

To Milton Eisenhower

January 21, 1947

Dear Milton:

David Owen reports that he had talked with you in Washington about
the interesting situation which has developed in the U.N. I think I know
something about the situation and Trygve Lie's problem. I hope very
much that you will be passing through Chicago and that I will have an
opportunity to talk to you about it before you reach a final decision. In
many ways I think it is a job of the utmost consequence and one for

which you have peculiar qualifications. I need not add that it would be a fascinating experience.[178]

With warm regards,

Sincerely yours,

Julius C. Holmes, who was being considered for the UN position that Stevenson refused, wrote Stevenson that the UN needed a Deputy Secretary-General to be a general manager for Trygve Lie. Holmes added: Incident[al]ly, you were the recepient of pretty high compliments from Senator Vandenberg when I talked with him the other day."

To Julius C. Holmes

January 27, 1947

Dear Julius:

Thank you for your "report" on your ventures chez Trygve Lie. Your conclusions about the necessity for a General Deputy coincide with mine. Indeed, we made this proposal originally in London more than a year ago. I suspect — not for repetition — that the Russians will vigorously oppose, for the present at least, anyone between [Arkady] Sobolev, Assistant Secretary General for Political and Security Affairs, and the Secretary General. In short, I have the impression that the position of Deputy has to be approached softly and sidewise, and I suspect that Lie is inhibited in talking about it to you and others whom he does not know well. But he has been quite candid with me, and I think he has in mind that for the present the job must be entitled Assistant Secretary General and must be a replacement for [John B.] Hutson, but this individual will serve as Acting Secretary General during his absence and will in due course assume full responsibility for general management and the coordination of the Economic and the Social Departments. With the passage of time I could envision the formulization of a position as Deputy Secretary General.

But these are the chances one must take, and meanwhile the present necessity is the tiresome job of putting the house in order, i.e. Hutson's job.[179] All in all, I think it has very attractive possibilities and I am delighted that you disclose some interest in it. I have no information what-

---

[178] Mr. Eisenhower replied on January 25, 1947, "I would welcome and profit by a visit with you. Thanks ever so much for your interest." He did not accept the position.

[179] Byron Price was finally appointed to succeed Mr. Hutson as Assistant Secretary-General for Administration.

ever as to developments subsequent to my short visit in New York, but I believe he has also in mind as a possibility Milton Eisenhower.

You can be sure that if I find a rich — or even a poor — client to send me to Washington that I will look you up.

With warm regards, I am

Sincerely yours,

P.S. I am glad Senator Vandenberg thinks so well of me. It is mutual.

President Peter Odegard of Reed College invited Stevenson to attend a conference on world affairs at Reed.

To Peter Odegard

February 4, 1947

My dear Mr. Odegard:

Nothing would please me more than to come to Reed for the Pacific Northwest College Congress and your invitation to speak with Mrs. Roosevelt at the public meeting on March 7th is most flattering. Unhappily, I have some law work and have also made some engagements in Chicago for about that time, which I cannot adjust.

I could not be more disappointed. And I don't want to miss the opportunity to record my enthusiasm for what the students at Reed have been doing to awaken interest and enlarge understanding of the most critical questions with which their generation will have to deal. . . .

Moreover, I hate to miss a trip to Oregon! And I hope you will remember me to my friends, Marshall Dana and Richard Neuberger, if and when you see them.

With every good wish for the success of this important project and my warm thanks, I am

Cordially yours,

To Arthur B. Perry[180]

February 18, 1947

Dear Mr. Perry:

I am more than a little flattered by your invitation to speak at Commencement for fifteen or twenty minutes. I have hesitated because I am planning to go to Princeton for my 25th Reunion the following week-end and I have had some misgivings about attempting both. But I have de-

[180] The original is in the possession of Milton Academy.

cided to risk it (Adlai to the contrary notwithstanding[181]), subject only to a fair warning to you that I am wholly inexperienced as a commencement speaker. I made a beautiful effort of this kind at a university out here last June and came away convinced that the only person in the sweltering hall who understood it was myself!

But if you cannot find a more reliable performer, count me in and cross your fingers. Be sure that I will try to ambush a client to pay my way. But experience to date is not reassuring!

With warm regards to Emily,[182] and our thanks always for all you have done for Adlai, I am

Cordially yours,

P.S. The date you use is Fri. June 6. But Sat. is June 7 — I hope that's correct.

Stevenson spoke to the Princeton Club of Chicago, February 21, 1947.[183]

Mr. Chairman:

Your flattering introduction is substantially correct as to the facts — I did serve with the Secretary of the Navy for three years; I did travel for the Navy, the FEA [Foreign Economic Administration] and the War Department, extensively in the Pacific, the Mediterranean, and the European theatres during the war, and I did work on the development of the U.N. in Washington, San Francisco, London and latterly I was a member of the U. S. Delegation to the General Assembly in New York.

But tho your facts are correct, your conclusions are not. The innocent might assume that after all this experience in war and peace that I had some of the answers, but I haven't — I'm as confused as you are — which of course has not deterred me in the least from making countless brilliant speeches from New England to Oregon in which I have reached all manner of conclusions — seldom consistent.

So, tho I am aware that the question of whether I should or should not make a speech here tonight has all but shattered the ancient harmony of the Princeton Club of Chicago, and I am indebted to those of you who have so vigorously advocated an opportunity for me to justify my ab-

---

[181] Adlai Stevenson III was a student at Milton Academy.
[182] Mrs. Perry.
[183] This speech was transcribed in 1959 from the original longhand text. Apparently Stevenson wrote out only the first part of the speech.

sence from these meetings for the last six years, I have also noted with alarm the sinister good will of some of my classmates. But they forget that after long experience in negotiation with Russians, Poles, and others I am too wary to be so easily trapped. I, too, remember the admonition of President Coolidge who said, "It is better to keep still and be thought a fool than to speak and remove all doubt."

And as I look into your bland, well fed and slightly flushed faces I also realize what an opportunity this would be to waste my precious wisdom on desert air. Indeed, a story Lord Halifax told one day in that famous Penthouse on top of the Fairmont Hotel in San Francisco takes on new and less humorous significance for me. . . .[184]

Indeed, as I look at you and reflect on the effort I was about to waste I think of the time I was walking along a street with a friend who was an actor. We stopped in front of one of those restaurants full of fish on a mound of ice that stare at you with cold, expressionless eyes. After a moment of hideous fascination my friend started and said, "My God, that reminds me, I have a matinee."

But much as I should like to get along to the worthwhile part of the evening I seem to be obliged to say something about the foreign business or else your President says I will have to pay for my dinner.

Now I've observed of late that all a speaker on international relations has to do is to talk darkly about the atomic bomb, vaparization [vaporization], bacteriological extermination, damn the sinister Russians, beat his breast self righteously and wind up with a prayer for the United Nations — and a five or six point program — five or six points depending on whether he thinks he can get away with an eloquent demand for economy, tax reduction and more free enterprise, coupled with emphatic insistence on an impregnable national defense in the atomic age.

It's a cinch, you can't miss. Your audience is spellbound. They thank you earnestly and nervously and walk off into the night with their apprehensions confirmed, their confusion enlarged and their perspective diminished.

It's tempting — but I am not going to risk it and in the two hours that remain to me I am going to try out on you some accumulated information about the Russians, all of it old and familiar, because our difficulties with the Soviet Union — the vicious circle of mutual suspicion between Russia and the West — are the basic obstacle to peace and security.

I'm like the old lady from Vt. who said — so I'm going to read to you from some disorderly notes. . . .

[184] He told a story at this point but only put selected words in the text to remind himself.

Stevenson introduced Mrs. Franklin D. Roosevelt to the Chicago Council on Foreign Relations on March 3, 1947.

The last time I appeared on this platform — a year ago this month — I had a less agreeable task. I had just returned to Chicago after six months in London at the Preparatory Commission and first General Assembly of the United Nations, and I harangued you about the organization of the United Nations, the state of the world generally, America's responsibilities specifically, — and sundry other small subjects!

You sat patiently and attentively for a very long hour, but I detected manifest relief when I finally assured you that I was going to go and sin no more; that I was stepping off this platform forever.

And here I am again — faithless, irresponsible, and very happy, because your officers have asked me to introduce Mrs. Roosevelt. I will avoid the temptation to enlarge on the *absurdity* of *my* introducing *Mrs. Roosevelt* to anyone anywhere. And I can't help recall the plight of the world traveller and professional lecturer who was deploring the fact that there was always someone in the front row who knew more about the place he was talking about or what he was talking about than he did. "My luck is so bad," he said, "that if I talked about life among the Llamasaries of Tibet, Marco Polo would be in the audience — or Mrs. Roosevelt."

No, there are too many Marco Polos in the audience. There is nothing I can tell you about Mrs. Roosevelt, much as I should like to try. But I do want to say, because I am very proud of it, that I have had the invigorating experience of serving with her for long, relentless days and nights, weeks and months, in the formative period of the United Nations, first at the General Assembly in London a year ago and then at the General Assembly in New York this fall. At both she was assigned the most difficult tasks as a senior member of the United States Delegations.

I have seen with my own eyes what many have said — that day in an[d] day out she carries a heavier schedule than most any man.

I have seen her conduct with patience, firmness, eloquence and dignity the long, long fight for the International Refugee Organization — the fight for the cherished right of political sanctuary for the thousands of refugees and displaced persons from northern and eastern Europe who do not wish to return to their native lands. And I have seen her win that exasperating battle against the bitter, implacable opposition of the Soviet Union, and emerge with even greater respect among the Russians and the eastern bloc.

I have seen something of the demands on her time by groups, individuals, public and private affairs.

I have seen personal mail delivered to her in baskets — mostly asking for help.

I have seen her work from early morning to midnight, day after day, and then go home with the next day's documents and come back early in the morning better prepared than anyone with half her load.

I have seen the faces of the crowds along the streets waiting for her to pass by.

But I have never seen her *impatient, undignified, thoughtless.* I have never seen her *too busy* for *courtesy,* or for someone who needed her.

There is a Chinese proverb, something like, "subdue people with goodness, people can never be subdued; nourish people with goodness, and the whole world is ready to be subdued."

With goodness an American woman has won the respect, the confidence and the love of more people, great and small, at home and abroad, than, I venture to say, any living person.

It is better to light candles than to curse darkness.

Mrs. Eleanor Roosevelt, United States member of the all-important Commission on Human Rights of the United Nations.

On March 3, 1947, the Canadian Undersecretary of State for External Affairs wrote Stevenson urging him to write a review article for the International Journal of the Canadian Institute of International Affairs *about the reports the Canadian delegation to the United Nations had submitted to Parliament.*

To Escott Reid

March 5, 1947

Dear Escott:

Your letter was a happy start for another winter day and I am glad to hear that the third volume of "Reid on U.N." is soon to make its appearance. You were good to think of me and I look forward to my copy eagerly. But I just can't undertake to do the review for the International Journal — which is a very ungrateful reaction to your flattering suggestion that I *could* do it properly.

I have, as usual, attempted to do too much of late, and this business of trying to earn an honest living again is interfering dreadfully with more important things — including this one! I am grateful to you for thinking of me and I only wish my time had been better allocated with a large item for contingencies.

I hope we will meet again, and I have thought longingly of the snows of Canada of late, as my neglected skis gather more and more of the dust of years.

I hope the Department will find something for me to do at the next assembly, which will give us more opportunity to collaborate, but I doubt if there will be places by that time for obsolete, obscure private citizens.

With thanks and warmest regards,

Cordially yours,

Stevenson spoke to the Immigrants' Protective League on March 12, 1947.

Over ten million people were herded into Germany and Austria during the war, most of them as slave laborers, some as prisoners of war, some as refugees from invading armies. Many died. When the Axis collapsed a counterwave took place and the Allied armies, with the help of UNRRA, returned nearly seven million to their homelands by rail, by truck, by foot, by air. It was the largest and quickest Volkermanderung of all time.

But a million would not return. 850,000 of them, including a large portion of women and children, are living in camps in the American, British and French zones of Germany. I should have said existing, for these displaced persons — D.P.'s they're called — are the saddest chapter in the epilogue of the war. And they have occasioned the bitterest and most prolonged controversy in the life of the United Nations. Driven into slavery by the Nazis, fleeing from persecution and invasion, these survivors who have suffered every abuse, every brutality and indignity, have still, after almost two years, had no chance to start again and rebuild their shattered lives.

The largest national group are Poles; many are Balts, from Latvia, Lithuania and Estonia which have been taken over by Russia. Some are Yugoslavs, and there are some other Eastern Europeans. For many reasons they do not want to return to their homelands. Some are anti-Communists who fear persecution at home; home to many is ashes and agony. Many are Catholics; about 20% are Jews — the wretched remnant of Hitler's massacre.

They have been rounded up in camps and cared for by UNRRA and private relief agencies supplied by the armies. But UNRRA will expire in

June, its mission completed, and this is not soldiers' work even if there were soldiers to do it. So what then? What to do about these unfortunates; how to support them, how to get them back to their own countries or how to get them resettled elsewhere; how to enable them once more to become useful, productive human beings; how to weed out the Quislings and the traitors? This was the problem that confronted the First General Assembly of the United Nations in London a year ago last month.

After prolonged debate there; then at a special international conference last July; then in the Economic and Social Council; the General Assembly in New York in December of last year, after some six weeks of almost continuous debate, finally approved the Constitution of the International Refugee Organization. Seventy-nine amendments to the Constitution were proposed in the Assembly, mostly by the Soviet Union and the Eastern countries of origin who sought relentlessly and tirelessly to compel the repatriation of political dissidents whom they seem to regard as war criminals or fascists. All these proposals were successfully resisted, largely under the leadership of the United States, represented by a great citizen and a great humanitarian — Mrs. Eleanor Roosevelt.

From the inception of the idea of an International Refugee Organization the United States, supported by Britain and France and China, has insisted that no one should be forced to return home against his will. And that principle of political sanctuary, which brought so many of our ancestors to these shores, was overwhelmingly sustained by the United Nations.

Now a Preparatory Commission to organize the I.R.O. is meeting in Geneva. Senator Vandenberg and Senator Connally introduced a resolution in the Senate authorizing American participation, and yesterday it was unanimously approved by the Foreign Relations Committee. The President has asked Congress for $75,000,000 for our share of the administrative and operational budget for the first year. The total budget is about $160,000,000 to feed, clothe, shelter, repatriate and commence the work of finding new homes, for 1,000,000 people. Lest America's share of 73 to 75 million appear very large it should be remembered that about two-thirds, 600,000, of these refugees in Germany, Austria and Italy, are the responsibility of the United States, and our contribution to the I.R.O. will actually be substantially less than the Army's expenditures have been. General Hilldring has testified that it will cost the United States $130,000[,000?] in the fiscal year ending June 30, compared to this contribution of $75,000,000 to the I.R.O.

All who know anything of this poignant problem fervently pray that the United States Congress will act promptly so that the organization will be prepared to take up its formidable burden the end of June. The other countries are waiting to see what we will do.

It is hoped that many of the Poles who are peasants and some of the Yugoslav peasants can be persuaded to go home. Of the remainder less than a third will be Jews. They will not return. There are too many mass graves in Eastern Europe. The Estonians, Latvians, and Lithuanians will not return to their Soviet dominated homelands. 700,000 is a minimum hard core that will have to be resettled somewhere soon, before human deterioration sets in.

That will be the great task of the I.R.O. The sooner this humanitarian task is completed, the sooner this sad legacy of the war is liquidated, the better it will be for the refugees, and for the world. As the greatest, richest and one of the most sparsely settled countries in the world, we can easily find homes and useful occupation for many of them. More than half will be women and children. All are reminders that "the evil men do lives after them."

On March 17, 1947, Stevenson spoke at a meeting in Chicago sponsored by the Jewish Welfare Fund Campaign. It was basically the same speech that he had delivered in Springfield, Illinois, on January 10, 1947, and had used on several subsequent occasions. By this time, however, President Truman had just requested Congress to provide economic and military assistance to Greece and Turkey. Stevenson added the following paragraphs as a result of the President's message.

The program for Greece and Turkey indicates the route we are taking for better or for worse to but[t]ress our firm diplomacy.

We can't be sure it will succeed. We can't be sure that what we do and when we do it won't be too little and too late.

But one thing most everyone will agree upon — that a full belly is a better defense against communism than an atomic bomb.

To John D. Black[185]

March 18, 1947

Dear Mr. Black:

I would appreciate it very much if you would take a few minutes to look at the enclosed statement of the U.S. Committee for the care of European Children. Appeals for relief purposes these days are appalling,

---

[185] Member of the Chicago law firm of Winston, Strawn, Black & Towner.

but to me the care and placement of these orphans of the war come first.

The Chicago Committee has received individual contributions from small amounts to several thousand dollars. I hope you will find it possible to help with this work.[186]

Sincerely yours,

To Alger Hiss[187]

April 9, 1947

Dear Alger:

I am prompted by the last of an interminable series of interviews with people — mostly young and very dedicated — to write you this note.

You know better than I how many promising young people feel that they want to make a career of some kind in the foreign field. Some — the one just now — are just beginning college after service abroad; some are finishing college; some are in graduate schools; some are confused fathers and mothers trying to help their children, etc., etc.

If my own futility is any measure, there should be somewhere a clearing house of information about the U.S. foreign service; exchange scholarships; foreign educational institutions (cf. Geneva Institute of International Relations); domestic institutions; summer study, travel and language facilities (cf. Experiment in International Living (?), Hubert Herring's Thing in Mexico); foundations (cf. Institute of Current World Affairs); corporations with foreign service training schools (cf. International Harvester), etc., etc. In short, some place or some cumulative booklet where these earnest gropers could find out what there is at all levels and how to follow it up.

If the Carnegie Foundation could assemble this sort of information, its name would be forever blessed — by at least one bewildered frontiersman!

Sincerely yours,

During the mayoral election Stevenson supported the candidacy of Martin H. Kennelly, a Chicago businessman untainted by the Democratic machine but supported by it. He easily defeated the Republican candidate, who was backed by Governor Dwight Green. Kennelly drew considerable support from independent and Republican voters.

[186] This is identical to many other letters Stevenson wrote to raise funds.
[187] President of the Carnegie Endowment for International Peace.

To Edward G. Miller, Jr.[188]

April 14, 1947

Dear Eddie:

I was delighted to have your letter this bright spring morning, and your surmise is correct. I called you while in New York in hopes that we might review the professional, political and international situation in a few minutes. I will try again the next time — if there is a next time!

I had not heard that you had been elevated to the status of partner, and herewith proffer my felicitations. I am agreeably surprised to note that you are still on your good behavior in spite of this minor alteration in your status. On second thought, I think I will not see you in New York, because I suspect that I would soon embrace your proposal that we take off for Brazil.

I have little to say on the local political situation, except that Kennelly's victory has reinvigorated the local democracy and suggested the revolutionary idea that you can do better with good candidates. Just how this affects me I do not know, except that people of good will continue to whisper in my shell-like ears.

Can't you contrive to come out here for a weekend in the country — at someone's expense!

Yours,

On a radio program on April 27, 1947, Stevenson debated Governor Kim Sigler of Michigan on the topic "Should the Communist Party Be Banned in America?" Only Stevenson's opening statement is reprinted here.[189]

Yesterday what we call democracy was challenged by Nazism and Fa[s]cism. We fought and won an awful war to destroy this menace. Today what we call democracy is challenged by another form of tyranny called Communism. The whole world is the battleground in this great twentieth century struggle for men's allegiance between those who believe the individual exists for the state and we who believe that the state exists for the individual.

Our own country is no exception; we are part of the battleground but we must prevail in the struggle here at home without sacrificing funda-

[188] Member of the New York law firm of Sullivan and Cromwell and a member of the U.S. delegation to the UN Conference in San Francisco in 1945.

[189] The text is based on a typescript of the public service debate series *Your Right to Say It,* sponsored by radio station WGN, Chicago.

mental personal freedom in the process, otherwise we will not win; we will lose, because it is precisely these personal freedoms that are our most precious heritage. The right to think, to say what we believe without fear of interference from the state. The difference is not the objective but the method; that is what our discussion is about tonight; whether to outlaw the Communist party is a good or bad method.

I think it is a bad method and I will tell you why. I will give you three reasons which seem to me convincing.

In the first place you would drive the Communist Party underground, and surely everyone knows it is best to keep your adversary where you can see him.

In the second place, it would be a confession of weakness. Democracy is strong; let's act that way. If we have faith in our system, surely we are not afraid to risk it in open competition with Communism.

And thirdly, suppression is a dangerous precedent. If in a moment of nervous anxiety we outlaw a political party to protect democracy, who knows what liberties may be sacrificed to the same end and then where is our freedom, our democracy. Let us not adopt Fascism to defeat Communism.

The ultimate test of such legislation, it seems to me, is whether it will increase the security of our democratic society or not. I am afraid it won't. Our own experience with the alien and sedition laws shows that suppression is not the best way to deal with such people. The Czarists tried to suppress revolutionary ideas. Many governments have tried to suppress radical political agitation but they only increased the effectiveness of the agitation and aggravated the tension and fear.

Suppression is the birthmark of a police state and we detest police states, be they Czarist, Communist, Fascist or what not.

The most dangerous Communist in this country, as Governor Sigler has said, is not the avowed one but those who work in secrecy to promote disorder, rebellion and violence. They are underground already. They despise democratic processes but if the rank and file of those who call themselves Communists want to use the ballot and behave like normal American candidates and enlist support publicly if they can, let them do so. Don't drive them underground to reinforce the sinister subversives. Keep them on top of the bed where you can see them. Don't push them under the bed where you can't see them. If we are afraid of them now when they are behaving like ordinary citizens trying to gain their ends, how will we feel when they are out of sight and working in the dark recesses of our society.

The reason many, probably most people call themselves Communists is not because Russia is still the symbol of a better world or because they know much about the theories of Marx and Lenin, it is because they are discontented. That is the cause of most dangerous political agitation. Discontent is the soil Communism cultivates. If you deprive these people of a chance to register their discontent, you redouble that discontent. You not only lose your chance to redeem them but many will say, "This country is lousy; we haven't a chance, we can't even vote for what we believe, let's try something else." And, presto, you have made a new group of dangerous hidden malcontents.

No, you catch more flies with honey than you do with vinegar. Moreover, if the party is banned, you will lose sight of the size of this group. There are only about sixty thousand Communists in this country; fewer per capita population than in Britain and the Dominions. But it is a good idea to keep track of them by leaving them on the ballot officially each time.

But even more important than these common sense reasons for opposing this legislation are some fundamental principles. This is the land of the free. We have faith in human wisdom and in the power of inquiry. Our great strength is that we can discuss openly anything within the law. Let's not plug up the safety valves. All the world is watching us to see how much validity there is in the principle of political freedom we talk so much about. Let's not get rattled in this great struggle of the century. Let's not wobble down the road of soulless conformity, for who can say where it will lead. More secret police, hysteria, witch hunts, laws forbidding revolutionary doctrines. Hitler burned the books of freedom. May the time never come when we can't read the works of Thomas Paine, the trumpeter of American revolution. No, let's not fall for the very methods of suppression we despise. Let's not throw out the baby with the bath water.

Suppression isn't the American way. It is wrong in principle and what is more, it won't work. You can't stop the spread of ideas by laws or by bayonets, but you can stop them with better ideas. Our idea is a better idea. Let's not lose faith in it. Let's fight suppression and fear and Communism with truth and freedom and positive democracy.

On May 13, 1947, Stevenson was the featured speaker at the Jefferson Day Dinner at Pontiac, Illinois. Only his introductory remarks are reprinted since the remainder of the speech was basically what he had said at Springfield, Illinois, on January 10, 1947.

I always wince a little when I get south of the Cook County line and am referred to as a Chicagoan. I suppose it's because, while I am as proud as anyone to be identified with Chicago, I don't like to feel disassociated with the downstate where I was raised and my family have lived for 115 years. Indeed, I don't feel in the least like a stranger in Pontiac, not only because I've been passing thru this city as long as I can remember, but because my great grandfather, Jesse Fell, once owned a substantial part of Pontiac and planted many of the older elms that line your streets. His interest in Pontiac property almost ended disastrously, because much of his land had been purchased originally by his predecessor in title from the guardian of a young man. A decision of the Supreme Court would have invalidated the original sale and Fell's title had not R. E. Williams, a Pontiac lawyer, proved that the young man had later confirmed his guardian's sale.

I wish we still had title to that property and I might be living down here among you embattled Democrats! But like all of Fell's land, I guess it was sold much too soon and much too cheaply for the enrichment of his great grandchildren!

It was this same ancestor of mine, Jesse Fell, who located the Illinois State Normal University and the Soldiers' Orphans' home in Normal. Then in 1869 he started to raise subscriptions here in Pontiac for a reform school. The citizens and supervisors subscribed a total of $90,000 and won the location of the school. Fell donated the original site of 64 acres, and also presented Pontiac with the land for a city park, which, I believe, was named in his memory in 1915. I don't know whether it is still named Fell Park; if it isn't, I think you ought to give it to me and I'll retire and move down here!

All of which is by way of introduction to a confession which I had better make before someone else does: that great-grandfather, Jesse Fell, was a staunch Republican! What's more — he was the first to propose Lincoln for the Presidency. Only this winter, on Lincoln's Birthday, his descendants presented to the Library of Congress in Washington Lincoln's autobiography in his own handwriting which he inscribed to Fell in 1859.

But I think you Democrats will forgive me for being proud of a Republican ancestor who supported Lincoln — and Pontiac! Anyway, the republicanism was soon diluted, because my Republican mother married my Democratic father, and in those days when a man and woman married they became one — and the man was that one; those dear, dead days!

But Dr. Von Ruden[190] and Bill Vicars [191] invited me to come down to

[190] Dr. H. A. Von Ruden, a Pontiac dentist and member of the Democratic State Central Committee for the 17th Congressional District.
[191] Administrative aide to Secretary of State Edward J. Barrett.

Pontiac for this Jefferson Day dinner not to discuss the old family real estate but international affairs, altho as you can see I've got myself into a frame of mind to do a much better job of contrasting the glorious past of the Republican Party in these parts and its inglorious present in all parts. But I can't do that, nor can I submit to the temptation to talk about the remarkable recovery of our Party since the dark days of last November. And what an opportunity that reversal in public esteem affords for moralizing on the fickleness of public favor, the dangers of over-confidence and the responsibility of our Party to lead the way compassionately and wisely, never forsaking the people, for whom the Republic exists, etc., etc. — all in the oratorical tradition of Jefferson Day speeches.

But I can't do that, because you see I've, unconsciously, become an expert on foreign affairs, and experts, as you know, are supposed to know more and more about less and less until they know everything about nothing. And I've arrived at that happy state without ever passing thru the process of knowing more and more. . . .

On May 20, 1947, Stevenson delivered a speech in Chicago entitled "Where Do We Go From Here?" to the 128th meeting of the board of governors of the Investment Bankers Association of America. The organization published the speech.[192]

I am going to resist the temptation to masquerade as a statesman. I am going to spare you my unimportant and irresponsible comments on the controversy Mr. Henry Wallace has stirred up.[193] Instead, I want to mention some things that seem to me both obvious and important to people who know that our destiny is shaped by greater forces than headlines.

During these past two years we have passed through successive waves of optimism and pessimism across the whole spectrum of emotion — from the happy illusion that the United States [Nations] was somehow a substitute for power politics and a guarantee of automatic peace, to

[192] Parts of this speech were repeated by Stevenson in "The Economic Crisis of 1948," in *Foreign Notes*, published by the Chicago Council on Foreign Relations, May 23, 1947, and in "Some Post-War Reflections," *Illinois Law Review*, Northwestern University, Vol. 42, No. 3 (July-August, 1947).

[193] Henry A. Wallace was forced out of President Truman's cabinet in September, 1946, over disagreement with the hardening of U.S. policy toward the Soviet Union. Wallace was critical of the Truman Doctrine since U.S. aid was unilateral and thus bypassed the United Nations. He was an opponent of Truman's "get-tough" policy with the U.S.S.R. over Greece, Turkey, Czechoslovakia and other issues. He feared the result would be a fatal arms race between the two superpowers — the U.S. and the U.S.S.R. — and concomitantly each side would be less able to solve world problems such as famine, hunger and disease.

periods of black despair, talk of another war, and visions of the ugly spectre of two evil old worlds in hostile balance instead of one bright new world. But in spite of all the emotional gymnastics of the past two years, it would seem that the American people have matured very rapidly; that there is now a general awareness that making peace is harder than making war, and the obstacles and hazards infinitely more difficult to understand and to evaluate; that the hard realities of international life are no longer the monopoly of any region or group; that this is an era of world revolution and reorganization that has few historical counterparts; and that America is in the world to stay, not because it wants to be, but because it knows it can't keep out.

Another major American decision has been evolving for sometime and culminated in the Greece and Turkey bill, which I suppose it is fair to say passed the Congress not because they liked it, but because they felt there was no safe alternative. From 1793 to 1917 American policy and legislation was based on three premises: (a) that wars were inevitable and a legal means of settling international disputes; (b) that since wars could be localized the United States should remain neutral; and (c) that international law protected neutral ships not carrying contraband and that, therefore, a policy of non-intervention and neutrality would not destroy our commerce. We sustained the doctrine of neutral rights with a fair degree of success for 100 years or more, although President Madison had to abandon neutrality and fight for our neutral rights in 1812; and, of course, the violation of our neutral rights by Germany was still President Wilson's ostensible reason for going to war more than 100 years later, in 1917.

Now we have rejected all three of the basic premises on which our policy has rested since Washington's neutrality proclamation of 1793. We no longer recognize war as a legal means of settling quarrels; we no longer believe that wars involving major powers can be localized; and we no longer believe that neutrality can be maintained even by abandoning neutral trading rights. We are on a new tack. We are attempting through the United Nations to settle international disputes at their inception, and we propose through the "Truman Doctrine" to intervene, unilaterally if necessary, at the request of the aggrieved, to support the principles of the United Nations Charter.

Assuming the conclusion that the United States is going to be a vigorous and permanent participant in world affairs is not premature, we see for the first time the world balanced between two non-European states, the highly developed United States, with old ideas, and the undeveloped Soviet Union with new ideas. Surrounding areas are attracted like satellites to these planets by dependence, by fear, by racial affinity. Large areas and populations are exposed to both magnetic fields. Russia has little and wants everything; the United States has everything and wants little. Both want peace and security — Russia, to bind up her awful wounds and to develop her vastness and wealth; the United States to enjoy hers.

Must these two galaxys of power and influence some day collide? If we were ants we would probably have to answer in the affirmative. But we are not ants; we are rational human beings who know that there will be no victors and no victory in another war, although people persist in talking about war as though it might again be a definitive solution of something. It would be healthy if the ancient concept of war as a decisive arbiter could be removed from contemporary thinking.

I suppose the root of this hostile drift in American-Russian relations is fear — fear of one another, fear of those ideas, old and new. Our old fear and mistrust of Bolshevism is aggravated by Russia's stubborn, acquisitive behavior. Russia's old fear of capitalist encirclement and counterrevolution is aggravated by a suspicion that we would have been glad to see Russia and Germany both bleed to death in the war. The Soviet press call us reactionaries and imperialists determined to dominate the world. We call them aggressors and imperialists determined to dominate the world.

And so it goes — fear begets fear, epithet begets epithet; the vicious circle tightens, the division between East and West sharpens — and the bystanders tremble. The arena is the United Nations, the Council of Foreign Ministers, many less publicized international meetings, and those great areas exposed to both gravitational pulls — largely Europe now, with, first, the Middle East and then Asia in the background.

How can we break this vicious circle of fear? How can we erase the tensions and get on with the business of redeeming this bloody century? With our technological and cultural achievements there's a golden age ahead. Can we get there — alive?

That's the question everyone, everywhere asks — and no one answers. That's the question our generation may be compelled to answer. Why can't we answer it quickly; sit down together and reason things out with the Russians and make a deal? Why can't we stop this dangerous, expensive, distasteful maneuvering for advantage? Why can't we exchange a great big loan for a permanent political and economic settlement as Henry Wallace suggests? [194]

[194] The Soviet Union requested a loan from the United States for reconstruction purposes. The heavy damage the Soviet Union suffered was described by Marshal Stalin at the Yalta Conference. After the death of President Roosevelt, the Russian request "somehow managed to get itself lost in the files of the Foreign Economic

Let me remind you that the Russians may mistrust us profoundly, and not wholly without cause in view of the many manifestations of our distaste for Communism and the Soviet system commencing with American armed intervention on Russian soil after the last war. But let me also remind you that the difficulty of dealing with the Russians which had been so conspicuous since the war is nothing new. One hundred years ago our ambassadors to the Czar's Court were having some identical troubles. Even when Russia was fighting for her very life the suspicion and distrust never subsided. Indeed, there has been far more contact and negotiation between the Soviet Union and the Western Powers since the war than there was during the war.

The Soviet and American Chiefs of Staff met only twice during the war — at Teheran and Yalta. Discussion, let alone agreement, about coordinated military plans was almost impossible, even when the Germans were hammering at Moscow. When Russian need was greatest it still took months and months of negotiation to blast a hole through the iron curtain in Iran for lend-lease supplies coming up the Persian Gulf. Although Stalingrad was tottering, they would not permit our ferry pilots to deliver fighter planes to the Red Air Force across the Bering Sea. Their pilots had to come and get them in Alaska, and few lend-lease planes reached the Eastern front until long after that decisive battle.

If even a superficial review of the past makes our present difficulties in the Council of Foreign Ministers and in the United Nations less surprising, they are still no less exasperating and perplexing.

Now, why is this? Perhaps at least a partial answer can be found in some elementary Russian characteristics. I suggest that the factors of Communist ideology, ancient Russian habits of thought, and the internal conditions there, in combination, have produced a suspicion, fear, and a missionary zeal that underlie our difficulties with the Soviet Union. These difficulties cannot be resolved by angry name calling and threats any more than you can break a colt by intimidation and roughness.

In the first place, Russia has never known peaceful, friendly neighbors. She has had to fight them all from the earliest times and the outside world has come to mean a hostile world. The external dangers of the past, real or fancied — and Germany and Japan were very real! — and the traditional fear and suspicion of foreigners has fitted nicely into Communist requirements of ruthless discipline and purity of thought.

In the second place, the dictatorship of the proletariat has functioned through decisions imposed from above, not from the proletariat. A mi-

---

Administrator . . . while Administration officials denied that it had ever been received," the New York *Herald Tribune* noted on March 3, 1946.

nority of trusted party members controls the will of the majority. The result is that opposition has always existed, and the internal security of the regime has been a constant preoccupation of the rulers in the Kremlin. But the Soviet Government naturally could not admit the existence of opposition. So the internal danger has been treated as a reflection of the external. Hence the purge trials, the talk of wreckers and saboteurs always as agents of foreign powers. The external enemy has been a convenient justification for the rigorous measures of protection against the internal one.

And bear in mind that the Soviets did not have to manufacture this fear psychosis. It was there, made to order, already. Czarist Russia was a police state.

Fear breeds abnormalities. A threat of persecution and apprehension runs through Russian literature. And there is a weird ancient superstition that Mother Russia's, Holy Russia's destiny is limitless. This messianic quality also fits nicely into the classical Communist concept of world revolution.

But I won't enlarge. The point is that we are not dealing so much with individuals as ideas. We are dealing on the one hand with ancient habits of thought and conceptions rooted in centuries of Russian life and history, and on the other hand with "the magic of a great idea."

Like all those who hold beliefs with deep-rooted, fanatic conviction, the Soviets will seek to propagate theirs without dilution or compromise. They are not hypocrites and the idea that we can somehow buy them out is insulting. They are not frivolous and the idea that we can somehow charm and talk them into acquiescence is foolish. Add to these ancient characteristics a philosophy that the ends justify the means, a conviction that Communist ends are good, and mistrust and fear of our powerful, hostile capitalist country, and I hope I have made it clear why some people are not too sanguine about an early and permanent general settlement on any acceptable terms.

But the prospect is not all discouraging. Historically, Russian diplomacy has been very flexible. They have always made sure they could retreat when they run into firm and final resistance. We have seen that repeatedly. In a military sense, also, their commitments never exceed their capacity. I hope, we, the United States, can match them in both respects!

Also history records the gradual cooling of the passions engendered by all revolutionary movements. As Carr puts it, "The tendency is for the revolutionary aspect to predominate in the earlier stages, the positive aspect in the later. Primitive Christianity was revolutionary until it had disrupted the old Roman civilization; then it created a new and positive world order of its own, and underwent a corresponding modification of its outlook. The Reformation began by being revolutionary and destructive, and ended by becoming the basis of a new social order."

Gibbons [Edward Gibbon] pointed out that there is but a short step between enthusiasm and imposture. Our own conversion from isolationism proves that facts and reason and time can revise a nation's approach to world problems.

Qualified observers say that the emotional power of Communist party doctrine in Russia is diminishing; that the urge for better relations with the outside world — for freedom from fear — is closer to the surface than we realize. The fact of a friendly world — if it is a friendly world — will gradually penetrate, will gradually dissipate the hard shell of fear.

The situation is not without hope and encouragement. But meanwhile we don't know what they want — just security or World Communism — and they won't oblige us with a bill of particulars. Perhaps they don't know themselves. But, after two years of painful, stubborn negotiation, it seems clear that they are determined to get all they can while they can, whatever the ultimate objective — defensive or offensive.

So, confronted with uncertainty of Soviet ambitions, the expansion of Soviet power, and the encroachment of Soviet ideas, our policy for world order and security is resistance and assistance. Resistance to further political expansion, because we know all too well that appeasement doesn't work; that you can't sacrifice principles and justice and retain leadership. If there are moderates in the Soviet hierarchy who are more concerned with security, recovery, and development than expansion, appeasement won't help them: it will strengthen those who insist on further adventures, just as it strengthened Hitler.

But, of course, political resistance alone is not enough. Political resistance without economic resistance won't suffice, because we've learned another lesson. At least I hope we've learned that prosperity, like peace, is indivisible; that you can't have an island of prosperity in an ocean of want; that given a choice between life and liberty, people will choose life, like most animals.

Order and security in the world will depend largely on those areas which have not made a choice between the old ideas and the new. Because ours is the only nation that has the *power* to *resist* and the *wealth* to *assist* the burden falls squarely on us. It will be expensive and it may not succeed. It won't succeed if it's too little and too late. But you can't succeed without trying — you can't win by default — and the cost of *not* resisting and assisting in the long run will make the cost of resisting and assisting now look like peanuts.

So I conclude, therefore, that the United States has made some historic decisions in these two years. Twenty-five years ago we would not even follow; today we are leading in the development of international concepts through the United Nations. We have given unmistakable evidence of permanent participation in world affairs. We are going to resist the spread of a new totalitarian threat to the peace. We are going to attack economic disintegration by collective action if possible, by individual action if necessary.

The real question is no longer so much *what* the United States will do, but *how* we will do it. Will we use our economic abundance boldly and to the full to attack the breeding grounds of desperate political solutions? As the Chinese say, "You can't carve rotten wood and you can't paint on walls of sand." Until Europeans can eat regularly and live decently, they are not going to think much about the place of the individual in the scheme of things.

Doesn't it boil down to this? Ideologies and systems have to stand a very practical test. First they have to produce results in the economic sense. Then peoples' inherent desire for justice, freedom, and security asserts itself and they have to meet that test. The danger is that if we fail on the first test we may not have a chance to prove the superiority of our system in the second.

And the ultimate question is whether an old, complacent, free Democratic economy can meet these new tests on the heels of a gigantic war effort. Can we again convert our thinking, our politics, and our economy to another all-out effort before we've recovered from the last one? Or are the Soviets right and is another depression in the United States inevitable? With it will the whole fragile house come tumbling down and result in (a) universal chaos, (b) the extinction of capitalism, (c) universal Communism, or (d) war?

Are they also right who reason that Britain must collapse before we become really aroused; that, confronted with assumption of her additional burdens in Germany and elsewhere, the United States will wobble and begin to pull out of Communism's path? Are they right who reason that with another severe depression in this country and the failure of Democracy to solve its economic and social problems, a man on horseback will ride in, millions will follow, just as they have elsewhere, and the United States will go Fascist, with war as the inevitable result? Is it probable that the Russians are far more afraid of us than we are of them?

We have made much progress in the last two years toward the liquidation of the awful legacy of the war, particularly in the development of international machinery. With the [International] Bank [for Reconstruction], the [International Monetary] Fund, the International Trade Organization, the Economic Commission for Europe, and other devices, we are getting ready to attack the economic roots of war. Mass starvation has been avoided and in spots economic recovery is well under way. But the world is still very sick and very receptive to the new ideas moving from East to West, including the idea that the old Western Democratic political and economic institutions are no longer capable of solving the problems of mass civilization. We must face the fact that Asia is in revolt and struggling to rid herself of her European masters at the moment of Europe's greatest weakness. A billion people are demanding a share in the fruits of the twentieth century. We must face the fact that there are only about 600,000,000 people in the world who share or know anything about the Western Democratic tradition, as opposed to 1,600,-000,000 who do not. We must face the fact that Russia is contiguous to a large part of these people and we are very remote. We must face the fact that at the present rate two-thirds of the population of Europe will be Slav in another generation.

And, we dare not overlook that with two world wars, major revolutions, and a shattering economic collapse mitigated only by wholesale departures from the individualist tradition, the concepts of Democracy and individual freedom which we have taken for granted for so long have lost much of their vitality and appeal, even in Western Europe where individualism was born. After the last war Democratic institutions sprang up everywhere. But they didn't last long. When they failed to solve their problems (and we didn't help much) dictatorships took over. And after this war, Democratic institutions didn't even spring up. The new political institutions in Europe more closely resemble collectivism than individualism. The contemporary trend away from individualism and toward totalitarianism is everywhere unmistakable. We cannot rest on our ancient laurels.

It's worth inquiring whether the flow of men and ideas from West to East which began in the Renaissance, the age of discovery, and the Reformation, has been arrested; whether the tide has turned after 500 years and the flow is now from East to West again; whether a new social order is in the making; whether it will be Democratic or totalitarian, or a synthesis resembling current European Socialism.

I think you will conclude that whether and how much of the Democratic tradition survives depends less on ideological sympathies and more on the positive economic and social achievements of the Democracies, particularly in those great areas that are caught between the two magnetic fields, East and West. We know that a full belly is a better defense against totalitarianism than an atomic bomb. We know that you can't stop ideas with soldiers; that in the long run there is only one defense against this creeping disease, and that's healthy flesh. To improve the well being of the masses is today a mission commanding the same kind of moral fervor that formerly went into the task of winning their souls. If that is what Henry Wallace is saying, I agree with him. But the patents on that idea were burned up in revolutions long ago.

That an economic crisis without precedent is developing with appalling rapidity is all too apparent. Germany and Japan, the big producers, are crippled. In the industrial countries production is still 20 per cent to 50 per cent below pre-war. The deficits of food, fuel, and goods have been supplied largely from this country. With our export balance reaching the disastrous figure of more than 8 billion this year, Europe's financial resources and gold reserves are vanishing.

Confronted with the exhaustion of Allied dollar resources during the war, we passed the Lend-Lease Act to defend our idea of the good life. From the day of surrender it has been obvious that the recovery of Europe was the next essential step in that defense, because hunger, want, and insecurity is our real enemy and he has many, many divisions in the field.

How to lick him — how to meet the economic crisis of 1948, for it must surely come with the exhaustion of the British loan, is this country's major foreign policy problem. Obviously our resources are not inexhaustible. We can't provide everything that is needed everywhere at once, if at all. How much we can spare, how to use it, where to use it, when to use it, is going to require bold, fast thinking, in which you gentlemen will have to participate; widespread public education, in which you will have a special responsibility; and a political courage that doesn't generally characterize national campaign years.

To conclude — to head off the collapse of Europe is the first step; to head off the collapse of the United States is the next step. Free enterprise didn't produce very enlightened economic leadership in the 1920's. But there's one more chance. If it succeeds the Democratic tradition will survive and Russia's fears and the present tensions will subside. But it will not succeed and the Democratic tradition will not survive if we unconsciously drift into collectivism to defend individualism — if we embrace Fascist totalitarianism to block Communist totalitarianism.

For the idea that the individual will is the supreme arbiter of human destiny and the individual conscience the ultimate moral censor — the idea that the state exists for the individual rather than the individual for the state — are the most precious ideas America has to defend. They *can't* be defended by mere words, by mere military power, by inaction. And they *won't* be defended by Fascism in any American disguise.

[405]

Stevenson received many comments on his speech "Where Do We Go From Here?" Benjamin V. Cohen, Counselor of the Department of State, wrote, "That was a ripping good speech." Assistant Secretary of State William Benton praised the speech, as did his assistant, Edward Moore. Benton asked Stevenson in his letter of June 20, 1947, whether he could be prevailed upon to return to the Department of State. Secretary of State George C. Marshall by this time had announced that if European nations would plan their recovery in common, they would receive speedy help from the United States.

To William Benton

June 24, 1947

Dear Bill:

Thanks for your flattering comments on that obsolete speech. Your judgment, combined with Ed. Moore's, persuades me that it was better than I thought! After groping around for months in these speeches it is very comforting to have the "Marshall Plan" finally enunciated.

As to the Department, I'll have to profess a persistent interest, but as I told you I don't feel that I should consider taking any permanent employment outside Chicago for the present. As for you, I earnestly hope, and even expect, that your reward is not far distant. More than that, with a growing public understanding of the information program, I think the time will come when your remarkable work there will get the recognition and appreciation it deserves. Then you can think of withdrawing!

Many thanks for your good letter, and let me know when you are hereabouts with a moment to spare.

Sincerely yours,

On June 27, 1947, Stevenson delivered a lecture at the Northwestern University Law School. Only the first part of his speech is reprinted since the remainder was basically the same as he delivered to the Investment Bankers Association.

I am, as you know, appearing here today with the greatest reluctance. I am the victim of shameless treachery by Dean [Leon] Green and his faithless faculty. The arrangement I had was to produce lecturers to present a competent, consecutive story of the structure, operations and objectives of the United Nations throughout the last academic year. It was never contemplated that I would have to give any of this series myself, but when Dr. [Adrian] Pelt, A.S.G., of the Netherlands, was unable to come here on May 6th to conclude the series as scheduled and I proposed to produce a substitute to talk about the Secretariat of the U.N., Dean Green declined and told me I would have to appear!

I waited until he left town and then his faculty, with equal bad faith, imposed this cruel and unusual punishment on me and on you. They may know the law, but in my judgment their view of equity is at least opaque.

I think it just as well that you know something of the character of the gentlemen to whose tender inconstancy you are exposed!

But I am going to have my revenge and the lecture I am going to give is an excellent example of how not to give a lecture. My last formal academic lecture was a classic example of what a lecture should be. It was on the Walgreen Foundation at the University of Chicago, in a very large hall. There were about 20 people there to hear my painfully prepared masterpiece. They said it was due to a sudden and violent storm!

At all events, I'm making no pretense at a lecture today. I'm not even going to talk about the United Nations — which is the only thing I know anything about! I'm going to mention some unrelated things in the international scene which I hope will be of interest. And I hope I don't end up by making a speech, after my usual fashion. Because I don't know what will happen, I am not going to risk the question that the old Texas lawyer asked the Supreme Court on his first and last appearance — "Do you gentlemen prefer the oratorical or the conversational delivery."

You will recall that the last speaker on this series was Prof. Philip C. Jessup, of Columbia. He was thereafter appointed to represent the United States on the Committee on Codification of International Law.

Development of International Law — The first step toward the development of international law under the U.N. was taken when the committee convened for its first session at Lake Success on May 12th. This committee has the formidable title of the Committee on the Progressive Development of International Law and its Codification. It was established by an Assembly resolution of December 15, 1946. Its function is not to discuss the substance of international law, but rather to consider the methods by which development and codification can best take place.

Under the League of Nations a long series of efforts toward the codification of international law was made, culminating in The Hague Conference of 1930. It is generally conceded that the results were disappointing. Many experts believe that this failure was due to shortcomings inherent in the method used, — the so-called "convention" method. A convention is a multilateral treaty negotiated at an international conference and then submitted to the signatory states for ratification. When ratified, it has the force of law as among the states which are parties to it.

At recent meetings, various members of the U.N. Committee on International Law pointed out that conventions may be of great value in developing *new* international law or extending international law into new fields but that conventions are not equally useful when the purpose is to bring together or "codify" *existing* international law. Several delegates, especially Professor J. L. Brierly of the U.K. and Professor Jessup of the United States, took the position that codification was essentially a problem of scientific "restatement," that it should be a project not for government representatives but for individual experts, and should be kept out of politics as much as possible. Dr. Brierly held the statements of existing law which these experts prepared should usually not be submitted to the General Assembly nor be embodied in conventions to be ratified by the states, since to do so would inevitably lead to their considerations as political issues. He argued that such a scientific restatement, even though not officially binding, would have great influence, for example, upon judges responsible for deciding law cases involving points covered in the scientific restatement.

Need I add that the Soviet representative opposed codification by scientific restatement holding that the traditional convention method was the only one acceptable to his government.

During the past two years international organization has been rapidly extended into wider and wider areas — economic, social and political. The frustration of our hopes for prompt political settlements has obscured this remarkable development of the machinery of orderly international living and retarded in its use.

But neither frustrations abroad nor preoccupations at home have retarded the growing curiosity about the new dimensions of our lives. The lively and sustained interest of the organized bar in the United Nations and its agencies is only one example of this anxious concern. Thanks to [the Law?] school, Rosenthal Foundation and to you for your interest and patient attention. And certainly lawyers, as the custodians of the legal tradition and as educated, privileged citizens whose influence is disproportionate to their numbers, have a responsibility to understand this process and these procedures whose success depends on a much broader popular base than governments.

If lawyers do not understand and cannot interpret the activities of a complex of deliberative bodies like the United Nations and its agencies, we cannot expect laymen to. If lawyers, with an understanding of legislative and judicial procedure at the level of single states, do not understand the difficulties of procedure and negotiation at the level of many states, we cannot expect laymen to. If lawyers are impatient and intolerant and ignorant about these first clumsy, faltering, awkward motions of complex, imperfect mechanisms, can we expect the rank and file to stand fast and keep faith? . . .

To Benjamin S. Adamowski

July 3, 1947

Dear Ben:

I do not want to be the last to congratulate you.[195] But I suspect there is a long line over there this morning, so I will content myself with this note until I see you. The Mayor, likewise, has earned emphatic congratulations on this appointment — and he will get mine!

Cordially yours,

To George G. Stoddard [196]

July 15, 1947

Dear Mr. Stoddard:

If none of your ancestors lived in Kentucky you are lucky! Mine did — and I seem to have a limitless supply of "Kentucky cousins" — mostly indigent.

The most recent "cousin" to show up is Miss Martha Hobson, personable appearing middle-aged daughter of a deceased former president of the McCormick Theological Seminary. She is a graduate of Bryn Mawr, has a Ph.D. in English from Northwestern, but, unhappily, she is a recently recovered invalid. I gather that she has emerged at last from a long period of kidney trouble and a series of operations, of which the last was something of a miracle, but a success. She is now fit again, but finds it very difficult to get teaching employment after her long period of inactivity.

Miss Hobson tells me that she thought she might find a position at the Navy Pier, but that her interview was not successful. She mentioned to me a Mr. Livingston Osborn, whom she hoped to see, and she seems to have picked up the idea that appointments there are "somewhat political."

At all events, all I could think of was to write you against the possibility that you could get sympathetic consideration for her at the Navy Pier. Her field seems to be English literature, particularly drama — and I gather that she has some talent for recitation and impersonation which she hopes to capitalize by putting on programs for clubs, etc., once she can get a job, get stabilized and some sense of security.

[195] Chicago Mayor Martin H. Kennelly had appointed Mr. Adamowski to the post of corporation counsel.
[196] President of the University of Illinois.

I have checked her physical condition with her physician, and some of her other statements elsewhere. I believe she has represented the situation accurately and if it were not for her feeling of desperate insecurity she could do useful work again.

Please forgive me for telling you about this case, but you know how you feel after you have talked to one of these unfortunates who is trying to rebuild a crumbled castle. If there is nothing you can do, don't hesitate to tell me so, but if there is the possibility of an opening for her it would be a godsend.

With warm apologies, I am

Sincerely yours,

Louis A. Kohn wrote letters and talked to innumerable people during the spring and summer of 1947 about running Stevenson for U.S. senator. Stevenson asked his old friend Hermon D. Smith to work with Kohn. Stevenson also enlisted the help of lawyer Stephen A. Mitchell, who formerly had been head of the French division of the Lend-Lease Administration and adviser to the Department of State on French economic affairs. It was decided to ask Loring C. Merwin, Stevenson's cousin and publisher of the Daily Pantagraph, *to send letters to downstate Illinois newspaper publishers about Stevenson. Merwin sent the draft of the letter to his cousin on July 17, 1947. He wrote: "For the purpose of this letter, at least, I thought it best not to complicate the matter by suggesting you might run for governor."*

To Loring C. Merwin

July 18, 1947

Dear Bud,

This is a superb letter. My face is very red — which has not deterred me from using my pencil freely — to make the sketch even more colorful! It is now accurate in probably only one respect — and I won't be disappointed if the reaction is quite negative.

. . . With warm thanks for your Intelligence Service!

Yours,

In 1939, Britain imposed restrictions on Jewish migration to Palestine and six years later prohibited immigration altogether. Large-scale illegal immigration continued, however, and occasionally the British intercepted ships carrying immigrants. Stevenson sent the following telegram to the Secretary of State.

To George C. Marshall

July 22, 1947

JUDGE HARRY FISHER AND COLONEL JACOB ARVEY PROMINENT CHI-
CAGO JEWS HAVE ASKED ME TO EXPRESS TO YOU THEIR GRAVE
ANXIETY LEST THE RECENTLY APPREHENDED JEWS BE RETURNED TO
EUROPE AND THEIR HOPE THAT BRITAIN WILL TAKE THEM TO CY-
PRUS. RESPECTFULLY.

*On July 24, 1947, Loring C. Merwin sent Stevenson a copy of the letter
he had just mailed to downstate editors and publishers suggesting
Stevenson for senator.*

To Loring C. Merwin

July 28, 1947

Dear Bud:

. . . The letter to the publishers was perfect — even accurate! I hope
it isn't a mistake and does not embarrass you. Dutch[197] is going away
until after Labor Day, so you might send the answers, if any, to Louis A.
Kohn, 231 South LaSalle Street, to be passed on to Dutch. I will tell
them both what you are doing — and my guess is that the answers will
dampen their ardor, not to mention mine which is already slightly moist.
Many thanks!

Yours,

P.S. I note that there is no letter to Decatur, which I suppose is a
deliberate omission.

*President Truman appointed Stevenson as an alternate delegate to the
second session of the UN General Assembly that convened in New York
on September 16, 1947. Secretary of State George C. Marshall, Warren
R. Austin, Herschel V. Johnson, Mrs. Franklin D. Roosevelt, and John
Foster Dulles were delegates. In addition to Stevenson, the alternate
delegates were Charles Fahy, Willard L. Thorp, Francis B. Sayre, and
Virginia C. Gildersleeve.*

*Senator Arthur Vandenberg wrote Stevenson on July 29, 1947: "I want
you to know — as a matter of record — that when I was asked for rec-*

[197] Hermon D. Smith.

ommendations in connection with the United States Delegation, I put your name down as a 'must.' I wish you were devoting all of your time to our foreign affairs at a high level in the State Department."

Porter McKeever, a staff member to the U.S. delegation, wrote Stevenson on July 28, 1947: "Just a note to tell you how glad all of us are that you are going to be on the General Assembly Delegation." He closed his letter by writing: "All of this should imply a warning to you that I am going to need all the help you will have time to give me during the Assembly."

When the appointment of Stevenson was announced, the Chicago Sun on July 24, 1947, stated: "Illinois can be proud to have contributed Adlai Stevenson to the cause of world organization for peace. And Mr. Stevenson can be proud to have gained a rare experience in constructive statesmanship which will make him one of the state's most valuable citizens."

When Stevenson visited Washington early in September, 1947, Secretary of State George C. Marshall offered him the position of Assistant Secretary of State for Public Affairs. By the time Stevenson wrote the following letters he was in New York City for the meetings of the General Assembly.

To Mrs. Edison Dick[198]

Dear Miss Janie:

Gen. [George C.] Marshall has just invested 1 hr & 20 minutes & Bob Lovett[199] 3 hrs & 20 minutes persuading me to take a certain job that leaves me a little full in the throat. . . .

P.S. After a few hours in the State Dept. I have a distinct impression that life at the General Assembly this time will resemble the third ring of purgatory. And the sun is shining outdoors! Why am I such a fool? Remember to answer that one!

To George C. Marshall

September 15, 1947

My dear Mr. Secretary:

I have thought and thought, or rather worried and worried!, and I have talked to my wife and friends in Chicago. I must decline, not alone with thanks, but with profound regret. As time goes on I may regret it

[198] The envelope is postmarked September 11, 1947. The original of this handwritten letter is in the possession of Mrs. Dick.
[199] Under Secretary of State Robert A. Lovett.

still more but I just don't see how I can move back to Washington on full time now with so many new commitments and so much "unfinished business" in Chicago.

Then too, I haven't quite the stomach for that job that I had a couple of years ago, which is not to say that I don't appreciate its importance. On the contrary, I think the understanding and respect you have for that job is an encouraging augury for the future. Perhaps my ardor for operating jobs has been diminished by intermittent tastes of diplomacy!

In any event I will continue to lecture around the Middle West and content myself with the thought that in a very small measure I am helping with the domestic education program.

I hope you won't write me off all together when other situations turn up where I might be of service because some day my situation may abruptly change. For the present I feel I cannot make such a major readjustment.

Sincerely yours,

To Mrs. Edison Dick[200]

Dear U.W.F.[201] —

It is very late. I've just come into my dark and dreary rooms after a long post facto discussion of Vyshinsky's speech and delegation strategy. I'm weary, my eyes ache & I'm still smarting under that two hours of garbage Vysh. hurled at us this afternoon. All evening I've tried to act & talk calmly, coldly and not lose sight of the *"forest for the* trees" — and now I want to burst loose with a torrent of profanity and abuse — No I don't. I want to go to bed and sleep.

I've even read the enclosure from the Chairman of the UWF of LF, and a very good letter in a noble, if slightly remote, cause it is too. Intelligent girl, I look forward to seeing her. . . .

P.S.S. I've declined the exalted job Marshall (I think he's a great man or almost a great one) thrust upon me. Today he passed a scribbled note of regret, on the back of an envelope, down the table to me. I think I'll keep it a long while.

During the Second General Assembly meetings Stevenson represented the United States in Committee 5 (Administrative and Budgetary) and

---

[200] The envelope is postmarked September 19, 1947. This handwritten letter is in the possession of Mrs. Dick.

[201] Mrs. Dick was chairman of the Lake Forest, Illinois, chapter of the United World Federalists.

in the First (Political) Committee on the question of membership. In addition, he and other members of the U.S. delegation devoted long hours to persuading a majority of the delegations to vote for an Interim Committee. This committee, or "Little Assembly," was to be available for summoning at any time when its parent body was not in session. It was to handle any matter referred to it by the General Assembly, but it had none of the enforcement powers of the Security Council.

Another important decision made by the General Assembly was the partition of Palestine into a Jewish state and an Arab state. Stevenson supported partition, as did the entire U.S. delegation, "a decision I have never regretted," he wrote later.[202]

STATEMENT BY ADLAI E. STEVENSON,
UNITED STATES REPRESENTATIVE IN COMMITTEE 5,
September 25, 1947[203]

I am going to confess — before my colleagues on this Committee discover it themselves — that I have had little previous experience with the work of this Committee. Indeed I must admit that in my long association with the United Nations I have avoided the administrative and budgetary business of the Assembly. My unhappy plight is not eased by the massive documents that confront us, nor by the warm esteem of so many of you for my friend and predecessor on this Committee, Senator [Arthur] Vandenberg. I wish he were in this seat now!

So you may be certain that I am more than sincere when I express my Delegation's gratitude to Mr. [Trygve] Lie and the Advisory Committee for their excellent reports which will guide us in our task.

I particularly wish to express the gratification of my Delegation with the progress made during this past year in strengthening the administration of the Secretariat. The United States Government is familiar with the almost insuperable administrative difficulties faced by the Secretary-General and his associates during the past two years. We wish to acknowledge publicly our appreciation of his efforts and achievements and to pledge our support of those measures which he has under consideration to further improve the efficiency and quality of the Secretariat's work.

Turning to consideration of the 1948 budget estimates, I wish to say again that my previous experience in the General Assembly has been with those Committees which promote, rather than control, expendi-

---

[202] Handwritten letter to Kenneth S. Davis, March 19, 1957, in the possession of Mr. Davis.

[203] The original is in the possession of the United States Mission to the United Nations.

tures. I believe that at least some of us who previously have not been concerned with the financial problems of the United Nations may not have fully realized the importance of the financial integrity of the Organization and the full and wholehearted financial support of every Member. This Committee, in the final analysis, has the heavy responsibility of reconciling and balancing the laudable program desires of the substantive committees of the Assembly and the several councils and commissions on the one hand, and the resources which the Organization has available to finance its varied activities, on the other, a point to which Mr. Lie referred yesterday.

The consideration of the budget for 1948 offers us an opportunity to achieve this end. The budget is the work program of the United Nations expressed in monetary terms. Some increase in the budget estimates for 1948 over this year should not surprise us, since the Secretariat's work load has steadily increased. To the extent that the increased budget reflects an increasing reliance upon the Organization in solving our common problems, the increase is to be welcomed. The United States will oppose, as I am sure all Members will oppose, any attempts to cripple the program of the Organization by denying sufficient funds for the effective conduct of its work.

At the same time the need for economical administration must be constantly present in our minds. Many nations are encountering extreme difficulty in obtaining dollars to pay their contributions. We must, therefore, support efficient practices and administrative expenses to fit the conditions in Member states. The budget must be divested of nonessential expenditures. The Secretary-General's statement to this Committee yesterday was particularly welcome to the United States Delegation because it assures us of the earnest determination in the Administration to observe all possible economies.

This committee is fortunate in having detailed recommendations from the Advisory Committee on savings which can be made without impairing the substantive work of the Organization. We are pleased to note that the Secretary-General feels able to proceed in most cases on the basis of these recommendations and even to report certain additional reductions in the light of his management surveys. The United States Delegation welcomes these proposed reductions by the Advisory Committee and the Secretary-General, which reduce the original budget estimates from $39,400,000 to $34,500,000.

During the course of the Fifth Committee's consideration of the budget we may find that certain additional reductions can be made. For example, the Advisory Committee reports that substantial savings could be effected by changes in the application of the rules of procedure concerning languages, by greater use of summary records in lieu of verbatim reports, and by a reduction in the number of documents printed in the official languages. Yesterday the Secretary-General pointed out that approximately $2,000,000 might be saved in 1948 if the language rules affecting the costs of translating, editing, and printing were modified. In order to take full advantage of these large potential savings, the United States Delegation recommends that a Subcommittee of Committee 5 be appointed to consider the Secretary-General's proposals and to submit definitive recommendations.

The experience of the Fifth Committee last year indicates that supplemental items will arise from decisions taken in other committees of the Assembly. Our Delegations must be diligent in carrying out the rule of procedure which requires that such matters come to Committee 5 for consideration of their effect on the budget before they are acted on by the Assembly. Our discussions of these questions will, of course, be limited to the budgetary implications of these proposals and should avoid reopening the questions of policy already dealt with in other committees of the Assembly.

Mr. Lie told us yesterday that a comprehensive work program has not as yet been developed for the United Nations as a whole or by the various organs. The Assembly might well request the Economic and Social Council, the Trusteeship Council, and the Security Council, to adopt each year, well in advance of the regular session of the General Assembly, a program for the coming year. If each Council could thus forecast its needs in an orderly fashion and with reasonable accuracy, the Secretary-General would be able to present a total program and budget based upon well considered and concrete plans. We should consider carefully the other steps suggested by the Secretary-General, by which better comprehensive programming might be achieved.

Closely allied to the budget is the size of the Working Capital Fund. The United States strongly favors the maintenance of the Working Capital Fund at its present level of $20,000,000 under the safeguards recommended by the Advisory Committee and the Secretariat. At the appropriate time we wish to introduce a slight modification in the draft resolution to authorize expressly the use of the working capital to finance the initial expenses of the Free Territory of Trieste.

The Committee on Contributions has presented its recommendations on the distribution among Members of the expenses of the United Nations for 1948. The United States maintains its conviction, as expressed by Senator Vandenberg in this Committee last year, that under normal conditions no one Member should contribute more than a third of the total administrative budget of the Organization. However, in many countries abnormal economic conditions still persist as a result of the war. Therefore, my Delegation is prepared to recommend to the United States Congress the continued payment, as a temporary measure for one more year, of 39.89% of the total contribution.

Of equal importance to the financial system of the United Nations is the organization and quality of the Secretariat. The Secretary-General has made substantial progress in the development of a highly qualified and truly international Secretariat. Much, however, remains to be done, as Mr. Lie himself indicated yesterday.

The United Nations was established at a time when it was exceedingly difficult to recruit competent personnel. As a result, some of the persons recruited were not well qualified. Under the circumstances this was unavoidable.

The Secretary-General has replaced some of the temporary personnel recruited in this initial period. His decision to go slowly in making permanent appointments is sound. The United States supports the recommendation of the Advisory Committee that the Secretary-General should reexamine the qualifications, background, and experience of every member of the staff, with a view to replacing those who do not fulfill the high standards contemplated by the Charter. In this review the major emphasis should be on the superior ability to perform the job as compared with other available persons. If such a program is to be successful any obstacles to the removal of incompetent persons must be removed, and Member States must cooperate with the Secretary-General to that end.

There is one problem on which I would particularly like to seek the opinion of the Committee. As a resident of the United States, it seems to me that the scale of allowances granted to United Nations employees in addition to their salaries is excessive. Because of its belief that the United Nations must be able to attract first-rate men and women to its services and its recognition of the difficulties of recruitment, the United States, together with other Members has supported generous salaries from the beginning. Likewise, recognizing the special problems facing persons who come from other countries, the United States has supported a number of special allowances designed to compensate for the financial disadvantages of expatriation. These include education allowances, installation allowances, installation grants, home leave expenses, travel and removal costs, daily living allowances for staff entering upon duty, and termination allowances.

During the past year, the Secretary-General has instituted a whole new series of allowances, some of which seem to overlap and duplicate other allowances and to be excessive in the light of the liberal salary scale. These include special expatriation allowances, rental allowances, a cost of living salary increase, life insurance contributions, and proposed increases in the children's and education allowances. The staff also receive additional benefits under the pension scheme, health insurance plan and welfare activities.

In the budget a total of $17,000,000 is requested for salaries, and nearly $7,000,000 more is requested for these other payments to the staff. The United States Delegation believes that the present salary scale, while very generous in comparison with the civil services of the Members, is satisfactory. We are disturbed, however, by the size of the additional compensation hidden in this array of special allowances. I wish to call your attention in this connection particularly to Appendix B of the Advisory Committee's report.

The United States Delegation believes that demands by some of the staff for what it regards as excessive allowances may be due in part to their failure to find adequate satisfaction and incentive in their work. Reductions in allowances and removal of unsuitable employees should be accompanied by greater recognition to the many members of the Secretariat who have given loyal and competent services. More effective supervision, training of employees, and measures aimed at securing teamwork and mutual understanding will all contribute to the esprit de corps as well as efficiency of the staff.

The Secretary-General yesterday called our attention to the necessity for improved coordination of the programs and financial administration of the specialized agencies. My Delegation considers this a problem of first importance, to which the Assembly should devote its most careful attention.

As Senator Vandenberg stated in this Committee last year, the financial aspects of the relationships between the United Nations and the specialized agencies are of over-riding importance to the future of the Organization. We must achieve a comprehensive system of international organization which, while maintaining a desirable decentralization of functions and activities, will at the same time work smoothly, harmoniously, and economically.

Our people, and I suspect yours, are confused by the number and complexity of the specialized agencies. Many feel, with some justification, that the various international organizations are not cooperating very well. The United States Delegation believes it imperative for the United Nations to exercise the leadership and to provide the coordination so clearly anticipated in the Charter.

To this end we hope that the Economic and Social Council will proceed immediately to obtain reports from the specialized agencies on their activities, to review these reports, and to make appropriate recommendations to the agencies and the Assembly. The General Assembly might well request the Economic and Social Council to assign the highest priority to the solution of this question during the coming year.

Budgetary and administrative coordination is the particular responsibility of the Assembly and of this Committee. In this field there is urgent need for closer relationships between the United Nations and the specialized agencies. As provided by the agreements, some of the specialized agencies have submitted their budgets to the Secretary-General for review by the Advisory Committee on Administrative and Budgetary Questions. However, I learn with regret that there was little consultation with the United Nations in the preparation of these budgets. In short, we do not yet have a comprehensive picture of the combined budget requirements of the United Nations and the specialized agencies.

My Delegation urges Members to recognize their own responsibility for implementing General Assembly action in this field. I suggest that we must all be vigilant in instructing our representatives to the specialized agencies to conform to the policies established by the United Nations, both with respect to program coordination and administrative and budgetary affairs. The United States intends to strengthen its own facilities for insuring a consistent approach to these matters by its representatives in the several organizations.

In conclusion, I should like to re-emphasize the intention of the United States Delegation to support the essential activities and programs of the United Nations. Except for the adjustments in the budget which I have mentioned, we see little possibility for further reductions without risking impairment in the services of an organization on which we all alike depend for security and a better future. In the English idiom such economies would be "penny wise and pound foolish."

To Robert A. Lovett

September 27, 1947

Dear Bob:

I have been disturbed by some speculative comment I have seen in the press about my being appointed to that post.[204]

I want you to know that if there has been any leakage — i.e., something more than normal speculation — that I had luncheon on Long Island on Sunday, September 14, at Gardner Cowles' house. Mr. [Bernard] Baruch was there and when he recognized me he talked in quite an uninhibited manner about the importance of my taking this job which

[204] Assistant Secretary of State.

he seemed to know all about. Several people overheard him. I have been embar[r]assed about this gossip because I know the chilling effect of shopping around. . . .

Sincerely yours,

To Robert A. Lovett

September 30, 1947

Dear Bob:

I am sorry to belabor you with another suggestion but I hear that Ed Murrow has quit his executive job with CBS [Columbia Broadcasting System] and started last night broadcasting for Campbell Soup. I should have little doubt that Mr. [William] Paley could get him released from this contract if need be. I also recall, from personal talks with him in the past, that his ultimate objective is education or Government service of some kind. I suspect he has developed some financial independence now and might be available.

He would have many of the qualifications you want and perhaps his ignorance of the [Capitol] Hill would not be wholly disqualifying because he has prestige and excellent personality. At least I felt it was worth while putting his name in your hat — in case you still have an empty hat!

Sincerely yours,

STATEMENT BY ADLAI E. STEVENSON, UNITED STATES REPRESENTATIVE IN COMMITTEE V, *October 9, 1947*[205]

Mr. Chairman:

After the speeches by the delegate of Poland, I find myself a little bewildered about the objectives of this Committee. I had thought that the job of this Committee in connection with the 1948 budget was to review the estimates with a view to fixing the amount of funds required under each section of the budget during the coming year.

However, in the light of some of the proposals of the delegate of Poland, one might conclude that we are also engaged in an effort to determine who the Secretary-General should employ and how he should organize and administer the Secretariat.

I submit, Mr. Chairman, that any move along the lines proposed by our colleague from Poland would represent an invasion by Committee V

[205] The original is in the possession of the United States Mission to the United Nations.

of the field of responsibility established for the Secretary-General by the Charter. He is "the chief administrative officer of the organization." It is his business to run the Secretariat — not ours, as the delegates of France and The Netherlands have pointed out.

What has been proposed by Poland seems to me irrelevant, and its implications are serious enough to warrant close consideration. In the first place, this document — report of the management survey — is before us for our information, *not for action.* The survey was conducted for the Secretary-General for his benefit, *not for this Committee.* I cannot see that the document has any place in our deliberations except to show us how the Secretary-General is able further to reduce his original estimates, i.e., Section 4, which figures are reproduced in Document 154 and 157, and have been before us for some time.

Mr. Aghnides[206] pointed out yesterday that the conduct of the management survey is strictly an internal responsibility of the Secretary-General. The Secretary-General initiated these surveys. They represent a commendable effort on his part to increase the efficiency of the Secretariat. That is what we all want. That these surveys have been of value to the Secretary-General is apparent from the fact that he finds it possible to carry out the work program with an additional reduction of a million dollars. At least, that's sufficient evidence of its value for me. But even if it resulted in no budget cuts, it would be most reassuring to know that the Secretary-General was alert to the possibilities of increasing the efficiency and economy of his large organization.

According to Mr. Lie, the management survey has indicated methods of improving the internal arrangements and procedures of the Secretariat, which will enable it to discharge its work load under this curtailed budget. If the Secretary-General is wrong in his judgment, let us call him to account a year from now when we have had opportunity to see the results. The test of any pudding is in its eating.

I protest that it is not the function of the General Assembly to examine all of the internal arrangements and procedures of the Secretariat and to try to tell the Secretary-General how to do his job. The function of the General Assembly is to tell him what services, projects, and other activities are desired, leaving to the Secretary-General the internal arrangements for providing these services and the selection of staff to perform them.

While the General Assembly should establish general policies governing the Secretariat such as those provided in the staff regulations and the financial regulations, it seems to us highly improper, on administrative as

[206] Thanassis Aghnides, chairman of the Advisory Committee on Administrative and Budgetary Questions.

well as constitutional grounds, for us to interfere in the job of the Secretary-General.

After examining the whole process by which the budget has been prepared, reviewed, revised and submitted to this Committee, I am convinced that the Secretary-General has acted in a diligent and praiseworthy manner.

This Committee should, in our opinion, strongly resist any attempt to embarrass the Secretary-General for his honest effort to effect economies in the budget and to correct administrative imperfections in the Secretariat.

For this Committee to demand the working papers of the Secretary-General — and that is what the management survey reports are — and to presume to suggest how his subordinates should be organized and do their work, would be a gross invasion of the Secretary-General's powers and an open invitation to Members to meddle in the day-to-day management of the Secretariat. It would be equivalent to a vote of no-confidence in the Secretary-General. Such action would undoubtedly dissuade the Secretary-General from making any more efforts to diagnose the defects of the Secretariat for fear of having his confidential files subpoen[a]ed by the Delegations. I feel sure that this Committee has no intention of placing the Secretary-General in such an intolerable position.

Whether or not the management survey has been a good survey is not germane to the work of this Committee. We are, of course, interested in knowing whether the Secretary-General has been diligent in his effort to place the affairs of the Secretariat on an effective and economical basis. The very fact that he ordered a survey is proof of such effort. Whether it is a good, a fair, or a poor job is for him — the responsible executive officer of this organization — to determine, not for us to whom he is responsible.

Therefore, Mr. Chairman, I am emphatically opposed to the demand of Poland that the survey documents be produced before this committee. If we were adopting a resolution on this subject my delegation would propose a resolution commending the Secretary-General for his initiative in taking positive steps, including the conduct of management surveys, to improve the internal organization and operations of the Secretariat and to find ways of carrying on the work of the Secretariat at less cost.

I note also that the delegate of Poland also proposed that the minutes of the Appeals Board be brought before the committee.

The Appeals Board minutes are even more confidential than the management survey documents. They are hearings in which employees appeal from disciplinary action. They are administrative details and so far as I can see have no place in this committee, unless we are going to attempt to run the Secretariat.

Mr. Chairman, I join with the preceding speaker, the Honorable Delegate of The Netherlands, and I will risk the guess that it is the consensus of the committee that we resume an orderly consideration of the budget figures prepared without further diversions.

STATEMENT BY ADLAI E. STEVENSON, UNITED STATES REPRESENTATIVE IN COMMITTEE V, October 14, 1947[207]

I should like to refer to two suggestions which were made here yesterday.

The Delegate of Canada suggested that the Secretary-General might make an annual survey in order to evaluate with more accuracy the effectiveness of the Information Program. My Delegation endorses that idea. We share Senator Lambert's[208] view that this Committee could, in the future, deal more intelligently with the information budget if it were in a better position to evaluate the effectiveness of the information Department's work. I say this without any illusions as to the difficulty of accurately appraising the effect of information work.

I should also like to refer to a remark made yesterday by our colleague, Mr. Roland Lebeau, of Belgium. I believe he said that in the present state of the United Nations, "publicity was more harmful than good." I am not sure I understood him correctly, but if I did I would agree with the reaction of the Delegate of Colombia. It seems to me that public information is important not only in reporting what the United Nations does, what it accomplishes (unhappily all too little thus far), but that even more basic is the worldwide understanding that the United Nations exists, that it *is* at work, that it is struggling patiently to find solutions. How can people believe if they do not know?

Moreover, we feel that the public is entitled to know about our failures as well as our successes. We are dealing with "information" as distinguished from "propaganda." We must report not only the good news but the bad news. I think that there are positive advantages in full information — the bad with the good. An understanding of the reasons for our delays and our failures is by no means only negative. The success of the

---

[207] The original is in the possession of the United States Mission to the United Nations.

[208] Senator the Honourable Norman P. Lambert, member of the Canadian delegation.

United Nations may well depend on public understanding of the reasons for these delays and failures, because ignorance and impatience are our great enemies.

With respect to the budget for the Department of Information, I remind you that in London the Assembly approved and sent to the Secretary-General for his guidance a report which stated that "the activities of the Department of Public Information should be so organized and directed as to promote to the *greatest possible extent* an informed understanding of the work and purposes of the United Nations among the peoples of the world."

I believe we are all agreed that this is a proper objective and that Mr. Cohen[209] and his assistants have sought faithfully to execute the program assigned to them. But I agree with the Delegate of Belgium that there is nothing sacrosanct about this assignment. It can be revised by the Assembly if need be. Yet it seems clear from our debate thus far that our disagreement is not in fact over the objectives of the information program, but rather over its scope, rate of expansion and expenses.

Many have said, and I agree with them, that we should make no further cuts, that public information is vital to the success of our enterprise, that now is the time to spend money on information when things are going badly[,] when there is cynicism, ignorance and impatience in the world; that when things are going well there will be less, rather than more, need for a comprehensive information program.

Others have said that the shortage of dollars, the widespread suffering and want in the world make it imperative that we put substantive things first and save every possible dollar. I agree with them too. And I suppose what we are all saying, in effect, is that people everywhere must have as complete and full information as we can *afford* to give them in this difficult time.

Now surely we can find in this Committee some intelligent, reasonable reconciliation between the anxiety to economize on the one hand, and the anxiety to keep the world fully informed on the other.

Surely if our objectives are identical we can find some intelligent meeting ground between those who insist on cutting the budget another $1,000,000 and those who insist on no more cuts whatever.

Because my Delegation feels that public information is of primary importance to the welfare of the United Nations, and because we also feel that it is highly desirable to reconcile, if possible, the sharply conflicting views that have been here expressed, I hope you will bear with me while I make some comments on the sections of the budget which were discussed yesterday.

[209] Benjamin Cohen of Chile.

In studying the new budget of the Secretary-General I note that a reduction of $935,000 has been made over the original estimates, but only $83,700 has been in staff costs. The reductions in publications, films, and other activities should I believe afford greater reduction in staff required to prepare and distribute these materials.

As to the Headquarters Liaison Services, we think there may be something to Mr. [Kenneth] Younger's criticism of this service, although it has been of very great assistance to us in this country. Certainly it should not undertake work which could be done by the voluntary private agencies. Certainly it should not compete to serve the public. Perhaps it *is* top-heavy and could be contracted, but we should be very unhappy to see it eliminated or crippled, not only because of the many services it renders in this country, but also because its work is becoming more and more useful to national and international organizations in other countries.

In the field of press services, the estimate submitted will provide for the continuance of the program at approximately the present level. The United States Delegation supports that appropriation. We feel that adequate service to newspapers, periodicals, radio commentators (all of which rely on this Division for current information) is the heart of any adequate Information Program. I hope all members of this Committee have had an opportunity to visit the Press Section of the Secretariat and to see for themselves what it is doing and how it is doing it.

The Publications Program has already been drastically reduced both by the Advisory Committee and the Secretary-General. It seems to us it now provides for almost the minimum of materials required for the use of the Organization itself, governments and private organizations and individuals. We are happy to note that substantial economies can be made by changing the frequency of publication and the character of the Bulletin. Perhaps some further economies can be effected by eliminating more of the less essential publications, such as pamphlets and leaflets without disproportionate risk to a vital service, although I confess it seems doubtful.

The program for posters and exhibitions might be reduced. I say this without underestimating the value, particularly in schools, of posters. As the Chinese say, "a picture is worth a thousand characters." But if we have to find further economies it may be that they can be found here with less damage than elsewhere.

The Radio Program will cost some $200,000 more than in 1947. This expenditure is required, I understand, to place the activities initiated in 1947 on a full-year basis. Although the Radio Program is primarily intended for overseas information it may be of interest to you to know that more than 100 radio stations in this country have found these programs sufficiently interesting to their listeners to pay the necessary connection charges to tap the transmission lines carrying these programs from New York to the broadcasting stations on the West Coast for relay to the Orient. Canada and the United States have been furnishing facilities for this radio program to the United Nations without charge; services valued in 1947 at some $300,000. My Delegation believes that this radio information service is one of the most effective information services of the United Nations and well worth its cost. We hope it will not be crippled.

The Motion Pictures Program seems to us desirable, but perhaps less imperative than the other major programs. In 1947 funds have been, or will be obligated, for twelve films. Eleven of these will be produced, I understand, under contract with private or governmental agencies. One of these films is being produced directly by the United Nations. My Delegation doubts the wisdom of such direct production and I am informed that no further production of this character is contemplated.

Of the $320,000 requested for films in 1948, less than $100,000 is requested for new production. The balance is required for the completion and distribution of the 12 films already started under the 1947 program, and for photographing, for historical purposes[,] proceedings of some of the organs and commissions. I suspect we can all agree that it would be shortsighted economy to withhold funds for the completion and distribution of the films in which we have already invested several hundred thousand dollars. Similarly, some funds might usefully be provided at this time for historical record purposes. But it seems to my Delegation that the production of three additional pictures next year could be deferred while the division finishes and distributes the work already in progress.

Now with respect to the Field Offices, or Information and Correspondent Centers, as they are called, which are referred to on page 120 of the Budget Estimates, it seems clear that if properly staffed they can strengthen substantially the Public Information Program by taking it to the people around the world. The location of the Headquarters in the United States places all other countries at a great disadvantage. The world-wide dollar shortage, high cable tolls, shortage of paper, etc., all make the distance factor even more significant than it would normally be. The Information Centers seem to us of first importance because they can assist all agencies of information in overcoming these handicaps. That they should be operated with scrupulous economy and as a supplementary service to local information services and facilities, and not in competition with them, I assume needs no repetition. It may be that one can criticize the distribution of these Centers, it may be that too many have been projected, it may be that it is not necessary to have one in Washington, but that they are of great potential value to public understanding of the United Nations around the world can hardly be denied.

In conclusion let me say again that cooperation through the United Nations for the maintenance of peace and security and for the improvement of the well being of mankind is a relatively new idea in our world, and, as many of you have so wisely said, the peoples of the world have a right to get, and we have an obligation to give the factual and objective information which is indispensable to the achievement of the aims of the United Nations. Ignorance and apathy are eternal obstacles to progress. They fear no weapon but knowledge.

I have not been very specific. But I hope I have made it quite clear that my Government attaches great importance to public information and to the program of this Department which has been doing no more than the General Assembly has instructed it to do. Under normal circumstances the United States Delegation would support the budget requested in its entirety.

But we cannot disregard the views expressed here which either put less emphasis on the priority of this program than we do or which reflect severe, I hope temporary, difficulties. I would hope that we could reach some agreement on a budget which would neither cripple this program, nor give it, in the judgment of any, a too disproportionate share of our total funds.

Picking out, therefore, what seems to us the less imperative aspects of the Department's work I should like to have Mr. Cohen's comments on:

1. The implications of postponing the new motion picture projects at a saving of $75,000 to $100,000.

2. The possibility of referring [deferring?] the poster and exhibition programs and even further reduction in pamphlet publication and the resulting saving, and

3. Whether there are not substantial further savings possible in staff costs as a result of the project reductions already made by the Advisory Committee of Experts and by the Secretary-General and resulting from the additional project reductions I have suggested this morning.

We can see in the foregoing possible total additional savings of from $200,000 to $350,000. But I want to make it abundantly clear that my Delegation does not feel that it can intelligently support these or any other reductions until we have the benefit of the views of Mr. Cohen, the Assistant Secretary-General in charge of the Department of Public Information.

Thank you, Mr. Chairman.

Hermon Dunlap Smith wrote Stevenson on October 6, 1947, that at the suggestion of Louis A. Kohn he had talked to Marshall Field about some stories in the Chicago Sun *about Stevenson for senator. The newspaper that day stated that Senator Scott Lucas could be the Democratic nominee for governor "if he likes. . . . Lucas' hand was seen in Saturday's statement by Adlai Stevenson that if offered the nomination for the U. S. Senate to run against Senator Brooks he would accept. Senator Lucas has made it clear that he prefers Stevenson to Paul A. Douglas of Chicago, whom many regard as the logical candidate to unseat Brooks."*

To Hermon D. Smith[210]

October 16, 1947

Dear Dutch:

I had hoped for a good talk about a variety of things, including a tentative proposal I have received to become Executive Head of the Chicago Board of Trade at an attractive salary. This in the *utmost confidence* and I will speak to you about it again later.

As for the Association of Commerce meeting, I cannot predict with certainty when this ordeal will end but certainly I will not be at large again before the middle of November. If they are really interested in such a meeting I would suggest not earlier than the last week in November.

Yours,

AD

On October 20, 1947, Clark M. Eichelberger, director of the American Association for the United Nations, Inc., wrote that Stevenson had just been elected to the board of the organization.

To Clark M. Eichelberger

October 22, 1947

Dear Clark:

Thank you for your letter. I have for the last year or so made a solemn pledge not to accept membership in anything! I am afraid the same must apply to the American Association for the United Nations. I am much flattered and honored by the election and my only reason for reluctance is that I take so much time out during the year that I really cannot afford any time for extracurricular activities during the period when I am trying

[210] The original is in the possession of Mr. Smith.

to practice law and doing some lecturing. I hope you will understand and if you merely want my name on the Board you are quite welcome but I can be of literally no help.

Faithfully yours,

To Emmett Dedmon[211]

October 16, 1947

Dear Mr. Dedmon:

Here it is — hastily written. But I did find time to read a little of the book.[212] I'm afraid it does not much resemble an orthodox book review and I hope you will take any liberties with it that you please.

There has been and will be so much about what this book says I thought I would explain *why* he wrote this kind of a book, and a couple of the less obvious things it brings out which are of basic importance historically.

Sincerely yours,

"SPEAKING FRANKLY"
By James F. Byrnes[213]

Speaking frankly, "Speaking Frankly" is not historical literature. Rather it is a simple, unadorned, candid, first person report of the quest for peace in the heartbreaking period since the war. And the reporter, Mr. Byrnes, was, himself, Secretary of State and the chief architect of American policy in the fateful two years following Roosevelt's death.

Much will be written about this book; it will be roundly criticized on many counts. But it will be read and reread in every chancellery in the world. It will be read by every thinking American who is confused by the past and anxious about the future. And they won't read it just because Mr. Byrnes' revelations and views are sensationalized in the press. They will read it because people read the news and "Speaking Frankly" is the history of yesterday today. It is almost spot news.

Nor will people everywhere read and quote and criticize and applaud this book just because it was written by James F. Byrnes — Congressman, Senator, Supreme Court Justice, "Assistant President" and Secretary of State, — but because it is the skipper's log of the first phase of the historic journey in which we are all engaged.

[211] Literary editor of the Chicago *Sun*.

[212] James F. Byrnes, *Speaking Frankly* (New York: Harper, 1947).

[213] Chicago *Sun*, October 26, 1947. Mr. Dedmon made a few minor changes in the review. We print the text that Stevenson sent to the paper.

Critics will say that this book does not analyze the forces at work in the post-war world, that it neglects economic factors, that it is superficial, that its style is defective, that it does not cover the United Nations during this interval, that reporting and opinion are mixed up together, etc.

To these criticisms, all of which are fair, I have this to say: Mr. Byrnes had to make an editorial decision at the outset. The material is so voluminous he had to decide whether to write slowly, laboriously a long "think" book worthy of one of the most experienced, shrewd and respected men ever to sacrifice health and fortune to his country, or whether to do a straight reporting job. He chose the latter. He chose to write a short, inexpensive, popular book.

Why? Because Secretary Byrnes believes that "if you are to have a lasting peace, it must be a people's peace. The people can exert their full influence in the conduct of foreign affairs only if they know more about them." So when he became Secretary of State he continued the system of background press conferences instituted by the U. S. Delegation at San Francisco. He broke down by patient pressure the traditional European resistance to public information. After every conference he reported first to the President and then by radio to the people. "Speaking Frankly" is Byrnes' last report to the *people*.

In time much will be said about a great failure and a great triumph of Secretary Byrnes — his *unsuccessful* effort to break the frustrating fear of a revived Germany by a four-power treaty of alliance which Stalin first embraced and Molotov, the villain of the piece, later scuttled, and his *successful* effort to reassure Europe that America would follow through when scepticism was high and hearts were low as our mighty army melted away. "Some of the people who yelled the loudest for me to adopt a firm attitude toward Russia, yelled even louder for the rapid demobilization of the Army."

And still more will be said about the gospel Byrnes never ceased to preach: that the charter of the United Nations itself imposes an *obligation* to take collective measures outside the United Nations if collective action against an aggressor within the United Nations is thwarted by the veto. "They (Russia) must learn what Hitler learned — that the world is not going to permit one nation to veto peace on earth."

But the conclusions, right or wrong, of the man who was there all the way will attract the most attention. "I do not doubt that (Russia's) ultimate goal is to dominate all of Europe." And if you find his opinions too depressing, don't stop. Read to the end. You may feel a little better, and you'll have something beside Russian behavior to think about. You'll have America's!

To Mrs. Edison Dick[214]

J — I'm back where we left off — waiting for dinner at Alicia's [Patterson], and if it isn't announced pretty soon I'll leave!

Its Sat. night — I've just come over here from a tedious day at Lake Success. Tomorrow morning I'm meeting Scott Lucas[215] at Locust Valley for a talk about the Democratic ticket & at this moment I've not the slightest idea what to say. Shall I agree to run for Senator: shall I agree only if he will run for governor, shall I make an effort to get the nomination or continue on the same path of casual indifference — which, unhappily, is the situation? . . .

P.S. Bedell Smith[216] from Moscow and Lew Douglas[217] from London have been here to report to the delegation this week. Its a solemn year — this year of decision & I wish you were spending all your time & energy on the Marshall plan — *so that someday we might have world govt.*

STATEMENT BY ADLAI E. STEVENSON TO THE SECOND REGULAR SESSION OF THE GENERAL ASSEMBLY ON THE U.S. PROPOSAL TO ESTABLISH A CEILING ON CONTRIBUTIONS TO THE UNITED NATIONS, NOVEMBER 3, 1947[218]

Our consideration of Chapter VII of the Provisional Rules of Procedure gives us an opportunity to consider the terms of reference of the Contributions Committee. As I stated during the general debate and again during the consideration of the report by the Committee on Contributions and as Senator Vandenberg, my predecessor, stated emphatically in this Committee last year, it is the conviction of the United States that no one Member should contribute in normal times (I repeat, in *normal* times) more than one-third of the cost of the administrative expenses of the United Nations. My Delegation agreed to a 39.89 per cent assessment for the United States last year and we have accepted the same assessment this year, not because we are willing to surrender the concept of a ceiling but only because we recognize the obvious fact that post-war economic difficulties continue to exist in other countries. Thus, we are

---

[214] The envelope is postmarked October 20, 1947. This handwritten letter is in the possession of Mrs. Dick.

[215] Democratic senator from Illinois.

[216] Walter Bedell Smith, U.S. ambassador to the Soviet Union.

[217] Lewis W. Douglas, U.S. ambassador to Great Britain.

[218] The original is in the possession of the United States Mission to the United Nations.

willing to assume temporarily a higher proportion of the costs of the United Nations than we think any one Member should assume under normal conditions.

Abnormal conditions will not, however, continue indefinitely. Therefore, we are anxious that the General Assembly recognize formally the principle that in normal times a maximum and minimum limit should apply to contributions for administrative expenses.

At present, Rule 43 of the Provisional Rules of Procedure directs the Committee on Contributions to "advise the General Assembly concerning the apportionment . . . of the expenses of the Organization among Members, broadly according to capacity to pay." The Committee has no other specific terms of reference, although the first part of the first session of the General Assembly drew the Committee's attention to considerations which were recommended by the Preparatory Commission. The Preparatory Commission had recommended that the Committee on Contributions be given discretion to consider not only all data which is relevant to capacity to pay, but also "all other pertinent factors."

My Delegation submits that the concept of the sovereign equality of Members is not only a "pertinent factor," but, next to capacity to pay, is the most important "pertinent factor."

In an organization of sovereign equals, in which each Member has an equal vote on program and expenditures, it seems to us inappropriate for any one Member to pay a preponderant share of the cost, and run the risk thereby of exercising a preponderant influence in the organization. Conversely, it is an unhealthy situation for the organization itself to be unduly dependent for financial support on any one Member. The Secretary-General stated last year in this Committee that such a condition would be unhealthy from the standpoint of the Secretariat.

The concept of broad financial support has been recognized by the adoption by the General Assembly, by implication, of a "floor" in the scale of contributions. Eight Members are each assessed .04 per cent although their relative capacities to pay are not all equal. The concept of broad support has not, however, been implemented by clear recognition of the principle of a maximum at the other end of the scale.

In recognition of this principle, the United States Delegation respectfully submits an amendment to the present Rule 43 of the Provisional Rules of Procedure revising the first sentence of Rule 43 to read, "The Committee on Contributions shall advise the General Assembly concerning the apportionment under Article 17, paragraph 2, of the Charter of the expenses of the Organization among Members, broadly according to capacity to pay, *taking into account the principle of sovereign equality of Members, and recognizing that under normal conditions maximum and minimum limits should be established for contributions for administrative expenses."*

This amendment, if adopted, would not determine the ceiling to be established but would permit the Contributions Committee to consider these factors in making its annual report to the General Assembly.

In addition to the reasons already stated, the United States Delegation believes that the proposed broadening of the terms of reference will facilitate the work of the General Assembly. It will ensure that the proposals of the Contributions Committee will be based on all of the factors which should be considered in the framing of a contribution scale rather than on only one of the pertinent factors.

Several delegations have inquired concerning the application of Rule 16 to the U.S. amendment. As this question may be raised by other delegations, I would point out that our proposal merely relates only to the terms of reference of the Contributions Committee and not to the scale of assessment. Further, I might point out that the agenda item under which this amendment is being proposed was placed on the agenda by specific action of the last General Assembly so that Delegations have had at least twelve months notice that the rules were to be considered at this session of the General Assembly. I would reiterate that this proposal does not affect the method of apportionment. It merely has the effect of broadening the factors which the Contributions Committee can consider in its deliberations.

Accordingly, I request your favorable consideration of this amendment to the terms of reference of the Contributions Committee. And I repeat that it fixes *no* ceiling — neither one-third as previously suggested by the United States nor 25% as suggested by Belgium, or any ceiling whatsoever — it merely directs the Committee on Contributions to bear in mind that this is an organization of sovereign equals and to bear in mind that under normal conditions, to preserve that sovereign equality, no member should have a too great or too small financial interest in the United Nations.

STATEMENT BY ADLAI E. STEVENSON IN COMMITTEE 1
OF THE GENERAL ASSEMBLY, NOVEMBER 7, 1947,
ON THE QUESTION OF MEMBERSHIP IN THE UNITED
NATIONS [219]

Mr. Chairman, at the risk of repeating what you already know, I hope the Committee will bear with me while I briefly review the recent history of

[219] Verbatim transcript from the files of the United Nations, New York.

the membership question. It seems to us that some perspective might be helpful and will demonstrate the necessity for action at this session of the General Assembly.

A year ago, Mr. Chairman, in debating the Report of the Security Council on the Admission of New Members, this Committee made clear its deep concern over the Security Council's action. Of eight applicants, only three had survived the Security Council's proceedings so that the Assembly could vote on their admission. Of the five rejected countries, three — Transjordan, Ireland — I beg your pardon, Dr. Evatt[220] — Eire — and Portugal, had been excluded by vetoes of the Soviet Delegate. Each of these three applicants, Mr. Chairman, received nine or ten votes.

In the Security Council the Soviet representative had been somewhat ambiguous, as has been pointed out here, in explaining his veto of Transjordan, but not in explaining his vetoes of the applications of Eire and Portugal. He had stated simply and clearly that they were based on the lack of diplomatic relations between the USSR and these two countries. These vetoes and the grounds given for them were criticized sharply in this Committee. Delegation after delegation stated its belief that these applicants were fully qualified under the Charter and deserved to be admitted. The Assembly adopted a resolution requesting the Security Council to re-examine all five rejected applications on their merits under Article 4 of the Charter.

Now, in these Assembly debates last year, the Soviet delegation came forth with a new reason for the Soviet vetoes of Eire and Portugal in the Security Council. The new reason was a vague and general charge that the conduct of these two countries during the war had not been satisfactory. This Committee rejected by a large majority the efforts of the Soviet delegation to write into the General Assembly resolution its new criterion of behavior during the war as a test of qualification for membership in the United Nations.

The Security Council accepted the General Assembly's recommendation to reexamine the applications. In the Security Council's proceedings, however, the Soviet delegate again vetoed the admission of Portugal, Eire and Transjordan, which were each supported by nine or ten members. The only difference was that his previous statements were somewhat amplified. As before, the Soviet representative in the Membership Committee of the Security Council, and in the Security Council itself, gave as one ground the lack of diplomatic relations with the Soviet Union. But, it was this time explained that diplomatic relations with the Soviet Union have some special significance in determining the qualifica-

220 Herbert V. Evatt, chairman of the Australian delegation to the General Assembly.

tions of a state for membership in the United Nations under Article 4 of the Charter. The reasons, however, for this special significance were not made clear.

The argument that Eire and Portugal had behaved badly during the war — an argument which this Committee of the Assembly had expressly rejected — was used as an additional ground for Soviet opposition in the Security Council. But, Transjordan, Eire and Portugal were, unfortunately, not the only states which were excluded by the Soviet Union vetoes in August of this year. Recommendations that Italy and Austria be admitted to membership at such time and under such conditions as the General Assembly might deem appropriate were defeated — Italy by a vote of nine in favor to one against; Austria by a vote of eight in favor to two against — the Soviet Union in each case vetoing the recommendations.

Now, in September of this year, after ratification of the peace treaties, Finland presented its application; the United States proposed reconsideration by the Security Council of Italy's application, and Poland, as Dr. Lange has said, proposed the admission of all five of the treaty states. Poland and the Soviet Union then called for a decision on these states *en bloc*, without consideration on their individual merits. The Soviet representative declared that he would vote for all five but would not permit the admission of any one state unless all five of the treaty states were admitted, a proposal which was characterized at the time as a horse trade.

When other members of the Council opposed Hungary and Bulgaria, the Soviet Delegate vetoed the applications of Italy and Finland, which each received nine votes. Mr. Chairman, of all the wrongful vetoes of membership applications, these seem to my delegation the most indefensible. Having clearly admitted that these two States meet the qualifications set forth in Article 4, the Soviet representative vetoed two admittedly qualified states because the other members of the Security Council did not deem the other three states, Rumania, Hungary and Bulgaria, qualified under the Charter.[221]

Now this, gentlemen, is the record of the consideration and the reconsideration of the applications of Italy, Eire, Portugal and Transjordan, and I submit that it is a melancholy record. My delegation believes that in the light of Article 4 of the Charter the continued exclusion of these states by the abuse of the veto cannot be defended. My Government is

[221] The deadlock on this issue between the Soviet Union and the United States was broken in December, 1955, in a "package deal." Sixteen states were admitted to membership: Albania, Bulgaria, Hungary, Rumania, Austria, Eire, Finland, Italy, Portugal, Spain, Jordan, Libya, Cambodia, Ceylon, Laos, and Nepal.

concerned, moreover, with the unfair and inequitable treatment of Austria, which was not an enemy state but a victim of aggression.

Finally, the exclusion of Finland by the use of the veto is in our judgment as unjustifiable as that of Italy. I shall set forth our views on these states in detail at a later stage in the debate. I shall also set forth our views as to the other rejected applicant states which we do not consider qualified for membership.

The problem before us now, however, arises from the unhappy fact that states have been excluded from the United Nations because the provisions of the Charter have not been applied by one member of the Security Council. Admittedly qualified states have been excluded for no sufficient reason. Other states have been excluded because they did not have diplomatic relations with the Soviet Union, or because it did not admire their behavior during the war.

The question as to what action the Assembly shall take in order to secure, if possible, the fulfillment of the Charter's terms is, of course, a serious one. My delegation does not doubt that some action by the Assembly is required. Although the United States delegation would be glad at any time to meet with the permanent members of the Security Council, as Dr. [Oscar] Lange of Poland has suggested, but we do not believe that such a meeting should affect in any way the General Assembly's consideration of a matter which vitally affects the whole of the United Nations, and not just the five great powers. Nor do we believe that any such consultation between the five permanent members should be limited to a consideration only of the applications of the five treaty states. We believe that it should consider at any such consultation not only the five, but all of the eleven applicant states.

So the question remains, what action in accordance with the Charter and what action we can take that is likely to be effective. In the various draft resolutions before the Committee, several alternative courses are in effect proposed, perhaps three. At the moment, I shall indicate only briefly the views of my delegation concerning them.

The first course is that proposed in the resolutions presented by the delegate of Argentina. These resolutions aim to solve the problem at one blow by admitting Transjordan, Eire, Portugal, Italy, Austria and Finland forthwith. I have already said enough to make it clear that my delegation warmly supports the admission of these states. However, these resolutions proposed by Argentina appear to us to involve formidable Charter difficulties. While we will give the most careful consideration to the closely reasoned opinion Dr. [José] Arce has presented, it seems to us that the history of Article 4, as Dr. Lange has pointed out, seems to us clearly to support the view that the General Assembly cannot admit an applicant without a recommendation in favor of admission from the Security Council. The General Assembly need not accept that recommendation, but it cannot admit a state without it.

This view, in our opinion, is strongly supported by the legislative history of Article 4, despite the very scholarly legal opinion for which we are indebted to Dr. Arce. Moreover, the practical construction given to this Article by the General Assembly and the Security Council in the adoption of their rules of procedure, and in their action concerning membership applications heretofore, is uniformly in support of the same view, that action by the General Assembly must be based on a positive recommendation from the Security Council.

The second course is that proposed by the Swedish resolution. That resolution declares the doctrine of universality, and recommends that the Security Council reconsider the applications of all the rejected states, regardless of whether or not these states are believed by the Assembly to meet the qualifications set forth in the Charter. I believe that the views of my Government on the so-called doctrine of universality are well known. We earnestly hope that some day all states will become members of the United Nations. We have made earnest efforts to achieve this in as large measure as possible. Universality is our ultimate aim, and I am sure the aim of a great majority of the other members of the United Nations.

But, since we act under the Charter, this universality must be the universality of qualified members, not blind universality regardless of the Charter. We look forward to the time when all states will qualify for admission under the Charter, when all states will be peace-loving, will accept the obligations of the Charter, and will, in the judgment of the Organization, be willing and able to carry out these obligations. This does not, however, enable us to evade the question presented by each application as to whether the applicant may fairly be said to fulfill the conditions set forth in Article 4.

Now, a third course is that proposed by the joint Argentine-Brazilian and Chilean resolution, and in a measure by the Australian resolutions. The United States delegation agrees with the substance of the joint Argentine-Brazilian-Chilean resolution as far as it goes. We feel, however, that it is not entirely complete. It does not provide any method for its implementation. It would be acceptable to us if it contained a clause requesting the Security Council to reconsider these applications in the light of the Assembly's declaration. The resolutions submitted by Australia contain this needed implementing clause. They have another advantage in that there is a separate resolution covering each qualified applicant. This is proper, as we should maintain the principle that each application should be considered on its individual merits.

The United States Delegation, therefore, gives its full support to the resolutions submitted today by the Australian delegation. In so doing, we believe we do not deviate in any way from the principles expressed in the Argentine-Brazilian-Chilean resolution. We note, however, that the Australian delegation has not submitted a resolution on Austria. We believe that, after considering the Austrian application, this Committee will wish to adopt a similar resolution respecting Austria.

In the Security Council reconsideration of the various applications, the United States will not presume to act as the sole judge of a state's qualifications. We will not obstruct a majority decision as to a state's qualifications. Accordingly, we are prepared to say to the delegate of Canada, that we welcome his suggestion that the great powers refrain from the use of their veto power in connection with applications approved by the Assembly. We accept his suggestion. The United States will not exercise its right of veto in the Security Council to exclude from the United Nations any of the present applicants which the Assembly determines are qualified for membership. The United States will go even further, and will accept the elimination of the veto in the Security Council in connection with applications for membership entirely.

In this Committee and in the Assembly, however, the United States will vote against the applications of states which it considers disqualified for membership.

Now, to summarize, Mr. Chairman, in the view of my delegation, a fresh approach to the problem of the rejected applications is necessary. That fresh approach can be made only in the Assembly. It is, therefore, our view that the Assembly should now take unequivocal action to state what applicants it deems to be qualified, and to recommend to the Security Council the reconsideration of those applicants, in accordance with the Australian resolutions relating to Italy, Eire, Portugal, Transjordan, and Finland.

Thank you, Sir.

On November 6, 1947, Hermon Dunlap Smith wrote Stevenson that in a talk with Milburn (Pete) Akers, editor of the Chicago Sun, Akers stated that Stevenson could get the nomination for governor and "wondered if this would not make sense. . . . The strongest team would be Douglas versus Brooks, and Stevenson versus Green." Akers remarked that a number of Democrats were afraid of having Paul H. Douglas as governor in Springfield. (He had fought the Democratic machine while he was in the City Council, from 1939 to 1942.)

To Hermon D. Smith[222]

November 13, 1947

Dear Dutch:

Thanks for your letter reporting your talk with Pete Akers. I am sorry to hear he has gone to Japan as I hoped to counsel with him when I returned. As I think I told you, he has suggested several times during the last six months that I not make myself unavailable for Governor. But I have never felt that it was my "dish" and still don't. However, perhaps I should not be too emphatic and I won't for the present.

I am coming out with General [George C.] Marshall and hope for a glimpse of you either before or after the meeting. I am glad you are going to give them a hand with it as it is a great effort for him, what with Congress reconvening on the 17th and his departure for London scheduled for the 20th. Also he plans to make it a "major" speech.

If anything develops on the Association of Commerce speech, I hope you will let me know in ample time. I am afraid Marshall will steal most of my thunder, but if they want me to speak I could talk with less inhibition about the Russian-American situation and so on. I think I will be back for keeps a little before the end of the month. . . .

Yours,

Ad

On November 1, 1947, Adlai T. Schuhnaier, dean of education at Vermont Junior College, wrote that he had been named for Stevenson's grandfather and inquired how the Stevensons pronounced "Adlai."

To Adlai T. Schuhnaier

November 14, 1947

Dear Dean Schuhnaier:

I was so glad to have your letter and to find another "Adlai." We are very few and aside from a first cousin and my own son, I know of only a few others.

We have always pronounced the name in my family as though it were spelled "Adlay," although in my grandfather's day many people pronounced it "Adlii."

I shall be interested in knowing what pronunciation developed in your family.

Sincerely yours,

[222] The original is in the possession of Mr. Smith.

STATEMENT BY ADLAI E. STEVENSON BEFORE THE 118TH PLENARY MEETING OF THE GENERAL ASSEMBLY, NOVEMBER 17, 1947, ON THE QUESTION OF MEMBERSHIP IN THE UNITED NATIONS [223]

I will not detain you long. This will just be a speech, but [not] a "pretty" one, like the woman —: mentioned by Mr. [José] Arce.

It has been asserted again that the unwillingness of the United States to agree to the admission of Albania, and the other treaty states, Bulgaria, Hungary and Roumania, results only from political motives, from our distaste for internal developments in those countries. We have made it quite clear in our statements on every pertinent occasion that we do not oppose the application of any country because of our distaste for its political regime, or our disagreement with its political philosophy.

The Charter requires the organization to exercise its judgment as to whether each applicant is able and willing to carry out the obligations contained in the Charter. In the cases of these applicants, Albania, Outer Mongolia, Bulgaria, Roumania and Hungary, we have raised objections which pertain clearly and directly to the obligations contained in the Charter. As representatives are well aware, a succession of international agreements has governed the relationships of the Allied and associated Powers most immediately concerned and the Governments of Bulgaria, Roumania and Hungary during this period of transition towards normal peaceful conditions in which those countries would be restored to membership in the community of nations.

As at this time, peace treaties are in force, peace treaties which specify clearly and explicitly that human rights shall be guaranteed in these countries, we have repeatedly stated — and I do so again — that specific acts of the regimes in Hungary, Rumania and Bulgaria have violated these treaty provisions.

These peace treaties are not of minor importance in the relations of the ex-enemy countries with other States, but are, on the contrary, basic to the relations of the ex-enemy States with a large portion of the international community. They are solemn international covenants. Important violations of their provisions are not mere matters of domestic concern. On the contrary, such violations necessarily cast serious doubt on the willingness of the violator to respect any international agreement.

I shall not weary the General Assembly with a long history of the

[223] Verbatim record, United Nations official records of the Second Session of the General Assembly: Plenary Meetings of the General Assembly, Vol. II, pp. 1074–1077.

details of these violations. In the First Committee I gave a summary of concrete steps which have been taken by the present regime in Roumania to stifle every kind of political or ideological freedom of expression. It is said that these steps, in Roumania and elsewhere, are nothing but the punishment by the people of fascists, traitors, quislings and "Benedict Arnolds."

This is just what has been suggested in all these cases, in all these countries, but it cannot escape notice that these so-called quislings, traitors and fascists have included the leaders of every important political party opposed to the minority groups that these parties include, in the case of each one of these countries, large democratic parties of long standing, which have been recognized as democratic and entitled to take part in the reconstruction of their countries; and that these alleged fascists have included men with longer, and more consistent, and more notable records of opposition to fascism than those of many other members of the Governments that have condemned them.

I do not need to give names. In short, these charges of fascism have been used as a cloak for a complete and ruthless extermination of all political or ideological opposition and dissent. We regret, therefore, that we cannot support these applications for membership, but I must emphasize again that the responsibility lies with the Governments themselves. We would welcome any change which would enable the United States to support these countries in their applications for membership.

We have heard a great deal, during the afternoon and evening, about Albania's qualifications. The United States respects the resistance of many Albanians as much as Mr. Vyshinsky does, but, without going into the Corfu incidents or any other questions regarding Albania's qualifications under Article 4, let me only say that, in the opinion of my delegation, Albania cannot qualify for membership now in view of the finding of the Commission of Investigation concerning Greek Frontier Incidents, concurred in by a majority of the Security Council, that Albania has extended assistance to the guerillas operating against Greece.

In these circumstances, we think that our refusal to consider Albania as a peace-loving State, qualified for admission, requires no further explanation and no apology.

We have heard a great deal, both here and in the First Committee, with regard to fascism. We should probably have as much trouble reaching a common definition of fascism as we evidently have in defining "peace-loving." To us the two worst features of fascism are, first, its totalitarianism or non-recognition of human or spiritual values outside the State, except as they may be conferred or allowed by the State; and secondly, its aggressive intentions towards its neighbors.

These features of fascism do not characterize Portugal, which in this discussion has been labelled as fascist with considerable warmth. Although the Portug[u]ese Government is authoritarian in form, it is no more objectionable in this respect than some of the Charter Members of the United Nations.

This afternoon Mr. Vyshinsky, in attacking the eligibility of Ireland as well as Portugal, gave us a new definition of "peace-loving." He said — and I hope I am quoting him exactly — that a "peace-loving" State is a State which fought fascism or assisted in that struggle. One could speculate over the position of the USSR itself under this definition, if it had not been attacked by Nazi Germany.

More interesting, however, is how this definition squares with Mr. Vyshinsky's enthusiastic support of ex-enemies that fought for fascism, not against it. Evidently Mr. Vyshinsky prefers a reformed enemy to a consistent neutral. Let me remind him that Portugal, which he attacked so vigorously, qualifies even under his definition of "peace-loving," because the air bases in the Azores were of great assistance to the Allied and associated Powers during the war. They helped thousands of my countrymen, including myself, to cross the Atlantic.

I shall not impose on the representatives a recital of the reasons why we have supported the admission of Italy, Finland, Austria, Ireland and Transjordan. As to the last, however, I must confess to getting more amusement than enlightenment from the vigorous assault on Transjordan's independence by the representative of the Ukrainian Soviet Socialist Republic.

We earnestly support the resolutions before the General Assembly which recommend a reconsideration of the application of Ireland, Portugal, Transjordan, Italy, Finland and Austria. We have supported these applications at every stage; we are convinced that all of these countries deserve to be admitted. It is our earnest hope that the adoption of these resolutions by the General Assembly will hasten the process of admission.

Let me conclude by saying again that the United States delegation will gladly consult with the other permanent members of the Security Council, in accordance with the Polish resolution which was adopted by the First Committee. I must say that Mr. Vyshinsky's attitude this afternoon does not give us much encouragement that such consultation will be productive.

Finally, I should like to repeat that the United States will not exercise its right of veto in the Security Council to exclude from the United Nations any of the present applicants which the General Assembly deems qualified for membership, and we would go further and would be willing to accept the complete elimination of the veto in the Security Council in connexion with applications for membership in the future.

Let me say again that, if there really is a sincere desire on the part of the other permanent members for consultation, with regard to membership, I submit that consultation with a view to an agreement among the permanent members to waive their right of veto on membership applications, would be most welcome to my Government, since the successful outcome of such a discussion and such an agreement would lead to a solution of this vexing membership problem, to the great good of the United Nations now and forever.

Sarah Bond Hanley of Springfield, long associated with Democratic politics in downstate Illinois, wrote Stevenson on November 8, 1947, that personally she hoped he would run for governor rather than senator "but I fear I shall not be consulted." Mrs. Hanley was then eighty-two years old.

To Sarah Bond Hanley

November 17, 1947

Dear Mrs. Hanley:

Once more I must thank you for the clipping and your good letter. I have been out of touch with things for so long that I hardly know what is going on, but I expect to be back in Chicago soon and I suppose I will have to deal with this problem finally before long.

Your many expressions of interest and enthusiasm are a comfort and even if the politicians do not consult you any more, I will!

Sincerely yours,

On November 18, 1947, Stevenson flew to Chicago with Secretary of State George C. Marshall. Many years later, Stevenson stated in an interview that at the 1947 meeting of the U.N. General Assembly he talked many times with Marshall about the issues he was handling for the delegation: "I always found General Marshall not only extremely attentive and extremely interested, but as precise and accurate about those matters which one wouldn't have thought were within his area of interest or particular competence. . . . His precision had impressed me during the war."

On the flight to Chicago, Stevenson and Marshall discussed politics and the rumors that the General might be the Democratic candidate for

President in 1948. "I told him," Stevenson recalled, "that while at that time I had never been in politics, I was fascinated about it and extremely interested, of course. I had never been in 'combat' politics. He unburdened himself in a most interesting way. He in the first place dismissed, as precisely and as finally and as conclusively and as briefly as one could possibly do it, any possibility of himself being considered. . . . And then we got on the subject of General Eisenhower and he explained . . . how he had counseled him to forsake any interest in politics or political preferment as inconsistent with the career of a professional soldier." [224]

Stevenson introduced General Marshall to the Chicago Council on Foreign Relations that evening.

Mr. Chairman:

Thank you, Mr. Chairman, for the privilege of introducing Secretary Marshall to my fellow townsmen. And let me, on their behalf, thank you Mr. Secretary, for coming to Chicago tonight, on the very point of your departure for London and the fateful meeting of the Council of Foreign Ministers.

But my task is an awkward one, Ladies and Gentlemen, because Secretary Marshall is not easy to introduce. I know from personal experience how much he dislikes unnecessary words, and that he dislikes encomiums even more. I'm tempted to let loose, for tonight I am not his delegate to the United Nations. He's our prisoner and I could take my revenge. But I'm going to be merciful.

I know why you are here. I know you've diverted these precious hours to come to Chicago, because your voice, your views in the Council of Foreign Ministers, in the United Nations, in all your myriad negotiations, even in the Congress, are no stronger than the voice and the views of the American people — a circumstance that makes your task no easier at this critical moment, and in competition with the representatives of a state and a system that need not listen to the voices and the views of its people.

I hear it said that too few of us appreciate the difficulties and the gravity of the situation that has arisen in barely two years of peace. On the one hand, the precarious balance in Europe can be preserved no longer without prompt and extreme exertions by the United States. On the other hand, the Government of the United States, already politically divided between a Democratic administration and a Republican Con-

[224] Interview conducted by Forrest C. Pogue, biographer of General Marshall, April 30, 1958. A recording of the interview is in the George C. Marshall Research Library, Arlington, Virginia.

gress, is now confronted with a Presidential campaign when political advantage and national interest may get confused.

Never before has our political system been subjected to such a severe test in the face of issues so formidable and risks of failure so great!

After the victory which was so largely your victory, at the pinnacle of a soldier's career with the thanks of the world ringing in your ears, you asked for the retirement and the rest you deserved.

But there is no rest for you yet. Your war is won. Your peace is not. Your problems are distracting; your responsibility appalling. But you will carry on. And you will prevail, because in peace as in war the people will not fail. They will understand the prize and its price. For many things are revealed to the humble which are denied to the great.

Ladies and Gentlemen: The Chief of Staff in the years of our greatest national effort; the Secretary of State in our year of decision — George C. Marshall!

To Olive Remington Goldman[225]

November 20, 1947

Dear Olive:

I went to Chicago on Tuesday with Secretary Marshall to introduce him and find your letter on my desk on my return to New York this morning. . . .

From what I gathered in my brief hours in Chicago, the ticket seems to be [Paul H.] Douglas–Meyer,[226] but my friends still continue to agitate and I have not called them off for the reason that it might be desirable for that group to develop some influence in the party councils for a later time.

They have urged me to make a few speeches in December after I return and I will do so, but I declined the invitation from the Ladies Garment Workers Union for the present because it seemed like a specialized group and, I must confess, I feel so tired that I did not relish the prospect of any more speeches for a while. If you think it desirable to cook up something around Champagne [Champaign]-Urbana, I will try to cooperate. The man to get in touch with is Louis A. Kohn, 231 South LaSalle Street.

Forgive this hasty note — I am overdue at Flushing already.

Sincerely yours,

225 Lecturer, teacher at the University of Illinois, and clubwoman active in many groups including the Chicago Committee to Defend America by Aiding the Allies and the Committee for the Senate's Win the Peace Now Resolution; unsuccessful Democratic candidate for Congress in 1946 and again in 1948.
226 Karl Meyer, head of Cook County Hospital.

P.S. When I say the ticket seems to be Douglas–Meyer, I do not mean to imply that I have anything from the "horse's mouth," but just a feel of the way things are going. And I cannot feel too disappointed.

STATEMENT BY ADLAI E. STEVENSON BEFORE THE 121ST PLENARY MEETING TO THE GENERAL ASSEMBLY, IN SUPPORT OF THE BUDGET RECOMMENDED BY COMMITTEE 5, NOVEMBER 20, 1947[227]

This item on our agenda represents the end of a very long and arduous journey by the Fifth Committee, and I should like, on behalf of the United States delegation, to express our full support of the budget which the Rapporteur of the Fifth Committee has just presented to us.

This budget has been exhaustively examined and reduced during the past nine weeks in the Fifth Committee. Never before, I venture to say, has so small a budget been reviewed so much by so many. It seems to my delegation, therefore, that we can vote the budget as a whole without further detailed discussion of individual items.

I know that other delegations will join with the delegation of the United States in commending the Secretary-General for his initiative and his continuous cooperation with the General Assembly in arriving at the final figure in this budget. The Secretary-General originally submitted figures estimating a grand aggregate of almost $39,000,000. The Advisory Committee on Administrative and Budgetary Questions, in the course of its extended hearings, reviewed each provision in the budget and recommended a reduction of over $4,000,000. Based upon these proposals, and upon further studies which were also initiated by the Secretary-General, he recommended at the beginning of the General Assembly a further reduction of nearly $1,000,000 over that proposed by the Advisory Committee.

Those of us who are familiar with budgetary practice in national legislatures appreciate that this was indeed a forthright and courageous act on the part of the Secretary-General. During the deliberations in the Fifth Committee the Secretary-General volunteered to make further adjustments, in view of the expressed desire of representatives to accomplish every possible economy. But he rightly defended, in our estimation, his estimates when he felt that any additional reduction would impair the effective operations of the United Nations.

As a result of this process of objective review and appraisal of the

[227] Verbatim record, United Nations official records of the Second Session of the General Assembly: Plenary Meetings of the General Assembly, Vol. II, pp. 1196–1198.

financial requirements, the budget has been kept below $35,000,000, even though more than $2,200,000 has been required for new programs adopted at this session of the General Assembly. If we add to the original estimates of the Secretary-General the subsequent estimates of the Secretariat to carry out the new programmes adopted at this session, we find that the total savings effected by the General Assembly are $7,000,000, which is an impressive accomplishment, the Members will agree. To keep the budget at this level, it has been necessary to reduce the meetings of commissions, committees, and of a number of special conferences, and to curtail projects and activities in which many Members have a great interest.

None of us, I suppose, is entirely happy about the outcome. Yet I believe we all agree that the spirit of compromise and the desire to find the best common ground, which have been demonstrated by the Secretary-General and his assistants and the Members of the Fifth Committee, have produced a sound budget, viewed in its entirety. While we believe that the budget, in the aggregate, is a very tight one, it does provide essential flexibility by authorizing the Secretary-General, with the concurrence of the Advisory Committee, to make transfers between sections of the budget and to use the Working Capital Fund, under safe restrictions, in meeting unforeseen and extraordinary expenses.

In some cases the funds voted in the budget may not be entirely adequate for the approved programme. In other cases the Secretary-General may find that he can effect economies which will produce a surplus. It is the hope of my delegation that the Secretary-General will be able, through continued improvement in the management of conferences and in the administrative work of the Secretariat, to absorb all unforeseen and extraordinary expenses within the total appropriations voted here, except perhaps those of a very exceptional character.

The Secretary-General was able during the current year, 1947, to meet through prudent management most of the unforeseen and extraordinary expenses out of his regular budget. We congratulate him for this accomplishment, and we look forward to and hope eagerly for his equal success during the ensuing year of 1948.

In conclusion, I should also like to express the warm appreciation of my delegation to the Advisory Committee on Administrative and Budgetary Questions for its assistance to the General Assembly during the current session. The chairman of this Committee, Mr. [Thanassis] Aghnides, and the members of this Committee have been of great help in finding effective and economical ways of handling the financial and administrative affairs of the United Nations; and they have also, I know, been a source of encouragement and support to the Secretary-General in his efforts to strengthen the Organization and management of the Secretariat.

Finally, let me suggest once more, in view of the very thorough scrutiny that this budget has already received, that it be adopted by the General Assembly as a whole.

On November 19, 1947, Secretary George C. Marshall wrote Stevenson: "I want you to know that I appreciate very much the excellence of the extensive arrangements that were made for the gathering last night." Marshall closed: "With my regards, and thanks also for the splendid work you have been doing in the United Nations General Assembly."

To George C. Marshall

November 24, 1947

Dear Mr. Secretary:

That you found time in your last moments to write me about the Chicago trip will make me value your letter the more. I know what an effort the journey and the preparation of that splendid speech took, and I hope it is some comfort to you to know that, quite aside from the national effect, the local impact was even more reassuring than I had foreseen. The very fact that you went to all that trouble has impressed many, many people in that area with the seriousness of the situation, and I am still hearing the repercussions.

Let me also thank you once more for the privilege of serving again on our delegation at the Assembly. My work is finished and I will be returning to Chicago tomorrow. And I will take with me an enduring memory of my association with you.

I know you will not hesitate to call on me if you think I can ever be of any service. If I can do it I will. If I can't, you will understand. I will be very discreet. And I suspect the time is not far distant when home and family will be moveable!

With warm thanks and loyal good wishes, I am

Faithfully yours,

To Mrs. Edison Dick[228]

J — Guess where I am. Right! Its 12:45, I leave for Chicago at 4:30, but I'm still "in the lines" at Lake Success listening to the Palestine debate.

[228] The envelope is postmarked November 25, 1947. This handwritten letter is in the possession of Mrs. Dick.

There was some hope that we would get to a vote this morning — a vote which may have much to do with the future of this organization — but we're still on amendments to the Sub-Com. report & at the moment they've [they're] all tangled up on the administration of the international city of Jerusalem. What sorrow, what eternal trouble that center and source of much of the world's culture has seen! . . .

First, my thanks for the first intelligent criticism I've had for a long while of that speech in Committee! You are right, dear Jane, it did have too much of sarcasm. Its a constant temptation & the provocation was great, but all the same I should have resisted. It doesn't help. There is a gentle way to be humorous — its the way you do it, the tone of voice etc. but I'm afraid this at the time & in the circumstances had no saving grace. . . .

I'm glad Ellen [Stevenson] seemed well — somehow she flourishes when I'm away. I must be a very exhausting husband.

I must go to the corridor for "conference." You write extraordinarily well. You think straight and say coherently what you think. . . .

Part Five

Election as Governor of Illinois
1948

When Adlai E. Stevenson returned to Chicago from the meeting of the General Assembly of the United Nations, Louis A. Kohn, Stephen A. Mitchell and Hermon Dunlap Smith intensified their efforts to gain Stevenson the Democratic organization's backing to run for the Senate. Stevenson, as well, consulted many people including Jacob M. Arvey, leader of the Cook County Democratic party.

After Christmas, Arvey told Smith and Stevenson that the Democratic organization would back Professor Paul H. Douglas for the Senate and Stevenson for the governorship. Stevenson pointed out that his experience was almost wholly with the federal government and foreign policy. Moreover, he observed, Douglas wanted to run for governor. Arvey explained that Douglas's record as a Marine wounded in the Pacific theater of the war and his spellbinding oratory made him a match for the World War I record of Senator C. Wayland Brooks. Another reason for the selection of Douglas was likely that the Democratic organization did not believe it could work with him on patronage. Between 1939 and 1943, as an independent New Deal alderman in Chicago's City Council, Douglas had been an able foe of the Kelly-Nash machine. Time noted on January 12, 1948, that every patronage Democrat "would have howled rebellion" if Douglas ran for governor.

When Stevenson asked Arvey if he would be free on patronage appointments, Arvey replied that he would not make recommendations on major appointments. On minor appointments, "we would hope that you would appoint Democrats if qualified. It would be your free choice." [1]

[1] Kenneth S. Davis, A Prophet in His Own Country: The Triumphs and Defeats of Adlai E. Stevenson (New York: Doubleday, 1957), p. 289. Davis interviewed Stevenson and Stevenson read the manuscript of Davis's book. Noel F. Busch wrote that Chicago's seasoned politicians figured if Stevenson "by any amazing chance . . . were to get elected, he could immediately be taught to play ball and that, if he proved inept, he could be readily dropped from the roster at the next election. The discoveries first that Stevenson had no intention of playing ball, and second, that

For the next three and a half days Stevenson pondered and analyzed the proposal. Hermon Dunlap Smith (a registered Republican) warned that the Democrats needed him that year: "If you say no when they need you, they won't take you when they don't need you." [2]

Stevenson replied that he wanted the support of Chicago's Mayor Martin Kennelly, who favored former Cook County State's Attorney Thomas J. Courtney, a foe of the Arvey organization, for the gubernatorial nomination. Smith argued that Kennelly would have to support him. But Stevenson expressed concern that unless Kennelly helped, the possibility of victory was endangered. (Kennelly did not mention Stevenson's name publicly until August, 1948, when he endorsed the entire Democratic ticket.)

Finally, Stevenson, with only a few minutes remaining to inform Arvey, told Smith, "Well, I guess you're right. It's now or never. I'll do it." [3]

Arvey wrote: "I am greatly amused at the stories that Adlai Stevenson was indecisive. He was not a superficial man. He insisted upon knowing everything about his subject. He did not do things impulsively. He did not make impulsive decisions, but wanted to know every facet of a problem before he decided upon action." [4]

Once Stevenson decided, he became utterly absorbed by the role of candidate. He was tireless, resourceful, and courageous. Although he made many speeches to the Democratic ward organizations of Chicago, he placed the focus of his campaign on reaching independents, independent Democrats, and independent Republicans. He concentrated on the corruption, the payroll padding, and the ties with gambling interests of Governor Green's machine. But, of equal importance, he urged the people of Illinois to remember their great traditions and vote for a respon-

---

far from being expendable he was the state's greatest political asset in a century was only made by them later on, and then with by no means unmixed delight." *Adlai E. Stevenson of Illinois* (New York: Farrar, Straus & Young, 1952), p. 95.

[2] Davis, *A Prophet in His Own Country*, p. 291. There was a widespread feeling among Democrats that they could not carry Illinois with Harry S Truman as the presidential candidate. A blue-ribbon ticket headed by Stevenson and Douglas would help but many believed they could not win either. Arvey denied, however, that they were selected as "sacrificial lambs." He wrote: "That there were many who doubted Stevenson's ability to win, and some who thought that he had no chance whatsoever, made it easier to procure an almost unanimous approval of his candidacy. The fact remains, however, that most members of the organization felt that we had a chance, a better than even chance, of winning." "A Gold Nugget in Your Backyard," in *As We Knew Adlai: The Stevenson Story by Twenty-two Friends*, edited and with preface by Edward P. Doyle, foreword by Adlai E. Stevenson III (New York: Harper & Row, 1966), p. 53.

[3] Davis, *A Prophet in His Own Country*, p. 291.

[4] "A Gold Nugget in Your Backyard," in *As We Knew Adlai*, p. 54.

sible government that would serve the public and guide the state to cope with problems of education, welfare, roads, industrial safety — and above all to end cynicism about politics and public service.

Hermon Dunlap Smith, Louis A. Kohn, Stephen A. Mitchell, and Edward D. McDougal, Jr., helped Stevenson form a nonpartisan Stevenson for Governor Committee and enlisted Democrats, Republicans, and Independents. Mrs. Edison Dick played an active role as cochairman of the Women's Division together with Mrs. Eric Stubbs.

Mrs. Ernest L. Ives helped organize the Women's Division in downstate Illinois. By the end of the campaign there were many independent groups for Stevenson around the state.

James W. Mulroy, former managing editor of the Chicago Sun and Pulitzer Prize-winning reporter, became the campaign manager. He had vast contacts with newspapermen and politicians. And he had tireless energy, imagination, and unfailing cheerfulness. "Mulroy aroused us to action," Mitchell wrote.[5]

Carol Evans, who had worked at the Sidley, Austin, Burgess and Harper law firm, joined Stevenson as his secretary. Paul H. Morrill, William S. Epple, Patricia Dowling, Marjorie Grigsby, Juanda Higgins, Marion Kirkland, Phyllis Gustafson and Janet Rosenstock were the principal staff members in the Chicago office. Volunteers, including William I. Flanagan, Mrs. James W. Mulroy, and Ben Hansen, worked long hours to assist the small paid staff.

We publish a selection from the letters Stevenson wrote and the speeches he delivered. He established a pattern for his future campaigns. By and large he wrote his own speeches. His old friend, Lloyd Lewis, Professor Walter Schaefer of the Northwestern University Law School and others submitted drafts for speeches or memoranda. But Stevenson seldom delivered such speeches without some rewriting. His associates in 1948 — and later — complained that he spent far too much time on his writing. While he agreed, he had too much respect for literary quality, for the use of words, to do otherwise. Moreover, he was determined to be his own man, to present the real man, not a myth manufactured by ghosts and public relations manipulation. Up to the last minute before he spoke, Stevenson rewrote and rewrote to achieve the proper nuances. Unfortunately, sometimes when he finished and a reporter asked to borrow the copy, Stevenson gave it to him. As a result, many times we do not have available the text he actually delivered. We indicate, however, whether the text used is that of the speech he delivered or whether it is based on an uncorrected carbon copy or press release. We found no text for speeches delivered to the Chicago ward organizations. Colonel Arvey

[5] "Adlai's Amateurs," in As We Knew Adlai, p. 75.

wrote: "I accompanied the Governor on several of his speaking tours through the Wards but cannot recall a single instance when he used a text. He was in the habit of having a little card with him on which he made one or two notes as a reminder of the subjects he wished to cover." [6]

The Stevenson papers used in Part Five are in the Adlai E. Stevenson collection, Princeton University Library, unless otherwise indicated. He probably wrote many handwritten letters and postcards while he was campaigning all over Illinois, but we have been unable to locate many of them. In these letters we have retained Stevenson's own spellings. Mrs. Edison Dick has submitted extracts to the editors from handwritten letters she received from Stevenson during the campaign. She has indicated with ellipses material that was deleted by her. The originals of all the handwritten letters are in her possession.

To Jacob M. Arvey[7]

December 23, 1947

Dear Colonel,

You asked me to ascertain the position of the Chicago Daily News. Lloyd Lewis talked yesterday with "Stuffy" Walters,[8] in Mr. Knight's[9] absence. Walters said that Knight would not commit himself as to what he might do and would make no primary recommendations. He added that it was no secret that Knight was "very friendly toward Stevenson." When Lewis asked him about their position on Major [Paul H.] Douglas, he replied that he could make no comment.

I am afraid this is about all we can get from the Daily News at this stage.

With warm regards,

Sincerely yours,

To Mr. and Mrs. Ernest L. Ives[10]

January 1, 1948

Dear Buffy & Ernest —

Well, I'm in it, after several dreadful days of indecision & stalling. I'm still a little stunned by the enormity of the task I've undertaken. Whether

---

[6] Letter to Carol Evans, October 1, 1968.
[7] The original is in the possession of Mr. Arvey.
[8] Basil L. Walters, executive editor of the Chicago *Daily News.*
[9] John S. Knight, publisher of the Chicago *Daily News.*
[10] This handwritten letter is in the Elizabeth Stevenson Ives collection, Illinois State Historical Library.

I've the strength, thick skin & capacity to at least make a good race I don't know, but at least I've got to try now for 10 fearful months.

If you want to send some money make the check to Hermon D. Smith, Treasurer and send it to him c/o Marsh & McLennan, 164 West Jackson Blvd. It might be more helpful know [now] to get things started than later.

And if you really *want* to do some work I suppose the most useful thing would be a biography. You might write such ancestral portions as you can with the material you have & it can be fitted into something more complete later.

I don't feel very gay this New Year's Day!

Hastily

AD

On January 7, 1948, Stevenson, Jacob M. Arvey, and other Chicago Democrats went to Springfield for a meeting of the Democratic State Central Committee. Stevenson, when informed that he was expected to speak, reminded Arvey that he had never made a political speech and suggested that James "Spike" Hennessy, publicity director for the Cook County organization, "dash off" something. Arvey suggested Stevenson try it and Hennessy would edit. When Stevenson returned he read what he had scribbled. "Editing was unnecessary," Arvey wrote, "because . . . we knew then that this was a new style in political speaking and it was bound to make an impression upon all those who heard him." [11]

The statewide candidates on the ticket in addition to Stevenson and Douglas were Sherwood Dixon, running for lieutenant governor; Edward J. Barrett, running for reelection as secretary of state; Ivan Elliott, running for attorney general; Benjamin O. Cooper, running for auditor; and Ora Smith, running for state treasurer.

Stevenson spoke to the Democratic State Central Committee on January 7, 1948.[12]

May I take this opportunity, first, to greet you all — and to tell you how much I appreciate the honor the State Central Committee of the Democratic Party has done me by endorsing me as its candidate for Governor in this fateful election year of 1948.

[11] "A Gold Nugget in Your Backyard," in *As We Knew Adlai*, p. 54.
[12] The text is based on a mimeographed copy of the speech.

I accept your endorsement sensible not only of the great and unde-served honor you have done me but also of your flattering confidence that my stable mates — and I know they will agree with me — and I can and will conduct the state campaign in a manner befitting the best tradi-tions of the Democratic party in Illinois. But even more than these, I am sensible of the solemn responsibility you have given me — a responsibil-ity not alone to you as the organized, militant shock troops of the Demo-cratic party in Illinois, who have carried the standards of the people's party for so long, in adversity as well as triumph, but also the responsibil-ity you have assigned me to the people of Illinois, regardless of party, who are not content with things as they are. And there are many of them. There are many people, Republicans and Independents as well as Demo-crats, thruout the state of Illinois, in the cities, on the farms and in the small towns, who know that all is not well in this state which Providence has so richly blessed with almost everything — except good government.

The crudest, old fashioned spoils politics in the state administration cannot be veiled by virtuous pronouncements forever. The masks are worn thin and the stark, ugly face of the state's affairs is all but apparent.

The people don't like what they've heard and they'll like it less and less as they hear more and more about what's been done and what's *not* been done in the last eight years. And then they'll size up Paul Douglas; my-self; Eddie Barrett (except they've already sized him up and approved him); Ivan Elliott; Sherwood Dixon; Fred Harrison; and Ben Cooper.[13] They'll look very good in contrast, and the Democratic ticket will be elected — in November! — with the help of many Republicans and In-dependents who think Illinois is entitled to something better.

And I want to win, not just because I'm a Democrat, not just because as a lawyer I like to win my cases, and not just because of the honor of governing this state in which my folks have lived for 115 years, but be-cause — and I know everyone in this room will agree with me — because I believe that we *must* and that we *can* give this state better, wiser, thriftier government. "Must," because I believe with all my heart and soul, just as you do, that we *must* meet the demands, the challenge of our time, and restore the people's faith in democratic republican govern-ment. I believe with all my heart and mind that as citizens of the Repub-lic, not as Democrats, but as citizens of the richest, strongest, healthiest Republic on earth, we must restore popular esteem and confidence in the democratic system at all levels — municipal, state and national.

[13] This ticket was finally approved with the exception of Fred Harrison, who was replaced as candidate for state treasurer by Ora Smith. Paul H. Douglas received the committee's endorsement for U.S. senator.

How else can we insure the survival of our free institutions when the winds begin to blow? If the people are cynical, suspicious and abused, if their confidence in their heritage is undermined by corruption, greed, excessive partisanship, we cannot be sure that they will withstand or even identify the demagogues and the false prophets of a better way who always march in the forefront of the reaction, be it of the right or left, be it fascist or communist, that will surely threaten us when the winds blow, and blow they surely will if we stumble headlong much further down this path of inflation, rising prices and corrosive, insensitive materialism.

But I had not intended to make a speech or preach a sermon. I wanted to say simply that I believe, as you do, that our form of government which has blessed our land and which has long been in the ascendancy thruout the world is now undergoing its severest test, is now being watched by millions of people the world over, some with malice but more with prayers.

I say simply that our system is on trial; that our example in the years immediately ahead of us will determine the shape of things to come; that unless we continue healthy, strong and free we will not win many converts; that unless we can lift the hearts of men, unless we can reawaken the hopes of men, the faith of men, in the free way of life, we will be alone and isolated in a hostile world.

Can we do this? Of course we can! And we will — with the enlightened leadership and the vision of the future of that humble, sincere, forthright man in the White House, President Truman.

But we in the state, like our great Mayor, Martin Kennelly in Chicago, who is shaping the new pattern for municipal government for all America, all of us, share the President's responsibility to make democratic government work, to prove that it is not obsolete, to demonstrate to the whole world that it can adjust to the changing needs of changing times, that it is not antiquated, moribund and decadent. There must be no rotten apples in the American barrel. I am proud to serve with you embattled Democrats who believe that democracy can survive its severest test and can bring hope, security and peace to men for centuries to come. I am proud that you enlisted me in the great work of lifting our beloved Illinois out of the morass and putting it in the forefront of exemplary state government.

I believe the people are wise and just; they are very tolerant, very forgiving. But once aroused by prolonged abuse they are merciless to their betrayers. It will not be enough to arouse them, it will not be enough to win the election. You have to deserve, you have to earn the people's confidence, not once, but constantly. That is what those who will be our opponents in the November campaign have forgotten. We will keep the people's confidence not by our words but by our works.

That, as I see it, is our goal. I am proud to be among you — to have a part here in Illinois in the everlasting struggle for the freedom and security of all the people.

On the day before his forty-eighth birthday Stevenson resigned from his law firm. He opened campaign headquarters at 7 South Dearborn Street, Chicago. Although an impressive number of Independents, Republicans and Democrats joined his Citizens' Committee, the campaign suffered from inadequate funds. This led to the scrapping of some plans for advertising and radio speeches and kept the paid campaign staff at a bare minimum.

To Walter T. Fisher[14]

January 21, 1948

Dear Walter:

I am advised that you have sent a contribution to the Committee, and I need not tell you how pleased and grateful I am.

I hope to Heaven that I can finance this thing, at least in some considerable part, through this independent Committee to reduce my reliance and sense of obligation to the organization. This for your information.

With warmest thanks,

Sincerely yours,
ADLAI

Stevenson asked his running mate, the candidate for lieutenant governor, for his ideas about the sales tax.

To Sherwood Dixon[15]

January 29, 1948

Dear Sherwood,

I have your very helpful memorandum on the Sales Tax question, which has been giving me so much concern. I am delighted to see some-

[14] A Chicago lawyer. The original is in the possession of Mr. Fisher.
[15] The original is in the possession of Mr. Dixon.

body in our group who is prepared to sit down and actually write something. Mostly we do nothing but talk!

I am collecting considerable material on this problem, and I hope out of it will come a position along the line that you suggest, which will be sound in fact and not politically distasteful here or downstate.

I will look forward to seeing you next week in Ottawa[, Illinois].

Sincerely yours,

To Francis Russell [16]

February 19, 1948

Dear Francis:

I am taking the liberty of introducing to you by this means Mr. Walter J. Orlikoski and Mr. Bernard J. Woods. Mr. Orlikoski is a valued friend and an Alderman of the City of Chicago who exercises a wide and wholesome influence in this community, and particularly among our huge population of Polish descent. Mr. Woods and Alderman Orlikoski are much interested in the development of an institution in Chicago to train people for service abroad in business as well as government. They have some plans which are well matured and they are anxious to talk with somebody in authority in the Department with a view to resolving various questions which you will quickly appreciate.

I will be grateful if you will see that they get into the right hands. As you well know, I have been anxious for a long time to see some of the current post war enthusiasm for foreign service captured before it is dissipated, and properly channelled. I know you feel the same way.

With warm regards, I am

Sincerely yours,

Stevenson opened his campaign in his hometown of Bloomington, with a speech to the Jackson Day Dinner on February 23, 1948.[17] *Mr. and Mrs. Ernest L. Ives held a large reception in the family home before the candidate delivered his speech.* Time *had stated on January 12, 1948: "Stevenson, who has never campaigned for office, planned no slam-bang fight. He would work hard, but quietly. Most of the fireworks would come from Douglas."*

But after listening to the Bloomington speech, Time *reported in its issue of March 8, 1948, that Stevenson's speech "made his fellow Demo-*

[16] Director of the Office of Public Affairs, Department of State.
[17] The text is that released to the press.

crats jump with joy. The speech was sometimes folksy . . . sometimes eloquent, always forthright. Stevenson laid into his rival . . . with one haymaker after another. . . . The diners went wild. 'Go get 'em Ad!' screamed jubilant party functionaries. When it was all over, veteran Chicago newsmen knew that a dazzling political star had been born."

The day after the speech John Dreiske wrote in the Chicago Sun-Times: "He was a smash hit. There once were those who gloomily opined he should not travel in the same caravan with Paul H. Douglas . . . because of the danger he would be eclipsed by that brilliant orator. Put away your handkerchiefs. Don't cry for Stevie."

I am grateful to you all for coming here to greet me today. Many of you are the oldest friends I have, and here in McLean County I have my earliest recollections. I suppose to most people few things are more precious than home. Although I have practiced law in Chicago for more than 20 years, except for intervals of government service, Bloomington has always been "home" for me. I was raised here in Bloomington. Here I received my early education and gained my earliest impressions. I would be too pious if I didn't admit that I also got into all sorts of trouble here as a boy — and I always suspected that some of you who are here tonight were more responsible for those escapades than I was. I hate to think how much property needed repair along Washin[g]ton Street the day after Hallow-e'en about 35 years ago — in spite of my efforts to restrain you!

Here, too, my family have lived and labored for generations. My great grandfather, Jesse Fell, settled here 115 years ago; my grandfather, Adlai Stevenson, for whom I was named, was a citizen of this community when he was elected Vice President of the United States; and here my mother and father were born, married and are buried.

I am fortunate to be able to come back to my old home to commence my campaign for Governor of Illinois, and I could think of no happier place to start this new endeavor in my life than Bloomington, and no more agreeable way to start than here among my oldest friends. And I haven't overlooked the fact that it has been a long time since so many people in this Republican community turned out to greet a Democratic candidate! It's very flattering to me personally, and very reassuring to me politically — and I hope you don't change your mind about me before next November!

Many of you have asked me how and why I became a candidate for Governor when I have never sought a public office before and wasn't even identified with the Democratic organization in Chicago. Well, the fact of the matter is, I didn't seek the job. The Democratic State Central Committee asked me to be their candidate for Governor. I don't know why exactly, but, of course, I think they showed very good judgment!

I was told that they selected me because they respected my record in private life and my public service in the war and the peace, knew I could win, and that as Governor I would be a credit to our party. I remember that one of the leaders said to me that the best government was the best politics, and that if any politicians were skeptical, Mayor Kennelly's conduct of Chicago's affairs was rapidly convincing them.

But if I haven't been in politics, I have been all around it, both Republican and Democratic. My great grandfather, a close friend of Abraham Lincoln, first suggested him for the Presidency. My grandfather, a Vice-President of the United States under Grover Cleveland, was defeated for Governor of Illinois in a Republican landslide by only a few thousand votes — just 40 years ago. And my father was Secretary of State (1914–1917) with Governor Dunne. So I have a bad case of hereditary politics acquired right here in McLean County.

But let me talk with you seriously for a few minutes, because neither as Democrats nor Americans can we afford to be indolent, indifferent or frivolous about the world, the nation or the state in which we live. I would like to talk about the tormented world in which we live and in which we as Americans and the most fortunate people on earth have such a stake, but my job is Illinois. They say a statesman thinks of the next generation and a politician thinks of the next election, and my job is the next election.

But as the world contracts, as what happens everywhere affects more and more what happens here, it bcomes more and more difficult to disregard the great forces at work in this revolutionary era.

The military victory of the Allies raised our country to heights never reached by any other people. This young nation of ours is marked by destiny to lead mankind in a forward march toward a world consecrated to the worship of the noblest ideals ever uttered by sage or prophet — the establishment of permanent peace and uncompromising justice. During the war we proclaimed this to be our goal, and since its ending we have been and are engaged in a struggle with those who challenge our ideals, who advance different philosophies of life and who press for revolutionary changes — a struggle upon the outcome of which depends the survival of democracy, personal liberty and human dignity.

In this struggle not only the Federal Government is engaged, but every State of the Union and each of us, individually, as well. It would be a sham and a mockery if while preaching the ideals of democracy and justice to others we failed to practice them at home. America would be unworthy of her consecrated destiny if while denouncing corruption, selfishness, prejudice and intolerance in other peoples we condoned such practices in any part of our land. Any State leadership which is not conscious of these self-evident truths has forfeited every claim to leadership or to public confidence.

These United States, including Illinois, have reached political maturity. The men and women who fought and suffered in the last two wars, the fathers, mothers, wives and children of those who have not returned from the battlefields will not tolerate public servants whose primary loyalty is to their political parties instead of their public trust. The resentment toward the present State leadership is mounting. Countless good Republicans throughout the State feel humiliated and indignant about the performances of their officials. Many have pledged me their support. More come every day. No better evidence of the unhealthy condition of that Party in Illinois is necessary than the degrading spectacle we recently witnessed in the shameless power politics, the over-the-counter trading and maneuvering by which the Republican candidates were finally elected. It looked like a "black market" in Republican candidates! And then look at the results! You'll hear more of that midnight double play — Lueder to Murray — for Auditor,[18] and that miraculous triple play — Cross to Wright to Green — whereby a Governor who detests third terms was able to run for a third term without primary opposition.[19] You will hear more of Government by stealth at midnight.

Ladies and gentlemen — and I don't care whether you're Democratic or Republican — we must recapture for Illinois the commanding and dignified position she once held among her sister states. She is entitled to it by virtue of the quality of her people, her wealth, her power and her exalted traditions. It can be done, but not with a party boss sitting in the Governor's chair — at least for a little while longer.

I don't mean to deprecate party leadership, but I insist that you can't be the Party boss and Governor at the same time without subordinating the State's interests to the Party's fortunes. The greater your success as a partisan boss, the more serious the sacrifice of the people's interests. And,

[18] Sinon A. Murray, a lobbyist and leader of the Republicans in Chicago's river wards, who worked in the office of State Auditor Arthur C. Lueder, filed to run for auditor five minutes before the deadline set by law, announcing at the time that Lueder would withdraw because of ill health. Lueder, who had had the endorsement of the regular Republican organization, did withdraw, and a day later another candidate for the office, Louis Yager of Litchfield, also withdrew, leaving Murray unopposed in the primary.

[19] Governor Green in his 1940 campaign had denounced President Roosevelt for running for a third term. Republican Lieutenant Governor Hugh Cross and State Treasurer Warren Wright announced their candidacies for governor, but, at the last minute, Green announced for a third term and the other two withdrew.

friends, the present incumbent of the Governor's office, who also pretended to detest machine politics with righteous fervor has become the master political machinist of all time.

If Illinois is to regain its rightful position among the States, if it is to assume a measure of leadership in the struggle against totalitarianism, the idolatry of materialism or any other evil "ism"; if it is going to aid in the just solution of our domestic problems — the first business on the agenda must be to banish from our capital the unconscionable spoils machine which is the negation of the democratic dream and which now holds the State in its grip. This machine must be destroyed beyond the possibility of repair. Its foundations must be uprooted and the earth scorched so that another can't be built in its place — whether it bears the trademark of the over-fed elephant or the lean donkey!

I want to say right now that this campaign is not just another quadrennial struggle to determine who dispenses the patronage. It is a campaign to revive the people's faith in the integrity of democratic government.

This task cannot be entrusted to a partisan overlord. Only men with the single loyalty to the highest interest of all the people of the state can be expected to perform that operation. I think we have on the Democratic ticket that kind of men. I say that not with shameless immodesty because I am on the ticket. I say it because if I didn't think it was so I wouldn't be on the ticket! And I didn't ask to be put on the ticket. And I have no ambition and no other interest in politics than to do what I can, with your help, to clean up Illinois, to administer its affairs in the interest of all the people, be they downstaters from whence I come or Chicagoans where I work, and to put Illinois in the forefront of the best governed states of this Republic.

The State of Illinois was, not so long ago, one of the most progressive commonwealths of the Union. It was often referred to as a great social laboratory. Its social legislation, such as The Juvenile Court Act, probation, etc., became models to be copied in virtually every state. The care of our dependents, the supervision and guidance of our wayward children, our educational system, were inferior to none. We have lost our preeminent position in this respect. So far as the quality of our government is concerned we are now regarded as among the backward States. With hundreds of millions in the treasury, our educational system is poorly supported by the state; juvenile delinquency has reached an appalling state; some of the most gruesome crimes are committed by mere children.

This need not be so. A proper regard for our responsibilities and an uncompromising determination to solve these problems will bring relief. But there will be no improvement without intelligent and devoted leadership and a large share of that responsibility falls on the Governor. But a Governor who is pre-occupied with his personal political fortunes and the fortunes of his political party has neither the time nor the vision, nor, if you please, the freedom and independence for such leadership. A governor who ignores the appeals of miners for protection while his mine inspectors are collecting campaign funds from the operators has, particularly after a tragic disaster, deprived us of any hope for disinterested leadership.[20]

The public welfare must be the first concern of every civilized State. I shall, as the campaign progresses, point out the indefensible neglect by the present State administration of its sacred trust in connection with our charitable and correctional institutions. The administration of these institutions should again become what they were in the past — a model for other States to follow.

None but the best qualified and properly trained personnel should ever be permitted to handle the intricate problems of the dependent human beings who have become wards of the State. Those who are chosen for these delicate tasks must be ensured tenure of office, ample compensation and encouragement to make of their work a life's career. No campaign fund solicitors belong.

This State should take a vow that there shall be no more "Centralia tragedies," and that whenever political favoritism has become a contributing cause, none of the guilty will go unpunished, no matter what their station in life or how high their rank or office.

The people of Illinois should not rest until the education of their children has been raised to the highest possible level. If the people of Illinois choose me for their Governor, I shall regard it as my solemn and agreeable duty to do all I can to achieve the mandate of our Constitution that there be in Illinois a "thorough and efficient system of free schools." Basic education is the condition precedent to a conscientious and responsible citizenry.

The welfare of the men and women who labor on the farm, in the factory, store or office must be the vital concern of every Governor and every legislator in the country. It is not true that the Federal Government alone carries the responsibility in this respect. The State, too, has responsibilities for preserving the social gains we have made — made, I remind you, largely under the leadership of two great Democrats — Woodrow Wilson and Franklin Roosevelt. I pledge myself to preserve

[20] This refers to the Centralia mine disaster of March 25, 1947, when an explosion killed 111 miners. Governor Green's mine inspectors had collected campaign funds from the mine operators and ignored violations of safety regulations. John Bartlow Martin, "Blast In Centralia," *Harper's*, March, 1948.

these gains inviolate, and to administer the State's responsibilities without fear or favor and with the scrupulous honesty of a public trustee.

Our State holds a commanding position in business and industry and its influence should be commensurate with the contributions it has made to the progress of the country. I would like to think we could set an example for other States to follow by developing machinery capable of harmonizing divergent interests. Employers and employees need not be forever at swords points. It is the duty of government to find the proper medium for agreement on bases which will guard all interests — for the sum of all interests is the public interest. I shall never renounce my belief that that is possible, practical and indispensable. And I shall never renounce my conviction that arbitrary power exists nowhere in a democracy — not even in a majority, be it a labor majority or a management majority!

Incidentally, I want to give this assurance to the businessmen of this State: as Governor I shall do my best to emancipate you from paying tribute, from political shakedowns by State employees, to which, as I am informed, you have been subjected in recent years. If I don't wholly succeed, let me know, because I want servants, not solicitors on the State payroll!

Perhaps it is because I come from this famous agricultural county; perhaps it is because, like most of you, I am interested in farming; perhaps it's because I worked in the Department of Agriculture in the depression 15 years ago, but whatever the reason I'm sure this audience will understand me when I say that I consider the contributions of the agricultural community to the well-being of our country the most important. They sustain us in war and in peace; today they are figuratively saving the world from chaos. If we who disintegrated the atom succeed in integrating humanity and saving the peace we will have the American farmer to thank most of all. Illinois, if not the greatest, is one of the foremost agricultural centers of the country and whether we live in the city or on the farm, the problems of the farmer — the producers of the basic wealth of the nation — must command the constant attention of the state as well as the Federal government.

Let me also say that after working in the city for a long time I have discovered no legitimate reason why the people of the great communities outside Chicago and the people of that city should not live in the friendliest cooperation, without suspicion, without fear and without jealousy of each other. Quite the contrary is true. We are so dependent upon each other that logic and reason cry out for harmony and mutual respect.

I have spoken of these things simply to indicate some of the problems with which we shall have to deal seriously and soon. They are by no means all. As this campaign progresses I shall discuss these and others at greater length. I shall have something to say about the sales tax and the accumulation of too much money in Springfield. I shall have something to say about pensions and the treatment of the old and infirm. I shall have something to say about housing, about conservation and about many of the responsibilities of the State to its people.

And most of all, I will never let up on my conception of honesty in public service. I shall remind you over and over again that the State budget has doubled since the last biennium of Henry Horner[21] — and the lustre of his memory grows brighter with each passing year. I shall inform you about the facts with regard to the State payroll — facts which I find are not easily available. But I venture to suggest that the State payroll has doubled since Horner's time. I shall remind you that if the Governor and his followers really want to save money for the taxpayer, they have plenty of work to do here in our own State of Illinois to stop gigantic waste and inefficiency — to use no sterner words — instead of spending their time and their eloquence in denouncing expenditures in Washington.

To paraphrase the title of a great American novel, "Look Homeward, Angel."

I will have much to say about bad government, inefficient government, corruption, coercion and the shocking extravagance and cynicism of this state administration. All this I will do frankly, forthrightly, and I hope in such language that every citizen shall be able to understand.

And in appealing for support to the Democrats, to the great host of unfettered Republicans, and to those who bear no party label, I make this solemn promise: As Governor I shall act as the servant of all the people, without regard to race, color, creed or political affiliation.

In conclusion, let me remind you that two great Justices of the United States Supreme Court, [Oliver Wendell] Holmes and [Louis] Brandeis, preached the doctrine that the various States should be the experimental stations where ideas looking toward greater progress should be tried out and their efficacy tested. I wholeheartedly agree with that proposition, and as the executive of this State I shall not hesitate to advocate forward-looking measures which hold the promise of leading our State to great and ever greater achievement. It shall be my constant aim to acquire and retain the confidence of the people of Illinois. I shall draw upon them for advice and participation in every endeavor looking toward the advancement of the welfare of this State and of our beloved country and, God willing, we shall make our full contribution to those efforts which will

[21] Democratic governor of Illinois, 1933–1940.

hasten the coming of the day when peace and justice shall be securely enthroned for us and for the generations to come.

On February 17, 1948, one of Stevenson's Princeton classmates wrote him soliciting funds for Princeton's Quadrangle Club and expressed the hope that the public, who did not know him like his Princeton friends, would nevertheless elect him.

To Charles M. Shipway

February 25, 1948

Dear Dope:

I was delighted to have your note this morning, and I feel like a dog not to send you, and at once, a handsome contribution to the Club mortgage retirement.

Unhappily, I have, after six years of starvation on a government payroll, now agreed to run for Governor, with the result that I am now more impoverished and the demands are greater than ever. Hence, you will have to excuse me — if you can!

Thank God, there are not many Princeton men in Illinois or I wouldn't have a chance of election. I am not sure how long I can fool the people out there anyway, but the less you tell them the better.

Sincerely yours,

To Beardsley Ruml

February 25, 1948

Dear Bee:

Thanks for your invitation to the meetings on March 19 and 20.[22] Unhappily, I will be in downstate Illinois at that time beating the bushes for this unknown character they have selected as the Democratic candidate for Governor. It has been a lot of work and a little fun, and the prospects are encouraging, but I see no prospect of getting East again for a long while, what with the job of making myself contagious to eight million voters and raising the money to do it!

On the latter count, if you run across any people in New York who are aching to contribute to my campaign fund I can assure you that their contributions will be most welcome.

Sincerely yours,

[22] Mr. Ruml had invited Stevenson to attend a conference.

To Sir Louis Spears

February 27, 1948

Dear Louis:

We were both delighted to have your note of February 18. I am glad you have met Ronnie's new wife and I agree that she is most attractive.[23]

I finally surrendered to the blandishments of the politicians and agreed to run for Governor on the Democratic ticket. Although I would have preferred to run for the Senate, it seemed that our prospects of electing either Governor or Senator would be vastly enhanced if I ran for Governor. Hence, the last minute switch.

I need not tell an old campaigner that it is a fearful chore in such an enormous state as Illinois, and particularly for one who is relatively unknown outside a small section of Chicago. On top of that my adversary has enormous financial resources and a huge political machine behind him.

I will be at work continuously on this business until the election in November, and meanwhile Ellen and the children seem to be getting along quite well but with infrequent glimpses of the old man. We had a comforting report on you and Mary[24] from Bayard Dodge and his wife who passed through here not long ago, but it was hardly the equivalent of a visit with you, and I wish there were some reunion for us all in prospect.

Ellen sends her love to you both.

Yours,

From March 1 to March 17 Stevenson toured downstate Illinois with Paul H. Douglas. Louther S. Horne wrote in the New York Times, *March 14, 1948, that Stevenson "is staging a lively pre-primary campaign." Horne added that observers with the Democratic caravan reported "that Mr. Stevenson's chatty, persuasive style of delivery and his infectious grin have introduced a 'new look' in Illinois campaigning that is winning audiences."*

While on this campaign tour Stevenson wrote to his old friend, Mrs. Edison Dick, cochairman of the Women's Division of the Stevenson for Governor Committee.

[23] Mr. and Mrs. Ronald Tree had told Sir Louis that Stevenson was running for governor.
[24] Sir Louis was married to Mary Borden, Ellen Stevenson's aunt.

To Mrs. Edison Dick[25]

. . . I've had not a moment, except at the price of some of these precious few hours of sleep, to report my recent adventures. At the moment I'm racing along from Galva to Peoria where we all join for our night meeting. Last night it was Rock Island — a big meeting — with a wild trip in the middle of it to E. Moline & a labor meeting. I made a good speech last night, if I do say so, & about the only good one so far, but it was too subtle & much of the satire went over the heads of the audience. I went to bed, however, with an unhappy feeling that you would not have approved — too much "unworthy" sarcasm about [Governor Dwight] Green. Indeed for the first time I'm glad you were not there — unless you too might have been contaminated by this tone!

There's so much to say & as usual no time. I've "born[e] the battle" rather better than I expected & if I only had a little more facility with the political manner of speaking — showmanship, oratory & the mysterious something that excites people — I would worry no more, except about the organization and financing jobs ahead. But I just haven't got that something — impress them, yes, but not excite them.

We wind up this travelling circus in Waukegan Mar 17. If otherwise unengaged why don't you and Eddie[26] come up & laugh at the trained seals — and listen to me stagger thru some words — contrived in mortal combat with nausea. . . .

To Mrs. Edison Dick[27]

[no date]

It's Sunday morning. I'm in an automobile driving from Danville where we spoke last night to Decatur to resume this fantastic ordeal. We've driven about 1350 miles since last Sunday, and I've spoken about 20 times, shaken hands with thousands of people and slept all too little.

It's been an amazing experience, and I've come to wonder how anyone can presume to talk about "America" until he has done some campaigning. Perhaps it's the secret, perhaps the curse, of American political success — the illusive business of finding your way to the heart of the average man — when there is no such thing — and, unhappily the human heart is often an organ encased in a pocketbook, and not a Bible or a textbook.

[25] The envelope is postmarked Peoria, Illinois, March 13, 1948. This handwritten letter is in the possession of Mrs. Dick.
[26] Mr. Dick.
[27] This handwritten letter is in the possession of Mrs. Dick.

I've seen Illinois in a capsule — the beauty of the south, the fruit belt, the coal fields, the oil fields, the great industrial area around East St. Louis — and everywhere the rich, black, fecund earth stretching away and away. It gives you a great feeling of pride and power. Shut your eyes a moment and let the fetid, hot places, the scorched islands, the arid, the cold, the small — all the places of the world where men struggle to live and love and breed — dance through your head — then open your eyes and look at Illinois, and murmur 'thrice blessed land' — and exult in the power, majesty, wealth, might — and tremble a little when a cigar-smoking pol says "Pardon me, 'Governor,' but ———," and quake as the visions die and *responsibility* engulfs you.

But I'm getting a little lyrical for a Democratic politician. . . .

Governor Green had not intended to campaign in the primary but as Stevenson's speeches attracted more and more attention he returned from Miami Beach. On March 13 he launched his campaign. He attacked Stevenson, stating his "chief claim to fame is as a sub-author of the United Nations' plan, the most dismal failure in the history of American diplomacy." Then, Green charged Stevenson was "on leave from the striped-pants brigade of the Roosevelt-Truman State Department." (Green ceased this line of attack when the Chicago Daily News published a picture of Governor Green wearing striped pants.)

The following speech by Stevenson was delivered in Waukegan, March 17, 1948. It is the text that he delivered with corrections inserted in longhand.

It was a little more than three weeks ago that our Democratic pre-primary campaign commenced at Springfield. At that time I expressed some of my diagnosis of the ailments of our beloved Illinois.

I said then that the people of Illinois would no longer tolerate public servants whose primary loyalty is to their political party instead of their public trust. I said that a man can't be a party boss and governor at the same time without subordinating the interests of the State to the fortunes of his party; that the greater the success as a partisan boss the more serious the sacrifice of the people's interests.

I said that our Governor, who once with righteous fervor and missionary zeal decried machine politics, had become the master political machinist of all time. I said that his State House gang had degraded and corrupted the public service of Illinois. I said that it must be destroyed.

And I told you that the next order of business would be to recover for

Illinois the commanding and dignified position she once held among her sister states.

That is a major operation — it cannot be entrusted to a political over-lord. It cannot be accomplished by men who are preoccupied with their personal political fortunes and the fortunes of a political party. They have neither the time nor the imagination, nor the freedom and inde-pendence, for such leadership. Only men with a single loyalty to the highest interests of all the people of Illinois can provide that leadership.

That, as I saw it, was the objective of the Democratic Party in Illinois in 1948. But that was more than three weeks ago. Meanwhile our cara-van has traveled thousands of miles through the wonderland of this vast and mighty state. We have visited 130 towns. We have talked with many people in all walks of life. And I have this to report to you: I made a mistake here three weeks ago. It is not alone the objective of the Demo-cratic Party in 1948 to root out the State House gang; to obliterate the machine; to give the people what they want and pay for — honest, ear-nest service; to give Illinois what it deserves — dignity and distinction.

It is not, I say, just the Democratic Party's objective in 1948 — it is everybody's!

Perhaps to be more accurate I should say it is everybody's objective except the gang's. But don't worry — we, the people, still outnumber them! And even some of the payrollers are mad because there are so many that don't have to do *any* work for their checks.

I have, therefore, something else to report. The citizens have had enough of this plunderbund. We will be elected in November, and we will start to work in January. But don't minimize the job of restoring this State to her rightful place among the best and most honestly governed in the Union after these spoilsmen get through.

In starting our caravan tour of the State we were told that Governor Green and his associates on the Republican State ticket would not stage a pre-Primary campaign. And I assumed that come early Fall the Gover-nor and I would discuss the record of his eight years in office and the programs on which each of us advocate.

Imagine my surprise therefore, when I was informed that the Gover-nor had changed his mind and had rushed into the political arena, mar-shalled his forces, and was marching on the "striped pants brigade" and the United Nations at the head of two thousand words.

I should have suspected something like this would happen. Recent biographies tell how at the age of four he beat out a false alarm from atop the fire tower at Ligonier, Indiana. This was a prophetic act, and he has now perfected the art of beating out false alarms. He has sounded the tocsin — again, come back to Illinois, jumped on his ghost writer and ridden off in all directions at the same time, over the State, the Nation and even the world, slashing at Stalin, Truman, Roosevelt, the New Deal and even me. He even did me the honor of calling me one of the "sub-authors of the United Nations" Charter — a distinction that has not received such exalted recognition before, and I'm blushing with pride and confusion — and prepared to accept your congratulations!

I've been tempted to ride after him in several directions. And the other night I did say that I would be glad to put on striped pants, a morning coat, spats and a black Homberg hat, and thus suitably attired, debate international questions with him in Florida, Arizona, California, or any place convenient for him. Of course, I would have to rent the equipment, unless he would loan it to me.

But, in Illinois I propose to stick to Illinois issues. I am not running against Mr. Green for Vice President. I am running against the kind and quality of government that Mr. Green's machine has given Illinois for the past eight years — and which they have so generously offered to give us for four more.

Fortunately, the assault doesn't wholly preclude the possibility of discussing Illinois with the Governor, because at Fairfield he said: "I stand upon my record for the last eight years. The issue is whether our State Government shall continue to be an honest, solvent, efficient and progressive representative government."

Now if we can stop right there we'll get somewhere and we may even be able to enlighten the people about Illinois. If the Governor will only stand right there I think we can develop for the people's enlightenment some sharp conflicts in our definitions of "honest" and "efficient" — words which I always thought had a meaning common to all of us. We'll have quite a bit to say about *that* record for the last eight years. We'll welcome a sober discussion of the continuation of that kind of "honest" government, because Illinois is ashamed of the quality of her government; ashamed of the antics of most of those who have assumed a public trust; ashamed of nothing for the people and everything for the machine — at the people's expense. And lest you think this is a personal indictment, I refer you to an editorial which appeared in the Chicago *Daily News* on June 27, 1947. It is the same indictment of the State House gang.

We are delighted that Governor Green has found urgent, personal political reasons to rush home and, like Paul Revere, ride through every village and farm to spread the alarm that the "New Deal bunglers and treasury raiders" are threatening the State. This from a man who asked for and obtained the first billion dollar budget in our State history. This from a man who has built up the most cynical and expensive political machine in the history of this State, if not of the country.

He said at Fairfield, and I quote: "The strategy of the New Deal campaign in Illinois is to promise state expenditures which necessarily must destroy our state solvency and impose new burdens on our people." This is certainly a devastating indictment of me, if true. But he doesn't say what these promises are. I have made none whatever. So ring up another false alarm, although we used to label that sort of thing falsehood, instead of false alarm!

Now the Governor says: "The Republican Party kept its promises. We did reduce the sales tax and we did balance the budget."

Let's look at the record.

Yes, he did balance the budget — and so has every governor since 1870. Under our Constitution he can't unbalance the budget. I refer the Governor to Article 5, section 18, of our State Constitution — and ring up another false alarm.

He says the Republican Party kept its promise to reduce the sales tax from 3% to 2%. More nonsense. Another false alarm. Let's turn to the record again.

I quote from the Act approved June 29, 1939, Illinois Revised Statutes, p. 2723, Amendment to the Retailer's Occupational Tax Act.

> "Section 2. A tax is imposed upon persons engaged in the business of selling tangible personal property at retail in this state at the rate of 2% of the gross receipts from such sales in this State of tangible personal property made in the course of such business upon and after the taking effect of this act and prior to July 1, 1935, and at the rate of 3% of the gross receipts from such sales on and after July 1, 1935, and prior to February 15, 1939, and 2% of the gross receipts from such sales after June 30, 1941."

Now, who signed that bill reducing the sales tax from 3% to 2%? Henry Horner signed that bill into law. It was reduced to 2% by a Demcratic legislature and signed into law even before the election of Mr. Green.

I find no legislation reducing the sales tax on the books signed by Governor Green.

The plain speaking, straight thinking Governor did not mention the fact in his opening campaign talk that he is on record as promising to remove the sales tax on food. What happened to that promise?

And what happened, by the way, to this promise to the miners? "The lives of the men, therefore, have been entrusted to the state. The only security you have depends upon absolute enforcement of these laws. To that end an investigation of why these laws have not been enforced should be made now, before a tragedy shocks the nation and before we may be called upon again to behold that silent line of loved ones crowded at the mouth of some mine, dreading the evidence of loss that may be brought up from below . . . I pledge to you that this law and all other laws protecting the health, safety and lives of the men employed in the mines will be enforced rigidly and thoroughly. In other words, to the letter of the law."

What happened to that promise? You know what happened to it. It blew up at Centralia, and the St. Louis Post-Dispatch wrote: I quote:

> "To say that the successor to Henry Horner has been a disappointment is to put it mildly — the consequences of political prostitution of the mine inspection service is of course common knowledge throughout Illinois. It is now widely known that the Green Administration carried the political lug further than any other predecessor administration by using mine inspectors to solicit campaign contributions."

Harper's Magazine has quite a bit to say on the same subject this month. Here's one paragraph from 27 pages on Centralia No. 5 and the Green Government of Illinois:

> "Here lies Green's responsibility — not that, through a secretary's fumble, he failed to act on the miners' appeal to 'save our lives' but rather that, while the kingmakers were shunting him around the nation making speeches, back home his loyal followers were busier building a rich political machine for him than in administering the state for him."

And speaking of solicitation of campaign contributions, every few days for the last two months we read something more about the gouge on employees of the state institutions in violation of the law — Pontiac, Jacksonville, Anna, Lincoln, Peoria, Manteno, and I don't know how many more. Yesterday the Chicago Daily News reported that the attorney for the Civil Service Protective Association would ask the State's attorneys to take action if Governor Green didn't. Is this honest, progressive government — or does this fall under the category of "I stand on my record"?

And now, at the risk of boring you, let's look at the record again — this time on the subject of schools.

Governor Green made the statement last week that State appropriations to the common schools for the present biennium amount to $81,700,000. To quote him, he said: "Let me repeat, these are facts that no amount of political distortion can obscure."

Now to be quite accurate — and I strongly recommend accuracy, but more of that a little later — the facts are, as I understand them, that at the last session of the legislature out of a total appropriation of almost a billion dollars for the biennium, only 65 million was appropriated to the common school distributive fund to help bear the expense of common school education. Now it's true that in addition to the 65 million, 16½ million was also appropriated, in part to take advantage of Federal funds, for special educational purposes, such as salaries for teachers of vocational courses, funds to help defray the cost of school lunches, help for physically handicapped children, truant children, etc. And I'm glad the Governor's scruples didn't deter him from accepting those Federal — New Deal — funds!

So, as I have said before, and say again, the state appropriated just 65 million dollars out of a one billion dollar budget for the distributive fund for common school education — or about 15% of the total cost of common school education.

The failure of the State to provide adequately for common school support does not arise from lack of resources. Our failure lies in the fact that our leadership in Springfield seems to give priority to appropriations for swollen payrolls and grease for the machine over appropriations for the education of our children.

Now I must resist the temptation to dissect a few more claims of meritorious achievement made by the State House Gang — the same gang, by the way, that cried out in anguish at the very thought that anyone could conceive of running for a 3rd term — that is, anyone on a Democratic ticket. Now they say they are indispensable; that the very survival of honest government depends upon a third term, and what's more they say it with a straight face!

But you'll forgive me if I can't overlook just one or two other omissions in this catalogue of Republican accomplishments. The Governor tells us, and I quote, "The state is now engaged in a broad program of construction and modernization of buildings at the State hospitals that care for more than 43,000 helpless wards, and this is being done on a cash basis."

I applaud the Governor and his party for getting this desperately needed program under way. But I see no reference in his speech to the report made by a legislative committee appointed to investigate the State Hospitals and signed by Reed Cutler, a Republican and chairman of the committee.

I wish I had time to read that document to you in its entirety. But I will only say here that the committee found conditions in our State hospitals reminiscent of the Black Hole of Calcutta — wards of the State living in some cases in fire-traps and in almost all cases under circumstances almost unbelievable in this enlightened age. Listen, I have time to quote but a few words of the official report:

> "We found hundreds of pounds of bologna, green with mould, not only on the outside, but all the way through, and not fit for human consumption; meat that was old, discolored and dirty coming from one or the other of these firms."

Mind you, these are not my words. They are the words of the report of the investigating committee. I could go on reading from this report about substandard food, and other purchases, even useless purchases, made by the State always from certain "favored firms" at wholesale, and at higher prices than the retail prices for the same articles. To quote one more sentence from the report: "It is indeed strange that the State of Illinois, purchasing in huge quantities, should pay higher prices for inferior quality goods than first quality goods would be purchased at retail." Is that what the Governor calls "honest," "efficient" government? Or is that simply more grease for the machine — at the taxpayer's expense.

Now, I feel that I'm just getting warmed up, at *your* expense! Bear with me just a few moments more. The Governor was kind to me in his Decatur talk. He pointed out that I couldn't be expected to be familiar with Illinois problems and in particular, the heroic work of the last General Assembly, because, he said, "I wasn't even in Illinois during most of the time the Assembly was in session." Well, Governor, I said I recommended accuracy. So I'll be very accurate. I was out of the State on business three days in January, four days in March and two days in May. In other words I was away 9 days while the Assembly was in session between January 8th and June 30th, or about five percent of the time. But he says I wasn't even in the State "most" of the time. Well, if five percent of the time is "most" of the time in the Governor's dictionary, I guess we know at last how he figures he's governing Illinois, "most" of the time!

Now here's another quote from that Decatur speech, "it is no wonder he knows so little about things that have been accomplished by the State government. For the last ten to twelve years he has spent so little time in Illinois he could not be expected to know about them."

"His interests have been elsewhere — in Washington and New York, in London and in Paris, on first this and then that assignment he received from various agencies and bureaus of the New Deal government in Washington."

He's doing better this time. He's exactly 38% accurate. But I didn't think I would be criticized for some service in the European Theater for the War Department. But perhaps Governor Green has overlooked the fact that the "bureaucratic bungler" who headed that Department in our greatest peril and to his everlasting credit was Henry L. Stimson — also a Republican.

Well, then — to make his statement 38% accurate — and I must account for some more time — and I spent some more time after the war working for some wild, irresponsible men named Secretary of State Stettinius, Secretary of State Byrnes and Secretary of State Marshall — and if they are "treasury raiders," "bureaucratic bunglers," "deficit spenders" and that most devastating of all Republican epithets "new dealers" — well, then count me in too! But, of course, it's possible the Governor hasn't heard of them.

Now I have a proposition for you. If, as Mr. Green implies with contempt, the New Deal of the immortal Franklin Roosevelt was without merit, if as he implies, it is a synonym for extravagance and waste, then I would nominate for charter membership, Mr. Green, his corpulent colleague, Si "Midnight" Murray, who works while you sleep, and all the rest of the plunder-bund. For to paraphrase the imperishable words of Churchill, to the shame of Illinois: never did so many — take so much — for so little!

But, and let me be deadly serious for a moment — there is one part of his speech I cannot treat with levity. He said, and I quote, "The United Nations is the most dismal failure in the history of the American Foreign Policy."

I would like to think these words were written by a "ghost writer" and pronounced by Governor Green gravely, but heedlessly. Because these are sensational words — terrifying words. These are not words that a sober, responsible man utters just to serve his personal political ambition.

I ask you to consider the effect of such a statement by the most exalted public spokesman in one of the most influential areas of the United States — the most fortunate country on earth, which, therefore has more at stake in the future peace and security of the world than any other nation on earth.

The United Nations is the law of our land! It is a solemn international treaty, in which to our everlasting credit, we took the initiative and the leadership. It was ratified by the Senate with the concurring vote of all the members of Governor Green's party save two.

It has been repeatedly declared by the President of the United States and the leaders of both parties as the cornerstone of United States foreign policy. It is the most recent and greatest effort to realize mankind's immortal dream of peace. It is the hope, the only hope, of countless millions. It is the last best hope for peace on earth.

But Governor Green, speaking as the elected political leader of 8 million thrice blessed people has seen fit to characterize it as a "dismal failure," presumably for no better reason than to do me some political injury.

I would hope, indeed I would pray, that we could discuss our intimate family problems in Illinois without such dangerous and irresponsible alarms.

Fortunately, no responsible Republican leader has ever whispered such a thing — Taft, Vandenberg, Dewey, Stassen, MacArthur, Joe Martin, not even the Vice-Presidential candidates! That the Governor of Illinois' shattering statement did not reverberate around this terrified world, that it didn't attract National attention, that it didn't even attract local attention, I can only attribute to the fact that nobody seems to care about our Governor's views.

Arthur Krock wrote Stevenson on March 6, 1948: "As a poor return for the interesting speech you sent me, I enclose one of mine. As I read your Bloomington oration, the thought occurred to me that, while what you have undertaken is a great work, I wish you had been speaking on world affairs as a candidate for the Senate."

To Arthur Krock

March 17, 1948

Dear Arthur:

I find your letter of March 6 on my return this morning from three weeks of campaigning through the state. I didn't know that you had been blessed with a copy of any of my recent political orations, but if I don't get more out of yours than you got out of mine — cut me off your mailing list!

Best to Martha.[28]

Sincerely yours,

Stevenson's boyhood friend Joseph F. Bohrer was extremely active in the campaign, and served as chairman of the McLean County Independent Voters for Stevenson.

[28] Mrs. Krock.

To Joseph F. Bohrer

March 18, 1948

Dear Joe:

I find your letter of March 12 on my return today from the caravan tour of the Wonderland of Illinois. I am much obliged for your suggestion about the Butler Bills[29] and I have encountered some indignation about the tax increase everywhere. The trouble is, I think, that it is less the fault of the bills and more the fault of the local taxing authorities and the Department of Revenue. I am trying to have some work done on this now with a view to working out some rational conclusions to place the blame where it belongs.

The downstate tour was much more of a success than any of us anticipated. There seems to be a general discontent with the present administration and more activity among the regular Democratic Organization in the various counties than for a long while . . . I think Lawrence Irvin is very anxious to set up downstate headquarters of the committee in Bloomington, and perhaps you can find a moment to talk with him some day.

I am frank to say I don't see what can defeat us except the national Democratic campaign. But perhaps I am getting a little foolishly optimistic.

Yours,

AD.

Stevenson spoke to the Jackson Day Luncheon in Chicago on March 20, 1948.[30]

I have never been quite confident that Old Hickory would approve of these Jackson Day affairs. I doubt if Andy Jackson would approve such expensive homage, and I doubt if he ever foresaw the day when so many members of the Party of the common man could afford $25.00 for lunch. I think he was more concerned with the day when the common man could not afford any lunch at all!

[29] Tax legislation bearing the name of Senator Walker Butler, Republican, passed by the Illinois legislature in 1945, and providing a mechanism for the enforcement of the law that property must be assessed at its full value. Stevenson discussed this subject in his speech of October 8, 1948, to the Illinois League of Women Voters, below.

[30] The text is based on a carbon copy of the speech.

But I am sure he would be relieved to hear that the Republicans don't have all the money. And I am sure he would approve the cause. Even if he had to be the excuse, I am sure he would approve as many gatherings as possible to strike a blow for the people. Because he knew that the little people are the only important people; that many things are revealed to the humble that are obscure to the self-righteous and the self-important.

A gifted successor in our public life who comes from the same part of the country as Andy Jackson is here today to join in our tribute. Senator [Alben] Barkley, of Kentucky, has for a lifetime preached and practiced the gospel we profess. During the years of our country's t[r]oubles, the years of depression and war, it fell to his lot to shoulder the frightening burden of legislative leadership with his great colleague in the White House. If there is but one aristocracy — the aristocracy of service — in our land, then Senator Barkley was the patrician brother of his colleague, Franklin Roosevelt.

I am proud to be able to call Senator Barkley my kinsman, and I am happy to be able to share this platform with him as your candidate for Governor.

This is the first opportunity I have had to meet you who represent the militant forces of the Cook County Democracy, and my first real chance to thank you for adopting me as your candidate for Governor of Illinois. It's an adoption I like more each week, because we Stevensons have been Democrats back to the days of Andrew Jackson. The Democratic Party has claimed us all — and it claimed us always.

I hope my adoptive parents will like it too and that none of you will have reason to feel that your confidence was misplaced.

I can only give you the best I've got — but I promise to give you all of it.

And that goes for the opposition. We'll give them the very best we've got — all of it.

I have one regret today. I know I've disappointed many of you. I regret that I could not appear before you in that mythical attire which has received so much publicity. The simple truth is that I do not own a pair of striped pants, and I hope it isn't true, as many seem to suspect, that Mr. Green is as uninformed about Illinois as he appears to be about the Federal Government and diplomacy.

The only pair of striped pants I ever expect to own is the pair I'll jerk off Mr. Green next November.

Moreover, it is apparent that he is already beginning to lose some of his garments. Having first announced that a Republican primary campaign [was] unnecessary, he suddenly rushed back to Illinois, marshalled his forces at Fairfield, Illinois, on March 10 and marched on the New

Deal and the United Nations at the head of thousands of words. Since then the august Governor has been racing up the turnpike with his shirt tail on fire.

While thanking you for adopting me as your candidate for Governor, I want to thank you also for enriching my life with a new and exhilarating experience. For three weeks I have travelled through Illinois with Paul Douglas, whose mind is as large as his heart and whose statesmanship as unmistakable as his integrity, with Sherwood Dixon, Eddie Barrett, Ivan Elliott, and Ben Cooper, whom by the way, they seem to prefer down-state to the Governor's corpulent colleague, Mr. Si (Midnight) Murray, of Chicago. I am proud to be associated with your candidates. They are the kind of honest, forthright, competent men the people want. They will stick to their jobs and kick the corruptionists down the State House steps, instead of inviting them to put their feet on the table.

But these men are also delightful companions, and together we have traversed the wonderland of this vast and mighty state from the Ohio River to Galena. The enormity, the wealth, the power of this thrice blessed land of Illinois fills you with pride — and with humility.

We visited 130 towns; we talked with many people in all walks of life, and you would be surprised how well the people of the farms and in the small towns, as well as the big cities, know that all is not well with Illinois which Providence has so richly blessed with almost everything but good government. Everywhere we had a warm, enthusiastic welcome, even in counties where the genus democratus is all but extinct. The response, the deep interest in the problems that affect us all so vitally, the simple decency and anxiety to rid this state of misrule and to regain our rightful position of leadership among the states, make it perfectly plain that the voters of Illinois want the doors of the State House reopened to the honest citizens and closed to the privileged and selfish — just as the White House doors opened and closed in the days of Andy Jackson.

Two things among the many I noted on this exhilarating journey I want to report to you, because they are peculiarly contributions of Chicago and you Democrats. No one thing ever endeared a city to more people than the Chicago Service Men's Center, which fed, clothed, entertained and nourished the spirits of hundreds of thousands of lonely soldiers, sailors and marines during the war. All the people of Chicago made that institution the success it was and lifted the hearts of countless service men and countless parents. But I think in simple justice first credit must always go to its founder — the man who conceived it, worked for it night and day, pouring into it his warm sympathy and executive skill — [former Mayor] Edward J. Kelly.

I also want to tell you that many Republicans and Independents added their enthusiastic support as we journeyed through the state. I detect a spirit not unlike that which swept our great Mayor, Martin Kennelly, into office a year ago. I believe he has contributed materially to the awakened spirit of non-partisan citizenship downstate. What you, the Democratic Party, have created here by his nomination and election has spread across the entire state and promises to become the pattern for party action and responsibility for years to come.

In 1946 the fortunes of our Party were low. Hamburger and pork chops seemed to be more important than men. The trend was away from us. Then you gentlemen had an inspiration which gave our state a new look, and its first fruit was Martin Kennelly as Mayor of our great Chicago. The whole country sat up sharply. It turned to look again, rubbed its eyes and applauded. Instantly the trend was checked. I predict that if we but hold fast to the course started with Mayor Kennelly the trend will be reversed to the discomfort of the lumbering, unregenerated elephant.

I believe, immodest as it may seem, that in the selection of your State and County candidates, including myself, you have been prompted by the same motives of public interest first, which led to the selection of the Mayor. I believe you selected us because you know that the Democratic Party must and can give this State a better, wiser and thriftier government.

That is why we will be elected in November. That is why we will have the support of many Independents and Republicans who in this day and age know that party loyalty is not a substitute for honesty or for loyalty to the people's interests.

But please don't misunderstand me. I am not opposed to party loyalty. I shall always defend the right of like-minded citizens to organize and support their political parties. I think the two party system has been the salvation of our democracy. I hope and pray that it endures and that we can avoid the multiple party system which has enfeebled popular government in other countries. Organized political leadership has been a blessing in our country. But I do despise corrupt machines, boss-controlled machines, because the boss uses the people to further the machine, instead of using the force and prestige of the organization to advance the welfare of the people.

And speaking of a political "boss," I must say that our satisfaction in getting the Governor home again is diluted only by some uncertainty as to whether he is running for Governor, for Vice-President, or for best dressed man of the year, or just running from force of habit.

It seems to me Illinois' misfortune is that the Green regime started out with its fingers on the public pulse and is winding up with its fingers in the public pocket.

There are apologists for the Green administration who maintain that it could be worse. I presume the yardstick of their appraisal is that none of the State House gang has gone to jail.

There are others who say that if this administration hasn't done anything, if it has been mediocre, uninspired — it is due to the war and not to bad intentions. I dispute this. It *has* done something, something very big; it has built up an enormous, omniverous machine.

Politics has come first — public service second.

Some folks have said to me, "Aren't you being a little hard on Green? After all, he is a pretty nice fellow; I know him and I know he is a nice fellow. . . ."

But you have to be more than a "nice fellow" to be Governor of Illinois. You have to fill a very big chair, and many people think his dimensions are not right for that chair.

The majority of the people in Illinois want a change. They have had enough. They are tired of extravagance, greed and graft. They are both amused and indignant with warnings that a change will result in exactly what the plunderbund in Springfield has already made an accomplished fact.

Only a few days ago the Governor of Illinois called upon the people of the state to count their blessings. Over a hookup of thirty radio stations he said that his kind of administration makes no headlines — that there is nothing sensational about the State government.

Isn't that the trouble?

Isn't its lack of inspiration, fearfulness of innovation and mediocrity the reason why the record of the State House machine is almost a complete blank?

As for myself, during the campaign I shall talk about Illinois, its problems, its needs and its hopes and aspirations. I shall talk about what our Party should do for the State, and make it clear that I shall always want it to render the highest type of public service. I shall always want its officeholders to realize that only by such service can they make their Party strong and increase its prestige and usefulness. Every great President, every great Senator, every great Governor and Mayor who has contributed to the well-being of our country was enabled to do so by a Party strong enough to elect him. I want no other system. But the Party that has given to our country, our state and our city such fine leaders must demand of every public servant it nominates and elects nothing less than service of the type envisioned by the best of our leaders.

With your help, I hope that Paul Douglas, our other candidates, and I will be able to contribute something to the distinction of our State. My prayer is that the contribution of each of us may be considerable.

Carl McGowan, who had worked with Stevenson in the Navy De-
partment during World War II, wrote on March 10, 1948, that he and
Mrs. McGowan had read "with real elation the account in Time *of your*
successful kick-off in the corn belt." He suggested Stevenson call on his
parents when he campaigned at Paris, Illinois.

To Carl McGowan

March 22, 1948

Dear Carl:

I was delighted to have your letter on my return from three weeks
campaigning downstate. It was a wonderful experience, and I am mortified to confess that I knew but little of Illinois before. Unhappily, I did
not get to Paris. Had I done so I would have called on your parents even
without your reminder. I suppose Paris will be on the itinerary some
other time, and I will not overlook a chance to see them and reveal some
perhaps obscure aspects of your otherwise estimable life.

The progress of the campaign so far is rather better than we had any
right to expect. We forced Green to come back from his vacation and he
is now campaigning violently and talking incessantly — something the
Republicans hadn't planned to do during the primary. I am back here in
Chicago now and start doing the wards tonight. It has been an exhausting business, but I have enjoyed it and I am learning slowly.

I hope all goes well with the baby, and give my love to Jodie.[31]

Sincerely,

To Mrs. Franklin D. Roosevelt[32]

March 24, 1948

Dear Mrs. Roosevelt:

The Democratic State Organization is most anxious to persuade you to
come to Illinois in September to address the State Democratic Convention, in Chicago. The idea, as I understand it, is to commence the last lap
of the state campaign with a bang-up mass meeting here — and you are
the best "bang" in the Party.

I told them I suspected you might be going to Paris for the General
Assembly about the first of September and might not return until after
the election. In that event they say they will advance the date of the
Convention to sometime in August, if you can come, in order to meet
your convenience.

[31] Mrs. McGowan.
[32] This letter is in the Franklin D. Roosevelt Library, Hyde Park, New York.

I am most reluctant to even suggest another chore for you. But I need not add that your presence here would be a tonic for all of us — and we have, as of now, a better than even chance of electing the entire state and county tickets, thanks to the support of many Republicans and Independents throughout the State.

Please do not hesitate to decline. I know how unmercifully burdened you are. But we all hope you can accept and will tell me what date would be most convenient.[33]

Faithfully yours,

Stevenson delivered the following speech at Centralia and in the surrounding area on March 24 and March 25, 1948.[34]

Tonight is the eve of an anniversary in Illinois — an anniversary that will live forever in the memory of southern Illinois. Tomorrow, March 25, is the anniversary of the Centralia mine disaster and the death of 111 men underground.

Harper's Magazine for this month, March 1948, and the Reader's Digest for April 1948, say: "One hundred and eleven men were killed in that explosion. Killed needlessly, for almost everybody concerned had known for months, even years, that the mine was dangerous. Yet nobody had done anything effective about it. Why not?"

If you are interested in Illinois you should read that article, because it tells you why not. It recounts in sequence all the reports that were made over a period of years by a conscientious inspector, Driscoll Scanlon, to the State Department of Mines and Minerals about that mine and what happened to those reports that the mine was unsafe. "Seldom has a major catastrophe of any kind been blueprinted so accurately so far in advance." There you can also read the letter the miners themselves finally wrote to Governor Green on March 9, 1946: ". . . this is a plea to you to please save our lives, to please make the Department of Mines and Minerals enforce the laws," and what happened to that appeal just a year before the disaster took place.

Let me read you just a sentence or so: Green "has governed but little, permitting subordinates to run things. Re-elected in 1944, he reached the peak of his power in 1946 when his machine succeeded in reducing the control of the Democratic machine over Chicago. Jubilant, Governor

[33] Mrs. Roosevelt declined the invitation because of her work with the United Nations, but she ended her letter of April 28, 1948, "With every good wish for the success of your state ticket."

[34] The text is based on a carbon copy of the speech.

Green handpicked a ward leader to run for mayor in April of 1947 and backed him hard." You remember who that was. His name was [Russell] Root. He was the man the Republicans selected to run against Martin Kennelly for Mayor of Chicago.

Then what happened. Well, you know. The mine inspectors were called into Springfield, at State expense, and told to go out and collect campaign contributions from the mine inspectors [operators].

As a miner said: "If a coal company gives a politician $1000 they're gonna expect something in return."

And, as the article says:

> "Here lies Green's responsibility — not that, through a secretary's fumble, he failed to act on the miners' appeal to 'save our lives' but rather that his loyal followers were busier building a rich political machine for him than in administering the state for him. Few mine inspectors went out of their way to look for trouble; some inspectors after leaving the Department have obtained good jobs as coal company executives. One inspector explained, 'If you tried to ride 'em, they'd laugh at you and say, "Go ahead, I'll just call up Springfield." ' One man said, 'It was a cozy combination that worked for everybody's benefit — everybody except the miners.' And the UMWA man on the Board did not oppose the combination. Nor did Green question it."

And, as the St. Louis Post-Dispatch says:

> "To say that the successor of Henry Horner has been a disappointment is to put it mildly — the consequences of political prostitution of the mine inspection service is of course now common knowledge throughout Illinois. It is now widely known that the Green administration carried the political lug further than any other predecessor administration by using mine inspectors to solicit campaign contributions."

Now let me read to you one more bit. These are Green's words as a candidate in 1940:

> "The lives of the men have been entrusted to the state. The only security you have depends upon absolute enforcement of these laws . . . before a tragedy shocks the nation and before we may be called upon again to behold that silent line of loved ones crowded at the mouth of some mine dreading the evidence of loss that will be brought up from below . . . I pledge to you that all laws protecting the health, safety and lives of the men employed in the mines

will be enforced rigidly and thoroughly. In other words, to the letter of the law."

And here's one other fact in this sorry tale that may interest you as taxpayers. In the interval from the Governor's eloquent pledge to enforce the safety laws to the letter to the day when that promise blew up at Centralia at the cost of 111 lives, the appropriation for the administration for the Department of Mines and Minerals increased from $260,000 for the last biennium of Henry Horner to $1,190,000.

It is the disease, not only the symptom, that must be eradicated. We must attack that malignant growth on the body politic, the cynical cold-blooded sale of privilege. And I hold that the Governor is responsible for the system whether he personally condones, actively solicits, or passively permits, the sale of governmental favors. There will be no bold and no furtive solicitation of campaign funds for me at the risk of human life in the coal mines or anywhere else. I want public servants — not solicitors.

And speaking of solicitation of campaign funds, it is only fair to say that the Illinois law did not forbid the activity disclosed by the Centralia disaster. It was a question of morality, not legality. But today, a year after, what do we see? We see this state machine extracting campaign contributions from even civil service employees of the state institutions — Jacksonville State Hospital, Anna State Hospital, Manteno State Hospital, Kankakee State Hospital, Peoria State Hospital, Joliet Penitentiary, Pontiac Penitentiary, Lincoln State School, etc. And this time in violation of the law which expressly forbids solicitation in any manner of campaign contributions from any civil service employee of the state.

Who knows, some day somebody may take a notion to enforce the laws of Illinois, and then some of the Green machine may really wear striped pants after all, but the stripes will be horizontal instead of vertical.

Stevenson's good friend John Nuveen, Jr., ran in the Republican primary against incumbent Congressman Ralph Church.

To John Nuveen, Jr.[35]

April 1, 1948

Dear John:

I am very hopeful that you can beat Church, whom I have known for a long time.[36] I wish there were something more I could do to help. I have

[35] The original is in the possession of Mr. Nuveen.
[36] Mr. Nuveen lost.

[489]

urged many people to vote in the Republican primary in the district. (Not to be published!)

If you can think of anything else I can properly do I hope you will let me know.

Sincerely yours,

ADLAI

Funds for the campaign continued to be a serious problem. Stevenson, however, refused to seek funds from sources which would expect a commitment in return.

His insistence that he be governor without strings was illustrated when two union men called on him. Jacob M. Arvey was present. They said they were ready to support him but wanted him to appoint a member of their union as director of labor. Stevenson told them: "I need your support. But I haven't made any promises about appointments, and I'm not making any. I may or may not pick a man from your union. Jack, here, hasn't asked me for such commitments. If he doesn't, why should you?" [37]

To Hermon D. Smith[38]

April 8, 1948

Dear Dutch:

In view of the present financial condition of the Committee, and in view of the difficulty of getting a proper finance committee organized, it seems to me we confront something of an emergency, which could be handled in the following manner:

I suggest that Henry Tenney,[39] and I hope he will feel disposed to do so, invite a few people to meet with him in his office or at luncheon, explain to them the circumstances with which you are familiar, i.e., that a proper finance committee has not yet been organized with a chairman, etc.; that meanwhile we have lived off of virtually unsolicited contributions; that a substantial amount of money is immediately necessary to bridge the interval until a proper solicitation for funds can be launched; that some money can be had and had quickly by personal solicitation of the names on the attached list and from such other sources as the people present will be familiar with. The situation, as I understand it, is briefly this:

---

[37] Davis, *A Prophet in His Own Country*, p. 294.
[38] The original is in the possession of Mr. Smith.
[39] Member of the Chicago law firm of Tenney, Sherman, Bentley & Guthrie.

Approximately $18,000 has been contributed so far; the bank balance as of today is approximately $800; the monthly payroll, even on the basis of the present limited staff is $1550; and we have contracted additional obligations which must be paid before May 1 of about $12,000. My assumption is that if some or all of the people he invites will personally solicit the names on the attached list and such other sources as occur to them, a substantial amount of money could be raised now when it is most needed and that then the Committee and the planning for a more deliberate and organized solicitation could be worked out more carefully and with some deliberation.

Please understand that I do not assume for a moment that all of these people will contribute or that all of those to meet with Henry will be able to come. But I am confident that from past expressions there is a considerable amount of money available within this group if they are approached personally and promptly with a statement that their help will be most useful now instead of later and that I am, of course, trying to avoid taking any money which would leave me with any possibly embarrassing commitments.

I am most reluctant to impose on Henry Tenney, but in your absence and in view of the present emergency, it would seem to me the best way to proceed at once.

I have checked those names on this list which have already made some contribution, since it was prepared before I went downstate the first of March.

Sincerely yours,

ADLAI

P.S. I would assume, of course, that Henry Tenney would explain that their activities in this connection would be entirely anonymous.

AES

CC TO *Henry F. Tenney*
    120 South La Salle Street
    Chicago, Illinois

Illinois's constitution was virtually unamendable. A constitutional amendment to be adopted had to have a majority of those voting at the election. Many people voted only for candidates and disregarded the separate ballot with the amendment. Many proposed amendments received a majority of the votes cast on the issue but not a majority of those cast in the election.

To the Illinois State Bar Association and the Chicago Bar Association

April 26, 1948

Gentlemen:

This is in reply to your joint letter regarding constitutional revision in Illinois.

I have long felt that this constitutes one of the most pressing needs of our state, a view expressed for many years by the leaders of the major political parties. It seems to me that the rigidity of our "unamenable" constitution which has often prevented the enactment of desirable legislation in Illinois can best be eliminated by a common non-partisan effort. As the Democratic candidate for Governor, it is my sincere hope that all political parties will join forces to accomplish speedily the required constitutional changes and to overcome the difficulties which have defied many previous praiseworthy efforts.

Any legislation looking toward constitutional revision will require a two-thirds majority vote of the Senate and House, and will call for the cooperation of both parties in the 1949 General Assembly. Furthermore, after the General Assembly has enacted the appropriate legislation it will still be necessary to surmount the obstacles that have frustrated all but three out of sixteen efforts to amend the Constitution since 1891. To avoid another failure, it is imperative that an intensive state-wide campaign be conducted to secure support for revision. In view of the constitutional procedure required to be followed, such efforts will have to continue until the goal is reached. However, I am certain that political parties and leaders dedicated to the public welfare will be eager to assume the task.

As in the past, apprehension over Cook County domination of the General Assembly will doubtless be invoked by opponents of constitutional revision. But there can be no danger of such domination in a Constitutional Convention in which downstate will be represented by the same percentage, i.e. more than 60%, as it now has in the General Assembly. Moreover, Cook County, I am sure, will support an equitable solution of the representation question.

By non-partisan methods, Missouri in 1945, and New Jersey in 1947, adopted modern constitutions, and I trust that it will be the high privilege of all parties and civic organizations to work together to achieve such a result in Illinois. Your Associations may well undertake the responsibility of bringing about a state-wide understanding which will facilitate, in the public interest, the solution of these important problems of government on a non-partisan basis. Please be assured of my whole-hearted support and my desire to participate in this vital project.

Respectfully yours,

Stevenson spoke to the Immigrants' Protective League of Chicago on April 15, 1948.[40]

I don't know whether I appear here today as a candidate for Governor or as a member of the Board of Directors of the Immigrants' Protective League, or as a member of the Chicago Committee on Displaced Persons, or as a plain citizen.

But I guess it doesn't make much difference, because people wiser in the ways of politics than I am, say a candidate can be nothing but a candidate, and the way I tie my necktie, whether I prefer jelly or jam, can win or lose votes. And I'm beginning to believe them. A few weeks ago some very political gentlemen took my manager aside downstate and asked him a little sheepishly if he had any objection to suggesting to me in some delicate, inoffensive manner that I wear a different hat.

I'm telling you all this just to get some sympathy for my unhappy and unfamiliar predicament. It's so bad that I can't even talk to old friends without my feeling that they feel that I'm trying to get their vote, or a campaign contribution. And, of course, the worst of it is that both are true! I've even detected an unnatural aloofness in my home, and my children say, "Hi, Governor," and then disappear with their hands in their pockets.

My advisers have been reminding me for some time — with a cheerful smile and a faint note of desperation — that a statesman thinks of the next generation, but a politician thinks of the next election, and that the next election is my present and exclusive business.

Thinking of the next election I could hardly pretend to be ignorant of the fact that there are some 700,000 foreign born in metropolitan Chicago, and perhaps three times that number of second generation citizens! In other words, about two-thirds of the total population hereabouts. They will have a good deal to say about whether I move to Springfield next January — in spite of its acute housing shortage.

So, of course, if I say anything nice about the foreign born here today — which I intend to do — it will be discounted as political vote-catching, and if I don't say anything nice my opponents certainly will and I'll lose some votes.

[40] The text is based on a carbon copy of the speech.

But all the same, I am glad to be here with you friends of the Immigrants' Protective League, of which I have had the honor of being a director for many, many years, and I feel a certain immunity because I have said the same things long before I was ever attacked by the vote-catching affliction from which I now suffer.

Of course, there is another hazard. And that is that whatever I say or don't say will be misinterpreted or misrepresented by the opposition. But I'm getting used to that. One day they charge me with wearing striped pants, because I was on the United States Delegation to the United Nations. And in my innocence I never realized that the Governor of Illinois was going to rebuke me for working for international peace and security.

Another day they charge me with having been out of the state quite a bit in recent years. And in my innocence I never realized that the Governor of Illinois was going to rebuke me for serving in the Navy Department during the war.

And now they say I'm a fraud and an imposter and don't even reside in Libertyville, and in my innocence it never occurred to me to tell the United States Post Office Department that they don't know their business or my correct address! [41]

After this meeting I don't know what the opposition will say. But I wouldn't be surprised if they said I was for cheap foreign labor! And I'll confess I am for *something* cheap in this country, but I would prefer something better than cheap politics.

I guess I'm too naive to be a good candidate, but I don't hesitate to say that I deplore the political practice of appealing to citizens on the basis of national origin rather than as Americans. I deplore the type of demogogic approach to national groups that resembles incitement to insurrection more than appeal to reason. Unhappily it is all too common in Chicago, and it seems to me both an insult and an imposition — an imposition because their hearts are full of the miseries of Europe; an insult because these people, whatever their origin, are Americans. They are Americans who want to respect and honor their chosen leaders. We who have been here longer and have had greater advantages have a responsibility to inform and not mislead, to educate and not incite these people to mistrust the government and the system they want to love and respect.

Must we forever foul our own nest; must we forever corrupt the mind and the spirit to serve personal ends? Must it be forever open season on the gullible and innocent? Are passion, prejudice and cupidity proper weapons of democracy? I prefer to believe that light and reason [are] the only hope for democratic salvation.

[41] The Republicans charged that he really lived in Vernon township and claimed Libertyville as home simply because it was a "symbol of American freedom."

Some day when I'm not running for anything I hope you will let me come back and tell you something more of what we all know — that the cynical exploitation of national feeling for partisan political ends is one of the most sinister disservices we can do the very thing we are fighting for all over the world — government by the free choice of the governed.

One of the many reasons I have so long respected the Immigrants' Protective League and its distinguished director, Mrs. Kenneth F. Rich, is that the League not only stands ready to assist the foreign born in this most cosmopolitan city with all their intricate problems, but also because its work is the antithesis of exploitation. The League helps to make these newcomers love and respect the land of their dreams; it helps them to believe that this country practices what it preaches; that there is truth in the professions of democracy; that there is equality under the law; that they are not second class citizens — and fair game for every designing promoter or politician. Lincoln said it in these words, and right here in Chicago, just 90 years ago:

> "We have among us . . . men who have come from Europe themselves or whose ancestors have come hither and settled here, finding themselves our equal in all things."

Another important, if less apparent, service the Immigrants' Protective League performs by its very existence and by meetings like this, is to constantly remind us all how much we owe the foreigner, the immigrant. The plains of the west and the forests of the far west were made productive by new citizens from Germany, Norway, Sweden, and other countries of Europe. The mines of Pennsylvania yielded their coal for the development of our industrial life to new citizens of Ireland, Poland and Lithuania. The steel mills, the mines, and the farms of Illinois owe much of their production to those men and women who came as new Americans to help develop our natural resources and enrich our life.

I like to recall that although only three Democrats have been elected Governor of Illinois since the Civil War, they were the best — and even Republicans will all admit they were among the best! — we have had. Peter Altgeld, Vachel Lindsay's "Eagle Forgotten" was born in Germany. Edward F. Dunne was but one generation removed from Ireland. Henry Horner's father was a native of Bavaria.

It was Altgeld who wrote in 1890 that "but for the assistance of the immigrant the election of Abraham Lincoln as President of the United States would have been an impossibility, and that had the cry, 'America for the Americans' prevailed as at an earlier period of our history, the 19th Century would never have seen the great free republic we see, and the shadow of millions of slaves would today darken and curse the continent." Because half the Union armies were either foreign born or the sons of foreign born immigrants.

And I like to remember that Governor Altgeld was a Protestant, Governor Dunne a Catholic, and Governor Horner a Jew. Here truly is the American story, written in the last fifty years here in our city of Chicago and here in our state of Illinois by these three men of diverse religions and cultures, but common ideals, one an immigrant and two the sons of immigrants, who brought to us so much and left so much behind for us.

During the war many of the men and women who were driven from their homes and came to this country for refuge with little but their souls and undernourished bodies found new lives here in Chicago. They joined the ranks of the professional men and women, the farmers, the workers, who before them had helped to build our land — yes, and to govern our land.

Many more who were persecuted or who are sitting listlessly and uselessly in the displaced persons camps of Germany and Austria pray that they too may have a chance to become Americans. They live in the shadow of fear that they will be sent back to their homelands, back to places horrible with memories, back to persecution, even death, because of their religious or political beliefs. We in the United States believe in sanctuary; indeed, we are one of the last great sanctuaries for the freedom-loving on this tortured earth. We have solemnly signed an international covenant recognizing the humane principle that these displaced people must not be compelled to go back to their homelands against their will. But it is not enough piously to accept the principle. We must practice what we preach. Our behavior must resemble our words. We must accept a share of these displaced people, and the sooner the better. We've been debating it for two years now.[42]

Those who want to keep the displaced persons out of the United States claim to do so out of regard for "enlightened self interest." They say sentiment has no place in the world of reality. I believe that a society without sentiment is either a doomed society or a society not worth living in. But we can discuss the matter on their terms.

I think western individualism, democracy, or whatever you choose to call what we have, is threatened not only by aggressive collectivism from without, but also by indifference, self-righteous complacency and conceit from within. There are fire hazards in our basement which our fine exterior cannot mask. And one of the worst of them is intolerance and preju-

[42] The Displaced Persons Act passed by Congress later in 1948 and amended in 1950 admitted four hundred thousand European refugees.

dice which contradict our whole history. During international conferences I used to think sometimes that other nationalities saw us better than we see ourselves.

Why is it that democracy has flourished nowhere as it has here? Is it our great natural wealth? Is it our climate? Does it thrive best on the English language? More than any of these, it is due to constant reinvigoration, self-appraisal and the brotherhood of diverse peoples. And all of these we owe to immigration.

English scientists are saying that the war's influx of Poles, Belgians, Czechoslovakians, etc., came just in time for that great people, bled white by two wars in a generation; people who have lived almost without immigration since the eleventh century — except for an occasional rich American girl!

It was not all charity that inspired the famous words emblazoned on the Statue of Liberty. "Give me your tired, your poor, your huddled masses yearning to breathe free, the wretched refuse of your teeming shore; send these, the homeless, tempest-tossed to me! I lift my lamp beside the golden door," is but half the story! The other half is, "Give them to me that I may live and grow strong — that in brotherhood I may resist the powerful poison of unbridled nationalism." Ancient Rome and ancient Greece succumbed at one time or another to the false god of national purity, and we may profit by their experiences. Yes, and by the experience of the last disciple of racism — Hitler.

It may be a bitter pill for the complacent, but it is also true that self-government is often more meaningful to the recent immigrants than it is to those who take its blessings for granted. The immigrant comes to our land with homely classic concepts of democracy. He is apt to know what too many of us forget; that no form of government demands such vigilance, such civic virtue, such public spirit and such intelligence. Without the challenge that is presented by the newcomer, complacency, cynicism, disillusion, might long since have transformed our society into a stagnant breeding place for totalitarian pests.

We have another reason to thank the "new citizens," the foreign born and their descendants. Their personal and family contacts all over the world form the best communications network we have for spreading the truth about America. They are a huge corps of unofficial ambassadors.

In saying, by implication at least, that diversity has been a blessing for this country, I don't overlook that it also presents awkward problems. But there is no novelty in pointing out that it is our very diversity of culture and sentiment that have made and enriched the American culture. And I hope it is equally well understood that there is no room in our country for diversity of allegiance.

The apprehension that prejudices aggravated by the post-war tensions in the world will infect our society with foreign loyalties is already disproved. In every period of national crisis the foreign-born, and those, who like the Nisei have been subjected to suspicion by reason of their descent, have demonstrated that the bonds which tie them to this country can withstand all the pulls of national origin when the chips are down. Give the immigrant a chance; lead him, don't herd him; educate him, don't incite him; and he will join in our laughter and tears, in our work and play, just as any other good citizen, and add strength to our free way of life!

I suppose by this time some of you suspect that I secretly favor unlimited immigration, or at least taking in all the displaced persons who are slowly rotting in Europe. I don't. But I do think there is room for a good many of them in this country, not only because it is humane to give them a chance, not only because it is politically wise to remove that dangerous tension from Europe, but also because we need them for the reasons I've suggested. And I remind you that for several years now there has been but little immigration into this country. Our laws set a limit of about 150,000 immigrants annually. Only a fraction of this quota actually entered during the war years, and even before the war our quotas were not being filled.

I hope and believe that Congress will not let another year go by without taking some action to rescue a portion of the 850,000 displaced persons, and half of them are women and children, from their "aimless character-deadening, skill-destroying existence." And I think it is high time Illinois took some positive steps to determine both our needs and our capacity to absorb some of these new immigrants. Lest certain circles suggest that I am talking through my hat — let me point out that seven states have officially recognized the need for further immigration. Iowa, Minnesota, Nebraska, North Dakota, South Dakota, Kansas, and Wisconsin, all have created official commissions on displaced persons for the purpose of studying the need for new immigration into their communities to rebuild their farms and rural life and to help meet the existing needs of the urban areas. In the states of New York, New Hampshire, New Jersey, West Virginia, Michigan, Missouri, Colorado, and Montana, action is contemplated leading toward the creation of official commissions.

In our neighboring state of Wisconsin, the Governor has appointed a State Commission on Displaced Persons composed of representatives of the church groups, labor, agricultural, civic, and social welfare organizations. This state body is working with twenty local Citizens' Committees on Displaced Persons. Together they are conducting a survey to ascertain the need for immigration and the places where people can best find re-settlement.

In Iowa, 21,000 people participated in a survey and expressed a positive need for new citizens in that state. There are at present housing facilities for more than 8,075 families in rural areas. There is additional promise of welcome and assistance for 1,450 displaced persons' families who have no relatives in Iowa but who could be assisted by citizen groups. Some of the jobs which need filling there are electricians, carpenters, gardeners, farm helpers and domestics.

A survey made by the University of Kentucky has pointed out that Kentucky can easily absorb 34,000 displaced persons over a four-year period.

The Minnesota Commission, one of the earliest to be appointed, found it necessary to give considerable thought to the indoctrination of its members. They are briefed in the problems of resettlement and in the facts which will be required to counsel and help newcomers to their state.

These are examples of the needs and the opportunities which are known to exist in this country. But Illinois, a great industrial and agricultural state, has taken no steps to ascertain whether it too can and should participate. One request for the appointment of an official State Commission on Displaced Persons has been made to the Governor, and other requests will go forward to him shortly. I hope he concludes to act promptly.

All of this may mean that cities in Illinois, large and small, will find it necessary to set up small groups from social agencies and religious bodies to help these new citizens make the adjustment. They will need opportunities to work and to live without fear. They will need friends to bolster their hopes in a new country and to relieve their fears. Very few of them will need what we call "relief." They know all about hardship and will not be readily discouraged in the struggle to provide their own living.

Many of the displaced persons are devout Christians who are seeking a new opportunity for the expression of their belief in God and in the brotherhood of man. A much smaller group is Jewish. They need the same chance. For nearly fifteen years these Jews have been denied the freedom to worship and to express their culture. The churches, then, will have a major responsibility for bringing these families and individuals new opportunities for living, to restore family life, and to revive the God-given rights of dignity and self-respect.

Let me close by saying that the world will more readily recover from the physical scars of war and revolution than it will from the deep wound to the conscience of mankind that this last great struggle inflicted.

We have heard much since the war about the responsibilities of leadership that have devolved upon us. Our responsibility in the realm of moral rehabilitation must not be overlooked while we talk of economic and political responsibility. But we can't lead from a weak hand or a weak spirit. The spirit is an eternal frontier, and we have some fresh pioneering to do on that frontier at home as well as abroad. The foreign born, those here and those to come, are an everlasting reminder both of our greatness and our shortcomings.

To Mrs. Walter T. Fisher[43]

May 3, 1948

Dear Catherine:

For the information of the League of Women Voters I enclose a copy of letter I have sent to the Chicago and State Bar Associations regarding constitutional reform.

It seems to me that the most statesmanlike and positive thing I can do is to invite Green to join me in an entirely non-partisan position in support of constitutional revision. I hope that the League will agree that this is a proper approach. I should be glad to discuss it with you and my reasons for proceeding in this manner at your convenience.

Sincerely yours,

To Adlai E. Stevenson III

May 4, 1948

Dear Bear:

I am most apologetic that I have not written you a full report of developments before this. After the primary on April 13 I had some more speeches and a great deal of work to do and once it was in hand I left for Southern Pines and stayed ten days with Aunt Buffie. I came back last Friday to find the family all well and Borden making a great deal of progress with Emily [Welles] and very little with his lessons. We have had a talk with the head master of Choate School and have decided to send him to Choate summer school and on to Choate in the autumn. I am afraid he has not made the most of his opportunities here — at least his academic opportunities!

The pre-primary campaign, as I told you in the airport, was a brutal business, and now I am off tomorrow for another trip downstate which

[43] President of the Illinois League of Women Voters. This letter is in the files of the League of Women Voters, Chicago Historical Society.

will keep me away most of May. I hope to be in Chicago, however, most of June, and I understand that you and Tim [Ives] will probably drive back together. I would like to arrange for you to go to the Republican National Convention in Philadelphia, which Tim is very eager to do, but I am not sure I can arrange to get tickets. At all events, I am confidently planning on your seeing part of the Democratic Convention with me in July. The summer plans are in a state of great confusion. I had so much hoped that we could go to a dude ranch for a while, but about the only opportunity would be right after your school and before the Democratic Convention. I probably will not be able to get away at all myself. If you have any ideas as to what you would like to do, let us know at your convenience. You could always go to Bloomington and have a few weeks' experience in the Pantagraph which might be desirable, and I have no doubt I could find plenty for you to do around my headquarters here in Chicago as the summer progresses. But I think Mother will want you to go away somewhere for a holiday. I only wish I knew what to suggest. Perhaps you would like to go to a ranch alone or with another boy for a while.

I am frank to say the most useful thing you could do would be to go to Mexico City to one of the summer schools, which would give you invaluable conversational facility with Spanish in a very short while, but perhaps due to the confusion this year that should be postponed for another year.

Be sure to let us know promptly when you hear anything from Princeton.[44] I have no idea when you are likely to hear and you might let us know that.

Love,

To Mrs. Martin D. Hardin

May 4, 1948

Dear Aunt Julia:

Yesterday I received from Buffie your utterly charming letter of April 29, and this morning your letter to me. I am more delighted to have stories of grandfather than I can tell you.

You would be surprised to find how many people recall him who are still active politically. Particularly in the rural downstate communities I invariably met some old fellows who voted for him in 1892, 1900 and 1908, and, of course, they all were intimate friends!

These new stories you have given me — I had heard only the one

[44] He entered Harvard University that fall, not Princeton University.

about Jeff Davis before — are delightful and I think some of them will be politically useful, the Peter Cartwright story particularly.

I wish so much that we could meet during the summer and perhaps if you go to Ephraim via Chicago perhaps you could let us know and stay a night with us in the country.

Affectionately,

To Sherwood Dixon[45]

May 7, 1948

Dear Sherwood:

I enclose an itinerary of my travels during May. I have had two profitable days in Peoria, and you will note that I start out again on Sunday for Kankakee. During the day I plan to meet people of all stripes around town through the good offices of some "non-partisan" citizens and meet with the Democratic organization for a little talk and question-and-answer symposium in the evening.

I hope you will be able to join me on some part of this trip.

Sincerely yours,

To Adlai E. Stevenson III

May 22, 1948

Dear Bear:

I have your good letter this morning, but I note that you say Mother is under the "disallusion" that someone is trying to persuade you to stay in Illinois this summer. I am sure Mother would be much disillusioned to find you misusing the word "illusion." That is a complicated way of saying that you meant that Mother is under the illusion.

I hope very much you can do just what you suggest — work a bit in the campaign headquarters and a bit at the Pantagraph, and maybe a little holiday too. I cannot yet tell about the GOP Convention but I doubt if I will be able to get you any tickets. However, I intend that both you and Tim [Ives] act as Sergeants-at-Arms at the Democratic Convention. Mother is thinking of going down to Massachusetts with Granny[46] on the third or fourth of June, and I fully expect to get there for your graduation on the 12th. She wants to go on to New York for a few days afterward but I will have to come right back. I have a speaking engagement in Peru, Illinois, on June 14. I can't tell you how delighted I was to

<hr>

[45] The original is in the possession of Mr. Dixon.
[46] Mrs. John Alden Carpenter.

hear Mr. Hewitt's[47] report on your examination papers. I hope and pray that the College Entrance Board will feel the same way!

Love,

P.S.   The Progressive candidate for Governor is Grant Oakes — President of the CIO Farm Equipment Workers Union. His Communist connections are notorious.

We did well in the primary. With almost no primary contests, the Democratic vote in Cook County increased by 6% over 1944 and 56% downstate — a total state increase of 17% against a total state increase for the Republicans of 14% over 1944. I am very optimistic. The hazards are Wallace,[48] Truman's unpopularity and the enormous and ill-gotten Republican campaign funds.

Stevenson spoke to the Democratic State Convention at Springfield, Illinois on May 27, 1948.[49]

I am proud to be the candidate of the Democratic Party for the exalted office of Governor of Illinois. I am proud to be associated with Paul H. Douglas and the other candidates whom you honored by nomination on the Democratic ticket at the Primary Election in April.

We did not enter this contest to lose. I expect to be Governor of Illinois. There are staggering difficulties ahead of us. Yet I know that with your tireless, united support we can give Illinois a clean, honest and progressive state government. With the help of an aroused and like-minded citizenry, regardless of party, we can restore to the people of Illinois the full enjoyment of their noble democratic heritage.

Our weapons in the arduous campaign ahead and in the trying years of responsibility to follow must be integrity and truth, respect for the ultimate judgments of the people, faith in our democratic institutions — faith that the people can govern themselves, faith that the best government will always be a government by the governed.

We meet today in our party's State Convention in our beloved old capital of Springfield, in accordance with the law and the practices established by our fathers long ago. So it has been for almost a century. The two great parties select their candidates to enlist the people's support at the polls in November by peaceful contest between men and ideas.

[47] Merritt A. Hewett, registrar of Milton Academy.
[48] Henry A. Wallace was unable to get on the ballot in Illinois as a candidate for President.
[49] The text is based on a carbon copy of the speech.

It is fitting that we do this. It is fitting that we meet as free men to participate freely in the deliberations of our freely chosen parties. It is peculiarly fitting that we do so in this 1948th year of the Christian era when so much of the modern world cannot do so; when a large segment of the human race has no free choices, no choices whatever; when the shadow of a medieval, pagan darkness is creeping across the earth, and tyranny, the most ancient form of government, again envelops so many of our fellow men.

Ours is a sad, disillusioned world. Too many people on this blood-soaked, battered globe live in constant fear and dread; fear of hunger and want, dread of oppression and slavery. Poverty, starvation, disease and repression stalk the world and over us all hangs the menace of war like a gloomy shroud. But everywhere people cling to their hope and their faith in freedom and justice and peace — though fear, anguish, even death, are their daily lot.

Why? Because the Master's teachings forever nourish the soul and the spirit of men. And westward the land is bright. Amid this mounting misery the United States is the symbol of hope. America stands out as an earthly paradise, a land of plenty where freedom, justice and democracy flourish, and no one rattles a saber and no one drags a chain. It is hard for us to realize that our example, our aid, our very existence is the hope of millions, silent, unseen millions, allied with us in the struggle with the new tyranny that may well decide the fate of the world for generations. Our best weapon in that struggle and our best hope for the peace which is the most important unfinished business of our generation is our own democracy, because our democracy rests on those eternal principles of justice, freedom and practical, concrete acceptance of the dignity and worth of every human being.

We must everlastingly preach our faith. But to preach the blessings of democracy and justice and purity of purpose without practicing them is hypocrisy. There must be no rotten apples in our basket. The failure to live up to our professed ideals in any part of the country, in any state, contaminates the whole and undermines the power and the prestige of the entire country on the world scene.

So, while we cannot afford to be indifferent to the central problem of peace, which concerns us all wherever we live, whatever our occupation, neither can we afford to be indifferent to our domestic well-being as a whole, or in any of its parts. And our job is the very large and vital part known as Illinois.

What do we see? We see a state administration that has been in office seven and a half years and has enjoyed, thanks to unparalleled national prosperity, undreamed of state revenue from taxation. Its opportunities have been many. Its declared purposes were good. What has it done? It has accomplished some things, some good things. I wish there were more. But, unhappily, its greatest achievement has been an enormous, rapacious political machine to serve the ends of political pirates in the State House, and the personal ambition of a boss who was elected to the office of Governor — and who occasionally doubles in that role, sometimes even here in Springfield!

But a man can't serve two masters. A Governor can't serve the people and a gang at the same time. If he does — the people suffer. If when this campaign is over there is an adult in Illinois who doesn't know what he has suffered during the past eight years, then it is my fault and it is your fault. It's our job as candidates and as the organized leaders of our party to tell the people the naked truth about their servants and their service, as well as to tell them what we hope to do for them. Then it is up to them to decide whether in this grave hour of conflict between the police state and the people's state they want honest, wholesome government in Illinois, or are content to languish four more years in political bondage to political brigands.

The sodden weight of this machine rests on the state like a heavy blanket — a green blanket. Corruption and moral poverty have invaded every department of the state government.

What about the payrollers one finds in every county who make no pretense of doing any work for the state — at the taxpayers' expense?

What about the Burnham Building purchase, the Wolf Lake land purchases, the Lee County land purchases? [50]

What about the Cutler Report on the state hospitals which said not a year ago: "It is indeed strange that the State of Illinois, purchasing in huge quantities, should pay higher prices for inferior quality goods than first quality goods could be purchased for at retail"?

What about the unhappy inmates of the mental institutions who have been guilty of no crime, yet, the report says, "their predicament in many

[50] According to the Chicago *Daily News,* which exposed these real estate purchase scandals, the state had purchased the Burnham Building (now the State of Illinois Building) at 160 North La Salle Street in Chicago, for $6 million after an option to buy at $4.85 million had been allowed to lapse. Even the lower figure was called excessive by independent appraisers. In his speech to the DeWitt County Fair on August 5, Stevenson charged that the state paid "as much as ten times the appraised value, until a Chicago paper exposed what was going on," at Wolf Lake in northern Illinois. The Chicago *Daily News* reported the price paid or contracted to be paid by the state Conservation Department for land was from four to ten times the valuation placed upon the property by the Chicago Real Estate Board of Appraisers. In Lee County, the state paid $7,000 over the agreed purchase price for a 480-acre addition to the Green River conservation area and shooting grounds, and Stevenson further charged that more was paid for the land than the owner received from the sale.

cases, is far worse than that of a person confined in any one of our penal institutions?"

What about the shakedowns of merchants and business men and licensed professions?

What about Centralia where 111 miners died while the inspectors were out shaking down the operators for campaign funds? And the cost to the taxpayer of that kind of protection for the miners increased from $260,000 to $1,200,000 since [Governor] Henry Horner. Medill and Weir[51] were indicted over a year ago and have not been tried yet. Why?

What about the demoralization of the civil service and the merit system for the protection, the efficiency and morale of the conscientious employees? And what about the collection of campaign contributions from civil servants in violation of the law?

Is no stone left unturned? Is no recess of the State unprobed? Is there no restraint, no timidity, no sanctuary from the merciless squeeze of this administration?

Thanks to the Chicago Daily News, the Chicago Sun and Times, the St. Louis Post-Dispatch and other fearless, independent newspapers who have told the story bit by bit, the people don't have to rely on us for their information about the bold effrontery of this organization which now asks for a four year renewal of its license. But as I said at the outset, I propose to do my best to inform the people of Illinois about the low estate to which their public affairs have fallen — at a cost of more than 500 million a year for the state government, and the highest local taxes we have ever seen. Yet we rely not alone upon the evil record of our opponents in asking for the suffrage of our fellow citizens. We rely on a positive program to restore the prestige and advance the welfare of our state.

Henceforth, as the campaign progresses, we shall present that program step by step. For we must recapture for Illinois the respect of the American people. We must restore Illinois to the place of vigorous leadership which she once enjoyed. Illinois can be a national example of enterprise and courage, a symbol of progress and probity, as Chicago is under a great Democratic Mayor, Martin Kennelly.

I have no ambition and no other interest in politics than to do what I can, with your help, to clean up Illinois, to administer its affairs in the interest of all the people, be they downstaters from whence I come or

[51] Robert Medill, director of the Department of Mines and Minerals, and Robert Weir, his assistant. For a discussion of the Centralia disaster, see John Bartlow Martin, "Blast In Centralia," *Harper's*, March, 1948, and "Who Killed the Centralia Miners," *Reader's Digest*, April, 1948.

Chicagoans where I work, and to put Illinois in the forefront of the best governed states of this Republic!

Stevenson's close friends Mr. and Mrs. Lloyd Lewis sent him a $250 check for the campaign. Stevenson returned it after tearing it into three pieces.

To Mr. and Mrs. Lloyd Lewis[52]

June 18, 1948

Dear Catherine [Kathryn] and Lloyd:

When the sheriff knocks on the door you will be summoned — just as I always summon you in desperate moments! Meanwhile, I will ask you to preserve the fragments of this generous gift against the time when I may ask you to piece it together for me. As a matter of fact, things are looking a little better. Otherwise I might be tempted to take advantage of your generosity. Meanwhile I will impose only on Lloyd's time and Catherine's extraordinary capacity for political agitation!

My love — my thanks — my God! what fellers you are!

ADLAI

The following memorandum was written to James W. Mulroy, Stevenson's able and dedicated campaign manager, and Louis A. Ruppel. Ruppel, between assignments as managing editor of the Chicago American *and editor of* Collier's *magazine, took over briefly while Mulroy was hospitalized for illness.*

June 20, 1948

MEMO TO MESSRS. MULROY & RUPPEL[53]

Edgar Mowrer has submitted
"McCormick's G-Men — Greed, Grime and Green!"

AES

Stevenson addressed the state convention of Young Democrats in Springfield, Illinois on June 26, 1948.[54]

[52] The original is in the papers of Lloyd Lewis, Newberry Library, Chicago.
[53] The original is in the Stevenson papers, Illinois State Historical Library.
[54] The text is based on a carbon copy of the speech.

Young Democrats — and old veterans — I greet you as young Democrats and "old veterans" because many of you cast your ballots four years ago from the four corners of the earth — from France, from Italy, from the far reaches of the Pacific — where you were winning the greatest victory over the greatest menace in history. I know you are fighting men and women because I saw you in those far-away places. I, too, was shivering in France on election day in November four years ago.

But your fighting didn't end when you came home. And I think that's why you are here today. Not just because you are young and believe in the people's party, but because you believe in doing something about the largest and most important business in which every American is engaged — government. I wish there were more like you in your generation. There must be if we are going to remedy the disrespect for politics and public office which has cursed the country of Jefferson and Washington. Surveys four years ago when you were fighting to preserve our political system disclosed that your elders — that seven out of ten adult Americans — thought so *little* of politics that they were definitely opposed to a son of theirs making a career of it. Fight *for* it, yes; but work *at* it, no!

In other countries a political career is a most honorable calling, but not in the land of Jefferson and Washington!

But you learned, perhaps in one of those far-away theatres of war, that people in a democracy cannot assert their rights vigorously and accept their responsibilities reluctantly. You also learned, thank God, that if people *neglect* their democratic *duties,* they may *lose* their democratic *rights.* For that's when those gentlemen elbow their way in the front door who are first hailed as "strong men," and then, too late, cursed as dictators.

But I won't go on. The argument is old and obvious: indolence and neglect are the deadliest enemies of democracy. Paradoxically and unfortunately those deadly sins are often most prevalent among the people who have the largest stake in a free country and have enjoyed its blessings most.

So I am delighted to see you here tonight — you veterans of the war of survival who have enough respect for what you fought for to put your shoulder to the wheel and make it work. With time, with patience, with incorruptible respect for yourself, for the people and for a people's government, you *can* and *will* help restore the lost respect for politics and public office in the land of Jefferson and Washington. If this is to be the century of American leadership, then the leadership of Americans must be the honorable calling the founders of a government by the governed meant it to be.

I've preached long enough, much as I would like to go on and talk about the future of our party whose leadership is even now passing to your hands. But there is something more important for you to do today than to listen to me. It is to listen to some remarks made this week by Governor Green, who heard his master's voice — McCormick's voice — and missed the bus in Philadelphia.[55] The Midwesterner will soon be coming back disconsolate to Illinois, to ask you for another extension of the lease on the mansion which he occasionally occupies in Springfield.

Here is a sample: The Keynote orator, Bertie's Boy, said: "The way to stop slavery is to build more freedom." As a great newspaper commented: "Those words have a fine ring, but they sound like a program to stop crime by ending violations of the law."

Here is another quotation: "The New Deal's rendezvous with Communism . . . supinely suffered Communism to master half of Europe." Rendezvous! Well, if those meetings with the Russians were "rendezvous," then Pete and I have different ideas of romance! And remember, I was there and he wasn't. He wasn't even in Springfield, and what, by the way, has the firm of McCormick, [Sinon] Murray and Green been saying during these last years? Was it demanding that the United States Army occupy all of Eastern Europe to keep the Russians out? Was it urging the government to increase the strength of our forces overseas, or was it demanding that the boys come home?

For that matter, what were Bergen McCormick and McCarthy Green saying when the Nazis were raping Poland and sweeping over Europe? Were they demanding conscription, preparedness, and weeping over enslaved Europe? Or were they saying that we have nothing to fear; that isolation and America First is the path to peace? But McCarthy Green didn't say anything at Philadelphia about a "rendezvous" with Fascism!

Yet the most amazing thing about the Keynote orator's damnation of our foreign policy wasn't in what he *said*, but in what the Convention *did*. On *Monday* he ridiculed and abused the New Deal and all of its works. But on *Tuesday* the Convention adopted as its own the whole structure of our foreign policy as designed by its great architects, Franklin D. Roosevelt and Woodrow Wilson!

On *Monday* Bertie's Boy makes a sarcastic remark about this "double

[55] At the Republican Presidential Nominating Convention, Governor Dwight (Pete) Green delivered the keynote address. It was a blistering attack on the New Deal and on the foreign policy of Roosevelt and Truman. The speech mirrored the views of Colonel Robert McCormick's Chicago *Tribune*. The day after the speech the convention adopted a platform that reflected instead the domestic and foreign policy positions of Governor Thomas E. Dewey. When Dewey was nominated, Green lost his bid for the vice presidential nomination.

talk of bi-partisan foreign policy." But on *Tuesday,* the Convention adopts a platform which says "we shall invite the minority party to join us in stopping partisan politics at the waters' edge!"

Not long ago the third-term candidate for Governor, exhibiting the same statesmanship and understanding of the world, said here in Illinois "that the United Nations was the most dismal failure in U. S. diplomatic history," and in his keynote speech on *Monday* he gave the United Nations no attention. But on *Tuesday,* the Convention said "We believe in collective security . . . We shall support the United Nations as the world's best hope in this direction." I might add that Woodrow Wilson and we Democrats were beseeching the Republicans to believe in collective security thirty years ago!

And I might further add that while the Republican bosses evidently strove hard for the "New Look" of liberalism, about the only thing new in the Old Guard was Herbert Hoover's soft collar! But it's a blessing for the country that McCormick, Murray and Green are retreating to Illinois to run for a third term, even if, as Republican candidate for Vice President, Mr. Green would have been a blessing to the National Democratic ticket!

There are a lot of other things about this keynote speech that amused me. Here's another. The Keynoter said: "The New Dealers opposed the tax cut on the ground that more money in the people's pockets would increase spending and inflation. We Republicans believe that more money in people's pockets is good for the people and good for the country." (He didn't explain how the Republicans are going to arrest inflation and high prices which are impoverishing the poor, nor when they propose to reduce the national debt.) But the hypocrisy about this chunk of demagoguery is that Illinois has accumulated a vast surplus, but has anyone heard Mr. Green say that a tax cut which would put more money in the pockets of Illinois people would be a good thing for Illinois people? Has anyone heard him propose a tax cut any time in eight long years — for Illinois?

What's sauce for the goose is sauce for the gander, or should be. Yet while he applauds a Federal tax cut when the Federal budget is only precariously balanced, he increases taxes in Illinois, which is rich — so rich that he evidently can afford to send public funds every month to hordes of faithful politicians who make no pretense of working for the state.

My time is short; just one more Green gag. The third-term candidate reached the summit of his eloquence when he said: "An honest nation deserves honest government through an honest party. It expects its government to tell the truth and all the truth, to keep its accounts as honest men keep their accounts, to make no promises it cannot keep; to keep those that it has made, and to match material with moral character." That's the best thing he said. I agree with every word of it. I am glad he said it. It took a lot of courage for him. At least, I assume he read it before he uttered it. Now let's apply it briefly to his own government of Illinois. Has it been honest? Has it made no promises it cannot keep? Has it kept the promises it made? What of its moral character? Or is this a new high for hypocrisy?

Listen to the people, not to me, for the answer. Everywhere you go they are complaining about the fungus that is smothering Illinois — Green fungus.

The business men of Illinois are crying for relief from the State House system of shakedowns which lies on free enterprise like a wet blanket.

Honest men want an end to the machine's brassy habit of demanding a slice when the State buys lands, or buildings, or even food for the State Institutions.

The honest, hardworking employees of the State plead for you to save them from the savage stickup men who collect for the Green machine, the stickup men who say "your money or your job."

Everybody, everywhere I have travelled throughout the state asks how long we must endure two governments in Illinois, the corrupt pedestrian government at Springfield and the ghost government of thousands of payrollers who "toil not, neither do they spin." And neither will they win!

The laboring man asks you to protect him from inspectors who are more concerned with politics than they are with law enforcement. If you doubt it, talk to the miners at Centralia where more than a hundred families lost their breadwinners while the mine inspectors were soliciting campaign contributions from the operators.

Ask a civil servant what has happened to the Civil Service and the merit system in Illinois.

Ask a sportsman how many game wardens there are in Illinois who have never been closer to a catfish than the truth has been to Sinon Murray?

While the people groan under the tax burden, the state rakes in tax money at an undreamed of rate, but there is no more money for the schools, for housing, for roads, for the impoverished towns, or the starving old-age pensioners.

And listen to the pitiful prayers of the families of the inmates of our hospitals for the mentally ill, who have committed no offense. Instead of the tender care they deserve they are treated worse than criminals in the penitentiaries. And don't take my word for it, read the report signed by the Republican chairman of the Legislative Investigating Committee appointed by the 65th General Assembly. That report will also describe for you how the Green gang buys inferior food for these helpless thousands and pays to favored firms more than you pay at retail for good food.

The ghosts of the men who died because the Governor's henchmen were too busy with politics to listen to their plea, haunt the State House, pointing phantom fingers at the windows and ask in threatening whispers, "Is there no right, no wrong; are there no guilty and no guiltless? Is this the way you keep your promises, Governor?"

While Governor Green of Illinois prates to the Republican Convention about truth, about honest government, about keeping promises, the sorry fact is that Illinois is one vast Centralia mine. Like those poor men, the whole citizenry begs for truth, for honesty and the fulfillment of promises.

This hypocrisy is too much for the unbossed Republicans as well as the Democrats and for all the good people who know that *party* loyalty is never a substitute for *public* honesty.

From Chicago and Galena, clear to Cairo, this kind of citizen is voting with you, joining hands with you, for like you, they want above all else, their home state to be what Boss Green, the keyhole orator, so eloquently proclaims for the nation and so audaciously denies to Illinois.

But the period of begging and pleading is nearing an end. The gang has sinned away its day of grace. The carnival of corruption is over. It is too late to make amends for eight years of broken pledges. He can promise to protect the laboring men, but Centralia is still there. He can promise to stay at home and stick to business, but Miami is still calling. He can promise to cut loose from the political brigands, but he's surrounded and there's no escape. He can promise economy, but the padded payrolls will still be there — because the *machine* is the master!

I have no doubt there are some in the gang who are so frightened by this hue and cry of the outraged public, so "deathly afraid," as the St. Louis Post-Dispatch said last week, "that if Dwight Green runs against Adlai Stevenson in November, Adlai Stevenson will be Governor next January," that they would like to slow down and play virtuous until after election. Some of them would like to put on the false face of reform for the time being, but the hungry horde of payrollers at their backs won't let them, so the Green machine goes careening on, fed with plunder from the pockets of the toiler and the cash registers of the honest businessman.

I can't find out what the State payroll is today. Perhaps candidate Green will make it public, because he said at Philadelphia "an honest nation expects its government to tell the truth, and to keep its accounts as an honest man keeps his accounts." If that's a good prescription for the nation isn't it a good prescription for the State? He also said that a Republican President "will remove every payroll parasite." That's a fine recipe for a Republican President — and also for a Republican Governor who promised us eight years ago to remove every unnecessary payroller. But instead, he doubled the payroll — He has given every honest, hardworking state employee a stand-in! He's shooting the works — double or nothing! Look into one of the State Departments today and you'll think you have blundered into a convention of baby sitters.

I can say with all reverence that I can't help but be glad that those two great men, Henry Horner, a Democrat, and Frank O. Lowden,[56] a Republican, are not here to behold the desecration of the high office they so nobly filled. But the rebellion that came within a whisper of beating him four years ago burns brighter and hotter and down at the end of the road is the barricade marked "November 2nd." The people of Illinois are ready to turn as they turned in 1912 and 1932 to the Democratic party to rescue them from an administration grown indifferent and contemptuous of the public welfare.

That's why our hour is coming, because Illinois wants no more of "gone goose" Green, to borrow a delicate epithet from the rich vocabulary of another Republican orator — Claire Booth [Clare Boothe] Luce. And when you and I are called to the State House next January we will attack our formidable task with the respect for public service and the sincerity of purpose that bring you Young Democrats here tonight. For Illinois needs the attention of honest, sincere, truthful men. Our roads, our schools, our cities, our institutions need our prayerful attention — every service of the state needs attention! The social gains of the Democratic era must be preserved and strengthened. Illinois, the land of Lincoln, Grant and Altgeld, must never be behind the procession in its respect for the civil rights of *all* our people, regardless of color, creed or class. The businessman, the working man, and the farmer, are entitled to the same consideration — no more, no less. Ours must be a government not just for labor, not just for big business, not just for agriculture, for the *public* interest is not just the *sum* of all *private* interests, it is the *paramount* interest. Ours must be a government — all-Illinois, for all-Illinois. And it must never again be a personal government, nor a gang government.

There will be no place for political tricksters. But there will be a large place for the advice and counsel of disinterested, representative men and women. We must counsel with farm leaders about the peril which hangs over Illinois and the nation — the erosion of our greatest asset — our black prairie soil. Honest labor leaders more interested in the wel-

[56] Governor of Illinois, 1917–1921.

fare of labor than in patronage, honest businessmen and employers more interested in progress than privilege, will enter the Governor's door where now pass in and out some people who shouldn't be *out* at all!

The world is troubled and frightened as perhaps never before. If there ever was a time for humanity in government, for plain, simple neighborliness among the citizens of a state, for forgetting of race prejudice and religious rivalry, for thrift and economy, for sane, forthright, hardheaded management, for unity and ever greater unity, it is now.

Illinois is in no condition today to endure another collapse like that of 1929. Respect for its state government is far lower than it was even in 1932, and some of you are old enough to recall our fears in those dark days, with the hungry and the dispossessed muttering in the streets. With wisdom, sincerity and energy we can so *strengthen* the people's confidence in our state government, we can so *fortify* our state finances, we can build such *trust* in order and democracy that our people can take whatever is in store and come up serene and steadfast in the old faith on which we have built so *well*, lived so *long* and prospered so greatly.

That's what must be done. And that's what we Democrats are going to do — because Illinois has had enough of greed, grime and Green!

To Mrs. Edison Dick[57]

Sunday midnight

J — I'm in Rock Island at last — the end of the worst campaign journey yet. Day before yesterday I was in Lawrenceville — the S. E. corner of the state — tonght in the N. W. corner. The trip thru Egypt[58] was a horror — a fever stricken horror. I can't remember such heat. . . .

Mayor Martin Kennelly's failure up to this point in the campaign to give Stevenson his support prompted the following letter.

To Hermon D. Smith[59]

July 6, 1948

Dear Dutch:

Further with reference to our talk of yesterday, my point was that it might serve some purpose for a small group of responsible people to call

[57] The envelope is postmarked Moline, Illinois, June 28, 1948. This handwritten letter is in the possession of Mrs. Dick.
[58] Southern Illinois.
[59] The original is in the possession of Mr. Smith.

on Kennelly and tell him that they are doing so on their own initiative to make it very clear to him that they support me for Governor. Possible names that have occurred to me are Ra[w]leigh Warner, Edison Dick, John Stuart, Lester Armo[u]r, Ralph Bard, Jim Oates, and Hughston McBain.

. . . I think my only other request of you before your departure for your holiday is to canvass the possibility of Renslow Sherer being chairman of the Finance Committee.

Yours,
ADLAI

P.S. The delegation calling on Kennelly should, of course, indicate that they are calling to express their support for me, and perhaps should imply naively that they would like his advice as to how they could help.
I will try to see John Stuart today.

A.E.S.

To James W. Mulroy[60]

July 6, 1948

Perhaps the underlined quotes from "Progress in Democratic Government," by Charles Evans Hughes, could be of some use for the Committee in literature or for speakers:

"He serves his party best who loves his country most." * * *

pp. 76 & 77:

"At times, not simply the interests of the people at large, but of the party itself, may justify the party man in acting independently of it. It is often the only available means of rebuke and of party discipline through which opportunity may be provided for a more healthful party life."

pp. 79 & 80:

"The actual administration of state affairs, however, rarely has any close connection with questions of national concern. A state governor may perform his duties for years without being called upon to deal in his official capacity with any question that may fairly be called national. And as the people become interested in state affairs, and local questions achieve prominence in their minds, inde-

[60] This memorandum is in the Stevenson papers, Illinois State Historical Library.

pendence tends to increase. They show a growing disposition to refuse to be influenced by the appeals of the national party to which they belong, and for local reasons to choose to state offices men of opposite national faith." * * *

"Illustrations are not lacking where the support of state governors to a considerable extent has been composed of men of all parties whose action with respect to state issues does not imply surrender of their party convictions or their national party relations. It cannot be doubted that this tendency to break away from national parties in state elections is deplored by the leaders of the national parties, or rather by those of the party which suffers the loss, as it is deemed to imperil the party integrity. These fears are often exaggerated as the voters show increasing capacity to discriminate between those elections in which really they are dealing with national issues, and those in which they are not."

pp. 120 & 121:

"It is most unworthy to take advantage, in self-enrichment, of the opportunities of our democratic life and to refuse to bear our share of its burdens. Against cupidity we must ever set up the standards of honour, and the more sincerely devoted one is to the cause of his party, the more steadfast should be his opposition to every effort to use party place for private gain. True loyalty to party is not loyalty to selfish manipulators. True devotion to the interests of party is not fealty to faction or to the personal ambitions of party managers. True party spirit is opposed to all the baneful practices which emasculate the public service and thus, dishonouring party, lose principles and statesmanship in low intrigue."

A.E.S.

To Walter V. Schaefer[61]

July 7, 1948

Dear Walter:

I had hoped to see you long before this, and now I am obliged to leave for the Convention before you return.

I have been hopeful that I could enlist you to do some "brain-trusting" on the issues. I have particularly in mind some good editorial work for which I am not well equipped and have too little time to do myself.

In August I will have to make a lot of speaking engagements and county fairs downstate, and then in September start the horrible grind of three counties a day. I am, of course, anxious to develop several general

[61] The original is in the possession of Mr. Schaefer.

speeches designed (1) for urban audiences, (2) for rural audiences, and (3) for labor audiences, combining a portion of denunciation of the Green record and constructive proposals calculated to appeal specifically to these several groups.

Then I had hoped to develop paragraphs which could be inserted from time to time for press release purposes, bringing in new matter as I travel along.

For examples of the positive type of thing, I think I should plug for constitutional reform, pointing out some of the reasons why it would be beneficial to all groups concerned, for taking the Department of Conservation out of politics, also perhaps the State Police, the Boxing Commission, and the Racing Commission, by extension of the civil service. The latter two, of course, are of particular interest in the cities. More state aid for the schools is something to which I am already committed. Some constructive suggestions on how to meet the problem of our rapidly deteriorating roads is essential. Then there is housing, which is of particular interest in the cities, and, of course, a myriad of other things, including the suggestion that thought should be given to another effort to remove the sales tax from food by legislation, enumerating the articles to which the tax should apply. The whole tax problem is a field in itself, and on which I am doing some work and will have some views. The Butler Bills are very unpopular downstate, but I cannot oppose them — merely suggest that more equitable ways can and must be developed to evaluate property.

On agriculture, we have to refer to the Democratic national record, of course, but there are also things that can be said about the state services which I have in mind.

This is just a crude and hasty outline of what my major problem is at the moment, and if you could find some time to help with sorting it out it would be invaluable. Merle Bergman[62] has a lot of speeches and drafts, together with material on a variety of subjects and is available to help you knit it together if you will have some time after you return.

Yours,

ADLAI

Many Illinois Democrats felt that President Truman as the nominee would take the ticket to certain defeat in November. Jacob M. Arvey and Paul H. Douglas joined with others from around the country in an attempt to draft General Dwight D. Eisenhower. Stevenson declined to

---

[62] G. Merle Bergman, a Northwestern University law student who did volunteer work in the Stevenson headquarters in the summer of 1948.

join this move. On the train to the Democratic Presidential Nominating Convention in Philadelphia, Stevenson told reporters, "Truman deserves our support in Illinois, and he will get it." At the Illinois caucus in Philadelphia, it was decided to give all the votes to Truman on the first ballot. Stevenson advised the delegates to "shake off the gloom about November" because "we're going to win."

As a member of the credentials committee, Stevenson led the struggle to bar the Mississippi delegation from the convention. The Mississippi delegates had announced they would not support Truman or anyone who supported Truman's civil rights program. When Stevenson lost in the committee, he tried to bring the issue before the convention. Senator Alben Barkley, who was presiding, refused to recognize the Illinois delegation. This did not, however, deter Stevenson from supporting Barkley for the vice presidential nomination and making the following seconding speech for him on July 14, 1948.[63]

Illinois is gratified by this opportunity to second the nomination of the brave and beloved Alben Barkley of Kentucky.

More than a hundred years ago the black prairie soil of Illinois was the goal of a great westering migration along the wagon roads and rivers. They came from New England, they came from the South. Many of them came from the "dark and bloody ground" of Kentucky. Those hardy, proud settlers, my own ancestors included, nourished Illinois in its infancy. They broke the prairie sod, and they laid the foundations of the Democratic faith in Illinois. They made only one mistake. They left Alben Barkley's for[e]bears home in Kentucky. But those Barkleys came as close to Illinois as they could, and his home town of Paducah is just across the Ohio from Metropolis, Illinois.

Kentucky was good to us in those early pioneer days. She endowed Illinois richly. And we of Illinois have even forgiven her for evicting all her Republicans — who also promptly came to Illinois.

And Kentucky is good to us now — good to Illinois — good to all of us — good to every human being who believes that the destiny of man is freedom, justice and opportunity for all. Because Kentucky has given us Alben Barkley!

We of this Convention cannot honor him. He has long since taken an exalted place among the inspired architects and incorruptible custodians of a people's government. As Americans, we thank Kentucky for the great Henry Clay, for [John C.] Breckenridge, for Ollie James, for others we could name, and now we thank you for Alben Barkley. While some forget that many things are revealed to the humble that are hidden

---

[63] The text is based on a carbon copy of the speech.

from the great, he has never lost touch with the humble, has never faltered, never turned aside.

Long before the great era of the Roosevelt Revolution was born Alben Barkley stood and battled with the stubborn courage we know so well for the New Freedom of another great Democrat, Woodrow Wilson. Thirty-five years a member of Congress; eleven historic years majority leader of the Senate — twice as long as anyone in history — he has fought courageously, courteously, eloquently, in the best tradition of our party and our country for his convictions, for our convictions, ever mindful that "those who treat politics and morality apart will never understand the one or the other."

In this Quaker City of Philadelphia I can say of Alben W. Barkley:

> *"None knew thee but to love thee*
> *"None named thee but to praise."*

My fellow delegates, Alben Barkley never surrenders! The Democratic Party never surrenders! We've just begun to fight! I am proud to be able to call him my kinsman.[64] We will all be proud to call him Vice President of the United States in the second administration of Harry Truman!

To John Stuart

July 17, 1948

Dear Mr. Stuart:

. . . I think it important for Mayor Kennelly to realize that a good many people of your kind are interested in my candidacy for Governor, and I am going to ask Laird Bell or someone to assemble a little group to call on him this next week to reassure him on that score. I hope you will be able to go along. I think it will help to loosen up the money situation, which has been difficult for me, once he takes some more positive steps to make known his support.

I am afraid I am imposing on you, but I am imposing on everyone these days, and getting highly insensitive!

My love to Mrs. Stuart.

Sincerely yours,

---

[64] Stevenson's paternal grandfather was a second cousin of Barkley's mother.

To Mrs. Kenneth F. Rich[65]

July 26, 1948

Dear Mrs. Rich:

I am taking the liberty of enclosing a letter from Lloyd Lewis about Betty Slovodka, who frequently "pinchhits" at our house as a cook or waitress. She is a remarkably competent woman and really beloved by everyone in our neighborhood. She is a naturalized Czech, and you will note from the attached most anxious about her son-in-law and daughter in Czechoslovakia.

If you have any suggestions as to how they could get to this country other than waiting for their turn on the quota immigrant visa list we would all be most appreciative. Also, if there is any other information you need I will be glad to get it from Betty.

I am going to be away until the end of the week but if during my absence you want to call my office and leave word, my secretary, Miss Carol Evans, will be glad to take any message.

Sincerely yours,

Stevenson spoke to the Soldiers and Sailors Reunion in Salem, Illinois, on July 27, 1948.[66]

Although you no longer reunite here once a year as soldiers and sailors, many of us here today *were* soldiers or sailors in the two world wars which have already made of our generation the bloodiest interval in the Christian era. As Americans we all better take stock of our national situation; we had best not forget those wars and what they cost in blood, treasure and disorder; we had best take our bearings and fix our course for the future as wisely and as farsightedly as we can in the clamor and confusion, the charges and counter-charges, the claims and counter-claims, of a national political campaign which seems to be sometimes better calculated to mislead than to enlighten the average voter.

I think of a cold, ugly day in the winter of 1943 when I stood in the Liri valley while our heroic army in Italy was creeping through the mud, snow and everlasting rain up that bloody road toward Rome. Ernie Pyle, whose simple, homely reporting of life with the GI's won him imperishable affection and fame, was standing next to me. I asked him, foolishly, what the GI on that rocky, rain-soaked front was thinking about. Was he

[65] Director of the Immigrants' Protective League.
[66] The text is based on a press release of the speech.

interested in the soldier vote controversy waging in Washington, was he interested in next year's elections back home, etc.? Pyle listened to me patiently for a minute, and then he said, "No, Mr. Stevenson, the GI is interested in only one thing." "What's that?" I said eagerly. "He's interested in finding a dry spot to put his wet bottom on, so as he can wring out his socks!"

That taught me a lesson in reality. But whatever the GI's and you and I may have been thinking about then we better think and think hard just what we really want now and how to get it. If we do, I know we'll all think alike — farmer, worker, housewife, businessman, Republicans, Democrats. Because in the last analysis we all want exactly the same thing — we want the peace and prosperity of the United States. Not peace *or* prosperity, but peace *and* prosperity. It's both or neither, because every bubble bursts, and without enduring peace there can be no enduring prosperity. Conversely, there can be no enduring peace without a healthy, strong, productive United States, on which the equilibrium of the whole world depends.

When you come right down to it, that's what we want, all of us. And where we disagree is how to get it. We've come a long way in the past fifteen years since those dreary days of apple vendors on the street corners and ten-cent corn in the stove.

Whether we like to or not, we must all thank Roosevelt and the Democratic party for giving the farmer and the working man a fair break, we must thank them for Social Security, for driving worthless, fraudulent stocks and bonds out of the market, for saving thousands of homes from foreclosure, for insuring bank deposits, and for a multitude of advances, not to mention the United Nations which the Republican Governor of Illinois characterized as the "most dismal failure in American diplomatic history," but which the Republican platform says is "the world's best hope" for collective security. And business too, big and little, on which we all depend, has profited richly from a better equilibrium in our national economy.

For three hot days and nights at Philadelphia the Republicans danced jubilantly on the grave of Roosevelt and in chorus denounced him and all his works. But did they propose the repeal of any of them? No, not one.

Perhaps the Roosevelt reforms were too costly, perhaps they could have all been done cheaper and more efficiently. I don't know. But I do know that we have pushed vigorously forward into the 20th Century and taken steps that enable us to face the future unafraid. As a Democrat I'm proud that my party took the lead, and I pay my respects to the many enlightened Republicans who stood up and were counted on the side of progress.

As one who struggled long and wearily in the post-war negotiations with the Russians, I thank God that President Truman has stood firm and taken a strong and positive position in the defense of the West against Soviet aggression. And I am proud that President Truman and the Democratic party have not wobbled on the issue of civil rights — the right to live, to work, to vote, and the full and equal protection of the law.

The Democratic party was tested in the Philadelphia furnace and it was not found wanting. It made its decision. It's going down the middle, between the stand-patters and the reactionaries on the right and the Communists and fellow travellers on the left — right down the middle road of sanity and salvation.

There's a story about a donkey between two stacks of hay that starved to death trying to make up his mind which to eat. But it will never be said that the Democratic donkey couldn't make up its mind in the crisis of 1948. It's going down the middle where it belongs, without equivocation or compromise — and let the chips and the radicals and the reactionaries fall where they may!

Maybe President Truman is saying "I'd rather be right than President." But the great mass of the people *want* what's right and *know* what's right. And that's why Truman and Barkley will be elected in November!

But I haven't mentioned the most important problem that confronts us in our common search for peace and prosperity — inflation. Some way must be found, and found soon, to arrest this whirling spiral of higher and higher prices. You can't outrun a pork chop. Prices will always outrun wages; a pork chop is faster on its feet than you are. Everyone agrees that the best remedy for inflation is more production. But we have got to deal with the economic facts of life. And unless we can find the answer with a Republican Congress the end is inevitable — collapse. And with collapse comes chaos, more and more Communism and, but for the grace of God, war.

So when you are grinning over your salary check, or farm prices, or scowling over the price of hamburger or machinery, think what it all means in the long run to peace and prosperity, and maybe pray a little for the wisdom and the guts of this Congress, and for the scrappy little President of the United States who lives with all these awful problems day and night.

But you, a free citizen of the United States, can't stop there. You better think a little about your place in all this. It's your Congress and your President. You elect them to represent you. And you'd better give a little thought to the quality of your local and state governments which condition the thinking of most of our people about all government. If our nation is sick in all or any of its parts it cannot be strong as a whole.

And our nation is very sick in the very large and very important part known as Illinois. The Republicans who are not on the payroll know it — and that's why the gang government in Springfield which has had our state in its grasp for the past eight years will be washed out of the State House in November. That's why Governor Green, the errand boy for The Chicago Tribune, will not get the third term he covets so dearly, since his hopes and aspirations for higher office far away from Springfield died abruptly in Philadelphia. With the delivery of his keynote speech, which bore little resemblance to the Republican platform, thank heavens, eight years of costly effort went up in smoke in Philadelphia and Green's mirage of Washington and the Potomac vanished — a view he obviously preferred to Springfield and the Sangamon [River].

He didn't even have the privilege of making his own choice. The Chicago Tribune decided for him.

A few days later The Decatur Herald asked "Who's Running This State?" and said that the three beneficiaries of the Republican convention were Thomas E. Dewey, Republican Governor of New York, Earl Warren, Republican Governor of California, and Adlai Stevenson, Democratic nominee for Governor of Illinois. It goes on to say:

> "Under the national convention spotlight with the nation's major league political writers and analysts looking on, Governor Green showed himself to be the compliant errand boy of Col. Robert R. McCormick, editor and publisher of The Chicago Tribune and foremost spokesman in the nation for isolation and reaction. The Illinois delegates and the people of Illinois, Democrats as well as Republicans, were shamed by the spectacle of the Governor of Illinois bowing to the demands of the embittered and frustrated Chicago publisher.
>
> "If Governor Green takes orders from Col. McCormick under the bright lights on a national convention floor, with hundreds of newspaper reporters looking on, we can imagine what happens when the Governor of Illinois is called into conference in Tribune Tower."

Thus the citizens of Illinois finally found out who runs the Governor, who runs the Republican party in Illinois, and just what their Governor was running for in 1948. Now we know. The Tribune has spoken. He is running for Governor — not for a first term, not for a second term, but for a third term. Although a few years ago he said he despised and detested third terms.

Perhaps now that there is no uncertainty about who is running for what, it will be possible for both candidates for Governor to discuss the government of Illinois and its administration.

Corruption, greed and self interest in the public service at the expense of the citizens of the state cannot be disguised forever, no matter how large, how powerful, how rich the machine is. Those individuals who have prostituted their public trust will be exposed and repudiated. I would call to your attention and to the attention of the Green gang, who do not represent the rank and file of the Republican party in Illinois, what a great Republican Governor, Frank O. Lowden, said thirty years ago.

> "There is a law older than any man has written, under the operation of which no human institutions can endure unless it renders a real service to mankind."

That's all we want. Republicans and Democrats alike want real service — honest, efficient, progressive service. And I ask this simple question: Has the Green government rendered a real service to mankind? Has it given you sound, honest, efficient service?

Is it sound to purchase property at inflated values for the enrichment of a chosen few? Is it sound to tolerate public servants who shake down merchants and businessmen for the benefit of the machine? Is the tax structure sound when farmers and property owners must pay burdensome and inequitable taxes on their land and buildings while other and greater wealth goes almost tax free? Is it sound to pile up millions and millions of your tax money in Springfield while denying help to impoverished towns, while denying our schools a share of the budget commensurate with the highest standards for modern public schools? Is it sound to permit the welfare institutions for the unfortunate to degenerate into unspeakable places of horror, inefficiency and corruption? And how about our horse-and-buggy Constitution adopted in 1870 which frustrates modern practices in every direction?

Bad government, ox-cart administrative practices, inefficiency, cynicism and corruption have become a habit in Illinois. Now is the time to break that habit. Illinois needs a face-lifting. But those old faces in Springfield don't lift — they enjoy feeding at the trough too well to clean it out and start again.

I could go on and on enumerating item after item — example after example of waste, extravagance and preferential treatment for the gang. But I think you are saying, "Yes, we know it's bad; we know that Illinois must have better government; we want Illinois to rise again and recapture its lost leadership. But what are you going to do? It is not so much what you are against, Mr. Stevenson, as what you are for."

Well, I'm going to ask you to listen for only a few minutes longer while

I mention just a couple of things that are crying for attention and what I would like to do about them.

A moment ago I mentioned the payroll in Illinois that is now swollen to fantastic proportions. In every county in the state I've seen what has happened to the payroll since the days of Henry Horner — and the name of that great Governor of Illinois becomes more lustrous with each passing year.

I don't know what the total state payroll is. In his keynote speech at Philadelphia, Governor Green said an honest nation "expects its government to tell the truth and all the truth, to keep its accounts as honest men keep their accounts." But evidently he believes in a double standard of public honesty and what he prescribes for a Republican President he does not practice himself. He won't tell us how many people he has on the payroll of the Green machine, even though it is your money, the taxes you pay on every loaf of bread and every bottle of milk, that pays them.

But one thing is certain. There are thousands of people on the state payroll who make no pretense of public service for which you pay them. One of the first steps should be to separate the sheep from the goats. The goats, of course, are 20,000 or more conscientious, sincere employees who keep regular office hours, do a day's work for a day's pay, and keep the state government functioning. The sheep are the thousands — how many I don't know and can't find out — who are taking a free ride on the state payroll without doing a day's work, or any work at all. In many cases they don't even report for work. They don't report for anything but political work.

Last week The Chicago Daily News printed a story about two Naval officers stationed at Great Lakes who are on the state payroll for $350 and $485 a month.

The State Constitution forbids employment by the state of Federal employees. And what public service are these men rendering the state while on full-time active duty with the Navy? I wish there were only two people on the payroll working for the Green machine at your expense, instead of working for you. But unfortunately, there are thousands.

As Governor of Illinois I can get the facts. And when I get them we are going to clean house. You are going to have public servants on the payroll instead of party workers. And you are going to save a lot of money which can be used for roads, housing, schools, tax reduction, and countless worthy purposes which are neglected in the present Governor's billion dollar budget.

I'll tell you something else I want to do which I am reminded of down here in Salem. The saddest thing that has happened in this state or any state in many years was the Centralia mine disaster. You know that sad story. All the world knows the story of Illinois' shame. It has been circulated to 12 or 13 million readers in eight or nine languages in one magazine alone — the Reader's Digest. Everybody knows how my opponent in a campaign message to the miners said: "The lives of you men have been entrusted to the state. The only security you have depends upon absolute enforcement of these laws . . . I pledge you that . . . all laws protecting the health, safety and lives of the men employed in the mines will be enforced rigidly and thoroughly. In other words, to the letter of the law."

What happened? An honest, diligent, fearless mine inspector, Driscoll Scanlan, made frequent reports on the dangerous condition of this mine. Nothing was done. Finally the miners themselves wrote a letter to Governor Green to remind him that for two years his Department of Mines and Minerals had ignored them. "In fact," the letter said, "this is a plea to you, Governor Green, to please save our lives."

But still nothing was done, and a year later the mine blew up. 111 miners died in that tragedy last year, including three of the four who signed that letter for the Union, and they left behind them 99 widows and 76 fatherless children.

Just before that mine exploded, Medill, the Director of the Department of Mines and Minerals, called in the mine inspectors, at state expense, and told them he wanted to defeat the Democrats and that all contributions they could collect would be welcome. But be it said to his everlasting credit that Driscoll Scanlan refused to go along. He thought his job was to inspect mines, not to solicit campaign contributions.

It's a sorry story of neglect, buck passing and political prostitution of a public service charged with the protection of human life. Medill and his assistant, Robert Weir, were indicted more than a year ago for "palpable omission of duty." They have not been tried yet. They may never be tried and the responsibility never fixed for this enduring stain on Illinois' name unless the voters of Illinois sweep out the Green gang, with its "Dear Bob" Medills, its "Sly Si" Murrays, and all the other political pirates that infest our state administration.

What this state needs is a strong dose of electoral DDT!

What am I going to do to see that Centralia never happens again under any administration, Republican or Democratic? I am going to do my best to take the mine inspectors out of politics. They must be put under civil service and removed from all possibility of political control or influence. They must enforce the law without fear or favor against mine officials and miners alike. And I am going to appoint a director of the Department of Mines and Minerals who is interested in the oil and coal industries and the men who work in them, not in politics.

Perhaps the present volunteer rescue team organization could be improved by establishing a few permanent full-time rescue teams. Perhaps the Mining Board should be reorganized to diminish the possibility of political interference. I don't know, but I am going to try to find out. And I do know that politics has no place in a public service charged with the protection of life itself.

In Pennsylvania the mine inspectors have been under civil service since 1870. It is time Illinois caught up with the procession, and if anyone opposes teeth for the mining laws and for their enforcement in Illinois I am going to expose them, whoever they are.

Down here in Southern Illinois where there are so many sportsmen I am always reminded that the Department of Conservation, charged with the management of our wild life resources, also needs considerable attention. Here again politics and corruption have done their ugly work. Wild life refuges have become political refuges. Ask a sportsman how many game wardens there are in Illinois who have never been closer to a quail than Ananias to the truth.

The Conservation Department bought land at Wolf Lake in northern Illinois, on the Indiana line, for ten times the appraised value. And they contracted to buy some more for five times the Real Estate Board's appraisal, but the Chicago Daily News exposed the deal in time. The Wolf Lake deal smelled so bad that even the fish, who can smell too, moved over to the Indiana side!

Over in Lee County the Conservation Department gave state funds to a Republican member of the Legislature to purchase some land for them. That was another odorous deal, because it turned out that the state paid more for the land than the owner received.

As Governor I am not going to tolerate such a system. It has been open season for politics in the Conservation Department long enough. The employees should be under strict Civil Service protection, instead of political protection. They should be chosen for their technical qualifications, not their vote-getting qualifications. I am going to consult the sportsmen's clubs and other interested groups. I am going to do my best to find a way to make this service which has so much to do with the healthy recreation and happiness of our citizens clean, efficient and economical. Other states have done it, and as in mine safety, Illinois must join the procession and move forward to better government and better service.

Better government, better service to the people who pay the bills and not to a political machine, is my ambition and I know it is what you and all decent citizens want and expect of public servants. I want to do my bit to improve the quality of self government here in Illinois where I have the opportunity because our form of government which has been in the ascendency for so long is now undergoing its severest test. It is being watched and measured by millions the world over — some with malice, but more with prayers.

I want you to help me, not alone at the election in November, but in the years to follow, because we can and we must meet the challenge of our times.

To William Benton[67]

August 2, 1948

Dear Bill:

I returned today from a trip through the fever-stricken prairies of Illinois and find a contribution from you to my campaign, forwarded by my friend Jim Alley, of New York.

I want you to know how very much I appreciate your generosity and your support. It was good of Jim to pass the hat around in New York, and nothing is more comforting than the help of some non-residents of Illinois.

Our state ticket is far ahead of President Truman and the political prophets seem to be reasonably confident that I will be elected if Truman does not run more than 400,000 or 500,000 behind Dewey in the state. It's an awful ordeal, but a great experience.

With warmest thanks for this further evidence of your good will, and with very best wishes, I am

Sincerely yours,
ADLAI

To Lloyd Lewis[68]

August 4, 1948

Dear Lloyd:

I find as a result of our meeting this afternoon that I am to speak for 10 minutes at the State Fair before Senator Barkley speaks. He will have 30 minutes and will probably use about 40 minutes.

I think this coincides with what I told you this morning, and if you can whip together anything it will be most welcome. But please don't feel it should take any priority against your other more important work.

Yours,
ADLAI

[67] Chairman of the board of the *Encyclopaedia Britannica*. The original is in the possession of Mr. Benton.
[68] The original is in the Lewis papers, Newberry Library, Chicago.

Throughout the hot summer Stevenson campaigned across Illinois concentrating particularly on county fairs. "We drove in the heat until we were exhausted; that is, everyone except Stevenson," Jack O. Brown wrote. "The man has the strongest self control, both mentally and physically, that I have ever witnessed. In my car he would sit by the hour with a fat brief case propped up on his lap, while he would draft his next speech or a few press releases. His writings were frequently interrupted by his own questions regarding a town or state institution we were approaching. He never missed a chance to acquire more facts and he was always exploring possible information by asking questions of anyone who was near him." [69]

Stevenson spoke at the De Witt County Fair, Farmer City, Illinois, on August 5, 1948.[70]

I am happy to have the opportunity to stand up here and talk to you for a very few minutes, because apparently most of the people in Illinois want me to be your next Governor — and I hope you will feel the same way about it. I can readily understand why they want a *new* Governor, but I am compelled to confess that my wife can't understand why they should want me! But I think she's going to vote for me just to help prove that the Governor has a governor!

Of course, I thought that was already pretty well known in the case of my opponent. If it wasn't, everyone found out at the Republican Convention in Philadelphia that Governor Green's governor is the Chicago Tribune. The Decatur Herald even said this about Governor Green and his governor in an editorial after the Republican Convention:

> "Under the national convention spotlight with the nation's major league political writers and analysts looking on, Governor Green showed himself to be the compliant errand boy of Col. Robert R. McCormick, editor and publisher of the Chicago Tribune and foremost spokesman in the nation for isolation and reaction. The Illinois delegates and the people of Illinois, Democrats as well as Republicans, were shamed by the spectacle of the Governor of Illinois bowing to the demands of the embittered and frustrated Chicago publisher.
>
> "If Governor Green takes orders from Colonel McCormick under the bright lights on a national convention floor, with hundreds of

[69] *Early Days and Late Hours with Adlai Stevenson* (pamphlet published by the author, 1956), pp. 10–11.

[70] The text is taken from a carbon copy of the speech.

newspaper reporters looking on, we can imagine what happens when the Governor of Illinois is called into conference in Tribune Tower."

That's only one reason why so many people from Rockford to Cairo — Republicans as well as Democrats — say they don't want any more of the Governor who wanted to be Vice President or Attorney General or most anything. That plan didn't work, and now that the Tribune has spoken, he is running for Governor, not for a first term, not for a second term, but for a third term, although a few years ago he said he despised and detested third terms. But that was when Roosevelt was running for a third term, and I suppose he just forgot to tell us then that he detested third terms for Democrats, but not for Republicans.

But there are many other reasons beside the third term why so many good Republicans seem to want a new Governor for Illinois. It's because they are honest and thrifty. They don't like waste and corruption. They don't like to see their tax money used to enrich the cynical political machine that has had the state in its grasp for the past eight years. And if you have any doubt about what's happening, look at the state payrollers in this and every county and compare their number with Governor Horner's administration. And I'm proud to say that that great Governor of Illinois was a Democrat!

Or, if you have any doubt, read the Cutler Report on the prices paid for goods and food of all kinds at the state hospitals. They pay more there, purchasing in huge quantities to feed more than 40,000 people, than you have to pay for the same articles of better quality at retail. And meanwhile these hospitals for the demented, the unfortunate and handicapped have degenerated into unspeakable places of horror, inefficiency and corruption.

Or, if you have any doubt about what's been going on, check up on the purchase of the Burnham Building in Chicago, or the purchase of land by the Conservation Department where they paid as much as ten times the appraised value, until a Chicago newspaper exposed what was going on. And it wasn't the Tribune!

But waste and corruption and the third term aren't the only reasons people want a new Governor. They don't think it sound for the state to be piling up millions and millions of government tax money in Springfield, while at the same time thousands of farm homes are still mudbound and three-fourths of our total road mileage is still supported solely from local property taxes; while at the same time our common schools beg in vain for a share of the state budget commensurate with the best standards for modern public schools; and while at the same time cities and towns all over the state are broke and unable to make ends meet as the cost of government continues to rise like everything else in this dangerous inflation.

Yet while the tax revenue piles up in Springfield at an unprecedented rate (in the first six months of this year about 12 million more from the sales tax alone than last year), the local taxes you farmers and property owners have to pay this year for schools, roads and local government services have gone up so far and so fast that people all over the state are groaning and growling.

Government is getting too expensive. Not much can be done to reduce the cost of the national government, even by Republicans, when about 80% of the Federal budget goes to pay for past wars and for present defense. But something can be done at the state level. And I say we must either reduce state taxes or use some of that revenue to relieve the burden of local taxes. I don't believe in hiding money away any more than I believe in throwing it away.

Moreover, I don't like to see so much money lying around with those kind of people in the State House in Springfield. And I know there are a lot of things we can do to reduce the cost of state government — the kind of things those fellows who have had their hands in the people's pockets so long can't do or won't do — the kind of things Mayor Martin Kennelly is doing in Chicago. And I hope you won't be offended if I remind you that he's a Democrat too!

For example, I mentioned the state payroll. I don't know what the total state payroll is. In his keynote speech in Philadelphia, Governor Green said an honest nation "expects its government to tell the truth and all the truth, to keep its accounts as honest men keep their accounts." But evidently he believes in a double standard of public honesty and what he prescribes for a Republican President he does not practice himself. He won't tell us how many people he has on the payroll of the largest political machine this state has ever seen, even though it is your money, the taxes you pay on every loaf of bread and every bottle of milk, that pays them.

But one thing is certain. There are thousands of people on the state payroll who make no pretense of public service for which you pay them. One of the first steps should be to separate the sheep from the goats. The goats, of course, are 20,000 or more conscientious, sincere employees who keep regular office hours, who do a day's work for a day's pay, and keep the state government functioning. The sheep are the thousands — how many I don't know and can't find out — who are taking a free ride on the state payroll without doing a day's work, or any work at all. In many cases they don't even report for work. They don't report for anything but political work.

As Governor of Illinois I can get the facts. And when I get them we are going to clean house. You are going to have public servants on the payroll instead of party workers. And you are going to save a lot of money which can be used for roads, housing, schools, tax reduction, and countless worthy purposes which are neglected in the present Governor's billion dollar budget. In short, we can have a lot more honesty, thrift and efficiency in our state government and the sincere conscientious employees of the state will welcome it most of all.

But you people are mostly farmers, and I wanted to talk to you about agriculture — the most important industry in our state on which we all depend, city and country, Republican and Democrat alike, for our well-being and prosperity. Yes, and I'll go further: on which the peace of the whole world ultimately depends, because hunger and want breed Communism, Fascism, rebellion and war.

But I'll confess it's hard for me to talk to you as farmers. I guess it's because I don't understand you farmers. Perhaps I should say *"us"* farmers, because my father was a farmer and I live on a little farm in Lake County, and operate a farm over in McLean County. I remember when I went down to Washington 15 years ago to work with the first boss of the Agricultural Adjustment Administration — and he was a Republican from Moline — corn was so cheap some of you were burning it for fuel, and the average annual income of an Illinois farm was around $400. In those desperate days you folks were mostly voting Democratic. But then after Roosevelt and the Democrats had given you farmers a fair break with a parity price support, soil conservation, rural electrification, benefit payments, farm loans, the reciprocal trade agreements act and farm prices had gone up and up, you voted for the Republicans, who never gave you anything but Hoover's ill-fated Farm Board!

I don't understand why people vote against their best friends, but if that was the only thing I didn't understand about politics I would be a lot more comfortable up here preaching to you this afternoon! But I think I do know something about you farmers, and I know you, like all the rest of us, are deeply concerned with the future peace and prosperity of the United States. I know you are the most independent, self-reliant people we have, and I thank heaven that we still have a lot of people like you who are not asking for more and more security and less and less work. I think all you are asking for is an exchange of goods between farm and city at a rate which will give the farmers who produce the food as good a life, on the average, as the city dwellers who eat it; and which allows farmers to maintain the soil in a state of permanent fertility.

That's what you want, that's what you now have, and that's what you must always have. And as your Governor I want to do my part to see that you have a fair break with the city dweller — not just because you are farmers, not just because agriculture is the most important industry in Illinois, but because our economic equilibrium depends upon it, and in turn the peace of the world depends on the health and strength of the United States. If we can't solve our own problems, we can't solve the problems of this tormented world. With economic collapse here will come chaos, more and more Communism abroad, and, but for the grace of God, war.

You have often heard the idea expressed that agriculture, industry and labor are interdependent and march along together or they wobble separately. But now we must recognize that there is a fourth leg to the stool on which our national economy rests — government.

In one sense we cannot avoid government partnership in business, for under our free enterprise system the government is by reason of its taxing power a preferred holder of especially preferred stock in every remunerative enterprise in this country. It declares its own dividend rate without assuming responsibility for management and for the most part without financial risk, except as its own "take" affects the soundness of the enterprise as a future source of tax revenue. In the interests of its own future dividend potential, government should encourage the wisest possible long-time use of all of our resources, human as well as material. That usually means free play of individual initiative, except where it runs counter to the public interest. When that happens government has an obligation to step forward and point the way toward a fair and equitable solution.

You have to reckon with government and government has to reckon with you. Soil conservation, as you well know, has become a national government concern and a state government concern in recent years. In my judgment it must inevitably become more and more government's concern and your concern. Why?

In the last 300 years the population of the world has increased more than 500%. Since the dawn of history man has probably destroyed as many productive acres as now exist in the world. Even a 2600 caloric diet for all people (a very meager diet by our standards) would require increasing present world food production by 110%. For each human being there are less than two acres from which food can be obtained, and 2-½ acres are needed to provide an adequate diet for each person.

In our country we have only a little more than three acres per person. And this picture is further darkened by soil and fertility losses. In the United States we have a rate of loss which is probably faster than that of any other region in the world, save South Africa. The amount and rapidity of our soil wastage is terrifying. Annual soil losses by erosion from our farm lands alone total about 3 billion tons, enough to fill a freight train which would girdle the globe 18 times! In a normal production year, erosion by wind and water removes twenty-one times as much plant food from the soil as is removed in the crops sold off this land. The dollars-and-cents cost of these losses is $3,844,000,000 annually — including the direct loss to farmers and the flood and erosion damages to highways and other facilities.

For all practical purposes, topsoil is irreplaceable. The average thickness of topsoil on virgin land was barely seven inches. In a very real sense we were only seven inches from destruction to begin with. We are closer than that now.

This, then, is the reality we have to live with; populations steadily increase; soil resources rapidly decline.

In the United States we now know *how* to lick the purely physical problem of soil and fertility losses, and even how to restore some fertility to depleted soils. Technicians have developed methods of control and good land use. They have shown many thousands of farmers how to diagnose the physical ills on their own farms. They have shown them how to use this diagnosis to shape an integrated conservation program tailor-made for each individual farm — a program employing whatever combination is necessary of terracing, strip-cropping, crop rotations, shifts in land use, and so on. Nationwide demonstrations have proved that this integrated program which reduces soil and fertility losses to negligible proportions also produces increased profits for the farm operator in the vast majority of cases. Far from costing him money, therefore, a properly installed conservation program makes money for the individual farmer — and does so within the first five years.

We in Illinois must take advantage of scientific farming and soil conservation. It is unfortunate that the physical problem is not the only problem, since that is readily capable of solution. The *social* problem of shaping a sound conservation program and policy, and of achieving quickly a nation-wide application of that problem yet remains. Despite the literally billions of dollars which have been spent in the name of conservation, especially since 1936, we are still a nation of wasters.

While we talk of farm prosperity with an eye on tomorrow, we must think about our farm problem with an eye on day after tomorrow, just as the politician thinks of the next election and the statesman of the next generation. And I am tempted to believe that economic aid to the individual farmer should be conditioned upon that farmer's establishing and maintaining a conservation program. In this manner he would be twice blessed — once by the payment and again by the good he does himself.

More important still, our state and nation would prosper proportionately. It is for good and substantial reason, therefore, that I favor strengthening our soil conservation laws, passed I remind you in the Democratic administration of Henry Horner, and encouraging the Illinois legislature in passing measures which will make the prevention of soil erosion a major agricultural project in this state.

While farming is an individual business, the success or failure of which depends largely on the farmer and his family, farmers operate in an economic and social environment which is profoundly affected by public policies. It is vitally important, therefore, that the public policies which we adopt be especially designed to encourage rather than to inhibit the natural growth of agriculture.

With this in mind I favor encouraging the efficient production of those farm products which consumers' demand in a free market make most profitable; and I favor the intelligent use of our farm lands so that production may be maintained or increased over a period of time as necessity warrants. The urgency of the situation makes necessary increased emphasis on research, education, and service activities in connection with effective soil conservation.

The interest of the farmer who is forced to seek high economic returns in the short run and the interest of the public in a continued and adequate food supply must be reconciled.

Reasonable stability in the general level of prices for farm products must be maintained without destroying the flexibility in individual prices essential to encourage different farm enterprises. Farming has suffered greatly from violent fluctuations in price levels since the beginning of World War I. Stability of price levels, of course, is a Federal government problem, since the management of government income, expense and debt, the expansion and contraction of bank credit and money supply, and the value of our currency in relation to foreign currencies, all influence the general level of prices and so influence the prices of individual farm commodities. But we in Illinois must likewise do our part.

We must discourage undesirable monopoly in every section of our economy including manufacturing, distribution, labor *and* agriculture. Agriculture is essentially a competitive industry and will prosper best when monopoly factors in all of our economic life are held to a minimum.

We must encourage efficiency and economy in the marketing, processing and distribution of farm products.

We must encourage the widest possible use of farm products with emphasis on the foods which add most to better nutrition. High level production, an efficient marketing system, a free and unrestricted market, and a reasonably stable price level will all aid in accomplishing our objectives.

We must encourage the continuation of the individual farm of economic size as the basic producing unit for most types of farming.

And we must continue in our crusade for better rural roads, for the extension of electricity to all rural areas where permanent farming can be expected to continue, for better common schools, and for better rural health and medical care.

In this field of public improvement we in Illinois with our enormous stake in agriculture cannot settle for half a loaf — we must attain the whole of it.

Stevenson spoke at the University of Illinois at Champaign-Urbana on August 10, 1948.[71]

. . . But I am happy to say that there is one institution of Illinois that has marched forward with the times and evokes the pride not alone of Illinois but of the whole nation. And I welcome this opportunity to pay my profound respects to the University of Illinois, and to its President, my friend, Dr. George Stoddard, its Faculty and the Board of Trustees. Together they have made — and I believe with the full cooperation of the Governor and the legislature — rapid strides toward the fulfillment of the promise envisaged by Dr. Stoddard when he said in 1946:

> "The University of Illinois is not only now a great University, but it can become the greatest of all State universities. In Illinois the State's educational resources are more nearly centered in this one institution than is the case in most other states. Here is a State University which has the physical and educational possibilities to become the greatest of them all."

And I firmly believe that this University will become the greatest of them all. If I have anything to say about it, it will! Somehow I have a strong impression that the state government has never taken full advantage of the resources of the university in the technical fields of research, nor for that matter the advisory services of all kinds. Although this is more of a threat than a promise to you faculty people, I feel that the state government and the University should work in a continual partnership to better

[71] The text is taken from a carbon copy of the speech. The first seven pages are omitted here since they repeat what he said at the DeWitt County Fair, August 5, 1948.

the quality of all our state services, and I will expect a lot of help from this great reservoir of wisdom and experience.

But the problem of education in Illinois is not confined to the University which, thanks to its President, Faculty and Trustees, has long since earned the generous sympathy and pride of the Legislature. There are also the fine state teachers' colleges and the great system of free common schools. I am proud to say that my great grandfather, Jesse Fell, was largely responsible for founding the first of these teachers' colleges — the Illinois State Normal University — in the town of Normal which he also founded.

In connection with these colleges I have noted the recommendation in 1945 of the Commission to Survey Higher Educational Facilities in Illinois that a State Board of Higher Education be established to assume responsibility for the state program of higher education, including the University of Illinois and the five teachers' colleges, and to replace the Board of Trustees of the Unversity of Illinois and the State Teachers' College Board.

This is an interesting suggestion and worthy of careful consideration. But it would seem to me desirable to avoid any risk that these colleges would lose their individuality and become merely feeders, almost junior colleges, to the University.

These colleges have been developing as regional colleges and expanding their programs to meet regional needs other than the training of teachers. Three of the teachers' colleges have become, in part at least, liberal arts colleges. Carbondale has changed its name to Southern Illinois University and now has three colleges. Considering the area which it serves and the scarcity of colleges in that area, it seems perfectly proper for it to develop in that direction.

Macomb and Charleston had their names changed to Western Illinois State College and Eastern Illinois State College. They no longer require their students to sign a pledge to teach, and they are going in the direction of general liberal arts training. And with the prospective huge increase in college enrollment it is doubtless a healthy development and will relieve the enrollment pressure on the University.

DeKalb and Normal have not yet moved in this direction and continue a strong tendency toward restricting their student bodies to persons definitely committed to teach.

All these schools give a Bachelor of Science degree in Education, and Southern, in addition, offers Bachelor of Arts degrees.

Some of them now offer graduate work leading to masters' degrees.

It is satisfying to know that the five schools comprising the former teachers' colleges and officials of the University meet regularly in a council of education and that no fundamental differences exist between the University on the one hand and the State colleges on the other.

Looking at the picture of education, primary and secondary, in Illinois, I was surprised to find that the State appropriated a total of approximately $82,450,000 for higher education in Illinois in the last session, and but $82,178,000 for common school education and all related services.

Now I don't believe for one minute that the 82 million dollars for higher education in the six state-supported institutions is excessive — but I do know that the 65 million dollars the State contributes to our common schools for strictly school purposes is not enough.

To maintain the distinguished position of the University of Illinois as one of the foremost universities of the world, it must have well prepared students. The product of our common schools must come to the University equipped to take full advantage of the educational opportunities offered by our several state-supported institutions of higher learning. After all, the principal purpose for which this great University exists is to provide advanced education for the children trained in our common schools.

We do not follow in Illinois the jungle doctrine of the survival of the so-called fittest; we follow, rather, the doctrine of fitting as many as possible for survival. From kindergarten to university, in technical schools, agricultural schools, vocational schools, continuation schools, professional schools, evening schools, adult classes and libraries, we open the door of opportunity to all. It should be our purpose to make sure that that door is kept open in all parts of the State for all of the people without discrimination on account of race, creed, color, social condition, geographical location or economic position.

We cannot afford to allow economic deprivation to make a mockery of opportunity for the people of any area of the state. We must so equalize our tax resources that school opportunity shall be equal for ambitious youth. We cannot afford to allow any portion of the state to suffer for lack of resources to maintain good schools.

Let me say that I hope to see and to play some part in the greater expansion of the physical and educational facilities of every one of the six state-supported institutions of higher learning. I hope that I, too, may play my part in removing the dependence of the common schools of this state from reliance on a single source of revenue — the over-burdened real property tax.

The combined resources of local communities, the state and the nation should be marshalled in support of education, not higher education exclusively. For good citizenship commences with good common schools.

Stevenson spoke at the Illinois State Fair in Springfield on August 18, 1948.[72]

I wonder how many of us here today remember that the Illinois State Fair represents the highest development of one of the oldest traditions of Western civilization. The tradition of the fair has resisted all the changes in our civilization. It remains today what it was in the fifth century in Europe, a meeting place for farmers and townspeople, for young and old.

By its nature the Fair has always been democratic. The rewards have gone to the best breeder of livestock, to the farmer who raised the best grain, to his wife and daughter who made the best pastry and wove the finest fabric. The prizes went to them not because they were born in the castle on the hill, but because they were the most proficient.

It was only natural that America should take this democratic custom to its heart; it was only natural that we should have built this custom into the magnificent state and county fairs which we have come to know. And this Illinois State Fair is the greatest of them all!

Like thousands of other boys raised here in central Illinois, a visit to the State Fair was my most exciting experience. Walking through these grounds I learned that I — and every boy in Illinois — was part of all this. I learned that Illinois was not only a great farm state, but also a great manufacturing and mining state, as well as the home of famous colleges and three of the great universities of the world. I learned that Illinois was a thrice blessed state.

I learned that here the steel plough that broke the prairie sod was invented; here was invented the wire fence which made it possible to raise corn and hogs side by side; that here in Illinois were established the stockyards, the packing house, the grain exchange; that here was created farm machinery that all people everywhere could use; that here in Illinois centered the railway system that has been the marvel of the world.

Perhaps I didn't realize then what I do now: that the most dramatic thing about this Fair is what it represents — the fruits of the hands and minds of a great people. And I'm sure I never thought then, when the political speeches my father always wanted to hear, seemed to me so deadly dull, that some day I would be standing up here committing the same nuisance and administering the same cruel punishment to a lot of innocent, happy boys!

But by immemorial custom Americans have made politics part of the pattern of the Fair. And a good thing it is too that the American farmer

---

[72] The text is from a news release of the speech.

sets aside a little of his midsummer holiday for politics, because government has more and more to do with his welfare. Here at the Fair he can see, hear and evaluate at least some of the men who seek public office. Great statesmen have come to plead their causes; famous demagogues and charlatans have come to weave their oratorical spells; and mediocre men have come with little but their plea for votes.

Yet they all come, because farmers are the most independent, self-reliant people we have; because agriculture is the basic industry on which the prosperity of Illinois depends; yes, and on which the economic and political equilibrium of the nation and the whole world depends.

And that's why I am here as a candidate for Governor. That's why all the Democratic state candidates are here, and also the great Senator Barkley of Kentucky, who for 35 years has fought the people's fight, in season and out, with a courtesy, courage and conviction that have won for him the respect and the love of friend and foe alike.

Kentucky was good to us in the early pioneer days. Many of her sons settled early Illinois. And now our southern neighbor, Kentucky, has given us — all of us who believe that the destiny of man is freedom, justice and opportunity for all — Alben Barkley, the next Vice President of the United States.

I am proud to call him my kinsman, not just because of his eminence, but because he has never forgotten that "those who treat politics and morality apart will never understand the one or the other."

Here at this magnificent demonstration of what we are today, is the moment to decide what we will be tomorrow. We cannot allow the yellow corn in these buildings to sell again at ten cents a bushel. We cannot allow that prize-winning hog and the farm that raised it to be sold again for the mortgage. And we cannot allow the rats of corruption and neglect to undermine the foundations of our state any longer.

I am going to be your next Governor; not because I possess any remarkable virtues and talents; but because the Green machine has given politics and greed the priority over public service and honesty — because the Green machine has treated politics and morality apart.

Each week brings some new revelation. A murder in Peoria reveals evidence of protection of gambling by state officials.[73] The St. Louis Post-

---

[73] In July, gangster Bernie Shelton was murdered in Peoria. St. Louis *Post-Dispatch* reporter Theodore C. Link, who unearthed an alliance between Governor Green's appointees and gambling interests, was indicted on charges of kidnaping, conspiracy, and intimidation against Peter Petrakos, the suspected "finger man" in the murder. (The indictment was dismissed in February, 1949.) Freedom of the press became an issue, and many newspapers which had done little to expose the graft and corruption Stevenson had been denouncing now began to attack the Green administration, and the disclosures turned many Republicans against Green and swayed many independent voters toward Stevenson.

Dispatch says that the Governor and Attorney General who want a third term "sit at the top of a state government which presides over a vast, undermining, corrupting underworld," and asks, "Are the people of Illinois going to take it?"

Tavern proprietors "fix" license revocation charges by regular monthly payoffs and contractors who would not make the ante the state demands even went to Washington to complain, The Post-Dispatch says.

Fraud and forgery of candidates' petitions by state employees are condoned by the State Treasurer and the Attorney General, the chief law enforcement officer of the state.

The machine purchases property for the state at grossly inflated values.

Naval officers are court martialled at Great Lakes because they are on the state payroll illegally. And I wish Governor Green dared tell you how many people there are on the payroll who make no pretense of earning the salaries you pay them. "What, you ain't on the payroll?" is a standing joke throughout the state.

111 miners die at Centralia while the mine inspection service is exploited for political purposes.

Even the civil servants have no security from the relentless shakedown for money for this rapacious machine.

Money piles up in Springfield like never before, and meanwhile the schools and local governments go hungry, although your property taxes have hit the roof. "Look at your tax bill, see red and feel green," somebody said.

This administration has spent more, taxed the people more, and done less for the people and more for the machine than any in our history.

People want something better than all this cynical costly, gang government. They want honesty and service most of all. And my colleagues and I are going to fumigate the State House and give it to you — or break our hearts in the attempt!

To Ronald Tree

August 20, 1948

Dear Ronnie:

I am taking the liberty of giving this note of introduction to Mr. and Mrs. James Edward Day. Ed has been associated with me in the law business here in Chicago for many years, except while he was doing a superb job for the Navy both ashore and afloat during the war. His wife is the daughter of Kenneth Burgess, formerly my senior partner and a leading citizen of Chicago.

They are on a brief holiday in England and Scotland, and I understand they are going to be visiting not far from you. I wanted them so much to see your beautiful place and your beautiful wife! — not to mention you.

My campaign is progressing even better than I had any right to expect, due largely to the widespread dissatisfaction with Governor Green's administration among Republicans as well as Democrats. If it were not a national election year it would be a cinch.

Ellen sends her best, and we will hope to see you here in the fall.

Yours,

Alicia Patterson and Adlai Stevenson had been friends since the mid-1920's. In July 1926, Stevenson went on a trip to Russia and Miss Patterson married and moved to London and later to New York. He did not see her again until he went to New York in 1946 as a delegate to the General Assembly of the United Nations, when they renewed their friendship. In 1948, and until her death in 1963, Miss Patterson (in private life, Mrs. Harry Guggenheim) was publisher of Newsday, *the Long Island daily newspaper.*

To Alicia Patterson[74]

[late August, 1948?]

Now I'm home with my horrible, bulging brief case and my bewitching John Fell. Ellen & Borden have gone to dinner parties & I should like to spend the sultry insect noisy night writing en[d]less thoughts to you and talking endless things with him. But I can't — with that ghastly brief case — and tomorrow — staring at me.

. . . My 4 counties a day itinerary for Sept. is almost complete and in a word I will be in Chi[cago] Sept. 12, 13 & 14 & thats all until Oct. Then I'll be working out of here until election. The 12th I'll be busy all day at the Riverview Democratic "picnic" where they expect to crowd in 200,000–300,000 people to raise money for the Cook County campaign. If you could come the night of the 13th it would be perfect.

Its as hard to stop this silly screed as it always is to say farewell. You were sweet to send the check to Jane [Dick]. She's still in the West, but due back soon I think, tho I wish you had sent this one to me. I don't want her to be sending in too many anonymous ones. The men collectors may wonder why they don't get at some of these mysterious sources!

As to the campaign — the breaks are all my way. Bad gambling disclo-

[74] This handwritten letter is in the possession of Adlai E. Stevenson III.

sures in Peoria county with Green's gang involved. The Post-Dispatch is doing a superb job for me with a burning editorial almost every day[75] — and now Fitz.[76] has gone to work with a magnificent cartoon. Charley Wheeler of the [Chicago Daily] News — the dean of political writers — thinks I'm going to win in spite of Truman and Green's money. Things are getting livelier & livelier — and why the hell do I want to win & get into that hideous mess for 4 years of solitary agony & heart break. . . .

A.

Stevenson spoke at the DuQuoin County Fair, DuQuoin, Illinois, on September 1, 1948.[77]

I am going to be the Governor of this great State. Not because of any remarkable personal virtues of mine, not even because this country is enjoying under a Democratic administration the greatest prosperity ever known to any people, with 61 million employed at high wages and national income over 200 billion, business earning more than ever before, and the farmers producing more abundantly and more profitably than ever before. We are going to win because the Republicans want a new Governor just as much as the Democrats.

People want a new Governor because two terms — eight years — is enough of the Green machine, which has taxed the people more, spent more and done less for the people and more for themselves than any previous tenants of the State House.

And you are paying for it all — you pay in sales tax, cigarette tax, and all the other state taxes, $45 a year for every man, woman and child. If you are the head of a family of four you are paying taxes to the state equivalent to a federal income tax on about $4,000 of income. And you know what has happened to your local taxes which have gone up so far and so fast everyone is groaning and grumbling. Someone said "when you look at your tax bill you see red and think of Green."

And still local governments don't have enough money to make both ends meet and maintain their services, while at the same time the state has been piling up a surplus of over 200 million of your money in Spring-

---

[75] As an example, the *Post-Dispatch* published an editorial on August 16 entitled "Now — Gov. Green?" which summarized disclosures of "intimate connections between Illinois officials and syndicated gambling" and asked: "Why is Gov. Green silent through all these disclosures? Is it because he is the chief beneficiary of syndicated gambling? Is it because the main gambling counties gave him the margin by which he was re-elected?"

[76] Daniel R. Fitzpatrick, St. Louis *Post-Dispatch* cartoonist.

[77] The text is based on a news release of the speech.

field! Until we can get a more fair and just system in Illinois some of the excess money in Springfield should be returned to relieve the burden of local taxes. I don't believe in hiding money away any more than I believe in throwing it away on a corrupt machine.

And people don't like a shadow government — Republicans don't like an errand boy governor. As The Decatur Herald-Review said about the Republican Convention:

> "Under the national convention spotlight with the nation's major league political writers and analysts looking on, Governor Green showed himself to be the compliant errand boy of Col. Robert R. McCormick, editor and publisher of The Chicago Tribune and foremost spokesman in the nation for isolation and reaction. The Illinois delegates and the people of Illinois, Democrats as well as Republicans, were shamed by the spectacle of the Governor of Illinois bowing to the demands of the embittered and frustrated Chicago publisher.
>
> "If Governor Green takes orders from Col. McCormick under the bright lights on a national convention floor with hundreds of newspaper reporters looking on, we can imagine what happens when the Governor of Illinois is called into conference in Tribune Tower."

And good, honest Republicans don't like this machine and the people who are running it any better than we Democrats.

The Greed Gang — no, I haven't a cold in my head! — the Greed administration has in the last eight long years become the most wasteful and corrupt political machine in the State of Illinois. It has persistently perverted its great responsibility. It has forfeited all claim to a third term.

Governor Greed and this callous, tyrannical, deceitful and extravagant machine:

(1) Has blocked adequate appropriations for the common schools to educate our children and protect our teachers.

(2) Has been indifferent to the needs of local governmental units in spite of excessive collection of state taxes.

(3) Has subsidized, at the taxpayers' expense, thousands of useless political payrollers.

(4) Is responsible for the loss of 111 lives in the Centralia mine disaster due to shocking neglect of duty.

(5) Our State hospitals have become patronage preserves. Political interference and gross neglect in the care of patients in the hospitals and the inmates of the state institutions have reduced them to unspeakable places of horror. The Legislative Committee appointed by the last General Assembly, dominated by Republicans, says in so many words that:

"The unfortunate inmates of our State Mental Institutions have, for a generation, been the most sadly neglected individuals in the State; they have been guilty of no crime, yet their predicament in many cases, is far worse than that of a person confined in any one of our penal institutions."

(6) Has paid sanctimonious lip service to the problems of housing for veterans but has left the tragic situation unchanged.

(7) Has cruelly ignored the fact that the cost of living has left our aged men and women below the level of decent subsistence.

(8) Its State officials have sold protection for liquor law violations and gambling. Shakedowns, graft and corruption all over the State in sales tax collections, contract awards and State purchases, have become the chief assets of the Green machine. The taxpayers have been defrauded in the Burnham Building, Wolf Lake and Dixon real estate purchases; civil servants are shaken down for campaign contributions in violation of the law; honest businessmen feel the squeeze; contractors for the State have to lay it on the line.

The other day The St. Louis Post-Dispatch, commenting on the evidence of bribery of state officials by the Shelton gang in Peoria, said:

"Dwight Green wants a third term as Governor. George F. Barrett wants a third term as Attorney General. Yet they sit at the top of a state government which presides over a vast, undermining, corrupting underworld. Are the people of Illinois going to take it?"

(9) The Green-Butler tax laws have been so administered that the burden on the farm owner, the small home owner and the building owner is more unfair than ever before.

(10) It has blocked all Democratic efforts to procure a Constitutional Convention — to modernize the archaic, expensive, inefficient government structure in Illinois, to restore more home rule to localities, to equalize the tax burden, to improve our judicial system, to diminish the fantastic multiplicity of governmental units in Illinois which are just about three times the national average, with all the attendant duplication of expense.

(11) It has failed to keep its solemn pledge to take the sales tax off food — a pledge made with a tongue in the cheek.

(12) It has destroyed the security and morale of civil service employees and used civil service and the merit system to build up a political machine instead of a career in public service.

(13) It has corrupted the Department of Conservation. There are more game wardens than rabbits in some counties.

(14) It has condoned forgery in the preparation of candidates' petitions.

We believe that Illinois can and must have honest, thrifty, clean government. We believe it can and must be restored to leadership among the states. We believe our State's reputation can and must be redeemed:

(1) We mean it when we say that government has no greater responsibility than our common school system. We believe in adequate appropriations for the schools.

(2) We mean it when we say the State should divert a portion of its excess revenues to assist localities — both rural and urban — and to relieve the overburdened taxpayers.

(3) We mean it when we say that politics must be utterly removed from mine inspection by placing mine inspectors under rigid civil service. We mean it when we say that the tragedy of Centralia must not be repeated.

(4) We mean it when we say there is no room on the public payrolls for employees who render no service to the state. It is hard enough in these days of the rising cost of living to balance the budget without subsidizing an army of payrollers. We mean it when we say we shall demand a full day's work for a full day's pay.

(5) We mean it when we say that public officials who profit from crime, vice and gambling should be exposed and subjected to the full penalties of the law.

(6) Shakedowns, coercion and all forms of tyranny and corruption must stop. The corruptionists must be routed out of the public service. Public office is not a hunting license, it is a public trust.

(7) We mean it when we say that the Department of Conservation must be removed from politics and must be reorganized so that it will serve its public purpose efficiently and without waste.

(8) We mean it when we say that the state civil service employees should have security and stability and that every extension of the merit system is a blow to bosses and machine politics.

(9) We mean it when we say that brutality must stop and that humane, modern conditions of care and treatment must be restored in the State hospitals for the mentally ill and the correctional institutions.

(10) We emphatically support legislation for a State Constitutional Convention.

(11) The allowance for our aged men and women should be increased to meet the demands of the increased cost of living.

(12) We mean it when we say that the Green-Butler assessment laws should be administered so as to remove inequalities and injustices in local taxation.

(13) Every effort must be made to bring about industrial peace between labor and management, but not at the price of the gains labor has made in both state and nation under Democratic administrations. We mean it when we say we will oppose any restrictive and repressive legislation affecting the rights of labor.

(14) We mean it when we say agriculture is the basic industry of Illinois. We favor strengthening the soil conservation laws and state services to farmers. The Illinois road system must be restored and improved from farm to highway to market.

(15) And we mean it when we say that people have had enough of the Greed Gang.

(16) And when we say we are going to be elected — we mean that too!

There is no date on the following handwritten letter. It may have been written on September 2, 1948, the day after Stevenson spoke at the DuQuoin County Fair. By this date, Henry A. Wallace, campaigning for the Presidency on the Progressive party ticket, had been denied a place on the Illinois ballot.

To Mrs. Edison Dick[78]

Thursday

J — I'm in Pinkneyville. The street is dancing in the heat. In a few minutes I leave for Vandalia. Yesterday it was Du Quoin, the day before Spring Valley — and so on and on to the end of time. I'm getting weary, nervous and car[e]less. . . .

Down here I'm very strong — not *some* Republicans but most all of them. Its Post Dispatch area. What with Wallace off the ticket it looks more and more certain now that the story of Green's iniquities is getting better known thruout the state. But I shudder at the thought of what I'll inherit & the corruption of ethics it will leave behind, even among the Democrats. . . .

p.s.s. I wasn't a bit satisfied with my radio recordings. No proper opportunity to edit the scripts. I hope you won't be too disappointed with them.

Stevenson was resting at his old home in Bloomington on a Sunday when he wrote the following letter to his running mate.

[78] This handwritten letter is in the possession of Mrs. Dick.

To Sherwood Dixon[79]

September 5, 1948

Dear Sherwood:

I'm stopping off here for one comfortable night on my endless quest and its the first opportunity I've had to write you since I heard about your mother's death in Shelbyville yesterday.

I am so distressed to hear of your misfortune and my thoughts are with you. I wish there was something I could do — but I'll content myself for the moment with adding your speech to mine!

With deep sympathy and my warmest regards to you and your wife —

Sincerely

ADLAI E. S.

Stevenson sent a campaign postcard with his picture on the front of the card to Alicia Patterson.

To Alicia Patterson[80]

September 5, 1948

Dear Miss Patterson:

This gentleman strongly recommends himself to the considerate attention of Mr. & Mrs. Albright,[81] residents of Ill[inois]. He also welcomes interviews by all distinguished newspaper women, particularly those re- siding on Long Island!

Four counties a day is fine education, but I don't recommend it for human beings —

ADLAI E.S.

Stevenson spoke at Brooklyn, Illinois, on September 6, 1948.[82]

The men who helped found Brooklyn some 111 years ago were of that handful who look beyond today and tomorrow and can see not alone what men are but what men are meant to be. Brooklyn, as places go in America, is not very big now. It was even smaller 75 years ago when it

[79] This handwritten letter is in the possession of Mr. Dixon.
[80] This handwritten postcard is in the possession of Adlai E. Stevenson III.
[81] Mr. and Mrs. Ivan Albright, Miss Patterson's brother-in-law and sister.
[82] The text is from a press release of the speech.

was incorporated. And yet, as things go in America, great principles seem to have a habit of taking root in small places, and in time, they cast their shadows over the land. That was true of a farming village called Lexington where political freedom was born in this hemisphere. It was true of a crossroads town called Gettysburg where human freedom was victorious. And it was true right here in Brooklyn, Illinois.

Here, in this place, your forebears and mine didn't merely establish another settlement in America. They established a *special kind* of settlement — one formed of people who by choice turned their backs on slavery and by choice accepted the risks of being free men. It is not an easy choice to make now. It was equally difficult then. There were doubting Thomases then as now who said that freedom was an illusion — that Egypt was preferable to a Promised Land that could be reached only by way of a desert. And even after the choice was made, those who travelled the underground route to this village ran risks and endured hardships as great as those faced by any man who escaped Hitler's Europe to join the legions of free men.

It is right and proper that we should recall the courage of the men who founded this community. It is right that we should honor them for choosing the risks of freedom. Their choice became that of the nation — and we are all in their debt because they made that choice. And yet, if our celebration of Founders' Day is to be something more than a festive occasion — if it is to penetrate and guide our deeper moods — then it is equally right and proper to ask:

What tasks should command our efforts today in the historic struggle to foster the growth of men *as* men?

The outline of that task was graphically expressed for me by a minister of your color. Before the Civil War, he said, a high wall was built around the Negro and the whites said to him: "You can't get out." But since the Civil War, the minister continued, the whites have built a high wall around themselves and said to the Negro: "You can't get in!" Will there ever be a time, the minister went on to ask, when we shall be able to live side by side without these prison walls?

My grandfather, Jesse Fell — a close friend of Lincoln and Elijah P. Lovejoy — helped tear down the walls the whites had built around the Negro. I would be unworthy of my heritage if in my own days I too failed to help tear down the walls whites have built around themselves. For that task summons us both — whites and Negroes alike. We have no strength to waste on the vice of bigotry and prejudice.

In this day in America, we have come to recognize that economic security and political freedom cannot be separated; that if one is sacrificed to the other, both are lost. The man who enjoys the rights of free speech, but is unemployed, will be tempted to give up that right if by suffering in silence, he can gain a little food for himself and his family. But the man who gives up his political freedom for economic security, loses the very means by which he can prevent that security from becoming the kind that prevails in a prison cell.

Americans, I say, have learned this to be so.

They have learned from the bitter experience of the German and Russian people, that anyone who gives up liberty for groceries, will have neither liberty nor groceries. They have learned, at the same time, that if groceries and the other necessities of life are not obtainable, then liberty itself soon collapses. From their experiences we have learned yet another lesson: that those who deny justice to others must soon lose it for themselves — that those who set one class or one race against another, will find themselves the ultimate victims of that action.

I am aware, of course, that proofs can be offered that Americans have not yet learned this lesson. I am aware of the existence in this country of sinister forces like the Ku Klux Klan and the Silver Shirts. I am aware of the Jim Crow laws and of the lynchings and discriminations at the polls. I am aware that men like Theodore Bilbo once sat in the Senate of the United States. I am aware that Henry Wallace, whose right to speak his mind, whatever his views, is the same as mine, has been egged and stoned; assaulted by men who claim Thomas Jefferson as their political patron saint. And Thomas Jefferson said, "I have sworn upon the altar of God eternal hostility against every form of tyranny over the mind of man."

I do not minimize any of these facts. They are all ugly sores on the body of our nation. They threaten not only Negroes, but they threaten every other citizen in the land. And the sooner that threat is met and mastered, the sooner we will be able to stand forth before the world as champions of human freedom, without exposing ourselves to the charge of hypocrisy.

Those of you who followed the proceedings of the Democratic National Convention know that the Democratic party had the courage to bring the issue of civil rights out into the open. We did not try to soft-pedal it. We did not seek refuge behind pious generalities as did the Republicans. We got down to cases. We felt that the time had come to cleanse our party of those men who mocked its ideals. And we *did* cleanse our party! [83]

[83] On the floor of the convention, Hubert H. Humphrey led a successful fight to have the strongest civil rights plank in the history of the Democratic party adopted. Then a number of Southern delegates marched out and formed the Dixiecrat party with Governor Strom Thurmond of South Carolina as the presidential candidate.

As an American, I am proud of President Truman for the courage he has shown on this issue. I was proud to have an active part in that fight as a member of the Illinois delegation to the convention. And I am proud of the Illinois delegation which, united all the way, led the fight all the way. I am proud that I belong to the Democratic party which has cleaned house and shouted to the nation:

The rights and safety and security of person belong to *all* Americans, not just to some of them!

The rights to citizenship and its privileges belong to *all* Americans, not just some of them!

The right to freedom of conscience and expression belongs to *all* Americans, not just some of them!

The right to equality of opportunity belongs to *all* Americans, not just to some of them!

But we did more than merely stomp and shout.

We wrote our demands into the Democratic platform. We affirmed our devotion to the principles of political liberty for all — the same principles which guided your forebears to this village. We pledged ourselves to embody those principles into positive federal laws. And we shall pass those laws when the Democratic party wins victory in November.

And here in Illinois the Democratic party has also spoken out for fair and equal treatment. I am going to be your next Governor and I am going to ask the next session of the legislature to pass a Fair Employment Practices Act to make our righteous proclamations of economic equality of opportunity something more than pious words.

But that is not all I propose to do. We have many laws on our statute books which protect the civil liberties of our citizens. But little has been done to enforce them. Our problem in Illinois is not so much new laws as enforcement of the laws we already have. They should be assembled in the Civil Rights Code and I think we should have a Civil Rights division in the Attorney General's office charged with their enforcement.

Successful self government depends on our enlightened, responsible citizens. And education is the basic requirement of a free and responsible citizenry. Negroes should have the same opportunity for education as anyone else, because they, like everyone else, must play a part in making democratic self-government work. If it fails, they and everyone else will slip back into slavery in one of its modern communist or fascist forms.

So I believe that we in Illinois can tolerate no discrimination in educational opportunity. All of our children are entitled to an equal start in life at the common school level. Steps must be taken to see that they have it. And we can tolerate no discrimination in opportunity for advanced education either. Access to advanced educational institutions must be on the basis of merit, not color or religion.

These are minimum needs. It is appropriate that such a program should come from Illinois. It is appropriate that this state where Lincoln grew to greatness should again point the way to the nation in bringing economic security and political freedom together as political objectives.

The Negro has many other concerns, I know. Let me mention one other that seems to me of first importance. I suspect that the hospital and health facilities to which the Negro has access without discrimination in our state are wholly inadequate. If this situation persists we must take legislative steps to remove the barriers and make the benefits of medical science available to all, for disease and misfortune know no color line.

In 75 years, an instant in history, the Negro in this country has made amazing progress in every field of human endeavor. His accomplishments against all obstacles is the best augury of what is ahead for your race. The future is bright. I wish we could hurdle time and be there tomorrow. We can't and any promise that we can and that I can do it would be a false promise.

We all dream, of course, of going to sleep at night and waking the next day to find that all the ills of the world are suddenly and miraculously cured. I wish that with a single stroke of the pen I could bring to this state the realization of humanity's highest aspirations for a life of dignity, a life of peace, plenty and order. But you and I know that things come to pass only by laborious, tedious, backbreaking and sometimes heartbreaking effort.

Instead of a promise of a miracle, I can promise you only that same laborious effort toward the ultimate goal of men — which is to live as brothers under the law of God. When Christ issued his injunction to men: "Be ye perfect," he knew that men were not perfect and that the fallabilities of our nature would prevent us from ever being perfect. But he also understood that the salvation of man lay in striving for perfection. And so it is in the political as well as the spiritual dimension of life. I mean here in Illinois to strive for perfection — and day in and day out, month in and month out, we shall lay brick against brick, plank against plank, to form the structure of life which will bring us a bit nearer to the society of our dreams.

Stevenson spoke at Mount Vernon, Illinois, on Labor Day, September 6, 1948.[84]

[84] The text is based on a copy corrected in Stevenson's handwriting.

On this day which is dedicated to the men and women who by their energy and skill have made the United States the marvel of history, it is fitting that we look briefly at the position which society has accorded to the laboring man.

That position has varied from one age to another. In the Middle Ages in Europe, several hundred years ago, long before factories existed or were thought of, the artisan occupied a place of dignity and respect in the community. He made his own products, and he marketed them himself. His skill and importance to the welfare of his fellow man were recognized — and the growth of the guilds made him a powerful, organized influence.

That situation changed with the machine age. The increased productivity made possible by the use of machines subordinated the position of the workman. Factories developed. Since the end product of the factory was the result of a combination of human effort and the use of machines, the machine and the man who made it work came to be regarded in the same light. The worker became a chattel; a commodity.

What the position of the working man was only a little over fifty years ago can be seen by the objectives for which labor was then pressing. It sought a 10-hour day, the abolition of sweat shops, the establishment of some restriction upon child labor and the abolition of imprisonment for debt. These goals have, of course, long since been achieved. Their accomplishment was the result of the banding together of laboring men into labor unions.

New objectives became important — compensation for injuries, improved safety of working conditions, the 8-hour day, the creation of labor departments in the national and state governments, and so forth. The first steps were taken toward the reestablishment of working men and women as human beings and not a commodity.

Fresh in the memories of all of us are the sweeping gains made by labor under President Roosevelt. The Wagner Act established as a matter of law the right to bargain collectively. The Social Security program provided old age insurance and insurance against the hazards of unemployment. The Fair Labor Standards Act put a floor under wages and a ceiling on hours of work. All of this extensive program was based fundamentally upon recognition of the fact that the labor force of the country is composed of human beings to be dealt with as such and not to be treated as a commodity.

The program made effective by President Roosevelt and defended by President Truman has been under attack since his [Roosevelt's] death. Whether those inroads will be checked depends on the kind of Congress you elect next November.

But I am a candidate for Governor of Illinois, and therefore it is fitting that I speak about those phases of state government which affect labor.

There is no more important part of the State Government than those departments which deal with employment. When I say employment, I mean everything connected with it, such as workmen's compensation, pensions, unemployment insurance, child labor, mine inspection, factor[y] inspection, minimum wage — all the State laws which affect *you,* if you are a working man, in your job, or when you are sick and can't be on the job, or when you get older and have to quit the job.

I want to talk to you briefly about labor in Illinois; not about federal legislation with which a Governor of Illinois has nothing to do; and not even about all the gains that labor has made under a Democratic national administration since a Democratic Congress recognized by law the right of labor to bargain collectively.

I want to confine myself to Illinois which is the job and the only job of a Governor of Illinois and I hope Governor Green will see fit to do the same altho he seems much more concerned with electing Dewey and national issues than Illinois.

The aspirations, in a word, of those who toil are *work, security* and *peace.* That's what labor wants. The opportunity to work depends on the economic health of this country, and I wish I felt some confidence that a Republican Congress would do something to arrest the spiral of inflation, the dangerous cycle of boom and bust, which may whirl this country to disaster, as it all but did after 12 years of Republican rule in 1932. For the inevitable end of inflation is economic collapse; and with collapse here at home comes not only untold suffering and dislocation at home, but chaos abroad, more and more Communism and, but for the grace of God, war itself.

But what about labor in Illinois? I see that Mr. [Reuben] Soderstrom, President of the State Federation of Labor, has personally endorsed Governor Green for a third term, although the Federation has not done so. Evidently Mr. Soderstrom has had a curious change of heart since 1944 when he said Green was "easily the worst Governor Illinois has ever had. . . ." He even referred to Green's administration as "a sort of nightmare, a bad dream."

I could go on. But why this change of heart? Has Green espoused the cause of labor? No, far from it. Has the Republican party? No, far from it. I won't speculate on the possible reasons which are well known to many of you for Mr. Soderstrom's change of heart. I'll stick to the record — the public record. I understand Mr. Soderstrom's public reason is that no legislation hostile to labor has been passed in this administration. But that doesn't seem to make much sense because I note Mr. Soderstrom has also said that "There is no anti-labor legislation on the statute books of the State of Illinois due to wonderful cooperation from Democratic legislators."

He might also have said that every important item of recent legislation beneficial to labor in Illinois was enacted under a Democratic Governor, the great and good Henry Horner — unemployment compensation, old age pensions, the eight-hour day for women, the occupational diseases act, and the minimum wage law.

In spite of this record, Governor Green had no trouble claiming that "during my administration more acts beneficial to labor were enacted into law than during any previous state administration." That's not surprising when you remember that he also claims that he reduced the sales tax from 3% to 2%, although that law was passed and signed by Henry Horner before Green was even elected! . . .

But what about me? What do I stand for as far as labor is concerned in Illinois?

I'll tell you in a few words.

(1) Last year 17,000 persons were killed on the job in the United States. Wage earners suffered more than 2 million temporary disabling accidents. Ninety thousand wage earners were permanently injured in a greater or lesser degree. And approximately 10% of all of those industrial deaths and accidents occurred in Illinois. The answer to this shocking situation is that greater attention to safety by both employer and employee is necessary. As Governor I propose to step up our accident prevention program.

There are only 80 factory inspectors, I understand, for some two million workers in 13,000 plants in Illinois. That number is too small; but even a small number of competent men, sincerely working at the job, could cut that appalling rate of industrial death and injury in Illinois. Any corrupt factory inspectors who are not on the job had better start looking for a new job — for Pete Green has petered out and I'm going to be the next Governor of Illinois.

(2) When I'm Governor, the Industrial Commission is going to be conducted for the benefit of employer and employee alike, and not for the benefit of politicians first and employers and employees second.

(3) It is clear to me that benefits under the Workmen's Compensation Act should be further increased in view of the inflation and general wage increases. An injured workman with a family should not be compensated on a lower comparative basis than the unemployed.

(4) Also, with a 35% increase in the cost of living since the present ceilings were adopted in 1945, the pitiful condition of some 125,000 old age pensioners must make anyone with a conscience stop and reflect upon the inadequacy of our aid to the aged. How many of us could keep body and soul together on an average of $10 a week?

My opponent has predicted that my administration will be extravagant. If it is an extravagance to be honestly and deeply disturbed by the circumstances under which our dependent citizens — both young and old — must subsist, then I am proud to acknowledge this extravagance. But I *wouldn't* be proud of using millions of public money to maintain a personal army of thousands of political payrollers who make no pretense of doing any work for the state. Nor would I be proud of inflated contracts and the waste of public money, when the aged and infirm are next to starvation.

(5) I believe in the principle that women are entitled to equal pay for equal work; and I believe we should reconsider our election laws in Illinois so that the polls would be open late enough to give every wage earner an opportunity to vote which is the most precious privilege of a free people.

(6) I believe that the state must exercise its influence and good offices to find solutions of the conflicts between labor and management. Industrial disputes are costly — to the working men involved as well as to the community. Production and ever more production means goods at lower costs to the consumers and everyone profits, labor as well as management, because labor is a consumer. The state government can assist in reducing disputes which cause work stoppages by providing arbitration and conciliation services.

(7) I intend to appoint as director of the Department of Labor someone from the ranks of labor with the courage and the capacity to administer our laws fairly and efficiently, and I shall *oppose without compromise the adoption of any laws in Illinois aimed to lessen in any respect the gains made by labor in its long years of struggle.*

But I shall not be "a labor governor," "an employer Governor," or a "farmer's Governor." I hope and pray that God will give me the strength and the wisdom to be a Governor for all the people. And one further word about Centralia. All the world knows the story of Illinois' shame. It has been circulated to 12 or 13 million readers in eight or nine languages in one magazine alone — Reader's Digest. Everybody knows how my opponent in a campaign message to the miners said: "The lives of you men have been entrusted to the state. The only security you have depends upon absolute enforcement of those laws. . . . I pledge you that . . . all laws protecting the health, safety and lives of the men employed in the mines will be enforced rigidly and thoroughly. In other words, to the letter of the law."

But 111 men died because these laws were not enforced and they died when the mine inspectors on the instruction of their boss were out soliciting campaign contributions from the operators — to beat MK [Martin Kennelly] for Mayor of Chi[cago]. . . .

Centralia No. 5 is a sorry story of neglect, buck passing and political prostitution of a public service charged with the protection of human life. Medill and his assistant, Robert Weir, were indicted almost 1–½ years ago for "palpable omission of duty." They have not been tried yet. They may never be tried and the responsibility never fixed for this enduring stain on Illinois' name, unless the voters sweep out the political pirates that infest our state administration.

What this state needs is a strong dose of electoral DDT!

What am I going to do to see that Centralia never happens again under any administration, Republican or Democratic? I am going to take the mine inspectors out of politics — all the way. They must be put under Civil Service and removed from all possibility of political control or influence. They must enforce the law without fear or favor against mine officials and miners alike. And I am going to appoint a director to the Department of Mines and Minerals who is interested in the oil and coal industries and the men who work in them, *not* in politics.

In Pennsylvania the mine inspectors have been under Civil Service since 1870. It is time Illinois caught up with the procession and if anyone opposes teeth for the mining laws and for their enforcement in Illinois, I am going to expose them, whoever they are.

In closing, let me say to you that I intend, as Governor of Illinois, never to forget that I represent and owe a responsibility to every resident of Illinois, irrespective of his or her political party. . . .

You can't have everything you want. But you can have honesty. You can have a lot more service for less money. Illinois doesn't have to be corrupt, backward and inefficient. And if our system and our free institutions are going to endure forever and meet the test of our times, Illinois cannot continue down the road of cynical corruption, backwardness and inefficiency!

On September 15, 1948, Stevenson's Bloomington friends welcomed him home with bands, a torchlight parade, floats, and a huge crowd to hear him speak.[85] *The politicians who visited from Chicago were impressed. When Stevenson went to bed that night he told his sister that*

[85] The text is based on a carbon copy of the speech.

this was the turning point of the election. The Chicago politicians for the first time offered him money for the campaign.[86]

I am here tonight, receiving honor at your hands, only because of what I owe to Bloomington.

Whatever responsibilities I have discharged, whatever positions have been assigned to me or offered to me have come because some people thought I had certain qualities that are not uncommon here in Bloomington. Other Bloomingtonians have represented these qualities far better. I know that as you know it. But there are attitudes bred in boys who walked these shaded streets — the ideals of the Middle West — neighborliness, friendliness, belief in the Republic, trust in the democratic principle — faith in the future — respect for the past — progress along the path that our ancestors blazed.

I am here tonight to own my debt, formally, to Bloomington. I am here tonight to tell you quite frankly and with all the sincerity that is in me, what an advantage it has been to me, privately and publicly, to have grown up in Bloomington.

What is unique and different and very dear to us may not be to others. I don't know whether Bloomington is — really — unique and different. But I do know that it is a truly American city. I do know that it is not too big, not too small — not too rich, not too poor, not too radical, not too conservative — a city half rural, half industrial — a city with all the modern devices but without the overcrowded lonesomeness of the great cities. Here in Bloomington there is progress without hysteria — the latest dish-washing machines and motor cars standing in the midst of a sea of growing corn.

You who are here tonight have come to this square to greet me as you have greeted other sons of Bloomington, not as political partisans, but as friends and neighbors — and that is precisely the way I join you. Whether we are the descendants of the pioneers who came here years ago, or whether we came at any time since those rail-splitting days, we are all the equal inheritors of the spirit that has typified Bloomington clear down the line today — the spirit that haunts this square tonight — the pure spirit of the American heartland.

As a boy I felt that spirit without knowing exactly what it was, and today, even now, none of us can say exactly what it is — but we know it is here — and we know when we are true to it and when we are not.

It is the midland concept of Americanism, progress coupled with

[86] Mrs. Ernest L. Ives, letter to Walter Johnson, December 31, 1968.

order, liberty without license, tolerance without laxness, thrift without meanness.

Here in Bloomington we want a better city, a better State, a better nation, a better world, but we measure our tomorrows by the standards of our ancestors sleeping under the sod, here in our midst. Our ancestors wanted a better world in their day. They wanted a better Bloomington because they knew that civilization never stands still, and that conscientious people must march forward or backward. There is no standing still. So it was in the quiet past when these sidewalks were planks and these streets were mud. And so it is in the turbulent present.

The lights on this old square were once flares blazing over coonskin caps — and then they were gaslights shining on hats of silk or straw, and then they were the new and naked electric bulbs shining on derby hats — and now they are neon and some of us no longer wear any hats at all — but it is only the lights that have changed — we, the people, have always been the same.

I can walk this square tonight and feel just as I felt forty years ago, thirty years ago.

How often in the dusk of evening in remote places at the end of bitter days of struggle and anxiety in war and peace I have sat and thought about the great, cool sanity that was lying on my home town among the cornfields. Back here, I knew, there was a great drive to win the war, a solemn determination to save democracy, an endless flood of materials and food, blood banks, Red Cross drives — war bond drives. Back home there was, I knew, a steady stream of young men waving goodbye — and back home there was that ticking of the telegraph bringing the news that one Bloomington boy after another would never be coming home at all.

But I knew no clamor of machines, no hurry of war work, no cheers for departing soldiers, no grief for boys that were forever gone, was interrupting the steady resolution, the calm determination, the wisdom, the horse sense of my home town people.

And I wished then and I wish now that I could always be like them in steadfastness, that I could always keep my head in a crisis, always represent, as they do, the real heart of America.

I have known many of the leaders, many of the so-called great and powerful of our time, both here and abroad. And I have Bloomington to thank for the most important lesson I have ever learned: that in quiet places, reason abounds; that in quiet people there is vision and purpose; that many things are revealed to the humble that are hidden from the great.

And my home town taught me that good government and good citizenship are one and the same, that good individuals make a good town — and that nothing else does. I learned that good communities make a good state, and nothing else can. I was taught here that what was wrong between private citizens is doubly immoral between public officials and private citizens.

These are not the only lessons I took away from Bloomington. Here I learned from my parents and my grandparents, from the immortal [Governor] Joe Fifer, the friend of my boyhood, and from many of you, that good government is good politics, and that public office doubled the responsibility that a man felt in his own home, his own neighborhood, his own town.

I hope and pray that I can remember the great truths that seem so obvious in Bloomington, but so obscure in other places.

If ever a man felt proud of his home town, it is I, and if ever a man wished that he could measure up to it in terms of self-respect, humanity and friendliness, I wish it tonight. I should be doing honor to you, not you to me.

To Lawrence Irvin[87]

September 16, 1948

Dear Lawrence:

I had wanted to call you this morning to thank you again for that extravaganza last night. I know how much of it reflected your energy and enterprise. I have about decided Bloomington is full of showmen, with you in the front rank!

With every good wish and my profound thanks, I am

Sincerely yours,

ADLAI

Stevenson spoke at Joliet, Illinois, on October 1, 1948.[88]

The third term candidate says the issue is honesty in government, and that Americans are tired of false promises. He must have given that speech without reading it. Because Dwight Green has made more false promises than Casanova or Don Juan, the gay deceivers.

[87] Secretary to the McLean County Democratic Central Committee. The original is in the possession of Mr. Irvin.

[88] The text is based on a carbon copy of the speech.

Back in 1940, pin-up Pete wooed and won Illinois with such promises as "I will remove every unnecessary payroll parasite" and "If you elect me Governor there will never be a Green machine."

By 1944 this sweet talk had lost its charm and this time he is not making many promises. There aren't any left. His only hope is to sneak up the back stairs in his stocking feet while old lady Illinois is in the parlor looking over that periodical visitor from New York, Mr. Dewey.

In the year when Governor Green made that promise to remove every unnecessary payroll parasite the great Governor Horner was still alive, and the record shows that Horner gave Illinois its best administration with never more than 24,000 employees.

Inside of eight years, Payroll Pete has added at least 10,000 to the payroll. That is only an estimate. Some say the payroll today is closer to 40,000. I can't tell you just how many there are because the third term candidate who says the issue is honesty in government won't tell it, although we are paying their salaries.

Some of the huge increase may be necessary because of the normal growth of Illinois. And doubtless many of the new employees are conscientious, sincere public servants. But, the Governor who promised to remove every unnecessary payroller and that there would never be a Green machine, has built up the largest political machine this state has ever seen. His gang has saddled the taxpayers with thousands of political locusts who make little or no pretense of performing any public service. Their only service is to the Green machine, yet we are required to pay them to ravage the public service, demoralize the conscientious, and spread contempt for public office and public office holders.

Clerks, newspaper publishers, even plumbers are on the payroll as beauty shop inspectors; dentists are legal investigators and bridge inspectors; Naval officers are court martialed because they are on the state payroll in violation of the law. George Chiames admits that he was on the payroll for $400 a month but denies that his job was to collect protection money from gamblers. He says he did nothing at all for his salary.

I have been in counties where they say the payroll has increased 400% since Henry Horner and it's still going up. Because of every kind of obstruction we have not yet been able to get the payroll complete for 1947, let alone the present figures.

I have challenged the Governor, who says the issue is honesty in government, to reveal the figures. He says his record is his platform. Maybe he will tell the people about his platform on the payroll in his next television seance.

But I doubt it. Actually, I doubt if Payroll Pete could tell us accurately even if he wished to. With new revelations daily about affairs in Illinois he is desperate. And now the gravy train is moving so fast I doubt if anyone knows how many are aboard.

Most recently, I hear that the election fixers are taking on scores of new party workers. They'll be paid from your pockets at an average of $250 apiece until election day. And they won't have to do anything but ring doorbells and ask you to vote for Green — the man who promised you he'd remove every payroll parasite and who now piously says the issue is honesty in government.

Sometimes I think that Governor Green's giant handouts have reached the point of diminishing returns. It's getting so the payrollers are falling over each other. They are ringing each other's doorbells and trying to talk each other into voting for the Republican ticket.

Before I close I would like to read two more of Promising Pete's vows. I want to repeat them because they explain why countless Republicans, who are sick of this verdant payroll paradise, are going to vote against Green and his pals next November.

Here is the first Green statement:

"We want no third term dictatorship in Illinois or in the nation."

And this is the other Green statement:

"We are in a fight to the finish to preserve the American form of government and our system of free enterprise. A third term would destroy them."

These solemn words, as you know, were spoken by Mr. Green during his 1940 campaign. He echoed the views of many sincere people of both parties who felt that a third term was wrong in principle. Candidate Green was one of the most eloquent exponents of that principle.

But principles went flying merrily out the window. Perfidious Pete resorted to a transparent political trick to force Hugh Cross, his own Lieutenant Governor from the primary last January. Thereby he deprived the many Republicans, who wanted their party leadership deloused, of any choice. And the Governor who said he detested third terms was enabled to run for a third term unopposed.

But the principles of many Republicans don't seem to be quite as flexible as those of Governor Green. So the Governor has been trying in this campaign to hide behind Tom Dewey, but I very much doubt if Green can make himself small enough or Dewey can make himself big enough to fool anyone. Illinois is ready for a bath. The people know it and that's why the state which gave Abraham Lincoln to the world will give Pete Green back to Miami Beach.

But there will be another job to do after that: To cut the deadwood out of the forest. We want in Illinois public servants, not political locusts. And we are going to demand and get a day's work for a day's pay.

Stevenson spoke to the Illinois League of Women Voters in Chicago on October 8, 1948, on the subject of constitutional revision for Illinois.[89]

I am about to talk of things many of you know more about than I. Sitting here I had a chilling recollection of a charity lunch long ago. Beside me was a formidable dour lady. Brightly I asked her if she came to such luncheons often. Disdainfully she said entirely too often. I recovered from the shock and politely asked her if she found them instructive. She replied — not in the least. When I recovered from that I finally renewed the attack and asked why she came so often if she disliked them so much, and she said to see if the speaker knows what the devil he's talking about.

I've never recovered from that chill — So uneasy I sat here and uneasy I arise before so many informed ladies. Maybe I can dismiss my sense of inadequacy with the remark of that Gilbert & Sullivan character in Ruddigore — You don't know what a poor opinion I have of myself & how little I deserve it!

There is no more appropriate forum for discussion of Constitutional revision in Illinois than a meeting of the Illinois League of Women Voters. I want to pay my respects to the League for its sustained and intelligent effort to give Illinois a modern Constitution. All of us recall your magnificent fight in the last session of the General Assembly for a Constitutional Convention — a struggle which failed by a narrow margin to secure the necessary two-thirds vote in the Senate and House to permit this all-important question to be submitted to the people for decision. May I say, simply, that if at first — or at last — you don't succeed, try, try again! In 1947 Senator [Abraham] Marovitz and Rep. [Paul H.] Ferguson both democrats introduced resolutions to call a const[itutional]. conv[ention]. which failed by a narrow margin.

But the issue of Constitutional revision transcends partisan political considerations, and on that score Governor Green and I are, I believe, in entire agreement. It can only be accomplished by the common effort of both parties, and no one knows better than you and your leaders, that the genuine and wholehearted support of the Chief Executive of the State spells the difference between success and failure in this high enterprise.

[89] The text is based on a copy corrected in Stevenson's handwriting.

Because of the active role of the League of Women Voters in the long fight for constitutional revision in Illinois, it borders on presumption for me to submit to you in detail my views as to why the present Constitution of 1870 fails to meet the needs of the State of Illinois today.

But at least some of the manifest deficiencies of our present Constitution have a significance which is so pervading in terms of public and private morality, as well as in terms of the efficiency and cost of government, that, although well known to you, they should not go unmentioned.

Perhaps the most significant among these major defects is the fact that failure to comply with the constitutional command of legislative reapportionment every ten years in practical effect results in the disenfranchisement of very large numbers of voters. Your own organization has pointed out the consequences of failure to observe the mandate of the Constitution. Senatorial districts in Illinois now vary in population from 74,000 downstate to 574,000 in Cook County. That means that 74,000 people have a voting strength in the selection of the members of the Legislature which is equivalent to that of 574,000 other people in the State.

At each session of the Legislature the members take an oath to uphold and maintain the provisions of the Constitution of the United States and of the State, and yet at session after session from 1901 until now — almost 50 years — the Legislature has failed to perform the duty imposed upon it by the Constitution. Resort to the courts has been unavailing. It has proved impossible to secure compliance with that flat command of the Constitution.

And the reason for this violation of duty by the Legislature lies in the Constitution itself. For the system of representation which it prescribes is based solely upon population and compliance with its command would mean dominance of the Legislature by Cook County. For 50 years the Legislature has been unwilling to concede that shift of control.

Another serious problem arises from the fact that the Revenue Article of the Constitution of 1870 saddles the State with a property tax structure which is literally impossible to operate today and which furthers, and indeed almost requires, widespread perjury and evasion. That article, like so many other provisions of our organic law, was designed to meet the needs of a rural economy. It was written at a time when real estate — land — was the principal form of wealth, and consequently it provided that taxes levied upon property should be uniform. The undeniable fact is that personal property — and I am thinking particularly of intangible personal property — stocks, bonds, bank deposits, etc. — cannot possibly be taxed upon a uniform basis with real estate. In the first place, a real estate tax rate applied to bank deposits or to bonds paying a low rate of interest would be confiscatory. In the second place, that type of property is mobile and it would be forced out of the state if a sincere attempt were made to tax it at a rate uniform with the rate imposed on real estate.

Even without any real effort to enforce the Constitutional requirement of uniformity, the flight of intangible personal property from Illinois before April 1st each year is enormous. That intangible property entirely escapes taxation in Illinois by the simple expedient of moving out of the State on the assessing date. It has been estimated that 60% of the total wealth of Cook County is represented by intangible personal property. Yet in the year 1946 all personal property, tangible as well as intangible, in Cook County paid taxes of only 41 million dollars as compared to real estate taxes of 175 million paid in the same year.

The situation is going to get worse instead of better. The Butler Bills, enacted in 1945, provide a mechanism for enforcing the command that property be assessed at its full value. All personal property, as I have said, cannot stand that type of assessment. I predict that as the valuation of property under the Butler Bills approaches full value, the demand will increase for constitutional revision to more nearly equalize the tax burden between tangible property (real estate, furniture, inventories, automobiles, livestock) on the one hand, and intangible property (stocks, bonds, insurance policies, etc.) on the other.

An inequitable system of taxation is a serious evil. But perhaps even more serious is the widespread evasion of the letter and the spirit of the law which follows in its wake. Public officials of necessity encourage and wink at violations of the requirement that property be uniformly assessed. Individuals owning bank accounts and securities are almost forced to violate the law, at least in part, to avoid confiscation of their property. Such a situation is absurd and can only contribute to disrespect for law with all its attendant evils.

Let me now call your attention to another major reason for constitutional reform in Illinois. The provision of the revenue article pertaining to municipal debt limitation has completely backfired in terms of the results which it seeks to achieve. It has resulted in the rapid multiplication of municipal corporations, many of which were created purely and simply to evade the constitutional debt restriction. Until the consolidation of school districts recently began to have an appreciable effect on the figures, Illinois had more than 15,000 separate municipal corporations with tax-levying powers, 400 of which are in Cook County alone. The total exceeds by 4,000 the number of governing bodies in any other state of the Union. In large measure this pyramiding of governments is forced by the requirement of the Constitution that municipal indebtedness may not exceed 5% of the assessed value of the property in the municipality.

Therefore, when a new municipal service is needed, a new municipal corporation is created to render it, so that it too can have the maximum debt limit. Lip service is thus given to the constitutional requirement, but in reality that provision which was intended as a brake on the cost of government has produced a directly opposite effect. The multiplication of governments, thanks to our ancient Constitution, is costing us a tremendous sum each year in duplication of administrative facilities and diffusion of governmental responsibility. And I need not remind you that as a by-product the task of the scrupulous voter has become almost hopeless due to the length of the ballot, because of the number of public officials you now have to elect to run all these governments.

I want also to mention the administration of justice which is of the utmost importance to all citizens. The lawyers of Illinois, speaking through the Chicago and Illinois State Bar Associations, have emphasized the need for Constitutional revision to enable the State to achieve modern methods of judicial administration. The pattern of our present judicial system originated in our Constitution of 1848, and the basic structure then established was carried over into the Constitution of 1870.

The lawyers of Illinois have found improvement of the courts by better methods of selection and tenure of judges obstructed by our Constitution. They have also found that the structure established a hundred years ago does not today permit the most effective utilization of the judiciary in the dispatch of the business of the courts today.

Moreover, types of litigation which were paramount in importance generations ago still engage the attention of the Supreme Court of the State to such an extent that it lacks sufficient time to consider other kinds of cases which raise the legal questions most significant today.

All of these considerations have moved the legal profession, whose natural conservatism is a by-word, to support most vigorously the cause of constitutional reform.

So much for the *need* for constitutional revision in Illinois. Significant matters which I have omitted will at once occur to you. As an example of less familiar matters, let me remind you that most of the more advanced and enlightened states have succeeded in taking the conservation of wild life and natural resources out of politics by creation of a commission with members appointed for staggered terms. But such a reform in Illinois, I am informed, is impossible under our Constitution.

There are, of course, many, many more, and *more* important examples, that could be cited. The amending procedure itself which has frustrated us for so long must be revised.

But the emphasis today, it seems to me, should no longer be upon the need, for that is not debatable; it should rather center upon the obstacles in the way of constitutional revision and the methods by which those obstacles can be overcome.

First, let's consider the objection that downstate Illinois will never stand for legislative reapportionment. That statement is undoubtedly true, I believe, if by legislative reapportionment is meant reapportionment in accordance with the method provided by the Constitution of 1870.

For that method would give Cook County complete control of both houses of the State Legislature.

But the problem of accommodating the needs of rural and urban areas in a legislative body is not new in American government. A similar problem was solved more than 150 years ago in the convention which drafted the Constitution of the United States. It has been solved in other states. It can be solved in Illinois. Cook County does not desire to dominate the State Legislature. And, more important, it could not secure that dominance even if it sought it. Delegates to a Constitutional Convention elected from the existing legislative districts downstate will control the Convention to exactly the same degree that they now control the State Legislature. And downstate is no more likely in a Convention to turn over control of the State Legislature to the City of Chicago and to Cook County than the Legislature has been willing to do during the past 50 years.

Realistically appraised, that supposed obstacle to a Constitutional Convention is almost insignificant. Two houses, following the pattern of the Federal Congress, have been suggested as a satisfactory solution; one elected on a population basis which might be dominated by Cook County, and the other on a geographical basis like the United States Senate which would be controlled by downstate.

The problem is not at the moment one of devising precise methods of accommodating the interests of both upstate and downstate. The present problem is one of understanding. Primarily, it is one of convincing the people of the State outside of Cook County that Chicago does not seek to take control, that it could not do so even if it wanted to, and that wholly practical means are available to protect both sections of the State.

The second obstacle is the fear that a Constitutional Convention might make it possible for Illinois to adopt a state income tax as some 32 other states have done. Those who base their opposition upon this ground are evidently willing to sacrifice all the benefits which would result from the removal of our Constitutional strait-jacket because of a single possible undesirable consequence. And that, it seems to me, is not sound thinking.

Obviously no one can now foresee whether or not a Constitutional

Convention would even propose a revenue article authorizing an income tax. And it is equally obvious that no one can now predict whether the General Assembly would ever levy an income tax if it was authorized to do so.

These opponents seem to overlook the fact that an income tax on corporation income and individuals engaged in business seems entirely possible even under the present Constitution.

Personally I see no present necessity for a state income tax — a field already preempted by the Federal government. And there are many cogent arguments against a state income tax even if there was any demand for one — Federal-state tax competition, duplication of machinery and services, and a large, expensive administrative machinery that might well become another breeding ground for corruption and abuse.

The pressing need today is for a revenue article which will permit classification of property so that all kinds of property, real and personal, tangible and intangible, can be taxed equitably. We need to be liberated from the unworkable requirement of uniformity.

Even if the Convention proposes to authorize an income tax, those who oppose it have an opportunity to express themselves in the referendum election on the adoption of the proposed Constitution. And if they should fail there, they still would have an opportunity to present their arguments to the Legislature if and when an income tax is actually proposed.

It seems to me, therefore, that there will be ample and timely opportunities to thrash out the income tax question. Moreover, there is no demand now for an income tax in Illinois, nor can the need for such a tax even be intelligently anticipated until a new revenue system has been adopted and tested by experience.

Hence, I conclude that it is very shortsighted to oppose all the needed constitutional reforms in Illinois merely because of a future possibility of an income tax. You don't cut off your nose to spite your face. And we need a new Constitution so badly and for so many reasons that I would glady even limit the Convention on the question of an income tax to allay fear and opposition on that score. The important thing now is to get on with the main show and not waste our time and substance in the sideshows.

A third important obstacle which must be surmounted relates more to the mechanics of revision than to matters of substantive change. I have in mind the requirement that any constitutional proposal submitted to the electorate must be approved by the majority of those voting at the election, as distinguished from a majority of those voting on the proposition itself.

In 1891 the Australian ballot Act outlawed the party ballots previously used and required that all ballots be prepared officially. The method of voting on constitutional proposals thereby became quite different from the method visualized by the framers of the Constitution of 1870. A vote for the party was no longer a vote for any constitutional proposal endorsed by the party. From that time on the Illinois Constitution has been virtually unamendable.

The factor of inertia has defeated effort after effort to amend the Constitution because the voter who failed to express himself on the issue was counted as voting against the proposal. Only two amendments have been adopted since 1891.

To call a Constitutional Convention, you must first have a two-thirds vote of both houses of the Legislature, and then approval by the people at a general election. As things now are the call must be approved by a majority of those voting at the elections, not just a majority of those voting on the proposition to call a Convention. It is evident from our prior experience with amendments that it will be very difficult indeed to surmount that hurdle.

There are two ways to do it. The first is an all out public information campaign to get the people to vote for a Convention, using every medium of public communication, and all the organized groups, including both political parties. Whether such a bi-partisan campaign will succeed is at best uncertain. But another method is possible: the legislature could revise the method of voting for a constitutional convention. At the 1945 session of the Legislature the "Party Circle" bills were introduced which would have accomplished this and have restored the method of voting on constitutional proposals to something approaching the method which the draftsmen of the Constitution had in mind.

All of us recall, and I know your League recalls with a special note of sadness, those Party Circle bills which were introduced with the support of the administration and passed by the Legislature only to be vetoed by the Governor upon the recommendation of Attorney General [George] Barrett who held that they were unconstitutional.

It is not my purpose to analyze for you the basis, or rather the lack of basis, for that opinion by the Attorney General, but it will interest you to know that the Supreme Courts of other states have found no constitutional objection to similar Party Circle bills.

The door is still open for the enactment of legislation which will permit the submission of a constitutional convention proposal to the electorate under conditions affording a fair opportunity for expression of the will of the people — legislation which will either correct the intolerable situation now in force which puts a premium upon inertia and apathy and counts silence as a vote against not only amendments to the present Constitution, but also a Convention to propose a new Constitution.

Finally, another important concern relates to the method by which a new Constitution would be submitted for ratification. Unfortunately, the notion prevails that there is something inherent in the convention method of revising a state constitution which requires the drafting of an entirely new Constitution and the submission of the same as a unit to the voters to be accepted or rejected in its entirety. That false notion must be completely discarded. Most states in adopting their constitutions have afforded the voters a choice between the old and the new with respect to each major revision. I cannot too strongly recommend that this organization and all other civic organizations which are seeking a constitutional convention, support a method of submission which will permit major revisions to be voted on separately. Otherwise the opposition to each part consolidates to oppose the whole and the prospect for ratification vanishes.

Finally, let me just mention the obstacle of attitude: I mean the reluctance to look squarely at the problem. That attitude finds expression in the myth that: "We get along all right under the Constitution of 1870." The complete falsity of that comfortable myth is apparent to everyone at all familiar with government in Illinois. The fact is, that we don't get along under the present Constitution at all.

We get along, not under the Constitution of 1870, but under a pattern of violations, evasions and subterfuges which make a mockery of the exalted principles which underlie constitutional government.

With the maturity of the State, shifts in population have made intolerable the system of legislative representation which was appropriate 78 years ago. And so for half a century we have tolerated flagrant violation of the basic American principle of representative government.

Economic developments since the Civil War days have completely shifted the relative significance of real estate and other forms of wealth. Our Constitution, geared to the economic needs of a community 78 years away by the calendar — and centuries away in terms of scientific and mechanical developments — requires that all property — real and personal — be assessed and taxed at uniform rates.

We don't honestly get along under that provision of our Constitution. We couldn't. Instead we are driven to tolerate an open system of private and official perjury and subterfuge.

Nor do the techniques of evasion and subterfuge end with the two fundamentals of representation and taxation. Their insidious influence spreads and crops out again in our patchwork of overlapping municipal governments by which, at an incalculable price in terms of expense, efficiency and responsibility, we sidestep a constitutional debt limit framed in terms of the governmental needs of the Civil War period.

It is no surprise to learn that the salaries fixed by the Constitution of 1870 for certain county offices are absurdly inadequate today. Nor is it any surprise to learn that a method has been devised, by the discreet use of expense accounts, through which the purpose of the Constitutional provision is completely thwarted.

In another environment, the energetic ingenuity we have developed here in Illinois to avoid the anachronisms of our Constitution might be amusing. But it cannot be amusing when it concerns basic principles of our form of government. A Constitution, as Americans look at things, is to be respected and obeyed, not evaded and flouted.

The system of public and private subterfuge, evasion and easy virtue which characterizes our efforts "to get along" under the Constitution of 1870 has a pervading effect upon political and governmental morality in Illinois. And its spread is as difficult to measure as it is to check.

Our basic problem in Illinois is better government at every level — city, county and state. The cost of all government during this generation has for the first time become a major charge on all business enterprise and every individual budget. We are not getting our money's worth. Illinois deserves better. Its basic charter of government must be one which promotes public and private integrity and efficiency and not evasion, extravagance and inefficiency.

I have been your ally in the past. I want to be allied with the League of Women Voters in this imperative reform in the future. We must lift the dead hand of the dead past from the throat of Illinois.

Stevenson delivered a radio speech at West Frankfort, Illinois, on October 20, 1948.[90]

I am an amateur in politics. I have never run for an office before, and I want to take advantage of this opportunity to speak over the radio here in West Frankfort about this campaign for Governor of Illinois, not so much as the Democratic candidate but as just another citizen.

Nothing has exhilarated me more in my brief experience in politics than the interest and, I hope, the support of people like yourselves all over the state — sober, sensible people who have nothing to gain from politics except community betterment.

Representative government cannot be wholesome, efficient and healthy at the top and corrupt, cynical and careless at the bottom.

[90] The text is from a carbon copy of the speech.

For my election I must rely in large measure upon the support of people like yourselves, who want nothing but the good of the whole, people who appreciate that the good of the whole sometimes transcends normal party allegiance.

This campaign is almost over. There are only 13 days left before the people of Illinois go to the polls to elect a President, a Senator, and a Governor and state administration in Illinois, as well as local tickets.

The issue in the campaign in Illinois was stated as follows by the St. Louis Post Dispatch on October 10:

> "Under Dwight Green, state administration in Illinois has become a sinkhole of bribery and payoffs, of lugs and shakedowns, of kickbacks and padded payrolls. For more than two months, one disclosure has followed another in a veritable procession of faithlessness."

It was stated as follows by the Chicago Daily News on October 7:

> "The Green administration is full of idle payrollers who make no pretense of working for their money. It nourishes a swarm of grafters, chiselers and racketeers who grow bolder every year. They threaten the moral health of the state — to say nothing of the State Treasury. To restore the moral vigor of the executive office is the outstanding issue of this state campaign."

It was stated 150 years ago by the great Edmund Burke, as follows:

> "When bad men combine, the good must associate, else they will fall, one by one, an unpitied sacrifice in a contemptible struggle."

Bad men have combined in Illinois, and it is high time that the good combined to restore the moral vigor of government in Illinois.

There are only 13 days left, but there is still time for Governor Green to answer the questions that people of all parties have been asking for so long. He has talked vaguely but eloquently of waste and bungling in Washington, of unity, of the virtues of the American home and of the perfidy of the man-eating shark. He says he stands on his record, but he has not said what he is going to do about the corruption, the broken promises, the maladministration and the machine-ridden government which has marked his record as Governor of Illinois.

What does Governor Green think about the disclosures in Peoria and Sangamon Counties, where it is commonly said that state officials have entered into a business partnership with the commercialized crime and vice lords? The Attorney General, the chief law enforcement officer of the state, appoints two of his own employees to conduct an investigation involving his own office. The Peoria Association of Commerce says the investigation is "headed up whitewash alley," but the Governor says he approves of this kind of an investigation of the alliance between crime and politics, whch he promised to end.

I have said that any state official who is corrupt and profits from lawlessness will be subjected to the full penalties of the law if I can get my hands on him.

The Governor says local law enforcement is none of his business and I agree that people should decide whether they want slot machines, bingo games and punch boards, but when the grasping fingers of large scale commercialized crime and vice reach into the state government and corrupt state officials it is very much the Governor's business.

Eight years ago Governor Green said we wanted no third term dictatorship in Illinois. This year he drove Hugh Cross out of the primary, depriving Republicans of any choice, so that he could run for a third term unopposed. People would like to hear what the Governor has to say about this abrupt change in his views on the third term.

We have the spectacle of an Attorney General whose employees are not only charged with selling protection to crime but who himself condones the refusal of his employees to testify before a grand jury in a forgery case (involving the petition of another Republican candidate for state office) on the ground that their answers might incriminate them. A lot of people would like to know what Governor Green thinks about this. And this Attorney General, George Barrett, is also asking for a third term, with more billboards scattered around the state and spending more money than all the Democratic candidates put together.

There is still time for Governor Green to tell the people what he thinks about Centralia No. 5, which blew up while his mine inspectors were shaking down the mine operators for campaign funds two years after his Department of Mines and Minerals had been notified by Driscoll Scanlan about the unsafe conditions in that mine and more than a year after the miners themselves had appealed to him to please save their lives.

There is still time for Governor Green to express his view about the trial of his Director of the Department of Mines and Minerals, Robert Medill, and Robert Weir, who were indicted 18 months ago for "palpable omission" of duty and have not yet been brought to trial.

There is still time for Governor Green to explain why it is costing the Illinois taxpayer $57,551 per mile for hard roads in Illinois in 1948 while it is costing the Iowa taxpayer only $27,685 per mile. And while he is at it, he might also explain why the Federal Government is investigating the stories of which we have heard so much about the kickbacks demanded from road contractors by the Green gang.

There is still time for the Governor to answer the questions of many honest, decent Republicans who don't like what has happened to the leadership of the Republican party in Illinois. The once great Republican party of Lincoln, Logan and Lowden has become the party of McCormick, Murray and Green — the party of the isolationist, reactionary publisher who called the tune for the Republican delegation of payrollers at Philadelphia while Governor Green acted as his compliant errand boy; the party of Sinon Murray, candidate for Auditor, friend and attorney for gangsters, whom Dwight Green once tried himself to have cited for contempt of court; the party of Pete Green who promised that there would never be a Green machine and has now built the largest, the most wasteful and rapacious political machine in the history of our state. The Republicans would like to know what he thinks of the Republican ticket in Chicago which the Better Government Association says is easily the worst ever presented to the voters of Chicago.

There is still time for the Governor to explain why he slashed 22 million dollars from the common school appropriation in the last session of the legislature and thus forced an increase in the crushing burden of local taxes in order to maintain our schools.

There is still time for the Governor to tell the people why his administration has increased the payroll of Illinois by 15,000 people since Henry Horner at an expense of millions of dollars to the hard pressed taxpayers, although he promised the people he would remove every payroll parasite.

There is still time for the Governor to explain why the Green gang's crooked friends receive higher prices for rotten food for the helpless thousands in our state welfare institutions than the price of good food at retail. And there is still time for him to tell us what he is going to do about brutality, maladministration, incompetence and neglect in the care and treatment of the 46,000 patients in our state hospitals.

There is still time for him to give us his views on the proper organization of the highway police which has tripled in size since Governor Horner's time, and why two carloads of state police watched nonchalantly from parked cars on the roadside last Memorial Day when Bernie Shelton and two of his gangster pals mercilessly beat a young veteran in Peoria.

He could also tell us what happened to his promise to take the Department of Conservation out of politics; why the state paid such exorbitant prices for the property at Wolf Lake. And he might also explain why the state paid six million dollars for the Burnham Building in Chicago after relinquishing an option for four and three-quarters million.

There is also time for him to explain what happened to his very well-phrased statement that "The merit system is no longer a subject for controversy. Since the power and prestige of a political machine is maintained by jobs, every extension of civil service is a blow to bossism." Thousands of honest, conscientious civil servants want to know why he threw this promise in the waste basket when he took the classification of jobs out of the Civil Service Commission and placed it in his own hands. They want to know why he piously declared his abhorrence of shakedowns of civil servants for campaign funds and then the employees from one end of the state to the other are squeezed, coerced and threatened to support his campaign for a third term.

There is still time for him to propose alterations in the administration of the Butler full assessment laws which have increased local taxes so much and so unfairly.

There is plenty of time, I say, too, for the governor who says his record is his platform, to answer these and many other questions about his record. But my guess is that you will not get behind the Green curtain, and that all you will hear is exhortations to vote the Republican ticket and vote it straight, so that you can have four more years of his brand of sound government in Illinois, while he talks of efficiency, honesty and economy. The only economy I've seen has been at the expense of the old age pensioners, the blind, the dependent children and the schools.

I will be elected governor because the questions can't be answered, because the Green machine has run its course, because even partisan Republicans say that to redeem the leadership of their once great party, they have to clean out to clean up. The tide has turned. Little by little, the story has reached the four corners of the state. In Chicago, he can't hide behind Governor Dewey, and even in the Republican strongholds downstate, word comes each day of the penalty in store for deceit, cynicism and inertia.

There are only three things which can save the Green gang. The first is a political miracle; the second, a tremendous stealing of votes; and the third, a Dewey landslide.

There will be no political miracles. The sordid story cannot be whitewashed. The wholesale vote thefts can be frustrated if we are vigilant. And even the propagandists of the Republican machine hesitate to prophesy a Dewey landslide in Illinois, thanks to the disclosures and magnificent campaign of President Truman.

All the billboards, all the radio speeches and all the political payrollers can't save the Green machine now.

[575]

So I will be the next Governor of Illinois. And I want to say a word to you about some of the things I hope to do.

Most of all, I want to restore — and I will need the help of all of you to do it — honest, decent government in Illinois. The people are entitled to an administration which places the public above politics. I hold out no hope for Utopia. I have no illusions about the difficulties and the obstacles. I will make no promises of achievements beyond my control.

But I can promise to give the people of Illinois my full time in running their business — the government of Illinois. I will not be travelling about promoting my political intention to move to Washington — I've already lived there five years — long enough.

I shall insist that the employees of the state give you a full day's work for a full day's pay. And I am serving notice on all of the political locusts whom you pay to campaign year in and year out for the Green machine to look for another job, because Pete has petered out and I want public servants and not political parasites on the payroll.

I shall insist that the civil service be respected. And I will fire the first official, be he Democrat or Republican, who interferes with an employee who is doing a good job.

I will insist on a hog-tight, politician-proof mine inspection service. No longer will the Department of Mines and Minerals be a political pasture. It is unthinkable that a service charged with the protection of human life itself should be susceptible to political interference from anybody. The operators and the miners alike will help me to remove this service from partisan political control and put it under a rigid foolproof civil service. No one can guarantee that there would never be another mine disaster in Illinois. But I can guarantee that the inspection service in the Department of Mines and Minerals will be charged with one responsibility, and only one. Never again, if I can help it, will the blood of a miner stain the record of an Illinois Governor — Democrat or Republican.

I will do my level best to squeeze the water and the waste out of our roads. When and where road repairs are made will be decided by needs and not politics. Nobody is going to take a bite out of the precious road dollar to enrich politicians and campaign coffers. And I am going to find out why it costs us twice as much to build hard roads in Illinois this year than it does in Iowa. And if the FBI does any investigating, *I* will be asking them and not someone else.

I am going to lift the pudgy hand of politics off the Department of Conservation so that our natural resources and wild life can be conserved for the benefit of the people and the sportsmen. The public are paying for fish and game and not for votes. I would like to see a Conservation

Commission administering this Department, as in many other enlightened states.

The honest, conscientious highway patrolman who is trying to do a professional job is going to be safe and secure under a merit system instead of at the mercy of a local political leader. Illinois is one of the few states which still retains a politically appointed state police.

I shall insist on adequate appropriations for the common schools. A good common school education for every child is the first essential to good citizenship, and it is an obligation of the state.

We must attack the administration of the full assessment laws which have resulted in such burdensome tax increases and such inequity and injustices. I will propose the creation of county supervisors of assessments to bring about uniformity and nondiscrimination within counties, which is now aggravated by the mysterious multiplier determined in Springfield.

I shall do my best to provide Illinois with a new and modern constitution, on which the solution of so many of our problems depends, and I shall ask for your help to thereby establish modern, efficient governmental machinery in Illinois.

I shall do my level best to humanize and modernize our state welfare institutions, where so many thousands of unfortunates are compelled to reside.

I shall squeeze the graft, the waste and the corruption out of state purchases, be it land, roads or bologna sausage, and I will fire the first official or contractor who cheats.

I want to say to labor that I think they have no other objective than all the other people — honest, decent government, and a fair break. I would resist any effort to impair or whittle away labor's hard won gains. I would demand an enlargement of our educational program for labor and employers alike to reduce the appalling industrial accident rate in Illinois. And I will do my level best to see that the Industrial Commission is administered for the benefit of the people and not the politicians or the lawyers.

I will not promise to reduce taxes. But if the streamlining of government, if the elimination of unnecessary payrollers, if the elimination of the "fix," will enable the state government to reduce state tax levies and at the same time render the needed services, I shall recommend tax reduction as soon as possible.

Lorna Underwood, Stevenson's close friend from the days he was a law student at Harvard University, wired him words of encouragement for his campaign.

To Lorna Underwood Carey[91]

October 21, 1948

My dear Lorna:

I have just opened a telegram from you and it gave me such a start that without even trying to refresh my memory about your address I am dictating this hasty note of thanks.

You warm my heart — which is battered beyond recognition! I am in the worst of my hideous and unfamiliar travail now, with the election just around the corner, and meetings every five minutes, no preparation, and stricken with terror!

I had a happy glimpse of Nina [Underwood] at the Democratic Convention in Philadelphia and we talked of you. Indeed, I was on the verge of jumping on a plane for Cape Cod and a tranquil afternoon by the sea as of long ago. But duty, political managers and a collapsed imagination drove me back to Chicago.

You were sweet to think of me and I only wish you were going to be presenting your good wishes in person.

God bless you — and my love,

AD

P.S. A hideous way to write. Forgive me but for heavens sake tell me where you are & where you will be, lest our paths might cross & we wouldn't know it!

To Lorna Underwood Carey[92]

October 31, 1948

Lorna —

Thanks for your sweet note — Red Bank reminds me of some happy moments long, long ago when fairy princesses gathered a soiled and weary traveller from Russia & spirited him away to Red Bank, rest, romance!

We must do something about our paths — Baltimore has been so far from mine for so long. But who knows — governors or defeated candidates must get about a bit & if & when I next come east will contrive an

[91] The original of this typewritten letter is in the possession of Mrs. George Sagendorph (Lorna Underwood). The postscript is in Stevenson's handwriting.
[92] This handwritten letter is in the possession of Mrs. George Sagendorph.

encounter, as you say, before all is lost — or all of us has withered —

Love
AD

p.s. I'm the bait on the right! [93]

On October 18, 1948, Newsweek stated: "You could tell an Illinois Democrat by his long face and doleful look even before you spotted his campaign button last week. . . . Illinois Democrats had written off Harry S. Truman long since." The report added that the Democrats had also given up hope for Paul H. Douglas, "although they continued to claim that Stevenson had an outside chance." On October 31, 1948, the New York Times reported: "The GOP is expected to retain the Senate seat and the Governorship."

On November 2, 1948, the voters of Illinois swept Stevenson into the governorship by the largest margin in the history of the state. He defeated Dwight Green by 572,067 votes. Paul H. Douglas defeated Senator C. Wayland Brooks by a margin of 407,728 votes, while President Truman won the state by 33,612 votes.[94]

Sixty per cent of the Democratic vote came from Cook County. But Stevenson won the downstate vote by a margin of 25,643 votes and carried 48 out of the 101 counties. On November 7, the New York Times commented: "Democrats and Republicans alike are apparently convinced that Governor-elect Stevenson . . . meant to carry out his campaign promise 'to return self-respect and morality to government in Illinois.'" And Newsweek on November 15 noted: "The friendly, earnest candidate visited almost every lunch wagon and curbstone from Little Egypt in Southern Illinois to the North Shore along Lake Michigan, making as many as a dozen speeches in a single night."

To Alicia Patterson[95]

[No date] [96]

Your precious letter[97] came yesterday, along with some thousands of wires etc which will paralyse me for days. . . .

[93] Stevenson enclosed a cartoon from the October 30 issue of the Chicago *Tribune*, showing him together with Paul H. Douglas, candidate for the U.S. Senate, and President Truman, as bait in the political ocean. Stevenson was labeled "One Worlder for Governor."

[94] *Blue Book of the State of Illinois 1949–1950* (Springfield, Ill.: Office of the Secretary of State, 1951), p. 745.

[95] This handwritten letter is in the possession of Adlai E. Stevenson III.

[96] Probably November 3, 1948, the day after the election.

[97] Miss Patterson's letters to Stevenson were not available to the editors, but she apparently wrote that she was about to visit Europe.

Things are rattling around here so I can't concentrate or write. . . . [Winston] Churchill, [Aneurin] Bevan et al are fine, but I'm going to try to find time to dictate a letter of introduction to Bill Stoneman & Wilder Foote who will really give you a look see at UN. I wish I had time to do the same re London, Berlin & Frankfurt — on the lower echelons. But I suspect Miss Patterson knows those echelons everywhere even better than I!

I carried Ill. by 565,000 plus — never anything like it in history — 515 000 ahead of Truman and 180 000 ahead of closest man on Democratic ticket. Now I'm really in trouble! . . .

To Harry S Truman[98]

November 6, 1948

Dear Mr. President:

I only want to express my thanks and respects to a gallant man for a gallant campaign.

I am at your service always, and God bless you!

Faithfully yours,

Walter Lippmann wired Stevenson on November 3, 1948: "My warmest congratulations. Nothing in the whole election gives me so much personal pleasure as your victory. Best wishes."

To Walter Lippmann [99]

November 6, 1948

Dear Walter:

I was delighted to have your flattering wire and you were good to think of me. I knew I was going to win, but the magnitude of the victory was a surprise, not to mention a record breaker.

I shall hope to see you before too long and tell you about my adventures in the jungle of Illinois politics. I have tried about everything now, and it's all been fun!

Ellen joins me in warm regards to you and Helen.[100]

Sincerely yours,

ADLAI

[98] The original is in the Harry S Truman Library, Independence, Missouri.
[99] The original is in the Lippmann papers, Yale University Library.
[100] Mrs. Lippmann.

To Mrs. Franklin D. Roosevelt[101]

November 6, 1948

My dear Mrs. Roosevelt:

Nothing has pleased me and flattered me as much as your cable of congratulations. Your thoughtfulness and consideration have always been beyond my understanding, and now I have an eloquent personal example of it. I only hope I can do half as well in my so-called "public life."

My thoughts and heart have been straying from the prairies of Illinois to the palaces of Paris much too often of late, but evidently the electorate didn't realize it!

With warmest thanks and affectionate best wishes, I am

Faithfully yours,

P.S. It's all your fault! You told me last fall to go ahead and have a try at it, and I have profited enormously from the experience quite aside from the amazing victory. So I am grateful to you on still another count!

A.E.S.

To James F. Oates, Jr.[102]

November 9, 1948

Dear Jim:

You were good to write me. I hope you will stand by to give me in confidence any suggestions at any time — particularly now, with respect to first class personnel — irrespective of politics — who might be available even for a limited term of service. I would like to do some drafting to get this thing started properly. Please give it some thought.

Yours,

ADLAI

To James Roosevelt

November 9, 1948

Dear Jimmie:

You were good to think of me and I appreciate your letter very much. I suspect that not a little of the President's unexpected success in California was due to you! [103]

[101] The original is in the Franklin D. Roosevelt Library, Hyde Park, New York.
[102] The original is in the possession of Mr. Oates.
[103] Mr. Roosevelt was California Democratic National Committeeman.

We have a great opportunity and I wish there was some way we could have a meeting like the British parties do to formulate a long term party program in general terms.

I shall hope to see you when you have a spare moment passing through Illinois.

Many thanks and warm regards.

Sincerely yours,

Former Secretary of State Edward R. Stettinius, Jr., sent Stevenson an additional contribution after election to help with any deficit. The Stevenson for Governor Committee raised $172,840.00 from December, 1947, to February 18, 1949. It spent during the same period $153,458.04.[104] The committee, however, had raised only about $107,000 during the campaign itself. After the election, the committee paid for research material to assist Stevenson when he took office.

To Edward R. Stettinius, Jr.

November 22, 1948

Dear Ed:

You're a great guy, as always! But I feel a little embarrassed about letting Virginia meet the Illinois deficit. Moreover, I feel as though you had been doing nice things for me for so many years now that it was time for a little reciprocity!

A thousand thanks and affectionate regards to you all — especially the twins! [105]

Yours,

To Mr. and Mrs. Ernest L. Ives[106]

[No date] [107]

Dear B & E —

The ill fated airplane journey ended in Richmond when word came that the Washington airport was closed in. Had we got off a little earlier we might have made it. Then a crazy taxi ride to the Ry station after hasty telephone calls to Wash. to rearrange appointments. But it turned

[104] Report of John Nagle, certified public accountant, Chicago, May 20, 1949.
[105] Wallace and Joseph Stettinius.
[106] This handwritten letter is in the Elizabeth Stevenson Ives collection, Illinois State Historical Library.
[107] The envelope is postmarked Chicago, November 24, 1948. This letter was written aboard the train from Washington to Chicago. Stevenson had just vacationed with his sister and brother-in-law at Southern Pines, North Carolina.

out to be the wrong Ry. station! We finally caught the train in the yards in a driving rain and reached Wash. at 2:30. So my day was shot and I decided to stay over today to make my visits and some more besides. I've accomplished something, I think, and talked with Truman by phone but didn't bother him with a call. Now I'm enroute for Chicago and the great travail, much refreshed — with the 3 Musketeers[108] in adjoining space! And still crowing over their days in S.P. [Southern Pines] & "Lord & Lady Ives" — the best hosts they ever met — and also cross examining me relentlessly. I had a wonderful visit & hope it didn't wear you both out.

Love,
AD.

To Alicia Patterson[109]

November 22, 1948

. . . This is a day to try men's souls — as we orators say. At 8 AM I left the Southern Pines airport in a private Beechcraft a friend loaned me to fly to Washington for my many appointments, accompanied by these leeches [George] Tagge of the Tribune & [John] Dreiske of the Sun-Times. At 10 we landed not in Nash[ville]. but in Richmond in black weather, Wash[ington]. was closed in. Then wild telephoning to cancel & rearrange appointments; taxis — not one but two because of asinine zone regulations — to the railroad station to catch a train for Wash. But it was the wrong station! Thence to the Ry yards to head off the train so the Gov. of Ill. could get aboard. And now its 2 PM & I'm locked up in a drawing room with these blood suckers and Wash. is still an hour away. My day is shot — my precious time wasted. . . .

Somehow this Gov. business seems a bit of dream to me yet, but I'll be in the exacting preparations when I get back up to my ears — staff, resea[r]ch, conferences, appointments to major jobs, patronage. Its a nightmare, but I could look forward to the Gridiron dinner in Wash. Dec. 11 and seeing you that night or the next night in Wash or N.Y. if only you got back in time. . . .

Monday Nov 22   En route to Chi; via Richmond — damn it!

---

[108] Chicago reporters. One of them, Charles Wheeler of the Chicago *Daily News*, told Mrs. Ives during the week's vacation, "With the plurality your brother got, he's going to be the next Democratic Presidential nominee." Elizabeth Stevenson Ives and Hildegarde Dolson, *My Brother Adlai* (New York: Morrow, 1956), p. 214.

[109] This handwritten letter is in the possession of Adlai E. Stevenson III.

To Lorna Underwood Carey[110]

[No date] [111]

Lorna dear —

I called you early and late at Pikesville 168 yesterday evening on the off chance that I might slip away and come over to see you. And now I'm off to Chicago and my travail after a week's "rest" in North Carolina hounded by three newspaper reporters from Chicago.

I'll be back in Wash[ington] in Dec. for the Gridiron dinner — the 11th — and some work. If circumstances permit I'll try again —

Love
AD

At this instant the train is standing in the Baltimore station!

Paul Scott Mowrer, Edgar Ansel Mowrer, Lloyd Lewis and other distinguished newspapermen resigned from the Chicago Daily News *out of disagreement with publisher John S. Knight. Mr. Mowrer wrote Stevenson from Paris, France, congratulating him on his victory and saying that he and Mrs. Mowrer were planning to live in New Hampshire.*

To Paul Scott Mowrer[112]

November 26, 1948

Dear Paul:

Ellen and I have read and re-read your good letter. Particularly, the part about coming back to New Hampshire. And then Edgar[113] showed up and spent a night with us and enlarged our knowledge about your plans.

Well, of course, I have ordered a new and more comfortable chair for the Director of Conservation and have posted your name on it. In due course I will arrange for wheels or sedan poles and black boys so you can be pushed or carried to the bank of every stream. Perhaps I'll get two chairs; maybe three, so we can take Hadley,[114] too!

Anyway, come on home. All is forgiven.

Love from Libertyville,

[110] This handwritten letter is in the possession of Mrs. George Sagendorph.
[111] The envelope is postmarked Chicago, November 24, 1948.
[112] This letter is in the Stevenson collection, Illinois State Historical Library.
[113] Mr. Mowrer's brother.
[114] Mrs. Mowrer.

P.S. I won by the largest plurality ever recorded in Illinois. God knows why.

Kenneth Younger, British Cabinet member, wrote Stevenson, November 9, 1948, that he was "very much missed" at the United Nations Assembly in Paris and congratulated him on his victory. He added that the unexpected triumph of President Truman, he thought, indicated that the Democratic party had become much more definitely the party of organized labor and of middle-class liberals.

To Kenneth Younger

November 27, 1948

My dear Kenneth:

I was delighted to have your letter, and you were good to think of me. My mind wanders all too often from the prairies of Illinois to the palaces of Paris and the halls of London. But I have inherited an appalling task here, and I suspect I will have to develop some new and rigid mental disciplines.

You are quite right about the danger of any hasty analysis of the elections. I had a rather special situation in Illinois which contributed to the largest plurality in the history of our state — and for a Democrat, when only three have been elected since the Civil War. But what you say regarding the national situation seems to be about right, subject only to the fact that the farmer voted Democratic, much to the bewilderment of the "experts." I can find no better explanation than that the farmer is enjoying high prices and concluded to let well enough alone. In him you had, of course, a very conservative ally which somewhat distorts the picture of an emerging coherent liberal party. And if President Truman had not carried Ohio, Illinois and Minnesota — all large farm states — he would have been defeated, even though the local Democratic tickets won. For example, here in Illinois, I had a plurality of 575,000 and President Truman won by only 33,000.

But forgive me for talking too much about something I know little more about than you!

I hope you are flourishing and I am sure you are doing a superb job. I wish I had some prospects of seeing you. Ellen sends her best.

Sincerely yours,

On November 19, 1948, Arthur Krock wrote in his column in the New

York Times *that Stevenson was being seriously looked at as a candidate for President in 1952.*

To Arthur Krock[115]

December 1, 1948

Dear Arthur:

Not less than twenty-five helpful people have sent me clippings from the world's greatest newspaper of November 18. Some have diligently pointed out that Arthur Krock is a columnist of wide repute; others that the New York Times is a very important newspaper; and the more sophisticated have suggested that perhaps I had overlooked your flattering remarks.

I didnt, although I have overlooked thanking you for them! [116]

Yours,

ADLAI

On December 14, 1948, Arthur Krock described in his column in the New York Times *Stevenson's background, his record in forming the United Nations, and his "unblemished reputation." Krock again noted that many prominent Republicans and Democrats saw him as a leading candidate for 1952.*

To Arthur Krock[117]

December 16, 1948

Dear Arthur:

I read the oracle of Washington's piece of December 14 with fear and trembling. Is anyone really looking me over? If so, the speculation will soon end!

But for the record:

Illinois — Plurality for President Truman	33,612
Plurality for Paul H. Douglas	407,728
Plurality for Adlai E. Stevenson	572,067

But what you overlooked, I think, or generously minimized, was that

[115] The original is in the possession of Mr. Krock.

[116] Mr. Krock replied on December 6, 1948: "I shrank from the telephone all the time you were here fearing you would reprove me for suggesting such a dreadful prospect to Ellen and you. But I am glad you took it so agreeably. I meant it most seriously, Adlai, and shall nudge the bill along from time to time."

[117] The original is in the possession of Mr. Krock.

Green elected Stevenson by the largest plurality in history, not Stevenson.[118]

Thanks again, and the Season's best.

Yours,
ADLAI

Stevenson's Princeton classmate Everett Case, president of Colgate University, wrote on December 15, 1948: "Arthur Krock has done one of his better jobs in articulating for readers of yesterday's Times *some of the things which your friends have been thinking about." He added that being president of a university was not so different from the State House "as one might imagine it to be."*

To Everett Case

December 22, 1948

Dear Ev:

Krock did nicely — and so did you! My only consolation in this hideous predicament is that it might be worse — I might have been a University President if I had had more brains!

Thanks for your letter — and the best of everything.

Yours,

On January 1, 1949, Stevenson and Allen Dulles delivered speeches as part of a ceremony commemorating the late President Woodrow Wilson.[119]

We have just celebrated the anniversary of Woodrow Wilson's ninety-second birthday. His stature today is higher — in our American as well as in world esteem — than at any time since he laid down the burdens of the Presidency.

Mr. Dulles will speak to you in a few minutes about the international side of Woodrow Wilson. It is, I think, part of the irony of history that Americans today think of him as first of all "the father of the League of

[118] Mr. Krock replied to Stevenson's letter on December 20, 1948, "It is all right for you to be as modest as all that, but I did not dream up the piece, as you eventually will discover."

[119] *Woodrow Wilson: Addresses upon the Occasion of His Ninety-second Birthday Anniversary, December 28, 1948,* with an introductory note by Julie d'Estournelles (Stamford, Connecticut: Overbrook Press, 1949), pp. 31–34.

Nations" — which was to have a successor in the present United Nations — for the reason that Wilson had correctly seen that there was a historic need for such an organization, no matter how difficult it might be to establish it. But the Wilson who was elected to the Presidency in 1912 had no specific program in foreign policy. He had become a national figure — as a scholar, as an administrator, as a candidate — on domestic issues. To Americans of that period he was the author of a book called *The New Freedom* — a collection of his 1912 campaign speeches which outlined a program that did *not* assume, with President Taft's conservative Republicans, that the best of all worlds would be a world in which government merely *policed* a competitive struggle of private interests and pressure groups. But it was a program that did not agree with Theodore Roosevelt's Progressive Party of 1912 *either*. It refused to accept Roosevelt's apparent belief that trusts and monopolies could be separated into goats and sheep, into bad trusts and good ones with corresponding distinctions in government policy and action. Theodore Roosevelt had argued for the acceptance of monopoly as an inevitable development, and proposed to regulate it. Wilson argued that there was nothing inevitable about such developments, and — following Justice Brandeis — that there were monopoly powers making for continuously more monopolistic development, which a creative government could curb. Government should not, he said, merely accept monopoly and regulate it, but it should constantly be concerned with the re-establishment of competitive conditions in which equality of opportunity could emerge with a new cutting edge.

Woodrow Wilson's *New Freedom* sketched a blueprint of American government that was positive and affirmative — that would change with changing economic, financial and technical circumstances but within which the creative energies of the people would be released in open competitive conditions and equality of opportunity. The subtitle of his book, *The New Freedom,* was "A Call for the Emancipation of the Generous Energies of a People." This was not socialism because it did not involve the continuous use of government authority in the detailed operation of the nation's economic life. But it was not the usual conservatism — "leaving things alone" — either. It involved the vigorous and creative use of the federal government's authority with the purpose, however, not of keeping the government *in* business, but of creating conditions which would permit full reliance on the competitive energies of equal opportunity.

He taught us to distinguish between governmental action that *takes over* the functions formerly discharged by individuals, and governmental action that *restores* opportunities for individual action. That is why he called his program the *New Freedom,* and that is why he always said that the only effective way to be a conservative regarding the essentials of the American way is to be a *progressive* in its *continuous* adaptation to changing facts and circumstances.

But long before Wilson made his mark politically as Governor of New Jersey and President of the United States, he had earned a reputation as a scholar. He had made his mark in 1885 with a thesis on our *Congressional Government.* He had stressed that "power and strict accountability for its use are the essential constituents of good government" and had pointed out that the conventional theory of the separation of powers between the executive, the legislative and judicial "parcels out power and confuses responsibility."

We have just had two years of experience with a Congress in the hands of one party and the White House in the hands of the other. Americans also remember the last two years of the Taft, Wilson and Hoover administrations as examples of the type of frustration which can result from our separation of the executive and legislative branches.

It is quite plain that nothing could discredit American democracy more than a complete paralysis in our governmental institutions in a time when provisions for swift and responsible adjustment to changing facts are essential to survival. In this sense the Woodrow Wilson of the League of Nations and the Woodrow Wilson of *Congressional Government* are indispensable parts of a single undivided whole. American democracy is no longer without rivals in the imagination of the world. The efficiency of our institutions in meeting the unparalleled challenge of the present world will be a vital factor in determining the success of our leadership in foreign policy. And to this day no political scientist and no statesman has more acutely analyzed our defects or charged our progressive course than Woodrow Wilson.

If we are to use government as an instrument with which we can *enlarge* freedom and avoid the creeping paralysis of bureaucratic control of the details of economic life, there is more to learn from Woodrow Wilson, who said that "the business of government is to organize the common interest against the special interests," than there is in all the communist and collectivist experiments of the current world scene. If our ears are attuned to the drumbeat of freedom, we should *not* ask: Should there be *more* government or *less?* And we *should* ask: How can we use government to make a new birth of freedom possible? For years to come people will be going back to Woodrow Wilson in search of the answer to that fundamental question for America.

To Alicia Patterson[120]

January 3, 1949

. . . Let me know as far in advance as possible when you are coming. I will have to be in Wash[ington] Jan 19, 20 & 21 arriving back here the 22nd for the inauguration monkeyshines. Evidently all the faithful are expected to attend.

Commencing Sunday of this week — the 9th — my address is Executive Mansion, Springfield, Ill — lest you've forgotten. . . .

I'm desperate — but no compromises yet! Difficulties that should make a volume on 'Innocents abroad in Politics.' Sometime I'll tell you about them — I hope. Meanwhile my hours are vanishing & I haven't even written my inaugural. . . .

A

[120] This handwritten letter is in the possession of Adlai E. Stevenson III.

Acknowledgments

We are most grateful to Adlai E. Stevenson's sister, Mrs. Ernest L. Ives, for her infinite patience and considerate help at all stages in the preparation of this volume. In addition to Mrs. Ives, Professor Stuart Gerry Brown, Edward D. McDougal, Jr., and Mrs. Edison Dick read the entire manuscript. The entire manuscript was submitted to the members of the Advisory Committee to *The Papers of Adlai E. Stevenson,* and their suggestions have been most helpful. Captain F. Kent Loomis, Assistant Director of Naval History, read Part I. Wilder Foote read Part IV. Their help is deeply appreciated.

Little, Brown and Company, Mrs. Eugene Meyer, Mrs. Marshall Field and the Field Foundation, Mrs. John French, Mr. and Mrs. Harold Hochschild, Arnold M. Picker, Robert S. Benjamin, Newton N. Minow, James F. Oates, Jr., Francis T. P. Plimpton, Benjamin Swig, Philip M. Klutznick, Mrs. John Paul Welling, William McCormick Blair, R. Keith Kane, Simon H. Rifkind, Wilson W. Wyatt, William Benton, Daggett Harvey, Mr. and Mrs. Edison Dick, William McCormick Blair, Jr., Lloyd K. Garrison, J. M. Kaplan, Jerrold Loebl, Hermon D. Smith, Edward D. McDougal, Jr., Glen A. Lloyd, Mr. and Mrs. Gilbert Harrison, Irving B. Harris, Edwin C. Austin, Archibald Alexander, Jacob M. Arvey, Paul Ziffren, Frank Karelsen, George W. Ball, C. K. McClatchy, Maurice Tempelsman, Barnet Hodes and Scott Hodes, generously provided funds to defray the editorial expense of this volume. The University of Hawaii kindly assisted in defraying the costs of typing the manuscript.

We are grateful to Roger Shugg, of the University of New Mexico Press, and Ned Bradford, of Little, Brown and Company, for their encouragement and support.

William S. Dix, Alexander P. Clark, and Mrs. Nancy Bressler, of the Princeton University Library, Paul Spence of the Illinois State Historical Library, and Paul Edlund and David C. Mearns of the Library of Congress, have been most cooperative. The Reverend Richard Paul Graebel,

John Bartlow Martin, Roxane Eberlein, Phyllis Gustafson, Margaret Munn, Judy Fresco, Juanda Higgins, Albert U. Romasco, Francis Nipp, Glen Holt, Paul Michael Green, Stephen Rautenberg, Gayle Nunokawa, Eric Sears, Colleen Wallace, Nancy Lee Dykes, and Carla Ley Fishman have helped us in many ways. Jo Ann Jay typed the manuscript with great care and skill.

WALTER JOHNSON
CAROL EVANS

Index

Academy of Political Science, 16
Acheson, Alice, 287
Acheson, Dean, 14, 66, 350–351; praise for AES's UN Preparatory Commission work, 287; letter to, 287
Act of Chapultepec, see Chapultepec, Act of
Adair, Lieutenant Commander Noah, 54, 58
Adamowski, Benjamin S., 8; letters to, 8–9, 408
Advisory Council for Italy, 197, 199
Africa, 139, 376
Aghnides, Thanassis, 421, 447
Aglion, Raoul, 345
Agricultural Adjustment Administration, 15, 532
Agriculture, U.S. Department of, 13, 17, 467
Akers, Milburn ("Pete"), 438, 439
Akers, Woodbury, 53
Alabama, U.S.S., 39, 45
Albania, 435n, 440–441
Albright, Ivan, 548
Albright, Mrs. Ivan, 548
Aleutian Islands, 136
Alexander, Major Archibald S., 171
Alexander, Henry Clay, 218
Algiers, 168, 169
Allen, General Terry, 224
Allerton, Robert, 102
Alley, James, 528
Allied and Associated Powers, 157
Allied Control Commission (ACC), 164, 171, 172, 173, 194, 195, 196, 198–203
Allied Military Government, in Italy, 171, 174, 177, 178, 179, 182–184, 193, 195
Allies, World War II, 35, 37, 116, 136, 139–140, 144, 198; ship and plane

production, 136–137; surrender of Italy, 163
Allison, John M., 331
Altgeld, Peter, 495–496, 513
Altmeyer, Arthur, 369
Amberg, Julius H., 158
"Amend the Neutrality Act," AES speech, 19–23
America First Committee, 47
American Association for the United Nations, Inc., 340, 428–429
American Bar Association, 16
American Broadcasting Company, 258; AES speech on General Assembly (October, 1946), 334–336
American Federation of Labor (A.F. of L.), 25, 306
American Judicature Society, 16
Americans for Democratic Action, 369
Anderson, Commander, 90
Andrews, General Frank M., 53, 54, 57; letter to, 60
Andrews, Walter G., 64
Angel, Zuleta, 336
antisubmarine warfare, 69–70; AES draft press statement on, 108–109
Arce, Dr. José, 436, 437, 440
Arends, Leslie C., 64
Argentina, 14, 44, 374, 375, 436–438
Arizona, U.S.S., 74, 101
armaments, 139, 143, 144
Armour, Lester, 220, 515
Armstrong, Hamilton Fish, 220, 221
Army Air Force Evaluation Boards, 217; AES mission to Paris and London for, 217–226
Army Medical Corps, 184
Army Specialized Training Program, 134n
Arnold, General H. H., 104